D1548550

The Papers of
Howard Washington Thurman

Volume 1

The Papers of
Howard Washington Thurman

VOLUME 1

My People Need Me, June 1918–March 1936

Senior Editor	Walter Earl Fluker
Managing Editor	Kai Jackson Issa
Associate Editors	Quinton H. Dixie, Peter Eisenstadt, Catherine Tumber
Advisory Editor	Alton B. Pollard III
Senior Advisory Editor	Luther E. Smith Jr.

The University of South Carolina Press

Published by the University of South Carolina Press
Columbia, South Carolina 29208

www.sc.edu/uscpress

Manufactured in the United States of America

18 17 16 15 14 13 12 11 10   09 10 9 8 7 6 5 4 3 2 1

Library of Congress Cataloging-in-Publication Data

Thurman, Howard, 1900-1981.
 The papers of Howard Washington Thurman / senior editor Walter Earl
Fluker ; associate editor Catherine Tumber ... [et al.].
    p. cm.
 Includes bibliographical references and index.
 ISBN 978-1-57003-804-4 (cloth : alk. paper)
 1. Baptists—Doctrines. 2. Theology. 3. Thurman, Howard,
1900–1981—Correspondence. I. Fluker, Walter E., 1951– II. Tumber,
Catherine. III. Title.
 BX6495.T53A25 2009
 280'.4092—dc22
 [B]

                                        2008052256

This book was printed on Glatfelter Natures, a recycled paper with 30 percent
postconsumer waste content.

This volume would have not been possible without the generous financial and material support
of the following contributors:
    The Lilly Endowment Inc.
    The Louisville Institute
    The Henry Luce Foundation
    The Pew Charitable Trusts
    The National Historical Publications
       and Records Commission

Contents

THE PAPERS

Chapter I. The Early Years   *1*

Chapter II. Morehouse College Years   *8*

Illustrations

PREFACE

You must wait and listen for the sound of the genuine that is within you.
When you hear it, that will be your voice and the Voice of God.

Howard Washington Thurman

Nearly thirty years have passed since these eloquent words ignited a passion within me that would spark a journey that would come to fruition in the production of this documentary edition. I am one of the many men and women who found in Howard Thurman a fount of inspiration and strength during a critical passage in our lives. Thurman and I met at a crossroads in our respective pilgrimages—he, a wise, old sage with little time left, and I, a struggling seminary student who had grown weary of abstract theological discussions that had become stale, irrelevant, and powerless. His wise counsel, his deep, penetrating silences, his wit and humanity—yes, his laughter—all these and more, provided for me an inner healing and new sense of direction that continues to this day.

I first became acquainted with Howard Thurman in 1972 when I served as a chaplain's assistant in the U.S. Army. It was my weekly responsibility to prepare the Sunday bulletin for the post chapel at Fort Riley, Kansas. The post chaplain regularly assigned selections from Thurman's small collection of meditations *The Centering Moment* for the back of the bulletin. With the exception of one other African American chaplain assigned to Fort Riley, I felt awash in a sea of white clerics and assistants whose religious experiences were foreign to my own. I had been brought up in a small storefront Baptist church on the south side of Chicago, where the faces and deep-structured issues of consciousnesses found little in common with the day-to-day routine of the military religious life and practice. Imagine my surprise and delight when I saw Howard Thurman's face on the back cover of *The Centering Moment*. When I read through the meditations, I was struck then, as now, by the quiet cadence and lofty idealism of Thurman's interpretation of the religious experience—always pointing inwardly and, yet, challenging the human spirit to soar higher into itself and the world of nature, people, and ideas.

I did not encounter Thurman again until the beginning of my seminary course on black preaching taught by Carl Marbury at Garrett Evangelical Theological Seminary in 1977. Dean Marbury introduced the class of budding homileticians to a variety of black preaching—but my experience in the class was marked by the evening when he asked students to listen to a long-playing album of "The Third Component," a sermon by Thurman. One year later, during my middle year, I was to meet the face of the words and the voice that had so enraptured me at Fort Riley and in the preaching class. Garrett's Church and Black Experience program held a consultation with Thurman in October 1978. I was selected as the student chaperone to pick up Thurman at the airport and deliver him to his hotel. Instead, we spent the entire afternoon discussing my plans for the future. Such was the generous and gracious spirit of this unusual man. He asked again and again in probing interrogatives that I later discovered were his hallmark, "Who are you, really? What are you trying to do with your life?" I answered matter-of-factly, in the forgivable arrogance of naïveté, "I want to change the church into a moral force for the transformation of society." His silences were gentle and mocking—and then he would ask again, "But *who* are *you*? Who do *you* seek to become?"

After that encounter in the fall of 1979, I was invited to the Howard Thurman Educational Trust in San Francisco as a part of the appropriately entitled "Footprints of the Disinherited," the first of three series of conversations between Thurman and ten African American students interested in religious vocation. There a company of my peers and I wrestled the angel with the flaming sword. Thurman began the first session with a three-hour reading of the Gospel of Mark with only one break. He asked us to abandon all theological presuppositions about what we had heard about Jesus and to imagine that we were somewhere else—maybe in a French villa or alone in a café and someone approached us and told us this story for the first time. Beyond the sweet-liquored words and long pauses that drew us into our own rhythms, I can only remember that I encountered Jesus as a radically free man. At the end of the week, we were changed—I was changed *forever*.

During my last year in seminary, Thurman and I exchanged letters regularly—I always asking the questions that he never quite answered—and he smiling gently through his written words. That last year in seminary was the hardest: I had to decide whether to pursue a PhD program in religion or to go another way. In the midst of this agonizing ordeal, I wrote a long letter to Thurman outlining my deepest fears and desires related to vocation. After what seemed a millennium, he replied in a two-page handwritten letter that was virtually impossible to decipher with doodles and tiny etchings within the margins. He suggested that my problem with choice was not for lack of opportunity but the converse, I had many options. In his inimitable prose, laying out for me the choices with which I was struggling, and finally suggesting that whatever decision I made that "You must *wait* and *listen* for the sound of the genuine that is within you. When you hear it, that will be your voice and the Voice of God." I didn't know how to respond to these words—but in that moment as I read them, tears of release flowed from a center within me that had already made the decision.

I chose to enroll in the PhD program in social ethics at Boston University. Little did I know then that only one and a half years later, he would pass on and that his wife, Sue Bailey Thurman, would donate a large portion of his papers to Boston University. Eight years later, I completed my dissertation, "A Comparative Analysis of the Ideal of Community in the Thought of Howard Thurman and Martin Luther King Jr.," at Boston University and began a pastoral and teaching career that led me from St. John's Congregational Church in Springfield, Massachusetts, to Dillard University as dean of the chapel and assistant professor of religion, where I preached every Sunday in the Lawless Memorial Chapel that was dedicated by Thurman in 1955. In 1987, I was appointed as an assistant professor of Christian Ethics at the Vanderbilt Divinity School, where I taught a regular seminar, first developed by the Reverend Kelly Miller Smith, on "The Religious Thought of Howard Thurman" and in 1988 hosted "America in Search of a Soul," a major convocation of scholars who studied the works of Thurman. Through the generosity of Vanderbilt University and the Mellon Faculty Fellowship, from 1989 to 1990, I spent an early sabbatical at Harvard College and the W. E. B. Du Bois Institute for African and African American Research with the intention of returning to my earlier research on Thurman and King. My plans were altered, however, when I met the late James Melvin Washington, a professor at Union Theological Seminary, who encouraged me to apply for a grant to the Lilly Endowment to publish a few essays and sermons from the Thurman corpus. I continue to be amazed at the fated steps of those who have simple intentions. Jacqui Burton, religion program director of the Lilly Endowment, responded positively. During that year, I accepted a new academic post as Martin Luther King Jr. Memorial Professor of Theology and dean of Black Church Studies at Colgate Rochester Divinity School, and in the fall of 1991 the Howard Thurman Papers Project was born. Rochester, New York, was not foreign territory for Thurman. He completed his seminary training in 1926 at the fabled Rochester Theological Seminary. Renamed the Colgate Rochester Divinity School / Bexley Hall / Crozer Theological Seminary, it was the home of the project until 1998 when I accepted my current post as professor of philosophy and religion, executive director of the Leadership Center and Coca-Cola Professor of Leadership Studies at Thurman's undergraduate alma mater, Morehouse College.

At the Leadership Center, Thurman's legacy continues as a critical resource in the development of curricular driven strategies linking spirituality and ethics for the preparation of leaders at local, national, and international levels. The remains of Howard Thurman and his beloved wife and partner, Sue Bailey Thurman, rest in a towering obelisk situated parallel to a statute of his younger visionary, Martin Luther King Jr. pointing to the future, but that future is best understood by remembering the past. During my first year on the campus of Morehouse, I stood one morning between these two monuments and realized that my work had come full circle—from San Francisco to Boston University to Colgate Rochester and to Morehouse, where it all began. *The Papers of Howard Washington Thurman* will challenge its readers to remember the story of Howard Thurman in the context of larger historical narratives which gave birth to the modern civil rights movement and impacted modern religious liberalism. The title of this volume, "My People Need Me," is taken from a letter written by eighteen-year-old Thurman to Mordecai Wyatt Johnson, which speaks to his early passion for justice and the uplift of his people. "My People Need Me" summarily defines Thurman's sense of calling that would propel him on a heroic journey from Daytona Beach, Florida, to his historic meeting with Mahatma Gandhi in 1936. It is our hope that in documenting Thurman's remarkable story we might also invite our readers to recommit themselves to the larger quest for character, civility, and community that marked his narrative.

WALTER EARL FLUKER, SENIOR EDITOR

OVERVIEW

This unprecedented collection of Howard Thurman's correspondence, publications, and speeches provides new insights on his life and times. Whether one has been familiar with Howard Thurman for decades or is just getting acquainted with him, this volume provides the most complete portrayal of Thurman to date.

Such a portrayal is important because although Thurman is increasingly acknowledged as a major religious thinker and activist of the twentieth century, he remains one of the least understood. Only a handful of scholars have completed extensive research and writing on Thurman. Others who consider Thurman to be a seminal religious thinker have reached this conclusion based on a limited number of publications and a limited awareness of Thurman's activism. The current volume presents a more fully textured Thurman and increases understanding about the man and his significance to history. A more comprehensive understanding of Thurman leads to a more comprehensive understanding of the ideas, organizations, and individuals he influenced.

Thurman's twenty-three books and numerous articles reflect his life and ideas and are intended for a wide and diverse readership on matters of the spiritual life, race relations, social justice, community, the church's mission, black spirituals, and the meaning of Jesus. In contrast, many of the documents in the current collection disclose some of his life events and thinking that were not intended for public consumption. Readers will come to know Thurman as the young student who is testing his abilities and discerning life's choices. The visitations of the Muse are evident in the poetry and fiction he writes. In seminary essays and speeches, he crafts his theological convictions and perspectives on sexual ethics. His letters speak about his struggles to meet basic needs and his caring for family and friends. Repeatedly his words show his frustration with racial injustice and his desire to improve life for black people. The longing of his young heart for guidance in his pursuit of vocational identity is palpable. In one of many letters to Mordecai Wyatt Johnson he expresses his admiration in a tone that clearly establishes Johnson's significance to him:

> In you I have ever seen what it was possible for me to become if I were willing to pay the price which you have paid. The best compliment that I have

received from any of my professors here came to me the other day thru a friend—This professor told my friend that I had a mind like yours. I actually blushed! (23 March, 1925)

Only in such correspondence do we come to understand Thurman's esteem and hunger for Johnson as a mentor.

New insights about the adult Thurman also emerge from these documents. We read his counsel to persons in crises and persons immobilized in their discernment process. His roles in social justice initiatives become evident. Lengthy and detailed memoranda, reports, and letters convey his rigorous administrative style. Intimate letters show Thurman as a devoted son, tender husband and father, and consummate friend. His many personal moods when confronted with disappointment, grief, success, and uncertainty and his ambitions, frustrations, and conflicts show as well.

Most readers of Thurman's publications have only had access to his books, which have remained available for purchase, but they alone are insufficient for tracking Thurman's thinking. His first book was published in 1944; his published articles began in 1922. If his books are the only sources for analysis, two decades of writings are lost to the interpretive task. The current volume now gives readers easy access to articles that are the building blocks to what is more fully constructed in his books.

Howard Thurman proclaims that any hope of a vital and fulfilled life, both personally and communally, requires a spiritually disciplined life in surrender to God. This leads him to address the significance of religious experience to personal and social transformations. The spiritual practices of commitment, growth, prayer, suffering, and reconciliation are integral to preparing for religious experience and responding faithfully to its insights. Throughout his life, Thurman emphasizes that an individual's proper sense of self, nourished by spiritual resources and the experience of caring community, is fundamental to the faith journey.

Thurman's focus on religious experience, spiritual practices, and a proper sense of self has so dominated most interpretations of Thurman that his commitment and witness to the systemic transformation of society are often lost. A phrase from his 1928 address "The Task of the Negro Ministry" makes this loss easy to understand: "The Spirit of Jesus grows by contagion and not by organization. One life aglow with the Spirit of Jesus is far more efficacious than a dozen organizational attempts to salvage society. In the final analysis a man's life is changed by contact with another life." And yet, the current volume shows Thurman as a national leader in the YMCA/YWCA student movement. He is the first African American to serve on the board of the Fellowship of Reconciliation, a peace-activist organization. His efforts organize black migrant workers in the segregated south, and he brings his eagerness to work with A. Philip Randolph to organize a mass meeting to protest social injustice. As the dean of two universities' chapels, he is enmeshed in the politics and procedures of higher education. He pioneers the founding of a church that aspires to break down the racial and cultural divides reflected in the membership and leadership of Christian congregations. After meeting with Mahatma Gandhi, Thurman travels throughout the United States and emphasizes how nonviolent protest is a powerful means for transforming racial injustice. He writes *Jesus and the Disinherited* as a book to empower those who are oppressed by the dominant forces of society. These and many other examples indicate that Thurman is deeply embedded in organizations and institutions to combat social ills.

The current and subsequent volumes not only disclose insights about Howard Thurman but also are a window on the issues, events, organizations, movements, institutions, and individuals of his times. A sampling of what is seen through this window entails the role of black colleges for the "uplift" of black people. The influence of India's independence struggle to the plight of African Americans is made explicit. Evident are the coping mechanisms of individuals and institutions during the Depression and World War II. The debate rages about communism and socialism as viable alternatives for improving the conditions of the poor and disinherited. Peace activists walk the fine line of aggressively opposing tyranny while affirming nonviolence. Religious leaders feel moral consternation after the United States uses atomic weapons against Japan. The ascendancy of the Civil Rights Movement in the United States eventually confronts Black Power as a competing social movement. Just a few of the prominent persons encountered through the window of Thurman's correspondence are Mary McLeod Bethune, W. E. B. Du Bois, Gandhi, James Farmer, Martin Luther King Jr., Muriel Lester, Benjamin E. Mays, Reinhold Niebuhr, Eleanor Roosevelt, Douglas Steere, and Channing H. Tobias.

The volumes also reveal Howard Thurman's complexity. Divergent perspectives are held in creative tension to portray reality and truth. He speaks of the transforming power of mystical experience and prophetic speech. He stresses the centrality of personality and the primacy of community to ultimate meaning. Affirming distinctive racial and religious identities is asserted to be essential to vital interracial and interfaith fellowship. The documents illustrate how such complexity served his character formation, ideas, and vision for an increasingly pluralistic world.

Thurman's complexity results from his reliance upon modern methods of critical reflection to pursue truth. In this sense, Thurman is a child of twentieth-century modernity. In asserting his convictions through writings and speeches, Thurman uses critical biblical scholarship, discoveries of science (and appreciation for scientific methods), social sciences, psychological analysis, and the relativity of historical interpretation. The documents disclose how Thurman's understanding of religion and life is indebted to the intellectual methods and resources of the modern era. The volumes, therefore, illustrate how intellectual streams of the modern era have nourished and informed his moral leadership.

Chapter I of the current volume covers Howard Thurman's early years in Daytona, Florida; chapters II through V his formal education and his leadership in the student movement and his early career as a pastor and professor. The volume culminates with his historic journey to India and his meeting with Gandhi. The subsequent volumes document Thurman's post-India years at Howard University as professor and chapel dean, his cofounding and leadership of the Fellowship Church of All Peoples in San Francisco, California, his tenure as dean of the chapel and professor at Boston University, his world-wide travels, through to his founding of the Howard Thurman Educational Trust.

The volumes can be read as a *documentary biography,* which the reader begins with the first document and reads sequentially. Or they can be used as a *documentary resource* for specific examinations of Thurman's life, relationships, and thinking. The editors selected documents and provided annotation to serve both reading approaches of systematic research or personal interest.

Extensive annotation provides a sense of context, an explanation of technical terms, an assessment of a document's importance to understanding Thurman's commitment and ideas, and the significance of persons, organizations, and events referenced. Considerable effort was expended to provide background information that increases the reader's ability to appreciate and interpret each document. This annotation, however, does not hijack the reader's opportunity to interpret the meanings and implications of documents, as the editors have endeavored to avoid imposing their interpretive renderings. The extraordinary quantity and quality of these documents and their annotation provide a long-awaited treasure.

At the end of his autobiography, Thurman wrote, "What I have written is but a fleeting intimation of the outside of what one man sees and may tell about the path he walks. No one shares the secret of a life; no one enters into the heart of the mystery. There are telltale signs that mark the passing of one's appointed days. Always we are on the outside of our story, always we are beggars who seek entrance to the kingdom of our dwelling place" (*With Head and Heart,* 270). Thurman realized that the sum of all the details of one's context, work, relationships, thoughts, and intentions neither defines an individual nor exhausts one's meaning. Something always remains beyond apprehension and comprehension. Something of each person is always elusive—always refusing to be a subject named, defined, and analyzed. These volumes do not presume to solve the mystery. This collection, however, is an invaluable resource for gaining greater insight into the power and possibilities of the mystery that is Thurman.

Luther E. Smith Jr.
Senior Advisory Editor

Acknowledgments

The Howard Thurman Papers Project was formally launched in 1991, but as early as 1979, two years before his death, Thurman took steps to preserve a documentary record of his life. He had, among other activities, arranged to have many of his audiotaped sermons transcribed and to have some of his friends and colleagues interviewed. Given the sheer bulk of the material, he was able to make only initial headway. After his death, Anne Spencer Thurman, who served as executive director of the Howard Thurman Educational Trust, published the first collection of her father's writings in *For the Inward Journey: The Writings of Howard Thurman* in 1984. In many respects, this current volume is a tribute to her and her early work of fulfilling her father's dream. Without Anne and Sue, this project would have never happened. Sue Thurman granted me written permission to publish Thurman's unpublished public writings as well as his correspondence, but her approval extends beyond the written word. Her imprimatur presents itself in every effort expended by the editors and me for the current volume to maintain the high quality of erudition and excellence that she sought in her own work and absolutely demanded of others. The letter of permission was written in consultation with Clayborne Carson, editor of the Martin Luther King Jr. Papers, a project that shares the peculiarly delicate task of publishing twentieth-century documents. I cannot begin to express my thanks to Clay, who also serves as a member of the Howard Thurman Papers Project Advisory Board, for his early support and guidance, which continue.

Since the deaths of Sue Bailey Thurman and Anne Spencer Thurman, Olive Thurman Wong has been a steady hand of support. As the eldest daughter of a well-known public figure and as a librarian familiar with the delicacy of documentary editing and archival management, Olive's sensitivity to the peculiar challenges of preparing documents for publication has been of inestimable value to the editorial team. Her continued support, direction, and prayers have sustained us during the latter years of the project. We also extend thanks to the grandchildren of Howard and Sue Thurman, Suzanne Vigil, Emily Wong, and Anton Wong, as well as great-grandchildren Phillip, Isa, and Ian Wong, whose lives bear the memory and the future of a legacy that will endure and continue to bear fruit and who represent what Thurman often called "the growing edge," the gentle reminder that the contradictions of life, even death, are not final. Special thanks to Carol Stewart, family member of Thurman's first wife, Katie Laura Kelley, who filled in many of the gaps in the Kelley family history for this volume.

During the early stages of the book's development, the Reverend Marvin A. Chandler, former executive director of the Howard Thurman Educational Trust and pastor of the Fellowship Church, provided encouragement and support. His successor at the Fellowship Church, Reverend Dorsey Blake, as well as the Fellowship Church family, continues in this role, making available to the project published records and materials that will be a major focus of volume 3 of the series. I am so appreciative of the support of the Thurman Library Board, including Johnny Parham Jr. and Roger Eaton.

The Howard Thurman Papers Project Advisory Board comprises some of the nation's most outstanding scholars, public intellectuals, documentary editors, and religious leaders. Board members have served in numerous capacities during the last thirteen years as advisors, diplomats, fundraisers, supporters, and friends. Among those whom I count as dear friends and cherished colleagues, the late James Melvin Washington and the late Samuel DeWitt Proctor deserve a special place of memory and tribute.

Since its inception the Thurman Papers Project has attracted financial support from a variety of sources. With its start-up support and subsequent grants, the Lilly Endowment has contributed the largest percentage of this support. Special thanks to Craig Dykstra, vice-president of religion, the Reverend Jean Smith, religion program officer, and to Jacqui Burton, who served as our first program officer at Lilly. Craig and Jean deserve special acknowledgment for their patience and faith when it appeared that the work would be interminable. James Lewis of the Louisville Institute for the Study of Protestantism and American Culture deserves special recognition. In the fall of 1994, I received a grant from the Louisville Institute supporting a sabbatical leave to work exclusively on the project, and since the spring of 2005, I have been the recipient of a grant for the present work on the volumes. The National Historical Publications and Records Commission (NHPRC) has awarded the project consecutive annual grants for the years 1994 to the present. NHPRC program officer Timothy Connelly has been a steadfast supporter every step of the way. In July of 1994 we received a three-year grant from the Pew Charitable Trusts, which was renewed. Joel Carpenter, now of Calvin College, was a veritable *angelos* who intervened on our behalf at a very critical period in our early existence. Finally, the Henry Luce Foundation, then under the presidency of John Wesley Cook, provided much-needed support for editorial assistance from 1998 to 2000. Now under the leadership of Michael Gilligan and with the assistance of Lynn Szwaja, our program officer, the Luce Foundation has also given us much-needed support for the completion of the volumes. Since 2005, Rev. Baxter Wynn has given generously in support of our undergraduate research assistants and interns.

The project has had two institutional homes, which also served as Thurman's undergraduate and graduate alma maters. From 1991 through June 1998, the Thurman Papers Project was sponsored by Colgate Rochester Divinity School / Bexley Hall / Crozer Theological Seminary in Rochester, New York. This early period provided a rich historical heritage as backdrop for our beginnings. Having access to the archives of the American Baptist Historical Society, a Howard Thurman Listening Room, and one the largest theological libraries at the time (and which held Thurman's official seminary transcripts, records, and other pertinent historical materials) made Colgate Rochester Divinity School an ideal setting for the first phase of our work. During this period, the project shared a special relationship to the Special Collections at Boston University, renamed in 2003 the Howard Gottlieb Archival Research Center to honor its founder. Gottlieb, who passed away during the writing of these acknowledgments, and his entire staff provided assistance and granted access and authority to catalogue the bulk of the then yet unorganized papers. Catherine Tumber, the first associate editor of the project, and I worked closely with Margaret Goosetray, who was available with wit and skill to answer our questions and to provide guidance during this crucial stage of work. The late George Makechnie, founder of the Howard Thurman Center at Boston University and close friend of the Thurman family, was an advocate for our work within the university and beyond, always demanding that we not forget the dream of community.

The project moved to Morehouse College in 1998. It is most appropriate that the Thurman Project is based at Morehouse College. As with Rochester Theological Seminary, Thurman was one of Morehouse's most illustrious alumni. The college established one of the first Howard Thurman Listening Rooms and named one of its buildings in Thurman's honor. The remains of Thurman and Sue are interred within the Howard Thurman International Memorial outside of the Martin Luther King Jr. International Chapel on the Morehouse campus. After publication of the documentary edition, the Leadership Center, where the Thurman Project is housed, will allow students, educators, politicians, theologians, business leaders, and laypeople to have access to Thurman Papers Project research and will provide a central location to explore the application of Thurman's ideals to the challenges and issues that confront twenty-first-century leadership. In addition, the Howard Thurman Educational Trust has been transferred from San Francisco to Morehouse College and will provide an excellent home for the ongoing legacy of Dr. Thurman.

Morehouse College has committed numerous resources to the Thurman Papers Project's in-kind support. The college is providing office space for the Thurman Papers Project free of charge and has committed its development and human-resources offices to the needs of the Thurman Papers Project. My special thanks to President Robert M. Franklin, former president Walter E. Massey, Willis B. Sheftall, Lawrence Edward Carter Sr., and Otis Moss Jr. for their support and faith in the dream of common ground that has inspired generations of Morehouse men and women and will continue to do so through the ongoing education, research, publication, and training that this project has produced. The Morehouse archives contain a wealth of Thurman-related documentary material, including the papers of Benjamin E. Mays, John Hope, and Martin Luther King Jr. I am tremendously indebted to Morehouse archivist Herman "Skip" Mason for his help with answering questions related to Thurman's student and teaching years at Morehouse that were critical to the completion of this first volume. On many questions related to deceased alumni, Henry Goodgame, director of alumni relations, as well as staff members Charles Fisher and Marilyn Bibby, were invaluable resources.

In 2000–2001 Morehouse College granted me part-time leave to teach courses and to conduct research at Harvard Divinity School and the Center for Public Leadership at the John F. Kennedy School of Government. Special thanks are extended to Professor David Gergen at the Center for Public Leadership, where Thurman's insights provided a critical resource for my work on ethical leadership, and to Preston Williams, whose invitation to come to the divinity school and to the wonderful students whose genuine interest in Thurman made my stay all the more exciting and enriching, I extend my heartfelt thanks. From 2004–5, I was fortunate to serve as a visiting scholar at Princeton Theological Seminary, where I conducted research and editorial review of this volume. My special thanks to Professors Peter J. Paris and Albert Raboteau, members of the Project's Advisory Board, who provided occasional opportunities to meet and discuss my research and editing for this volume. From 2003 to 2006, I served as visiting scholar at the Columbia Theological Seminary in Decatur, Georgia. The seminary generously provided office space, library privileges, and a wonderful staff that made our many and sometimes seemingly impossible tasks possible. Special thanks to former president Laura S. Mendenhall, D. Cameron Murchison, dean of faculty and executive vice-president, Tim Browning, Robert Thomson, Randall Tyndall, and Kim LeVert.

Over the years, we have maintained a supportive relationship with the publisher of our edition, the University of South Carolina Press. Barry Blose, our first acquisitions editor, was instrumental in helping us to craft the scope and content of the edition. It has been a pleasure working with all of the press staff members, including Curtis Clark, Jim Denton, and Linda Haines Fogle, as well as the copyeditor, Mary Lou Kawaleski.

Our success as a documentary editing project is measured not only by the publication of these volumes of Thurman's collected works but also by the tireless efforts and uncompromising commitment to intellectual integrity of the team of editors who have guided its work. Among these, I am honored to acknowledge Catherine Tumber, the first associate editor of the project, who anchored our work in Rochester. We devoted a great deal of time in the first several years of the project to the archival arrangement, description, and preservation of Thurman's papers. Until 1994, the collection was divided. Boston University has been in possession of approximately two-thirds of the papers since 1984. At Boston University, Catherine arranged all of this material into series of writings, correspondence, and subject files, and wrote a thirty-page inventory for the 1984 gift. The rest of the material remained with the Thurman family in San Francisco until January 1994 when most of it was given to Boston University. Catherine also arranged for the donation of Sue Bailey Thurman's papers to Boston University and completed the work of processing them. During her tenure, the project researched and copied documents from most of the major collections we consulted. Catherine and I also coedited a commercial trade volume, *A Strange Freedom: The Best of Howard Thurman on Religious Experience and Public Life,* published by Beacon Press in July 1998. Martin E. Marty, renowned historian of American religion, wrote the foreword.

Kai Jackson Issa, who now serves as the project's managing editor and associate director, has lifted our present phase of the work into a new orbit. Since 2003, Kai has not only provided the bulk of the editorial work on the volumes but also has managed the day-to-day operations of the project with astounding success. Her background in cultural studies, feminist thought, and institutional development and her gifted literary expression combine to offer a distinctive angle of vision. Given the increasing demands of the project and its strategic role in the development of the Leadership Center at Morehouse College, Kai's contributions have been more than remarkable.

I cannot say enough for the meticulous care and attention to detail that all the editors of this volume have provided. Quinton Dixie and Peter Eisenstadt have been with the project since its early years in Rochester. These extraordinarily talented and faithful colleagues deserve star billing. Quinton's passion for research and accuracy and his profound knowledge of the history of the black church were distinctive contributions to the volume. Peter's fine historical eye and relentless pursuit of the facts surrounding Thurman's student papers and the India Delegation were extraordinary. Luther Smith, my longtime colleague and friend, serves as senior advisory editor of the volumes. Luther's germinal work, *Howard Thurman: The Mystic as Prophet,* remains the authoritative text on Thurman's thought. Beyond his voluminous commentaries on documents collected for this series, his graceful spirit and generous wisdom guide us beyond the immediate tasks to the larger reason to which we devote our energies and skills.

Since the project's early years in Rochester, producer and documentary film-maker Arleigh Prelow has played a leading role in the collection and digital prepa-ration of Thurman photographs that appear in the volumes. Her upcoming feature-length film on Howard Thurman is a culmination of years of research of archives and stock footage housed throughout the U.S. and the world.

I am very grateful to key Atlanta institutions and partners that assisted us in our work for this volume. The Robert W. Woodruff Library, which serves the Atlanta University consortium of institutions, including Morehouse, deserves special recognition. Heartfelt thanks go out to library C.E.O. Loretta Parham, and head of archives and special collections Karen Jefferson, for their years of unwavering support. I am also grateful to Taronda Spencer (Spelman College), Brenda S. Banks (Georgia Archives), and Randall K. Burkett (Emory Univer-sity). Other institutions, archives, libraries and individuals that were instru-mental in assisting our work include Clifford Muse and Jo-Ellen El-Bashir (Moorland-Spingarn Research Center); Barbara Porter (Abingdon Press); Betty Layton (American Baptist Historical Society); Betty Clements (Claremont School of Theology); Margaret Nead (Colgate Rochester Crozer Divinity School); Donzella Maupin (Hampton University Archives); Haverford College Archives; Allen Borque (Harvard Cabot Library); Ken Grossi (Oberlin College Archives); Rev. Graylan Scott Hagler (Plymouth Congregational United Church of Christ, Washington, D.C.); Diana Lachatanere (Schomburg Center for Research in Black Culture); Carolyn Baker (Shaw University Archives); Mary Beth Sigado (Swarthmore Peace Collection); Union Theological Seminary Archives; the University of Massachusetts; Martha Lund Smalley (Yale University Library); and Dagmar Getz (YMCA Archives, University of Minnesota).

The process of securing legal permissions to publish involved tracking down the surviving heirs for individuals long deceased, and I am indebted to permis-sions coordinator Michelle Meggs for spearheading this effort. While arduous, our permissions work gave us a wonderful opportunity to connect with the family members of Howard Thurman's various associates, all of whom expressed enthusiastic support of the project. I am greatly appreciative to Frank Courtright, Karl Drake, Helen S. Horn, Nancy Kester-Neale, Converse Hunter, H. Christo-pher Luce, Bernice Mays-Perkins, Christopher Niebuhr, Karen Day Selsey, and Hugh Van Dusen.

A host of others have made invaluable contributions along the way. Mentors and friends such as James H. Cone, Dwight Hopkins, Edward Kaplan, James Earl Massey, Cornel West, and David Wills at various stages of the development of the project found ways to encourage our work. JoAnn Lahmon and Martha Wiggins assisted in the transition to Morehouse College and restructured the strategic processes of the project in its new home. Other editors who have worked with project over time include: Carolyn Denard, Laura-Eve Moss,

Clarissa Myrick Harris, and Alton Pollard. Special thanks to Michael Joseph Brown, Christopher H. Evans, Sudarshan Kapur, and Ralph E. Luker, who provided their expertise in difficult sections of consultation on these volumes. We are indebted to Marc Korpus for designing the "Journey of the Negro Delegation in South Asia" map that accompanies the India, Burma, and Ceylon section. I deeply appreciate all of the dedication and hard work of our research associates: Jamison Collier, for his technological and research expertise, Tami Groves, for her careful genealogical research, LeRhonda Manigault, Josiah Robinson, and Reginald Williams, for stellar research overall, as well as Lauren Frazier, Jacqueline Forbes, Carey Gifford, Marquis Hwang, Yantee Neufville, and Warren Watson; Morehouse research assistants Malcolm Gossett, Brandon Jackson, and Nathaniel Johnson; and staff members LaKetha Hudson, J. Alisa James, Michael Sauter, Joyce Sheffield, and Ruby Williams.

Finally, I would like to thank my family. My late father-in-law, Melvin Hampton Watson, and my late mother-in-law, Agnes Regina Watson, were close personal friends of the Thurmans. Dating back to his student days at Morehouse College, my father-in-law was a protégé of Howard Thurman. Their special relationship extended beyond Morehouse to Howard University and later to San Francisco, where Dr. Watson lived with the Thurmans while completing his doctoral studies. I owe special thanks to the Thurmans for introducing the Watsons, who made it possible for me to meet the most important person in my life, Sharon Watson Fluker. Her support of my work in these volumes and her love have been the steadying forces in the long days and nights when I was unsure that it would all come to pass. Sharon and our two sons, Clinton Rahman and Hampton Sterling, have given more to me than I can ever express in words alone.

WALTER EARL FLUKER, SENIOR EDITOR

LIST OF ABBREVIATIONS

The following abbreviations describe original documents, and the acronyms describe the locations of documents or are organizations.

COLLECTIONS AND REPOSITORIES

BTP-GEU	Bailey-Thurman Family Papers, Emory University Special Collections, Atlanta, Ga.
DAF-GAS	Deceased Alumni Files, Spelman College, Atlanta, Ga.
MWJ-DHU-MS	Howard University, Moorland-Spingarn Research Center, Washington, D.C.
HTC-MBU	Howard Thurman Collection, Boston University, Boston, Mass.
HTPP	Howard Thurman Papers Project, Morehouse College, Atlanta, Ga.
JLH-GAU	John and Lugenia Hope Collection, Woodruff Library, Atlanta University Center, Atlanta, Ga.
RB-NN-SC	Ralph Bunche Papers, Schomburg Center for Research on Black Culture, New York Public Library, New York, N.Y.
RJ-PHC	Rufus Jones Collection, Haverford College, Haverford, Pa.
LAF-OO	Student Leadership Alumni Files, Oberlin College, Oberlin, Ohio
WEBD-MU	W. E. B. Du Bois Collection, University of Massachusetts, Amherst, Mass.

ABBREVIATIONS USED IN SOURCE NOTES

Format

A Autograph (manuscript in author's hand)
H Handwritten (manuscript in hand other than author's)
P Printed
T Typed

Type	*Version*	*Signature*
L Letter/memo	c Copy (carbon)	I Initialed
At Audio tape	d Draft	S Signed
D Document	f Fragment	Sr Signed with representation of
Fm Form		author
f Fragment		

Graduation photograph, Florida Normal and Industrial Institute, May 1919. Courtesy of the Thurman family and Arleigh Prelow/Howard Thurman Film Project

Biographical Essay

Howard Washington Thurman was born on November 18, 1899, the second child and only son of Alice (Ambrose) and Saul Solomon Thurman. He spent his childhood from early infancy in Daytona, Florida, but he was probably born in West Palm Beach, Florida, where he was living in June 1900 when U.S. census enumerators recorded his family, consisting of himself, his older sister Henrietta, then three years old, and his Florida-born parents, Alice, born in July 1872, and Saul Solomon, born in July 1850.[1] At the time of the census, Alice, born in July 1872, was twenty-seven years old, and Henrietta was three. Saul Solomon was listed as a laborer, working on the Florida East Coast Railroad.[2] According to the 1880 census, Saul Solomon was born in Florida in July 1850, making it likely that he had spent his early years enslaved, which Thurman never made mention of in any public accounts of his father's life.

While Thurman perhaps knew little of his father's early experiences, he grew up in a community where the vast majority of the older residents (that is, almost everyone over the age of thirty-five when he was born) would have spent time in bondage, and he was profoundly shaped by the experience of American slavery through the witness and influence of his maternal grandmother Nancy Ambrose, who lived in Daytona with Thurman, his mother, and sisters for most of his early life. Known as "Lady Nancy" by her neighbors, she was a well-respected midwife in the community who also worked as a laundress. Grandma Nancy was the dominant person in young Thurman's life, and he fondly remembered her in his 1979 autobiography as "the anchor person in our family" and one who was "fearless" and "embraced life with zest."[3] The 1880 census indicates that Nancy Ambrose was born in 1842 or 1843 in or about the town of Moseley Hall, a community in Madison County, Florida near the Georgia border.[4] Her husband, Howard Ambrose, for whom Howard Thurman was named, was eighteen years older than his wife and had died long before his grandson was born.[5] According to the census records, Nancy and Howard Ambrose were farming land in Moseley Hall. They had eight children, ranging from Sarah, aged sixteen, born before emancipation, to Emily, aged two months. Thurman's mother, Alice, was eight years old at that time.[6]

Madison County before the Civil War was classic plantation country, with a cotton economy dominated by middle-sized and large estates. Nancy almost

Nancy Ambrose, circa 1930. Courtesy
of the Thurman family and Arleigh
Prelow/Howard Thurman Film
Project

certainly spent her youth on the plantation owned by John C. McGhee, who by
the eve of the Civil War was the second-largest slaveholder in Madison County.
His personal estate was valued at $70,000 and encompassed ninety-nine
enslaved women, men, and children, including an eighteen-year-old girl who
fits the description of Thurman's grandmother Nancy.[7]

Nancy Ambrose's roots were in South Carolina, the birthplace of both her
parents and her husband.[8] According to Howard, she had some Seminole
ancestry (*WHAH,* 13).[9] During the pre–Civil War period, large numbers of
South Carolinians, slave owners and their slaves, had moved to Madison
County. In 1850, two-thirds of the thirty-three large planters in the county
were from South Carolina.[10] South Carolina's black population, because of its
large number and a surge of slave arrivals just prior to the ending of legal
importation, had a distinctive culture, heavily influenced by African culture
and religion.[11]

Thurman wrote in his autobiography that his grandmother spoke very little
of her experience as a slave. Every year in late summer Thurman would accompany Nancy in what he called "Grandma's pilgrimage" to visit her eldest daughter, Mary, in Madison County, where the citified Thurman would enjoy exotic

feasts of gopher, coon, and possum. Thurman wrote that although this was in the vicinity of the slave plantation of his grandmother's youth, "She never spoke of it; she did not point out landmarks. . . . She granted to no one the rights of passage across her own remembered footsteps" (*WHAH*, 231–32).

Her general reticence to speak about her early life made the rare exceptions all the more memorable to her grandson. One story of her childhood that Nancy Ambrose often told her grandson was the rare visit to her plantation by a black preacher who had a different style and message than the usual fare on Sunday of exhortations to docility and obedience delivered by white ministers. At the end of his long sermon, during which he would energetically reenact the Passion of Jesus, he would directly address the congregation, telling them, "You are not niggers! You are not slaves! You are God's children!" (*WHAH*, 20–21). Thurman related that his grandmother did not permit him to read to her from the Pauline epistles because of Paul's notorious injunction for slaves to be obedient to their masters. Thurman's critique of the political complacency of Paul would be a major theme in his pivotal 1949 work, *Jesus and the Disinherited.*

Thurman learned an entirely different lesson about religion from his father, Saul Solomon, whom he remembered as a large, robust man. On his father's sojourns to Daytona after spending weeks away from his family laying railroad track, he would always stop in a local barbershop for a haircut and shave before returning home. Saul was an independent thinker who was suspicious of organized religion and whose limited collection of books included the works of the nineteenth-century American agnostic Robert Ingersoll.

In 1907, when Howard was seven years old, Saul Thurman died of pneumonia. On 5 August 1908, Thurman's younger sister, Madaline Mae, was born. In this difficult period and throughout Madaline's childhood, Thurman was charged with her care: "I could always calm Madaline in her distress, help her to sleep when she was restless. I combed and braided her hair, changed her clothes, and served in general as her nursemaid" (*WHAH*, 253). Thurman never minded the arrangement, and throughout his lifetime they would share a close relationship. Madaline, an accomplished pianist who earned a degree from the Oberlin Conservatory, would contribute to the care of Thurman's two daughters during his years at Howard University.

After Saul's death, Thurman's mother, Alice, whom he described as a quiet, devoutly Christian woman, went to work as a domestic for a white family in downtown Daytona. The work required her to be away from her children for long periods of time, and Thurman remembers that it was rare when she could enjoy a Sunday with her family. Shortly after Saul's death, Alice married Alex Evans, who was a skilled machinist in a sawmill in Lake Helen, Florida.[12] The family enjoyed some measure of material comfort and stability, residing in a small house owned by the mill. After Evans's death in 1910 Thurman, his mother,

Alice Thurman Sams, circa 1940.
Courtesy of the Thurman family and
Arleigh Prelow/Howard Thurman
Film Project

and sisters had to return to the family home in Daytona. By 1914, Alice had
married James Sams, her third and final husband. Thurman remembered his
mother as one who possessed "a deep inner sadness that I could not, as a boy,
understand" (*WHAH*, 12). A pivotal moment occurred in his childhood when
the depth of her faith was revealed to him. He recalled looking up into his
mother's face as they watched the wonder of Halley's Comet's appearance in
1910. Though he was fearful that the comet would drop out of the sky, his mother
assured him, "Nothing will happen to us, Howard. God will take care of us"
(*WHAH*, 15–16).

Saul's death, which Howard witnessed while standing at his father's bed-
side, was devastating and traumatic for Thurman. In *Footprints of a Dream*,
another memoir, he recalls his father "was the first person I had ever seen die.
. . . His magnificent chest showed the pressure from his lungs, as he fought for
air. Up from his throat came the guttural noises which in our community was
called the 'death rattle.' At length my mother said, 'Saul, can you hear me?' He
nodded his head. Continuing, she said, 'Are you ready to die?' With an effort
supreme, he said, "All my life I have been a man, I am not afraid of death, Alice.
I can stand it" (*Footprints*, 15).

Thurman's mother and grandmother were members of Mount Bethel Baptist Church, located in the Daytona neighborhood of Waycross, one of the two
black churches there, the other being Mount Zion African Methodist Episcopal

Thurman and unidentified young
women, circa 1918. Courtesy of the
Thurman family and Arleigh Prelow/
Howard Thurman Film Project

(AME). Because Saul was not a member of any church, many did not regard him a Christian, and the family's pastor refused to consent to hold his funeral service at their church. It was only at the insistence of Thurman's grandmother, who made an appeal to the deacons' board, that the family received permission to use the church for the funeral service. A traveling evangelist, Reverend Sam Cromarte, preached Saul's funeral and seized the opportunity as an occasion to illustrate the fate of those who died "outside of Christ." Thurman says, "I listened with wonderment, then anger, and finally mounting rage as Sam Cromarte preached my father into hell" (*WHAH, 6*).

Thurman's revulsion at the church's treatment of his father led to a lifelong skepticism of dogmatic religious claims and a rejection of the narrow definition of righteousness and salvation in organized religion. After his father's death, Thurman swore that he would never have anything to do with the church. But the examples of his grandmother's and mother's faith proved too great, and at twelve years old, he joined Mount Bethel. In the church, Thurman found a context through which he could pursue and actualize what he would later call "the hunger of the heart,"[14] which he would always balance against his father's skepticism and his own determination to be true to his experience against the claims and demands of external authority.

Thurman's independence was apparent from the beginning of his active religious life. The deacons of Mount Bethel Baptist Church refused to accept his membership because he had not recounted, to their satisfaction, his conversion experience, as was customary. But the deacons had not counted on Grandma Nancy. When Thurman went home to tell his grandmother of the deacons' rejection, she went right back to the meeting. As he remembered it, "She took me by the hand—I can still see her rocking along beside me—and together we went back to the meeting, arriving before they adjourned." She challenged the deacons, "How dare you turn this boy down? He is a Christian and was one long before he came to you today. Maybe you did not understand his words, but shame on you if you do not know his heart" (*WHAH*, 18). She demanded that her grandson be accepted for membership, and he was.

His grandmother's advocacy notwithstanding, Thurman's ambivalence with the church remained. Thurman wrote that his call to the ministry was mitigated by "a vague feeling that somehow I was violating my father's memory by taking leadership responsibility in an institution that had done violence to his spirit" (*Footprints*, 17). It was not until Thurman was a senior in college that he would resolve the uneasiness caused by this unsettling memory. A catharsis came unexpectedly after seeing the man who preached his father's funeral: "In some strange way this experience gave me my release" (*Footprints*, 18).

Whatever his unresolved doubts, Thurman's experience of baptism and later of discipline by a sponsor[15] in the church had an inestimable impact upon his sense of self by belonging to a community of people who cared for him. He explains the meaning of these early church experiences:

> In the fellowship of the church, particularly in the experience of worship, there was a feeling of sharing in primary community. Not only did church membership seem to bear heavily upon one's ultimate destiny beyond death and the grave; more than all the other communal ties, it also undergirded one's sense of personal identity. It was summed up in the familiar phrase, "If God is for you, who can prevail against you?" (*WHAH*, 17)

Church membership was particularly important to an adolescent as shy and awkward as the young Thurman, who, by his own estimate, was somewhat overweight, pigeon-toed, and ungainly: "My company was not welcomed by girls nor by the boys in choosing sides for games." Living in a household of women, he acutely felt the absence of a father or elder brother as a defender. "I was ever haunted," he later wrote, "by a feeling of awkwardness in all my relationships, I felt clumsy. As I walked, it was as if my feet felt fearful of being together." There was possibly an additional, deeply private source of Thurman's unease—rumors that Saul was not his biological father. Thurman never alluded to these rumors, although interviews with surviving family members in Arleigh Prelow's documentary film *Howard Thurman: In Search of Common Ground* suggest that Thurman was aware of the conjectures and intimations surrounding his father.[16]

As a loner Thurman's personal difficulties experienced in his early childhood contributed greatly to his close identification with nature and his need to develop his inner world. Young Howard was a keen observer of nature and the ways in which his natural surroundings spoke to a mystery beyond what he experienced in his tightly segregated community and the formal religious settings of the church. In speaking of the assurance and immunity that his companions from nature offered him, Thurman said in his autobiography, "I felt rooted in life, in nature, in existence" (*WHAH*, 8).[17] Of particular prominence was a huge oak tree in his backyard, which he referred to in later life as his "windbreak against existence."[18] He yearned for the self-sustaining autonomy that would allow him to remain resilient and firm in the face of adversity meted out triplefold in his shifting family circumstances, a hostile racist environment, and his personal quest for identity and become, in the words of one of his favorite biblical passages, "like a tree planted by the waters."[19]

Daytona, Florida, founded as late as 1876, saw its population increase from 300 in 1880 to 3,572 by 1910, with over half of the population being African Americans.[20] The circumstances of the Ambrose family's migration from Madison County to Daytona are unknown, but they were following a well-trod path. The growing citrus industry lured many to the area. The opening of the Florida East Coast Railroad around the turn of the twentieth century further accelerated the economic growth of Daytona, which, in addition to its agricultural output, became increasingly popular as a winter resort.[21]

Thurman grew up in Waycross, one of the three all-black communities in Daytona, the other two being Newton and Midway. He and his family lived in a small, two-story clapboard house at 516 Whitehall Street.[22] Thurman recalled that the people of Waycross transcended racial segregation and poverty through caring and sharing in community. He described his neighborhood as an "extended family,"[23] where all children were under the general supervision of the adults. A large population of black homeowners resided in Waycross, and there were a handful of thriving black businesses, as well as professionals such as doctors and teachers in the community. The Florida East Coast Railroad ran down the middle of Waycross, with the community's two churches, Mount Bethel Baptist and Mount Zion AME, on opposite sides of the tracks. A Daytona directory of 1900 includes the following positive, if somewhat paternalistic, portrait of the town's black community:

Here we see colored men, women and children at every step decently clad, healthy in look and well behaved. Within a mile are their houses on the west side of the railroad, Midway and Waycross, both promising settlements. Midway is quite a new settlement, having a good church building, etc. Waycross has a population of 300, two good, large well built nurseries, a public school and kindergarten, drug store, grocery store, Masonic and Odd Fellows lodge. . . . There is abundant proof that it is a fairly industrious population, self-supporting.[24]

One factor that probably attracted blacks to the area was that, for a small southern town at the height of the Jim Crow era, Daytona had a record of relatively moderate race relations. The first sustained settlement in the area was a freedman's colony set up by an abolitionist ex-Union officer in 1866. This failed, but a substantial African American population was in the area when Daytona was incorporated in 1876, and most of the founders were from the north. The racial climate was further influenced by the presence of the wealthy white northern "snowbirds" who resided in Daytona Beach during the winter months and were a main driver in the local economy. Among this group of northern residents was James Gamble, a millionaire entrepreneur (of Procter and Gamble fame), who would provide financial support to Thurman throughout his high school and college career. Many northern whites played a prominent role in Daytona's civic and cultural affairs. Northern women founded the Palmetto Club, a civic and philanthropic women's group that established a kindergarten for black children, which Thurman attended. As Thurman wrote, "The tempering influence of these northern families made contact between the races less abrasive than it might have been otherwise" (WHAH, 9).

From Daytona's founding, African Americans were able to vote and wield influence in local elections in the city. A black barber was elected to the Daytona City Council in 1898, the year before Thurman was born. The city administration was usually attentive to requests by black constituents for improvements to their neighborhoods. By 1905, both Waycross and Midway had black police officers. The city built new school buildings, cement sidewalks, and storm sewers in the black neighborhoods. Blacks played an important role in forcing a retreat of the Ku Klux Klan from Daytona politics, and black support was crucial to the success of Edward H. Armstrong, mayor of Daytona Beach from 1927 to 1938. As late as 1940, Ralph Bunche, in *The Political Status of the Negro in the Age of F.D.R.,* reported that Daytona Beach was the only large city in Florida with effective black voting.[25]

Despite some liberal voting policies and politics, the Daytona of Thurman's early years was a Jim Crow town in the deep south, with the schools separate and unequal, restricted areas, and the full regimen of racial segregation and discrimination. As it grew in size in Thurman's youth, Daytona became more hostile and restrictive to blacks. This was in part because of an influx of white southerners who came to outnumber the northern white founders of Daytona. The newcomers were largely successful in their efforts to make Daytona comport more fully with southern mores on segregation. One observer remembered that between 1902 and 1906, "colored" and "white" signs were erected in Daytona.[26] Thurman's autobiography places the change somewhat later but with the same trajectory:

> Daytona Beach (not Daytona itself) and Sea Breeze were exclusive tourist areas, located across the Halifax River from Daytona. I could work in Sea Breeze and Daytona Beach, but I was not allowed to spend the night there, nor could I be seen there after dark without being threatened. During those years, we were permitted to enjoy the beaches and to swim in the ocean—even these were later to be limited to whites only—but these areas were absolutely off limits after dark.
>
> The white community in Daytona itself was "downtown," no place for loitering. Our freedom of movement was carefully circumscribed, a fact so accepted that it was taken for granted. . . . Thus, white and black worlds were separated by a wall of quiet hostility and overt suspicion. (*WHAH,* 10)

Thurman's boyhood in Daytona taught him many lessons, most obviously the meaning of growing up poor and black in a profoundly unequal and segregated society. But there were deeply affirming lessons as well. Blacks in Daytona were not prostrate but participated in the political and civic society on their own terms. There were examples for Thurman, female as well as male, of successful, educated blacks achieving success within the broader society outside of Waycross without abasing themselves before whites and while remaining true to their own heritage.

Of his role models, possibly none was as important or enduring as Mary McLeod Bethune, founder of the Daytona Educational and Industrial Training School for Girls.[27] Bethune founded the school in 1904 with five students under the most humble circumstances, with supplies she scavenged from the city dump, groceries donated from neighbors, and proceeds garnered from selling her sweet potato pies. Thurman was aware of her struggles in starting the school and knew of her unrelenting faith that enabled her to realize the vision of creating a center of quality education for young Negro women in the south. Many of the city's wealthy winter residents regularly visited the school and became key contributors. Thurman recalled hearing of her trials and victories when Bethune spoke at her Sunday-afternoon temperance meetings attended by whites and blacks: "The very presence of the school, and the inner strength and authority of Mrs. Bethune, gave boys like me a view of possibilities to be realized in some distant future" (*WHAH,* 23).

Thurman considered Bethune a family friend—she and his mother were acquainted—and from this beginning, Thurman developed a lifelong friendship with the educational leader. Thurman's second wife, Sue Bailey Thurman, would become the first editor of *The Aframerican Woman's Journal,* the official publication of the National Council of Negro Women, founded by Bethune in 1935. In 1955, he would deliver the eulogy at her funeral, remarking, "Her life was involved with my own life as long as I can remember my own life."[28]

Outside his family context and Bethune's stellar example of leadership, two individuals in Daytona's black community served as important models for Thurman during his early years. Thornton L. Smith, Thurman's cousin, who had been a baseball player in the Negro Leagues, was an independent businessman and community leader who owned and operated a confectionary and sub-post office.[29] According to Thurman, Smith was "his own man," one who had played an instrumental role in defeating the Ku Klux Klan's control of the city of Daytona in the early 1920s. John T. Stocking, one of the few African American physicians in Daytona, treated both black and white patients, including Thurman's family. Significantly, Stocking refused to join either of the black churches in Waycross, much to the community's disapproval. He encouraged Thurman in the advancement of his education and urged him to pursue medical training. Thurman refers to both Smith and Stocking as his "masculine idols in those early years" (*WHAH,* 21).

Education was the chosen way to advance in the world for Thurman. If this fit in with the dominant theories of black uplift, it also came from a deeply personal source. His grandmother Nancy, illiterate all of her life, had a great appreciation for education. Like many who were enslaved, the denial of education to her as a young girl made her realize that her lack of education was another tool of oppression and sign of her bondage. She told her grandson that when she was enslaved, the daughter of her mistress tried to teach her to read. When the mistress discovered this, the little girl was chastised and sent to bed without supper. Nancy Ambrose believed all her life that there was something "magical" and profoundly transformative about education. Thurman's formal education began with Julia Green, teacher of the local kindergarten donated by the Palmetto Club. Afterwards, Thurman attended the only local black public school, which was in Newton and extended only to the seventh grade. In his autobiography, Thurman states that he was the first African American to matriculate beyond this social restraint and that his principal, R. H. Howard, volunteered to teach him the eighth grade. Thurman excelled in school despite the strains of having to help his mother financially support their family, which included working in a fish market. The stress of maintaining a grueling schedule of work while pursuing his education would manifest in bouts of physical and emotional breakdown, and this pattern of work and exhaustion recurred throughout his career. Thurman completed his grammar-school education with an average in the high 90s,[30] receiving the first certificate of promotion given to an African American in his county. Shortly after his promotion, Thurman states in his autobiography, an eighth-grade level was added to the public school (*WHAH*, 13–14).

Upon his graduation from the eighth grade, Thurman was accepted at the Florida Baptist Academy in Jacksonville, one hundred miles north of Daytona, one of only three high schools for African Americans in the state at that time.[31] Thurman recalls that with very little money and his few personal possessions packed in a ragged trunk, he boarded a train for Jacksonville. He relates a poignant moment of being helped by an unknown man at the train station on his way to school, when he did not have enough fare to send his trunk:

> I sat down on the steps of the railway station and cried my heart out. Presently I opened my eyes and saw before me a large pair of work shoes. My eyes crawled upward until I saw the man's face. He was a black man, dressed in overalls and a denim cap. As he looked down at me he rolled a cigarette and lit it. Then he said, "Boy, what in hell are you crying about?"
>
> And I told him.
>
> "If you're trying to get out of this damn town to get an education, the least I can do is to help you. Come with me," he said. (*WHAH*, 24)

After leaving that day for Jacksonville to pursue his education, Thurman would never again live in Daytona for any extended period of time, but it was nevertheless a place where he would periodically return throughout his career, often at his friend Mary McLeod Bethune's invitation to speak at her college. In 1963, Thurman returned to Daytona Beach when the mayor declared a "Howard Thurman Day" and presented him with the keys to the city: "The fourteen year old boy whose broken dream was restored at that station some fifty years before returned with his family to receive the keys to the city. A brass band came out to meet us, and many friends from surrounding cities and the community of Bethune Cookman College attended the gala reception that evening, among them my kindergarten teacher."[32]

Thurman proved to be a brilliant student at the Florida Baptist Academy, earning grades in the high 90s.[33] The school's rigorous curriculum included three years of Latin and one year of Greek. Thurman also was developing into an outstanding youth leader, serving as president of his school's YMCA branch in 1917, his sophomore year. During the summer of 1917, while he was in Jacksonville working as a substitute bookkeeper at Florida Baptist, tragedy struck when his older sister, Henrietta, died from typhoid fever. Due to their age difference and Henrietta's regard for him as the "little brother," they had never been close, Thurman recalls. She was, by his account, a gifted pianist and artist, and she had also left home to pursue further study.[34] At the time of her death, she

Thurman (seated in front to the far right) and other participants in the YMCA Student Conference, Kings Mountain, North Carolina, summer 1918. Courtesy of the Thurman family and Arleigh Prelow/Howard Thurman Film Project

was nineteen years old and married to a man whom Thurman had never met. On the day of her death, Thurman recalls, he had an overwhelming impulse to pray. While in prayer, his vision of Henrietta's suffering moved him to tears, and soon after his meditative moment, a messenger knocked on his door to deliver a telegram from his mother informing him of Henrietta's dire condition. By the time he arrived in Daytona, she had died (*WHAH,* 254). Thurman speculated that his occasional, yet powerful, clairvoyant experiences may have had some connection to his being born with a "veil"—remnants of amniotic film over the infant's face—a sign in African American folk belief that the individual would be endowed with the ability to tell the future. As a result, Thurman's ears were pierced at birth, for, "No parent wanted a child so endowed. It spelled danger and grief. If the ears were pierced, however, the power of the gift would be dissipated. How deeply I was influenced by this 'superstition' I do not know" (*WHAH,* 263).

In 1918, Thurman's senior year, Florida Baptist Academy moved to a 114-acre, former plantation property in Saint Augustine, Florida, and changed its name to Florida Normal and Industrial Institute. That summer, Thurman represented his high school at a student army training corps sponsored by the U.S. government at Howard University in Washington, D.C. The purpose of the corps was to train a select number of young black men to qualify for positions as noncommissioned officers. In 1940 Thurman would write in his essay "A 'Native Son' Speaks" that it was only in World War I that blacks first became aware of their American citizenship, and for "one breathless, swirling moment he became conscious of being a part and parcel of the very core of the nation.[35] How Thurman felt about his military training at Howard is uncertain, but he took it and the attendant responsibilities very seriously. In his autobiography, Thurman relates that after returning from Howard, his duties at Florida Industrial were equivalent to the dean of men, and he had to supervise the dormitory and was able to study only after lights out at 10 p.m.

Thurman's academic career at Florida Baptist was characterized by a drive and ambition to succeed to the point of physical and mental exhaustion. In the letter introducing himself to Mordecai Wyatt Johnson, Thurman wrote proudly of his grades (99 percent in grammar school and averages of $95\frac{2}{5}$ percent, 98 percent, and $94\frac{2}{5}$ percent at the Florida Baptist Academy), the various part-time jobs he worked to earn his tuition and living expenses (pressing clothes, working in a bakery), and having to walk five miles a day to and from school.[36] His sterling grades exacted a physical price. In his autobiography, Thurman writes that he became valedictorian, carrying an extra course load by dint of staying up half the night studying. During his graduation reception he collapsed while giving a speech, and though he stayed to deliver the valedictory address, his mother insisted that he return home to Daytona for recuperation. A week after graduation he wrote to his high-school English teacher Ethel Simons, whom Thurman credits with nurturing in him an appreciation of literature and poetry and "a feeling for the poetic line."[37] In the letter, he told her that his doctor had diagnosed him with high blood pressure and that he had accumulated a "big big bill to Dr. Sleep."[38] Thurman rested at home for a few weeks and returned to Jacksonville to work in a bakery in order to earn enough to attend Morehouse College in Atlanta, Georgia, in the fall.

There was a very good reason for Thurman's striving for academic success. The valedictorian from a Baptist secondary school received a partial scholarship to Morehouse. Without this assistance, Thurman would not have been able to go to high school or college, because, as he wrote to Johnson in 1918, his mother, with other children to provide for, was only able to provide "her prayers." Thurman continued his determined quest for academic attainment at Morehouse, winning an academic scholarship in each of his years in college.

Thurman's tenure at Morehouse from 1919 to 1923 marked a crucial period in his intellectual, aesthetic, and spiritual development. His four years at Morehouse represent his introduction into a new world of ideas that would whet his intellectual appetite and encourage him to pursue higher learning beyond the limited expectations imposed by the greater society. The college's rich fraternal atmosphere and

Thurman and Morehouse
friends, circa 1922.
Courtesy of the Thurman
family and Arleigh Prelow/
Howard Thurman Film
Project

the stimulating intellectual climate found a willing and enthusiastic participant in the searching spirit of the young poet, scholar, and preacher, who in his senior yearbook profile used the words from Shakespeare's famous love poems to describe himself, *"A spirit all compact of fire,* not gross to sink but light and will aspire."[39]

Thurman attended Morehouse during the presidential tenure of Dr. John Hope, the first African American president of the institution. The college has a long, distinguished history of developing African American men into leaders. Founded in 1867 as the Augusta Institute in the basement of the Springfield Baptist Church in Augusta, Georgia, the oldest independent African American church in the United States, its primary mission was to prepare black men for ministry and teaching.[40] Hope, who served as president from 1906 to 1931, was a Phi Beta Kappa graduate of Brown University and encouraged an intellectual climate comparable to what he had known at his alma mater. "His Phi Beta Kappa key, worn from a chain on his vest, was the first I had ever seen," Thurman recalls (*WHAH,* 35). In the dominant black educational debate of the era, between Booker T. Washington's view that education for African Americans should emphasize vocational and agricultural skills and W. E. B. Du Bois's insistence on academic education, Hope was firmly on the side of the Du Boisians and worked throughout his presidential tenure to expand the college's academic offerings and increase its physical facilities.

Beyond the very practical reasons for his academic exertions in Florida and at Morehouse, Thurman was responding to a specific cultural and religious imperative that called on young blacks to push themselves to attain excellence within the academy. Black colleges in the early twentieth century were suffused with the broad but difficult task to define an ideological current that is usually called the "ideology of uplift," a set of ideas that suggest a certain degree of group responsibility for the social welfare of the entire race. Advocates of the ideology disagree to what extent it is a movement of the masses or a movement on behalf of the masses. The concept is most frequently associated with W. E. B. Du Bois's notion of the "talented tenth," meaning that as the elite class of the race climbs, it is able to lift the other classes from their lower moral, political, and economic status.[41] From the Reconstruction period through World War II, racial uplift was thought to be a way to ameliorate race relations because once white Americans realized that blacks were working to improve their own condition, there would be no reason to maintain their racist beliefs and practices.

The primary institutions for training race leaders were black colleges and universities. At institutions like Morehouse and Spelman colleges, young black students aspired for a way out of the social misery that was drowning the hopes of many of the race's young people. Even as these students, who like Thurman were the children and grandchildren of former slaves, sought new possibilities for themselves, they interpreted their acquisition of middle-class values and desires through the lens of racial advancement and social responsibility. All of this resulted in a "politics of respectability," which not only demanded that black elites play a critical role in the self-help efforts of the masses but also displayed a certain kind of class bias that betrayed the "civilizing effects" of higher education.[42]

Thurman is squarely located within this tradition of racial uplift. He was educated at institutions formed around the notion of a few high-achieving students gaining an education they could then share with the masses. Although Thurman did not come from a family of means, he believed that education was the way out of poverty. Efforts like his attempt to get Hope to establish a scholarship fund at Morehouse,[43] providing lodging and money for students while he taught at Howard, and his establishment of the Howard Thurman Educational Trust in his later years all are a part of Thurman's commitment to give back.

At Florida Baptist and again at Morehouse, uplift was translated into a combination of moral and intellectual seriousness, personal rectitude, and a religiously based commitment to service. Thurman had a profound sense of the obligation his education had created. As he writes in his autobiography, "I was profoundly affected by the sense of mission the college inculcated in us.... We were inspired to keep alive our responsibility to the many, many others who had not been fortunate." This idea is probably most clear in his Emancipation Day oration "Our Challenge," an interesting, though an intellectually and rhetorically immature effort, delivered in early 1922.[44]

Addressing the needs of racial advancement was not limited to his college oratory. Outside of his formal instruction in high school and college, no institution was more important to Thurman in his formative years than the YMCA. The YMCA provided an avenue for black leadership, for critical interracial contacts, and for connections to modern and international trends in Christian thought and practice. Thurman would remain close to the YMCA and its kindred and associated organizations through the time of the Negro Delegation to India in 1935–36. Although the YMCA sanctioned segregation within its organizations and failed to challenge the country's prevailing Jim Crow practices, it nevertheless provided a significant vehicle for African American leadership development in the early twentieth century. Historian Nina Mjagkij notes that YMCA associations served as "sanctuaries that preserved African-American manhood and prepared men and boys for their leadership in the struggle for equality."[45]

Through the end of World War I, black students participated in YMCA national events through the segregated Colored Work Department. The Kings Mountain Student Conference, first instituted in 1912, was among the largest and most celebrated of these events. Held in the summer at Lincoln Academy in Kings Mountain, North Carolina, the conference was a gathering of young men and faculties from black academies and colleges across the American south. The conference was intended "to promote a positive, aggressive and efficiently constructive religious leadership among the students in schools and colleges for the education of colored youth,"[46] and it provided a forum for the established and emerging black religious leadership of the early twentieth century to interact, discuss, and debate with a Christian emphasis the most pressing racial issues.

Thurman attended his first Kings Mountain conference in the summer of 1917 as a high-school sophomore. As president of the YMCA at Florida Baptist, he was undoubtedly among the youngest of the delegates present, the majority being college-aged students from such premier institutions as Morehouse, Tuskegee Institute, Talladega College, and Hampton Institute. By the following year, the conference had enlarged significantly, and its theme was driven by the moral and spiritual urgency of the World War. The conference bulletin stated that the events of the war "have repeatedly uncovered the presence of evil in our modern world—forces that make mockery of civilization by using its finest achievements as instruments for the destruction of humanity."[47] There were ten days of discussion and prayer with student leaders and contact with national and international leaders in Christian activist circles. The days were highly structured, with morning Bible study and classes such as "Social Service and Association Method" taught by Channing H. Tobias, international secretary of the YMCA. Thurman and Tobias would develop a lifelong personal and professional association. Significantly, the Kings Mountain Student Conference is where Thurman first met YMCA leader and field worker Max Yergan and where he no doubt heard about Yergan's travels to India and South Africa.

By far the person who made the biggest impact on Thurman at Kings Mountain was Mordecai Wyatt Johnson, the former student secretary of the international committee of the YMCA (a position he had resigned in protest against discrimination in the organization), and since 1917 minister at First Baptist Church in Charleston, West Virginia. Johnson was quickly developing a national reputation as one of Black America's most brilliant orators and religious leaders. As Thurman wrote in a 1918 letter, Johnson "made a deeper impression upon my life than any man at the Conference last year or this year."[48] Thurman found in Johnson a perfect model for his growing desire to pursue a career in the ministry. The two men had much in common and would follow a similar path.

The 18 June 1918 letter from Thurman to Johnson is the earliest document in the entire corpus of Thurman's papers. The letter reveals the yearnings and ambitions of Thurman, then a junior at Florida Baptist Academy, and his commitment to pursuing a religious life in service to others. Written during the same summer that he would undergo training for the student corps at Howard University, he expresses a reluctance to get drafted: "As you know, the war is on and young men are being snatched daily. I am patriotic; I am willing to fight for democracy, but my friend Rev. Johnson, *my people need me.*"[49] Given that sponsorship by a prominent individual was critical for one's advancement during the period, Thurman's contact with Johnson was key. Thurman begs for Johnson's mentorship: "Please take a personal interest in me and guide me and God will reward you." He pours out his heart in the letter, sharing his dreams of education, leadership, and his desire to minister, "Listen while I tell you my soul."

> I want to be a minister of the Gospel. I feel the needs of my people, I see their distressing condition, and have offered myself upon the altar as a living sacrifice, in order that I may help the "skinned and flung down" as you interpret. God wants me and His precious love urges me to take up the cross and follow Him.

Thurman was one of the many outstanding students to benefit from Johnson's personal tutelage. His reply to Thurman's heartfelt letter speaks volumes to the long and fruitful relationship they would share in the years to come as colleagues and as molders of a new generation of leaders of the race: "I am glad that my words at Kings Mountain influenced you for good. Such testimonies as yours are the most precious rewards of my work. May God bless you and make you His minister indeed!"[50]

Hope, another important mentor, had a reputation for ruling Morehouse with an iron fist, insisting that students live by the Morehouse code of behavior, which prohibited drinking, swearing, cardplaying, and interactions with women without a chaperone. Thurman credited Hope with the foresight to create an environment whereby young black men could experience themselves as human beings with dignity and worth and their minds as their own. Living amid an Atlanta that, as Thurman writes in his autobiography, denied "our manhood, and that of our fathers," he was very impressed by Hope's habit of addressing all Morehouse students as "young gentlemen," which did much to instill a strong sense of self-worth that set Morehouse men apart. Significantly, Hope instituted the requirement that a student compose and memorize an original oration before an audience of the entire student body and faculty for each of his four years. If a student forgot so much as a word of his oration, he was required to repeat the exercise until he delivered it perfectly. "We learned to think on our feet and extemporize," Thurman remembers, "Later, during my early post-graduate years, members of the audience would frequently come up to me after one of my talks to say, 'You're one of John Hope's men, aren't you?' The Morehouse training was unmistakable" (*WHAH*, 37).

Hope, along with Samuel Archer, academic dean of the college, filled the faculty of Morehouse with some of the brightest young talents in African American intellectual life, many just a few years older than Thurman and his classmates. Thurman credited Benjamin E. Mays with awakening in him an interest in philosophy, which Thurman saw as the ability to engage in a critical analysis of the underlying presuppositions of society. The noted black sociologist E. Franklin Frazier was a Howard University graduate from whom Thurman took a course in social origins. In his autobiography, Thurman tells the story that after his return from the Columbia University Summer School of 1922, evidently feeling full of himself and sure of his mastery of sociology, he dominated the classroom proceedings to such an extent that an exasperated Frazier told Thurman one morning, "'I am the teacher and you are the student. From this day forward you are not to speak a word in this course, not even to answer "present" when the roll is called. Understand?' And with that, he proceeded with the lecture" (*WHAH*, 41). Another confrontation between Frazier and Thurman, in which Frazier, a professed atheist, taunted Thurman's religious beliefs, was recalled by a Morehouse classmate in 1938:

> I remember how Dr. Frazier would ridicule certain Scriptural stories with bitter sarcasm, and Howard Thurman would be moved to such a point that he would fold his arms, look up to the top of the ceiling, and audibly groan. Dr. Frazier, who knew that he was actually "torturing" Thurman, would "turn up the heat," and glance smilingly at him. Thurman argued with Frazier when he first came to the college, but naturally, the powerful Dr. Frazier

was too much for any student to cope with. Subsequently, Thurman would allow his challenges to go unanswered.[51]

Thurman's main focus of interest as an undergraduate was in sociology and economics and in exploring contemporary social, economic, and political realities. Although he had acknowledged his call to ministry as a high-school student, interestingly, he took only one religion course at Morehouse. Coming to terms with the poverty and distress he saw outside of the halls of Morehouse seems to have been his most pressing intellectual and spiritual concern. Morehouse College was in the heart of Atlanta's south district, surrounded by one of the most destitute, impoverished black neighborhoods in the city. Unlike the relatively self-confident black community of Daytona, black Atlanta must have struck Thurman as having few defenses against the racist brutality around it. In his 1929 essay "'Relaxation' and Race Conflict," Thurman used the Atlanta slums to illustrate his contention that "a sense of helplessness and despair is apt to work its way into the very soul" of a "stigmatized minority group."[52] Mays wrote of Morehouse in the early 1920s, "Howard and I were both determined that lynching, segregation, and degradation would not beat us down."[53] Thurman expressed himself similarly, "We were black men in Atlanta during a period when the state of Georgia was infamous for its racial brutality. Lynchings, burnings, unspeakable cruelties were the fundamentals of existence for black people. Our physical lives were of little value. Any encounter with a white person was inherently dangerous and frequently fatal. Those of us who managed to remain physically whole found our lives defined in less than human terms" (*WHAH*, 36).

During his time at Morehouse, Thurman rarely expressed this rage so directly, and the college's curriculum encouraged students to channel their rage into constructive ways of dealing with social problems. Although Thurman often wrote that he majored in economics, Morehouse did not offer a pure economics major for the 1923 graduating class. During his years at Morehouse, Thurman took courses in economics, money and banking, sociology, and social origins. In his autobiography, Thurman pays special tribute to Lorimer Milton, who taught the course in money and banking and went on to a career as a successful banker. Milton had little interest in religion or social issues as such and tried to persuade Thurman to pursue a career in business. While this did not interest Thurman, he appears to have been deeply interested in acquiring practical knowledge of how the world of business worked and how economic realities shaped social interactions.

Another teacher who greatly inspired Thurman was Garrie Ward Moore,[54] professor of sociology and economics and director of the Atlanta University School of Social Work. Thurman's transcript indicates that he took at least two courses from Moore. The two men seemed to have had a great deal in common.

They were from Florida, had attended Baptist schools, were active in the YMCA, and were Morehouse men. Moore was scheduled to spend the entire 1922–23 academic year at Columbia, presumably working on a doctorate, where he remained until his untimely death in March 1923. He was the teacher Thurman most had in mind when he said in his autobiography that his Morehouse instructors "placed over our heads a crown that for the rest of our lives we would be trying to grow tall enough to wear" (*WHAH*, 41).

Thurman's interests in social and political matters were not limited to the classroom. He had been active in the debating society from his freshman days, though traditionally only the seniors made the final team. The topics debated included the establishment of unemployment insurance, ending immigration, and nationalization of the railroads, and that chosen for Thurman's year as a senior debater—"Resolved: That the United States Should Subsidize Her Merchant Marine"—strikes modern ears as perhaps a bit uninteresting. But this was not how it seemed when at a debate at Fisk University the college president had arranged for an all-white panel of judges, outraging Mays, the coach of Morehouse's debating team. As he related in his autobiography, "I was furious, but I was powerless. I told Thurman and Nabrit [James Nabrit, later president of Howard University], that they had no choice either: they *had* to win that debate! When the judges gave the decision to Morehouse, I was (and still am!) accused of making one flying leap from the first floor of Fisk University Chapel to the rostrum to congratulate Nabrit and Thurman." Even a debate on the future of the merchant marine could become part of the fight against white supremacy.[55]

Thurman continued his affiliation with the YMCA and by 1922 had become president of the Morehouse Association, accompanying Hope to city YMCA branch meetings and as a Morehouse delegate attending a national convention in Cincinnati, Ohio. By far, the YMCA was the most active organization at Morehouse, providing opportunities for students to work in various churches and Sunday-school programs throughout the city. Thurman recalls, "These churches welcomed us not only because, as Morehouse men (and some of the pastors had been Morehouse men), we provided leadership and inspiration to the youth, but also because our presence was sometimes an inspiration to the congregation as a whole" (*WHAH*, 35). In the summer of his freshman year, Thurman first put his ministerial training into practice by serving as the supply pastor of his home church, Mount Bethel, in Daytona, while its pastor, Reverend Arthur L. James, was away completing coursework at the University of Chicago. Under James's guidance, Thurman preached his trial sermon before his home congregation, which gave him a conditional license to preach.

Through his involvement with the YMCA, Thurman also began to move in the wider world of the student Christian movement. Thurman evidently joined the Fellowship of Reconciliation (FOR), the leading Christian pacifist

Morehouse class of 1923, May 1923. Thurman is standing in the back row, sixth from the left. Courtesy of the Thurman family and Arleigh Prelow/Howard Thurman Film Project

organization of the time, as an undergraduate. The American branch of the FOR had been founded in Garden City, New York, in 1915, and soon included under its banner many who shared its general ideals of pacifism, anti-imperialism, a critique of the excesses of capitalism, and the search for a modern Christianity that was compatible with these positions. Thurman writes in his autobiography that in the FOR he found "a place to stand in my own spirit—a place so profoundly affirming that *I* was strengthened by a sense of immunity to the assaults of the white world of Atlanta, Georgia" (*WHAH*, 265). In FOR, Thurman would discover the possibility of genuine collaboration with like-minded whites, uncovering that "the vast possibilities of reconciliation between black and white all gave me the feeling of knowing a 'secret'" (*WHAH*, 266).

In the Morehouse yearbook of 1923, excerpted in the current volume, Thurman is listed as one of the three pacifists in his graduating class, and his lack of comfort with the military can be glimpsed as early as his 1918 letters to Johnson, in which he worries about getting drafted. The 1923 Morehouse yearbook also points to the popularity of socialism among Thurman's peers, with fourteen students identifying their political affiliations as socialist, Thurman likely among them. This moderate, non-Marxist socialism claimed by Thurman and his classmates

Morehouse senior yearbook photo-
graph, spring 1923. Courtesy of the
Thurman family and Arleigh Prelow/
Howard Thurman Film Project

involved less an overthrowing of capitalism than its reform in ways developed in
the social thought of John Dewey, who became a major influence on Thurman as
an undergraduate. For example, a paper Thurman wrote for Frazier on the profit-
sharing system at men's clothing manufacturer Hart Schaffner Marx suggests an
interest in a progressive, reformed capitalism (*WHAH*, 41). Although overtly
political themes rarely appear in Thurman's early writings, the thrust of much of
his thinking was that to end the oppression of blacks in the United States, one
must reform American society as a whole. The roots of this world view can be
found in the broad, encompassing education Thurman encountered in and out of
the classroom during his years at Morehouse.

Thurman's career at Morehouse was a remarkable success. Much as at Florida Baptist Academy, he was driven to succeed in as many arenas as possible,
and it is hardly surprising that he was voted the busiest student and was also
acclaimed in the *Torch*, the Morehouse College yearbook, as "the personification of the Morehouse Ideal."[56] Among his accomplishments, Thurman was
class president, valedictorian, commencement speaker, editor of the literary
magazine and the senior annual, Morehouse representative to the YMCA,
president of the Atlanta Student Council—which comprised the Atlanta area
Negro colleges—and a member of the varsity debating team. Unlike some of
those who outshine their classmates, Thurman was genuinely well liked and
was seen as a wise and sympathetic confidante. The *Torch* speaks of Thurman as
"the repository of many student problems."

Thurman could have pursued almost any professional course of his choosing, and Hope offered him an instructorship in economics at Morehouse and the chance to validate his degree at the University of Chicago. Thurman turned down Hope's offer and instead chose to attend Rochester Theological Seminary. Over the course of his years at Morehouse, Thurman had refined his conception of Christianity. It was one that fully embraced the modern world and contemporary thought and was passionately concerned with the social condition of blacks, along with the underprivileged throughout American society. It did not take refuge in fundamentalist theological currents of his day. The *Torch* describes him as "brainy and sympathetic he is our ideal of a minister, one who shall furnish us with a rational and practical christianity." The characterization was prophetic, for Thurman would spend the rest of his life trying to create a sympathetic and rational Christianity.

Thurman entered Rochester Theological Seminary in the fall of 1923. Founded by German Baptists in 1850 concurrently with the University of Rochester, the seminary was known for its modernistic liberalism,[57] academic rigor, and commitment to the Social Gospel, which placed Christianity in the service of social and economic reform. Its most distinguished faculty member was Walter Rauschenbusch, one of the founders of the principal social-gospel movement of the early twentieth century, who was professor of church history at Rochester from 1902 until his death in 1918. Johnson, Thurman's mentor, had been a student of Rauschenbusch. Although the renowned theologian died five years before Thurman arrived at the seminary, the institution still bore Rauschenbusch's imprint.

Unlike many seminaries in the early twentieth century, racial integration at Rochester was not strictly forbidden. Nonetheless, according to Thurman, the school only allowed two black students to attend the seminary at a time.[58] He described his early days there as "the most radical period of adjustment of my life up to that moment" (*WHAH,* 46). In stark contrast to Thurman's years at Florida Baptist Academy and Morehouse College, at Rochester he lived for the first time in a community of white men. The intensity of this setting had a radical impact on the ways in which he had previously related to whites. Thurman's early experiences of segregation and the toll of racial violence had inculcated in him an ethic of indifference for all white people. It was not until his experiences in seminary that Thurman began to examine this moral indifference (*WHAH,* 43–44). He recalls, "Until I went to Rochester I had accepted the fact that I was a Christian, a practicing Christian. I believed sincerely in the necessity for loving my fellow man. It was a serious commitment; however, it had not ever occurred to me that my magnetic field of ethical awareness applied to other than my own people" (*WHAH,* 51). This searching would lead to genuine friendships with his fellow white students.

Thurman's studies at Rochester Theological Seminary reaped high dividends in respect to his religious and intellectual development. Despite initial anxiety about his ability to "hold his own," Thurman excelled at Rochester. His habits of voracious reading only intensified with the presence of a full seminary library of books that had been unavailable to him at Morehouse's modest collection, and he undertook a punishing study schedule that left him with little leisure time. Among other courses in his first year, Thurman took "Hebrew History, Literature and Religion" and "Jewish Life and Thought," taught by Earle Cross, and "Psychology of Religion," taught by Henry Burke Robins. Both Cross and Robins were at the forefront of theological liberalism of this period, and Thurman's marks were among the highest in their classes.

Thurman's seminary years ushered him into a public career that would continue throughout his long and fruitful ministry. Though he was not yet ordained in the ministry, his main speaking venues were in Baptist churches in the Rochester and surrounding western New York areas. Programs and church bulletins from the period reveal his popularity as a speaker on matters of race as well as his developing theological perspective. During his first semester, Thurman delivered the address "Thinking Black" at the First Baptist Church of Penfield, New York. In his second semester, he addressed the Dewey Avenue Union Church of Rochester on the topic "The Faith of the American Negro," which had recently been used as the title for a well-publicized address by Johnson.[59] Thurman later delivered variations of the same talk at the Brick Presbyterian Church of Rochester and the First Baptist Church of Lockport.[60]

A church bulletin from First Congregational Church of Rochester dated 2 March 1924 urges members to "come early" to hear Thurman, "the noted colored preacher" and "very prominent educator." The bulletin states, "If you would know first hand information concerning the colored race, and the great ideals among American Negroes do not fail to be present next Sunday. The pastor was advised by prominent folk who know and have heard Mr. Thurman that he can not be advertised too much."[61]

Thurman conducted his speaking engagements amid Rochester's hostile racial climate that was further agitated by the presence of the Ku Klux Klan, which flourished in upstate New York during the 1920s. Thurman recalls in his autobiography that Klan members would regularly attend his speeches, even on one occasion going so far as to threaten the pastor of the church from which Thurman was scheduled to speak. Thurman was not to be intimidated, and he delivered the address with the pastor's support.[62]

Thurman's influence in the most prominent national white student organizations and his friendships and alliances with white student leaders grew during this period. His association with the white national student movement was undergirded by a theology that had as its basic premise the equality among individuals. Thurman's first published work on matters of religion and race, "College and Color,"[63] appeared in the *Student Challenge*, the official organ of the Student Fellowship for Student Life-Service, a national organization for students who had chosen to commit their lives to the service of Christianity. In the essay, Thurman advocates a "Christian way in race relations" on American college campuses in which "sympathetic understanding" produces mutual respect. He also lays the foundation for his lifelong quest for common ground by emphasizing the need to search for similar qualities among the races instead of highlighting differences. Thurman continued his involvement in the Fellowship of Reconciliation during his seminary years and served as a delegate representing Rochester Theological Seminary at the 1924 Quadrennial Conference of the Student Volunteer Movement held in Indianapolis.

The 1920s saw a great deal of interracial cooperation in the YMCA movement. All the southern states established interracial committees during the decade, and although no change was made in the YMCA's segregationist policies in its branches until 1946, black students enthusiastically welcomed dialogue. Interracial dialogue led African American students to call for a merger of black and white student work in 1923, a move that threatened the power of the Colored Work Department. This caused a rift between black students and professional leadership, which was evident in the overall tenor of the YMCA's Twenty-First National Conference on Colored Work of the Young Men's Christian Association, held in Washington, D.C., 21–23 October 1925, at the Twelfth Street YMCA and John Wesley AME Zion church. Thurman, the only student on the program, addressed the student section on the topic "The Christian Emphases." His 1925 article, "Negro Youth and the Washington Conference,"[64] based on the address, emphasizes the impact of the conference on Negro students. Most important, he subtly notes that although the leadership's concern about their inability to draw Negro youth toward YMCA work as a profession may be warranted, it must be coupled with a critique of their effort to make the work appealing for students.

During the summers of 1924 and 1925, Thurman worked on the ministerial staff of the First Baptist Church in Roanoke, Virginia, under the supervision of Reverend Arthur James. Among his many duties, Thurman oversaw the Daily Vacation Bible School Program with the assistance of Morehouse classmate Clarence J. Gresham. Through the planning of James and Thurman, First Baptist was able to help create one of Roanoke's first black newspapers, the *Roanoke Church News*. In "The Sphere of the Church's Responsibility in Social Reconstruction,"[65] published in the paper in July 1924, the influence of Social Gospel theology on Thurman's theological perspective is clear.

During Thurman's second year at Rochester, his fame as a speaker on race and religion and his prominence in national student movement circles solidified.

This year marked a flourishing of his personal relationship with whites. At Rochester, he was roommates with Seldon Matthews and David Voss, an intentional move that was borne out of his commitment to putting interracial theological perspective into practice. In his memoir, *Tales out of School,* Thurman's classmate Kenneth Cober recalled that Thurman's room was often the gathering place where Rochester students came to debate far-ranging religious and social topics of the day:

> About once a week, Howard would invite the boys on our floor to meet in his room for a devotional experience which he led. He would read some scriptures, interpret what he read, and pray. Then we had a period of meditation interspersed by other vocal prayers. In one of these sessions, I had the strong feeling that it was not Howard Thurman, but Jesus Christ, so much did his thinking emulate that of the master. I have never had another experience like that.[66]

The Brick Presbyterian Church of Rochester and the First Baptist Church of Lockport were among the prominent white congregations that invited Thurman to speak. At both, he delivered variations of his popular address on "The Faith of the American Negro."

Thurman's popularity as a public speaker was matched by a budding career as a writer addressing Christian social issues. "The Perils of Immature Piety"[67] was published in the May 1925 issue of the *Student Volunteer Movement Bulletin,* the official organ of the organization of the same name that recruited and trained undergraduate students for foreign mission appointments. In the article, Thurman denounces spiritual immaturity in the future leadership of the church. In January 1925, six months prior to his ordination, Thurman's essay "Let Ministers Be Christians" was published in the *Student Challenge.*[68] Drawing upon his seminary experiences as well as his student ministry work in Roanoke, Virginia, Thurman argues that when race relations are the issue, many professed Christians divide their ethical praxis into separate and unequal categories. Instead of serving God in Christ-like fashion, he asserts, ordained ministers often serve the interests of the racial status quo. The most emotionally charged of Thurman's seminary-period writings, the essay questions the limited application of the ideal of Christian brotherhood.

In the summer of 1925, Thurman applied to his home church in Daytona for permission to be ordained by First Baptist Church in Roanoke, Virginia, pastored by Reverend James. Thurman's request was a tacit snub of his home church, and the pastor refused to consent, most probably in reaction to the snub and out of his objection to Thurman's embrace of liberal theology. Few clues as to motives and responses are available; Thurman states simply in his autobiography, "The minister there refused."[69] Thurman subsequently joined First Baptist, where the date was set for convening an ordination council. On 2 July 1925, Thurman wrote to Johnson, asking that he preach the ordination sermon: "I want you to come to preach my ordination sermon. It is useless for me to try to say why. You know what you have been to me and I want you to come."[70] However, due to Johnson's prior commitments and the short notice, he was not able to come.

On 2 August 1925, Thurman was officially ordained. Reverend Samuel A. Owen of Memphis, Tennessee, another mentor and Morehouse graduate, traveled to Roanoke at his own expense to give the sermon of ordination. In a style that would be characteristic of Thurman's pastoral work, the ordination departed from the customs of the period and his denomination. Thurman wrote and read his own statement of faith and initially refused to take part in the laying-on-of-hands ceremony, judging it "altogether too old-fashioned." During the ordination his examiners, composed of ministers from various churches in the Roanoke area, challenged his modernist theology, their questions, according to Thurman, "running the gamut of religious doctrine within the scope of Virginia Baptist orthodoxy" (*WHAH*, 57). In his autobiography, Thurman refers to the transcendent significance of the moment of ordination, particularly the laying-on-of-hands ceremony, for his own spiritual journey: "Ever since, when it seems that I am deserted by the Voice that called me forth, I know that if I can find my way back to that moment, the clouds will lift and the path before me will once again be clear and beckoning" (*WHAH*, 58).

One of the major intellectual influences on Thurman during his years at Rochester Theological Seminary was a course he took at Columbia University in the summer of 1922 while still a student at Morehouse. The "Reflective Thinking" class, taught by E. A. Burtt, was Thurman's first formal introduction to philosophy, and he later recalls it as the most significant single course he ever took.[71] The course introduced him to the work of John Dewey, which he describes as one of the intellectual turning points of his life. Dewey believed that all thinking was inferential, and scientific or reflective thinking consisted of subjecting those inferences to rigorous challenge. In *An Introduction to Reflective Thinking*, this type of thinking was applied to any potential problem, of increasing complexity, from purely scientific inquiries to complex social and religious matters, with each chapter serving as a case study of another example of reflective thinking. For Dewey and the authors of *Introduction*, the use of a method of reflective or scientific thinking could unify all of the disparate realms of science, culture, and nature under a common understanding. This was the lesson that Thurman took from Dewey:

> It was an analysis of reflective thinking as process. It examined a basic methodological approach to problem solving in all fields of investigation, from simple decision-making to the understanding and treatment of disease and the most confused patterns of human behavior. This course established

for me a basic approach that I would use not only in my subsequent work as a counselor but also in thinking through the complex and complicated problems I would encounter in my personal life and as a social being. As a tool of the mind, there is no way by which the value of this course can be measured or assessed. (*WHAH, 44*)

Dewey wrote little on religion, though, and Thurman's most extended attempt to apply Deweyian "reflective thinking" to religion was in one of his most challenging (and troubling) student papers, "Can It Be Truly Said That the Existence of a Supreme Spirit Is a Scientific Hypothesis?"[72] Dated December 1925, Thurman's paper contrasts the formation of scientific knowledge about the solar system by contrasting the Copernican and Newtonian hypotheses (a subject that Burtt discussed in his 1924 *The Metaphysical Foundations of Modern Physical Science* and was likely to have covered in the 1922 Columbia course) with the knowledge of God. In his paper, which reflects aspects of a neo-Kantian as well as a purely Deweyian epistemology, Thurman argues that the scientific method simplifies the confused nature of external reality into quantifiable and testable hypotheses, but all knowledge gained in this way is necessarily provisional and cannot provide information about the ultimate nature of the physical universe. In the second half of the paper, he argues that only in the realm of religion is certain knowledge perhaps attainable through the possibility of experiential knowledge of God through heightened states of divine awareness. Thurman's paper set out several themes that he would return to throughout his career, a measured and rationalistic approach to knowledge claims on the one hand and holding out the possibility of nonrational knowledge of divine reality on the other.

What makes "Can It Be Truly Said" problematic is that the essay is heavily plagiarized from several sources. The first half of the essay, in which Thurman discusses the formation of scientific hypotheses, is largely constructed from two sources, the textbook *An Introduction to Reflective Thinking* and an essay by C. A. Richardson, "Scientific Method in Philosophy and the Foundations of Pluralism," published in *Philosophical Review* in 1918.[73] The second half of Thurman's essay is less plagiarized but relies for its structure and some of its contents on Charles Allen Dinsmore, *Religious Certitude in an Age of Science* (1924). There is no reason to doubt the sincerity of Thurman's argument in this essay, but there are also no grounds for disputing that Thurman's failure to indicate a number of verbatim quotations was at the least misleading to potential readers. Thurman's essay has a number of explicit quotations, some of them short, some of them extensive, suggesting his awareness of the convention that quoted material should be indicated in the text. Most of the plagiarized passages were expository, taking the argument forward, such as discussing the Copernican or Ptolemaic world views, rather than summary statements, which Thurman often ended with explicit quotations from his sources. Rather than paraphrasing the expository passages, Thurman simply quotes them, verbatim and uncredited.

It is unclear why Thurman engaged in plagiarism. What is certain is that he did not try to bury his plagiarism too deeply. The plagiarism is easy to trace through the references he provided at the end of the essay, which consist of works that his instructor, George Cross, was undoubtedly familiar with and perhaps recommended that Thurman consult. Probably the most likely explanation is the common excuse of an overworked student looking to cut corners. He was not a poor student and was certainly capable of providing an adequate paraphrase for the passages in question. But the paper has in places a somewhat thrown-together feeling, and perhaps Thurman was pressed for time.

This paper is also the best surviving evidence of Thurman's work with the systematic theologian Cross,[74] Thurman's most important teacher at Rochester. Cross taught Thurman during his last year and a half at Rochester. Thurman says that Cross "had a greater influence on my life than any other person who ever lived. Everything about me was alive when I came into his presence" (WHAH, 41). Thurman took three required courses from Cross: "The Christian Doctrine of Man and His Salvation," "The Christian Doctrine of God," and "The Christian Finality." The two met frequently on Saturday mornings for private conferences in which Thurman raised questions that arose from the weekly lectures. Here Thurman would air his disagreements with Cross, who would listen patiently and then proceed to "reduce my arguments to ash" (WHAH, 43).

Another major connection in Thurman's intellectual odyssey took place during his seminary tenure. In 1925, at an informal retreat in Pawling, New York, he was introduced to the writings of Olive Schreiner. A fellow participant, George Collins, read a selection entitled "The Hunter" from Schreiner's Dreams. This was the beginning of a lifelong spiritual and intellectual relationship with the South African writer. A critical question for Thurman in his initial investigation of Schreiner's life and writings was, "How could a white woman born and reared in South Africa think as she thinks and feel about man as she felt?"[75] Thurman never quite resolved this question nor the issue of Schreiner's use of derogatory language to describe black South Africans.[76] Despite these concerns, Schreiner served as a fountain of inspiration for Thurman in his search for "common ground." Two significant themes in Schreiner also can be found in Thurman's thought: the unity of all life and the redemptive role of the solitary individual and his or her responsibility to lay the foundation for the collective destiny of humanity. Thurman was also influenced by Schreiner's frequent use of parables, her feminism, and her pacifism, as well as her social progressivism and her determined religious unorthodoxy. The first evidence of Schreiner's influence on Thurman was in his 1926 seminary thesis "The Basis of Sex Morality: An Inquiry into the Attitude toward Premarital Sexual Morality among Various Peoples."[77] Schreiner's Woman and Labor is cited in the thesis, and both her feminism and her commitment to sexual freedom are the work's dominant themes, and indeed, perhaps it was his reading of Schreiner that led to his choice of this topic. Completed in April 1926, the thesis also evidences the strong influence of his work with Cross, his familiarity with John Dewey, as well as dominant trends in social, sexual, and behavioral psychology. In the work, Thurman addresses the issue of changing sexual mores in the post–World War I 1920s. Thurman also draws from the work of George Coe, most notably his 1925 work *What Ails Our Youth?*, raising the need for the development of a "valuational consciousness," an impetus to correct social behavior resulting from one's self-awareness as a child of God, a theme that would recur as a focal point in Thurman's later writings. Published in the current volume are Thurman's table of contents, which outlines the substance of the entire thesis, and excerpts from sections I, II, and III, which contain his main ideas and arguments. In brief, section I traces the history of "orthodox" sexual practices back to their origins in ancient and medieval religious and social practices. Section II relates women's increasing independence and the "youth revolt" against authority to the growth of world democracy. In section III, Thurman discusses the role of the individual in the formation of sexual conscience. He argues that while one's standards may be socially conditioned, premarital chastity is an individual matter. Additionally, he contends that premarital sexual activity, when it embodies "spiritual unity," is not immoral.

Toward the end of his last year at Rochester, Thurman met with Cross to share his future plans of marriage and to pastor the Mount Zion Baptist Church in Oberlin, Ohio. At Oberlin, he also planned to study with Edward Increase Bosworth and Kemper Fullerton. Cross unveiled his own plans for Thurman's future at their meeting, which later proved a source of encouragement and bewilderment for Thurman. He said to his brilliant young student:

> You are a very sensitive Negro man, and doubtless feel under great obligation to put all the weight of your mind and spirit at the disposal of the struggle of your people for full citizenship. But let me remind you that all social questions are transitory in nature and it would be a terrible waste for you to limit your creative energy to the solution of the race problem, however insistent its nature. Give yourself to the timeless issues of the human spirit. . . . Perhaps I have no right to say this to you because as a white man I can never know what it is to be in your situation. (*WHAH*, 60)

Thurman says that he "pondered the meaning of his words, and wondered what kind of response I could make to this man who did not know that a man and his black skin must face the 'timeless issues of the human spirit' together."[78] Thurman understandably found Cross's remarks somewhat patronizing, but Cross had touched upon a critical tension within Thurman that can be seen in much of his early work, that of a politically engaged young man angry at the racist

Rochester Theological Seminary class of 1926, spring 1926. Thurman is standing
second row, fourth from the right. Courtesy of the Thurman family and Arleigh
Prelow/Howard Thurman Film Project

society in which he was living and at the same time a committed Christian
seeking the necessary calm to think and write about the "timeless issues of the
human spirit." In his mature writings, Thurman found a number of ways of
bridging the distance between the varying demands of religion and politics,
looking for ways to write about the consequences of racial prejudice in ways
that transcend the political particulars and open to broader religious and spiritual questions. One can glimpse him working towards his eventual synthesis in
many of the works in this volume. Cross also told Thurman that he was going to
find a teacher abroad for him, but these plans were never realized. Cross died
early in 1929 before finalizing the arrangements.

   In May 1926, Thurman graduated valedictorian from Rochester Theological
Seminary out of a class of twenty-nine students. As was the common practice in
many American theological schools of the period, Rochester made a distinction
between graduating a student and conferring the Bachelor of Divinity. The major
requirement for this degree was the presentation of a thesis, and Rochester Theological Seminary usually directed its students not to complete the theses during
their senior year so as not to interfere with course work and to encourage a student's scholarly work in the early years of their pastorate. Thurman's completion

Katie Laura Kelley, circa 1924.
Courtesy of Olive Thurman Wong and
Arleigh Prelow/Howard Thurman
Film Project

of the thesis within his senior year and the conferring of the Bachelor of Divinity by graduation, therefore, was a distinctive and rare accomplishment, one not even achieved by his mentor Mordecai Wyatt Johnson, who graduated from Rochester in 1916 but did not receive the Bachelor of Divinity until 1920.

Two days before he was to assume the pastorate at Oberlin, Thurman married Katie Laura Kelley in LaGrange, Georgia. Thurman writes about Katie only briefly in his autobiography, but the impact of her illness and death were devastating and one of the greatest personal difficulties he had to endure. Born 4 September 1897, Katie was twenty-six months older than Thurman, the eldest of five children born to Charles H. Kelley, a prominent educator in LaGrange and a Morehouse alumnus, and Frances, an alumna of Spelman. Katie graduated from Spelman High School in 1916 and from the Teacher's Course at the College in 1918, one year before Thurman entered Morehouse.

After graduating from Spelman in 1918, Katie moved to Birmingham, Alabama, to work as a teacher in the public schools. Her first assignment was teaching the third grade, and she enthusiastically reported in a letter to Lucy Tapley, "I have on roll already fifty-five very active little folks."[79] By 1920, however, Kelley had left the teaching profession and moved from Birmingham to Chicago, where in the spring semester of 1921 she enrolled in the Divinity School at the University of Chicago, though she later returned to Atlanta to start training for a career in social work.

Kelley's chosen path in social work addressed the eradication of tuberculosis, a leading public-health threat to blacks living in the city's overcrowded, poverty-stricken communities. In 1921, Kelley was employed as a visiting health educator for the black branch of the Anti-Tuberculosis Association in Atlanta,[80] founded in 1915 under the leadership of Lugenia Burns Hope, wife of Morehouse President John Hope and a prominent social reformer in her own right who organized the Atlanta Neighborhood Union. John Hope served as the association's first chairman. By the time of Katie's employment with them, the association had already distinguished itself as a citywide operation that improved the health of its black citizens. By 1924 she left Atlanta to direct an anti-tuberculosis center at the Municipal Health Department in Morristown, New Jersey, where she remained until 1926, a month before her marriage to Thurman.

Thurman and Kelley may have become acquainted in 1921, when she returned to Atlanta to work with the Anti-Tuberculosis Association. She was also enrolled in the Atlanta School of Social Work, where Thurman's Morehouse professors E. Franklin Frazier and Garrie Ward Moore were on faculty. According to Kelley family lore, the two were introduced by her younger brother, Charles Kelley Jr., Thurman's Morehouse classmate and friend.[81] Thurman accompanied Charles to LaGrange on several occasions and became a favorite in the Kelley family household. Impressed by the young Thurman's ambition and intellect, Charles Kelley Sr. offered personal encouragement and some financial support to Thurman during his college career.[82] Although his autobiography does not mention his future wife (who was relatively nearby in northern New Jersey) in this context, he notes that he took frequent trips to New York City during his Rochester years to experience the cultural attractions of the city, seeing Walter Hampden star in *Hamlet, Othello,* and *Merchant of Venice,* Blanche Yurka in Ibsen's *Wild Duck,* and Anna Pavlova in Tchaikovsky's *Swan Lake* (*WHAH,* 53–54).

Howard and Katie's wedding was an intimate family affair held on Friday, 11 June 1926, in the Kelley family home at dawn. After a family breakfast following the ceremony, the newlyweds boarded a train bound for Oberlin, Ohio, where Thurman had accepted the pastorate at Mount Zion Baptist Church. The festivities were timed so that they could arrive in time for Thurman's first pulpit appearance that Sunday morning. Thurman would reflect on the magic of that day, "I well remember the softness of the rising sun reflected in the mysterious beauty of Katie's eyes" (*WHAH,* 65). By the time of their marriage, Katie was already in fragile health from what would prove to be tuberculosis, which she had more than likely contracted during her anti-tuberculosis work.

As pastor of Mount Zion in the "town and gown" environment of Oberlin, Thurman had access to an intellectual and religious climate that engaged his own critical questions regarding the role of religion and social change. At Oberlin, Thurman began to fully develop his talent and genius for sharing his inner spiritual life with his congregation. Thurman initially approached his position in Oberlin with the intention of trying, as he reflected in his autobiography, to "re-educate" his congregation in a way that emphasized rational understandings of Christianity. His efforts, which included introducing modern biblical translations into services, were met with resistance from the congregation. Thurman also organized classes on Negro history and current political and social problems. He also, dabbled in theatrical direction.[83] He restructured the communion service, stressing the roots of the Eucharist in pre-Christian totemic sacrifice, and opened up the ceremony to those outside of church membership. Thurman not only lectured his Oberlin congregation on the virtues of religious modernism but also sought to encourage, both in himself and his congregation, ways to work beyond the difficulties in publicly expressing "the utterances of the inner spirit." In time, he learned how to communicate to his congregation by deemphasizing lecturing and communicating "the meaning of the experience of our common quest and journey" (WHAH, 73).

The quest for genuine religious expression was an on-going challenge for Thurman. In "The Perils of Immature Piety" published in the *Student Volunteer Movement Bulletin* in 1925, he had critiqued empty spiritual posturing, or "the use of words without adequate experience," and any religious experience that did not "synthesize *all* of life." In "Finding God,"[84] written in 1927 while at Oberlin, he once again railed against religious expression based on formula and routine, emphasizing the need to root one's discourse on the authentic experience of God and to express this experience to others. The shared recognition of the inadequacy of religious expression becomes a common bond: "Human need is infinite, but when I respond to it to the limit of my power and become thereby painfully conscious of my own inadequacy, I seem to send my soul through the air and the sky and the sea in quest of an infinite energy that I may release for an infinite task."

Word of this creative young pastor reached beyond the Oberlin community, and Sunday morning worship at Mt. Zion became a gathering place for people from diverse racial, religious, and class groups. Thurman discovered, through the experiences of worship and pastoral care, an inner unity of fellowship that went beyond the barriers of race, class, and tradition. This was most acutely manifest in his inner life of prayer and meditation. One Chinese gentleman who regularly visited the worship services commented, "When I close my eyes and listen to my spirit I am in a Buddhist temple experiencing the renewing of my own spirit." Thurman remarked, "I knew then what I had only sensed before. The barriers were crumbling. I was breaking new ground. Yet, it would be years before I would understand the nature of the breakthrough" (WHAH, 73–74).

During this Oberlin period, Thurman continued to engage a frenetic pace in his speaking and lecture engagements. He was a featured speaker in the annual conferences of the YMCA-YWCA at Lake Geneva, Wisconsin. Increasingly, he was engaged to speak at predominantly white colleges, including Syracuse University (1925), Iowa State Teachers College, the University of South Dakota (1926), and Vassar (1928). In 1927, he was invited to speak at the Baptist Young People's Union in Nashville, which he turned down in favor of preaching a series of sermons at the National Baptist Convention in Detroit at the behest of the influential Baptist leader Nannie Burroughs. That same year he also preached the commencement sermon at Spelman College. In a 1927 letter to Lucy Tapley, Katie reveals her difficulties with adjusting to the demands of being a pastor's wife: "It has been difficult for me to enter whole heartedly into the new responsibilities of home-making and the pastorate."[85] She attributes her difficulty to her health, which was even more strained by Oberlin's harsh northern climate.

One of the attractions of Oberlin for Thurman was that it permitted him to continue his studies at the Oberlin School of Theology, and he registered for, though never completed, an STM (Master of Sacred Theology). While in Oberlin, he made a special study of the treatment of the "suffering servant" passage in Isaiah (52:13–53:12) with Kemper Fullerton, an Old Testament expert, in a private seminar. Thurman remarked that this was a "great creative adventure" and that since the seminar he had "never since lost sight of the far-flung mystery and redemption of the sacrament of pain" (*WHAH*, 70).

Thurman also studied briefly with Edward Increase Bosworth, a New Testament scholar and author of many popular works circulated by the YMCA. However, Thurman had decided shortly after arriving in Ohio that he would not pursue a PhD, as he explained in a letter to Johnson in 1926. Evidently this decision was not final, though, and he considered the possibility of a PhD as late as 1929. He eventually decided that, as he writes in his autobiography, "If I were to devote full time to the requirements of a doctoral program, academic strictures would gradually usurp the energy I wanted so desperately to nourish the inner regions of my spirit" (*WHAH*, 76).

On 9 September 1927, Thurman wrote to Johnson that he was "going through a veritable upheaval in my thinking."[86] How Thurman's thinking was transformed at this time is unclear, though he was beginning to state themes with greater clarity and force. In "Higher Education and Religion," published in 1927, Thurman decries contemporary Christianity in general and the black church in particular for what he called "spiritual cockiness," the simultaneous "sense of inferiority as life is squarely faced" and "a sense of superiority as things religious are in question."[87] Thurman saw a preening otherworldliness and a callow materialism as reinforcing the worst traits of contemporary Christianity.

In both "Higher Education and Religion" and "The Task of the Negro Ministry" (1928),[88] Thurman argues that the apocalyptic heritage of the black church, with its emphasis on the supernatural and the unworldly, left it ill-equipped to deal with either the spiritual or practical realms of existence. Thurman sought, as he articulates in "The Task of the Negro Ministry," the need for a "creative synthesis" between religion and science, so that folk traditions did not stunt the possibilities for both intellectual and spiritual growth. When a well-meaning sociologist advised Thurman that blacks needed to enrich themselves and "learn to speak the language of economic power and control," Thurman responded that the "religion of materialism" is soul-killing and "means death." Of the sterility of much contemporary religious discourse and the vainglory of contemporary church life, he wrote, echoing Nietzsche, "People always build their temples to their dead Gods." Thurman's response to the situation was to posit an alternative Christianity that would "demolish the artificial barrier between religion and life." This would involve a synthesis of science and religion, a recognition of the ethical demands on religious belief, and the rejection of religious certitude and dogma.

In the 9 September 1927 letter to Johnson, Thurman perhaps expressed himself more clearly than he did in his published writings, lamenting to his mentor, "We are clothed and fed by a vast system built upon deceit and adulteration." Society was largely defined by falsehood and pretense. Sincerity about religious belief in a society founded on lies and deceit was impossible without addressing the root problems. Membership and participation in a particular church deprived "an individual of the keen obligation to be increasingly exercised about being Christian." While working towards redress of concrete issues in the short term, religion had to generate the release of "such a grand swell of spiritual energy that existing systems will be upset." He concludes that the task of black religious leadership is to encourage the cultivation of spiritual power over "the demand for things," to draw practical ethical meaning out of personal piety, and to ensure that the spirit of Jesus is not overshadowed by Christian institutions.

During the Oberlin period, Thurman discovered that the sermon series was a creative forum for expressing his ideas. He preached a number of sermons in which he tried to expose medical quacks and hucksters, drawing on the text (modified from I John) that "Knowledge and understanding casteth out fear." Thurman recalled that his series met with much opposition from his congregation, many of whom used the household remedies described in the volumes. Nevertheless, Thurman stated that "a surprising number" did review the scientific exposé of quackery published by the American Medical Association that he made available to them. Undoubtedly, Thurman's interest in the subject was fueled by his wife's illness.

With a rising reputation as a preacher and a religious thinker, Thurman's services were much in demand for a more prestigious position than the Oberlin

Olive, Katie, and Howard
Thurman in LaGrange,
Georgia, circa 1929. Courtesy of
Olive Thurman Wong and
Arleigh Prelow/Howard
Thurman Film Project

congregation. He was considered as a replacement for Johnson at the First Baptist
Church in Charleston, West Virginia. Robert Russa Moton, the president of
Tuskegee Institute, asked Thurman to become its chaplain. Additionally, by the
fall of 1928, both his alma mater, Morehouse College, and Howard University, now
under the presidency of Johnson, were vying for his services. Thurman rejected
Johnson's offer and accepted a joint position at Morehouse and Spelman. At Morehouse, he taught philosophy and religion, and at Spelman, he taught the Bible as
living literature and served as religious advisor to students and faculty. Besides his
teaching and advising, he also took responsibility for a number of the chapel services at both institutions. The decision to return to Atlanta was largely because of
the deteriorating health of Katie. By the time they joyously announced the birth of
their daughter Olive Katherine Thurman—named after Olive Schreiner—on 5
October 1927, Katie's health was already in decline. Despite the optimism she
expressed in a 1928 letter—"the old strength returns in great surges,—it almost
frightens me sometimes.—My general condition is favorable,—most favorable;
and the building process goes on!"[89]—that same year, doctors advised Katie to
return to the south. She went with her child to LaGrange to convalesce, spending
many months in the McVicar Training Hospital on the Spelman campus.

   In the fall of 1928, shortly after his return to Atlanta, Thurman gave his most
extended lecture series to date, five connected sermons on "The Message of the
Spirituals," delivered at Spelman College.[90] This would be a theme Thurman
returned to time and again, culminating in the 1947 Ingersoll Lectures on

"Immortality of Man," later published in *Deep River* in 1955. The sermons spoke to the ways in which slaves tried to use the spiritual power of their faith as a means to better understand and survive in the conditions of their bondage. Underlying much of Thurman's thinking in the mid- and late 1920s was the search for ways to combine an authentic spiritual inwardness with full engagement with the world.

Thurman's thinking along these lines first received a jolt when back at Oberlin he read *Finding the Trail of Life*, a short book by the Quaker scholar Rufus Jones. Thurman wrote in his autobiography that after reading the volume he "knew that if that man were alive, I wanted to study with him."[91] Jones, who taught at Haverford College outside of Philadelphia, was a distinguished scholar of mysticism and had long been writing about many of the issues that concerned Thurman. He was also a denominational leader in the Society of Friends and helped organize the American Friends Service Committee during World War I, updating the historic Quaker testimony against war.

While still at Oberlin, Thurman wrote Jones at Haverford, and despite the Quaker institution's policy against admitting blacks, Jones nevertheless invited Thurman to come to the college.[92] Thurman recalled that in Jones's reply, "He did not comment on whether I would be admitted, but rather expressed interest in my plan" (*WHAH*, 74). After teaching one term at Morehouse and Spelman, Thurman arrived at Haverford in January 1929 for a semester of study. Thurman studied with Jones on a special grant from the National Council on Religion in Higher Education. This grant was primarily for doctoral students, but an exception was made for Thurman (*WHAH*, 76). He attended all of Jones's lectures in philosophy and was a special student in a seminar on the medieval German mystic Meister Eckhart. He was given special reading assignments and met for weekly conferences with Jones. Thurman also had access to Jones's extensive library on mysticism, which was one of the most comprehensive in America. Thurman referred to the period of study with Jones as "a watershed from which flowed much of the thought and endeavor to which I was to commit the rest of my working life." The study with Jones marked less a dramatic turning point than an intensification and a clarification of his developing thought: "These months defined my deepest religious urges and framed in meaning much of what I had learned over the years" (*WHAH*, 77).

Jones provided Thurman with a critical methodology to explore his belief that one could devote oneself to the ultimate concerns of the human spirit without neglecting the pressing moral issues of society. With Jones, Thurman was able to more clearly define the relationship between the interiority and the public experiences of religious life. The distinctive feature of Jones's mysticism is that it provides the basis for social transformation. During his stay with Jones, Thurman wrote papers on Spanish mysticism (presumably figures such as Saint Theresa of

Avila and Saint John of the Cross), the seventeenth-century French religious writer Madame Guyon, and Saint Francis of Assisi. But true to Jones's own predilections, the two spent much time discussing the contemporary ethical implications of the mystic experience and their relevance for war and peace, international conflict, and poverty. This was an area in which Jones, as a frequent traveler to Europe on matters of war and peace for the Friends, had vast experience. Their conversations did not focus much on racial matters, and Thurman writes that Jones "somehow transcended race" (*WHAH*, 76). Thurman, however, had no problem in applying insights gained from his study with Jones to the condition of blacks in America but perhaps with a greater sense of the more general implications of racial persecution and subordination, themes he would develop in years to come. The deeper lessons learned from the study with Jones needed time to fully gestate. Save a short review in 1934 of Mary Anita Ewer's *A Survey of Mystical Symbolism*, Thurman spoke or wrote little about mysticism until his late-1930s lecture series, which included "Mysticism and Social Change."

Katie's illness hung heavily over the early years at Morehouse and Spelman. Despite some temporary recoveries, her prognosis steadily worsened, and she died in Atlanta on 21 December 1930. Her body was taken home for burial in LaGrange. In the immediate aftermath of Katie's death, Thurman continued his grueling schedule of speaking engagements and teaching, but her death hurled Thurman into deep depression. Exhausted, emotionally and physically, he managed to teach the second semester, but when June finally came, he took a leave of absence and traveled to Europe, seeking the solace of the sea and of being a stranger in a foreign land, alone with his thoughts. He journeyed to London, Scotland, Paris, and Geneva, Switzerland, and spent the bulk of his leave in Scotland, where he lived as a paid guest with a crofting family on a sheep ranch (*WHAH*, 82–83). Upon his return to Atlanta for the fall of 1931, Thurman found the atmosphere dispiriting. From the time of his undergraduate study he had been depressed by the racial atmosphere in this deep-south city, and this sense was no doubt enhanced by the years he had spent in the north in Rochester and Oberlin. In his autobiography he claims that it was while teaching the "Bible as Living Literature" at Spelman that he was first struck by the ideas he would develop as "Good News for the Underprivileged" and *Jesus and the Disinherited*: "The racial climate was so oppressive and affected us so intimately that analogies between His life as a Jew in a Roman world and our own were obvious" (*WHAH*, 79). It was in Atlanta in 1932, in a lecture on "The Kind of Religion the Negro Needs in Times like These" that Thurman first spoke on the religious significance of Jesus being a member of a "despised circumscribed minority group."[93]

Thurman had known Sue Bailey, who would become his second wife, since their days as students at Spelman and Morehouse. Bailey was the YWCA's National Secretary for Colleges in the southern region, and in this capacity she

Sue Bailey Thurman, circa 1935.
Courtesy of the Thurman family and
Arleigh Prelow/Howard Thurman
Film Project

scheduled speakers for the YWCA's black student conferences.[94] Howard Thurman was among the most sought-after speakers on the lecture circuit and by her admission among the most difficult. Bailey later recalled, "I would arrange his lectures, and it seemed as if he was never satisfied with the location, the length of time he was given to speak, or anything. He would say, 'We start at seven o'clock sharp,' and that would be it. We did it for him because we knew he had something to say that we couldn't get from anyone else."[95] Bailey recognized that the source of much of Thurman's disposition was the recent death of his wife. At some point in 1931, when both were attending a meeting at Spelman, Bailey was asked to substitute for a canceled speaker. Both sat on the dais, and during the program, Thurman passed her a note, asking her to join him the next day for breakfast. Bailey visited his home, located on Ashby Street next to campus, and noticed that all of the shades were drawn. She let all the shades up. "What happened was truly symbolic," Bailey recalls. "It was time to let the light back into his life" (*Sue Bailey Thurman*, 7).

Sue Bailey was a woman of considerable ambition and intellect. Born Susie Elvie Bailey in Pine Bluff, Arkansas, on 26 August 1903,[96] she was the youngest daughter of Reverend Isaac G. Bailey, who had been a member of the Arkansas legislature during Reconstruction, and Susie Ford Bailey, a teacher. The Baileys were well-known educators, founding and operating the Southeast Baptist Academy in Dermott, Arkansas, a school for black children. After her father's death in 1914, her mother carried on the work of the Southeast Academy, and she would become renowned for inspiring the educational aspirations of several generations of black youth in Arkansas. Like Katie Kelley, Sue attended Spelman's preparatory school and teacher's college, graduating in 1921. At Spelman, she developed a great appreciation for the arts, and in 1920 she served as club editor of the Spelman-Morehouse literary journal, the *Athenaeum,* when Thurman was publishing his poems and short stories there. According to Bailey, she did not become acquainted with Thurman until the fall of 1921, after her graduation, when she had to complete additional courses in math, Latin, and French in order to gain admittance to Oberlin College. Ironically, their friendship developed in the course of reading and critiquing letters to and from other people they were dating at the time.

Bailey entered Oberlin College in the fall of 1922. She distinguished herself as a student leader, breaking the color barriers to become the first black president of the international club and cochair of the World Fellowship committee of the YWCA. In 1926, Bailey graduated with a Bachelor of Arts in music, earning a bachelor's degree in liberal arts after an additional summer study. On her graduation day from Oberlin, she and Thurman's first wife, Katie Kelley, crossed paths in a dormitory: "I passed Katie in the stairwell, and we had a brief chat—we had never been together alone before. I think of that time often. What would we have said, if we had known we would share motherhood to our little daughter, Olive, in years to come?" (*Sue Bailey Thurman,* 5).

Sue entered the education field, and she was hired on the music faculty of Hampton Institute (now Hampton University), a historically black college located in southeast Virginia. Bailey taught music, directed a YWCA program for girls, and worked on developing a music curriculum that could be implemented in the black southern schools. In the fall of 1927, Bailey, along with her Hampton colleague Louise Thompson, were among the few faculty to support the historic student strike at Hampton. The impetus for the strike was the Massenburg Bill, passed the year before by the Virginia legislature specifically to end integrated seating at Hampton's public auditorium. Another impetus was the general paternalism of Hampton's administration, most of whom, including the institution's president, were white. Hundreds of students initially supported the strike and it lasted several weeks. In the end, five students were expelled, twenty-nine were suspended, and thirty were classified as "temporarily ineligible." In 1928, Bailey and Thompson left Hampton for New York City, where they became roommates and close friends. After reporting on the Hampton events for the YWCA in New York City, Bailey was invited to join the organization as a national secretary, where she was charged with continuing her work with Hampton students and on a wider scale. By the time she met Thurman again in 1931, she was a nationally known speaker and organizer in the black student Christian movement, with a hectic schedule of travel and speaking that rivaled her future husband's.

The engagement and marriage of Thurman and Sue Bailey were accompanied by the careful and elaborate ritual that had become typical for middle-class black weddings. Their betrothal was formally announced on 2 May 1932, as "an event of decided interest to smart Atlantans," in the words of the *Atlanta Daily World,* thereby putting an end to "weeks of persistent rumor to that effect." The announcement was made at the "artistically appointed residence" of Mr. and Mrs. F. A. Toomer, the latter a friend of Sue Bailey from their high-school studies together at Spelman. The engagement dinner was a six-course meal featuring "alluring molds of ice cream in the shape of pink wedding slippers." The motif was carried out even in the evening's sugar cubes, which were embossed with the initials "B-T" in pink. In the words of the *Atlanta Daily World:*

> The dining room was a setting of beauty, with its color scheme of pink and white. The table was overlaid with a cloth of Madeira and filet lace combined, which veiled an undercover of pink. In the center was a pink glass bowl holding a pink tulle ribbon containing maidenhair ferns. On each side of the bowl was placed a pink candle in a pink holder and extending from one candle to the other was pink tulle ribbon containing the words "Bailey-Thurman" in gold letters.

The article promised the forthcoming wedding "of the prominent couple will be an event of the early summer."[97]

The wedding took place on 12 June 1932, at the end of a YWCA and YMCA conference at Kings Mountain in North Carolina, a conference that would mark the end of Sue Bailey's work as a YWCA national secretary. The wedding was the subject of two lengthy articles in the *Atlanta Daily World.* The wedding service was clearly very important to Thurman. With its combination of thoughtful readings, appropriate music, and meditation, appealing to the intellectual, the emotional, and the spiritual, the wedding service was in many ways similar to the chapel services Thurman would hold at Morehouse and Howard in the 1930s.

A sudden downpour forced the transfer of the ceremony indoors at the last minute, but the ceremony went off as planned. It was divided into three parts, the first to consist of readings by Thurman on the theme of love, read by Thurman, beginning with Langston Hughes's poem "The Negro Speaks of Rivers" and concluding with the familiar passages on love from 1 Corinthians 13:4–7. One account described Thurman's reading as being in "one of his characteristically mystic attitudes," reading Hughes's poetry "as only Howard Thurman can read it."[98]

The second part of the ceremony was musical. A thirteen-person chorus sang several selections. Chorus members included Marion Cuthbert, Frank Wilson, and Herbert King, concluding with the latter singing a bass solo on "Drink to Me with Only Thine Eyes."[99] The final part of the wedding service, as Thurman announced at the beginning of the ceremonies, would largely consist of silence.

Sue Bailey entered, with the chorus singing the wedding march from *Lohengrin* ("Here Comes the Bride"), with Thurman's daughter, Olive, as the only brides-maid, festooning the path with garlands of flowers. The couple stood and knelt before a floral altar for an extended period of time, and then Thurman offered a final reading from the opening of Tennyson's "In Memoriam," a classic poem of mourning that was, perhaps, a quiet tribute to Katie Kelley. The couple exchanged vows, and Thurman's longtime friend Clarence J. Gresham pronounced them husband and wife. Of Sue, Thurman would reflect in his autobiography, "She related to me as a person, as a man, giving to me at my center a life of heart that made the whole world new" (*WHAH*, 84). Sue assumed the care and mothering of her stepdaughter, and on 8 October 1933, the new couple's daughter Anne Spencer Thurman, named after the African American poet, was born.

By the time of his second marriage, Thurman had emerged as one of the lead-ing young preachers of his time, a legend among African Americans, and with growing fame among whites. By the summer of 1928 Thurman was already being described in the *Pittsburgh Courier* as "an outstanding pulpit orator and one of the greatest thinkers of this age."[100] His reputation as a mystic, years before he spoke extensively on mysticism, often preceded him. In 1929, he was described as speaking with "his dramatic and mystic conceptions."[101] A February 1932 talk that "held his audience spellbound and awed" was described as being delivered with "the characteristic mysticism and philosophy that pervades his innumerable addresses and public contributions whenever he appears on a public program."[102] In the 1930s, Thurman was variously described in print as "Howard Thurman the Great," as "the idol of colored and many white students throughout America," and as delivering one of his "characteristically profound and inspiring addresses."[103] After he served in 1932 as conference leader for the annual YMCA student confer-ence in Asilomar, California, launching him on a month-long speaking tour at universities, student conferences, and churches in the southwest, one white admirer wrote to him, calling him a "dreamer" in touch with the "sore spots of life" who embodied an ideal model of an "at one" personality.[104] At about the same time Reverend William J. Faulkner, pastor of the historic First Congregational Church of Atlanta, Georgia, wrote Thurman after an appearance that "God is bountifully blessing you as a teacher and prophet in pointing the way to the light for our people in these troublous times."[105]

By the time of their wedding, Thurman had accepted the invitation of his old friend and counselor, Mordecai Wyatt Johnson, who was then president of How-ard University, to become a faculty member of the School of Religion.[106] Thur-man's uneasy relationship with Spelman's president Florence Read undoubtedly contributed to his decision to leave Atlanta. The two had clashed early in his tenure over his schedule and the use of his free time. The deeper issue between them, which evidently grew into a deep enmity, was that he felt she was subtly

Howard Thurman (fourth from right) with Howard University ushers, circa 1935. Courtesy of the Arleigh Prelow/Howard Thurman Film Project

Sue Bailey Thurman and Anne Spencer Thurman, 1934. Courtesy of the Thurman family and Arleigh Prelow/ Howard Thurman Film Project

patronizing to her students. Thurman felt that the women at Spelman "lacked models for themselves as black women" (*WHAH*, 79), an assessment not unlike Sue Bailey's experience with the Hampton student strike of 1927.

In the fall of 1932 Thurman arrived at Howard to assume a position in the School of Theology, which included responsibilities for services at the university's Rankin chapel. This opened a period of fourteen years that would be one of the richest in his adult life.[107] During his years at Howard, Thurman became, if anything, more visible than he had been previously, touring the United States and Canada on behalf of progressive Christian organizations and speaking at colleges and universities and both black and white churches. It was a time of great political unrest in the United States, and like most Americans he watched the unfolding of the Great Depression in the early 1930s with a great sense of anger at the failures of the United States to take care of its own citizens and the persistence and in some ways the intensification of racism in the United States.

It is never easy to write about Thurman's political commitments, because he shied away from writing or speaking about them in specific terms. But it is clear that Thurman was never as politically militant as he was during the mid-1930s. When he invited Francis Henson, a leader in both the student division of the YMCA and the socialist party to speak at the chapel at Howard in 1934, he told him that he did not want him to focus on religion "in any formal sense" but rather the "spiritual significance that may be found in the struggle for a better and more clean-smelling world."[108] Thurman's politics were in the 1930s those of a moderate socialist, convinced that capitalism had failed and that an alternative was needed but stayed clear of Marxism in any systematic way. He was suspicious of President Franklin D. Roosevelt and the New Deal, particularly during his first term, but wrote approvingly to his Howard colleague Ralph Bunche in November 1934, after the latter's sharp critique of the New Deal, especially in its treatment of racial minorities.[109] He remained active in the Fellowship of Reconciliation (FOR) and was a pacifist, opposed to war and to American rearmament, though viewing events in the revived European dictatorships with growing unease. This was all background to what proved to be one of the greatest adventures of his life, his trip to South Asia in 1935–36.

One of the great experiences and challenges of Thurman's life was the chance to head the four-person Negro Delegation, consisting of Thurman and Sue Bailey Thurman and Methodist minister Edward Carroll and his wife, Phenola Carroll. The delegation left New York City on the *Ile de France* in September 1935. On the four-month tour Thurman spoke at least 135 times in over fifty cities, to a variety of audiences ranging from intimate prayer sessions to public meetings with over four thousand persons in attendance and on a variety of topics ranging from the theology of Saint Paul to the educational philosophy of Booker T.

Washington. Thurman met with average Indians of all religious backgrounds as well as some of the leading figures in Indian cultural and political life, including Rabindranath Tagore and Mahatma Gandhi.[110]

The selection of the members of the Negro Delegation became a major intrigue and threatened to derail the entire tour. Its various twists and turns are explored in the main headnote to the India documents that follow in the current volume. From the beginning, Thurman's view of the purposes of the delegation remained consistent. Although he was tactful and diplomatic, he was determined to be an active and forceful chair of the delegation and not to let the largely white committee dictate to him the agenda or purposes of the "Pilgrimage of Friendship" to India. He approached the tour with some skepticism of the relevance of the student Christian movement. For Thurman, two of the main spiritual issues of the time were the political, economic, and racial realities of 1930s Depression-era America and the need to craft a Christian message that rejected fundamentalist and other dogmatic sectarian appeals. The India trip gave him an opportunity to address and link both concerns.

The political connection between the oppression of blacks in the United States and the freedom struggles of the people of India was one of the reasons that A. Ralla Ram, the head of the Student Christian Movement in India, Burma, and Ceylon proposed the sponsorship of a Negro Delegation, arguing that "since Christianity in India is the 'oppressor's' religion, there would be a unique value in having representatives of another oppressed group speak on the validity and contribution of Christianity."[111] Although the delegation was cautioned by the committee not to speak on Indian politics, many who heard the delegation, from average listeners to Gandhi himself, drew the obvious connections between the two situations.

Thurman's other main worry about the Negro Delegation was about the version of Christianity it would convey. He was concerned, as were the tour's American organizers, that it not become an occasion for evangelizing. This proved one of the major problems in the tour. In numerous stops, the sponsors and audiences were surprised and somewhat upset that the talks and sermons did not touch on traditional Christological themes. Thurman did speak in numerous talks about the role of the Christian faith as a bulwark for personal and spiritual endeavors as well as on the significance of the Negro spirituals and other religious topics. However, Thurman's major apologetic task in India was the defense of Christianity against its numerous and articulate detractors. In an encounter early in the tour, a law student in Colombo challenged Thurman in attacking Christianity as a religion for imperialists and slave masters. Indian students frequently confronted the delegation with questions about the Scottsboro case, in which black teens were unjustly accused of raping two white young women while riding a freight train in the South, and other incidents of racial injustice in the United States.

A highlight of the tour was Thurman's meeting with Bengali scholars Rabindranath Tagore and Kshitimohan Sen near Tagore's university ashram in Shantiniketan, near Calcutta. Thurman, who had been an admirer of Tagore's for some time, quoting one of his poems in "The Perils of Immature Piety" (1925), found Tagore a profound but somewhat distant spiritual presence. As Thurman recounts in his autobiography, during their conversations, "I felt his mind was going through cycles as if we were not even present. Then he would swing back from that orbit, settle in, take us into account again, and sweep out" (*WHAH*, 130). If Thurman remembered the meeting with Tagore as a mild disappointment, claiming that at no point was there the "kind of identity with him that I later felt in Gandhi's presence," he had a very different reaction to Kshitimohan Sen (1880–1960), a distinguished scholar of Hinduism and Indian religion and the head of Visva-Bharati's division of Oriental studies.[112] In his autobiography, Thurman describes their meeting once they overcame their defensive support of their respective religious traditions as "the most primary, naked fusing of total religious experience with another human being of which I have ever been capable. It was as if we had stepped out of social, political, cultural frames of reference, and allowed two human spirits to unite on a ground of reality that was unmarked by separateness and differences. This was a watershed of experience in my life. We had become a part of each other even as we remained essentially individual. I was able to stand secure in my place and enter into his place without diminishing myself or threatening him" (*WHAH*, 129).

Thurman found Gandhi to be a much more engaged presence than Tagore. His meeting, the first significant meeting of Gandhi with prominent African Americans, was a major step in the introduction of Gandhian ideas of nonviolence to the struggle for racial equality in the United States. The meeting also had a great personal significance for Thurman. In Gandhi, a pacifist who had spent his life combining his burning sense of political injustice with a profound spiritual calling, Thurman found a personal example for emulation. If Gandhi's religious experience, rooted in his native Hinduism, sought a religious canopy that could encompass all of India, Thurman was searching for an analogous way to universalize his Christian-rooted religiosity.

Thurman's spiritual epiphany took place about ten days before his meeting with Gandhi, in Peshawar (now in Pakistan), while the delegation spent the morning visiting the nearby Khyber Pass. Although this was an area famous for border skirmishes and clashes—and it remains a violent part of the world today—Thurman saw beyond the violence. Gazing out into the distance of the vast frontier, he saw as far as Afghanistan while a long camel train bearing cargo passed close by. It was a moment of vision for Thurman that held in its

Negro Delegation at a train station (from third from right, front row, Howard Thurman, unidentified woman, Sue Bailey Thurman, Phenola Carroll, Edward Carroll), October 1935–March 1936. Courtesy of the Thurman family and Arleigh Prelow/Howard Thurman Film Project

Negro Delegation resting (Howard Thurman, top, Phenola Carroll, to right, Sue Bailey Thurman, right front), October 1935–March 1936. Courtesy of the Thurman family and Arleigh Prelow/Howard Thurman Film Project

Howard, Sue (in black with pearls), and Edward Carroll (next to Thurman) with unidentified persons in India, October 1935–March 1936. Courtesy of the Thurman family and Arleigh Prelow/Howard Thurman Film Project

very core the possibility of true human community. As Thurman writes in his autobiography, he had to find a way to "answer the persistent query of the Indian students about Christianity and the color bar" (*WHAH*, 136).

> Here was the gateway through which Roman and Mogul conquerors had come in other days bringing with them goods, new concepts, and the violence of armed might. All that we had seen and felt in India seemed to be brought miraculously into focus. We saw clearly what we must do somehow when we returned to America. We knew that we must test whether a religious fellowship could be developed in America that was capable of cutting across all racial barriers, with a carry-over into the common life, a fellowship that would alter the behavior patterns of those involved. It became imperative now to find out if experiences of spiritual unity among people could be more compelling than the experiences which divide them. (Footprints, 24)

This vision was one Thurman would explore and attempt to answer for the remainder of his public life and ministry, leading to his work with the Fellowship Church and beyond. In some ways the vision at the Khyber Pass provided Thurman with a way to respond to the challenge first posed to him by George Cross, a way to be true "to his Black skin" while fearlessly addressing the "timeless issues of the human spirit."

NOTES

1. U.S. Bureau of the Census, *Twelfth Census of the United States, Population Schedule, Dade County, Florida* (Washington, D.C.: GPO, 1900), Roll T623_167. Census records list Thurman's birth as 18 November 1899, but then erroneously calculate his age as four months old. Instead he would have been approximately seven months old by June 1900. To our knowledge, Thurman never publically identified his place of birth, but stories of his West Palm Beach birth seem to have been widely known in the 1930s. In 1937, Clarence Walker, principal of the Industrial High School Negroes in West Palm Beach, wrote to Thurman, "My attention has been called to the fact that this town has the honor of being your place of birth." Thurman's reply to Walker neither affirmed nor contradicted the claim. See From Clarence Walker, 2 January 1937 and To Clarence Walker, 14 January 1937, HTC-MBU: Box 21.

2. In his autobiography, Thurman recalls that his father "worked on a railroad crew laying the track of the Florida East Coast Railroad from Jacksonville to Miami, and would come home every two weeks." See *With Head and Heart: The Autobiography of Howard Thurman* (New York: Harcourt, Brace, 1979), 4. Hereafter referred to as *WHAH*.

3. Ibid, 20–21.

4. U.S. Bureau of the Census, *Tenth Census of the United States, Population Schedule, Moseley Hall, Madison County, Florida* (Washington, D.C.: GPO, 1880), Roll T9_130.

5. Thurman's one known discussion of his grandfather (almost certainly his maternal grandfather, Howard Ambrose) came in the course of a speech in India when he mentioned that despite the brutal oppression of slavery, many slaves managed to excel in arts, handicrafts, and other artistic and intellectual pursuits. A newspaper account of the speech notes, "Dr. Thurman was deeply moved when he made a brief reference to the life of his grandfather, who as a slave had been a calculator on an American estate." "The Three Faiths of the Negro: Brief in His Ability, in Life, and in God," *Times of (Bombay) India,* 21 February 1936. Presumably Howard Ambrose was a person with considerable mathematical abilities that were used in the business of the plantation. Some slave calculators, prodigies who were able to swiftly solve difficult mathematical problems in their heads, were exhibited by their slave masters and became minor celebrities. See Sidney Kaplan and Emma Nogrady Kaplan, *The Black Presence in the Era of the American Revolution* (Amherst: University of Massachusetts Press, 1989), 167–70.

6. U.S. Bureau of the Census, *Tenth Census,* Roll T9_130.

7. U.S. Bureau of the Census, *Eighth Census of the United States, Hamilton, Florida* (Washington, D.C.: GPO, 1860), Roll M653_107; *1860 U.S. Federal Census - Slave Schedules,* Madison County, Florida, M653. Thurman mentions the name of his grandparents' master as "old man McGhee." *Jesus and the Disinherited* (New York: Abingdon-Cokesbury Press, 1949), 30.

8. U.S. Bureau of the Census, *Eighth Census of the United States,* Roll M653_107; *1860 U.S. Federal Census - Slave Schedules,* Madison County, Florida, M653.

9. However, this might be inconsistent with her South Carolinian lineage.

10. Clifton Paisley, *The Red Hills of Florida, 1528–1865* (Tuscaloosa: University of Alabama Press, 1989), 147.

11. See Ira Berlin, *Many Thousands Gone: The First Two Centuries of American Slavery* (Cambridge, Mass.: Belknap Press of Harvard University Press, 1998), 307–316, 319–324.

12. U.S. Bureau of the Census, *Thirteenth Census of the United States: 1910—Population* (Washington, D.C.: GPO, 1910), Roll T624_168. Alex Evans is listed as head of household with Alice named as his wife and Howard, Henrietta, and Madaline as children.

13. Howard Thurman (HT), *Footprints of a Dream: The Story of the Church for the Fellowship of All Peoples* (New York: Harper, 1959), 15. Hereafter referred to as *Footprints*.

14. HT, *For the Inward Journey: The Writings of Howard Thurman. Selected by Anne Spencer Thurman* (San Diego, Calif.: Harcourt, 1984), 275, 279–80.

15. A *sponsor* is a more experienced spiritual mentor under whose tutelage a newly baptized member is placed.

16. Arleigh Prelow and InSpirit Communications, *Howard Thurman: In Search of Common Ground* (forthcoming). Prelow's film also treats the paternity issue as a rumor in the community that deeply affected Thurman in his formative years.

17. In reference to his affinity with nature, Thurman reflected, "When I was young, I found more companionship in nature than I did among people." *WHAH*, 7. See also Lerone Bennett, "Howard Thurman: Twentieth Century Holy Man," *Ebony*, February 1988, 76. Bennett describes Thurman as a "loner, a brooder, a sensitive suffering spirit who sought solace in the woods and on deserted beaches and communicated with forces that are not visible and audible to other mortals."

18. HT, "Windbreak against Existence," *Bostonia* 34, no. 2 (1960): 8.

19. Jeremiah 17:8.

20. Leonard Lempel, "The Origins of the Civil Rights Movement in Daytona Beach," (working paper, Daytona Beach Community College, Daytona Beach, Florida, 1993), 5. During Thurman's boyhood, Daytona included the community west of the Halifax River. In 1926, the municipalities of Daytona, Daytona Beach, and Seabreeze merged to form the current city of Daytona Beach.

21. Leonard Lempel, "African American Settlements in the Daytona Beach Area, 1866–1910," in *Proceedings from the Florida Conference of Historians* (Orange Park, Fla.: Florida Conference of Historians, 1993), 109.

22. At some point, the home's address was changed to 614 Whitehall. The house was restored in 1987 and was listed in 1990 on the National Register of Historic Places. See Sale Gardner, "Vision Helps Accelerate Thurman Restoration," *(Daytona) News-Journal*, 6 September 1987, 1–2F; Lois Kaplan, "Dr. Thurman's Legacy," *Daytona Morning Journal*, 1 July 1985, 1.

23. For discussion of the concept of *extended family* in the black community, see Robert B. Hill and Lawrence Shackleford, "The Black Extended Family Revisited," in *The Black Family: Essays and Studies*, ed. Robert Staples, 2nd ed. (Belmont, Calif.: Wadsworth, 1978), 201–6; and Andrew Billingsley, *Black Families in White America* (Englewood Cliffs, N.J.: Prentice-Hall, 1968).

24. *Polk's Daytona Beach City Directory* (Jacksonville, Fla.: Polk, 1900), 2–3.

25. Ralph J. Bunche, *The Political Status of the Negro in the Age of F.D.R.*, ed. Dewey W. Grantham (Chicago: University of Chicago Press, 1973), 280–82, 451–54. For more on the politics of Daytona Beach, see Lempel, "Origins" and "Race and Politics in Daytona Beach, Florida, 1876–1937" (unpublished draft, May 1995).

26. Lempel, "Race and Politics," 8.

27. *Mary McLeod Bethune: Building a Better World, Essays and Selected Documents*, eds. Audrey Thomas McCluskey and Elaine M. Smith (Bloomington: Indiana University Press, 1999).

28. "Eulogy for Mary McLeod Bethune," audio recording, HTC-MBU.

29. Smith's confectionary is listed in *Daytona Beach and Seabreeze City Directory*, (Jacksonville, Fla.: Polk, 1914), 199.

30. See volume appendix for Thurman's academic transcripts.

31. The school was established in 1892 in the basement of the Bethel Baptist Church through the support of the American Baptist Home Mission Society (ABHMS) and the Baptist General State Convention for the express purpose of educating new generations of freed women and men.

32. Thurman would last meet Julia Green in 1963 on Howard Thurman Day in Daytona Beach, where "seeing her again after so long a time and on that particular occasion was a high-water mark in my life." *WHAH*, 14.

33. See volume appendix for Thurman's academic transcripts.

34. Thurman stated that she went to Fessenden Academy, a church school in Ocala, Florida. *WHAH*, 253–54.

35. Howard Thurman, "A 'Native Son' Speaks," *The Advocate*, 17 May 1940, to be printed in volume 2.

36. See To Mordecai Wyatt Johnson, 18 June 1918, printed in the current volume.

37. Their correspondence, included in the current volume, reveals a close friendship between teacher and student that continued throughout her life. See Elizabeth Yates, *Howard Thurman: Portrait of a Practical Dreamer* (New York: John Day, 1964), 45–46; and Hermia Justice, "Listening to My Mother: Ethel Simons Meeds," *The Listening Ear: A Newsletter of the Howard Thurman Educational Trust* 19 (Spring 1989): 3, 7.

38. See To Ethel Simons, 4 June 1919, printed in the current volume.

39. Shakespeare, *Venus and Adonis*, 145; italics added. The full line is, "Love is a spirit all compact of fire."

40. Edward A. Jones, *Candle in the Dark: A History of Morehouse College* (Valley Forge, Pa.: Judson Press, 1967), 10–11. The Augusta Institute moved to Atlanta in 1879, changed its name to the Atlanta Baptist Seminary, and later relocated to its present site in 1885. In 1897, Atlanta Baptist Seminary became Atlanta Baptist College.

41. Actually, Henry Lyman Morehouse, corresponding secretary of the American Baptist Home Mission Society and the one for whom Morehouse College is named, used the term in 1896 before Du Bois made it popular. See James M. McPherson, *The Abolitionist Legacy: From Reconstruction to the NAACP* (Princeton, N.J.: Princeton University Press, 1975), 222. See Kevin Gaines's treatment in *Uplifting the Race: Black Leadership, Politics, and Culture in the Twentieth Century* (Chapel Hill: University of North Carolina Press, 1996), 31–78, where he traces the genealogy of uplift and illustrates how it began first as "theology of liberation" for freedmen and women, to over time develop its own elitist sentimentality rooted in moral and classist ideology.

42. See Evelyn Brooks Higginbotham, *Righteous Discontent: The Women's Movement in the Black Baptist Church, 1880–1920* (Cambridge, Mass.: Harvard University Press, 1993) and Walter Earl Fluker, "Recognition, Respectability, and Loyalty: Black Churches and the Quest for Civility," in *New Day Begun: African American Churches and Civic Culture in Post-Civil Rights America*, ed. Drew Smith (Durham, N.C.: Duke University Press, 2003), 121.

43. See Proposal for Negro Scholarship Fund, [1922–23?], printed in the current volume.

44. "Our Challenge," February–March 1922, printed in the current volume.

45. Nina Mjagkij, *Light in the Darkness: African Americans and the YMCA, 1852–1946* (Lexington: University Press of Kentucky, 1994), 129.

46. See "Program of the 1918 YMCA Kings Mountain Conference," YMCA Archives, Special Collections, University of Wisconsin, Madison, Wisconsin.

47. Ibid.

48. To Mordecai Wyatt Johnson, 18 June 1918, printed in the current volume.

49. Italics added.

50. From Mordecai Wyatt Johnson, 8 July 1918, printed in the current volume.

51. Gamewell Valentine, "Themes and Variations," *Atlanta Daily World,* 31 May 1937. This anecdote raises the interesting question whether Thurman retained a relatively traditional view of the accuracy and historicity of the Bible during his Morehouse years (he became a passionate champion of modernist exegesis during his years at Rochester Theological Seminary) or whether he was objecting to Frazier's mocking tone and felt Frazier was not giving Biblical accounts the dignity they deserved. Valentine was a 1924 graduate of Morehouse and his consistent misspelling of *Frazier* as *Frasier* is corrected in the transcription.

52. " 'Relaxation' and Race Conflict," 1929, printed in the current volume.

53. Henry James Young, ed., *God and Human Freedom: A Festschrift in Honor of Howard Thurman* (Richmond, Ind.: Friends United Press, 1983), xiv.

54. Garrie Ward Moore (1892–1923) was born in Genoa, Florida, and graduated from Florida Institute in Live Oak (1909) and Atlanta Baptist (1912). He spent the 1912–13 academic year at Columbia University and New York School of Social Work and was the first Morehouse graduate to have his degree validated by that institution. He spent the summers of 1913–17 and 1919–22 in New York working on a master's degree, which he earned in 1923. While at Columbia, Moore wrote what appears to be an expanded version of his Columbia BA thesis entitled "Study of a Group of West Indian Negroes in New York City," Columbia University Archives, New York, N.Y.

55. Benjamin E. Mays, *Born to Rebel* (New York: Scribner's, 1971), 93.

56. *Torch,* Morehouse College Yearbook, 1923, printed in the current volume.

57. See Kenneth Cauthen, *The Impact of American Religious Liberalism* (New York: Harper, 1962) and Gary Dorrien, *The Making of American Liberal Theology: Idealism, Realism and Modernity: 1900–1950* (Louisville: Westminster John Knox Press, 2003).

58. *WHAH,* 46.

59. Johnson delivered this speech at his commencement at Harvard University in 1922, where he completed his requirements for Master of Sacred Theology. The speech was published that same year in the *Nation,* 19 July 1922.

60. "Biographical Scrapbook 1923–1929," Research Files, Howard Thurman Papers Project, Morehouse College (HTPP).

61. "Bulletin First Congregational Church of Rochester," 2 March 1924, Research Files, HTPP.

62. The Klan's presence in New York State peaked from 1920 to 1925, and it declined sharply thereafter. In 1923 an estimated two hundred thousand Klan members were in the state, with the membership concentrated on Long Island and in upstate cities, with particularly strong chapters in Binghamton (the site of the state headquarters) and Buffalo. *The Encyclopedia of New York State,* ed. Peter Eisenstadt (Syracuse, N.Y.: Syracuse University Press, 2005), s.v. "Ku Klux Klan."

63. "College and Color," April 1924, printed in the current volume.

64. "Negro Youth and the Washington Conference," December 1925, printed in the current volume.

65. "The Sphere of the Church's Responsibility in Social Reconstruction," July 1924, printed in the current volume.

66. Kenneth L. Cober, *Tales Out of School* (Cortland, N.Y.: Cortland, 1995), 22.

67. "The Perils of Immature Piety," May 1925, printed in the current volume.

68. "Let Ministers Be Christians," January 1925, printed in the current volume.

69. *WHAH,* 57.

70. To Mordecai Wyatt Johnson, 8 July 1925, printed in the current volume.

71. *WHAH,* 44. The course used two texts, John Dewey, *How We Think* (Boston: Heath, 1910), and Laurence Buermeyer, et al., *An Introduction to Reflective Thinking* (New York: Houghton Mifflin, 1923). The latter volume was cowritten by nine members of the Columbia Philosophy Department. E. A. Burtt, later a professor of philosophy at Cornell University, in *The Metaphysical Foundations of Modern Physical Science: A Historical and Critical Study* (New York: Harcourt, Brace, 1924), critiqued the limitations of empirical knowledge of nature from an implicitly religious vantage, in a manner Thurman would similarly employ in his later works.

72. "Can It Be Truly Said That the Existence of a Supreme Spirit Is a Scientific Hypothesis?" fall 1925, printed in the current volume.

73. C. A. Richardson, *Philosophical Review* 27 (1918): 227–73.

74. For Cross's impact upon Thurman, see Luther E. Smith Jr., *Howard Thurman: The Mystic as Prophet* (Washington, D.C.: University Press of America, 1981).

75. *WHAH,* 60. From that time, Thurman collected Schreiner's writings, and in 1973 he edited and published the anthology *A Track to the Water's Edge: The Olive Schreiner Reader* (New York: Harper and Row, 1973). In the work, Thurman commented, "It seems that all my life I was being readied for such an encounter. Through the years I have secured all available works of this gifted woman. Her ideas have influenced my thought at a very profound level." xi.

76. HT, *A Track to the Water's Edge,* xii. Although Thurman believed Schreiner was sensitive to the issues of indigenous South Africans, she still reflected her times, and he was appalled by her use of the term *nigger* in some of her writings. Ibid., xxix.

77. "The Basis of Sex Morality: Inquiry into the Attitude toward Premarital Sexual Morality among Various Peoples," April 1926, printed in the current volume.

78. *WHAH,* 60. The impact of Cross's advice, though not fully realized at that moment, became in time a driving principle for decision making in relation to social action for Thurman. Smith discusses the significance of this occasion and its relation to Thurman's baptism. See Smith, *Mystic as Prophet,* 24.

79. Katie Kelley to Lucy Tapley, 18 September 1918, Deceased Alumnae Files, Archives, Spelman College.

80. Jacqueline Rouse, *Lugenia Burns Hope: Black Southern Reformer* (Athens: University of Georgia Press, 1989), 82. Rouse incorrectly identifies Kelley as Katherine Kelley. See also Louie D. Shivery, "The History of Organized Social Work among Negroes in Atlanta, 1890–1935" (master's thesis, Atlanta University, 1936), 53.

81. Charles Kelley Jr. (1902–56) served as associate professor and chief of the radiology division at Howard University's College of Medicine and chief of radiology at Freedman's Hospital in Washington, D.C. He completed his undergraduate training at Morehouse in 1924 and graduated from Howard University School of Medicine in 1929.

82. Kai Jackson Issa interview with Olive Wong Thurman, 3 October 2003, Oral History Collection, HTPP.

83. "Oberlin College News," *Pittsburgh Courier,* 19 March 1927. This article mentions that Thurman had directed two plays performed by the Dunbar Forum, presumably an amateur African American theatrical group: "The cast was well chosen and the performance creditable to its director."

84. "Finding God," 1927, printed in the current volume.

85. Katie Thurman to Lucy Tapley, 9 April 1927, printed in the current volume.

86. To Mordecai Wyatt Johnson, 9 September 1927, MWJ-DHU-MS: Box 178.

87. "Higher Education and Religion," November 1927, printed in the current volume.

88. "The Task of the Negro Ministry," October 1928, printed in the current volume.

89. Katie Thurman to Lucy Tapley, 9 April 1927, printed in the current volume.

90. "The Message of the Spirituals," October 1928, printed in the current volume.

91. Rufus M. Jones, *Finding the Trail of Life* (New York: MacMillan, 1926). This volume was an autobiography, focusing on childhood years, his love of the spiritual dimensions of nature, and his growing appreciation for a nondogmatic conception of nature and was a possible model for Thurman's own autobiography. It says little about mysticism.

92. *WHAH*, 74. Haverford College, founded in 1833, admitted its first black student in 1926, did not have a black graduate until 1949, and would have no more than one or two blacks per class until the late 1960s. "Quaker Influence on the History of Haverford College," http://www.Haverford.edu/aboutHaverford/quaker/history.edu; conversations with Associate Dean Philip Bean, June 2005.

93. "27 Club Forum Draws Mammoth Crowd in Spite of Rain; Thurman Speaks," *Atlanta Daily World,* 24 February 1932.

94. Thurman and Sue Bailey had frequently met at conferences in the intervening years, such as the YWCA student conference in 1929, the Kings Mountain retreat that same year, and a joint meeting of the YMCA and YWCA at Atlanta University in 1930. "YWCA Holds Conference in Atlanta," *Pittsburgh Courier,* 29 January 1929; "Student Confab Opens," *Pittsburgh Courier,* 15 June 1929; "Georgia Y Conference Closes Two-day Meet at Atlanta U," *Pittsburgh Courier,* 29 March 1930.

95. Trudi Smith, *Sue Bailey Thurman: Building Bridges to Common Ground* (Boston: Boston University, Thurman Center, 1995), 7. Hereafter referred to as *Sue Bailey Thurman.*

96. Some evidence suggests that Sue Bailey may have been born in 1901. See "Sue Bailey Thurman," DAF-GAS.

97. "Thurman-Bailey Engagement Is Announced," *Atlanta Daily World,* 5 May 1932.

98. Lucius L. Jones, "Society Slants," *Atlanta Daily World,* 14 June 1932.

99. Other choristers included Frankie Adams, Frances Lawson, Dolores Mitchell, Marjorie Stewart, and Mrs. W. A. Fountain Jr., along with Ned Pope, John Knox, and Juanita Paschal Toomer. "Thurman in Charge of Own Wedding Ceremony," *Atlanta Daily World,* 15 June 1932.

100. "Y Workers to Meet July 6–21," *Pittsburgh Courier,* 23 June 1928.

101. "YWCA Holds Conference in Atlanta," *Pittsburgh Courier,* 29 January 1929.

102. Jones, "Society Slants," *Atlanta Daily World,* 24 February 1932.

103. Jones, "Society Slants," *Atlanta Daily World,* 7 October 1932; Gamewell Valentine, "Themes and Variations," *Atlanta Daily World,* 6 March 1938; "Ministers' Confab at Shaw Closed by Thurman," *Atlanta Daily World,* 20 August 1932.

104. Earl Alcorn to HT, 23 February 1932, HTC-MBU: Box 1.

105. From William J. Faulkner, 21 April 1932, printed in the current volume.

106. From Mordecai Wyatt Johnson, 8 October 1932, printed in the current volume.

107. Thurman's work and years at Howard University are discussed more fully in the biographical essay in volume 2 of *The Papers of Howard Washington Thurman.*

108. To Francis A. Henson, 18 October 1934, printed in the current volume.

109. To Ralph Bunche, 9 November 1934, printed in the current volume.

110. *The Papers of Howard Washington Thurman* uses his familiar title *Mahatma*, a Sanskrit word meaning *great-souled* as Gandhi's first name instead of Mohandas.

111. Committee on the Negro Delegation to India, Minutes, 13 March 1934. HTC-MBU: Box 136.

112. In his letter to philosopher W. E. Hocking of 29 May 1936, printed in volume 2, Thurman refers to his meeting at Shantiniketan with "Dr. Sin." In his autobiography he writes of "Dr. Singh," the "head of the division of Oriental studies," at Shantiniketan. *WHAH*, 129.

Editorial Statement

The array of Howard Thurman materials from which documents have been chosen for publication in *The Papers of Howard Washington Thurman, June 1918–March 1936* is considerable: public statements, sermons, lectures, speeches, articles, book reviews, interviews, recorded comments, unpublished manuscripts, student papers, essays, course syllabi, published articles, and more. The quantifiable universe of the Thurman papers, including subject files, consists of approximately 150,000 documents. Entered into the project database are over 58,000, of which 2,800 are public writings. Approximately 250 (about 9 percent) of these writings were selected for the documentary edition. Of the 57,000 letters from and to Thurman on file, approximately 600 were selected for publication.

This documentary edition spans 1918 to 1981, from Thurman's formative period and tenure at Howard University, his founding of the Fellowship Church in San Francisco, his tenure at Boston University, through to his work as director of the Howard Thurman Educational Trust. The volumes are arranged chronologically and each includes a critical introduction, chronology, selection of photographs, appendix, and an index.

The documents selected are those that in our opinion best represent Thurman's thought and his activities. Some published writings are included if they were obscurely published and not included in Thurman's later collections of sermons and essays. This includes almost all of Thurman's publications from the period covered in the current volume. Several unpublished writings are included as well, notably the three extant student papers from Thurman's work at the Rochester Theological Seminary, Rochester, New York. Several journalistic accounts of Thurman's speaking engagements are also included. Incoming and third-party correspondence are included if they provide important historical context and provide insight into Thurman's personality and dealings with other persons.

ANNOTATION

The editors of *The Papers of Howard Washington Thurman* have, in keeping with current documentary editing practice, followed a policy of parsimony in our annotation strategy. Annotations for prominent persons are kept to a minimum, and well-known political events or institutions are not described. For persons, places, or things we were, after extensive research, unable to identify, we have left without annotation. Annotations focus on Thurman's biography, and discussions of theology are limited to the effort of evoking Thurman's intellectual and religious world at the time of the document's composition.

However, to adequately treat some aspects of Thurman's life and career has meant more ample annotations here. The existing biographical treatments of Thurman are thin, and there has never been a comprehensive biography of Thurman. Although the current documentary editing project is not a substitute for the unwritten biography, a great deal of original and painstaking research was undertaken into a number of aspects of Thurman's life, and this is frequently reflected in annotations.

The best account of Thurman's life remains his autobiography, *With Head and Heart*. This will remain *the* essential source on Thurman's life, but like many autobiographies, it recounts many events that took place decades before its writing, is without footnotes or other documentation, is selective in its choice of topics, and on some subjects, especially his relations with his close associates, is at times less than fully candid. *The Papers of Howard Washington Thurman* provides an alternative source for Thurman's biography, confirming, amplifying, modifying, and in some cases challenging the accounts in *With Head and Heart*.

The lack of a previous scholarly biographical treatment has led the editors in some cases to provide comprehensive accounts of certain aspects of Thurman's career at considerable length. In the current volume a separate introduction describes his role as the chair of the Negro Delegation to India, Burma, and Ceylon in 1935–36, with documents ranging from 1934 to 1938; the documents on the aftermath of the journey of the Negro Delegation are included in volume 2.

TRANSCRIPTION

In preparing annotations and transcriptions, general editorial principles established in other documentary editing projects are followed, and we acknowledge a special debt to *The Papers of Martin Luther King Jr.* and the project's senior editor, Clayborne Carson. For general editorial principles, we rely on *The Chicago Manual of Style*.

Silent editorial corrections are made in cases of malformed letters, single-letter corrections in typescript (presumed to be typographical errors), and the transposing of two characters.

An author's use of hyphens and dashes is replicated with some modifications: end-of-line dashes are silently deleted unless the usage is ambiguous, hyphens between numbers are changed to en dashes (–), and em dashes (—), which appear as long dashes in many original manuscripts, are regularized.

Footnotes in the original text are now endnotes and are referred to with superscript symbols in the transcription. Endnotes in the original are still endnotes, with the exception of Thurman's master's thesis. Here Thurman's endnotes are indicated in footnotes to avoid confusion with the editors' annotations.

Strikeovers and insertions in such minor cases as correcting a misspelling or adding an overlooked connective word are not reproduced. When significant, insertions (usually handwritten) are indicated by placement in curly braces ({}) and placed to replicate the original document as much as possible.

The line breaks, pagination, and vertical and horizontal spacing in the original document are not replicated.

The underlining of book titles, court cases, or other words and phrases in typescripts is reproduced in the document.

Indiscernible words or segments of an original document or recording are indicated by the terms *illegible* or *inaudible,* respectively, in italic type and placed within square brackets, such as [*inaudible*] or [*illegible*]. Conjectures of unclear text or audiotape are indicated in the same way and are accompanied by a question mark. If the extent of illegibility is known, it is noted, such as [2 *words illegible*].

Illegible crossed-out words are indicated with the phrase and square brackets [*strikeover illegible*]. If the strikeover is by someone other than the author, it is not replicated but is described in an endnote.

If the remainder of a document is lost or unintelligible, the condition is described as [*remainder missing*].

Printed letterheads are not reproduced. Any significant information in the letterhead is explained in the headnote or in an endnote. On occasion, however, document facsimiles, including letterheads, accompany the transcribed version.

Signed, original documents were selected in preference to copies. Signatures are reproduced in the following manner: [*signed*] name. For example, Sincerely, [*signed*] Mordecai Johnson

Mordecai W. Johnson

If the closing includes neither a signature nor a typed name but based on surrounding correspondence the editors could determine the letter's author, the name is placed in square brackets. If the name is typed but is not accompanied by a signature, it is described as [*unsigned*].

The date of the document is reproduced on the line below the title, and the place of origin is indicated on the next line below the date. If the editors have taken an educated guess at the place of origin, it appears italicized in brackets.

Place names in the United States are identified by state, and Canadian places are identified by province. Localities elsewhere in the world are identified by their current country. Well-known cities are not further identified. The annotations use the historically appropriate name and orthography. Current names are indicated by, for example, [now Sri Lanka]. This form also indicates current forms of institutional names.

References to secondary works in the annotations follow *The Chicago Manual of Style*.

SOURCE NOTES

Source notes are in two parts (separated by a period and a space) at the end of each document. The first part is an abbreviated description of the document's format, script, version, and signature, as applicable (all categories may not pertain to all documents). The second part indicates the location of the original document. The majority of documents in the current volume come from the Howard Thurman Papers at Boston University, which is designated HTC-MBU. Thus, a letter handwritten and signed by Thurman might look like this:

ALS. HTC-MBU: Box 8.

The *A* stands for autograph, the *L* for letter or memo, and the *S* for signed.

For a previously published document printed in the current volume, the location of the initial printing is indicated in the source note.

HOWARD THURMAN CHRONOLOGY

The following chronology extends through March 1936 and is compiled from Thurman's correspondence, scrapbooks, and writings as well as secondary accounts of his engagements in newspapers. Undated items appear before dated items within their designated month and/or year. For more details of the South Asia trip 21 October 1935 to 1 April 1936, see "Detailed Schedule of the Negro Delegation to South Asia" in the current volume.

1842 OR 1843
Nancy Ambrose, Thurman's maternal grandmother, is born into slavery in Madison County, Florida, on a plantation owned by John C. McGhee. During her grandson's early years, she resides in her daughter's home. Nancy lives to the age of ninety-three.

1850
July
Saul Solomon Thurman, Howard Thurman's father, is born in Florida.

1872
July
Thurman's mother, Alice Ambrose, is born in Moseley Hall, Florida.

1897
April
Thurman's older sister, Henrietta, is born.

4 September
Katie Laura Kelley, Thurman's first wife, is born in LaGrange, Georgia.

1899
18 November
Howard Washington Thurman is born in Florida, probably in West Palm Beach. The Thurman family would soon return to Daytona, where Thurman would spend the majority of his boyhood and adolescence.

1903
26 August
Sue (Susie Elvie) Bailey, Thurman's second wife, is born in Pine Bluff, Arkansas.

1907
Saul Solomon Thurman dies of pneumonia.

1908
5 August
Thurman's younger sister, Madaline Mae, is born in Daytona, Florida.

1909
Alice Ambrose Thurman marries her second husband, Alex Evans. He moves the family to Lake Helen, Florida, where Evans works in a sawmill.

1910
Alex Evans dies. The family moves back to Daytona by 1912.

1913
Thurman joins Mount Bethel Baptist Church in Daytona and is baptized in the Halifax River.

1915
Because there is no eighth grade for black children in Daytona, Thurman studies independently with the principal of his elementary school, R. W. Howard, and passes his eighth-grade examination. He is the first in his community to do so.

Fall
Thurman enrolls in the Florida Baptist Academy of Jacksonville (after fall of 1918, becomes Florida Normal and Industrial Institute and moves to St. Augustine). He lives with a cousin in Jacksonville and does chores in exchange for room and board.

1917
Summer
Thurman's older sister, Henrietta, dies of typhoid fever in Daytona.

1918
19 May
Katie Laura Kelley graduates valedictorian from Spelman Seminary in the teachers professional course. She begins work as an elementary school teacher in Birmingham, Alabama.

Summer
Thurman attends the Student Army Training Corps at Howard University in Washington, D.C. He returns to St. Augustine, Florida, to teach skills to his high-school classmates.

1919

28 May

Thurman graduates valedictorian from Florida Normal and Industrial Institute (formerly Florida Baptist Academy) and receives a tuition scholarship to Morehouse College in Atlanta, Georgia.

September

Enters Morehouse College.

December

Thurman's "Sunrise," a poetic narrative, is published in the Spelman-Morehouse literary journal, the *Athenaeum*.

1920

Spring

Serves as chaplain of the Pi-Gamma Literary Society.

May

Wins the Edgar Allan Poe short story contest at Morehouse and a cash prize of $40.

Receives a Morehouse scholarship for the first-ranked student in the freshman class.

Sue Bailey graduates from Spelman Seminary High School.

Summer

Thurman serves as supply pastor of his home church, Mount Bethel Baptist Church, while the pastor, Reverend Samuel Owen, is attending the University of Chicago.

Fall

Early in his sophomore year, Thurman is appointed literary editor of *The Athenaeum*, an honor usually given to seniors.

1921

May

Receives an academic scholarship for the second-ranked student in the sophomore class and wins the F. J. Paxon prize for oratory and elocution.

1922

2 January

Delivers the address "Our Challenge" before the Pi-Gamma Literary Society emancipation celebration. The talk was later published.

May

Receives an academic scholarship for the first-ranked student in the junior class and is awarded the Willard Chamberlain Scripture Reading prize.

Sue Bailey leaves Spelman College to attend Oberlin College in Ohio.

May–July
Thurman lives with a cousin in Cleveland, Ohio. Works and studies philosophy on his own at the Seventy-ninth Street branch of the Cleveland Public Library to prepare for his summer classes at Columbia University.

July
Enters summer program at Columbia University, taking two philosophy courses, "Reflective Thinking" and "Introduction to Philosophy," and one government course, "American State Government."

   Drafts a proposal to John Hope for a college scholarship fund to assist black men.

Fall
Joins the debating team at Morehouse coached by Benjamin E. Mays.
   Serves as president of the YMCA branch at Morehouse.
   Becomes an assistant to Morehouse Dean Benjamin Brawley.

1923
21 March
Garrie Ward Moore, one of Thurman's mentors at Morehouse, dies suddenly at the age of thirty-one. Thurman would coauthor a tribute to him in the senior yearbook.

May
Morehouse's first senior yearbook, the *Torch*, is published. Thurman serves as editor and cowrites the senior-class poem.
   Awarded the Starks prize (best man of affairs).

30 May
Graduates Morehouse College as valedictorian and delivers the valedictory address at commencement.

September
Enters Rochester Theological Seminary in Rochester, New York. George Cross, professor of systematic theology, would become his primary advisor.

2 December
Delivers "Thinking Black" address at First Baptist Church in Penfield, New York.

28 December–1 January
Serves as a delegate at the Ninth International Student Volunteer Convention in Indianapolis, Indiana.

1924
9 February
Preaches at First Congregational Church, Perry Center, New York.

17 February
Delivers "The Faith of the American Negro" sermon, Dewey Avenue Union Church, Rochester.

9 March
Preaches at First Congregational Church in Rochester.

April
"College and Color," Thurman's first published work on religion and race, appears in *The Student Challenge*, the official organ of the Student Fellowship for Student Life Service.

Summer
Works on the ministerial staff of the First Baptist Church of Roanoke, Virginia, under the supervision of Reverend Arthur L. James. Works in the Sunday school and directs the Vacation Bible School program for three hundred children between the ages of seven and twelve.

July
Publishes "The Sphere of the Church's Responsibility in Social Reconstruction" in the *Roanoke Church News*.

12 October
Preaches "Temptations of Jesus" at the Dewey Avenue Union Church in Rochester.

16 November
Delivers prayer for the "Universal Day of Prayer for Students," sponsored by the World Student Christian Federation, at Union Theological Seminary Chapel in New York City.

1925
17 January
Delivers the address "Creative Idealism" at Asbury Methodist Church in Rochester, New York.

7 February
Delivers "Creative Idealism" address at Conesus Community Church in Rochester.

11 February
Speaks at Brick Presbyterian Church in Rochester.

29 March
Delivers "The Value of Silence" address and preaches "The Faith of the American Negro" at First Baptist Church, Ithaca, New York.

5 April
Preaches on "The Gift of the American Negro" at First Baptist Church in Lockport, New York.

19 April
Delivers "The Faith of the American Negro" address at the YWCA in
Rochester.

May
Publishes "The Perils of Immature Piety" in the *Student Volunteer Movement
Bulletin.*

Summer
Joins the First Baptist Church of Roanoke after his church in Daytona, Florida,
denies him permission to be ordained by another church. Works at First
Baptist as director of religious education and as pastor's assistant.
    Attends retreat in Pawling, New York, for the national board of the YWCA.
There he is introduced to the work of the South African writer Olive Schreiner.

2 August
Ordained as Baptist minister in the First Baptist Church of Roanoke by
Reverend Samuel Owen.

10–13 September
Attends general conference of the Fellowship of Reconciliation at Swarthmore
College in Swarthmore, Pennsylvania. The conference theme is "Peace or War
in the Pacific." Rufus Jones speaks at Sunday workshop "Utilizing Spiritual
Resources."

4 October
Delivers address "What Shall I Do with My Life?" at Delaware Street Baptist
Church, Syracuse, New York.

5 October
Delivers sermon "The Widening Horizon" at the Syracuse University Chapel.

October 21–23
Attends and delivers "The Christian Emphases" address in Washington, D.C.
at the twenty-first National Conference on Colored Work of the YMCA.

25 October
Delivers "Friendship" sermon at South Baptist Church in Newark, New Jersey.

November
Becomes a member of the executive committee of the Student Volunteer
Movement of America.
    Becomes a member of the National Council of Fellowship of Reconciliation.

15 November
Delivers address "Negro Spirituals" at First Baptist Church, Lockport, New
York.

Winter
Invited to preach and later to become pastor of Mount Zion Baptist Church in Oberlin, Ohio.

December
Publishes "Negro Youth and the Washington Conference" in *The Intercollegian.*

1926

24 January
Delivers address "Youth Movement in America" at Lake Avenue Baptist Church in Rochester, New York, as part of the Christian Endeavor meeting.

14 February
Delivers "The Faith of the American Negro" address at First Baptist Church in Evanston, Illinois, as part of the Young People's community-service program "A Fine Arts Worship Service: For Racial Understanding."

14 March
Delivers sermon and address at South Baptist Church in Newark, New Jersey.

Completes his Bachelor of Divinity thesis, "The Basis of Sex Morality: An Inquiry into the Attitude toward Premarital Sexual Morality among Various Peoples and an Analysis of Its True Basis."

9–11 April
Featured speaker and participant in the second annual New York State Student Conference in Dansville, New York, sponsored by the Student Christian Association of New York. The conference theme is "A Unified Life," and Thurman delivers the address "The Meaning of Faith."

25 April
Delivers address at the High School Girls' Conference at the Caledonia Avenue YMCA branch in Rochester.

Sue Bailey, one of the earliest African Americans to matriculate at Oberlin Conservatory, graduates with a Bachelor of Music.

18 May
Graduates from Rochester Theological Seminary.

11 June
Marries Katie Kelley one week following graduation from seminary in an early-morning ceremony at her home in LaGrange, Georgia.

13 June
Undertakes his first Pastorate at Mount Zion Baptist Church in Oberlin, Ohio.

September
Enrolls in postgraduate studies at Oberlin Graduate School of Theology. Studies Old Testament with Kemper Fullerton and New Testament with Edward I. Bosworth.

3 October
Delivers "Characteristic Christian Life Attitudes" sermon at Iowa State
Teachers College in Cedar Falls, Iowa.

12–17 October
Attends Ohio Baptist General Association meeting at Third Baptist Church in
Youngstown, Ohio.

28 December–1 January
Featured speaker at the National Student Conference in Milwaukee, Wisconsin. Speaks on "Finding God" and leads discussion groups.

1927
"Finding God" speech appears as chapter five of *Religion on the Campus,*
edited by Francis P. Miller.
  Delivers the address "Christian, Who Calls Me Christian?" at YMCA
meeting in Indianapolis, Indiana.

23 February
Delivers chapel-program address at Iowa State Teachers College, Cedar Falls,
Iowa.

26 February
Delivers keynote address at the YWCA High School Girl Reserves Mid-Year
Conference in Niagara Falls, New York.

March
Directs the Dunbar Forum at Oberlin High School in two plays, *Siles Brown*
and *Peter Stith,* by recent Oberlin graduate Randolph Edwards.

1–27 August
Conference leader and speaker at the third annual Summer Conference on
International, Economic-Industrial and Family Relations and Educational
Method at Hillsdale College, Hillsdale, Michigan.

21 September
Delivers address at the fall dinner of the Men's Club of Christ Methodist
Episcopal Church in Pittsburgh, Pennsylvania.

5 October
Daughter Olive Katherine Thurman is born.
  Publishes "Higher Education and Religion" in the *Home Misson College
Review.*

13 November
Delivers "Barren or Fruitful?" sermon at United Church (Congregational) in
Oberlin, Ohio.

27 November
Delivers address at the YMCA Older Boys' Conference, Western New York, in Olean, New York.

2–4 December
Delivers "Christ, the Hope of the World" address and leads devotions at the twenty-fifth annual Western New York State Student Volunteer Conference at Rochester Theological Seminary, Rochester, New York.

4 December
Delivers "Christian, Who Calls Me Christian?" address at the Elizabeth Street YMCA in Rochester.

5 December
Delivers address for the Saint Antoine, Detroit, Michigan, YMCA branch evening event themed "What Shall We Do about the Race Situation?"

1928
12 January
Delivers address "The Meaning of Religion in the Modern World" at McKinley Memorial Presbyterian Church, Champaign, Illinois.

13 January
Delivers "What Religion Has to Say to the Modern World" at the Wesley Foundation Inter-racial Commission dinner in Champaign.

Delivers address at a joint meeting of the cabinets and commissions of the YMCA and YWCA, Champaign.

Delivers "Deep River" address at the All-University Service, University of Illinois auditorium, Champaign, sponsored by the YMCA and YWCA and university churches.

14 January
Preaches at University Baptist Church, Champaign.

Delivers address for the Councils of Campus Churches, First Congregational Church, Champaign.

Spring
Receives fellowship from the National Council on Religion in Higher Education to study with Rufus Jones; resigns from Mount Zion Baptist Church.

12 March
Delivers sermon on Jeremiah 17 at Vassar College, Poughkeepsie, New York.

16 May
Delivers address at the supper conference of the Inter-Racial Council and Liberal Club at Ohio State University, Columbus.

10–20 June
Participates in the Eagles Mere Student Conference in Eagles Mere, Pennsylvania, jointly sponsored by the YMCA and YWCA.

20–24 June
Featured speaker at the Ministers' Conference of Hampton Institute, speaking on "The Problems of Youth."

July
Teaches at the YMCA Chesapeake Summer School at Bordentown Training and Industrial School, Bordentown, New Jersey.

Fall
Moves to Atlanta, Georgia, to accept a joint appointment to Morehouse and Spelman colleges in philosophy and religion.

5–10 September
Delivers sermons at the twenty-eighth annual session of the Women's Convention, auxiliary to the National Baptist Convention at Lampton Baptist Church, Louisville, Kentucky.

October
Publishes "The Task of the Negro Ministry" in *Southern Workman*.

15–19 October
Delivers five sermons on Negro spirituals at Spelman College, which are published in the fall in the *Spelman Messenger*.

December
"Peace Tactics and a Racial Minority" is published in *The World Tomorrow*. A slightly different version of the essay is published the following year as "'Relaxation' and Race Conflict" in *Pacifism in the Modern World*.

1929
14–18 January
Guest speaker for Religious Emphasis Week, Alabama State Normal School, Montgomery, Alabama.

19 January
George Cross, Thurman's primary mentor and Rochester Theological Seminary professor, dies.

20 January
Delivers address at a mass meeting for Montgomery citizens.

   Delivers "What Jesus Means to Me" address at Women's College, Alabama State Normal School, Montgomery.

28 January
Invited to Tuskegee Institute to speak at the Christian Association dinner;
meets George Washington Carver.

1 February
Arrives at Haverford College, Haverford, Pennsylvania, for the spring semester
to study with Rufus Jones.

Spring
"The Significance of the Cross in Our Times," a chapel talk at Spelman
College, is published in the *Spelman Messenger.*
   Delivers address "Am I Getting an Education?" at chapel assembly, Bennett
College for Women, Greensboro, North Carolina.

14 April
Delivers sermon at First Baptist Church in Roanoke, Virginia.

28 April
Delivers sermon at Rankin Memorial Chapel, Howard University, Washington, D.C.

31 May–1 June
Returns to Atlanta to participate in the Spelman College commencement
program.

15–22 June
Conference leader at the Asilomar Student Conference of the YWCA, Asilomar, California. The conference theme is "Toward an Understanding of Jesus."

25 August–1 September
Leads sunset devotion "Deeper Meanings in Life Experience" at the Hazen
Conference of the National Council on Religion in Higher Education, Lisle,
New York.

1930
19 October
Preaches "From Hour to Hour, Be Awake" at Sunday service at Vassar College
Chapel, Poughkeepsie, New York.

26 October
Preaches "From Hour to Hour, Be Awake" at Fisk Memorial Chapel, Fisk
University, Nashville, Tennessee. Delivers address at student forum with A.
Philip Randolph.

7–8 November
Delivers address at the eleventh annual YMCA State Inter-Racial Conference,
Trinity Methodist Episcopal Service, Louisville, Kentucky.

21 December
Katie Kelley Thurman dies.

1931
1 January
Delivers address at Bethune-Cookman College, Daytona, Florida, in celebration of the sixty-eighth anniversary of the Emancipation Proclamation. Mary
McLeod Bethune serves as mistress of ceremonies.

18–22 January
Featured speaker during Howard University's Week of Prayer. Preaches at
Howard's Rankin Chapel.

22 February
Preaches at Fisk Memorial Chapel, Fisk University.

29 March–5 April
Leads YMCA Lenten Series at Saint Antoine Street branch, Detroit, Michigan:
"An Almighty Affection" (March 29), "Jesus and Temptations" (March 30),
"Jesus and His Enemies (March 31), "Jesus and His Friends" (April 1), "Jesus
and Women" (April 2), "Jesus and God" (April 3), and "The Power of the
Resurrection" (April 5).

26 April
Delivers address at Brick Presbyterian Church in Rochester, New York.

Summer
Travels to London, Scotland, Paris, and Geneva, Switzerland, for rest and
renewal.

11 November
Delivers the eulogy "And Ghosts Will Drive Us On" for good friend Juliette
Derricotte, former YWCA secretary and dean of women at Fisk University.
Derricotte, injured in a car accident, died on November 7 in Dalton, Georgia,
after being denied medical treatment in a white hospital.

14–15 November
Featured speaker at the Atlanta Student Conference, sponsored by the interracial student group, the Atlanta Intercollegiate Council. Delivers the
addresses "Finding God in the Whole of Life" (November 14) and "I Am in
Quest of God" (November 15).

4 December
Directs a production of *Macbeth* at Sale Hall, Morehouse College.

26 December–2 January 1932
Serves as a YMCA student-conference leader at Asilomar, California.

1932

2–21 January

Tours California and Arizona as guest speaker and preacher at various university, YMCA, and YWCA venues. His speaking tour includes California stops at Santa Barbara, Mount Hollywood Congregational Church (Los Angeles), Twenty-eighth Street (Colored) YMCA (Los Angeles), Pasadena Presbyterian Church, Pomona College, La Verne College, and Scripps College (Claremont), University of Redlands, UCLA, Long Beach, Stanford University, San Jose, San Francisco Theological Seminary, College of the Pacific (Stockton), University of California at Berkeley, Berkeley YMCA, First Baptist Church, Berkeley, and Occidental College (Los Angeles); and the University of Arizona at Tucson.

February

Addresses twenty-seven club forums in Atlanta on "The Kind of Religion the Negro Needs in Times like These," an early version of "Good News for the Underprivileged."

March

Accepts position at Howard University, Washington, D.C., as professor of Christian theology in the religion department and as dean of Rankin Chapel.

May

Delivers commencement address at Morehouse College.

11 May

Addresses Atlanta branch of the National Alliance of Postal Employees at the First Congregational Church on the future of the Negro race in America.

June

Delivers three lectures at YMCA-YWCA Colored Students Conference at Kings Mountain, including "The Deeper Meaning of Negro Spirituals" and "The Blind Man Stood on the Road and Cried."

12 June

Marries Sue Bailey at Kings Mountain, North Carolina.

1933

8 October

Daughter Anne Spencer Thurman is born.

1934

March–April

The National YMCA and YWCA International Committee, on behalf of the World Student Christian Federation, invites Thurman to be chairman of the four-person Negro Delegation to India, Burma, and Ceylon.

16 May

Sue Bailey Thurman is invited to join the delegation to India.

1935

March

Sue and seven-year-old stepdaughter, Olive, travel to Mexico for an extended stay as guests of the Mexican YWCA leadership.

April

Thurman delivers two lectures at the Intercollegiate Missionary Conference at Gammon Theological Seminary in Atlanta, Georgia: "Can We Be Christians Today?" and "The Missionary Spirit and World Peace."

May

Addresses the Organization of Teachers of Colored Children in the State of New Jersey at Atlantic City, New Jersey.

Summer

"Good News for the Underprivileged" presented at the Annual Convocation Lecture on Preaching at Boston University and printed in the summer 1935 issue of *Religion and Life*. This forms the basis of *Jesus and the Disinherited* (1949).

21 September

The four members of the Negro Delegation on the Pilgrimage of Friendship to India, Burma, and Ceylon—Howard and Sue Thurman and Edward and Phenola Carroll—embark on the *Ile de France* from New York Harbor for Le Havre, France. Accompanying the delegation are Thurman's sister Madaline and his children, Olive and Anne, who would reside in Geneva, Switzerland, for the duration of the tour.

1 October

The members of the Negro Delegation leave Marseilles, France, for the voyage to Colombo, Ceylon, making ports of call in Port Said, Egypt, and Djibouti, French Somaliland.

21 October

The Negro Delegation arrives in Colombo for a three-week tour.

7 November

The Negro Delegation arrives in Pudokotah, their first stop in India.

29 December–9 January 1936

The Negro Delegation travels to Rangoon, Burma.

1936

16–17 January

The Negro Delegation meets with poet Rabindranath Tagore at his university in Shantiniketan, near Calcutta.

7 February

The Negro Delegation tours the Khyber Pass, near Peshawar.

21 February
In Bardoli, the Thurmans and Edward Carroll meet with Mahatma Gandhi.

8 March
Their work completed, the members of the Negro delegation embark from Colombo, Sri Lanka, to return to Europe and the United States.

The Papers of
Howard Washington Thurman

Volume 1

Howard Thurman, circa 1930. Courtesy of the Thurman family and Arleigh Prelow/Howard Thurman Film Project

CHAPTER I

The Early Years

~ TO MORDECAI WYATT JOHNSON
18 JUNE 1918
JACKSONVILLE, FLA.

Howard Thurman's earliest extant correspondence is this letter of introduction to Mordecai Wyatt Johnson, who would become Thurman's closest mentor during his early career. The inspired Thurman introduces himself to Johnson after hearing his address at the annual YMCA student conference for students of black colleges and normal schools held at Lincoln Academy[1] in Kings Mountain, North Carolina.

Mr. Tobias[2] knows me, also Rev. Samuel A. Owens[3] and Prof. Joseph A. Grimes[4] your schoolmates.

Rev. Mordecai Johnson,[5]
Charleston, West Virginia.

My dear Rev. Johnson:—
Do not be surprised at hearing from me, for I, at the Student's Conference of 1917, let you slip into my heart and occupy the place of a precious friend and as long as memory reproduces pictures, to me, you shall be a living inspiration. I admired your eloquence, bowed humbly before your sympathy, and rejoiced to know that you <u>cared</u>. I wanted to know you and wanted you to know me; I longed for a cheering word from a man like you; I yearned to tell you {of} my hopes, ambitions and discouragements, but each time something hindered, something caused me to be denied that coveted privilege. I attended the last conference but, as you remember, you were only there a few hours. I stood in the dark fully 45 minutes waiting an opportunity but Mitchell of Morehouse seemed to have had a monopoly on your time.

Listen while I tell to you my soul. My home is in Daytona Florida but I attend the Florida Baptist Academy of Jacksonville as you note. I am 18 years old. My father has been dead 11 years. He died leaving 3 small children for my mother to rear. God bless her holy name, she did her best. She toiled morning noon and night that we may be permitted to go to public school. I finished the public school, that is, during my last year I ran a fish market, studied my lessons at the market [*illegible*] went to the school to recite them, immediately thereafter reporting to my job. It was thus, that I [*strikeover illegible*] completed my grammar school education with an average of 99% receiving the first Certificate of Promotion given to the colored people of my County. During the early summer I told mother of my desire to continue my education. Her reply was this, "Son you may go but I cannot do anything for you financially, for I must care for your sisters." I told her that I did not expect anything of her only her prayers. The fall came, I had no money and scarcely sufficient clothing for the winter. I made arrangements with a cousin in this city to let me room with him. He did so and I played off on my insurance agent in order to get railroad fare to this point. I came here, ate an average of one square meal a day and walked to the Academy to school, a distance of 2 ½ miles. On Saturday I worked from 7 a.m. to 8 p.m. for 50¢. During the week I pressed clothes in the neighborhood for 25¢ per suit. My average scholarship for that year was 96 ⅖%, which was the highest in the school; I won the scholarship medal. The next year I boarded in at reasonable rate, working half of my schooling. My average scholarship was 98%. (highest) Last year the same conditions prevailed my average 94 ⅖%. I want to be a minister of the Gospel. I feel the needs of my people, I see their distressing condition, and have offered myself upon the altar as a living sacrifice, in order that I may help the "skinned and flung down" as you interpret. God wants me and His precious love urges me to take up the cross and follow Him. I want advice from you as to how to direct my efforts. I am scheduled to finish here next year. As you know, the war is on and young men are being snatched daily. I am patriotic; I am willing to fight for democracy, but my friend Rev. Johnson, my people need me. I want a thorough training for my work which would necessitate my taking a college course prior to Theology, would it not? If I do by the time that I am in Junior College, providing the age limit remains as it is I ~~shall~~ will be drafted. Hence my training cut off. What would you advise me to do? Please take a personal interest in me and guide me and God will reward you, for you are God's trustee. Believe me when I say that you made a deeper impression upon my life than any man at the Conference either last year or this year. I am hoping that you will not misunderstand me. I come to you {for guidance}, I have no real guide but Jesus but in some things I believed that He intended for his "Watchmen" (your expression) to point out the way.

Doubtless when this reaches your home you will be in Harpers Ferry.

I thank you for your sermon, "Thy kingdom come. Thy will be done, in earth as it is in heaven." Also for your famous "Skinned and Flung Down."

Please pray for me because {almost} on every hand I am discouraged in my choice of the Ministry. Sometimes I think nobody cares but thank God, Jesus does, mother does and I believe you do.

Awaiting an early reply, I am,

Yours very sincerely,

[*signed*] Howard W. Thurman,

Fla. Baptist Academy.

ALS. MWJ-DHU-MS: Box 178.

NOTES

1. Lincoln Academy was a normal and industrial school for black students founded in 1888 by the American Missionary Association.

2. Channing Heggie Tobias (1882–1961) received his AB from Paine Institute (now Paine College) in 1902 and BD from Drew University in 1905. In 1911, he became secretary of the Colored Department of the National Council of the YMCA and was a strong advocate for the organization's desegregation. In 1946 Tobias left the YMCA to become the first African American director of the Phelps-Stokes Fund, an organization that supported black education. He also served as a trustee of Howard University and chairman of the board of directors of the NAACP from 1953 to 1959, receiving the NAACP's Spingarn medal in 1948.

3. Samuel Augustus Owen (1886–1974) was pastor of Thurman's home congregation, Mount Bethel Baptist Church, Daytona, Florida, from 1917 to 1930. Like Mordecai Wyatt Johnson, he was a 1911 graduate of Atlanta Baptist College (now Morehouse College). From 1923 to 1971, Owen was the pastor of Metropolitan Baptist Church in Memphis, Tennessee. He also served as the president of Roger Williams University. Owen Junior College (since 1968 LeMoyne-Owen College), organized in 1954 by the Tennessee Baptist Missionary and Educational Convention, is named in his honor.

4. Joseph Grimes was one of Thurman's teachers at Florida Baptist Academy. Grimes attended Morehouse briefly. He received his BA in history from the University of Iowa (1934) and his MA in history from the institution (1935).

5. Mordecai Wyatt Johnson (1890–1976) was born in Paris, Tennessee, was educated at Roger Williams University (a high school) in Nashville and Atlanta Baptist College, graduating in 1911, and had his degree "validated" at the University of Chicago in 1913. At Rochester Theological Seminary, he received a BD (1916) and earned an MST from Harvard Divinity School (1922). He served as student secretary of the International Committee of the YMCA in 1916 but resigned less than one year later due to the failure of YMCA leadership to challenge discriminatory hotel arrangements for a national conference in Atlantic City, New Jersey. Even after his resignation, Johnson continued to speak at YMCA national student conferences. From 1917 to 1926, he was the pastor of First Baptist Church of Charleston, West Virginia. In 1926, he was chosen as president of Howard University, becoming the institution's first black president. During his presidency, Johnson supervised Howard's growth into a major university and center of African American intellectual life. His forceful managerial style was controversial and had both ardent supporters and opponents within the Howard faculty. In 1960 Johnson retired from Howard. He was one of the leading orators of his time and spoke frequently on matters of racial

discrimination and intolerance and the evils of colonialism. See Richard I. McKinney, *Mordecai: The Man and His Message, The Story of Mordecai Wyatt Johnson* (Washington, D.C.: Howard University Press, 1997).

🐦 FROM MORDECAI WYATT JOHNSON
8 JULY 1918
CHARLESTON, W.VA.

Writing to Thurman at Florida Baptist Academy, Mordecai Wyatt Johnson responds to his questions about the preparation required for ministry, encouraging him to become a well-educated thinker and leader of his people.

My dear Mr. Thurman:

I thank you heartily for your recent letter. I have read the story of your aspirations and your strivings with great interest and sympathy. Your industry, your perseverance under difficulty, your reverence for your mother, and your yearning to serve mark you as a God-chosen man.

By all means go on with your preparatory and college work. Meanwhile make yourself more and more acquainted with the history and biography of the Bible and with the teachings of Jesus and of Paul. It will be far better for you to enter the ministry after you have completed a college course than to make a short cut, putting a shallow course in theology on top of your preparatory work. As young as you are you should set before you the ideal of thorough preparation—a first class college course plus a first class theological training. You will be able to do this, I judge, before you are twenty-six years of age.

Keep in close touch with your people, especially with those who need your service. Take every opportunity to encourage their growth and to serve them. School yourself to think over all that you learn, in relation to them and to their needs. Make yourself believe that the humblest, most ignorant and most backward of them is worthy of the best prepared thought and life that you can give.

It is not necessary that you delay the actual work of preaching until you have completed your courses. You may have yourself licensed to preach at any time, by your local church. Rev. Alfred C. Williams,[1] now pastor of the Sixteenth Street Baptist Church of Birmingham, Alabama, began pastoring when he was about your age; but he continued with his work. When he graduated from Morehouse College he was pastor of a church in Atlanta. Many young men pastor churches while they are doing their theological work. I did that in Rochester.[2] Prepare! Prepare! This is the one and only word for you. You need have no fear about work; you will find plenty to do both while you are in school and afterwards.

Do not allow the prospect of being drafted to deter you from your work of preparation. There are three years yet before you will be called. It is possible that the war will be closed before that time. If, however, the war continues and you are called, you will have the joy of giving your country a superior type of service such as college men can give, and you will return from the war prepared to take your place again in the higher college classes with an early prospect of being one among the few well trained thinkers and leaders who will have the destiny of our people in their keeping.

I am glad to learn that my words at Kings Mountain in 1917 and 1918 influenced you for good. Such testimonies as yours are the most precious rewards of my work. May God bless you and keep you and make you His minister indeed! Sincerely yours,
[*signed*] Mordecai W. Johnson
P.S. Under separate cover I am sending you a brief history of the People of Israel as set forth in the Old Testament. You will find it to your advantage to cultivate the historical perspective[3] that such books can give.
M.W.J.

TLS. HTC-MBU: Box 8.

1. Reverend Alfred C. Williams (1883–1964) received his BA from Atlanta Baptist College (1912) and his MA in philosophy and religious education at the University of Michigan (1928). He served as pastor of the Antioch Baptist church in Atlanta, Georgia, until 1912. In 1913 he led the Mount Nebo Baptist Church in Pulaski, Florida, and was the pastor of the Sixteenth Street Baptist Church of Birmingham, Alabama, from 1916 to 1920. He left there to go to Detroit, Michigan. See Christopher M. Hamlin, *Behind the Stained Glass: A History of Sixteenth Street Baptist Church* (Birmingham, Ala.: Hill, 1998), 21–22.

2. While a student at Rochester Theological Seminary, Johnson served as student pastor of the Second Baptist Church in Mumford, New York, from 1914 to 1916.

3. Johnson's reference to a "historical perspective" probably reflected his interest in the "higher criticism," that is, the careful study of the historical roots of Christian and Jewish religious texts and his concern that his young correspondent does not fall into an uncritical or sentimental Biblicism.

🦋 To MORDECAI WYATT JOHNSON
17 JULY 1918
JACKSONVILLE, FLA.

Thurman expresses his appreciation to Johnson for his encouraging words and declares his willingness to undergo rigorous preparation for the ministry.

Rev. M. W. Johnson,
First Baptist Church,
Charleston, West Virginia.

Rev. Johnson:—
Your very inspiring favor also the book came in due course of mail. Permit me to assure you that those thoughts of encouragement which you so beautifully

tenderly encouched in your letter are most thoroughly appreciated. Never before had I arisen to the full consciousness of the responsibilities which must of necessity devolve upon men, if I must preach the gospel. God knows that I thank you and it is my prayer that you feel always a personal interest in me and that it is my pleasure to have you advise me at any time.

I get the weekly editions of the "Standard," "Watchman-Examiner," and the "Journal and Messenger," these, I find, are very helpful, for our leading ministers contribute {to them} articles of sterling worth.[1] I have studied, most carefully, Bosworth's "About Jesus" and a portion of Wilson's, "The Christ We Forget;" {et al} what else do you suggest?[2]

I noted with much interest what you said about my beginning to preach. I am away from home working at the school, hence I cannot be licensed by my church until early fall. When you write, please explain to me how to make my application.

Thanking you for the gift of the book and assuring you that I am already an earnest student thereof, I am,

yours very truly,

[*signed*] H. W. Thurman

ALS. MWJ-DHU-MS: Box 178.

1. The *Standard, Watchman-Examiner,* and *Journal and Messenger* were among the leading mainstream Baptist periodicals of the time. The *Standard* was a semi-monthly publication of the Baptist General Conference out of Arlington Heights and Evanston, Illinois, that began in the early 1900s. The *Watchman-Examiner,* a northern Baptist weekly, had arguably the largest circulation of any Baptist publication, with the exception of Sunday school literature. Considered to be a "journal for all Baptists," it was widely read by both black and white Baptists in the south. The *Journal and Messenger* was a weekly serial published from the 1800s until 1920.

2. Edward Increase Bosworth (1861–1927) wrote *Thirty Studies about Jesus* (New York: Association Press, 1917). Bosworth was a popular writer on Christology and many of his writings became standard texts of the YMCA and YWCA. While Thurman was pastor of Mount Zion Baptist Church in Oberlin, he studied the New Testament with Bosworth at the Oberlin Seminary. *WHAH,* 60, 70–71. Philip Whitwell Wilson (1875–1956) wrote *The Christ We Forget: A Life of Our Lord for Men of Today* (New York: Revell, 1917).

❧ TO ETHEL SIMONS
4 JUNE 1919
DAYTONA, FLA.

Less than one week after his graduation as high-school valedictorian, Thurman writes to his English teacher Ethel Simons from his home in Daytona. The letter offers evidence of Thurman's recent struggles with his health, brought on by the strain of a punishing work and study regimen.

Dear Miss Simons:[1]

Your spark of sunshine came just in time to cheer me up and make me feel real happy. I thank you for it—may I—anyway, I take the liberty.

I am resting now. Last night I was in bed before dark. You should see me—no collar, no socks, just loose sleeping, eating and having a good time. I went to the doctor, he says that I had cheated Somnus—that I owed a big big bill to Dr. Sleep. My blood pressure is too high, other than that I am all right. I am planning to remain here until the last of next week. I am not decided as to the summer.

Not long since I was telling my mother how much you really meant to me. I will not tell you all that I said because you may not believe me—just like you. I will say this much, I miss you and I find myself actually wishing to be in your company. Write me as often as you can and feel like it. Your letters mean much to me.

I was sorry to leave without seeing you but I hope to see you either in St. Augustine or Jax.[2]

All right now, please do not mark this letter up and send it back with this inscription: Rewrite and Put in Book E.M.S.

I am feeling fine to-day.

I have already bought and read June's issue. I have a copy of "Rubáiyat of Omar <u>Khayyam</u> {sp?}" and Florence Barclay's "The Wheels of Time."[3]

I have one or two things that I must say to you sometime.

Write when you feel like it.

Mother and sister send best of regards.

Yours What?

[*signed*] Howard Thurman

Can you read it?

ALcS. HTC-MBU: Box 198.

---

1. Ethel Simons Meeds (1887–1990) received her BA (1909) and MA (1910) from Benedict College in Columbia, South Carolina. Simons had high regard for Thurman and followed his career, on occasion attending his lectures. Hermia Justice, "Listening to My Mother: Ethel Simons Meeds," in *The Listening Ear: A Newsletter of the Howard Thurman Educational Trust* 19 (Spring 1989): 3, 7.

2. Jacksonville.

3. Edward Fitzgerald (1809–83) translated *The Rubáiyát of Omar Khayyám* (1859), a loose translation of quatrains by the Persian mathematician, astronomer, and poet Omar Khayyám (1044–1123) that became one of the most popular books of Victorian poetry. Florence L. Barclay (1862–1920), an English author who wrote love stories with a religious emphasis, published the novella *The Wheels of Time* (New York: Crowell, 1908).

CHAPTER II

Morehouse College Years

❧ TO ETHEL SIMONS
9 OCTOBER 1919
ATLANTA, GA.

Early in his first semester of study at Morehouse College, Thurman proudly updates Simons on his academic progress.

Dear Miss Simons:—

Your letter was sent to me from home. I also received your card. I thank you for taking the time to write me.

I am at Morehouse. I made straight Freshman without a condition. Because of your fame as an English teacher rather your thoroughness I should say, I made Brawley's English 5 the hardest course on the hill.[1] Just think, a young man come here from Lincoln University the other but notwithstanding the fact he had completed his Freshman work there, he was not admitted into English 6 but instead was admitted into English 5, And that on condition. You have helped me Miss Simons—your life has at least blest me if none other. I see now {as never before} that truly you are a good teacher in English.

From time to time I shall write you about conditions and also send a paper to you, occasionally, from my English. Dean Brawley is indeed an authority. It is an inspiration to be under him.

Within the last week I have had a very sad experience. It took only the gut of a man to stand such. Maybe when I have time I shall tell you about it.

I keep very busy. My head gave out the other day. I am trying to be careful. I am studying English 5, Greek 2, History I, French I Bible IV.

Answer when you have time.

From your friend,

[*signed*] Thurman

ALcS. HTC-MBU: Box 198.

1. Benjamin Griffith Brawley (1882–1939) was a noted educator and author who was professor of English at Morehouse from 1902 to 1910 and 1912 to 1920. He served as dean of the college from 1920 until his death in 1939. Brawley received his first bachelor's degree from Atlanta Baptist College (1901) and a second from the University of Chicago (1906). He received his MA from Harvard University (1908) and his PhD in literature from Shaw University (1927). Brawley taught at Howard University from 1910 to 1912. He also taught at Shaw University and served as president of the Association of Colleges of Negro Youth (1918–20). After being ordained in 1921 he served as pastor of the Messiah Baptist Church in Brockton, Massachusetts (1921–22). His books include *History of Morehouse College* (Atlanta, Ga.: Morehouse College, 1917), *The Negro in Literature and Art in the United States* (New York: Duffield, 1930), and *A Short History of the American Negro* (New York: Macmillan, 1931).

To Ethel Simons
13 July 1920
Daytona, Fla.

Thurman writes to Simons at the close of his freshman year at Morehouse. The development and maturation in his use of language are readily apparent. Thurman also alludes to his first experience in ministry serving as the supply pastor of his home church in Daytona, Florida.

My dear Miss Simons:—

Your card received. All of my themes are with my books at Morehouse. As for that old oration I do not know where it is. I cannot remember the part that you copied for me—I only know the quotations that I used. Now if I can help you any by writing a theme or trying to write another Valedictory, let me know and I shall be happy to do so.

Accept my congratulations on attending the {Michigan} University. I am sure that it will prove helpful to you. Florida for you next year?

I am at home. I accepted the work here as supply pastor[1] of my own church. Rev. Owens is away attending University of Chicago until October 1. I am here holding this big job down as best I can under God.

My year at the college was quite successful. I won first scholarship with an average of 92 6/9%. I won first prize $10.00 Edgar Allen Poe Short Story contest for the best original short story. I split first prize with a senior college man for the best literary production entered in the college paper or magazine ($6.25 prize being $12.50). I am Literary Editor of our magazine for next year an honor in years previous only given to senior college men but under God, somehow they gave it to me. I am also secretary to the Life Work Council and have charge of the Educational Work of our Y.M.C.A. I give the honor to God who strengtheneth me.

I am working, working, working. I preach real hard too. I must do my best even tho it is against my health.

Let me hear from you.

Very Sincerely

[*signed*] Thurman

P.S. Where is your brother now & how is he? I have themes of 3rd year high school. [*illegible marking*]

ALcS. HTC-MBU: Box 198.

1. A *supply pastor* is a lay preacher primarily responsible for preaching in the absence of a congregational pastor. Traditionally the supply pastor does not perform sacramental ordinances.

❧ THE *ATHENAEUM* WRITINGS
DECEMBER 1919–FEBRUARY/MARCH 1921

Thurman had several creative outlets during his undergraduate years at Morehouse College, which he used to hone his writing and public-speaking skills. One of them was the Athenaeum, *the literary journal for Morehouse College and Spelman Seminary that was published from May 1898 to March 1926. Thurman claims that most students dreamed of the day they might get a poem, short story, or essay published in the* Athenaeum, *and during his four years in college the journal published his writings from each genre. "Sunrise" was Thurman's first publication. As a young boy he was profoundly moved by the majesty and power of nature, whether experiencing the frequent violent storms and hurricanes that lashed Florida's east coast or, as in this case, a placid sunrise. The sentiments expressed in the poem "The Flag" reflect Thurman's youthful patriotic feelings and, unique among his writings, express a willingness and eagerness to serve in the military. The poem "Mother" no doubt was inspired by Thurman's close relationship with his own mother. The poem extols the virtues of truth and steadfastness that his mother demonstrated so admirably during his childhood. In the poem "Night" Thurman pays moving tribute to the feminine, transforming power of the night and its alignment with the transcendence of God.*

Thurman served as literary editor of the Athenaeum *in his sophomore year. "The Letter," published then, shows Thurman's literary interest in male/female relationships—in this case the unrequited love of a young man for a woman he met in his youth. The story's main character, after many years, writes confessing his true love for his now-married sweetheart through a standard plot device in romantic fiction, the compromising and embarrassing letter, which becomes the vehicle for both revealing, then concealing, the truth. Sue Bailey, who would become Thurman's second wife in 1932, is listed in this issue of the* Athenaeum *as club editor. The final selection of his* Athenaeum *writings is the serial short story "The Ingrate." Only the final installment of the story is extant.*

SUNRISE

Calm, calm is the sea. Silently the waves roll gently upon the shore, advancing little by little until soon for miles the beach will be covered by the high tide. How sweet the gentle breezes blow! Quietness reigns; nature seems to be hushed in silence only to be broken by the faint ripple of the waves or the distant sound of some crowing cock warning the world that day is about to break.

Dark is the morning; a gentle dimness spreads itself over the starry elements. Look! Along yon eastern horizon the dawn of day is coming. Before the fast approaching light darkness gathers its diamond studded robe about itself and hastens noiselessly away with a poise as magnificent as that of a prince. In clear outline is seen the lighthouse which for years has cast its beacon light over sea pointing out the way for the weary traveler.

But look! A certain sector of the eastern horizon seems to increase in brightness. Strong bright rays mark a distinct outline on the clear skies. Brighter and brighter these become until there appears a segment of the brilliant, blazing, dazzling sun. Up, up, slowly out of the sea it rises, filling all the earth with brightness and sunshine. All nature is happy; even the sea makes its billows heave and plunge with more precision along the shore. Unconsciously we exclaim: "Truly, this is the beginning of a perfect day."

H.W.T., '23.

Athenaeum 22 (December 1919): 30.

THE FLAG

> To thee, O Flag, I lift my voice,
> In joyous echoes ring;
> Thou art my nation's own great choice.
> To thee my praise I bring.
> Thy stars upon a field of blue
> Thy stripes of red and white
> Combine to make an emblem true
> Which thrills me with delight.
>
> No price too dear to pay for thee
> Thou proud America's guide;

Then can I fail to fight for thee
 And in thy love confide?
Under thy guidance I was born
 To live to fight to try;
Through thick and thin from morn to morn
 Standing for thee, I'll die.

If to protect thee I am called
 I go with willing heart,
Though with my love my soul's enthralled
 I'll gladly do my part.
To thee "Old Glory" I pledge my all
 Whatever that may be;
If for thee on the field I fall
 I've lived and died for thee.

Athenaeum 22 (January 1920): 57.

MOTHER

Thou, angel dear, God gave to me,
 Fresh from his heart of hearts divine,
The purest love He gave to thee
 To make thee sweet, hallowed, sublime;
The price thou paidst to give me birth
 The sorrows, pains, the silent sigh,
Were kin to heaven more than earth,
 And God kept watch lest I should die.
Thy tender cry, thy earnest plea
 Goes up to God from day to day;
With gracious love He watches me
 And always answers when I pray;
With gentle care He takes my heart,
 And resting in His fond embrace
The curtains slowly drift apart,
 And in His soul I see thy face.

H.W.T., '23   Athenaeum 22 (February 1920): 64.

NIGHT

The sun has kissed the earth farewell
 Some other worlds its tale to tell,
Behind a cloud it slips away
 And marks the dying of the day.

The soft and gentle breezes blow—
On distant plains the cattle low;
Now all is still—a death-like calm
Spreads ev'rywhere its healing balm.

But hark! who in the distant way
Has ushered out the dying day?
She moves—she covers ev'rything
A train of stars she proudly brings.

A spell is thrown o'er land and sea
From all mankind there comes a fee;
She reigns upon a throne of might
Her king is God; her name is Night.

Athenaeum 22 (March 1920): 76.

THE LETTER

Attorney Sylvester Hart sat in his room in the hotel looking over the daily paper. Suddenly he threw the paper down, rose and nervously reached for his hat. He repeated aloud, "Dr. H. S. Smith has sold office and practice to Dr. L. James."

He sat again. From his pocket he took a copy of the letter he had just sent by a messenger to Marion. Half aloud to the empty silence of the room he read:

"Dear Marion:

"For a long time I have been writing this letter. Today for some reason I am rewriting it just as it is.

"Lose yourself in the fond reflections of the past. Now do you remember when we first met—you as the tourist, I as the guide? Can you delve deep enough into the labyrinth of a memory-infested past to recall the day that I took your little brown fingers into my horny hands and helped you over the rocks just below the hotel? That day as I looked at your tall graceful form, strange emotions took possession of me. In your dark brown face with its beautiful nose and spirituelle eyes, I saw life, hope, faith, love, God! It was then that I realized that with you life to me would be as one sweet song pervading all the world.

"The season at the hotel closed. You and your mother left. Well do I remember how I sighed and tears made little furrows down my dark, dusky cheeks. The silent throbbings of my heart kept time with the tearful cadence of my longing soul. I was dissatisfied, unhappy, miserable, suffering from the disease of lost love.

"And you know the difference in our standing in life prevented our ever entertaining a hope of marrying each other. I, a poor, untutored guide for the tourists of a mountain hotel; you, the proud, beautiful, aristocratic daughter of a wealthy widow. Ah, what an unfortunate contrast! Yet because of the sympathy of your cousin, the doctor, whom I met the day you left, I have kept track of you all the intervening years. This has made life bearable for me even though I have not seen or heard from you directly.

"Pardon such outbursts of sentimentality as you find scattered through this letter, for at times I am seized with an uncontrollable longing and craving for you, my soul's joy. If I thought that you did not continue to care, if I thought that our friendship was buried beneath the crumbling ruins of a forgotten past, if I thought that you merely regarded our relation as one of the shifting scenes of your early experiences, I would pray for death and that speedily. O, that you were near me!

"As a direct result of your advice to me I have become educated. In my chosen profession I have made a name for myself. Doubtless you have read of my most recent success before the Superior Court. I owe it all to you; for it was you whom I promised that at the close of the season I would go to school.

"I married; not the woman whom I loved—I love only you.

"I have kept this letter as long as I can, so I send it to you today. I could not risk mailing so I came to the city where I could have a local messenger deliver it to you before you ended your visit with your cousin, the doctor. It is not best that I see you.

"From Sylvester."

As he finished reading the copy he put it back into his pocket and rushed out of the room slamming the door behind him. Soon he arrived at the address of Marion's cousin. He was met at the door by a stranger who introduced himself as Dr. James. He explained that Dr. Smith had sold his practice and left the city.

"Did you receive a letter addressed to Miss Marion Zone, in care of Dr. H. S. Smith?" said Attorney Hart.

"I did, and there it is," said Dr. Smith, pointing to the letter which was lying on his desk.

"May I have it please?"

"What right have you to it?"

"I sent it here a few minutes ago by the messenger and as Dr. Smith is not here I want it so that I may direct it to Miss Zone as soon as I find out her whereabouts. Upon what grounds do you object as you are not Dr. Smith nor are you Miss Zone?" asked the attorney angrily.

Dr. James turning around opened the door and called his wife. During the intermission the attorney with back turned was looking out of the window into the street. He was wondering just what to do. It was clear that he was in the clutches of this strange man. While he was thus buried in thought the door was silently opened and the doctor began:

"Dear, here is a letter which this gentleman sent to you by a special messenger not knowing that Dr. Smith had sold out to me and that you were my wife. He now wants the letter. I refuse to give it to him. Now, in order to prevent suspicion please read it that we both may hear."

Hearing this the attorney turned quickly around, looked directly into the face of the woman whom he loved. He stood as though he were turned into marble—then his large, athletic body trembled not unlike a leaf. Reason, Judgment, Decision all left him. Cold chills wrapped their freezing folds about his heart. Startled, shocked, almost horrified, he seemed to have felt his very soul moving silently up the dark passage of his expanding throat—he choked,—happily for him Marion broke the silence.

"Dr. James, I cannot read this letter as you request. Each of you has a claim— he that of the youthful love of a maiden; you that of the ardent love of a woman." Saying this she tore the letter into bits while both of the men looked on in blank amazement.

H.W.T., '23.

Athenaeum 23 (November 1920): 6–8.

THE INGRATE

Mrs. Wall awoke with an idea. In the early afternoon she began moving. Each load was carefully inspected by a guard who was stationed at the gate. After a series of trips the house was emptied of everything except her husband, an old fashioned trunk and herself. While the baggage man was on his way with the last load of furniture, she resolved to carry out her plan. She opened the door of the cabinet and told her husband to get quickly into the trunk.

Yawning lazily, he said, "What do you want with me?"

"What do I want?"

"Yes; just a little while ago you refused to let me get out of here, now you tell me to move in a hurry. You are changing like the moon."

"Mr. Wall, please do not remain there arguing with me. Move quickly or all is lost. Is it that you do not believe that I am asking you to do the best thing, after all that I have already passed through? For Goodness sake, move!"

Realizing that he stirred his wife considerably, he lost no more time—stiff, faint and weary, he suffered himself to move.

On the porch Mrs. Wall was stopped by the guard who ordered her to open the trunk. Her countenance fell—she felt that she had failed. The hint of distrust which her husband had manifested in her project loomed before her. Again she saw the expression which he had just shown her. Tears came to her eyes but the fervency of her desires for her husband's safety caused them to evaporate on the very threshold of her eyelids. Happily for her the guard was called away by a fomenting riot. They escaped.

When the draperies of night had fallen and all nature was hushed in silence only to be broken by the chirp of the cricket or the distant lowing of some far-off cattle, Mrs. Wall sat thoughtfully on the steps of her temporary home, while her husband was making his way to the city of Washington on a fast-moving express.

In a few days, she sold all of her furniture and bade farewell to the cursed town that had robbed her of her youth and glory, simultaneously making her a victim of gray hair, sunken eyes and a furrowed brow. Arriving at the city of Washington, she went to the address of her husband. Instead of finding him she found this note which he had left with his landlady.

"Dear Wife:
   I have one fairer and more attractive than you. I left today for Philadelphia.
   John."

She read aloud and the rest was silence.

Athenaeum 23 (February/March 1921): 73–74.

❧ KATIE KELLEY TO LUCY TAPLEY
16 MAY 1921
CHICAGO, ILL.

Five years before her marriage to Thurman, Katie Kelley wrote to Lucy Tapley, president of Spelman College, about her plans to prepare for a career as a social worker and her interest in working with the colored branch of the Anti-Tuberculosis Association of Atlanta. Kelley had previously taught in the public schools of Birmingham, Alabama, and was living in Chicago, where she was enrolled at the University of Chicago Divinity School.[1]

3256 Rhodes Ave.,
Chicago, Ill.,

My dear Miss Tapley:[2]
   Just after mailing your letter, I received a letter from Miss Lowe, Secretary of the Anti-Tuberculosis Association,[3] informing me that I had been accepted for the work which Miss Dukes[4] has. I have been anxiously waiting to hear from you before I accepted any offer. President Hope was in the city a few weeks ago and he told me of the opportunity which the work offered in Atlanta. My people are exceedingly anxious for me to be nearer home next year.

   I am even more anxious to continue my study, but I see in this opportunity a remarkable chance to render service, and at the same time be in position to help my people and myself. If I am there I want to arrange to continue my study of sociology at Morehouse College, if possible, with the hope of continuing the study here again, probably in a year or two.

I really want an opportunity to talk with you fully about my plans, and I do feel that the Lord will open the way for me to accomplish much of what I desire.

Please send me a reply by return mail, for I must write Miss Lowe this week.[5] With deep appreciations,

I am

Yours most sincerely,

[*signed*] Katie Kelley

ALS. DAF-GAS.

1. Kelley did not receive a degree from the University of Chicago. Her transcript indicates that she took courses about the Reformation and science of missions and in public speaking during the 1921 spring quarter only. Katie Kelley, University of Chicago alumni archives, Chicago, Illinois.

2. Lucy Hale Tapley (1857–1932), an educator and mentor to generations of Spelman women, was one of the most distinguished presidents who shaped the college during its first half century. President of Spelman College from 1910 to 1927, she had been on the faculty since 1880 as a teacher of English and arithmetic. Under Tapley's administration, the school's name was changed from Spelman Seminary to Spelman College in 1924. Florence Read, *The Story of Spelman College* (Princeton, N.J.: Princeton University Press, 1961), 187–209.

3. Under the leadership of Lugenia Hope (1871–1947), a prominent social-reform activist who was the wife of John Hope, the branch was founded in 1915 as an outgrowth of the all-white Atlanta branch. John Hope was its first chairperson. Lugenia remained active in the association throughout its existence. Jacqueline Rouse, *Lugenia Burns Hope: Black Southern Reformer* (Athens: University of Georgia Press, 1989), 80–82.

4. Carrie Dukes, a Spelman graduate, was an educational agent of the Anti-Tuberculosis Association, Atlanta branch. According to Rouse, she was the first black paid employee in the association. *Lugenia Burns Hope,* 82.

5. Tapley replied to Kelley, expressing disappointment that Kelley did not want to continue teaching but nevertheless encouraging her interest in anti-tuberculosis work. Lucy Tapley to Katie Kelley, 23 May 1921, DAF-GAS.

✌ To JOHN HOPE
20 JUNE 1921
DAYTONA, FLA.

From his home in Daytona, Thurman writes to John Hope, congratulating him on opening the first summer-school program at Morehouse College. In the letter, Thurman is optimistic about his academic progress despite unnamed personal difficulties.

My dear President Hope:—[1]

Accept my congratulations for successfully opening the first Summer School of Morehouse College! It is my prayer that it will prove a genuine asset both to the college and the race. Again, congratulations!

My work here moves along with an air of progress. I believe that the trend of fundamentals is forward notwithstanding blunders, mistakes, back sets and the like. Hence my conclusion with reference to my work.

I thought that my Sophomore year was pregnant with experiences sufficiently exacting to fit me for many of the battles of my early years. But I find that they were but the calm before the storm through which I am now passing. I rejoice, however, that I have a deep consciousness that God is with me.

I pray for you. The magnitude of the responsibility which is yours, sleeping or waking, moves me with prayerful compassion as I think on it. Courage,—Decision,—Judgment—God and all His attributes—That these may never leave you is my prayer.

Very sincerely,

[*signed*] Howard W. Thurman

P.S. Will you kindly send me one of the late catalogues? HWT

Catalogue Mailed[2]

ALS. JLH-GAU: Box 22.

1. John Hope (1868–1936) was one of the leading black educators in the early decades of the twentieth century and a key figure in the era's civil-rights struggles. Born in Augusta, Georgia, to a white father and black mother, Hope received his BA from Brown University (1896), and in 1898 he took a teaching position at Atlanta Baptist College, becoming its first black president in 1906. He remained president of the college, later renamed Morehouse College, until 1929, when he was named president of Atlanta University.

2. "Catalogue mailed" was added presumably on receipt of Thurman's letter.

FROM JOHN HOPE

28 JUNE 1921

ATLANTA, GA.

John Hope responds to Thurman with kind words of advice and encouragement.

Mr. Howard W. Thurman,

516 White-Hall St.,

Daytona, Fla.

Dear Mr. Thurman:

Your kind inspiring letter of June 20th was duly received and read with much comfort. I want to thank you very much for writing. The burdens are heavy but it is the part of a man to bear burdens, and I had rather early experiences along that line. While unpleasant things are occurring and the burden is galling the neck we may sometimes wince and wish that we did not have them but when we have carried these burdens a certain distance and find ourselves released we frequently become aware that we have gone a journey and arrived at a more prosperous outlook. I want to say to you that you are mentally and spiritually endowed to feel things very keenly and you will no doubt always have burdens and sorrows, if not your own somebody else's, but you must develop good cheer and great hopefulness as it is going to be your business in life to impart inspiration and to bring relief.

I have just heard this morning through Mrs. Bethune[1] that my dear friend, President N. B. Young,[2] has been removed from his position. I deeply regret this and could not feel it more if it had come to a brother of mine. I hope the people of Florida can bring it to pass that President Young may be called back even if he does not stay but a day.

With kind regards, I am

Sincerely yours,

[unsigned]

TLc. JLH-GAU: Box 22.

1. Mary McLeod Bethune.

2. Nathan Benjamin Young (1862–1933) was born into slavery in Newbern, Alabama, and educated at Talladega College (AB, 1884) and Oberlin College (AB, 1888; AM, 1891). In 1892 he was hired by Booker T. Washington to head the academic department at Tuskegee Institute, leaving in 1897 over Washington's effort to weaken the school's academic component. Named president of Florida A&M College, Young made an effort to increase the academic curriculum there but ran into opposition from both white politicians and some black Washingtonians who claimed that Young was moving away from the vocational purpose of land-grant colleges. He was fired in 1922 (and not, as John Hope prematurely tells Thurman, in the summer of 1921), though by the time of this letter he was already embroiled in difficulties. After leaving Florida, Young served two terms (1923–27, 1929–31) as president of Lincoln University in Missouri, where his tenures were also characterized by conflicts over his efforts to improve the academic standing of a vocationally based land-grant institution. Raymond Wolters, "The Travail of Nathan B. Young," in *The New Negro on Campus: Black College Rebellions of the 1920s* (Princeton, N.J.: Princeton University Press, 1975), 192–229, and Nathan B. Young, "These Colored United States: Florida," *Messenger,* November 1923.

꽃 FROM CLARENCE J. GRESHAM

29 DECEMBER 1921

SAVANNAH, GA.

Writing from the American Red Cross U.S. Marine Hospital in Savannah, Georgia, where he was being treated for an ankle injury, Clarence Gresham,[1] a classmate of Thurman's at Morehouse, expresses his deep affinity for his friend.

My beloved Friend,

Only a few lines. We are somewhat disturbed here today as one of the employees was found to have a very dangerous case of Small Pops.[2] They have quarantined our floor I hope I wont take it.

I know you had a fine Xmas. Van[3] informed me of the trip you were to take.

It gives me much real joy to see you very active in the college affairs. This greaved me much last term because such wonderful talent was not in use. I am very proud that our friendship has reached such proportion that even the thought of a breach is unthinkable. I really believe that my success in life depends on my relations with you, God and myself alone being excepted.

Oh how I wish I could hear your oration New Year night. You will not forget to keep it I will see it when I return.

Just when I will return is still unknown to me.

Best regards to the fellows and my sincere prayer for you.

Sincerely Yours,

[*signed*] Clarence J. Gresham.

ALS. HTC-MBU: Box 191.

1. Clarence James Gresham (1898–1985) was a native of Atlanta, Georgia. He graduated from Morehouse College Academy in 1918 and Morehouse College in 1923. For the next three years Gresham attended Oberlin Graduate School of Theology, and following his completion of the BD he was named interim pastor of First Baptist Church of LaGrange, Georgia. In 1926 he was professor of biblical literature in the School of Religion at Morehouse. He served as pastor of Ebenezer Baptist Church of Athens, Georgia, from 1937 to 1952. In 1958, Gresham began his pastorate of Shiloh Baptist Church in Atlanta, where he remained until his death.

2. Here *small pops* refers to "smallpox."

3. George Jackson Van Buren, a Morehouse classmate of Thurman who graduated from the institution in 1923, attended summer session at Columbia in 1922.

❧ "Our Challenge"
FEBRUARY–MARCH 1922

The annual Emancipation Celebration was the signature event of the Pi-Gamma Literary Society of Morehouse and Spelman colleges. Two addresses were given, one by a student from Morehouse, the other by an alumnus selected by the student body. Thurman delivered "Our Challenge" on 2 January 1922, and it was later published in the Athenaeum. *Emancipation addresses to commemorate the January first anniversary of the Emancipation Proclamation were a well-estab-lished tradition in early twentieth-century African American oratory, one in which the speaker had to balance the progress made by African Americans since 1865 against the distance to travel to reach full equality. The piece is a typical student effort, in very ripe rhetoric, a glimpse of a master orator learning his craft.*

Physical slavery is no more. No more too the frantic wail, the awe-inspiring groan of black men as they crouch and cower beneath their master's lash. When Lincoln signed the Emancipation Proclamation the die was cast for physical slavery within the United States of America. Notwithstanding the fact that our chains have been loosed, every black man in America finds himself chained and fettered by certain racial characteristics which have their origin in a past external environment but their perpetuation in a present subjective environment. We have been told that our progress is unparalleled in history; we have been told that our loyalty is unsurpassed from Bunker Hill to Carazel; we have also been told that we are a peculiar people ordained of God to bring salvation to the world. All this, too often. The effect has been decidedly unwholesome. Instead of inspiring us to higher heights, to greater effort, these things have tended to make us fold our arms in complacency and satisfaction. We have become intoxicated with our own progress, we have fallen asleep, now we are dreaming, yes, in a nightmare and the world is working.

While we are thus sleeping, our thoughts, our attitudes, our ideas and in many respects, our destinies, all, are being shaped and planned by those who love us not. The result is that although our chains have been loosed, our minds have been more securely bound. The calamity of it all is, however, our psychic slavery is so complete, our sleep so sound, our last waking impression so satisfying, that though we are victims, we do not realize it.

The problem of arousing our people to possess the land of their possibilities is complex in its nature and perplexing in its solution. For, as we have said before, there are certain racial characteristics which conspire to hinder our advance and to perpetuate that form of psychic slavery of which we speak. In this, fellow-students, we find our challenge.

We have carried to the extreme the philosophy of the eternal Now. We have transliterated, rather than interpreted the teachings of Jesus relative to the eternal present. We have a predisposition to have no place in our philosophy of life for future responsibility. In Africa we were supplied with a cheap plenteous food and a hot climate. The result was, as a matter of survival, we developed a rather shiftless, desultory nature and almost no sense of responsibility for the future. Why should we have thought in terms of the future when in the present we were supplied with all our needs not as a result of much effort on our part, but largely as a gift of nature? We came to America as slaves. The southern white man, our sometime master, exacted of us regular labor, but we became his responsibility to feed, to clothe, to care for. Hence, for ages past in Africa and for more than two hundred years in America, we had no need to develop a sense of responsibility for the future. We have been dependent upon the white man so long for the necessities of life, we have been compelled to look to him so long for succor and for aid that to the masses of our people he partakes of the nature of a god, to be honored, adored, feared and obeyed. We have been nurtured into the belief that his will must be our pleasure and his wish our sincere desire. In this state of darkness, of corrupt belief and false conception of things that are, the masses of our people live and move and have their being.

As students, that is, as students of meager means, we have been literally stormed into developing a sort of responsibility, at least, for the immediate future; but we are held mercilessly in the thraldom of shiftless and desultory habit. This finds expression among us in our desire to get by, to skim over, or to half do our job. These things must also pass away if we would survive.

It is true that we have made some progress, that we have blazed some paths, that we have paved some highways, but the tasks, the great big achievements of our race lie in the future. For indeed "the present is big with the future."[1]

In our struggle for existence in the American civilization, our salvation depends upon our independency, our organization, our keen sense of responsibility for the future, and our jam-up efficiency, along all lines temporal and spiritual. It seems amazingly peculiar, but strikingly true, that our ideals are but the visual manifestations of our greatest needs. Let us therefore acknowledge the existence of our ideals or of our needs, and with that fervor which only the great big human soul which we possess can know, let us develop for ourselves an emotion of these ideals. Then, as teachers and prophets of a new era, let us go forth wherever black men live and suffer and eject into the masses this same emotion. Through a series of slow and painful processes, we, the victims will soar higher, higher and higher, above the sordid ruins of our hinderances and set our ownselves free. No one can do this for us! We have been freed, now let us be free. In the judgment hall of our own race consciousness we must be victims or victors forever. Thus will the burning worlds of our economic depression flee and lighten through immensity, will the judgment fires kindle about the pillars that stay race prejudice and rolling their smoke and flames upward, fire the entire civilized dome, and then, and only then, will the car of Negro freedom, physical and psychic, rumble on forever, over the bleak and dismal loneliness of an exterminated slavery.

Athenaeum (February–March 1922): 49–50.

1. From Gottfried Wilhelm Leibniz (1646–1716): "The present is big with the future and laden with the past."

∾ "PROPOSAL FOR NEGRO SCHOLARSHIP FUND"
[1922–23?]
[ATLANTA, GA.?]

This undated document addressed to John Hope was most likely written during Thurman's junior or senior year at Morehouse College. The proposal calls for the establishment of a scholarship fund for black male students to pursue advanced degrees, presumably at predominantly white institutions at which they would have their degrees validated, and then "return to some designated Negro college" to teach. Thurman conceived this as an effort in black self-

advancement and wanted to solicit contributions from the black community until the principal of the fund reached one million dollars. This was in contrast to contemporary scholarship programs for black students, such as the Julius Rosenwald Fund or John F. Slater Fund or the later United Negro College Fund, which all relied heavily on contributions from wealthy white patrons. Thurman's proposal perhaps reflects the influence of Lorimer Milton,[1] a proponent of black economic advancement, who was one of the most successful black entrepreneurs in Atlanta. Milton taught Thurman economics at Morehouse, and he was one of Thurman's favorite teachers.

There are several reasons to plausibly assign this document to Thurman's undergraduate years. During his junior year at Morehouse, Thurman had made a similar proposal to James Gamble of the soap manufacturer Procter and Gamble, Thurman's benefactor since high school. In his proposal to Gamble, which is known about only from Thurman's autobiography, he suggested that Gamble establish a fund that would provide loans for teachers in black colleges to support their studies for advanced degrees.[2] Other factors supporting an early dating include stylistic elements, such as his address to "President Hope," a salutation not found in his later correspondence with John Hope, and a certain immaturity in style and content, including limiting the scholarship fund to males.

On some level, Thurman's concern with a Negro scholarship fund reflects the difficult financial circumstances of his own academic career, where his ability to attend college hinged on his winning very competitive scholarships. If Thurman rarely returned to explicit self-help schemes such as the one outlined here, the emphasis on developing and encouraging sound moral leadership among black college students would remain for Thurman a lifelong concern.

It shall be incorporated under the name of the "Negro Scholarship Fund." The fundamental purpose of the fund shall be, to promote and encourage higher education among Negroes:

1, To make it possible for talented Negro men to pursue advanced courses along special lines until [*word missing*]

2. To especially aid Negro men who are looking toward the teaching profession that they may specialize at some designated institution. Said men will be under obligation to return to some designated Negro college or colleges as professors thereby simultaneously raising the standard of said college or colleges. The ultimate aim of such will be to bring the blessings of higher education within the reach of the average Negro youth.

SUPPORT.

It is my plan to use as a working principal the amount that is placed on interest plus the {accrued} interest. In the event that I can have a sum sufficient say $100,000.00 as a working principal it will be possible for me to function with the fund using the interest on the said amount, at least until it is possible to add very materially to the principal. By soliciting {regular} contributions from among my people both from individuals and organizations, it will be possible to steadily increase the principal until it amounts to $1,000,000.00.

CONDITIONS.

1. Men must be of good moral character.
2. Men must present {satisfactory sufficient}[3] evidence of scholarship and inability to meet financial needs.
3. Men must be willing to obligate themselves to return the amount advanced without interest after <u>he</u> is out and earning {a ~~living~~ money.}[4] This does not apply to prospective teachers.

REMARKS.

It is not the aim to defray all of the expenses of a man but instead to bring up the deficit remaining after the savings from the summer's earnings. In the event that a {man boy}[5] is being supported both by his efforts and those of his parents in a school of lower ranking and it is proved necessary to his best development to matriculate in a larger school ~~with~~ having greater facilities and advantages, the fund will supply whatever excess over the rate at the said ~~lower~~ school of lower ranking.

Men must be at least of Freshman College grade.

President Hope, will you kindly look this over and think it through? I assure you that whatever suggestions that you make will be most thoroughly appreciated and most gratefully received.

Oblige,

[*signed*] H. W. Thurman

ALS. HTC-MBU: Box 179.

1. *WHAH*, 42. Lorimer Milton (1898–1971) became president of Citizen's Trust Bank in Atlanta in 1926. Under his direction the bank became one of the country's premier African American economic institutions.

2. *WHAH*, 25–26, 237–38. Thurman states that Gamble turned down the proposal, saying he had recently set up a similar arrangement with the YMCA.

3. Curly braces are Thurman's.

4. Curly braces are Thurman's.

5. Curly braces are Thurman's.

🐟 THE *TORCH:* MOREHOUSE COLLEGE YEARBOOK
1923
ATLANTA, GA.

The Torch,[1] published by the Morehouse class of 1923, was the college's first senior yearbook, and Thurman served as editor. The yearbook included biographies of each class member, the class poem, which Thurman cowrote, and student profiles—both humorous and prophetic. Thurman wrote many of the lively biographies and no doubt contributed to the class profiles. The Torch *provides an endearing portrait of Thurman. He was at once the brilliant philosopher and writer of his destiny but also the good humored, ambitious, sometimes stubborn class leader whom his friends admired and affectionately called "Dud."*

HOWARD WASHINGTON THURMAN
"Dud"

> *"A spirit all compact of fire*
> *Not gross to sink but light and will aspire.[2]"*

Born in Daytona, Fla., November 18, 1899; Florida Normal and Industrial Institute, 1919; Freshman: first scholarship, Edgar Allen Poe Short Story Prize, Athenaeum Literary Prize, Y.M.C.A. Cabinet, Glee Club, Pi Gamma, Chi Delta Sigma; Sophomore: second scholarship, Paxon Prize Oration, literary editor, *Athenaeum,* Y.M.C.A. Cabinet, class president, chaplain Pi Gamma, Chi Delta Sigma, Hamlet; Junior: first scholarship, Chamberlain Scripture Reading Prize, student orator Emancipation Day, representative to National Y.M.C.A. Conference, Cincinnati, Ohio, Y.M.C.A. Cabinet, alternate debater, *Othello,* Program Committee Pi Gamma; Senior: first scholarship, president Y.M.C.A., president Atlanta Student Council, varsity debater, editor-in-chief Annual, summer session Columbia University (1922), valedictorian. Commencement speaker, class poem, assistant to the Dean.

Scholar-Christian-Man. Slow in speech, large in stature, with long dangling arms, "Dud" is a striking figure in any group. The personification of the Morehouse Ideal a genuine christian. His big heart and massive brain have been the repository of many student problems, only to be solved and settled. Brainy and sympathetic he is our ideal of a minister, one who shall furnish us with a rational and practical christianity. Holder of the two highest offices of the class, president and editor-in-chief of Annual, varsity debater, winner of a different prize every year, president of Y.M.C.A., orator, writer of class poem, actor, student's unanimous choice to National Y.M.C.A. Conference, Cincinnati, Ohio, he has won the confidence and respect of entire school. His effect on other students as president of Atlanta Student Council—A.U., Morehouse, Morris Brown, Clark and Gammon—assistant in dean's office, honor student, valedictorian, commencement speaker, "Dud" is our most brilliant classmate. This annual, the creature of his hands, ably attests the literary ability of our friend and brother who soon leaves to win higher honors in Rochester Theological Seminary.

CLASS POEM

> We came,
> From hamlet, burg and urban heights afar
> Where open hearth and flickering torch
> Or harnessed lightning shed its rays.
> We dreamed,
> We yearned, we hungered long and oft
> To see our magic hopes become our own;
> At last with cheeks aflush
> Courageous, unafraid
> We came.
>
> II
> We grew.
> The pains of grilling toil,
> The pangs of failing grades
> The aftermath of vic'tries won
> We know.
> Thru long hurrying years—
> This place our nursery
> Our fostering Mater,
> Thru long swirling years
> We grew.
>
> III
> We go.
> The mystic hand has marked the end.
> It is the beginning.
> Sons—loyal triumphant,
> Prepared at thy shrine
> We go
> Fond Mater to reflect the halo
> Which thy face hath shed—

On the heights, in the valley, pursuing the gleam
Where'er it lead,
We go.[3]

IN THE CLASS OF '23 WHO WERE

The tallest? Riley heads the ticket with Morris and Maxwell tying for second place.

The shortest? Holmes can kiss a rat without stooping, while neither Johnson, Gentry brothers, or Davis would dislocate hips in doing same.

The fattest? Per square inch Johnson, but in toto Perkins wins the rag.

The Biggest Crab? "G. T." Tillie, Lord Byron triumvirates of Tireless crabdom with Sledge as patron saint.

The greatest grind? Van Buren wins the knitted bathtub by unanimous acclamation.

The most popular? Frank leads the procession while Brooks marks time with us—"Gab" and Dr. Puck vie for rable chieftainship.

The best dresser? Who is that coming so gladly arrayed? Jimmie, of course with Kack in the distance.

The best natured? Gab's on the mountain peak while we crown the slopes.

The best looking? The idol of the ladies, the envy of the men "Gab" has no peer. Samson, the delicate aristocrat is his chief rival.

The biggest eater? Harper, the indefatigable dilating food enveloper has never had his hunger appeased. Dr. Puck crowds him for his honors while Kack and Jack make deadly inroads on all viands. "Dud" is a noble contestant.

The best athlete? Sledge with basketball, football and track is slightly in the lead of Dunson with basketball, baseball and track laurels.

The best football player? "Pap" Gentry, All-Southern, All-American of course. Mack and Puck come in for their share.

The most efficient? Jimmie, of course.

The heart breakers? Kack, Frank and Jimmie, the heroic triplet, to be sure. Samson would be, but—

Those seen least at chapel? Harper, Lee, James hold chapel with the ladies. Lord Byron answers the Angelus in College Park.

The most versatile? Skeeter is the cat's noodle of versatility—football, basketball, track, soloist, musician, orator, dramatist, poet, scientific boaster. Dunson and Hope get honorable mention.

Those who loaf most? Slick, the U.K.O.L. (uncrowned king of loafers) James is his faithful cupbearer, Holland his courtier and Lee his queen.

Those who slept most? Riley dying from sleeping sickness and G. T. is his faithful nurse superintended by the orthodox Kack.

The optimists? Van Buren hopes when hope is dead and Alexander helps Hope.

The pessimists? Sledge, Brooks, Tillie tussle for first place, while Puck and Lord Byron hold their coats.

The Robert Hall Pests? GAB.

The tight-wad? A Lemon.

The least understood? Pete, the Holy Brick.

The quietest devil? Sig—himself.

The neatest men? Gresham has the laurel while Frank, Sig and Snells support his antics.

The greatest pluggers? H & H. Hope and Huggins, hand in hand by themselves.

The most sanctimonious? Rev. Perry, Riley, Thurman and Lemon.

The most orthodox? It must be Kack and his table mate Rev. Perry.

The most radical? Did you say Puck and Crawford? certainly.

The busiest? Debating, teaching, preaching, editing the Annual, managing the "Y" and office work give "Dud" the hand-painted, cutglass comb. Crawford is a distant second.

The biggest feet possessors? Maxwell covers the territory while the editor plays tag.

The woman haters? Father Pete, the Living Rock.

The slowest? If Calhoun and Bridges drove an ice wagon it would be mistaken for the city sprinkler.

The stingiest? Crawford the Silas Marner of '23.

The brokist? Parks is 100%, while our good friends Lee, Gurley and Puck are 95% or better.

The champion borrowers? Frank holds the torch so that Harper and Dunson may see how to find Puck who is looking for James and Lee.

The biggest boaster? Alfred Joseph Jackson—Rigell, Steve himself.

The biggest flatterers? G. T. and Lee.

The most independent? Jimmie wears no man's collar.

The noisest? Gab and Jack.

The greatest nuisances? Brooks, Jack and Dunson. The three mosquitoes.

The quietest? Gresham and Lemon.

The orators? Holmes, Jack and Dud.

The biggest head? James holds first place while Jimmie and Dud follow his lead.

The biggest baby? Dunson.

The most dignified? "Dud."

The most conceited? Dunson.

12[4] *What does Morehouse need most?* Departmental Classification; $2,000,000 endowment; Administration Building; men like "Dud"; organized alumni; more classes like '23; more profs with better salaries; better culinary;

The Torch; Grand Stand; larger Library; greater emphasis on scholarship and debating.

13 *Political preference?* Twenty-two Republicans; fourteen Socialists; three Indeterminists; one Bolshevist.

14 *Religious preference?* One Pagan; one Presbyterian; one Catholic; four A.M.E.; one Primitive Baptist and all the rest dyed-in-the-wood-Baptist.

15 *Favorite amusement?* Hobnobbing with the Spelman girls; dancing with A.U. belles; shooting hot air; throwing the bull; "ain't no such animal"; bossing.

16 *Hardest course in college?* Physics II; any of McKinney's courses; Calculus; Money and Banking.

17 *Easiest courses?* Geology; History of Ed.

18 *Most enjoyable course?* Ethics; Music Appreciation; Sociology and Psychology.

19 *Most beneficial course?* Sociology.

20 *Morehouse greatest asset?* President Hope; class of '23; Science Building; "Spelman ladies"; college spirit; good scholarship; christian principles; men; Dean and Kemper Harreld.

21 *Views on schools for Boys and Men?* Great; get tired of seeing them; creates manhood; as for rest see editors privately.

22 *Faculty Czars?* Harvey, by far; Milton; McKinney and Latson.

23 *Faculty Democrats?* Dean; Tillman; Mays; President; Warner; Pap Johnson; Dansby.

24 *Student Instigators and Politicians?* Patrick; Ellis; Puck; J. B. Harris.

25 *Student Pacifists?* "Ed"; "Dud"; Riley.

26 *General Advisers?* "Popper Hooks"; Riley; Jimmie; Sam Johnson; "Dud."

27 *Ideal Professor?* President Hope.

28 *Ideal man?* Dean Archer.

29 *Ideal Morehouse man?* Late Garrie Moore.

30 *Greatest Events of 1923?* President's Silver Wedding Anniversary. 25th year at Morehouse, graduation of class of '23; Presentation of Sun Dial; Publication of the *Torch*.

AWARDS WON BY CLASS OF 1923

Edgar Allen Poe Short Story Prize
Howard Thurman, 1920
Willis James, 1921
Edward Hope, 1922

Chamberlain Scripture Reading Prize
Howard Thurman, 1922

*Chamberlain Scripture
Recitation Prize*
Charles Holmes, 1923

Pozon Prize Oration
Howard Thurman, 1921
Charles Holmes, 1922

Chemistry Prize
Edward Hope, 1922

Athenaeum Literary Prize
Floyd Crawford, 1920
Howard Thurman, 1920

General Scholarship
Freshman Year
1 Howard Thurman
2 Edward Hope

Sophomore Year
1 William Payne
2 Howard Thurman

Junior Year
1 Howard Thurman
2 William Payne

Senior Year
1 Howard Thurman
2 William Payne

---

1. *Torch*, 1923, Morehouse College Archives.

2. William Shakespeare, *Venus and Adonis*, 1.145.

3. Cowritten by Thurman and William Kenneth Payne; also published in *Athenaeum* (May 1923): 190–91.

4. Numbers 1–11 were not reproduced.

CHAPTER III

Rochester Years

❧ ROCHESTER THEOLOGICAL SEMINARY NOTEBOOK: "VIRGIN BIRTH"
[JANUARY–MAY 1924?]
ROCHESTER, N.Y.

*"Virgin Birth" is taken from one of Thurman's notebooks during his years at
Rochester Theological Seminary. The notebook contains a typed version of the
paper and under the heading of "Virgin Birth II" typed notes about early
Christianity and Pauline theology. This paper was probably written for Henry
Burke Robins's spring 1924 course, "Psychology of Religion." It is not known if
this version of the paper was submitted to the course instructor. The unusual
orthography of the paper suggests that it might have been typed by a second
party from Thurman's handwritten draft.*

*"Virgin Birth" illustrates Thurman's developing critical skills in theological
reflection. He uses contemporary works of evolutionary anthropology, which
argued for a sharp difference between the mentality of primitive and advanced
societies, to explore the idea of the virgin birth of Jesus as a residue of mythological thinking. Thurman argues that most primitive cultures fail to understand the
connection between coition and pregnancy, treating all human births as being in
some sense "miraculous." In time more-sophisticated civilizations like the ancient
Greeks and Hindus restricted the doctrine of virgin birth to persons of great
significance. Thurman argues that the doctrine of the virgin birth of Jesus should
be classified as mythology, akin to similar stories told of Zeus, Krishna, or Isis.
Overall, Thurman aligns himself with the modernist project of freeing the truth of
Christianity from the mythological accretions of traditional doctrine. The
opening quote from Edward Carpenter indicates Thurman's familiarity, before
his initial encounter in 1925 with the works of Olive Schreiner, with the circle of*

British writers advocating free thought and sexual freedom, including Carpenter,
Schreiner, and Havelock Ellis.

"The vision of a perfect man hovered dimly over the mind of the human race on its first emergence from the purely animal stage; and a quite natural speculation with regard to such a being was that he would be born from a Perfect Woman—who according to very early ideas would necessarily be the Virgin Earth itself, mother of all things. It was a wonderful Intuition, slumbering as it would seem in the breast of early man, that the Great Earth after giving birth to all living creatures would at last bring forth a child who should become the Savior of the human race."[1]

Spring with its bursting buds and blooming flowers must have made profound impression upon primitive man. But an even greater impression was made by the actual coming into life of one of his kind. It was well nigh impossible for him to connect births with sexual union. The space of time between the copulative union and the consequences is so long that the two events would not necessarily appear to men of very low mental development as cause and effect. Immediate results, and they alone strike savages of the most primitive type as connected with their antecedents. Even today, certain aboriginal Australian natives believe that births are caused by the entrance into prospective mothers of ancestral spirits and have no connection with union of the sexes. Some anthropologists seem to think that this idea was once common to all mankind in the animistic stage of culture, and this is highly probable when we think of our ancestors even in those days, as little better, mentally, than animals, who certainly, cannot connect the gratification of a transient passion with its long subsequent, and not inevitable result.

As Redgrove points out, The Aruntos of Australia believed that conception was occasioned by the common passing near a churinga—a peculiar shaped piece of wood or stone, in which a spirit child was concealed, which entered into her. Here we might possibly locate the primitive roots of Phollic Cults—while as yet phollus is unconnected with fertility.[2]

There was also a widespread notion that women conceived by the wind. Hiawatha was said to be the son of the West wind, and many other mythical hewes[3] owed their existence to that wind, or to the east or south wind.

Natives of Mesopotamia and Egypt have for hundreds of years, artificially fertilized their dates and palm trees by brushing the pollen of the male palm on to the ovaries of the female date. Only recently did they learn that the process they were helping to carry out was sexual. It was thought to be a process to keep some evil spirit from eating up the small dates.

Even in England, recently, it was customary to root up the male of hop plants as useless encumbrances, and it was not until numerous experiments had been made, that the hop growers were persuaded to believe that the wind-borne pollen of the male hop was necessary for full development of female fruit.

In some parts of Germany the "Yule Straw"[4] was, and perhaps, is bound round fruit trees, for purpose of fertilizing them; the origin of the custom and of other similar customs to which we have referred, being doubtless connected with sympathetic magic.

But let us return to the apparent facts of vegetable reproduction. Men eventually began to notice the constantly recurring and apparently miraculous death and rebirth of vegetation, the dead seed sown in the womb of the earth and called to life again by the rays of the sun. Earth had to be regarded as real Mother, and the Sun as real Father.

Myths were inevitable. Oldest stories about Isis were that she had no partner. She lived a lonely life among the marshes. There without any male assistance, she gives birth to a son. It is probable that the idea behind this is derived from apparently immaculate birth of vegetation from seeds. It was thought that vegetation required only moisture for purpose of reproduction. Hence the Goddess of fertility conceiving amid the ponds and marshes and hence, too, the stories of the first creation taking place in the damp shores of the ocean.

Spontaneous generation was believed in until most recently. St. Augustine in "City of God" describes the peopling of some islands with animals spontaneously generated. The fact about the fertilization of the Queen Bee was not discovered until the 18th Century.

It was thought that eels were metamorphosed hairs dropped into ponds from tails of horses. There are some communities in America where it is believed that a strand of horse hair left for a certain period in rain water will turn into a snake.

What do these facts point out? They demonstrate very clearly that the most elementary physiological facts are very easily misunderstood or overlooked until their real nature is explained by scientific observers, and that in very primitive times myths could very easily arise which—in case of all myths, would survive long after the natural course of events was fully understood by most men.

The inhabitants of Asia Minor, Dyria, Babylonia and Egypt were, in the first century of our era, no longer ignorant of many of these things pointed out above. But they inherited myths which arose in a transitional period. They would not invent entirely new myths of that kind but they would accept, repeat and reapply old myths invented by their less well-informed ancestors.

The essence of all Virgin-birth legends is the failure or inability of primitive man to recognize the necessity for a woman to have intercourse with a male in order to bring about conception and child-birth.[5]

This is the permanent primitive element in the idea. At first it was universal—slowly but surely it became more and more restricted until at length it was only used as the explanation of the origin of an individual of great significance. Of course a part of the idea may date back to that matriarchal period, when descent was reckoned always through the maternal {line} and the fatherhood in each generation was obscure or unknown or commonly left out of account.

The permanent element to which we referred, with its restricted application, has enjoyed a world wide dissemination. Zeus, Father of the Gods, visited Semele, in the form of a thunder storm; and she gave birth to the great saviour and deliverer Dionysus. Devoki, the radiant Virgin of the Hindu mythology became the wife of the God Vishnu and bore Kirsha the [*word missing*] and prototype of Christ. The Egyptian Isis, with the child Horus in her [*word missing*], was honored centuries before the Christian era and worshiped under the names of "Our Lady," "Mother of God" etc. The old Teutonic Goddess Hertha was a Virgin, but was impregnated by the heavenly Spirit. The Scandinavian Frigga, in much the same way, was caught in the embrace of Odin, the All-father, conceived and bore a son, the blessed Bolder, healer and savior of mankind. Tuetzolcoatl, the saviour of the Aztecs was the son of Chimalman, the Virgin Queen of Heaven.[6]

Legends have grown up around many great men. These legends as to birth always have our permanent primitive element. Buddha (Gautowa) was given birth to by Maza an immaculate virgin, who conceived him through a divine influence. The facts are—Gautowa was the son of a Hindu rajah named Suddhadana, and was born, in the ordinary course of nature in 563 b.c. He did not claim to be a God, neither did either he himself or his disciples claim that his birth was miraculous.

When Zingis Khon,[7] the Mogul, had conquered a great part of Asia and became master of a formidable and aggressive empire and a {terror} to the whole Eastern world, his courtiers evolved for him a geneology which traced his descent seven generations back to an immaculate Virgin. He received Title Son of God. Familiar!

About 2000 years before Christian era Metumua, the Virgin, Queen of Egypt was said to have given birth to the Pharoah Amenkept III, who built temple of Luzor, on the walls of which were represented:

1. The Annunciation—The God Poht announcing to the Virgin queen that she is about to become a mother.
2. The Annunciation—The God Kneph (Holy Spirit) mystically impregnating the Virgin by holding a cross, the symbol of life, to her mouth.
3. Birth of Man-God.
4. Adoration of the newly born infant by Gods and men, including 5 kings (magi?) who are offering him gifts. Cross again appears as a symbol.

From these illustrations and many others, like unto them we see how widely disseminated and persistent has been this man-God legend. It remained for the

Gnostic philosophers and early theologians to repeat and reapply an old myth to the interpretation of the matchless life of Jesus of Nazareth, the Son of God. It is apart from the purpose of this paper to trace the Gnostic Doctrine of the Spiritual Virgin Births, through the Catholic doctrine to the Protestant doctrine. It is simply my purpose to trace the permanent primitive element in this doctrine that has its roots back in the dim shadows of a misty antiquity.

SUMMARY IDEA.

The Virgin Birth of Christ is a Doctrine of the Catholic Church and of most Protestant Churches. It has its origin in a time when primitive man was unable to recognize the necessity for a woman to have intercourse with a male in order to bring about conception and children. This idea became more and more restricted in the light of an ever advancing Learning until it permanently established itself in the desire of men to glorify with mythical origin anyone of their number who proved to be a saviour and born to them. Born in error it has been perpetuated by adjusting itself to a universal human craving normally to glorify its hewes but to express its gratitude to those rare spirits who have in one way or another striven to be saviours of their race.

TD. HTC-MBU: Box 178.

1. Edward Carpenter, *Pagan and Christian Creeds: Their Origin and Meaning* (New York: Harcourt, Brace, 1920), 161. Edward Carpenter (1854–1929) was an English socialist, feminist, and pacifist. His *Intermediate Sex: A Study of Some Transitional Types of Men and Women* (London: Sonnenschein, 1908) was the first widely circulated defense of homosexuality in English, and his *Pagan and Christian Creeds* (London: Allen & Unwin, 1920) was an explicitly anti-Christian work, denying the historicity of Jesus and arguing that Christianity would be supplanted by the "great World-Religion," an amalgam of eastern and pagan religious practices.

2. H. Stanley Redgrove, *Bygone Beliefs Being a Series of Excursions in the Byways of Thought* (London: Rider, 1920).

3. *Hewes,* which appears twice in this typescript, both times as an apparent substitute for *heroes,* is perhaps the result of errors made by a typist who had problems interpreting Thurman's original handwritten manuscript.

4. Mainly a European Christmas tradition, yule straw was spread on the floors of Christians to simulate the manger, Christ's first resting place.

5. Many anthropologists of the early twentieth century believed that the connection between copulation and pregnancy was beyond the reasoning abilities of those in primitive societies. Thurman would have encountered this belief in Carpenter's *Pagan and Christian Creeds* (159), and it was accepted by many of the leading lights of the field, including James Frazer and Bronislaw Malinowski. Thurman offers it in the strongest possible version, claiming that ignorance about the nature of conception was at one time "universal." By the 1930s, anthropologists were increasingly interpreting the so-called virgin birth accounts as religious and symbolic rather than as literal accounts of the birth process. The theory of a widespread ignorance of the birth process has few if any adherents today. For an account of this

episode, see Edmund Leach, "Virgin Birth," in *Genesis as Myth and Other Essays* (London: Cape, 1969), 85–110.

    6. Thurman's examples here are similar to those in Jocelyn Rhys's text, *Shaken Creeds: The Virgin Birth Doctrine, a Study of the Origins* (London: Watts, 1922).

    7. Ghengis Khan was a Mongol, not a Mogul (or Mughal) ruler.

ᘯ "COLLEGE AND COLOR"
APRIL 1924

"College and Color" was published in Student Challenge, *the official organ of the Student Fellowship for Student Life-Service, a national Christian student organization founded in 1922. Thurman frankly discusses the casual racism faced by African American students in white colleges and the predominantly white student Christian movement. Some of the stories related by Thurman have the feel of personal reminiscences. He is scathing in his condemnation of whites who have a merely intellectual understanding of the race problem. In the essay, Thurman advocates a "Christian way in race relations" on American college campuses in which "sympathetic understanding" produces mutual respect. He concludes that only through personal interaction conducted outside of the limitations of social conventions on race can students of different races come to truly treat each other as equals. He also draws upon the work of George Coe,[1] a pioneer in the fields of psychology of religion and religious education, who was a major influence upon Thurman's intellectual development during his seminary years.*

Not long ago I spent a weekend with a friend at whose church I was scheduled to speak. My presence in the home was quite a curiosity to his four year old daughter. She had never seen my like before.

    I made several friendly overtures and at length she said, "Have a seat over there," pointing to a large Morris chair. As soon as I was seated, she jumped into my lap, took both of her hands, rubbed them on my face and then examined them to see if any of my color had been removed. Discovering no change in my face and no stain on her hands, she asked with great earnestness and anxiety, "Are you black all over?"

    "Yes."

    "Are you black under your collar?"

    "Yes."

    "But I know you don't have black feet?"

    "Certainly."

    "Did you have to be black? Why aren't you white like Daddy?"

After this grilling cross examination our friendliness increased and when I left the home, as far as I could see her from the distance, she was waving a fond good-bye to the human being she had discovered under a black skin.

Ruth's first reaction was one of shyness mingled with fear. My overtures assured her that I was harmless and friendly in spirit. A relationship of primary contact established, she proceeded to a firsthand investigation of the phenomenon. Her first problem was whether my color was genuine or artificial, and whether it covered my entire body. "If he is the same color all over, he must be different from Daddy." The next step was to see if I had chosen my color or if I had had no choice in the matter.

Convinced that I was black and had always been black, she dismissed that difference as beside the point and began to appreciate that part of me over which she felt that I had a measure of control. In other words, she judged me by the qualities which I had in common with her father and not by our differences. In a very fundamental way Ruth's attitude was one of sympathetic understanding which led to a very real respect for my personality.

The heroic absence of this attitude both on our campuses and in our national life is the very crux of racial conflicts. I state as my thesis that the Christian way in race relations is the way of sympathetic understanding—which leads to respect for personality.

By sympathetic understanding I do not mean a patronizing attitude or anything that is cheap and sentimental. Nor do I mean an attitude that is so swollen with condescending pride that its stench is intolerable. But I do mean an attitude which says that a man of another race is essentially myself, and that I feel toward him fundamentally as if he were myself. His needs and cravings and the drives which lie behind his actions are similar to mine in their essentials.

It is more or less a truism that an idea held in mind tends to express itself in action. Especially is this true if the idea carries with it an emotional fringe. We cannot properly appreciate and understand what is going on in objective experience unless we somehow get back of it to the great world of ideas—intangible, unseen—which controls human activity. As Mumford in his *Story of Utopias* points out, "Man walks with his feet on the ground and his head in the air; and the history of what has happened on earth—the history of cities and armies and all things that have had body and form—is only one half the Story of Mankind."[2] For the other half we must address ourselves to the realm of ideas which lie behind deeds and actions.

The first question we raise, then, has to do with what is going on in the mind of the Negro student on your campus in the face of discrimination and prejudice. What is going on in his mind when during the opening days before seats are assigned, all the chairs in his immediate vicinity are marked by an invisible,

"UNCLEAN"? What is going on in his mind when purchasing his theatre ticket he hears two students, perhaps classmates, debating as to whether they shall buy orchestra seats or seats for "Nigger Heaven"?[3] What is going on in his mind when from the lecture platform there comes the eternally humiliating joke at the expense of the entire Negro group? What is going on in his mind in the face of blatant outbursts of "white supremacy"?[4]

The second question has to do with the primary reactions and the more or less permanent attitudes towards this student on your campus. These first reactions generally run something like this, "Here's a place where I'll get some good jokes"; "I wonder how that happened," etc. But whatever the temporary reaction is, the permanent attitudes fall under certain general groupings most of which are suggested by the following statement given by a recent graduate of an Eastern university: "I have the greatest admiration and respect and sympathy for those of their race who can lay a straight course and keep to it with a brave heart in the face of everything they must suffer. The Jew's life is hard, but it is much easier than the Negro's. In our graduating class in high school there was a fine colored girl who was going on to college. The other people ridiculed her almost openly and no one marched with her. It roused Blank terribly and she went to the principal and had him change the line so that she would be with the girl. I do not know whether I could have done that."

The first attitude suggested is one of interest. Sometimes this takes the form of simple toleration. One student expresses it this way, "These people feel that to condescend to smile, 'Hello' or wave 'Good-bye' adds to the sum total of their humane tendencies. . . . Back of this garb lies every emotion ranging from genuine hatred to total indifference."

Sometimes this interest takes the form of paternal protection. Here is a man who dares to face ridicule in order to shelter an "unfortunate," just as a plantation owner defends a peon on his farm. In such a relationship the designated protege becomes the "underling" and all signs of manhood vanish. Sometimes the motives underlying such assumptions are genuine, but pity always weakens and embarrasses.

There is another type of interest that tries to impress one with a high sense of fairness which really does not exist. The stock approach is the famous, "I have no prejudice," as if mere words meant much. I am reminded of the adage, "Beware of the man who sells you a pig in the market-place in the name of the Lord."

Finally there is that interest manifested by those whose actions are determined by a fine sense of fair play. Contact with that kind of student is as invigorating as a refreshing shower in the midst of a tropical summer. There is nothing sentimental about that kind of relationship; it is simply a case of man meeting man and appreciating the fine qualities of each. This type of person is not bound by traditional attitudes or by group complexes, but his actions are based upon a high sense of honesty and fairplay. Of such is the Kingdom of Heaven.

There are those who are indifferent or thoughtless. They float easily down the stream of accepted opinion and think that it is the way of life. Their point of view is the right one and nothing counts save themselves and their immediate interests. Whatever the prevailing attitude is, it becomes theirs and that settles it. One such student writes, "I have never thought seriously about my attitude. Such terms as 'Nigger,' 'Nigger Heaven,' were current on my campus when I entered college. It never occurred to me to think what effect they had on colored students."

The final group may be thought of as those who are hostile. It is this type that intentionally and maliciously brushes against the Negro student in the corridor, steps on his foot, makes wretchedly nasty statements about his race and his women, and in general seeks every opportunity to humiliate and embarrass. One thing in their favor is their utter lack of hypocrisy; there is no room to question approaches because they are not.

Underlying all of these attitudes, save one, there is the steady, unswerving hand of tradition and custom. It is not a question of what is right, or of what ought to be, but it is simply a question of what has been and what the particular environment will endorse. Any attitude, regardless of its basis, which strangles personality and inhibits its highest growth and development is wrong. For a Christian believer to have that kind of attitude is a crime against God.

Professor Coe in his *Social Theory of Religious Education* summarizes the situation as follows: "When we who pray to God as Father, and call humanity a family, and exalt the idea of service, nevertheless take unprotesting comfort in the anti-domestic unbrotherly, castelike inequalities of opportunity that prevail in the world, then, however unconscious we may be of compromising our religion, we actually become teachers of an anti-Christian ethic."[5]

If the college bred student does not treat members of other races as individuals, respecting their personalities, what can be expected of the great masses who never come under the stimulating influences of collegiate life? If we do not find tolerance in the colleges and universities, where liberal thoughts and democratic ideals are supposed to be fostered, where shall we go?

In too many instances the issue has been side-stepped. There are some questions that are supposed to be settled, but when a man dares to examine their foundation, to actually take the light of investigation down into the cellars of these settled issues, he finds cobwebs, scorpions, snakes and old baby bones. The sight of these things either frightens him, or fills his soul with righteous zeal to have a house cleaning. The Discussion Groups at the Student Volunteer Convention in Indianapolis[6] sent many brave hearts into the cellar of a "settled" race issue. The undergraduate life of today and the national life of tomorrow will be greatly influenced by their reaction to what investigation has revealed.

I do not argue for special favors or for special treatment on the campus. Any such action is pauperizing, to be sure. My contention is that we should be given all of the privileges and freedom of regular matriculated students, no more, no less. The institution of which I am now a part does that.[7] This means that purely on a basis of merit, if that is the criterion, we should be admitted into every activity of college life. We should be dealt with as students, not as *Negro* students. This can only come to pass when there is an official and group attitude of sympathetic understanding expressing itself in respect for personality. This attitude should obtain in dealing with all races—What a hard time Jesus of Nazareth would have if he matriculated at one of our colleges today!

May I suggest a principle of action for the individual student? *Think of the other fellow as essentially yourself and feel towards him fundamentally as if he were yourself.* College life should be very conducive for this kind of development because of its opportunities for primary contacts. It is only in a relationship of primary contact that the individual emerges.

Peace in America and peace in the world depends upon this kind of fellowship. College life is pregnant with opportunities which make for peace, fellowship, brotherhood—the day of delivery is now—whether on your campus these opportunities are born dead, feeble, or full of vigor and promise depends upon you!

Student Challenge 2 (April 1924): 1–2.

1. George Albert Coe (1862–1951) received his AB from the University of Rochester (1884) and entered the School of Theology at Boston University but abandoned his plans to enter the parish ministry and shifted his emphasis to philosophy and scientific method. He received his STB (1887), an MA in philosophy (1888), and his PhD (1891). In 1903, Coe became a founder of the Religious Education Association. In 1909, he was named a professor of religious education and psychology of religion at Union Theological Seminary in New York City and was elected president of the Religious Education Association. While at Union he wrote his most significant works, *The Psychology of Religion* (Chicago: University of Chicago Press, 1916) and *A Social Theory of Religious Education* (New York: Scribner's Sons, 1917). In 1922 he moved to Teachers College at Columbia University and authored *What Ails Our Youth?* (New York: Scribner's Sons, 1925) and *Law and Freedom in the School* (Chicago: University of Chicago Press, 1924) before his retirement in 1927.

2. Lewis Mumford, *The Story of Utopias* (New York: Boni & Liveright, 1922), 12. Lewis Mumford (1895–1990) was a lifelong opponent to urban overdevelopment and wrote extensively about the effect of buildings on the environment and quality of life.

3. The term *Nigger Heaven* refers to a designated place, usually the balcony, where blacks were forced to sit.

4. Here Thurman is marking *white supremacy* as a term propagated by the early twentieth-century eugenics movement.

5. Coe, *Social Theory of Religious Education,* 43.

6. Thurman is referring to the 1924 Quadrennial Conference of the Student Volunteer Movement held in Indianapolis, Indiana, where he was a delegate representing Rochester Theological Seminary.

7. At this time Rochester Theological Seminary had an unofficial policy of admitting only two blacks per year, and sleeping quarters were racially segregated. During Thurman's

second year, the policy of segregated dorm living was broken when Thurman moved in with two white roommates. *WHAH*, 46–52.

꙳ "The Sphere of the Church's Responsibility in Social Reconstruction"
July 1924
Roanoke, Va.

During the summers of 1924 and 1925, Thurman worked on the ministerial staff of the First Baptist Church in Roanoke, Virginia, under the supervision of Reverend Arthur L. James, former pastor of Thurman's home church in Daytona, Florida, and a family friend whom he affectionately called "Cousin Arthur." Among his many duties, Thurman oversaw the daily vacation Bible school program with the assistance of his Morehouse classmate and friend Clarence J. Gresham. The Roanoke Church News, *among the earliest of black newspapers in Roanoke, was published monthly by the Men's Club of the First Baptist Church. James established the newspaper when he first arrived in Roanoke in 1919 and edited it until his retirement in 1957.[1]*

In this brief article Thurman argues, as many in progressive circles did, that the Treaty of Versailles after World War I was an imperialistic victor's peace that would foster international instability. Thurman also argues that the religious and moral institutions that proved powerless to prevent the war or conclude a just postwar settlement were not in a position to claim the ethical high ground. Demonstrating the influence of the Social Gospel on his thinking, he claims that whatever the future holds, the church must embrace social transformation as well as individual salvation.

Up to 1914 the world was fast asleep having for its cozy bed the cradle of a crusted, but internally seething volcano. In a united chorus illusioned hosts sang with Pipa, "God's in his Heaven, all's right with the world."[2] The air was full of echoes of peace and brotherhood, but in the hearts of men forces were at work which were soon to break loose into the most terrific and bloody carnage the world has ever seen.

The war came. For four long, weary years this second Horseman of the Apocalypse swam across Europe in a sea of blood tieing laurels on his brow with heart strings.[3] Men were awakened from their dreams of peace and brotherhood into the stark reality of fiendish hate and destruction.

At length a so-called peace was obtained. The victors were about like other victors. They had only past records to go by and so in their deliberations they followed ancient precedents. They readjusted geography to their own pleasure.

Professor Adler in his Hibbert Lectures for 1923 has summed up the situation and its moral challenge as follows: The horror of the recent war is still felt in our bones, and yet it seems as if mankind could not take to heart the most drastic lessons, the most condign punishments. For alongside of the pacifistic currents, preparations for new wars to be conducted by still more terrible methods are proceeding apace. Above all, there is one fact that strikes the observer: the so-called moral forces seem to have failed in the great crisis through which the world is passing. Religion was powerless to stay the carnage. Indeed, many of its representatives fell in with the prevailing fury, and on their part added fuel to the flames. Allah is said to have laughed aloud in his Mohammedan heaven when the news came that Christian preachers on the one side were proclaiming a Jehad or holy war against their Christian brethren on the other side. Again, the prayers for peace that were prescribed and recited in many churches were spoken into the wind; they had no effect upon the combatants.

"Immediately after the war the task of reconstructing human society was uppermost in people's minds. But the task remains, as necessary, as urgent, as ever."[4]

The conditions resulting from the world war are but a part of the great task of social reconstruction. Our whole social order is shot through with many inherently vicious principles working themselves out in a thousand human ills presenting constant challenge to that institution founded upon Him who "went about doing good."

THE AIM OF THE CHURCH

That the Church has a very definite responsibility in the face of the conditions outlined above is obvious. But just what this responsibility is, no one seems to know. In this regard there is a vast medley of confusion. In an attempt to locate this responsibility the first question that must be asked is, What is the aim of the Church? Is its goal characterized by concreteness and definiteness so that though its ideals have their heads in the clouds, their feet are planted steadfastly in the great world of human experience?

Even the leaders of the Church are far from agreed as to just what its business in the world really is. Many believe that its only aim is to save the individual soul—to give men a sample bliss capsule so as to fire their souls with earnest zeal for the life to come. Jesus is a mistake when he is taken out of sacraments and altars and becomes the daily companion in the home, in business, and in life generally, they seem to think. They insist that the Church's aim alone is to save men's souls, but it has nothing to do with economic ills, political corruption and social injustice.

Roanoke Church News, July 1924, 1.

1. See Eunice R. Poindexter, *Journey of Faith: A History of First Baptist Church, Roanoke, Virginia* (Roanoke, Va.: First Baptist Church, 1983).

2. From Robert Browning, *Pippa Passes,* 1,1.7–8.

3. Rev. 6:1–8.

4. Felix Adler, *The Reconstruction of the Spiritual Idea: Hibbert Lectures, Delivered in Manchester College, Oxford, May, 1923* (New York: Appleton, 1924), 1–2, 4. Felix Adler (1851–1933) was the founder of the Ethical Culture movement, a nontheistic offshoot of Reform Judaism that emphasized social responsibility.

❧ "Let Ministers Be Christians!"
January 1925

Most strongly in Thurman's early period, the following essay questions the limited application of the ideal of Christian brotherhood. Published in the Student Challenge *six months prior to his ordination, the essay seems to draw upon Thurman's seminary experiences as well as his student ministry work in Roanoke, Virginia. He contends that when race relations are the issue, many professed Christians divide their ethical praxis into separate and unequal categories. Instead of serving God in Christ-like fashion, ordained ministers often serve the interests of the racial status quo.*

A friend of mine invited me and a missionary on furlough to go out to dinner with him. When the missionary found that I was a Negro he informed my friend that he was not on the mission field at present; he was on furlough. The invitation was unceremoniously declined.

A young woman who is planning to go to Africa as a missionary said to an acquaintance of mine, "I can't understand why I am going to Africa as a missionary; I hate 'Niggers.'"

"Let me shake hands with you, Brother. I am from Texas but since I have been here I have understood Jesus Christ better and I can say the truth when I call you 'Brother.' I have a long way to go yet and I need your help." Such were the honest words of one who was entering into a larger life than anything he had ever known.

I was present at one of the meetings which formally closed a city-wide evangelical campaign in Atlanta when a rather elderly gentleman who was leading the devotions made this significant confession: "For a long time I have been struggling with this thing. At last I am convinced that there is no other way. . . . They (Negroes) are our brothers."

I

These four incidents illustrate, in a very real sense, what to my mind is the most fundamental and tragic fallacy in our particular brand of religion which we surreptitiously label "Christianity." I refer to the failure to recognize that to follow Christ means that *all* of life, not a segment here and there, must be increasingly permeated with the Spirit of Christ. There is no such thing as Christian living or even full time Christian service, for that matter, apart from the ordinary business of living. Our "Christianity" has been so shut up in water-tight compartments that scarcely a drop of it has been allowed to seep through to give strength and vigor to the thirsty, dying plants of Brotherliness in the garden of every day living.

II

Much of this false emphasis, this blind-alley sight-seeing, can be traced to the door of the ministry. The people in the pew have been given a comfortable, one-sided gospel by those who stand in the shoes of prophets but who utter the soft, satisfying words of the Status Quo. The minister is in direct apostolic succession.[1] Not only is he to encourage, to comfort, to inspire and to bless; but he is dedicated, also, to serve as the gad-fly to a slothful, thoughtless, sin-bespattered generation. His must be the Voice of God that calls the peoples to repentance and challenges them to a higher life in experience than they have achieved already. Above all he must urge men by precept and example and teaching to see life whole and to make it increasingly Christian by actually following Jesus both in attitudes and achievement.

The attitude of the minister must forever be the attitude of Christ; the attitude of every Christian must be the attitude of Christ. He must recognize and emphasize:

1. The sacredness of human personality.
2. The interdependence of men.
3. Supremacy of righteousness as the quality of life which gets Divine approval.
4. The necessity for all acts to be motivated and actuated by passionate good-will or love.

The Story of the Good Samaritan is a matchless example of the Christian attitude *geared to the road of life.* Even he who runs may read; much of the hell in the world and especially in America is *deliberate*!

III

"In so far as ye did it to one of these brothers of mine, even to the least of them, you did it to me."[2] This applies to all men, not to Nordics alone. God identified with human life! Who dares preach and teach and live such a revolutionary gospel? Do those words mean that every time a negro is lynched and burned God is lynched and burned? Do they mean that God is held as a peon in certain parts of this land of "Liberty"? Do they mean that God is discriminated against, segregated and packed in Jim Crow cars?

A friend of mine, a senior in a southern college, walked into a white church in his college town to worship. He was seated in the very rear of the church. At length one of the ushers approached him and inquired as to whether he had come to bring a message from the janitor.

"No. I came in here to worship God."

"Well, you will have to take a seat up in the back of the gallery."

The young man walked out. In telling me about it he had said that it was strikingly pathetic that when a negro and a white man were on their knees shooting dice, they were two common gamblers, but a negro and a white man could not kneel together to pray to a common Father without the definite drawing of lines.

Did Christ walk out of that church when my friend left? "In so far as you did it to one of the brothers of mine, even to the least of them, you did it to me."

IV

No man has larger and more significant opportunities to do and to suggest the Christian act than the minister. Let us consider a pastorate, say, in the South and raise a few significant questions about the opportunities that obtain there. The city is a typical southern one with a negro population of 40 per cent.

1. When the minister is invited to address the Rotary Club just on the eve of a campaign for summer amusements for the neglected children of the city, will he dare to urge them to include *all* of the children in his plans? Will he have courage enough to point out to these men that a large percentage of their money is made from negro patrons and for that reason, if for no other, negro children, always the most neglected civically in the community, should be included?

2. There are several members of the City Council in his church. Will he dare to say to them that they are un-Christian if they do not use all of their influence to provide sanitary living conditions and good streets and lights for what is popularly known as the negro section? Will he dare point out the fact that the negro taxpayers defray a pro rata share of the city's expenses while, for the most part, their benefit and protection therefrom are reduced to a vanishing quantity? Or will he pass by "on the other side,"[3] afraid that he might offend?

3. A member of the State Legislature is one of his trustees. Will he dare tell this man that he is an offender against God as long as he is silent while there remain written on the "statute books" of the state laws of discrimination and segregation; as long as he does nothing toward remedying the awful educational disadvantages and chaos due to no schools, poor schools, poorly paid teachers and the like?

4. In his program of religious education will he have the courage to deliberately include the teaching of brotherliness toward the negro neighbor as an

integral part of religion? Or will he just dwell on glittering generalities about loving all men?

5. Will his sermons ever include a bold courageous stand on the question of race-relations in the local community or will he pussy-foot and wabble by the truth in the name of Jesus of Nazareth?

These and many other practical things a minister must do if he would be truly Christian and lead others to try to achieve that quality of life. As a general thing, very little has been done. Jesus is still unknown in this land that is covered with churches erected in his honor—*absente Christo.*[4]

For the salvation of the world depends upon individuals who are willing to pay the debt they owe to their dignity as human beings by fighting out the battle within themselves until they possess their own souls."[5]

To your tents, O Israel![6]

Student Challenge 3/4 (January 1925): 1, 14.

1. Common among Protestant denominations that do not have episcopacies is the belief that ordained clergy are in direct apostolic succession. This is not to say they attempt to trace the laying on of hands from their own ordination back to the first-century founders of the faith but that their calling to the preaching and pastoral ministry is in line with that of the Apostles.

2. Matt. 25:40.

3. Luke 10:31–32.

4. The phrase *absente Christo* is Latin for *Christ is not there.*

5. From John Middleton Murry, "Religion and Christianity," in *To the Unknown God: Essays Towards a Religion* (London: J. Cape, 1924), 203.

6. 1 Kings 12:16.

❧ To Mordecai Wyatt Johnson

23 March 1925
Rochester, N.Y.

By the end of his second year at Rochester Theological Seminary, Thurman's reputation as a speaker in national student Christian circles already had begun to flourish. Thurman hopes to visit his mentor Johnson during the summer to discuss his future plans.

300 Alexander St.
Rochester, N.Y.

My dear Rev. Johnson,

Your letter came at a time that I most needed the lift which it gave. I am very grateful for it.

I am indebted to you for the vision to do some of the things that I have been privileged to do in these parts. In you I have ever seen what it was possible for me to become if I were willing to pay the price which you have paid. The best compliment that I have received from any of my professors here came to me the other day thru a friend—This professor told my friend that I had a mind like yours. I actually blushed!

Next Sunday I go back to Cornell University for two addresses—the following week I am in New York City and April 10th I am to address the National Presbyterian Student Assembly meeting at University of Mich. Despite my going around I have tried to keep up a splendid average in my class work.

My plans for the future are far from being determined. I do need some real advice or some give-and-take conversation with someone like you. I shall spend the summer at Roanoke, Va—that is, after I return from Kings Mountain and Talladega.[1] I am wondering if it is possible for me to make contact with you at some point before next fall. I am a Senior next year and several matters about further work etc. must be worked out—if I am to get aid from this end. (I neglected to say that I shall be working at the First Baptist Church at Roanoke until Sept. 1. If there is no other way I would be willing to come to Charleston from Roanoke during the middle of ~~the~~ {any} week after my vacation school closes—providing I would not have to lose too much time on the train and could return before Sunday.

With every genuine wish for you and the work to which you are so thoroughly committed,

~~I am,~~

Very sincerely yours,

[*signed*] Howard Thurman

Rev. M. W. Johnson

Charleston WV

ALS. MWJ-DHU-MS: Box 178.

1. Thurman is referring to the annual black college and normal-school student conferences: the YWCA student conference that met at Talladega College in Alabama and the YMCA student conference held at Kings Mountain in North Carolina.

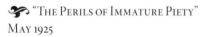 "THE PERILS OF IMMATURE PIETY"

MAY 1925

In the following article, published in the Student Volunteer Movement Bulletin,[1] *Thurman denounces spiritual immaturity in the future leadership of the church. Criticizing efforts to escape reality by artificial means, Thurman insists on the integration of all aspects of human existence, including one's devotional life, into the concept of Christian service. The article is remarkable for Thurman's discussion of the power of language as a means of articulating and furthering the*

Christian message. Of particular note is his insistence that words and spiritual practices be appropriate to the time in which they are used and expressive of their speaker's authentic experience. The article is also notable for the first indication of Thurman's interest in eastern religion and the works of Rabindranath Tagore.

Wherever groups of students are gathered together in the name of Christ, one theme constantly recurs throughout the entire deliberation—Spiritual Power, the Lack of It or How Best to Generate It. Slightly less than a year ago a group of students and adult leaders in conference at Delaware Water Gap[2] reached the significant conclusion, with practically no dissenting utterance, that the greatest and most imperative need on the campuses with which they were conversant, was personal spiritual power in the lives of student leaders and followers. As a result of this wide-spread and utterly recognized need, a medley of reactions have taken place. I shall suggest two.

1. The looking to the past as the Golden Age in Christian student activities. "If we could possess the spiritual power and certainty of the men of the student generation of thirty years ago." "If we could couch our message in the same dynamic terms which they used." And we waste our energy by sliding around these slippery "if's."
2. The tendency to place a halo around our heads, a kind of shekinah,[3] which, for want of a better term, may be called immature piety. In time, it is *the use of words without an adequate experience* or the *assumption of an attitude that has little basis in fact.*

We shall dismiss the first reaction by simply asserting that to the Christian student the Golden Age is in the future. If we are just as good as the students of past generations, it means that we are worse than they were. In order to be as good as they were we must be better; for apart from us they cannot be made perfect. Again, it must also be kept in mind that every generation must hear the message of the Kingdom of God in its own language.

The second reaction is at once the theme of our discussion. There are two fundamental perils of immature piety: Superficiality and Spiritual Sophistication.

Superficiality: The problem which this student generation seems to be conscious of facing is the obvious failure to achieve in its experience the quality of life which is in harmony with the highest and best that it knows. It is the same problem of which the Apostle Paul is conscious when he says, Brothers, I for one do not consider myself to have appropriated this; my one thought is, by forgetting what lies behind me and straining to what lies before me, to press on to the goal for the prize of God's high call in Christ Jesus.[4] In attempting to define the problem we have called it a lack of personal spiritual power. In a desperate effort to find solutions many things have been seized upon as genuine panaceas.

The Morning Watch:[5] Let me urge at once that I do not for a moment underestimate or undervalue the psychological and spiritual values involved in the careful developing of a genuine devotional life. A great cloud of witnesses bear testimony to the dynamic power of the Morning Watch. I do feel, however, that students, under the influence of a wide variety of stimulants, have resorted to the Morning Watch as a kind of fetish. It has been used as a part of a religious formula, the manipulation of which will net a certain result—Spiritual Power. At most, the Morning Watch is but an instrument, a vehicle—the significant factor is the man and his needs. Unless the Morning Watch is a necessity to my well being, and unless it fits into a need the consciousness of which is imperative, no amount of exhortation or logic can give it a permanent place in my life. Many students have turned away from it with a keen sense of disillusionment, because it has been sought for itself alone and not as a means to fellowship with the Unseen in response to the deepest urge of the human spirit.

Twentieth Century Monastic Concept: There are others who say, Give yourself to God—this is the way to a genuine solution of the problem. If a student does this, he will find welling up in his own life the living water which will overflow to meet the needs of a tired, weary, thirsty world. Thus, in our own times, there has arisen a new emphasis upon going into "full time Christian Service" as over against secular activities.

The confusion arises when an attempt is made to find out just what is meant by giving one's self to God in the sense of full-time Christian service. Does it mean the *act* of group participation or membership? Does it mean the conformity to some objective standard in a way that is acceptable to a particular group? Does it mean to be "Christian" in my choice and practice of a vocation to the utter disregard of my own personal life? In fine, are life and "full-time Christian service" two separate things for the Christian or are they fundamentally the same? It seems evident that, for one reason or another, we have made the giving of one's life to God a monastic ideal resulting in the drawing of sharp lines between our personal lives and practice and the religion which we feel to be at work only in a particular type of service.

I had a friend in college who early in his life had literally set himself aside for "full time Christian service." There was one thing about him that always puzzled me—he was a great college politician who resorted to any kind of trick to get his man elected. One day I asked him how it was that he could resort to such unfair methods and at the same time feel that *he* was set aside for "full time Christian service." "But that's different," he said: "when I get ready to play politics I put my religion in my trunk." Superficial distinction resulting ever in paucity of spirit.

Dedication to God is worthy and is demanded of all, but not in the sense that such a dedication divorces one from the obligation to carry out its implication in the common walks of life and daily experience. Any conception of "full time Christian service" that does not synthesize *all* of life around that ideal is barren. In the normal workings of life, in the commonplace experiences of ordinary living, in the simplest daily contacts, we must find God—we must find the spiritual power the need of which we feel so sorely.

Imitation: Conscious imitation of a person or of persons whom we feel to have achieved in their lives the quality which we need in our own lives is a very real temptation. Whatever such persons suggest to us, we do. There is much to be said for such an attitude. "If I could be like him"—"If I could live the victorious life as she does." Doubtless from the lips of each of us these words have fallen as here and there we have met someone who radiated from his very countenance the living power of God! In making such utterances we forget the great span of experience that separates them from us. We are utterly unmindful of the price that such persons have paid for the faith that is in them. By imitation we try to assume a thing the power of which we recognize, the need of which we feel, but the clue to which we do not have.

A few days ago I heard a gentleman say in an address before a body of clergymen: I am weary of listening to echoes from the pulpit—I want to hear a *Voice*. I think he struck something fundamental. The presentation of words without the possession of the experience which the words imply is another way of assuming an attitude which does not grow out of the richness of our own lives. As long as we merely try to imitate someone else in our devotion, our piety and our living, so long will we be superficial, ineffective and incomplete. I must know for myself the raison d'etre of the faith that is in me. I must live deeply and effectively all phases of my life if I would know God. I must be most myself if I would know what it means to follow Jesus. "Only, we must let our steps be guided by such truth as we have attained."[6]

Spiritual Sophistication: "He also told the following parable to certain persons who were sure of their own goodness and looked down upon every body else. "Two men went up to pray in the temple: one was a Pharisee and the other was a tax gatherer. The Pharisee stood up and prayed of himself as follows: I thank Thee, O God, I am not like the rest of men, thieves, rogues and immoral, or even like yon tax gatherer: Twice a week I fast; on all my income pay tithes. But the tax gatherer stood far away and could not lift up even his eyes to heaven, but beat his breast, saying—O God, have mercy on me for my sins. I tell you, he went home accepted by God rather than the other man: for everyone who uplifts himself shall be humbled and he who humbles himself will be uplifted."[7]

There is an old German fable which goes something like this: A little seed began suddenly to give signs of life and it shot up through the hard crust of the earth and it spread forth its roots, rejoicing in the sunshine, crying aloud in its joy—I am a tree! But there came floating by a voice which said: "The wind shall rock thee and great storms tear thy very roots and the winter's frost shall bite thee and many winters and summers pass over thee as the years roll along ere thou canst call thyself a tree!"

I am wondering if an attitude like this is not responsible for much of the blandness among the Christian students on our campuses. Why is it that so often the biggest and most outstanding men and women on our campuses are not challenged by the faith which we profess to have? Is it because our zeal is not born of knowledge and insight that we repel men rather than attract them by what they call our "super-goodness" or "spiritual sophistication"? Is it because we seem to *drag* God into everything rather than to find Him as a part and parcel of all experience?

> "I laugh when I hear that the fish in the
> water is thirsty.
> You do not see that Reality is in your
> home, and you wander from forest to
> forest listlessly!
> Here it is, the truth! Go where you
> will from Benares to Malthurs;[8] if you
> do not find your soul the world is un-
> real to you.
> O Friend! hope for Him whilst you
> live, know whilst you will; for in life
> deliverance abides. . . .
> Kabir[9] says: "It is the Spirit of the quest
> which keeps: I am the slave of the
> spirit of the quest."[10]

Student Volunteer Movement Bulletin (May 1925): 110–13.

1. The *Student Volunteer Movement Bulletin* was the official organ of the Student Volunteer Movement for Foreign Missions. Founded in 1886, the organization grew out of an undergraduate Bible study conference held the previous summer at the Mount Hermon School in Northfield, Massachusetts. The organization recruited and trained undergraduate students for foreign-mission appointments. It was very successful until the 1920s, when student enthusiasm for the work waned.

2. Thurman refers to a national student conference held at the Delaware Water Gap, now a national recreation area located along the New Jersey and Pennsylvania banks of the Delaware River.

3. The word *shekinah* is a Hebrew term for *divine presence.*

4. Phil. 3:13–14.

5. A reference to organized morning prayers or devotions, corresponding to the practice of evening prayer, or vespers.

6. Phil. 3:16.

7. Luke 14:11.

8. In the original poem, *Malthurs* is *Mathura.* Benares, now called Varanasi, and Mathura are major Hindu pilgrimage sites in North India.

9. Kabir (1440–1518) was an Indian religious poet, born in Benares. Originally a Muslim, he became a mystic in the Hindu tradition, opposing both the caste system and image worship. His work combined elements of Islam and Hinduism, and he preached the essential unity of the two religions.

10. *Songs of Kabir,* trans. Rabindranath Tagore (New York: Macmillan, 1915). Thurman combines two poems from Tagore's *Songs of Kabir.* The first section reproduces poem 43 in its entirety. The second section, beginning "O Friend!" is from poem 3, with the elision as indicated.

🖎 To MORDECAI WYATT JOHNSON
8 JULY 1925
ROANOKE, VA.

Thurman asks Johnson to preach at his upcoming ordination. In the summer of 1925, Thurman applied to his home church in Daytona for permission to be ordained by First Baptist Church in Roanoke, pastored by Arthur L. James. Upon the refusal of his home-church pastor—for reasons not fully determined— Thurman joined First Baptist, and the date was set for convening an ordination council there. Possibly because of prior commitments and the short notice, Thurman's request could not be met.

208 Patton Ave. N.W.
Roanoke, Va.

My dear Mr. Johnson,
    From many sources have I heard about your excellent address delivered the day after I left Rochester. Down at the University of Pa. a fellow told me that it was the only one that competed seriously with Fosdick.[1] I thank God for His power that is released in you from time to time.
    The Church here is going to ordain me. The service is planned for the first Sunday in August—Aug. 2nd. I want you to come to preach my ordination sermon. It is useless for me to try to say why. You know what you have been to me and I want you to come. If that date is not a good one—make your suggestion. It must be not later than the 5th or 6th of August. Now, I am anxious for you to come to give me that "kick off"—Will you? I have arranged for expenses, in fact, it is with the hearty approval of the pastor that I am asking you. If you prefer a formal letter from him it can be forthcoming.
    Shall tell you about my conference experiences when you come.
    May I hear from you by return mail as this must be arranged this week?
With every gracious wish,
As ever your friend,
[*signed*] Howard Thurman

                              ALS. MWJ-DHU-MS: Box 178.

1. Harry Emerson Fosdick (1878–1969), a 1903 graduate of Union Theological Seminary, was pastor of First Baptist Church of Montclair, New Jersey (1904–15), First Presbyterian Church in Manhattan (1919–25), and Riverside Church (1925–46), and was a professor at Union Theological Seminary from 1915 to 1946. Fosdick was the most prominent liberal Protestant minister in the early decades of the twentieth century and a leader in the fight against fundamentalism.

To Mordecai Wyatt Johnson
28 August 1925
Roanoke, Va.

Thurman drops a note to Johnson after visiting him and attending services at his church in Charleston.

208 Patton Ave. N.W.
Roanoke, Va.

My dear Friend,

Just a hurried note to express my genuine appreciation to you and your good people for the very unusual experience which was mine. It has actually happened. It meant more to me than you can perhaps imagine to see you "at home." I tried to observe everything and to hear all that came in reach. I thank God for the privilege.

I leave here Monday a.m. for Lake Geneva to attend Fellowship Conference. I hope to reach Rochester about Sept. 20.

Juliette Derricotte[1] of Y.W. wrote me a letter this week—she expressed herself in no uncertain terms about the very fine piece of spiritual work God did through you at Talladega.

Lest I forget—I thank you for taking me to the home of the Brownleys—I have never had a more delightful stay in any home anywhere. Kindest regards to your family.

Your friend
[*signed*] Howard Thurman

ALS. MWJ-DHU-MS: Box 178.

1. Juliette Aline Derricotte (1897–1931) was born in Athens, Georgia, and graduated from Talladega College in 1908, becoming the college's first female trustee in 1920. She served as a traveling secretary for the YWCA (1908–19), was a representative at the World Student Christian Federation (WSCF) meeting in 1924 and 1928, and traveled to India as a representative of the WSCF (1928). In 1929, she became the dean of women at Fisk University. Her life ended tragically following an automobile accident in Dalton, Georgia, when she was refused admittance to a well-equipped white hospital in Dalton and lay unattended for six hours in a private home before being sent to a Negro hospital in Chattanooga, Tennessee. Derricotte died there, and her unjust death drew national and international

attention. Jessie Carney Smith, *Epic Lives: One Hundred Black Women Who Made a Difference* (Detroit, Mich.: Visible Ink, 1993).

🦕 "CAN IT BE TRULY SAID THAT THE EXISTENCE OF A SUPREME SPIRIT IS A
SCIENTIFIC HYPOTHESIS?"
FALL 1925
ROCHESTER, N.Y.

Written in the first semester of Thurman's senior year at the Rochester Theological Seminary, this paper survives in a corrected typescript. The paper is the most important evidence known of Thurman's work with George Cross,[1] his primary advisor. Thurman took a three-semester sequence with Cross in systematic theology and wrote this study on the philosophical grounds of religious belief for the second of these courses, "The Christian Doctrine of God 2."[2] Thurman selected the topic from a list of sixteen possible term-paper topics provided by Cross, all of which concerned analyzing conceptions of God.[3] The paper provides an important glimpse of Thurman's development as a religious thinker, his evolving views on theology, his contact with pragmatism and Deweyism, and his earliest comments on nonrational and essentially mystical ways of obtaining knowledge of God.

The paper also offers important evidence of the influence of the summer course in philosophy Thurman took at Columbia University in 1922, which he regarded as "perhaps the most significant course I ever took."[4] Thurman argues in the paper that all scientific knowledge is hypothetical and provisional, drawing broadly on the neo-Kantian perspective of George Cross and perhaps that of the instructor in the 1922 summer course, E. A. Burtt, whose best-known work, The Metaphysical Foundations of Modern Physical Science *(1925), argues that a priori philosophical conceptions were crucial to the scientific breakthroughs of the seventeenth century. Drawing on works in the philosophy of science in the early twentieth century, Thurman argues that conclusions about the ultimate nature of the physical universe go beyond science and enter into the realm of faith. In the second half of the paper Thurman argues that empirically grounded religious knowledge is possible, unifying the subjective experience, objective reality, and the necessary connection between them, concluding that knowledge, rather than faith, provides the surest avenue to a complete experience of the Supreme Spirit.[5]*

What makes "Can It Be Truly Said?" troubling is the evidence throughout the paper of unacknowledged attributions and, at points, systematic plagiarism. Whether George Cross read this version of the paper can not be determined. The paper is ungraded, and there are no substantive comments by Cross on it. However, there are handwritten corrections interpolated throughout the text, which represent the work of either Thurman or Cross (or possibly both). The handwriting of the corrections appears similar to that of the autograph on the title page, both presumably written by Thurman.[6] There are also, though, several proofreading markings that appear to be made by an outside hand. It is impossible to determine the source of the handwritten marks, but it seems likely that either this version of the paper was read and copyedited by Cross, or contained last-minute proofreading by Thurman before its submission.

In the first half of the paper, Thurman considers the nature of the scientific hypothesis. The plagiarism in this part of the paper is drawn from two sources. The technical details on the Ptolemaic and Copernican hypotheses are drawn from chapter 3 of Laurence Buermeyer, et al., An Introduction to Reflective Thinking (1923), one of the textbooks Thurman used in his 1922 summer-school course at Columbia University.[7] In his discussion of the nature of a scientific hypothesis, there are several unacknowledged borrowings from a 1918 article published in Philosophical Review by C. A. Richardson, "Scientific Method in Philosophy and the Foundations of Pluralism,"[8] a largely neo-Kantian effort to establish a scientific epistemology and basis for religious knowledge. There are fewer unacknowledged appropriations in the second part of the paper, but the argument and in places the wording closely follow Charles Allen Dinsmore's 1924 work, Religious Certitude in an Age of Science.[9] Thurman depends on Dinsmore for the structure and details of the argument, and the paper concludes with a long quotation from Religious Certitude.

Thurman in 1925 was familiar with the two main scholarly devices for indicating the quotation of a secondary source: the use of quotation marks and for longer passages the use of indented paragraphs. He uses both methods in "Can It Be Truly Said?" and his other contemporary student papers. Depending on how they are enumerated, there are about thirteen instances of textual appropriations in this essay, ranging from a sentence to a paragraph, as well as instances of unattributed quotations borrowed from Dinsmore's Religious Certitude. All the instances of textual appropriation are indicated in the annotation, and handwritten markings are indicated in curly braces or are footnoted.

Scheme of Development.
I   What Is a Scientific Hypothesis
    How arrived at
    An examination of two hypotheses
        Ptolemaic
        Copernican
    The test of a   scientific hypothesis
    The marks of a good   "   "
    The limitations of a   "   "
II The Existence of a Supreme Spirit
    Basis of the idea
    How the idea is arrived at
    Comparison with scientific hypothesis
        Points of agreement
        Points of difference
    Relative merit of the two beliefs
    The test of the belief
    Summarizing quotation

Before we examine the idea of a supreme spirit to see whether or not it is a scientific hypothesis it becomes necessary to inquire into the nature of a scientific hypothesis. What then is a scientific hypothesis? In order to answer this question we must trace the steps by which the scientist arrives at what he calls a scientific hypothesis. At once we notice that the scientist attacks his problem in bits. The problem arises because of the action of certain sense-data. As far as possible the problem is isolated, and an attempt is made to clarify the conceptions relative to the problem with a view of determining by continued analysis, the true source of the perplexities underlying the particular problem. In any particular investigation the generally accepted body of knowledge, however poorly organized, is used. For the most part{,} it is very disorderly and confused; hence the immediate task of analysis is to resolve the data into a definite number of propositions arranged in logical sequence. The data is sense-data and is delt with on the supposition that certain universally valid and inclusive principles exist—for example, certain primitive logical truths which we may call {"}laws of thought{"}; principles of causation, conservation of energy, and perfect elasticity of other. For purposes of emphasis I shall repeat myself at this point using slightly different language. Practically all of the immediate facts of existence are confused, disorderly and complex. If the scientist would attempt to deal with them as they are, it would be a mere waste of time and effort. It is for this reason {that} the aim of the scientist is to reduce all phenomena to such definiteness as to render them amenable to mathematical treatment.[10] This is done by introducing certain concepts such {as} atoms and electrons in physics.

The desire to render the data amenable to mathametics is due to the certainty of mathametics. But we must not overlook the fact that the certainty is placed originally in the postulates, axioms and definitions of mathametics. From the above it is clear that the total approach of the scientist is conceptual. It is on the basis of certain fundamental concepts that he conducts his investigation.[11]

It becomes necessary at this point to examine in outline two great scientific hypotheses, one of which was discarded for the other: the Ptolemaic or Geocentric Hypothesis and the Copernican or Heliocentric Hypothesis.[12] There are certain observed facts of astronomy which even the most casual observation of the sky can establish. When we look into the sky we see numerous points of light which appear from time to time in different directions from the earth and which change their positions with regard to each other as well as the earth. The lights and their varying directions form the immediate facts for the astronomer.[13] An analysis of these facts yields the following results:

1, The so-called fixed stars including the sun and the moon appear to rotate about the earth once every day; rising in the East and setting in the West.[14]
2, But certain of the light spots are not fixed and they change their positions every day with reference to the other stars. These are called wonderers or planets.[15]
3, The moon, while sharing in the daily rotation of the celestial sphere, appears to lag behind it somewhat, so that it rises about fifty minutes later every day. In the course of about a month it has traversed a complete circle about the sky, and the celestial sphere has gained upon it one entire rotation. The sun also travels in a great circle around the sky, losing four minutes upon the fixed stars each day. So that at the end of a year it has returned once more to the same relative position.[16]
4, The planets form circles similar to the sun and moon from west to east The motion appears to be more erratic; there seems to be a backward and retrograde motion at times.[17]

The first attempt at a systematic ordering of these observations was made in the second century before Christ by Hipparchus.[18] Later he was followed by the great Ptolemy of Alexandria. Simply outlined, the Ptolemaic Hypothesis or "Mathematical Composition" as he called it, is as follows:

1, The earth is an unmoving sphere at the center of things.[19]
2, Around the earth there circle the moon, the sun and the planets and outside was the sphere in which were fixed stars.[20]
3, These circlings were {are} not at the same rate; stars rotate fastest{;} then the planets{,} sun{,}and moon.[21]
4, Backward motion of planets was accounted for by a double orbit system in which the planets moved. This situation was met by the use of Epicycles.

The rival hypothesis to the one outlined above was the work of a Polish mathematician whose name {was} Copernicus. The outline is as follows:

1, The sun is at the center of things.
2, Around the sun there circle the earth and the planets.
3, Erratic Planetary motion is due to the motion of the earth. The earth is moving more rapidly than the planet and overtaking them. Few Epicycles.

The Copernican Hypothesis was accepted over the Ptolemaic. Why? It was found that the former theory was less awkward and less cumbersome than the latter with its ponderous epicycles. While the latter covered all of the observed facts it was not fruitful and suggestive with reference to unknown or unobserved data. Those observations raised two questions, what are the tests of a scientific hypothesis? What are the marks of a good scientific hypothesis? In answering these questions with reference to the two hypotheses under consideration, two courses are open: One could proceed to elaborate each hypothesis, to see what further consequences each would imply if it were true and then to investigate with a view to finding out if these further consequences did take place. Or one could observe some new fact that could not be satisfactorily accounted for by one of the hypotheses and which would disprove it. These are the two ways in which all scientific hypotheses are tested. There is ever this double process of elaboration and development to discover the utmost possible bearing and of constant reference to observable facts. If the hypothesis is true, then certain things must follow. Do they? Such and such phenomena are observed. Does our theory explain them? In natural sciences, as we have pointed out above, the first developement is made possible by mathematical calculation. If such and such a theory is true, then these equations hold, and from them we can deduce other equations which lead to other conclusions. If the conclusions prove true in experiment, then the original theory has been verified.[22]

From the above it seems to be reasonably clear that a scientific hypothesis depends upon scientific experimentation for its validity.[23] It has a very definite method of verification. Given the heliocentric hypothesis the astronomer by the use of mathematics and the telescope can check the implication of his belief. This is also true in other phases of natural science. The assumption given, it is considered valid when checked by certain facts. Essentially, scientific experimentation is a sense experience dealing with sense-data.

The marks of a good scientific hypothesis are as follows: It is simple. It covers all of the facts. It is fruitful and suggestive. It explains in the sense of description. Hence a scientific hypothesis is a affirmation or belief which as a working basis for the scientist is simple, inclusive, fruitful and explanatory.

What then are the limitations of a scientific hypothesis, if any? In the first we note that an hypothesis is built upon the partial observations of a system and with that data, limited as it is, an attempt is made to describe the system as a whole. Fallibility is inevitable unless it be assumed that the system is capable of complete description in general terms. But any system comprising subjects of experience cannot be so described, for the subjects in the experiences of each are essentially individual and unique. Therefore, an infallible hypothesis could not be formed unless we knew all the facts, past present and future, and then we would have merely a narrative of these facts and not an hypothesis.

Again, we have [no] reason to assume that laws which have held in the past will continue to hold in the future, unless along with it there is the assumption of some principle like that of induction which depends upon some a priori[24] principle of probability. We may know that a hypothesis is false if it is contradicted by some fact but we can never know absolutely if it is true. It is always more or less probable, the degree of probability depending upon its applicability to the facts observed up to that time. "Thus any final belief as to the constitution of the universe cannot depend on scientific knowledge but must be based on faith."[25]

To recapitulate, the scientific hypothesis lays stress upon the objective side of experience not in relation to the subject, but considered per se and therefore in abstraction from the subject. It takes into account certain concepts whose validity depends upon the degree to which they can be applied to the objects of experience apart from the subject. When objective sense data are per se there is simply the fact that certain sense-data are invariably followed by certain other sense-data. In the future sequence there is found no hint as to the reason of this sequence or invariance nor is there disclosed a warrant that it will continue to hold in the future. Probability is all that can be secured on that basis. If provisions are made for the consideration of the subject implied in the experience of sense-data, then certain concepts of purpose and meaning must be introduced which would be without significance except in application to the subject. We are now ready to consider whether or not the idea of the existence of a Supreme {Spirit} is a scientific hypothesis.

In order to properly[26] evaluate the idea of the existence of a Supreme Being with a view to determining whether or not it is a scientific hypothesis, we must examine the basis upon which such an idea rests for its validity. In an article in the Harvard Theological Review on the "Task of the Religious Thinker," Daniel Evans rightly points out the experiential basis of religion. Since the center of religion concerns itself with the idea of God, the basis of such an idea must be experiental. I quote:

> Man finds himself on this earth, with powers of mind which make it pos-
> sible for him to be acted upon by the powers of the world, and in turn to
> react upon them. This action and reaction gave him his experiences on the
> various levels of consciousness, to[27] the lowest sensuous to the highest spir-
> itual plain. The highest experience arises like the lowest from the sense of

reaction of forces upon him and his reaction upon them in feeling, thought and conduct. He feels himself in relation with super-sensible reality. There is another presence than the world and human beings which disturbs his soul with deep feeling, high thought, and great projects. He has the sense of dependence upon this great reality for his existence and for his larger and deeper life, He feels himself held in moral subjection to a higher authority than his own will or the wills of his fellow beings. He is bound in obedience to a moral authority that searches his very soul, and has the august right to command him to live for the best. He realizes that he is not here for his own private interests, but in the interest of the Divine Being in whom he lives and before whom he stands. . . . He finds that he may have fellowship with this Divine presence; that there may be an interchange of thought and a communion in which he finds the joy of living and the inspiration for his high endeavor. These religious experiences take their rise here and now in the hearts of men. They are the ultimate facts of our religious life. . . . These religious experiences, taken in their general features, are not peculiar to one man or to a group of men, nor to one nation nor one period in the history of the world. They are, on the contrary, human, universal, and persistent.

The steps by which the man of religion arrives at his idea of the existence of a supreme spirit seem to group themselves in outline:

"There are in our world, both the subjects and the objects of experience. Between these there is at least formal unity. If the subject can interpret the object which is, in truth, the objects method of self-revelation as well, then there must be a unity of relationship between them.

The explanation or interpretation of this unity must be in terms of a Being with whom this unity must ultimately rest. The significance of our interpretation must also rest in such a Being.

Such a development at once reveals purpose. There must of necessity be a deeper unity than of relationship—it must be a unity of design. This introduces simultaneously the element of conscious will.

The Being with whom the unity of the subjects and the objects of experience rests must be creative and as such must express Itself in the PROCESS as well as the objects of creation. Reality is of such that it is identified with this process as well of such that the creative will of the Being can express itself in creations.

This Being must be personal therefore, and its highest ends must be in terms of values or character. He must be good. If the highest {ends} are moral they must have to do primarily with human beings, the highest subjects of experience. The relationship between human beings and this Personal Being must be fundamentally one, not so much of Creator and creature, but of personality, hence human personality becomes the key to the interpretation of the Being of whose plan and purpose it is such a significant part.

This Being is a creative spirit not a static infinite. Every process of his creative will is a perfect process, within the limits inherent in the things created. In process he is infinite and perfect—the act itself is perfect, the full untramelled expression of the act depends upon the nature of the things created.

Now that we have traced the steps in outline by which the man of religion arrives at his idea of the existence of a supreme spirit we must address ourselves to the question, What does this idea have in common with a scientific hypothesis and at what points do they differ, if at all? There are two fundamental points that are common to both: They both take into account the world of objective experience and they both rest upon faith.

The idea of the existence of a supreme Spirit must have an objective necessity. The fact that men must live in a universe places upon them the obligation to understand it. An insight into the objective reality of our interests and experiences must be obtained. Every experience must be in a kind of context of meaning; it cannot be known apart from that context and it can only be finally known when that context in its entirety is read and understood.

A word with reference to faith as the common quality. A scientific hypothesis is a scientific belief, it is assumption, it is a faith.[28] The idea of the existence of a Supreme Being is an assumption, it is a belief, it is a faith.[29]

At what points then do the two differ? We have seen how the scientist uses faith throughout; from a confidence in the general trustworthiness of the sense perceptions to the dependableness and capability of the external world to be interpreted, he runs the entire gamut. Yet it is true that he is dealing with external phenomena and modes of behavior but not with meanings and ultimate realities. This is as far as his hypothesis can legitimately carry him. In the very nature of the case the scientist must deal with the objects of experience only; while the affirmations of the man of religion deal not only with the objects but the subjects of experience. And at no point is this truer than the affirmation that has to do with the existence of a Supreme Spirit. It seems, therefore, that the idea of the existence of a Supreme Being or Spirit is more than a scientific hypothesis.

In the discussion having to do with the limitations of a scientific hypothesis, it was pointed out that if provisions were made for a consideration of the subjects implied in the experience of sense-data, then certain concepts of meaning and purpose must be introduced which would be without significance except as applied to the subjects. But the moment we begin to talk about purpose and meanings in the sense of values, we are outside of the realm natural science and its hypothesis. Since the assumption of the existence of a Supreme Spirit must of necessity deal with the objects and the subjects of experience, it cannot be confined within the limits of a mere scientific hypothesis. This assumption employs a much larger portion of nature and human nature in its sweep and it touches a wider environment.[30] There is a realm that is above sense phenomena. It is a realm of values and meanings and it is this realm that gives significance to what is disclosed in the purely sense field of objective experimentation. Man's interest in the objects of experience has its roots in something deep within him. It is this something interpreted in terms of varied interests that places a halo over the sense-data with which science deals. Science, with all of its hypotheses and the like, becomes the hand-maid and the servant of religion. Touching this point in his letter to Kingsley, Huxley said,[31]

> The more intimately I know the lives of other men (to say nothing of my own) the more obvious it is to me that the wicked does not flourish nor is the righteous punished. But for this to be clear we must bear in mind what almost all forget, that the rewards of life are contingent upon obedience to the whole law—physical as well as moral—and that moral obedience will not atone for physical sin, or vice versa.
>
> The ledger of the Almighty is strictly kept, and everyone of us has the balance of his operations paid over to him at the end of every moment of his existence. The absolute justice of the system of things is as clear to me as any scientific fact. The gravitation of sin to sorrow is as certain as that of the earth to the sun, and more so—for the experimental proof of the fact is in reach of us all."[32] This is more than agnosticism.

The validity of the faith that there is a supreme spirit is determined by whether or not it will stand the test of experience. We have seen that it gives significance to what science does; but this is not enough. Here it is not out of order to make my appeal to the religious experience which I know the best. By living on the basis of that faith I find that I am coming increasingly to a quiet confidence in its genuineness and validity. There are times when I am supremely conscious that I make contact with SOMEBODY and I know that I am not alone. Slowly there is taking place in my life a transformation which is more in keeping with the highest things that I think and feel. With my total personality I do not only say, "I believe" but when I am most myself I say, "I know." I find that I am a part of a great company. The ultimate test of the validity of the great affirmation is in the quality of life which it tends to produce and this brings with it an assurance that the man of science can never have. William James said, "By being religious we establish ourselves in the possession of Ultimate Reality at the only point at which reality has been given us to guard."[33] WE DROP INTO OURSELVES TO FIND THE RAISON D'ETRE OF OUR AFFIRMATION AND WE SPEND THE REST OF OUR LIVES SEEKING A VERIFICATION WHICH WILL COVER THE TOTAL RANGE OF ALL OUR EXPERIENCE.

I cannot do better than to summarize our discussion by quoting ~~two~~ {three} paragraphs from the McNair Lectures for 1923:[34]

Men need God, they trust him, they seek to learn his will and obey him. The steps one takes in solving his religious problems are much the same as those he takes in solving his scientific problems. In science we trust our sense perceptions and the conclusion of our intellect. In religion we trust our spiritual intuitions and the validity of the claim of our moral and emotional natures—{"}and the validity of our sense perceptions{"}[35] (Mine). Religious faith is our reason acting bravely in the presence of life's gravest problems. It is a valor of soul which makes ~~his~~ us commit the highest in ourselves to ~~the~~ what we believe is the Highest in the universe.

To give unity to our faith and thought we conceive the Supreme Power which science recognizes and the supreme worth which ethics knows to be manifestations of the one Reality from which all things proceed. We assume that goodness and righteousness are not human conventions, but are expressions of the character of God. . . . To us the loftiest spiritual being in humanity—must be God manifest in the flesh. . . .

To christians the fullness of that glory is seen in Jesus Christ. Because the light which issues from his mind solves our most vital problems, because his spirit, whenever it is reproduced in men, brings the redemption which is humanity's greatest need, we believe that we have found a manifestation of the Everlasting Reality. This light is the true light, not an illusion, not a temporary flash of splendor, but the steady shining of the Ultimate Truth.

BIBILIOGRAPHY.

Dinsmore-McNair Lectures for 1923
Harvard Theological Review
    Volume I: Task of Religious Thinker—Evans[36]
        "   II: Some Problems in Science of Religion—King[37]
King,—The Development of Religion[38]
Philosophical Review
    Volume 27: Scientific Method in Philosophy—Richardson
MacIntish—Theology as an Empirical Science[39]
Munro et al.—Reflective Thinking[40]
Various lecture notes and reactions thereto
                                    TD. HTC-MBU: Box 177.

1. George Cross (1862–1929) was born at Bewdley, Canada West (now Ontario). While serving in a series of Canadian pastorates, he acquired his education from the University of Toronto (BA, 1888), McMaster University (BTh., 1894; MA, 1895), and the University of Chicago (PhD, 1900). In 1901, he was appointed to the chair of history and church history at McMaster. In 1912, after three years at the Newton Theological Institution in Newton

Center, Massachusetts, he came to Rochester Theological Seminary as professor of systematic theology, remaining until his death in 1929. His books include *The Theology of Schleiermacher: A Condensed Presentation of His Chief Work, "The Christian Faith"* (Chicago: University of Chicago Press, 1911), *What Is Christianity? A Study of Rival Interpretation* (Chicago: University of Chicago Press, 1918), and *Creative Christianity: A Study of the Genius of the Christian Faith* (New York: Macmillan, 1922).

2. *Rochester Theological Seminary Bulletin* 4 (January 1926): 46.

3. Many of the suggested topics were studies of the theologies of specific individuals, such as John Calvin, René Descartes, Immanuel Kant, John Wesley, Josiah Royce, and William Ernest Hocking. Other topics included comparisons of mysticism with Deism, contrasting the Unitarian and Jewish views of God, a study of the religious value of pantheism, and a paper speculating on the effects on Christian faith of demonstrating that Jesus was mythical. HTC-MBU: Box 178.

4. *WHAH*, 44. Thurman was inspired to take the Columbia summer course by Garrie Moore, his instructor, and shared a room in Harlem for the summer with his Morehouse classmate George Van Buren.

5. For Cross's negative comments on the limits of the cognitive usefulness of mysticism, see *What Is Christianity?* 83–86.

6. The bottom of the title page has the following autograph:

Department of Theology
Dr. George Cross
Howard Thurman

7. Laurence Buermeyer, et al., *An Introduction to Reflective Thinking* (New York: Houghton Mifflin, 1923).

8. Richardson, "Scientific Method in Philosophy and the Foundations of Pluralism," *Philosophical Review* 27 (1918): 227–73.

9. Charles Allen Dinsmore, *Religious Certitude in an Age of Science* (Chapel Hill: University of North Carolina Press, 1924). Charles Allen Dinsmore (1860–1941) was an expert on the religious thought of Dante and was pastor of the First Congregational Church in Waterbury, Connecticut, from 1905 to 1920.

10. Richardson, "Scientific Method," 236: "The immediate facts of nature are confused, complex, and loosely ordered. Any attempt to deal with them as they stand, for the purpose of calculated interference in the course of events, will be foredoomed to hopeless failure. Consequently, physics introduces such conceptions as those of a material particle and aluminiferous ether, in order to coordinate the phenomena, so as to render them amenable to mathematical treatment."

11. Richardson, following some early twentieth-century philosophers of science such as Ernst Mach and Pierre Duhem, treats atomic particles as hypothetical constructions rather than real physical objects: "Even should the material particles of physics actually exist (and this seems very doubtful) we could not know of their existence." Richardson, "Scientific Method," 233.

12. The Ptolemaic hypothesis is a mathematical model of a geocentric universe that received its most complete statement by the Alexandrian Greek astronomer and mathematician Claudius Ptolemy (100–170 A.D.). The Ptolemaic system persisted, with minor adjustments, until supplanted by the hypothesis of a heliocentric universe, proposed in a posthumous work by the Polish astronomer Nicolaus Copernicus (1473–1543).

13. Thurman's account of the Ptolemaic and Copernican systems is derived from Buermeyer, et al., *An Introduction to Reflective Thinking:* "All that we can really see when we look at the heavens is a number of spots of light, which appear from time to time in different directions from the earth, and which change their position with regard to each other. The varying directions of these light spots form the only immediate facts for the astronomer." 37.

14. "The great body of so-called fixed stars, together with the sun and moon, appears to rotate about the earth once a day, rising in the east and setting in the west." Ibid., 38.

15. "But certain of the light spots are not fixed, and change their positions with relation to the other stars. These are, besides the sun and the moon, those called planets or wanderers." Ibid., 38–39.

16. "The moon, while sharing in the daily rotation of the celestial sphere, appears to lag behind it somewhat, so that it rises about fifty minutes later every day. In the course of approximately a month, it has traversed a complete circle about the sky, and the celestial sphere has gained upon it one entire rotation. Though it is not so easily observed, the sun also travels in a great circle around the sky, losing four minutes upon the fixed stars each day, so that at the end of a year it has returned once more to the same relative position." Ibid., 39.

17. "The planets, while in general performing similar circles from west to east that require greater or less time, seem to possess a much more erratic motion." Ibid., 39–40.

18. Hipparchus (160?–127? B.C.) was a Greek astronomer and mathematician who made fundamental contributions to the advancement of astronomy as a mathematical science and to the foundations of trigonometry. In Buermeyer is: "The first attempt at the systematic ordering of these observations was made in the second century B.C. by a Greek named Hipparchus." Ibid., 40.

19. "He placed the earth as an unmoving sphere at the center of things." Ibid., 40–41.

20. "Around the earth there circled the moon, the sun, and the planets, and outside of all was the sphere in which were fixed the stars." Ibid., 41.

21. "These circlings were not at quite the same rate; the stars rotated fastest, then the planets, the sun, and the moon." Ibid.

22. "Two courses were open. One could proceed to elaborate each theory, to see what further consequences each would imply if it were true, and then to investigate whether these further consequences actually did take place. Or one could observe some new fact that could not be satisfactorily accounted for by one of the theories, and which would thus disprove it. These are the two ways in which all scientific hypotheses are subjected to scrutiny and testing. Whenever a new theory is propounded, there is carried on this double process of elaboration and development to discover its utmost possible bearings, and of constant reference to the observable facts. If it be true, then such and such things must follow. Do they? Such and such phenomena are observed. Does our theory explain them? In the natural sciences this first development is made possible largely by means of mathematical calculation. If such and such a theory is true, then these equations hold, and from them we can deduce other equations which lead to the following conclusion. If that conclusion prove correct in experiment, the original theory has been verified." Ibid., 54.

23. Handwritten bracket mark follows the word *validity*.

24. Handwritten underline.

25. "An hypothesis passes from necessarily partial observations of a system to a description of the system as a whole in space and time, and is therefore inevitably fallible unless the system be assumed capable of complete description in general terms. . . . We could not

form a unique and infallible hypothesis unless we knew all the facts, past, present and future, and then it would no longer be an hypothesis, but a mere recital of those facts. . . . We have no reason at all to assume that laws which have held in the past will continue to hold in the future, unless we also assume some principle, such as that of induction, which depends on a priori principles of probability. Hence, though we may know an hypothesis to be false if it is contradicted by any fact, we can never certainly know it to be true. All that can be said is that it is more or less probable, the degree of probability depending on its applicability to the facts observed up to that time. Thus any final beliefs as to the constitution of the universe cannot depend on knowledge alone, but must be based on faith." Richardson, "Scientific Method," 237.

26. There is an editing mark to indicate transposing *to* and *properly*.

27. The word *to* is circled. The correct word is *from*.

28. This is not quite what Thurman argued earlier in the paper, where he claimed that scientific hypotheses are true to the extent of the "applicability to the facts observed up to that time" and could only yield probabilities, not certainties, but certain or final knowledge about "the constitution of the universe" must reside in faith.

29. "We claim that the difference between the results of scientific experimentation and religious experience is not the difference between knowledge and faith, but between two different kinds of knowledge, each resting on faith, each established on experimentation after its own kind." Dinsmore, *Religious Certitude*, 73–74.

30. "Religion employs a larger portion of human nature in the discovery of truth than does science, and she believes that she touches a wider environment." Ibid., 74.

31. Thomas H. Huxley (1825–95) to Charles Kingsley (1819–75), 23 September 1860, *Life and Letters of Thomas Henry Huxley*, ed. Leonard Huxley (New York: Appleton, 1900), 1.233–39. Huxley was an English scientist who was best known as a vociferous defender of Darwin's theory of evolution and the coiner of the term *agnosticism*. Charles Kingsley was a leading Victorian novelist and social critic and a prominent Protestant controversialist. Thurman is arguing that Huxley's assertion of the existence of a "realm of values and meanings" beyond empirical verification was essentially a declaration of a personal religious faith, whatever doubts Huxley may have had about the existence of a deity as such. Thurman borrowed the Huxley quotation verbatim from Dinsmore (*Religious Certitude*, 78), who had excerpted this section from the much-longer letter by Huxley.

32. Huxley and William James, qtd. in Dinsmore, *Religious Certitude*, 78, 93. Thurman follows Dinsmore's argument closely in contending that religion provides certain knowledge and not what Dinsmore castigates as the "weaker words" of "faith" and "belief" (79). Yet Thurman's notion of a "Supreme Spirit" seems more personal and experiential and further removed from conventional Christian categories employed by Dinsmore.

33. William James, qtd. in Dinsmore, *Religious Certitude*, 93. James, *The Varieties of Religious Experience* (1902; repr., New York: Library of America, 1987), 448.

34. Dinsmore's *Religious Certitude in an Age of Science* was the McNair lecture for 1922, not 1923. The McNair Lectures is an annual series of lectures held at the University of North Carolina, Chapel Hill, on the relation between religion and science and formally begun in 1906 from a bequest made by the Reverend John Calvin McNair (1823–58) of the class of 1849.

35. The underline is handwritten.

36. Daniel Evans, "The Task of the Religious Thinker," *Harvard Theological Review* 1 (October 1908): 455–76.

37. Irving King, "Some Problems in the Science of Religion," *Harvard Theological Review* 4 (January 1911): 104–18.

38. Irving King, *The Development of Religion: A Study in Anthropology and Social Psychology* (New York: Macmillan, 1910).

39. Douglas Clyde Macintosh, *Theology as an Empirical Science* (New York: Macmillan, 1919).

40. Buermeyer, et al., *An Introduction to Reflective Thinking*.

❧ "Negro Youth and the Washington Conference"
December 1925

In this article, which appeared in the national YMCA monthly the Intercollegian,[1] *Thurman reports the activities of the Twenty-First National Conference on Colored Work of the YMCA held in Washington, D.C., on 21–23 October, 1925, at the Twelfth Street YMCA and John Wesley AME Zion Church. In 1925, interracial dialogue led black students to call for a merger of black and white student work, a move that threatens the power of the Colored Work Department. This causes a rift between black students and professional leadership, which is evident in the overall tenor of the conference.*

Thurman, the only student on the program, addresses the student section on the topic "The Christian Emphases" and in his article on the impact of the conference on Negro students. He notes that while the leadership's concern about its inability to draw Negro youth toward YMCA work as a profession may be warranted, it must be coupled with a critique of its effort to make the work appealing for students. Thurman also suggests that while Africa is an attractive field, colonialism deters students from pursuing a career of missionary service there.

"Of the calling of conferences there is no end." Such is the cry that arises from many quarters during these days of manifold activities in the interest of the Kingdom of God Some conferences are called; others are inevitable because of a particular development or growth. Of the latter type was the Twenty-first National Conference on Colored Work of the Young Men's Christian Association held in Washington, D.C., October 21–23. Delegates from all parts of the United States were in attendance. They came from varied walks of life and represented well-defined opinions with reference to the place and the function of the Brotherhood of which they felt themselves so much a part.

The program built itself around two general themes: Personnel, and Unoccupied Fields. In the discussion on personnel it was generally assumed that an adequate presentation of life work was being made to our youth, and especially to our students. The growing tendency on the part of our students to invest their lives other than in what is usually thought of as Christian vocations was viewed with grave concern. As a student, however, I looked in vain for someone to examine the present presentation of life work and see if it were really adequate. Does it actually challenge or is it too artificial and impotent to move youth to invest its life along the lines which it would sanction as being Christian? Despite the fact that certain student attitudes toward the question of life work were condemned, small room was given for the actual voicing of student opinion. Of course, one must realize that this was not a student conference.

There were numerous charts on display which showed the very great advance that the Association had made in many fields. It was all the more significant, therefore, that the conference, in the face of such progress, turned itself to a careful consideration of the great stretches of untouched areas where the Association must function if it is to meet the greatest need of the group. This involved a careful consideration of certain urban and rural conditions with reference to their effect upon the present status of our men and boys. Two unoccupied fields were staggering in their appeal: Africa, and personal dynamic faith in God.

Bishop Alleyene[2] of the A.M.E. Zion Church of America made a brilliant plea for a sympathetic understanding of African culture and life. He was persistent in his demand for an interpretation of African needs in terms of one's personal responsibility. The address was inspirational and authoritative but it did not come to grips with some of the practical difficulties which stand squarely in the way of our youth as they attempt to invest their lives among their people who, while they are so far away, are yet so terribly near. I refer, primarily, to barriers erected by certain governments that have raped the continent and its people through so many weary bloody years.

Bishop Vernon[3] of the A.M.E. Church, also a Bishop of Africa, told in dramatic fashion the work that is being done by Yergan[4] in South Africa. We rode and tramped with Max Yergan over vast stretches of South Africa as he met small and large groups here and there; as they caught from him with abiding enthusiasm a spark of recreative power; as, in his wake, there dawned into their souls a fervid consciousness that they were an indispensable part of a great world Brotherhood. Over and over it sounded: "Men must go to South Africa to conserve the power that God is causing to be released through Yergan's work; they must go to other parts of Africa that the same things may be done!"

There is little doubt that the meditations conducted by Dr. Mordecai Johnson gave us glimpses of unexplored areas of our personal religious lives. In a convincing manner he pointed out the weaknesses of the civilization of which we are a part, and, as the prophet of a new era, challenged us to become a part of a community of love which is gradually growing up in our midst. In the closing address our section of the Brotherhood was warned against placing its confidence in the wealth, the machinery, and the organization of which it is more and more a part. Again, a Voice came down the centuries, "O men, how little you trust Him." The man of real power is the man who lives the life of the spirit and who consecrates himself and all that he possesses to the progressive expansion of the sway of God in the world. This is the great adventure; this is a life at its best.

Intercollegian (December 1925): 77–78.

1. The *Intercollegian and Far Horizons,* a monthly magazine featuring student journalism, was published under a variety of titles by the National Council of Student Christian Associations and the Student Volunteer Movement for Foreign Missions in New York until June 1951.

2. Bishop Cameron Chesterfield Alleyne (1880–1955) of the African Methodist Episcopal Zion Church was a native of Bridgetown, Barbados. After receiving an undergraduate education from Naparima College (1903) at Port-of-Spain, Trinidad, he entered the United States and studied for one year at Tuskegee Institute. Alleyne was ordained deacon in 1904 and an elder the following year. He pastored several congregations until his 1916 appointment as editor of the *AME Zion Quarterly Review.* In 1924 Alleyne was consecrated bishop, the first resident bishop of Africa for the AME Zion Church. He remained at that post until 1928, when he returned to the United States.

3. Bishop William Tecumseh Vernon (1871–1944) was the forty-fifth bishop of the AME Church. Born in Lebanon, Missouri, Vernon was educated at Lincoln University and Wilberforce College. After his conversion and licensing to preach in 1896, he joined the Missouri Conference and was appointed president of Western University in Quindaro, Kansas. Vernon became active in Republican Party politics while in Kansas and was eventually appointed register of the U.S. Treasury by President Theodore Roosevelt. He served as president of Campbell College in Jackson, Mississippi, from 1912 to 1916 and was the bishop of South Africa from 1920 to 1924.

4. Max Yergan (1892–1975) was a senior secretary of the International Committee of the American YMCA from 1920 to 1936. Born in Raleigh, North Carolina, he graduated from Shaw University in 1914 and received an MA from Howard University the following year. In 1915 Yergan was an international secretary for black YMCA work. During World War I he served in India and Kenya, organizing YMCA units among the Indian and African troops in the British Army. Following the war he spent sixteen years in South Africa where he continued to work primarily among black South African students until his retirement from the YMCA in 1936. See David Anthony, *Max Yergan: Race Man, Internationalist, Cold Warrior* (New York: New York University Press, 2006).

❧ To Thomas W. Graham
9 January 1926
Rochester, N.Y.

Having accepted the pastorate at Mount Zion Baptist Church in Oberlin, Ohio,
Thurman writes to Thomas W. Graham, dean of Oberlin's Graduate School of
Theology, requesting special status as a postgraduate student there. In the fall of
1926, his "independent investigation" of the religious experience would begin
under the guidance of Kemper Fullerton, Edward Increase Bosworth, and
George Fiske. Thurman maintains that his interest in obtaining a doctoral
degree is of secondary importance and would decide not to pursue a doctorate
during his years at Oberlin.

Dean Thomas W. Graham[1]
Oberlin Divinity School
Oberlin, Ohio

My dear Dean Graham:
    In a conference with Professor Fullerton[2] of your faculty it was suggested
that I correspond with you relative to some special work that I am desirous of
doing in the Graduate School of Theology next year.
    I am a graduate of Morehouse College, Atlanta, Georgia, and am a senior in
the Rochester Theological Seminary of this city. I have accepted the pastorate of
the Zion Baptist Church of Oberlin and am interested in doing some independent
investigation under the guidance of perhaps two professors of your faculty. I went
over my plan rather carefully with Professor Fullerton. He was of the opinion that
it would require a special ruling of the faculty if such work were to count towards
an advanced degree. I am writing you, therefore, to find out if it will be possible for
me to do the kind of thing I have suggested here. I may add that the matter of the
degree is secondary; if I can get the work that is the major consideration.
    Such details as the transcripts of my college and seminary records can be
attended to as soon as my semester's work is completed.
Very sincerely yours,
[*signed*] Howard Thurman

                                                    TLS. OO-LAF.

    1. Thomas Wesley Graham (1882–1971), professor of homiletics, served as the dean of
the Oberlin Graduate School of Theology from 1923 to 1948.
    2. Kemper Fullerton (1865–1941) served as the Finney Professor of Old Testament Lan-
guage and Literature at Oberlin's Graduate School of Theology from 1904 to 1934. His books
include *Prophecy and Authority* (New York: Macmillan, 1919), *Studies in the Psalter* (Chicago: University of Chicago Press, 1910–11), and *The Truth about the Bible* (Chicago: American Institute of Sacred Literature, 1923), which he coauthored with Edward I. Bosworth.

🐿️ "The Basis of Sex Morality: An Inquiry into the Attitude toward Premarital Sexual Morality among Various Peoples and an Analysis of Its True Basis"
April 1926
Rochester, N.Y.

Thurman's Bachelor of Divinity thesis, like his other extant student papers, shows his awareness of what he calls here "the great gulf between the religion of the 'old Folks' and the religion of the youth" with Thurman's allegiance to the latter clear.

Modernist theologians had distinctive views on social ethics. In the general culture at the time, one of the most discussed subjects in the 1920s was the changes in sexual mores and the increasing acceptance of premarital sex among well-educated young people. Thurman notes that this was the most heated topic of debate at many of the student Christian meetings he attended.[1] The paper represents Thurman's effort to analyze an important contemporary problem that he felt was not being adequately addressed in the religious literature.

The thesis demonstrates much continuity with the thinking of George Coe, most notably his 1925 work, What Ails Our Youth? *In the first section of his paper, Thurman traces conventional sexual morality, taboos, and prohibitions back to their origins in ancient and medieval religious and social practices. Thurman argues that conventional religious morality and orthodoxy have played a major, negative role in reinforcing the taboos against premarital sex. In his extensive review of the marriage laws in the United States, Thurman sees a connection between the laws on premarital sexual behavior and antimiscegenation statutes.*

The analysis of the contemporary changes in sexual morality was uncompromisingly feminist, arguing that conventional abhorrence of premarital sex was a product of male domination of women, linked to the social custom of condoning male extramarital encounters, while harshly punishing similar activities by women. The double standard was collapsing, Thurman argues, under the impact of the worldwide social upheaval caused by World War I, which helped accelerate trends toward increasing higher education, voting rights, and economic independence for women.

In the final section, Thurman argues that while behavioral standards are broadly socially conditioned, premarital chastity is ultimately an individual matter. Thurman's argument, somewhat colored by the romantic pansexualism of Havelock Ellis, Olive Schreiner, and other early twentieth-century writers on sexual topics, claims that the human understanding of sexuality, newly liberated from societal restraints, would soon undergo a transformation. He concludes that premarital sex, when conducted between two committed parties, could be a genuinely spiritual experience. While Thurman's thesis is confined to questions of sexual behavior, his argument prefigures later themes in his treatment of the responsibility of the individual, claiming that when a person "has to stretch himself out of shape" to conform to society, he becomes immoral.

In the current publication of Thurman's thesis, symbols are used instead of numbers for his original endnotes, and his original endnotes are now in footnotes. The editors' comments are in endnotes, as is the convention in the current volume. Thurman's first section is without annotation, the bibliography is moved from the beginning of the thesis to the end, and the page numbers in Thurman's table of contents are deleted.

Contents

Introductory Remarks
 I. A Survey of Certain Past and Present Attitudes
   A. Uncivilized Peoples
   B. The Ancient Hebrews
   C. The Mohammedans
   D. The Greeks
   E. The Romans
   F. Early Christianity through the Reformation
   G. The Present Orthodox Attitude
     1. Social Sanctions
     2. Religious Sanctions
     3. Psychological Sanctions
   H. The Basis of the Various Attitudes
 II. Significant Factors in the Modern World
   A. The Demand for Freedom on the part of Women
     1. Increase in Education
     2. The Recent War
     3. The Ballot
     4. Economic Independence
   B. The Revolt of Youth
     1. Loss of Faith in Certain Old Sanctions
     2. Loss of Sense of Wrong in Matters Relating to Sex
     3. Women Become Self-assertive

III. The Basis of Sex Morality
    A. True Basis of Sex Morality is in the individual
    B. Individual Is in Social Relation
    C. The Ground of the Social Attitude
        1. Two Fundamental Considerations
            a. Sex Urge Must Be Understood
            b. No Inherent Conflict between Individual and Society
        2. Social Disapproval Is the Result of Racial Experience
            a. Pre-marital Unchastity Involves Irresponsibility
            b. There is Group Sense of Home-forming Tendensy
        3. The Significance of the Child
        4. Rising Estimate of Personality
        5. Temporary Relations Devoid Spiritual Quality

The Good Life: Introduction

Our inquiry is divided into three chapters. The first chapter is a review of the attitude taken toward pre-marital unchastity by various groups of peoples or different periods in time and in stages of cultural development. The chapter ends with an outline of the present orthodox and conventional attitude known as "Mrs. Grundy's" position. Such a review reveals the fact that social disapproval of pre-marital unchastity is not the work of one generation or of one particular cultural group. It represents the general experience of the human race.

The second chapter is a discussion of the reaction of the two groups most effected by pre-marital chastity or unchastity—Women and Youth. The changing of the status of women has made the reaction on their part to laws which were enforced upon them from men from above, very acute and articulate. The important factors in this shift are outlined. The raison d'etre of the reaction of youth is summarized in terms of a change of mind on the part of youth, and the factors which make that change pronounced are determined.

The third chapter examines the true basis for society's disapproval of pre-marital unchastity and discusses why such basis is valid in our modern world.

I. A Survey of Certain Past and Present Attitudes

A. Uncivilized Peoples*

The East African Borea and Kunama tribes do not regard it as in the least disreputable for a girl to become pregnant nor do they punish or censure the seducer. According to Warner in MacClean,†

---

*In this discussion I am using as a source, "History of Human Marriage," Vol. I, Chap. 4, and "The Origin and Development of the Moral Ideas," Vol. II, Chap. 42, by Westermark.

†Compendium of Kafir Laws, page 63. Quoted by Westermark.

"Seduction of virgins, and cohabiting with unmarried women and widows, are not punishable by Kafir laws, neither does any disgrace attach to either sex by committing such acts."

In the Solomon Islands, it is said, "Female chastity is a virtue that would sound strangely in the ear of the native—for two or three years after a girl has become eligible for marriage, she distributes her favors amongst the young men of the village." In the Malay Archipelago intercourse between unmarried people is very commonly considered neither a crime nor a danger; and the same is perhaps even more generally the case among the uncivilized races of India and Indo-China. Murdock writes of the Point Barrow Eskimo,

"Promiscuous intercourse between married and unmarried people, or even among children, appears to be looked upon simply as a matter for amusement. As far as we could learn, unchastity in a girl was considered nothing against her."

Pre-nuptial unchastity is by no means applicable with all groups of primitive peoples. There are those among whom unchastity before marriage is a disgrace. Among the Karaya, a Brazillian tribe, virginity is said to be highly esteemed and sexual intercourse out of wedlock to be severely punished. During the nine years' stay of Appun in Brazil, he only heard of one illegitimate child. When one of the Chi-chimes of Central America marries, a bride who proves not to be a virgin may be returned to her parents. Westermarck cites several instances of this general type among the American Indians.

Among the East African Takue a seducer may have to pay the same sum as if he had killed the girl. If a man among the Beni Mzab tribe seduces a girl he has to pay 200 francs and is banished for four years. Among the Kafir, Gaika, and Bantu peoples, fines are levied and offenders punished for pre-marital unchastity. Before the coming of the white man, the Australian Marousa tribe, Lower Darling, had very strict laws, especially those "regarding young men and women. It was almost death to a young lad or man who had sexual intercourse till married." The same is true among various tribes in western Victoria.

B. The Ancient Hebrews

Among the ancient Hebrews, pre-marital unchastity from the point of view of the maiden was disastrous. In the strands of the oldest document J[2] we find that it is not prohibitive for men to have pre-marital relations with harlots: Gen. 38:15ff. Here it was all right for Judah to have had relations with a harlot but when it was discovered that she was a widow then the situation was different. When the word came to Judah as to what his daughter-in-law had done, he "bring her forth and let her be burnt'" In the next oldest document E[3] there are very specific regulations. Exodus 22:16–17:

"And if a man entice a virgin that is not betrothed, and lie with her, he shall surely pay a mohar* for her to be his wife. If her father utterly refuse to give her unto him, he shall pay money according to the dowry of virgins."

Hence we see that seduction of a girl is penalized by enforced marriage of the couple, with the father having the privilege of objecting, but price must be paid in all events. In D[4] there is the following, Deut. 22:13–21:23–29:

"If any man take a wife and go in unto her, and give occasions of speech against her, and bring up an evil name upon her, and say, I took this woman, and, when I came to her, I found her not a maid: then shall the father of the damsel and her mother, take and bring forth the tokens of the damsel's virginity unto the elders of the city in the gate: and the damsel's father shall say unto the elders, I gave my daughter unto this man to wife and he hateth her; and, lo, he hath given occasions of speech against her, saying, I found not thy daughter a maid; and yet these are the token of my daughter's virginity. And they shall spread the cloth before the elders of the city. And the elders of the city shall take that man and chastise him; and they shall amerse him in an hundred shekels of silver, and give them unto the father of the damsel, because he has brought up an evil name upon the virgins of Israel: and she shall be his wife and he may not put her away all his days. But if the thing be true, and the tokens of virginity be not found for the damsel: then shall they bring out the damsel to the door of her father's house, and the men of the city shall stone her with stones that she die: because she has wrought folly in Israel, to play the whore in her father's house: so shalt thou put evil away from among you. . . . If a damsel that is a virgin be betrothed unto an husband, and a man find her in the city and lie with her; then ye shall bring them both out unto the gate of that city, and ye shall stone them with stones that they die; the damsel, because she cried not, being in the city; and the man, because he hath humbled his neighbor's wife; so thou shalt put away evil from among you. . . . If a man find a damsel that is a virgin, which is not betrothed, and lay hold on her, and lie with her, and they be found; then the man that lay with the damsel shall give the damsel's father fifty shekels of silver, and she shall be his wife: because he hath humbled her, he may not put her away all his days."

In this document a definite price is set and this price may be different from the bride price—the father has no power of refusal. When a girl is betrothed she has changed ownership from father to husband. Unchastity is punishable with death. In the P[5] document there is no regulation; the one exception being in Lev. 19:20–22. Here the priest atones for the deed that is done.

*Mohar or bride price.

C. *The Mohammedans*

"Throughout the Mohammedan world, chastity is regarded as an essential duty for woman."*

For the most part unchastity is punished with death. It is expected that the man will remain chaste. In "Old World Traits Transplanted," Park and Miller cite a case of one Asman Assen who learns that his daughter is pregnant. This man drags the daughter out into the woods and breaks her neck. On being questioned the mother said:

"My daughter was killed by my husband because marriageable, she became pregnant. I informed him of what had happened. He assured himself of the girl's condition and then decided to kill her according to our custom."†

Woman has a decidedly inferior position and at the same time she is the tool of men. Mohomet writes,

"When any one of them has tidings of a female child, his face is overclouded and black, and he has to keep back his wrath. He skulks away from his people for the evil tidings he has heard."‡

Lecky makes a very discriminating comment upon the Mohammedan attitude,

"If Mohammedans people paradise with images of sensuality, it is not because these form their ideals of holiness. It is because they regard earth as the sphere of virtue, heaven as that of simple enjoyment."§

D. *The Greeks*¶

The Greek woman was protected and the ideal for her was chastity. The same type of protection was given to daughters as was given to wives. The virginity of the daughters of Greece was expected. Lecky states,

Among the Greeks and Romans it was customary for the bride to be girt with a girdle which the bridegroom unloosed in the nuptial bed.**

Westermark says that chastity was the preeminent attribute sanctity ascribed to Athene and Artemis, and the Parthenon or virgin's temple was the noblest religious

---

*Westermark, Origin of Moral Ideas, Vol. II, p. 428ff.

†Park and Miller, Old World Traits Transplanted, p. 15.

‡Quoted by Parsons, The Old Fashioned Woman, p. 8.

§Lecky, European Morals, Vol. II, p. 112.

¶Lecky, European Morals, Vol. II, Chap. 5.

**Lecky, European Morals, Vol. II, p. 338.

edifice of Athens.* Chastity was not regarded as the highest good for men. The marvelous significance and influence of the Greek artesan show how generally accepted her position was; and the very nature of the case, being allowed more freedom or development and growth, she occupied an increasingly large place in life of Greece. Even Socrates instructs the artesan Theodata as to how to make herself even more adorable. He tells her that she should shut the door against the insolent, should look after her lovers in sickness and should love tenderly those who love her.† Full details as to the place of the courtesan and the type of unchastity which existed in Greece can be found in many of the writings covering the period.‡

E. The Romans§

In the most sacred orders of Rome, the Flowers of Jupiter and the Vestal Virgins typified the two prevalent ideals with reference to sex. The two orders had many things in common but there was one important difference. The former was representative of Roman marriage in its strictest and purest form; the latter was the type of virginity and the chastity the sacred ones was guarded by most terrific penalties.¶

In summarizing what happened to the ideals of purity in the Roman Empire, Lecky says,

> An inundation of Eastern luxury and Eastern morals submerged all the old habits of austere simplicity. . . The vast multiplication of slaves, . . . the games of Flors, in which races of naked courtesans were exhibited, . . . the influx of the Greek and Asiatic heterae who were attracted by the wealth of the metropolis; the licentious paintings which began to adorn every house . . . had all their part in preparing those orgies of vice which the writers of the empire reveal.**

Most significant of all perhaps, was the change in the form of marriage. Marriage was looked upon as a simple civil contract, entered into for the happiness of contracting parties. It could be dissolved at will. This led to a wild unrestrained type of Free-love that has rarely been equalled in any age.†† there were

---

*Westermark, The Origin and Development of Moral Ideas, Vol. II, p. 429.

†Xenophon Memorabilia, III 2.

‡The Deipnosophists of Athenaeus, Young's Translation Vol. III and the Dialogue of Lucretius concerning Courtesans.

§Lecky, European Morals, Vol. II, Chap. 5.

¶Lecky, European Morals, Vol. II, p. 315ff.

**Lecky, European Morals, Vol. II, p. 320.

††Lecky, European Morals, Vol. II, p. 324ff.

many examples of wonderful fidelity among whom Carolina and Seneca, and Paetus and Arria will always be remembered.

There were teachers who recognized that chastity for men [*illegible*]. Epictetus said to his disciples,

> "Concerning sexual pleasures, it is right to be pure before marriage, as much as in you lies. But if you indulge in them, let it be according to what is lawful."*

Rufus felt that no union of the sexes other than marriage was permissible. Most decidedly was this emphasis felt in the rise of Neo-Platonism and kindred philosophies. Plato was in favor of a law which would make it prohibitive for a man to touch anyone of the free-born or noble group except his wife (of course this would not apply to slave women). He felt that the citizens should be as chaste as birds that only mated in due season and remained attached for life. He regarded the body with its passions, as essentially evil, and all virtue as purification from its saints. This made for a stricter view regarding pre-nuptial unchastity.

F. Early Christianity through the Reformation

The early Church Fathers taught the excellence and superiority of virginity and chastity. I shall mention two specifically and refer to a third. St. Ambrose writes,

> "Virginity has brought from heaven that which it may imitate on earth. . . . They who marry not nor are given in marriage are as the angels in heaven. Who, then, can deny that this mode of life has its source in heaven?"†

He does not condemn marriages as such, but considers it a lesser evil. He quotes Paul in I Cor. 7:38,

> "He who giveth his virgin in marriage doeth well, and he who giveth her not doeth better."‡

Jerome recognizes marriage, for he says,

> "not that married women are, as such, outside the pale; they have their own place, the marriage that is honorable and the bed undefiled. (Heb. 13)"§

Virginity, with him, is the greatest good. The flesh is evil.

---

*Westermark, The Origin and Development of the Moral Ideas, Vol. II, p. 430.

†Re Virginibus (Nicene and Post-Nicene Fathers, 2nd Series, Vol. X, p. 365ff. Chap. 3).

‡I Cor. 7:38, New Testament.

§Epis. 22 (Nicene and Post-Nicene Fathers, Vol. III).

"Job was dear to God, perfect and upright before Him; yet, hear what he says of the devil, "His strength is in the loins, and his force in the naval.""

Commenting further, Jerome says,

"The terms are chosen for decency but the reproductive organs of the two sections are meant."

The fall of man was the loss of virginity:

Yet should we not weep and groan when the serpent invites us, as he invited the first parents, to eat forbidden fruit, and when after expelling us from the paradise virginity, he desires to clothe us with mantles of skin. . . .

Again he says,

To show that virginity is natural while wedlock only follows guilt, what is born of wedlock is virgin flesh, and it gives back in fruit what in root it has lost. . . . I praise marriage but it is because it gives me virgins.

In Augustine's Confessions and various passages in The City of God he takes a most definite position with reference to the sin all sex relations. Man fell through sex; it is evil.

Among the pronouncements of the early church councils, marital chastity is ideal and the relation of the sexes of wedlock is carnal. I select for citation the Synod of Elvira 305–6 a.d. There are several references to sexual intercourse out of wedlock as a carnal sin and special provisions [illegible] for restoration. Canons 12, 13, 14, 15, 30, 31, et al. Canon 14 is very instructive:

If a young girl who has made no vows has committed a carnal sin, and if she marries him with whom she has been led away, she shall be reconciled at the end of one year etc. This because she has violated only the marriage law, the rights of which she usurped before they were conferred upon her.*

Nothing is said of the man, pre-marital chastity for the woman is emphasized.

With its emphasis upon virginity and chastity, celibacy is the religious ideal. There was considerable discrepancy in Christian doctrine and practice. Immorality looming on the horizon and sexual vice was openly accepted.†

Lecky summarized the situation as follows,

The character of the seducer and especially of the passionless seducer who pursues his career simply as a kind of sport, and under the influence of no stronger motive than vanity or a spirit of adventure, has for many centuries

---

*Hefele, History of Christian Councils to A.D. 325.

†Lea, History of Sacerdotal Celibacy.

been glorified and idealized in the popular literature of Christendom in a manner to which there is no parallel in antiquity.*

The Reformation made at least one very significant concession to the actual relation between the ideal of chastity and the fact by making marriage permissible between groups for whom it had not been. As a result of the Reformation there were legal enactments making unchastity a crime.[†]

Westermark reacts to the total situation as follows:

> "it seems to me that with regard to sexual relations between unmarried men and women Christianity has done little more than establish a standard which, though accepted perhaps in theory, is hardly recognized by the feelings of the large majority of people—or at least of men—in Christian communities and has introduced the vice of hypocrisy, which apparently was little known in sexual matters by pagan antiquity."[‡]

G. The Present Orthodox Attitude

In our present society there is a certain well-defined orthodox attitude taken toward pre-marital unchastity. At no point is this attitude more clearly set forth than in the various statutes of the several states.[§] Fornication is defined as sexual intercourse between unmarried people. In twelve states, Arizona, California, Delaware, Kansas, Louisiana, Maryland, Missouri, New York, Oklahoma, South Dakota, Tennessee and Vermont, fornication is punishable by law. (Up to age 21.) Most of these laws in the remaining thirty-six states apply to men and women. It is interesting to point out that in Virginia and West Virginia the law reads,

> "Illicit intercourse between an unmarried man and a married women is fornication in the man."

From the woman's point of view this is adultery.

The next set of statutes worthy of examination are those which have to do with the age of consent for sexual intercourse. In all of the states in the Union there are laws regulating the age of consent. There is a wide difference in many of the states, however.

> "In Georgia, for example, the age of consent is fourteen years, whereas in Tennessee, 'unlawful intercourse with a female child between the ages of twelve and twenty-one constitute a felony, if the female is not a bawd, lewd

---

*Lea, History of Sacerdotal Celibacy, p. 346.

† History of Crime in England II, p. 182 and 582. Quoted by West.

‡Westermark, The Origin and Development of the Moral Ideas, Vol. II, p. 434.

§The Laws of Sex, Hooker, p. 144ff.

or kept female.' In South Carolina the age of consent is fourteen years, in Rhode Island, fifteen years, in the District of Columbia, sixteen years. In Alaska and Hawaii girls are protected only until they are twelve years old, whereas in Colorado and Washington both boys and girls are protected until their eighteenth year."

In all of the states the laws apply to the 'carnal knowledge' of girls under certain ages but nothing is said of the 'carnal knowledge' of a boy under a certain age. It is certainly true that boys are raped many times over but from the point of view of the law this is impossible.

In seventeen states the lowest age at which a female can make a valid contract except marriage is 18; while in the remaining states it is 21. But in Kentucky, Louisiana, Maryland, Mississippi and Virginia a child TWELVE years old may marry with parental consent; in one state the age is thirteen; in 10 states fourteen; in 10 states fifteen; in 9 states sixteen; and in 5 states eighteen.

> "Thus it is seen that marriage which is without doubt the most important relationship into which a girl can enter, becomes valid from the age of twelve years and upward, whereas all other contractual rights are invalid until she reaches at least the age of eighteen."*

There are twenty-nine states which have laws prohibiting the intermarriage of races. This fact has very significant bearing upon our inquiry because in those states fornication is not illegal above certain age limits. If the law does not recognize the existence of a marital relation, then the law cannot recognize sexual intercourse as a possibility. It exposes the girls of the minority group to the lustful ravages of men in the majority group.

It seems reasonably clear that the aim of society from the point of view of the statutes is to protect the virginity of unmarried women. Chastity is the ideal and sexual intercourse outside of wedlock is illegal. We shall now turn to conventional society to see if we do not find there the very same feeling that we see reflected in the statutes.

In its attempt to protect the virginity of its women there are certain sanctions that society has developed, violation of which it punishes with its disapproval. I have rather arbitrarily divided them into three general groups, the artificiality of limitation of which are clearly recognized: Social Sanctions, based upon certain differences in the more restricted sense; Religious Sanctions; and Psychological Sanctions.

*Hooker, The Laws of Sex, p. 121

Social Sanctions

In the first place we note that conventional society places its approval upon the separation of the sexes. This separation is very old indeed. We take the position that the fundamental thing that lies back of this separation is based upon certain genuine and more or less psychological differences between men and women:

Organic Differences.

There is the difference in generative function. This has its basis in the purely organic differences in the bodies of men and women. Havelook Ellis in Man and Woman, points out their primary and secondary differences. We need not list them here; it is sufficient to rest our case with fact of generation. Perhaps the most impressive thing at this point is the fact of menstruation with all that goes with it.

More or Less Psychological Differences.

The Vaertings in their very excellent volume on "The Dominant Sex," point out with reasonable clarity and conviction that:

> "the contemporary peculiarities of women are mainly determined by the existence of the Men's State, and that they are accurately and fully paralleled by the peculiarities of men in the Women's State."*

Granted that this observation is true, it is our purpose to set forth these differences from the point of view of the present orthodox attitude.

Stated succinctly, men and women live according to different standards. As we interpret these standards their aim is to protect the virginity of women. We may even call them aids to Chastity:

1. The work of woman is in the home. She is to bear and rear children and to give to the world motherly and wifely affection. The result is, she is dependent; and if dependent, then inferior.

2. Woman's associations with men must be according to certain fixed standards. She may receive her callers at certain conventional hours and there is a code of conduct which she must strictly observe. If she goes out at certain times she must be chaperoned.

3. Women must dress in such a way as not to appeal to the lower natures of men—hence the emphasis upon the use of the corset the long dress and the like. She must not expose her body by crossing her legs in the presence of men. In fine, she must not make herself liable to advances. Along with this came the taboo on smoking and drinking and boisterousness in general. She must not become 'common.'

*Vaertings, The Dominant Sex, p. 13.

4. It was what Elsie Parsons calls a 'Sex Dialect'.* No 'decent' woman is supposed to know anything about prostitution nor to mention it. Even the name of her sex organs is only known to her—the body is to be kept out of sight. She must not use the word 'pregnant'—she must say 'limb' not 'leg'. The use of the word 'sexual' is tabooed also. She must not swear or even use 'darn'. When she uses a salutation it must be formal and more conventional than that of a man. It is out of such a wilderness of confusion and ignorance as this that a woman is supposed to get her knowledge of life. In Miss Davenport's book titled Salvaging of American Girlhood[†] she records the type of questions that high school graduates and prospective teachers asked in a certain experiment that she conducted. Let me list a few of them:

> "Can a man tell that a girl is menstruating by feeling her pulse or looking into her eyes?
>
> Does washing or destroying the napkins while a girl is menstruating increase the flow or make the period longer?
>
> Since women have the menstrual flow to relieve their passions, and men don't, isn't it necessary for men to have intercourse to relieve theirs?
>
> If a man uses a cover in intercoursing with a woman will he get consumption?
>
> Why do boys have to have sex intercourse after they are fourteen do they get consumption if they don't?
>
> Is siphilis caught by sex intercourse during menstruation?
>
> Is it true that if a man is very passionate during intercourse the result is a girl?
>
> Why does a girl feels so ashamed because she menstruates?
>
> Why is sexual intercourse considered sinful?
>
> Is there any man good enough for any girl to go with?"

Commenting further on the tragic ignorance et al. growing out of the conventional attitude, Miss Davenport says,[‡]

> "One wanted to know why she fainted either the first day before the menstrual flow came on–that as a rule this happened. Another asked if it was 'normal' for the bowels to move at the time of menstruation. She said that hers never did and she sometimes went two weeks this way without bowel action–was this 'natural' or did it show something was 'wrong?'"

---

*Parsons, The Old-Fashioned Women, p. 149.

†Davenport, Salvaging of American Girlhood, p. 185.

‡Davenport, The Salvaging of American Girlhood, p. 189ff.

Religious Sanctions

Here we are thinking primarily of the stigma of sin that has been attached to the whole question of sex and the remarkable influence of the ideal of chastity upon subsequent generations. At this point the attitude which we pointed out with reference to the church fathers has persisted:

The Flesh is sinful.
The Fall of Man was a fall from chastity.
The Ideal Life is the Chaste Life.

In a pamphlet entitled, The Garden of Eden and the Sex Problem,* the author says,

"The third chapter of Genesis is purely an allegory dealing with the sex organs, sex life, and sex relationship and with such an interpretation we find it to be harmonious and logical.... The Garden is the Human Body, and the trees of the garden are the various organs of the body, and the tree in the midst of the garden is the organ in the midst of the body, namely the life organ or generation organ. The serpent...represents lust. The lust in Adam is represented as the Voice of the serpent, persuading Eve to yield herself to the desires born in the sex organs of both. The sex act became the so-called sin. Until this time, Adam and Eve, not having partaken of the fruit of the tree in the midst of the garden; did not know shame. After having done so, belief of wrong produced consciousness of wrong."

The sinfulness of everything having to do with sex is the very essence of orthodox religious teaching along this line. Without a possible exception more than ninety young women at one conference last summer said to me that they were taught that is was evil to even discuss sex under any condition and the 'marriage relation was a concession made to the flesh.' The conventional attitude taken toward unchastity is inevitable. IT IS VERY SIGNIFICANT THAT THE CONVENTIONAL ATTITUDE HAS NOT BEEN ONEN WHICH RECOGNIZED THE SACREDNESS OF SEX BUT ONE WHICH SAID THAT SEX IS 'UNCLEAN', 'SINFUL', 'NASTY', IT IS UNGODLY.[†]

Psychological Sanctions

The differences in sex which have been outlined above have made for certain definite psychological attitudes which have acted as guards against pre-marital

---

*Davenport, The Garden of Eden and the Sex Problem, p. 3f.

†Simple mention should be made of a type of Biblicism based upon a proof text method which places the ban upon pre-marital sex relation by an appeal to scripture. As typical of this, see article by Burling in "Biblical World" Vol., 43, p. 92f.

unchastity—I do not refer here to the strictly religious influences. These attitudes have taken the shape of a certain fundamental fear of social disapproval:

1. Society condemns illegitimate children, children born out of wedlock. As a result of this condemnation there has arisen a fear of pregnancy which often inhibits pre-marital sex relations. The act itself is not the issue but the consequence of the act for an unhealthy interpretation of the act. The consequence is read into the process.

2. Society condemns venereal diseases. There is pity and tolerance for any victims of disease but when it comes to these venereal diseases there is condemnation and positive disapproval. As a result of this attitude, at least partially so, there has arisen a fear of disease which is operative in preventing pre-marital unchastity.

3. Society says that it is immoral to indulge in sexual intercourse outside of wedlock. It places its approval upon virginity in its women who belong to a certain class. To be known as a woman who has had relations with men is to lose something without which society will not 'respect' her. As a result of this there has developed a fear for the loss of status. The good girl, the honored girl is the girl who has not known a man. Chastity is idealized. But let us keep the question of status in mind.

So much for the ideal standard and its basis. We must now raise the question as to whether the facts accord with the standard and at what points there is wide divergence. The first thing that comes to our notice is that prostitution has flourished and in many instances has been encouraged for two very definite reasons: 1, It protects the virgins and those who belong to a certain status; 2, It makes provisions whereby men may satisfy themselves without entailing responsibility or loss of standing to women. These two are but phases of the same attitude. The recognition of these two kindred facts on the part of the government was very evident during the recent Mexican war as well as during the world war. It was during the Mexican war that the U.S. Government actually shipped women in.* Another such plan was being contemplated in connection with the cantonments but it was dismissed when at the meeting Dr. Abraham Flexner declared, "There is no use discussing regulation. The public will not tolerate the 'open' recognition of prostitution. It is very interesting that he said "open" recognition of prostitution. A careful study of the Vice Reports of Syracuse, Chicago, New York, Philadelphia, and Minnesota will reveal without question the actual situation with reference to the place of the prostitute in contemporary life and how she is patronized by many of the "Defenders of the Chaste." This situation is possible because of the duo-standard of morality with references to men and women as we have been setting it forth in the conventional attitudes.

*Hooker, Laws of Sex, p. 259f.

I need only to mention the large number of illegitimate children that are born and have been born annually, the ideal of chastity to the contrary notwithstanding.*

In order to sum up the present orthodox attitude we may state it as follows: Pre-marital chastity is the ideal for women. Pre-marital unchastity is winked at in men. Pre-marital unchastity for women of a certain 'lower' status is winked at. The sanction for premarital chastity is found in certain religious, social and psychological attitudes. In the main, the authority is external and objective and makes for artificiality.

H. The Basis of the Various Attitudes

Before closing this section it is necessary to examine cursorily what seems to be behind this feeling that sexual intercourse between unmarried people, if both parties consent, is wrong. Westermark† accounts for it as follows:

> "If marriage, as I am inclined to suppose, is based on an instinct derived from some ape-like progenitor, it would from the beginning be regarded as the natural form of sexual intercourse in the human race, while other more transitory connections would appear abnormal and consequently be disapproved of. I am not certain whether some feeling of this sort, however vague, is not still very general in the race. But it has been more or less or almost totally suppressed by social conditions which make it in most cases impossible for men to marry at the first outbreak of the sexual passion. We have thus to seek for some other explanation of the severe censure passed on the pre-nuptial connections.
>
> "It seems to me obvious that this censure is chiefly due to the preference which a man gives to a virgin bride...It partly springs from a feeling akin to jealousy toward women who have had previous connection with other men, partly from the warm response a man expects from a woman whose appetites he is the first to gratify, and largely from an instinctive appreciation of female coyness. Each sex is attracted by the distinctive characteristics of the opposite sex, and coyness is a female quality... Conspicuous eagerness in a woman appears to a man unwomanly, repulsive, contemptible. His ideal is the virgin; the libertine he despises.
>
> "Where marriage is the customary form of sexual intercourse, pre-nuptial incontinence in a woman, as suggesting lack of coyness and modesty, is therefore apt to disgrace her. At the same time it is a disgrace to, and consequently an offence against, her family, especially where the ties of kinship are

---

*Parker, What Becomes of Unmarried Mothers? (Pamphlet)

†Westermark, The Origin and Development of the Moral Ideas, Vol, II, p. 454ff.

strong. Moreover, where wives are purchased, the unchaste girl by lowering her market value, deprives her father or parents of part of their property. . . .

"The men, by demanding that the women whom they marry shall be virgins, indirectly give rise to the demand that they themselves shall abstain from certain forms of incontinence."

Continuing the discussion further Westermark makes the point that unchastity is regarded as an offence against the parents (among savages) rather than an offense against the girl. The harm done to the girl is very often over-looked. And that is essentially true in the contemporary orthodox attitude. The wrong is done against society; while the woman is hardly taken into account even in the case of rape. Then there is the responsibility attached to the off-spring that may come from illicit union. Mathus* feels that the essential cause of the attitude taken toward pre-marital unchastity is here:

"It could not be expected that women should have resources sufficient to support their own children. When therefore, a woman had lived with a man who had entered into no compact to maintain her children, and aware of the inconvenience he might bring upon himself, had deserted her, these children must necessarily fall upon the society for support... The offence is besides more obvious and conspicuous in the woman, and less liable to any mistake. When the evidence was most complete, and the inconvenience to the society at the same time the greatest, there it was agreed that the largest share of the blame should fall."

We must conclude that sexual intercourse between unmarried people is regarded as being wrong from a variety of points of view and for perhaps, very different reasons. From our survey of the field it is clear that unchastity for unmarried women is wrong. The authority for such a conviction seems to be external and is not a part of the inherent respect for personality which one indi-vidual should hold for the other. The appeal has not been made to an inner response of the individuals but to a medley of external prohibitions and supersti-tions. It is built upon a false conception of sex and upon a false conception of woman. That there should be a revolt is inevitable and there may be factors in the modern world which have made this revolt possible and effective. It is with these factors that we concern ourselves in the next chapter.

II. Significant Factors in the Modern World

In John Stuart Mill's essay "In Defense of Women,"[6] he takes the position that women should be allowed larger educational advantages, the right to enter industry and the professions and to play a direct part in politics. In making this

*Malthus, Population, Book III, Chap. 2, p. 279.

pioneer venture in defending women, Mill did not fail to recognize the full significance of motherhood with all that it means.* Since the writing of this essay during the middle of the nineteenth century, there has been an increasing sentiment among English speaking peoples in favor of a fuller and richer and more varied life for women. In creating this sentiment women themselves have played no small part. They have revolted against the selfishness, injustice and the domination of the "Man's State." Her inferiority assumed, woman's work was prescribed, her place was given her and she was told to remain quiet and let men run things. Well might the women of yester-year have said of men what Ulysses said of the people over whom he ruled: "A savage race, That hoard, and sleep, and feed and know not me."[7]

At no point has the domination of men been more disastrous than in the conventional attitude toward pre-marital unchastity. The reaction of women to this domination at this point has been very significant because it reveals just what is taking place in the shifting of the status of women. The Woman's Movement has had as its primary emphasis in this changing of status. At the present time there are three outstanding phases of this Movement: (1) A form of Socialism. It demands an equality of men with women and would have a public recognition of motherhood regarding it as a public duty worthy of being rewarded by the state. H. G. Wells and Bertrand Russell are the leading contemporary exponents of this view.[8] (2) Free Love. It would make marriage the result of a common decision to live together, and separation would be by common consent. W. L. George expounds such a view.[9] He would destroy all vestiges of the male monopoly. Further, he believes that there is something deep in the hearts of men and women which would urge them to live together in couples. (3) Complete Economic Freedom of women. This view is identified with Charlotte Perkins Gilman.[10] She would give sexual relations a secondary place and would have a keen division of labor, so that experts would do the home duties, care for the children and the like.

According to the classification given by Wadia in his Ethics of Feminism,† there are four basic conceptions which are at the bottom of the Feminist Movement—Freedom; Independence; Labor; and Individuality.[11] In the discussion which follows this classification, these four conceptions overlap so manifestly that they may all be grouped under Freedom with the other three as expressions of this Freedom. We shall discuss, therefore, this developing freedom on the part of the women with relation to the conventional attitude toward pre-marital unchastity.

---

*Mill, In Defense of Woman, Chap 2.

†Wadia, The Ethics of Feminism, Chap. 1.

A. Freedom: The Demand for Freedom on the Part of Women

It is impossible to separate the struggle for freedom on the part of women from the general wave of democracy that has swept across the world. This struggle grew out of a demand for equality. There are several factors which have been at work to make this demand more acute and imperative:

1. Increase in Education

Women had been segregated and been kept in ignorance so long that at first, their approach to education, wherever opportunity was afforded, was with the avowed purpose of proving that women could become educated. It became a matter of sex-vindication. This attitude has been largely dissipated because of the presence of an increasingly large number of women in the various institutions of learning. At first, men offered very stern opposition to this invasion of women and it is not entirely gone. There are many hospitals that will not take female internes and a few medical schools that will not admit women—this, from one field alone. Now this opposition has served to stimulate the struggle and to make the demand for freedom all the more exaggerated. As a result of the exaggerated idealization of freedom as a goal, the tendency has been to use freedom, when acquired, rather recklessly. The table below shows the increase in attendance of women in institutions of learning in America.

Teachers in Colleges and Univ. Students in Prep., Col, Grad, Prof. Schools

	Men	Women	Men	Women
1890	6,834	1,084	106,618	53,831
1900	14,546	3,674	136,297	60,866
1910	21,813	2,854	200,339	73,745
1920	34,111	8,771	334,226	187,528

Pct. of collegiate and resident graduate students

	Men	Women
1910	65.1%	34.9%
1920	62.3%	37.7%

Along with this developing freedom there has come what may be thought of as a flagrant disregard for certain conventional standards of morality which do not longer seem binding upon women. With the possible exception of the prostitute and of what Olive Schreiner calls the Parasitic Woman,* no group of women have been so adept at breaking conventions.[12] It is among educated women that we first find a developed aversion to motherhood and the ordinary grind of home

---

*Olive Schreiner, Women and Labor.

life. It is among them that association with men becomes the most unconventional, and petting and spooning are interpreted in terms of the acceptable. It is this group of women who first lifted the discussion of sex out of the vulgar classification and made it acceptable material for mixed conversation.

2. The Recent War

It is most natural that during a situation of crisis there would be a general breakdown of customary standards of morality. We should not be surprised, therefore, if in the sex morality of unmarried people we should find such "disintegration." The general condition has been aptly described by Edith Sellers in Nineteenth Century and After:*

> You forget that a new state of things has arisen, one in which mothers are practically helpless. In Pre-war days girls, as boys, were dependent on their mothers for years after they began earning their own living. They must pay heed to what she said, because they must live with her, as they had not money to defray the cost of living elsewhere. But all of that has changed now when, instead of earning 7s. or 8s. a week, they are earning 25s., 30s., 30s., 40s. or more, and the father is perhaps a thousand miles away. With such wages as she has now, a girl is dependent on no one; not only is she self-supporting, but she has money to spare, to give away. She can therefore betake herself off at a moments notice.[13]

When we add to this unique economics situation the many inducements to temporary relations, we can get some idea as to the peculiar strain that was placed upon an objective morality. This point is brought out very clearly in a discussion of the "Changing Moral Standard" by Gotto in the October issue of Nineteenth Century and After:

> A girl of 19, who entered a country house party, when asked by her hostess where she was staying the week before, answered glibly, in a mixed company, "Oh, I was at —— and had a topping time"; openly boasting of promiscuous immorality during the visit. That such an announcement could be made without the majority of those present feeling that anything out of the ordinary had occurred, shows that the social customs and traditions are altering rapidly in a most undesirable direction.
>
> Consider also the well-educated business girl who telephones for information as to where facilities for treatment of venereal diseases can best be obtained "because I was kind to a friend who came home on leave the other day and now my fiancé is reaching London next week and we are to be married." Or, the domestic servant who writes for information of the same

*Edith Sellers, The Nineteenth Century and After, Oct. 1918.

nature in great distress, because she cannot imagine "who I got it from as all my boys are such nice boys and it is not as if I was such a bad woman"; all indicate the changing standard.*[14]

Cases of the above type could be multiplied. It seems very clear that the freedom that had already begun to come into the lives of women was greatly increased by the war. It made the shift from a Pain Economy to a Pleasure Economy[15] rather suddenly, resulting in a certain amount of unrestraint. Men had retained the right to control their bodies as well as the bodies of women, and this is one of the rights that is being challenged by the rising tide of freedom.

3. The Ballot

The disfranchisement of women has been the most outstanding example of the exercise of the male right. It meant that women were not the equals of men and that they were to be classified with children, with prisoners and with the insane. It made it necessary for women to resort to a wide variety of tricks to get their wills translated into law.

The granting of the ballot to women meant at least three very definite things. (1) The recognition of the equality of women and men. (2) Opportunities for political advancement and control. (3) Women have a larger share in the destiny of offspring. The latter is important for our purpose. It is too early in the political life of women to ascertain even what may be done in the future. But it is not unreasonable to believe that future legislation will make ample provisions for motherhood, and the changing of present statutes so as to recognize a woman's right over her own body.

4. Economic Independence

This factor has been touched upon in the discussion as to the influence of the war. But there are factors to be considered in this particular which are more or less independent of the war. Prior to the war the number of women in industry was already on the increase. The feeling of independence as contrasted with the old feeling of dependence and inferiority has had a very direct effect upon the attitude taken toward sexual morality. Women are increasingly economically independent and accordingly postpone marriage until such a time as proves itself to be advantageous to them. As a correspondent writes, "Women, many of them, are caring less and less about marriage. It seems so unnecessary now, in an age where we are so free in thought and all, and get work which makes us independent."

Because a woman pays her bills, she decides where she shall live and under what conditions. Since she controls her living she also controls her body. If she

*Gotto, "The Changing Moral Standard," in the October issue, 19th Century and After.

controls her body, then, she feels as if she can do with it what she pleases. Her position is that society does not have a right until she commits an act which is more strictly social, that a sexual act, per se, is not a social act but it does become one when it results in procreation. In the conception of a child a woman commits a social act. It is at this point that society comes in. Society has something to say as to the condition under which it will welcome a new citizen into the world. But as long as the woman safeguards herself at that point, society becomes impertinent when it interferes with her personal independence.* Ellen Key says the whole of sexual morality revolves around the child.[16]

A physician correspondent in a large Western City gives a typical case out of the numbers recorded in her very large practice (exclusively among women):

> Day before yesterday another bride came into my office—married a week ago—she was five months pregnant. I asked her why she did not marry before—"Oh," she said, "I did not want to. I wanted to work and I knew he would not want me to if he knew that I was pregnant and I was married to him. So I just waited." They had been intimate for over two years and had thought nothing of it.

B. The Revolt of Youth

Last summer I spent more than twenty-five days in daily and intimate contact with several hundred young college men and women. We discussed everything from birth control to the planetary hypothesis. Over and over again I was impressed by the seriousness of the groups for the most part and for the almost flagrant disregard which they held for anything which savored of external authority. There was nothing that was more bitterly assailed than the present conventional attitude taken towards questions of sex. The hot spot was; "Why is it wrong for me to have sexual intercourse? What makes it wrong? If the essence of marriage is love, then why is love not sufficient ground for sexual intimacy? If my sexual appetite is a normal thing, why is it not moral to satisfy that appetite, making immorality synonymous with over-indulgence?"

What has happened to these young people that they are raising these questions in mixed groups with utter frankness and candor? Professor Coe in his little book, What Ails Our Youth?[†] has analyzed the present conditions of youth as follows:

1. Youth's outlook upon life is being transformed by the enormous increase in man's control over nature.

2. The changed status of the female in our society creates new problems for the youth of both sexes.

---

*For this discussion, see Ellis' Studies, Vol. 6, p. 417ff.

†Coe, What Ails Our Youth?

3. In the life of youth human contracts have vastly increased, and they have largely shifted <u>from domestic to non-domestic types</u>.

4. Our industrial civilization itself is ailing, and it communicates its ailments to the young people.

(1) Our industry approaches nature as an invitation to secure income.

(2) The mechanization of men.

(3) This mechanization creates a chasm between work and leisure, and sends men in search of exciting pleasures to offset the deadening routine.

(4) The drawing of a large number of women in industry with the resulting change in their outlook upon life.

5. Our young people have been plunged into these conditions without having opportunity for education appropriate thereto.[17]

In addition to these factors as outlined by Prof. Coe, something else has taken place. There is an increasing recognition of the great gulf between the religion of the "old Folks" and the religion of the youth. I do not mean this in any general sense. In the public schools, for instance, a child is being taught the evolutionary hypothesis, he is being taught physical geography, he is being taught civics and the basis of civil conduct. But at home and in Sunday School he is being taught certain things which are a direct contradiction to the things which he learns in public school. The young fellow concludes that the public school is right, and the Sunday School and the home are wrong. Once such an attitude is assumed, the tendency is throw over all the values which are in the Sunday School and in the home. Hence there is a revolt against the domination of these two factors. The college man faces the same situation to a greater extent perhaps. The total result of such a situation is the undermining of the sanction of religion for conduct.

Of course we could enumerate many things that have influenced youth and made the present situation possible, but we shall content ourselves with the above analysis and raise a much more important question. What effect have these factors outlined above had upon the outlook of youth upon life and more especially upon sex morality?

1. Loss of Faith in Certain Old Sanctions

It has caused youth to lose faith in the old sanctions and the people who epitomize them. Under this heading I shall quote just one of the many cases that fill the pages of the Revolt of Modern Youth, by Lindsey and Evans:*

> A high-school girl came to me recently for advice. She came of her own accord. I had never seen her before. She said that she had a personal problem which she could not talk over with her parents because if they knew

---

*Lindsey and Evans, The Revolt of Modern Youth, p. [1]53ff.

about it they would no longer be capable of acting like reasoning beings. It was one of those matters which parents are likely to consider a closed subject, not open to debate because it had only one side instead of two.

Her father, formerly wealthy, had lost his money. Now she would have to leave school and go to work. She had taken a position but had later given it up; and recently a wealthy man had asked her to become his mistress. What she wanted from me was an opinion of the wisdom of such a course. Should she accept the offer or look around for some other kind of job?

All this she put to me calmly as she would have discussed with her mother the choice of two ordinary positions, of the sort that would involve no question of conventional morality.

"You see," she explained, "I can't ask my parents for an opinion about this because they would merely rave. They would consider it immoral for me to think of such a thing, or to debate in my own mind. But I don't think it immoral to try to think straight, do you? Why should I take their word in such matters, as if they knew all? I can think of reasons why I might become that man's mistress and be no worse than I am now."

"You have a perfect right to reason about the matter," I told her. "And you have a right to decide the question for yourself—I am not shocked at your question and I certainly do not propose to throw a fit. . . . You are to decide this for yourself; and I will neither interfere with you nor violate your confidence.

"Now as to your question: Do as you think best. Follow your own judgment. Be this man's mistress if that's what you want to be. But first, let's you and me consider the facts and see if this is, after all, what you want, or do you merely think you want it."

Then I showed to her, as cogently as I could, what seemed to me the folly of what she was contemplating. In conclusion I said to her, "Don't try to decide this offhand. Think about what I have said, and see if my reasoning does not appeal to you after you have cooled off. If it doesn't, do as you think best; and if you go to this man, and he doesn't treat you right, come to me and I'll wring his neck."

She thanked me, departed, and in due time came to a reasoned decision, not to accept the man's offer.

Now what I want to make clear is this—the usual way to treat young people when they try to think about such things is to shriek at them hysterically and say you shan't, you mustn't, this isn't debatable, it's a sin, you'll get into prison, you'll go to Hell and other similar bunk.

Why is it wrong? Why isn't it debatable? Why is it a sin? In God's name, give them the facts, all the facts we have, and let them decide it for themselves. Maybe we are not so dead right as we think.

If our system of sex ethics can't survive that free and open encounter between truth and falsehood, then it doesn't deserve to survive; and any moral code that has to be bolstered up by taboos and dogmatic affirmations isn't worth preserving. If our conventions are any good, let them come out and fight.[18]

2. Loss of Sense of Wrong in Matters Relating to Sex

This loss of faith in the sanctions has made for active sex experimentation without the old consciousness of sin and wrong. In a private interview with the general secretary of Social Service Bureau of Rochester, New York, he told me of many cases that had come to his attention which substantiated the fact above. For example, a young high-school girl dropped her vanity case on the floor in the presence of her mother. The jar caused the spring to be released and the case opened. Among the things that fell out were two condums. Her mother was terribly alarmed. The girl said, "Oh, that's all right, all the girls carry them for fear that the fellows may not have a supply when we go out."

In a certain high school in ———, thirteen girls in the senior class were dismissed because they were pregnant. One afternoon a mother with her daughter were walking out and they happened to pass one of these girls. The mother remarked, "My, but it is a pity about those girls. I feel so sorry for them." Thereupon the daughter replied, "So do I. It seems to me that they should have known enough to make the men use condums. I always do."

A medical correspondent writes as follows:

Mrs. ——— age 22—white—fine-looking girl—very well dressed. Patient happy. No sign of remorse—I expected nothing—seemed happy to have a child. Normal labor, Nov. 7. Patient said to me, Dr. ———, do you know when we were married? It was October 2nd. I said, "Why my dear child, why didn't you get married before when you knew you were pregnant? You were marrying into a fine family and marrying a fine fellow." "Oh," she said, laughing as if it were a huge joke—"I did not like to tell him, he kept asking me if I was and I said, 'Well I like your nerve.' Finally I thought I had better tell him. This happened when he came to visit me down East last winter."

Upon quizzing I found that they had been living as man and wife for about two years and thought nothing of it, and were perfectly true to each other in this relation. Here is utter frankness in a girl who is a nice girl and the fellow is a nice fellow from a nice family. He thought everything of the girl and would not have missed the baby for anything. It seems to indicate very free relations outside marriage. It seems to me young people do not regard marriage very sacredly; if there is a child coming they try to legalize it. They begin petting parties very early and even develop these further. They do not seem to think anything of them.

3. Women Become Self-assertive

With the passing away of the feeling of sin with reference to pre-marital unchastity, women are increasingly becoming the active partners. Last fall in an interview with a young woman at a conference at Swarthmore College, PA (She is not a student there but was attending a conference), she told me how reluctant her friend had been in making any advances and that it was through her urging and guidance that they began to have intercourse with each other. She wanted to know if I thought that there was error in what she had done, in the light of some things she had heard me say. Her position was that she believed that where there was love, there should be no limits. They could not be married for at least a year and it was wrong to punish their bodies by not going the limit when they met each other.

Judge Lindsey* cites several cases making the same point. He speaks of one father who did not know what to do with his son because the girls come by the home and whistle for him to come out and meet them. He quotes the statement of a high school boy,

> I didn't go after her. She used to stop her automobile and ask me to take a ride. I felt like a fool if I said I wouldn't go with her.

Then there is this rather illuminating case on one Ellen who made an agreement with five other girls that before the summer vacation was over they would have a sex experience and the beginning of the year to compare notes. This particular girl selected a very fine fellow to take out to dinner to a questionable restaurant and while there she seduced him to his own utter astonishment.[19]

I have noticed an appreciable change in the attitude of young fellows towards the girl who has had sex experience. I have been surprised to find such a large number of college men who do not count it "against a girl" to go the limit in petting. It seems that men are being democratized at this point.

From the above it seems clear that the revolt of youth has been influential in undermining the basis of the conventional attitude toward pre-marital unchastity. The old appeal to external authority is gone and in the presence of a complex modern world some kind of morality based upon self-judgment must be brought to the front if we are to find our way out. The thing that gives us courage in the situation is the fact that the youth are trying to find a way out. As Coe points out,[†]

> It is probable that both sexes, on the whole, are meeting these difficulties; as well as we have the right to hope. Indeed, if we reflect upon the evasive

*Lindsey and Evans, The Revolt of Modern Youth, p. 90ff.

†Coe, What Ails Our Youth? p. 7.

treatment of sex by the present older generation, its false modesty, its double standard, its complaisance toward legalized lust, and its cruelty toward some forms of unlegalized sex-relations; and if in addition, we bring to mind the innate power and versatility of the sex-drive, surely we shall be surprised, not at the increasing unconventionality of speech and conduct, not at the increase of "petting," not at the rapid growth of divorce, not at the possible increase of illicit sex-intercourse, but rather at the general self-restraint and foresight that we witness among our emancipated youth. In the sense that they're struggling and to some extent floundering in the presence of an unsolved problem, something does ail them, but it is less a disease than an incident of social growth.[20]

We have seen that the conventional attitude toward pre-marital unchastity with its appeal to external authority had made for a situation so utterly untenable that some kind of reaction was inevitable. We have shown how this reaction, aggravated by certain factors in the modern situation, took the form of a change in the status of women on the basis of larger freedom; and a revolt of youth against external authority. It now remains for us to set forth what we believe to be the basis of a true sex morality in the light of what is actually taking place in the modern world.

III. The Basis of Sex Morality

A. True Basis of Sex Morality Is in the Individual

We set down this statement as a general proposition: The true basis of pre-marital chastity is within the individual. The authority for the conduct of the individual must be within, if such conduct is to be moral. We state as a corollary to the above proposition, the authority within the individual is largely derived from and is a part of the social situation in which the individual functions. The social sanctions for conduct become valid for the individual only when he recognizes their validity and affirms them within himself. We may even agree with John Dewey* that morality is essentially social, yet it is in the individual's "valuational consciousness," to borrow a phrase from Professor Coe, that the standards of the group are finally tested. Therefore, when we say that morality is social we mean that the <u>ground</u> of morality is social. Whatever sanctions society may evolve must be verified by the individual before conduct, as a result of them can be moral. It is inevitable that we conclude on this basis that before there can be a perfect life or before there can be perfect conduct there must be perfect knowledge.

In considering the bearing of such a position upon the question of pre-marital unchastity, two fundamental things must be done:

---

*Dewey, Human Nature and Conduct: Morality is Social.

1. The sex urge must be more thoroughly understood and appreciated. Sexual energy is fundamental to human beings as well as to the animal creation. Modern biology and physiology have shown with scientific precision how utterly diffuse sexual energy is throughout the entire human organism. It is automatically generated and registers in all phases of organic activity. The physical and psychological welfare of the individual is delicately dependent upon the generation and release of sexual energy. How important this is in the life of the child, for instance, has been set forth in that monumental work of Moll's Sexual Life of a Child.[21]

In Ellis's Little Essays of Love and Virtue,* he shows how society has sought to appropriate the sexual energy in individuals:

> The process by which this fundamental sexual energy is elevated from elementary and primitive forms is termed sublimation, a term originally used for the process of raising by heat a solid substance to the state of vapor. In the sexual sphere, sublimation is of vital importance because it comes into question throughout the whole of life, and our relation to it must intimately affect our conception of morality. . . . Throughout life, sublimation acts by transforming some part at all events of the creative sexual energy from its elementary animal manifestations, or at all events into finer forms of sexual activity, form[s] which seem to us more beautiful and satisfy us more widely. Purity, we thus come to see is, in one aspect, the action of sublimation, not abolishing sexual activity, but lifting it into forms which our best judgment may approve."[22]

We must not overlook the fact, however, that sublimation is only a part-way house in an attempt to appropriate sexual energy. It has very definite limitations and when they are exceeded the result is an abnormality.

Sexual intercourse is one of the chief methods whereby nature disposes of sexual energy. When this fact is clearly understood the unwholesome idea of the act will be undermined. Simultaneously with the coming of a fuller understanding of the place of sex in life must of necessity come a more thoroughgoing appreciation of the body. Physiological Chemistry and in recent times Behavioristic Psychology have revealed to us the relation between the glands of the body and various bodily functions. Especially is this relation discoverable between the development of the glands and the sexual life and generative functions. In the life of woman this relation is very pronounced. Perhaps the thyroid gland has been studied in this connection more than any other.

> The thyroid gland is closely associated with all the variations in woman's organism. To so marked an extent is this the case that Meckel long ago

*Ellis, Little Essays of Love and Virtue, 50–51.

remarked that the thyroid is a repetition of the uterus in the neck. The fact that the neck swells in women in harmony with the sexual organs seems to have been an observation made in very early times. All sexual activity in women is accompanied or preceded by hyper-activity of the thyroid. The thyroid swells at the first menstruation, and not uncommonly it increases to some extent at every menstruation. . . . Catullus refers to the influence of the first sexual intercourse in causing swelling of the neck, and it is a very ancient custom to measure the necks of newly married women in order to ascertain their virginity. This custom has not yet quite died out in the south of France. Heidenreich found that a similar swelling occurs in men at the commencement of sexual relations.*

B. Individual Is in Social Relation

2. There need be no inherent conflict between the highest interest of the individual and the highest interest of the group of which the individual is a part. If a normal individual has to stretch himself out of shape in order to be proper and acceptable to society, then the standards of society are such that the individual becomes immoral in conforming to them. On the other hand a blatant individualism which tends to disregard the relation of the individual to society makes the individual immoral. It must be in relation to society that the individual discovers what is the criterion of conduct for him.

A child becomes human in a social situation. The ego comes to itself in the alter.

This social reference of the ego abides, however distant or self-assertive the ego may become. It is by cooperation and clash of wills that I come to assert my will as my own, and it is by thinking of myself from other's standpoints that I acquire an opinion of myself. . . . Thus man is by nature social. Self-consciousness is _per se_ social consciousness, and individuality is in itself a social fact. Conversely, society, as distinguished from herds, rises in and through the individuating process, that is, through the increasing notice that one takes of another as an experiencing self. Neither term then—society or individual—is static; neither merely imposes itself upon the other, but the two are complementary phases of one and the same movement.†

C. The Ground of the Social Attitude

In a previous section of our discussion it was pointed out that there is a growing feeling on the part of some people that the sexual act is not a social act, _per se_. But it becomes a social act only when it issues in procreation. If procreation were

*Ellis, Man and Woman.
†Coe, Psychology of Religion, 142ff.

rendered impossible or at any rate improbable in any given situation, then society has nothing to say as to the rightness or wrongness of the act.

It remains as it began, a private act between two individuals. When society is called upon to welcome a new citizen, then the act becomes social. The fallacy in this argument is fairly obvious. If society is concerned with the bringing of a child into the world, then it must be concerned not only with the parties to the act but it must be concerned with every act of sexual intercourse. One sexual act may render the individuals who plan at some future time to procreate a child incompetent. If every sexual act has possibilities of procreation, then, if for no other reason, society must safeguard every act.

Upon what basis, therefore, can the authority of society which determines under what conditions it will endorse sexual intercourse be legitimately defended. Does it have any valid ground which can be sustained in our modern world?

In the first place we must recognize the fact that the failure of society to put its approval upon pre-marital sexual relations is not the work of one single generation. The first section of our inquiry has made this clear. The reasons, valid today, for such an attitude are not far [to] seek:

1. Premarital sexual intercourse involves irresponsibility in the persons so engaged. The act may issue in offspring or it may issue in disease, and if either, the group has no way of holding the individuals responsible for such consequences other than by registration. Society is against any one who is unwilling to shoulder his share of responsibility. Irresponsibility develops into license when it is deliberate. And license makes for the destruction of the finer experiences of which a sex relation is capable. All along there has been this groping toward an attitude which recognized the sacredness of sex and the consequent need for meeting certain requirements before the right is granted and approved. Such a feeling is valid for these times which recognize the normalcy of sex and which attempt to give it its true place in life. Such knowledge calls for fuller responsibility, for control, for restraint, for discipline. Especially are these needful because of the clash of cultures and social heritages incident to a shrinking world.

2. There is a group sense of the worth of the home-forming tendency in its members. Homes are demanded by society because there must be children in order to perpetuate the group. Illicit relations tend to break down the basis of love between individuals and thus render the formation of a home increasingly impossible. Of course there may be private vows but the vowers are not protected fully until the vows have social approval. The individuals make the vows, and society strengthens the vows by cooperating with its approval. It must be kept in mind that no human being is perfectly moral but each requires the backing of the group.

The value and the significance of the child is one of the outstanding facts of our age. With the emphasis upon the place of the child in the modern world, it is but natural that the circumstance and conditions under which the child is born and reared must be more carefully guarded. Pre-marital unchastity with its underlying tendency toward irresponsibility and license undermines the stability of the home and endangers the life of the child. I recognize the fact that there may be many relations intimate and beautiful outside of wedlock but as yet society has not approved of such relations and the offsprings are branded undesirables. They do not have a fair chance. It is interesting that many such couples marry in order to "legalize" the child.

Not only is society's attitude the result of the funded experience of the race but today it has added value due to the rising estimate of personality* and the higher evaluation of the sex act. It is hardly necessary to labor with the first reason. It may be pointed out, however, that the point at which the greatest injury is done to personality as a result of pre-marital unchastity is found in the fact that sexual intercourse when carried on without social approval results in a sense of shame. This means that the personality of the persons participating has been thwarted or warped. This feeling is largely neutralized or offset when the two parties truly love, are fully matured and find that immediate marriage must be postponed. We are thinking here of the general situation. Another factor to be considered is this; If a couple develop certain habits incident to cohabitation and one of the members withdraws, then under the urge that is not being met promiscuity is the natural result. Along with promiscuity will come unrestrained indulgence and all that goes with it.

Temporary relations are usually devoid of the spiritual quality which makes a sexual act significant. By the use of the term "spiritual" I do not mean any mysteriously supernatural qualities. I use the term here to distinguish it from the purely animal impulses or qualities and to cover all the higher mental and emotional processes which in human evolution are gaining greater power. It includes all that makes pleasure more than mere animal gratification. There is a classic passage on this point in the introduction to Olive Schreiner's Woman and Labor:[†]

> That as humanity and human societies pass on slowly from their present barbarous and semi-savage condition in matters of sex into a higher, it will be found, that over and above its function in producing and sending onward the physical stream of life (a function which humanity shares with the most lowly animal and vegetable forms of life, and which even by some noted thinkers of the present day seems to be regarded as its only possible function), that sex and sexual relation between man and woman have distinct esthetic, intellectual, and spiritual functions and ends, apart entirely from physical reproduction. That noble as is the function of the physical

*Felix Adler, Reconstruction of the Spiritual Ideal.

†Olive Schreiner, Woman and Labor.

reproduction of humanity by the union of man and woman, rightly viewed, that union has in it latent, other, and even higher forms of creative energy and life—dispensing power, and that its history on earth has only begun. As the first wild rose which hung from its stem with its center of stamens and pistils and its single world of pale petals had only begun its course, and was destined, as the ages passed, to develop more and more, stamen upon stamen to develop into petal upon petal, and to assume a hundred forms of joy and beauty.

And it would almost seem, that, on the path toward the higher development of sexual life on earth, as man has so often led in other paths, that here it is perhaps woman, by reason of those very sexual conditions which in the past have crushed and trammeled her, who is bound to lead the way and man to follow. So that it may be that at last, sexual love—that tired angel who through the ages has presided over the march of humanity, with distraught eyes, with feather-shafts broken, and white wings drabbled in the mires of lust and greed, his golden locks caked over with the dust of injustice and oppression—till those looking at him have sometimes cried in terror, "He is the Evil not the Good in life" and have sought, if it were possible, to exterminate him—shall yet, at last, with eyes bathed from the mire and dust in the stream of friendship and freedom, leap upwards, his white wings spread, resplendent in the sunshine of a distant future—the essentially Good and Beautiful of human existence.[23]

Pre-marital relations leave small room for the realization of such possibilities because of their insecurity. When through constant and intimate association with one another there has grown up between two individuals a true fellowship, then there is brought to the sexual act a funded experience of rich contact and association. Under such experience the sexual act becomes the highest compliment that the two individuals of different sex can pay to each other. When it is indulged in on any other basis it becomes a violation.

Christianity has looked with disapproval upon pre-marital unchastity because it violates its conception of the good life, the pure life. In order for such a position to be valid today, the good life has to be redefined. In the past it has been built upon the assumption that as a result of original sin, human nature is impure, bad, lustful in the foul sense. The flesh became synonymous with the evil. Hence the good life is to suppress and ignore the flesh. Today, as a result of the development of various sciences and an enlightened interpretation of Jesus and his teachings, we are recognizing the fact that to be human is to be good. The flesh instead of being the great destroyer of the Spirit is the great vehicle whereby the Spirit expresses itself. The good life is the life in which there is perfect harmony, perfect coordination, unity.

What effect must such an interpretation have upon the sexual life? The sexual life makes for impurity not because it asserts itself but it makes for impurity when it is given an abnormal and unnatural expression which undermines control and harmony within the individual. For the child this means that provisions must be made whereby the sexual energy will express itself along lines which do not injure the further development of the organism. For the youth it may mean early marriage and control after marriage. It means to recognize that

> sex intercourse is the great sacrament of life, he that eateth and drinketh unworthily eateth and drinketh his own damnation; but it may be the most beautiful sacrament between two souls that have no thought of children.[24]

It becomes necessary at this point to make a further statement with reference to what was said above about the re-interpretation of Jesus. The present emphasis in this particular is more moral and less theological. Jesus interpreted purity in terms of the heart, in terms of motives and desires. Such an interpretation becomes even more significant as we apply it to the realm of sexual relations. The pure man is not necessarily the man who has not had sexual intercourse with a woman, the pure woman is not necessarily the woman whose hymen is yet intact. It may be that such individuals are merely obeying the letter of the law, yet are carrying around with them hearts that have indulged in all of these things.[25] This throws a very penetrating light upon all auto-erotic practices yielding practically the same pleasurable sensations without the consequent risks.*

If two normal responsible unmarried adults, on the basis of spiritual unity, finding that from their point of view marriage for them must be postponed over a period of years, indulge in sexual intercourse as an expression of the sacred vow which between them is, such individuals may not be immoral. Spiritually they are one already; for spiritual companionship is the relation of personalities as a whole, and in the sex relation it is not just the intellect of the man that is to be mated with the intellect of the woman, but the integral man to the integral woman. And while this relationship does require the development of personality on either side (the manifestation of worth in terms of value), nevertheless it implies fundamentally, and before all and above all, respect for personality, and discarding of either by the other is contrary to such respect.† Instead of such an attitude encouraging promiscuity it would make it increasingly impossible. The good life is the unified life, the undivided life, and it has no particular reference to social approval or disapproval other than what is normally included in the conception of the undivided life.

---

*Studies made by K. Davis, Auto-Erotic Practices, Parts I and II.; and Ellis, Studies in the Psychology of Sex, Parts I and II.

†Adler, The Reconstruction of the Spiritual Ideal, p. 111.

With all the mistakes and the experience of the past from which to draw, with all the funded knowledge concerning life and the human organism at its disposal, with all the courage and frankness so characteristic of these times may we dare believe with Olive Schreiner that the history of sex with its great power and its beauty of holiness is still in its infancy.

finis.

BIBLIOGRAPHY

All American Conference on Venereal Diseases—Report 1924 (Pamphlet).

Adler, F. The Reconstruction of the Spiritual Ideal. New York: D. Appleton Co. 1924.

Annals Number 166—Social Work with Families, 1918.

Anthony, K. Feminism in Germany and Scandinavia. New York: Henry Holt & Co. 1915.

Biblical World, vol. 43, E. Bualing.

Blanchard, P. The Adolescent Girl. New York, Moffat Yard & Co. 1920.

Breckenridge, S. & Abbot, E. The Delinquent Child and the Home. New York: Russel Sage Foundation, 1912.

Bridgeport Vice Report, 1916.

Carpenter, E. Love's Coming of Age. London: Methuen & Co. 1924.

Carson, W. E. The Marriage Revolt. New York: Hearst International Library Co., 1915.

Calcord, J. C. Broken Homes. New York: Russel Sage Foundation, 1919.

Conference of Social Work, Kansas City. The Unmarried Mother. 1918.

Conference of Social Work. The Home. 1925.

Crawley, E. The Mystic Rose. New York: MacMillan Co. 1902.

Davenport, F. F. The Salvaging of American Girlhood. New York: Dutton & Co. 1924.

Davis, K. Study of Certain Auto-Erotic Practices, Vols. I and II. Pamphlets 1925.

Densmore, E. Sex Equality. New York: Funk & Wagnalls (no date).

Dewey, J. Human Nature and Conduct. New York: Henry Holt Co. 1922.

Ellis, H. E. Little Essays of Love and Virtue. New York: Doran Co. 1922.

   Men and Women. Chas. Scribners Sons, N.Y. 1914.

   Studies in the Psychology of Sex: The Evolution of Modesty; Sexual Inversion; Analysis of the Sexual Impulse; Sexual Selection in Man. Erotic Symbolism; Sex in Relation to Society. Philadelphia: F. A. Davis Co. 1924.

Finot, J. Problems of the Sexes. London: D. Nutt Co. 1913.

Foerester, F. W. Man and the Sex Problem. New York: F. A. Stokes Co. 1912.

Gallicnan, W. M. Psychology of Marriage. New York: F. A. Stokes Co. 1918.

Garden of Eden and the Sex Problem and advertising pamphlet.

Gwynne, W. Divorce in America. New York: MacMillan Co., 1925.

Hall, W. S. Sexual Knowledge. Philadelphia: J. C. Winston Co., 1916.

Hooker, Edith. Laws of Sex. Boston: R. G. Bodger, 1921.

Hefele, J. History of Christian Councils to A.D. 325. Edinburgh, 1872.

Herbert, S. Fundamentals of Sexual Ethics. New York: MacMillan Co., 1929.

Howard, W. L. Sex Problems in Work and Worry. New York: E. J. Clode, 1905.

Journal of Social Hygiene—Files.

Key et al. The Woman Question. New York: Boni Liveright & Co., 1918. The Renaissance of Motherhood. New York: Putnam's Sons, 1914.

Kneeland, G. Commercialized Prostitution in New York City. New York: Century Co., 1913.

Lancaster Vice Report, 1913.

Lay, W. A Plea for Monogamy. New York: Boni & Liveright, 1925.

Lea, H. C. History of Sacerdotal Celibacy. New York: MacMillan Co., 1907.

Lecky, W. E. History of European Morals. Vols. I–II. London, 1869.

Letourneau, C. H. The Evolution of Marriage. New York: Scribner's Sons, 1911.

Lindsey, B., and Wainwright Evans. The Revolt of Modern Youth. New York: Boni Liveright Co., 1925.

Mecklin, J. M. Introduction to Social Ethics. New York: Harcourt Brace Co., 1920.

Mill, John S. In Defense of Women. (Essay).

Nicene and Post-Nicene Fathers. 2nd series. Vol. X. St. Ambrose—De Virginibus; Jerome—Epistle 22.

Park, R. E., and H. A. Miller. Old World Traits Transplanted. New York: Harper & Brothers. 1921.

Parker, E. A. What Becomes of Unmarried Mothers? Pamphlet.

Parson, E. W. The Old Fashioned Woman. New York: G. P. Putnam's Sons, 1913. Fear and Conventionality. New York: G. P. Putnam's Sons, 1914.

Philadelphia Vice Report. 1913.

Popenoe, Paul. Modern Marriage. New York: Macmillan Co., 1925.

Rappaport, P. Looking Forward. Chicago: Chas. H. Kerr, 1913.

Red Plague—Transactions of Commonwealth Club of California, 1911.

Royden, A. M. Sex and Common Sense. London: Hurst and Blackett, 1922.

Schaff, P. History of Christian Church. Vol. V. New York: Scribner's Sons, 1907.

Schreiner, O. Woman and Labor. New York: F. A. Stokes Co., 1911.

Social Evil in Minneapolis. 1913.

Social Evil in Chicago. 1911.

Syracuse Vice Report. 1913.

The Bible.

Waertings, M. The Dominant Sex. London: Allen Unwin, 1923.

Wadia, A. Ethics of Feminism. New York: Geo. O. Doran Co., 1923.

Watermarck, E. The Origin and Development of the Moral Ideas. Vols. I & II. New York: Macmillan Co., 1906.

History of Human Marriage. Vols. I, II, III. London: Allerton Bock Co., 1922.

Xenophon's Memorabilia. III.2.

Young's Translation, Volume III. The Deipnosophists of Athenaeus; Lucretius Concerning Courtesans.

Magazine Articles.

Allen, A. W. Boys and Girls. Atlantic Monthly, 125:796–804, June, 1920.

Biblical World, Vol. 43, articles by Burling.

Carter, J. F., Jr. These wild young people. Atlantic Monthly, 126:301–4, Sept. 1920.

Deranged manners are reflected in the passing of the parlor. Literary Digest. 62:40, July 19, 1919.

Foglegle, W. I. Undangerous ages; some arresting discoveries concerning the ideals of our supposedly wild young people. Outlook, 130:379–80. March 8, 1922.

Frankau, G. Can the modern girl love? Forum, 68:917–22. Nov. 1922.

Gerould, K. F. Reflections of a Grundy cousin. <u>Atlantic Monthly,</u> 126: 157–63, August, 1920.

Gwynn, S. On being shocked. <u>Living Age,</u> 322:281–83, August 1924.

Lovejoy, O. R. Youth and some of its perils. <u>Missionary Review of the World,</u> 46:509, July, 1923.

Modern Youth and Its Ways. <u>Living Age,</u> 307:45–50, Oct. 2, 1920.

<u>Nineteenth Century and After,</u> Oct. 1918.

Society's need for Restating the sex Ethic. <u>The Shield,</u> H. Northcots Feb. 81–94, 1919.

Howard Thurman, B.D. Thesis, Rochester Theological Seminary (Colgate-Rochester Divinity School), 1926.

1. For an account of the new sexual attitudes, see Paula S. Fass, *The Damned and the Beautiful: American Youth in the 1920s* (New York: Oxford University Press, 1977).

2. In the nineteenth century, a number of prominent biblical scholars proposed that the Torah, the first five books of the Hebrew Bible, was composed from several distinct sources, later redacted to form the canonical text. The so-called "documentary hypothesis," associated with German scholar Julius Wellhausen (1844–1918), identified four main sources for the Torah. J, the Jahwist source (from the German spelling of "Yahweh") and E, the Elohist Source, were both named for the characteristic name used for God in the source. The J and E strands comprise the bulk of the books of Genesis and Exodus, as well as a portion of Numbers. D, the Deuteronomist Source, was the main source for Deuteronomy, while P, the Priestly Source, was the basis of Leviticus. By the time Thurman attended Rochester Theological Seminary, the documentary hypothesis would form the basis of his study of the history of the Old Testament.

3. Elohist Source.

4. Deuteronomist Source.

5. Priestly Source.

6. John Stuart Mill, *The Subjection of Women* (New York: Appleton, 1869).

7. Tennyson, "Ulysses," 1.14–15.

8. Herbert George Wells (1866–1946) was an English novelist, journalist, and historian who was most famous for his works of science fiction. Wells espoused a feminist critique of the social order in works including *Mankind in the Making* (London: Chapman & Hall, 1903) and *A Modern Utopia* (London: Collins, 1905). Bertrand Russell (1872–1970) was a British philosopher, logician, essayist, and social critic best known for his work in mathematical and analytic philosophy. In the 1910s and 1920s Russell wrote often against conventional sexual morality, and these writings culminated in his *Marriage and Morals* (New York: Liveright, 1929), published several years after Thurman's thesis.

9. Walter Lionel George (1882–1926) was an English writer born in Paris, France, and educated in Paris and Germany. He was the author of *A Bed of Roses* (New York: Modern Library, 1911), *The City of Light: A Novel of Modern Paris* (New York: Brentano's, 1912), *Caliban* (New York: Harper, 1920), *The Confession of Ursula Trent* (London: Chapman & Hall, 1921), and *One of the Guilty* (London: Chapman and Hall, 1923).

10. Charlotte Perkins Gilman (1860–1935), an American writer, economist, and lecturer, was a significant early theorist of the feminist movement. She authored over two hundred short stories and ten novels. Gilman's best-known treatise is *Women and Economics* (Boston: Small, Maynard, 1898), in which she attacked the division of social roles, arguing that

only economic independence could bring true freedom for women and equality between husbands and wives.

11. Ardeshir Ruttonji Wadia, *The Ethics of Feminism* (New York: Doran, 1923), chapter 1.

12. Olive Schreiner, *Women and Labor* (New York: Stokes, 1911), chapter 1. Schreiner argues that throughout human history, one of the chief manifestations in the material advancement of civilizations has been the parasitic woman, whereby "social conditions tend to rob her of all forms of active conscious social labor, and to reduce her, like the field-bug, to the passive exercise of her sex functions alone." 76–77.

13. Edith Sellers, "Boy and Girl War Products: Their Reconstruction," *Nineteenth Century and After* 84 (1918): 109.

14. Sybil Gotto, "The Changing Moral Standard," *Nineteenth Century and After* 84 (1918): 725.

15. The phrases *pain economy* and *pleasure economy* were introduced by the American economist Simon N. Patten (1852–1922) in *The Theory of Social Forces* (Philadelphia: American Academy of Political and Social Science, 1896).

16. Ellen Key (1849–1926) was a Swedish author, social critic, and a pioneer in the field of early childhood education. She argued that women are primarily fit for motherhood and deplored feminist claims to equality in the labor market. Her ideas regarding state child support influenced social legislation in several countries. Among her best-known works published in English are *Love and Marriage* (New York: Putnam's, 1911) and *The Century of the Child* (New York: Putnam's, ca. 1909).

17. George A. Coe, *What Ails Our Youth?* (New York: Scribner's, 1924), 3, 5, 7, 10–13.

18. Ben B. Lindsey and Wainwright Evans, *The Revolt of Modern Youth* (New York: Boni and Liveright, 1925). Judge Ben Lindsey (1869–1943) was in 1900 the founder in Denver, Colorado, of one of the first juvenile court systems in the United States. His best-known work in the area of sexual morality, published shortly after the completion of Thurman's thesis, is *The Companionate Marriage* (1927, also with Wainwright Evans), which advocated a new form of marriage, permitting young childless couples to divorce simply by mutual consent.

19. Lindsey and Evans, *Revolt of Modern Youth,* 90.

20. Coe, *What Ails Our Youth?*

21. Albert Moll, *The Sexual Life of a Child* (New York: Macmillan, 1912). Moll (1862–1939) was among the major founders and promoters of sex psychology alongside Havelock Ellis and Sigmund Freud. A physician from Berlin, he organized the International Society for Sex Research (1913) and the International Congress for Sex Research in Berlin (1926).

22. Havelock Ellis, *Little Essays of Love and Virtue* (New York: Doran, 1922), 50–51.

23. Schreiner, *Women and Labor,* 20–21.

24. Olive Schreiner, qtd in Havelock Ellis, *The Erotic Rights of Women and the Objects of Marriage: Two Essays* (New York: Women's, 1921), 69.

25. Most likely a reference to the Sermon on the Mount, which says, "Everyone who looks at a woman with lust has already committed adultery with her in his heart." Matt. 5:28.

CHAPTER IV

Early Career

↝ FROM MORDECAI WYATT JOHNSON
22 SEPTEMBER 1926
WASHINGTON, D.C.

Johnson congratulates Thurman on his marriage and requests a copy of Thurman's thesis from Rochester Theological Seminary. He also informs Thurman of his recent appointment as president of Howard University, raising the possibility of Thurman eventually joining him on the Howard faculty.

Rev. Howard W. Thurman
143 Groveland Street
Oberlin, Ohio

My dear Dr. Thurman:

While I was in Europe Mrs. Johnson forwarded me a fine letter from you. Somehow it has been mislaid. I remember one or two things, however.

First of all, let me congratulate you upon your marriage to so excellent a companion. You will be happy and immensely serviceable I know.

While I was in Berlin I had a talk with Mr. D~~iesmann~~{eissmann}[1] in which he mentioned his coming to Oberlin and the possibility that he might see and talk with you. I told him something about your record at Rochester. I was very eager to talk with him at length on New Testament questions, but there were so many around that I could not do this. I wish it were possible for me to hear his lectures at Oberlin.

The title of your thesis at Rochester interests me greatly. Is it possible for me to secure a copy of it, for even a few days? I see that you are driving directly to the heart of real questions.

As you already know, I have accepted the presidency of Howard University. This step was not taken without some very great pain on my part. It remains yet to be seen whether I shall be able to do a greater work here for the Master and his people. One of my hopes is that some day I may have you here with me. Does it ever occur to you that you would like to become a teacher in a first class theological seminary?

The Rev. Mr. Ketcham who is one of your white ministerial associates at Oberlin was with us in the Eddy Seminar.[2] You will find him very eager to cooperate with you.

With cordial regards and best wishes to Mrs. Thurman and yourself, I am Sincerely yours,
[*unsigned*]
KEB

TL. MWJ-DHU-MS: Box 178.

1. Adolf Deissmann (1866–1937) was a German biblical scholar and theologian who taught for many years at the University of Berlin. His works include *Bible Studies* (Edinburgh: Clark, 1909) and *The Religion of Jesus and the Faith of Paul* (New York: Doran, 1926).

2. The Eddy Seminars were tours of Britain and the Continent conducted by Sherwood Eddy (1871–1963) from 1921 through 1957. Eddy was a longtime leader of the YMCA and the Student Volunteer Movement and an advocate for interracial religious cooperation.

To Mordecai Wyatt Johnson
22 September 1926
Oberlin, Ohio

Thurman writes a congratulatory note to Johnson upon his recent appointment as the first black president of Howard University. Thurman's own emergence as a religious leader and public figure is also increasingly evident, and he may have been a candidate to replace Johnson as pastor of First Baptist Church of Charleston, West Virginia. However, the church remained without a pastor until the arrival of Vernon Johns in 1927.

My dear Mr. Johnson,

First of all let me send to you my personal felicitations—I greet you now as President Johnson. And you have my prayers and my generous interest!

How I wish I could see you for a good long talk.

Will it be possible for you to come this way at all during the winter? I am just out of Cleveland by 1½ hours. I wish the students here could hear you and what a joy it would be to have you in our home! Please let me know if there is the barest possibility.

I heard from Mr. Clark relative to the possibility of a visit to Charleston as a possible candidate.

Things are opening up in a way which is positively embarrassing. I spent all of August in Y.W. Conferences in Wisconsin (Lake Geneva). Next month I go to

State Teachers College of Iowa as college preacher and out in South Dakota on similar errand in November. I can leave my church only one Sunday in the month during the winter. I thank God for it all. And you must have your share too—because of what your life means to me.

I know you are busy but will you drop me a line sometime?

My wife joins me in generous wishes for your new work.

Very sincerely yours,

[*signed*] Howard Thurman

President M. W. Johnson
Washington, D.C.

ALS. MWJ-DHU-MS: Box 178.

 "FINDING GOD"

1927

"Finding God" appeared in 1927 as a chapter in Religion on the Campus, *a collection of essays presented at the annual National Student Conference of the YMCA and YWCA at Lake Geneva, Wisconsin.[1] This article strikes a characteristic theme that would appear in many of Thurman's writings in the late 1920s that there is no division between God and human experience, and to partake of the unity of God would lead men and women into community with one another.*

> I am tired of sailing my little boat,
> Far inside the harbor bar;
> I want to go out where the big ships float,
> Out on the deep where the great ones are.
> And should my frail craft prove too slight
> For storms that sweep those billows o'er,
> I'd rather go down in the stirring fight
> Than drowse to death by the sheltered shore.[2]

Students of this generation are protesting in telling fashion against the bondage of formulae. Yet almost in the same breath there comes a series of questions. Tell me exactly how I can find it. Outline for me the steps. Point out for me the way along which I must go if I may find that for which my heart hungers.

And out of the heart of life I seem to hear a voice which says, "No one can give to you the answer to your questions, but you must live into that answer."

As for myself, I seem to be as a child who walks along the seashore, admiring the pretty pebbles scattered here and there, while the vast ocean of truth stretches out before him, boundless and unexplored. I seem to catch up in my own experience the words of Tennyson, "But what am I, an infant crying in the night, an infant crying for the light, with no language but a cry."[3]

What I shall say to you, therefore, this morning is but a confession of faith and a sense of the direction toward which when I am not myself I seem to go.

The quest for fulfilment is perhaps the most real quest in all the world.

When the Latin poet Horace[4] says that he was not able to sleep because of the pressure of unwritten poetry; when Bunyan tells us in his prologue that he had to put aside the work that he was doing on some sermons and other serious tracts in order to write "Pilgrim's Progress"; when Walter Hampden[5] says that he had to play Hamlet in order to keep a contract with his soul; when a reviewer writes about a concert which Paderewski[6] gave after his five years' dip into politics, "I am confident that I am not listening to a musician who is attempting to play a tune, but I am in the presence of a great catholic spirit which somehow is trying to express itself in a strange, mighty combination of rhythm and tone"; when another critic writing about Roland Hayes[7] says, "When I hear him sing, I know that I am sitting in the presence of one who sings because he must"; when Ulysses says, "I am a part of all that I have met, yet all experience is an arch where through gleams that untravailed world, whose margin fades forever and forever as I move";[8] when the Apostle Paul says, "Woe is me if I preach not the gospel";[9] or when Jesus of Nazareth on that memorable morning in Palestine says, "The spirit of the Lord is upon me because He has anointed me to preach the gospel to the poor";[10] all of these, each in his own way, is expressing the inner urge which drives him on, and he has no choice but to go, and it may be that the quest for fulfilment is the quest for God; and it may be when I have found that for which my heart hungers, I have found Him.

We have listened from this platform to words which point out essentially the ground or the affirmation which Jesus of Nazareth made about God. We have heard it affirmed that it was His faith and the faith of the speakers, that at the heart of this universe there is personality which is at once the source of life and the goal of life. If that affirmation is valid, then a series of things must follow therefrom, and it is along the line of these that I think the quest for fulfilment, the quest of God, drives one.

First of all, if God is the source of all of life, if out from Him emanate all creation, then there must be an underlying unity for all of them, and wherever one digs in honestly, living up to the limit of the light that one has at the particular time, one does make contact with that unity.

Last Christmas morning I sat before a fire listening to a man from Calcutta, India, tell me a very, very strange but fascinating story. He has been in America fifty-seven years. The first Christmas that he spent in this country he lived at the home of the president of one of the large railroads in America. A few days before this man had thrown the Christmas tree and the decorations over the fence into an alley, and on this particular day about which my friend was talking, some ragged boys in the street had crept up the alley to get the tree and the decorations. As my friend from India looked out at them, he said something happened to him, something like a flash of blinding light, and he saw very clearly what he would have to do if he remained in America another Christmas.

Without saying anything about it, he made his plans, and the next Christmas in the basement of this man's house he had a Christmas tree, and all the ragged boys around in that community were brought in; and for twenty-two years in that city in Texas where he lived, he had this tree.

He has been living in my village now for twenty-five years and every year he has had his tree for the boys in the community who would not have a tree. Last Saturday there were thirty-two of them, six of whom had parents who had once come to this tree to receive gifts, the only gifts that were theirs. As he talked to me about it, he said, "I am not particularly a religious man, but I have learned how to live, and I have found that life for me is conditioned by the kind of life that the boys in this community have, and to me God is very real."

If there is the unity of which we are thinking, the next thing which comes out of that is an essential kinship of all the creations of all the people in the world, and if that kinship is true, is genuine, then I can never be the kind of person that I ought to be until everybody else is the kind of person that everybody else ought to be. When Jesus of Nazareth says, "I came to seek and to save the lost,"[11] He is not only thinking about the need that a certain group of people will have for the kind of life which is his, but he is also reminded of the fact that not only do the lost need him but he needs the lost, and He will never be what He ought to be until they are what they ought to be. It seems to me that what the church tries to say about salvation is that the lost, whoever they are, need to become sensitive to His spirit, yes, but more than that, God needs them, and God will never be what He hungers to be in His world until these people are what they ought to be.

For better or for worse I am tied by the fact of the source of life to all the rest of the people in the world. There is something that each one has to say to me that will make of my life what it cannot be unless that person says it. So I go to the mission field not so much because I am sure that I have something necessarily to give to the person beyond the waters, something so high and so holy, something so different from that which he has, but I go because he has something for me that I must have if I am to be what I ought to be. I put up hospitals for him, I establish training schools for him, I build colleges for him, in order that I may release his bonds and put him in a position to give me the thing that I must have in the world.

If I need everyone else, then by the same process I must be sensitive to the needs of other people.

"O God," I cried, "Why may I not forget?
These halt and hurt in life's hard battle
    Throng me yet.
Am I their keeper? Am I to suffer for their sin?
Would that my eyes had never opened then!"
And the thorn-crowned and patient one replied,
"They thronged me too, I too have seen."

"Thy other children go at will," I said, protesting still,
"They go unheeding. But these sick, these sad, these blind and
    orphaned,
Yea, those that sin, drag at my heart.
Why is it? Let me rest, Lord. I have tried!"
He turned and looked at me, "But I have died."

"O God, I brought not forth these hosts of needy creatures,
    struggling, tempest-tossed;
They are not mine."
He looked at them the look of one divine.
He turned and looked at me, "But they are mine."
"O God," I said, "I understand at last.
    Forgive me,
And I will henceforth bond-slave be
To thy weakest, vilest ones,
    I will not more be free."
He smiled and said, "It is for me."[12]

Sensitiveness to the needs of others. Human need is infinite, but when I respond to it to the limit of my power and become thereby painfully conscious of my own inadequacy, I seem to send my soul through the air and the sky and the sea in quest of an infinite energy that I may release for an infinite task.

Finding God, finding fulfilment in a world like this, I must have demands within myself for the kind of energy that God releases, and that energy must be with reference to a need which calls it forth and which will not let me rest until I find it. This is what Jesus is thinking about, I believe, when He says, "You are to be congratulated if you feel a deep sense of moral and spiritual inadequacy, for yours is the kingdom, the rule, the presence of God."[13] Jesus stands with patient and quiet smile at the gates of the twentieth century, waiting till this lagging student generation catch up with him. Then he will lead the tired and the famishing into his city of love.

    Francis P. Miller, ed., *Religion on the Campus: Report of the National
Student Conference, Milwaukee, December 28, 1926 to January 1, 1927*
        (New York: Association Press, 1927), 48–52.

1. Francis P. Miller, ed., *Religion on the Campus: Report of the National Student Conference, Milwaukee, December 28, 1926 to January 1, 1927* (New York: Association Press, 1927), 48–52.

2. Daisy Rinehart, "The Call of the Open Sea," in *Vagrant Verse,* ed. John C. Lebens (St. Louis, Mo.: Avalon, 1926), 28–29.

3. From Tennyson, *In Memoriam*, Canto 54, verse 5.

4. This is Quintus Horatius Flaccus, known in English as Horace (65–8 B.C.).

5. Walter Hampden (1879–1955) was one of the leading dramatic and Shakespearian actors of his time. In his autobiography, Thurman states that during his years at Rochester Theological Seminary (RTS), he took trips to New York City where "I managed to see Walter Hampden in the entire Shakespeare repertoire." *WHAH,* 53. During Thurman's RTS years Hampden appeared on Broadway in the title parts of *Othello* (1925), *Hamlet* (1925), and *The Merchant of Venice* (1926).

6. The Polish pianist Ignace Jan Paderewski (1860–1941) was one of the most popular classical musicians of his era, especially in the United States. From 1919 to 1922, he served the newly independent nation of Poland in a number of capacities, including prime minister and ambassador to the League of Nations. He resumed his concert career in 1923.

7. The tenor Roland Hayes (1877–1977) was the first African American concert performer to enjoy an international career. Born in Curryville, Georgia, after attending Fisk University and a stint with the Fisk Jubilee Singers, he relocated to the Boston area in the mid-1910s.

8. From Tennyson, *Ulysses,* lines 18–21. In the original:

> I am a part of all that I have met;
> Yet all experience is an arch wherethro'
> Gleams that untravell'd world, whose margin fades
> For ever and for ever when I move.

9. 1 Cor. 9:16.

10. Luke 4:18.

11. Luke 19:10, "For the son of man came to seek and to save what was lost."

12. Lucy Rider Meyer, "The Burden" (1904). Lucy Rider Meyer (1849–1922) was an American social worker, educator, poet, hymnist, and missionary in the Methodist church. Meyer was a forerunner of the deaconess movement in the Methodist Church. She served as principal of the Troy (Methodist) Conference Academy in Poultney, Vermont, and as professor of chemistry at McKendree College in Illinois. In 1885, she cofounded with her husband Josiah S. Meyer, who was a Methodist Episcopalian minister, the Chicago Training School for City, Home and Foreign Missions in Chicago (which later became Garrett Theological Seminary), where she served as principal until 1917.

13. Matt. 5.

🐦 FROM MORDECAI WYATT JOHNSON
2 APRIL 1927
WASHINGTON, D.C.

Even as Thurman is gaining a reputation for innovative and interracial worship experiences at Oberlin, he maintains ties with his black Baptist heritage. Two major groups affiliated with the National Baptist Convention, the largest black denomination in the country, are interested in inviting Thurman to speak. Johnson encourages him to accept the engagements.

Rev. Howard Thurman
143 Groveland Street
Oberlin, Ohio

My dear Mr. Thurman:

I have recently had two distinguished visitors at my office, both of whom are anxious to secure your services in connection with national meetings of the Baptist Denomination. The first of them was the Reverend Mr. Jernagin,[1] President of the B.Y.P.U.[2] and Sunday School Convention. This convention meets in Nashville, Tennessee in June. He wishes you to be one of the principal speakers at that meeting.

The second visitor was Miss Nannie H. Burroughs, Secretary of the National Woman's Baptist Convention.[3] Miss Burroughs is hoping to be able to have a profound spirit of worship developed at the meeting of the Woman's Convention in connection with the National Baptist Convention in Detroit in September. She wishes you to conduct a morning service of worship every morning during the Convention. She will write you indicating the nature of the service, the honorarium, etc. I greatly hope that you may find it possible to accept both of these engagements. Both of these bodies are in need of such spiritual vision and understanding of worship as you are able to give. I covet for them your services.

With cordial regards and best wishes, I am
Sincerely yours,
[*unsigned*]
Mordecai W. Johnson

TLc. MWJ-DHU-MS: Box 178.

1. Reverend William Henry Jernagin (1869–1958), a native of Mississippi, was educated at Meridian Academy, from which he received an honorary DD degree. He taught in Mississippi public schools, was licensed to preach at Bush Fork Baptist Church in 1890, and was ordained in 1892. Jernagin organized the Young People's Christian Education Congress of Mississippi in 1902, was for a time the president of the National Race Congress of

America, and served as the pastor of Mount Carmel Baptist Church of Washington, D.C., from 1912 to 1950.

2. BYPU is the acronym for Baptist Young People's Union.

3. Nannie Helen Burroughs (1879–1961) was a prominent religious leader, educator, and social activist. In 1909, she founded the National Training School for Women and Girls in Washington, D.C., a leading educational institution for Negro girls in the early twentieth century, which Sue Bailey Thurman attended. In 1966, the school's name was changed to the Nannie Helen Burroughs School, and it remains in existence. One of the founding members of the Women's Convention Auxiliary to the National Baptist Convention in 1900, Burroughs served as corresponding secretary for forty-eight years and as president from 1948 until her death.

✎ KATIE THURMAN TO LUCY TAPLEY
9 APRIL 1927
OBERLIN, OHIO

Katie Thurman writes to Spelman President Lucy Tapley of her new role in Oberlin and her continuing health problems.

Dear Miss Tapley:

I am very happy to have a part in Founder's Day efforts of this year.[1] I shall hope as the years go by to increase my pledge of five dollars to one more substantial and more in keeping with my desire to share with Spelman—even as I have received.

This has been a year of many adjustments for me.—A leftover condition of my illness of two years ago has made it difficult for me to become acclimated to conditions in Oberlin. Thus it has been difficult for me to enter whole heartedly into the new responsibilities of home-making and the pastorate. With the coming of the warm weather, however, I begin to feel the old "go." I am confident that the greatest struggle for my health is passed.

I hope that I may be able to visit you before the year is over. There are many experiences which I would like to share with you, and it will be great just to come back to witness the marvelous advancements.

With kindest personal regards to you and Miss Lamson,[2]

Lovingly yours

[*signed*] Katie K.—T.

ALcS. DAF-GAS.

1. This annual event, celebrating the founding of Spelman and cofounders Harriet E. Giles and Sophia B. Packard, included an alumnae fundraising effort.

2. Edna Emma Lamson, dean of the college.

꩜ To Mordecai Wyatt Johnson
20 September 1927
Oberlin, Ohio

Thurman expresses strong disillusionment with the corruption of society, which he writes can only be challenged effectively by a "grand swell of spiritual energy." He is equally troubled by Christianity's seeming inability to establish an effective social witness. His mention of having read Katherine Mayo's Mother India *is the earliest letter in the collection that indicates his interest in the social and political conditions of India.*

My dear Mr. Johnson:

I was very glad to get your letter.

Please do not forget to send me a copy of your June address.

For several days now I have been greatly in need of some good fellowship with you. I have been working on this problem: Why is it that the hundreds of students who have been sent out from the "great heights" of our various conferences during the last decade have carried into their common tasks so little of the quality of the New Society? In other words what happens to them as well as to countless others who at times are greatly exercised about <u>being</u> Christian in the early days? (This is not stated clearly but you see it.) In attempting to grapple with this problem I have been working thru 4 very significant volumes—"The Tragedy of Waste," Chase; "Your Money's Worth," Chase & Schlink; two volumes from the American Medical Ass. Press—"Nostrums and Quackery." When I finished these I read Upton Sinclair's "Oil."[1] After going thru this material I have a growing conviction that we are fed and clothed by a vast system built upon deceit and adulteration. And it almost seems futile to talk to people about sincerity, about purity about honesty when they are eating, seeing, reacting to a mighty array of lies! Of course this is not the whole story. I believe with all my heart that our task is twofold—seek how ~~to~~ we may ~~plumb the deep of our spirit~~ release to the full our greatest spiritual powers, that there may be such a grand swell of spiritual ~~power~~{energy} that existing systems will be upset from sheer dynamic—and make whatever temporary adjustments as may prove helpful in relieving intolerable situations until there is a genuine uprooting. But more of this when I see you—the new kind of education has a very "Jesus" contribution to make to this whole problem.

The second thing that is giving me much thought is the question of Church membership. This may be a very premature judgment but it is a fact of my thinking and reflection just now: There <u>seems</u> to be something about joining a church which deprives an individual of the keen obligation to be {exercised} increasingly about being Christian. Those in my church who <u>seem so to be</u> are those who apparently have transcended the church. Perhaps ~~this~~ Jesus was wisest when he rested his case with the "contagious spirit" rather than a scheme or plan of salvation.

Forgive me if I weary you with my ranting.

I go South to Talladega for a week in late December or early January—my plan is to come by Washington to see you and Mrs. Johnson.

The work here's doing very well.

Have you read May's "Mother India"?[2]

Mrs. Thurman joins me in best wishes to you and Mrs. Johnson.

Very truly yours

[*signed*] Howard Thurman

ALcS. MWJ-DHU-MS: Box 178.

1. Two themes predominate in Thurman's reading list: (1) exposure of the general public to the often fraudulent nature of government and corporate entities and (2) a call for the public to awaken and act. Thurman's readings are Stuart Chase, *The Tragedy of Waste* (New York: Macmillan, 1925), Stuart Chase and F. J. Schlink, *Your Money's Worth: A Study in the Waste of the Consumer's Dollar* (New York: Macmillan, 1927), Arthur Joseph Camp, *Nostrum and Quackery: Articles on the Nostrum Evil and Quackery and Reprinted from the American Medical Association Press* (Chicago: Press of the American Medical Association, 1912–36), and Upton Sinclair, *Oil! A Novel* (New York: Boni, 1927). Thurman states that he used Camp's *Nostrum and Quackery* in his first sermon series.

2. Katherine Mayo's examination of social conditions in India, while paternalistic and controversial, remained broadly authoritative for years to come. See Mayo, *Mother India* (New York: Harcourt, Brace, 1927).

✐ "HIGHER EDUCATION AND RELIGION"
NOVEMBER 1927

In the following article, published in the Home Mission College Review,[1] *Thurman reflects on the role of apocalyptic black religion in forming the critical consciousness of black college students and questions the effectiveness of otherworldly religion in enabling intelligent black youth to grow into spiritual maturity. Here, the acquisition of higher education becomes a source of conflict and racial bitterness in young people who have been taught to seek their rewards in the life after death. At the same time, however, Thurman criticizes the belief that the goal of black education should be the attainment of "economic power and control." Viewing materialism as a religion in its own right, he characterizes it as poisonous for the African American community. This article is remarkable for Thurman's emphasis on salvific themes in black culture and for his insistence that materialistic culture cannot "save" troubled black humanity.*

Even the most superficial observer of the youth of our day finds that perhaps the most significant issue with which we are faced is that of arriving at some sort of helpful relationship between young minds and the claims of religion. What I shall say in this paper is not altogether true of any particular individual but is true in varying degrees of most of the youth of our time. Some one may suggest that only a few are thoughtful. That may be true. May it not be, however, that the thoughtful few will determine, for the most part, our controlling religious concepts for to-morrow?

I

We have as our heritage to-day a religion which is pretty largely apocalyptic. The procession of early Negro preachers found themselves leading their hosts through a wilderness of suffering, oppression, and cruelty. The odds appeared to be so overwhelmingly against them that there was well nigh nothing in the contemporary situation worthy of salvaging. Therefore, with marvelous insight, these prophets of patience turned their attention to the hope beyond this world and found great refuge in the promises of the Holy Book. Here we find apocalypticism at its best. God is the Real, the present world can give no peace. The slave who died in Christ would rise to "shout all over God's heaven."[2]

When such a view is carried to an extreme, as in times of great agony, at least two weaknesses reveal themselves in all of their ugliness and terror. In the first place such a view is characterized by a lack of confidence in man's ability to achieve and to develop.

> So runs my dream; but what am I?
> An infant crying in the night;
> An infant crying for the light,
> And with no language but a cry.[3]

With reference to an outlook on life, such a view develops a sense of insignificance and inferiority which may be easily confused with a certain kind of humility or immature piety.[4] It deprives individuals of the necessity of learning how to live, how to grow, and how to be at home in this world. It makes one less interested in changing conditions and in seeing God as One who is at work making the kingdoms of this world to become His Kingdom.

In the second place, such a view has encouraged the idea that there is a barrier between life and religion. Of course, among all Christians in all ages this view has been rather prevalent. There are certain things that are regarded as religious, having to do with God; and other things that are viewed as life; and it is felt that never the twain do meet. The manifestations of religion under such circumstances tend to be more theological than ethical. A fellow student in college clarified the issue rather successfully upon being asked how could he harmonize his immoral political tactics with his Christian life. He said, "When I get ready to play politics I put my religion in my trunk." Carried to extreme the result is a kind of "spiritual cockiness." In these two paragraphs we are dealing with what may be termed a double shield: one side reveals a sense of inferiority as life is squarely faced; the other reveals a sense of superiority as things religious are in question. Interestingly enough, Jesus found more of the symptoms of religion among the unwashed sinners of his day than among the rank and file of the professedly religious.

I shall mention in passing at least two very significant contributions which the apocalyptic faith made to our religious life.

1. It made for the development of creative and vicarious imagination under the ægis of religious symbolism.
2. Under the powerful influence of religious zeal and emotion, it made bearable an otherwise unbearable series of experiences without attempting to justify them.

II

Higher education, with its new view of the world and of life, has had and is now having a very marked effect upon our youth who have been brought up in the kind of religious atmosphere about which we have been talking. It has taken a number of years for higher education to make its impact upon the religious life of our youth. The young people themselves have been so occupied with the needs of their own people and how these needs may be met that there has been little time for rationalizing their religious outlook. Further, religion has been so much a part of the immediate life of the group that it has been very difficult to look at it objectively.

What is there in higher education that is producing a conflict in the minds of our youth? In the first place there is available a new body of factual materials. To cite a few examples: A careful and critical study of history would take slavery out of the realm of providence and discover its place amid the play of social forces and economic laws. Or, the physical world is very old and man's stay upon the earth is relatively short to date. This means that man is not a finished product but is a growing developing creature, and "it does not yet appear what he shall be."[5] Or, the increase in knowledge has made for a new sense of the worth and significance of the individual Negro. He has demonstrated his ability to master knowledge. Along with this awakening has come a profound group consciousness which would have been inevitable under any circumstance. Often this consciousness results in profound bitterness and cynicism because of the injustice of the present order, and there is little left of the apocalyptic hope to comfort and to bless. Many are saying that the group has been given a kind of religion that points from this world while their neighbors have secured more than a gentleman's share of this world's goods.

Therefore, in this condition, our youth are liable to be swept away by the religion of materialism which at present finds so many devotees in American life. Stated in baldest terms, its creed is: No sin, no future life, no sacredness of life, nothing but the survival of the fittest and every man for himself. It operates upon the theory that human life is cheap and that the most permanent thing in this world is economic power and control. This seems to express itself in the wild scramble of churches for dollars with which to erect temples, drives for greater economic security, and the like. Is the purpose of life

> To turn out typewriters,
> To invent a new breakfast food,
> To devise a dance that was never danced until now,
> To urge a new sanitation, and a swifter automobile—
> Have the life-surging heavens no business but this?[6]

The other day I was talking with the head of the department of sociology in a very influential college in the Middle West. After discussing at length the problem of economic control and its significance for the freedom of thought and speech, he gave me some advice for my own group. "The thing that you need to tell young Negroes is to get money. They must learn to speak the language of economic power and control, that is, the language of the American white man generally." "But," said I, "are you sure that with economic control in our hands we shall act any differently from the way the people act about whom you have been talking? The only people who are going to save our civilization, if saved it can be or ought to be, are those who have learned to *live* so as to reveal the superiority of the human spirit to the domination of things. Our experience has taught us that. But we are rapidly forgetting it as we embrace the religion of materialism, a religion that has already made you drunk with power and might. Your soul is dying, being crowded out of breathing space. We are yet sensitive, we are yet alive; but your suggestion means death, and that speedily."

III

What then is to be done if a helpful relationship between our growing young minds and the claims of religion is to be developed? I make four suggestions in as many sentences.

1. We must refuse to be caught in the current demand for things and find our security in the reality of God and the spiritual tasks to which He has set our hands.

2. We must put vast faith in the contagion of the spirit of Jesus rather than in the building of organizations to perpetuate his spirit.

3. We must seek to demolish the artificial barrier between religion and life.

4. We must not allow any phase of human knowledge to remain outside of our province, but must provide a creative synthesis, in the light of which all the facts of science or what not, may be viewed.[7]

Home Mission College Review (November 1927).

1. Edited by Benjamin Brawley, this bimonthly journal was sponsored by the American Baptist Home Mission Society (ABHMS) and the Women's American Baptist Home Mission Society. Morehouse and Spelman were among the ten ABHMS-supported Negro colleges and universities in the south, and together the schools produced *Home Mission College Review,* whose central offices were at Shaw University in Raleigh, North Carolina.

2. The phrase *shout all over God's heaven* is from the Negro spiritual "Heab'n, Heab'n." See "The Message of the Spirituals," October 1928, printed in the current volume.

3. Tennyson, *In Memoriam,* canto 54, stanza 5.

4. See "The Perils of Immature Piety," May 1925, printed in the current volume.

5. I John 3:2.

6. James Oppenheim, "As to Being Alone," in *Songs for the New Age* (New York: Century, 1914), 7.

7. For elaboration of these themes, see "The Task of the Negro Ministry," 1928, printed in the current volume.

🖎 LESTER A. WALTON, "NEGRO MINISTER FILLS PULPIT AT VASSAR: REV. DR. HOWARD THURSTON IS FIRST OF HIS RACE TO DO SO"
1 APRIL 1928
NEW YORK, N.Y.

Thurman's 12 March 1928, sermon at Vassar College was widely covered in the press. This account was published in the New York World. *The reporter, Lester A. Walton,[1] incorrectly identifies Thurman as Thurston[2] and, more than likely, was not present to hear the address but rather drew on other published articles about it. Nonetheless, Walton captures the historic significance of the event and the content of Thurman's address. Thurman's refusal to be typecast in his Vassar appearance is perhaps indicated by his lack of attention to specifically racial questions, while in lauding the late socialist Eugene V. Debs to his wealthy listeners, he made clear his refusal to temporize with any audience. Thurman, who preached at Vassar that moral action cannot be divorced from religious grounding, later reworked this sermon on Jeremiah 17:6–8 for publication in 1932 under the title "Barren or Fruitful?" (in chapter V of the current volume). Thurman had previously spoken on this topic at the Syracuse University Chapel, likely in October 1925, and at the Iowa State Teachers College in October 1926.*

Dr. Henry Noble MacCracken,[3] President of Vassar College, is known as an uncompromising foe of intolerance. He enjoys a reputation for consistency in that he practices what he preaches.

His latest public slap at bigotry and illiberality was in having Rev. Howard Thurston, a Negro minister of Oberlin, O., fill the pulpit at Sunday morning services.

The spectacle of a Negro preaching the Word of God to members of the faculty and the students of Vassar was unprecedented. It had never happened before in the sixty-seven years of the institution's history.

Nowadays the appearance of Negro men and women speakers at leading colleges and universities is not unusual. They are usually invited to discuss some phase of the race question. But the Rev. Howard Thurston went to Poughkeepsie to talk on theology and not racial progress, disfranchisement, Jim Crowism or the migration.

The Rev. Dr. Thurston, in his early thirties, is a graduate of Morehouse College, Atlanta. Two years ago, after finishing the Theological Department at Rochester University, he was called to the pastorate of the Zion Baptist Church, Oberlin. He is black and of unmixed blood, is six feet tall and weighs nearly 200 pounds.[4]

Last summer Dr. MacCracken attended the Negro Baptist Convention[5] at Detroit and heard the Rev. Dr. Thurston preach a sermon that deeply stirred a large audience.[6] It was delivered with dignity, yet forcefully and eloquently. The President of Vassar made up his mind he would have the young Negro minister speak at chapel when the first opportunity presented itself.

At Vassar the Rev. Dr. Thurston took his text from Jeremiah, chapter 17. He contrasted people living on barren ground and who inhabit the parched places in the wilderness with those living like a tree planted by the waters.

In alluding to the characteristics of the former or those who do not live with God, the speaker said they were not bad and may be good. He quoted Prof. Rauschenbusch, who said, "Some people are very good but not good enough to disturb the devil."

People in this category are careful observers of the moral teachings of Jesus Christ but not of the religious teachings, it was asserted. They have a high grade of intolerance. As an illustration the Rev. Dr. Thurston cited the parable of the Pharisee and the publican—the former who would let God know how good he was and who left the temple the same as he entered, while the latter was forgiven.

The promise of those who live apart from God is built on a false sense of security, the speaker pointed out. He recited the parable of the young man who went to Jesus asking for the secret life eternal. He had broken all the commandments. Jesus replied that since he had been taking chances with his security he could also take chances with Him.[7]

Those living like a tree planted by the waters have a personal dedication and devotion to things and deeds and look upon life not from their own level but from a higher level. They see God first and all life becomes clear.

Such people have an almighty affection which is not a cheap, blind sentiment, but a certain intelligent and undisturbed mind. For perfect love is perfect knowledge. Reference was made to the mother who, because of her love for her child, has understanding knowledge of him.[8]

The speaker recited the parable of the woman taken in adultery being brought before Jesus, who took her as she was and treated her as what she ought to be.[9] He said people living with God have an unaffecting sympathy, and told of a man who was in prison with Eugene V. Debs, as having said the late Socialist leader was "the only Christ I ever saw."[10]

"Disregarding political or religious opinions, one must realize there was something to Eugene V. Debs," he declared.

Commenting further on people living like a tree planted by the waters, the Rev. Dr. Thurston said they showed a willingness to suffer in order to make the unideal situation ideal. They have a simple trust in God.

New York World, April 1, 1928.

1. Lester A. Walton (1881–1965) was one of the leading African American journalists of his era and a longtime managing editor of *New York Age.* Walton became the first black journalist hired by a major New York City newspaper when he joined the *New York World* in the 1920s. From 1935 to 1945, he served as a United States minister to Liberia.

2. Walton might have confused Thurman with Howard Thurston (1869–1936), a famous magician and stage illusionist.

3. Henry Noble MacCracken (1880–1970), president of Vassar College from 1915 to 1946, was one of the leading liberal educators of his generation, a strong supporter of women's suffrage, and of interracial and interreligious dialogue and cooperation.

4. Though Thurman had an imposing pulpit presence, he was only five feet eight in height.

5. The National Baptist Convention USA, Inc.

6. Thurman spoke on "The Inner Life" in Detroit on 9 September 1927. *Journal of the Twenty-seventh Annual Session of the Women's Convention Auxiliary to the National Baptist Convention Held with the Second Baptist Church, Detroit, Michigan, September 7–13, 1927* (Nashville, Tenn.: Sunday School Publishing Board, 1927), 327.

7. Variations of this parable appear in Matt. 19:16–30, Mark 10:17–31, Luke 10:25, and Luke 18:18–27.

8. This is likely a reference to one of Thurman's favorite passages from Olive Schreiner's *From Man to Man; or Perhaps Only . . .* (New York: Harper, 1927), 158.

9. John 8:3–11.

10. Eugene V. Debs (1855–1926), a five-time Socialist Party candidate for president, was the leading figure in the American socialist movement in the first two decades of the twentieth century. Arrested for sedition in 1918, he garnered almost a million votes in his final presidential bid in 1920 while under federal incarceration. The personal appeal of Debs, whose speeches were often laced with Christian imagery and who had acquired the image of a saintly, "Christ-like" figure, extended far beyond the ranks of the committed socialists.

⁊ To Mordecai Wyatt Johnson
23 May 1928
Oberlin, Ohio

Because of Katie's declining health, Thurman chooses not to accept Johnson's offer of a faculty position at Howard University's School of Religion in the fall of 1928. Instead, he accepts a joint appointment at Morehouse and Spelman colleges in Atlanta in order to be nearer to the Kelley family home in LaGrange, Georgia, where Katie was recuperating with their daughter, Olive.

My dear Mr. Johnson

After going thru the whole matter of coming to Howard next year I have decided against it. Until we are surer of Mrs. Thurman's health I must ~~ren~~ work either in Atlanta or nearer there than Washington. For the immediate present I shall accept and offer to attempt to develop the spiritual tone of the students at Spelman and Morehouse. My plan is to begin there in the fall and work until December or January and then study for the rest of the year, providing Mrs. Thurman's health permits. I tell you the details of my plans because first of all you are my friend.

Sometime I do want to come to Howard providing you remain there. Will you keep that in mind?

I thank you for your quiet confidence in me. One of the greatest personal favors that life has given me came the day you first touched my life and shot it thru with a strange new glory. Thank you—thank God.

Let me hear from you.

Please remember me to the entire family.

Very truly yours
[*signed*] Howard Thurman

ALS. MWJ-DHU-MS: Box 178.

⁊ Katie Thurman to Florence M. Read
18 July 1928
Oberlin, Ohio

Before the Thurmans move to Atlanta, Katie writes to Florence Read, who succeeded Lucy Tapley as president of Spelman, and expresses buoyant optimism about her health and her new role as a mother.

Dear Miss Read:[1]

I am sending a wee-wee line to report of the substantial gains which are coming to me during these days of resting and waiting.—The old strength returns in great surges,—it almost frightens me sometimes.—My general condition is favorable,—most favorable; and the building process goes on!

Mr. Thurman says so often in his "Love Series" that the little things done <u>out</u> of the line of conventional duties,—the small favors which folks don't <u>have</u> to do— these count most,—make the lasting impression. And that is what I want to say to you in appreciation.—Most of all I am grateful for the flowers, the muse (?), the frequent little visits and the <u>smiles</u>—'specially the smiles! You have surely tied the Thurmans to you, forever.

Baby Olive is a great benediction. In so many ways we are growing together these days.

I am <u>so</u> happy for all that is coming to our Spelman.

Love to you and to the dear Miss Carpenter.

[*signed*] Kate Thurman.

ALcS. DAF-GAS.

1. Florence Matilda Read (1886–1973) was born in Delevan, New York. A Mount Holyoke graduate (1909), she served as president of Spelman College from 1927 to 1953. She also served as secretary of Atlanta University from 1929 to 1953 and as acting president of Atlanta University from 1936 to 1937 during the interim period between the death of John Hope and the election of his successor. Read was the last white president of Spelman and one of the last white presidents of any prominent black college. Thurman in his autobiography was unusually outspoken in his criticism of what he felt was Read's condescension toward blacks and black education. *WHAH*, 79–80.

"THE MESSAGE OF THE SPIRITUALS"
OCTOBER 1928

Probably the most significant legacy of the black church for Thurman was the Negro spirituals, which were a touchstone of his faith throughout his career. As early as 1925 Thurman spoke to a church audience on the topic. His first extended essay on the spirituals appeared in the Spelman College alumnae magazine, Spelman Messenger, *in the fall of 1928. This was an abstract, of his own devising, of five chapel talks he delivered the week of 15–19 October 1928, each devoted to a different spiritual. Many of Thurman's readings of the spirituals were incorporated into his later writings on the subject, especially his article* "Religious Ideas in Negro Spirituals" *(1939) and the extended consideration of specific spirituals in* Deep River: An Interpretation of Negro Spirituals *(1945).[1]*

"The Message of the Spirituals" was a significant contribution to the ongoing efforts in the 1920s to rehabilitate the poetic, musical, and religious significance of antebellum slave songs.[2] Thurman wrote in 1975 that one of the main reasons for his interest in the spirituals was to address "a generation which tended to be ashamed of the Spirituals, or who joined in the degrading and prostituting of the songs as a part of conventional minstrelsy and naïve amusement exploited and

*capitalized by white entertainers," a concern made explicit here in his comments
on "Heab'n, Heab'n."³ Thurman's readings in "The Message of the Spirituals" are
generally more traditionally Christian and sermonic than his later writings on
spirituals. For example, "My Soul Is a Witness" (significantly the only spiritual
in the 1928 article that Thurman does not consider in his later writings) is largely
concerned with ways to revitalize the missionary enterprise.*

*Unlike many of his contemporary and subsequent writers on spirituals,
Thurman is consistent in his emphasis on the theological implications of Negro
Spirituals while not neglecting their poetic, musical, specific historical origins, or
political implications. He has little interest in viewing the Negro Spiritual as an
exemplification of a distinctive African American religiosity or in emphasizing
the overt political content of slave songs. Instead, Thurman emphasizes the
relevance of the spirituals as religious documents, the product of the subtle and
sophisticated search of antebellum slaves for sacred wisdom amidst extraordinarily distressful circumstances. Thurman illustrates how the primacy of
religious experience provides the basis of hope and the tools for survival in an
otherwise hopeless situation.⁴*

(In the morning chapel service the week of October 15–19, 1928, Reverend Howard Thurman discussed in outline the religious message of five of the Negro
spirituals. At the request of the editor, Mr. Thurman has prepared an abstract of
each of these illuminating talks.—The Editor.)

For today and at the chapel hour each morning this week it is my plan to discuss, in outline, the religious message of five Negro "Spirituals." We think of the
"Spirituals" as creative music. But the religious message which they brought to
the people who first sang them is either forgotten or lost in the beauty of the
melodies for which they are distinguished. It is our purpose during these mornings together to attempt a rediscovery of the religious message.

FOR TODAY LET US CONSIDER: JACOB'S LADDER:

> We are climbin' Jacob's ladder,
> We are climbin' Jacob's ladder,
> We are climbin' Jacob's ladder,
> So'dier ob de cross.

> Ebery roun' goes higher an' higher,
> Ebery roun' goes higher an' higher,
> Ebery roun' goes higher an' higher,
> So'dier ob de cross.

We are climbin' Jacob's ladder,
We are climbin' Jacob's ladder,
We are climbin' Jacob's ladder,
So'dier ob de cross.

This "spiritual" has its background in the Genesis story of the dream of Jacob. Jacob has cheated his brother of his father's blessing and has swindled him of his birth right. As revenge, Esau is seeking his life. The harvest time for Jacob has come. In order that he may be saved from his brother's wrath, Jacob's mother spirits him away and gives to her husband a spurious reason for their son's disappearance.

After travelling a day's journey Jacob lies down to sleep, using a stone as a pillow. As he sleeps, he dreams. In his dream he sees a ladder stretching from "earth to heaven" and on this ladder angels are ascending and descending. When he awakes he is convinced that despite his sin and his own straitened circumstances, God is there and He cares.

It is impossible for us to know the particular situation which gave rise to this "spiritual." But there are three things about this experience of Jacob's which would make a tremendous appeal to the slaves and which would bring to them strength and assurance.

First: Jacob's future was most uncertain. He was going to a strange land, a land crowded with many experiences, new and hazardous. The future of the slaves was equally uncertain and hazardous. Tomorrow, and tomorrow, and tomorrow was fearful to contemplate. Yes, the future for them was most perilous and uncertain.

Second: Jacob could not turn back. Because of dishonorable deeds the bridges behind him were burned. Future uncertain, past impossible! The singers of this song could not turn back, although for an entirely different set of reasons. An immediate past crowded with tragedy, tragedy, tragedy, the thought of which would fill the soul with horror. Yes, for them the past was impossible!

Third: Jacob's present circumstances were crushing and depressing. Apparently there was not a redemptive element in the present situation. How true was this of the slaves! Driven and herded together like cattle, felled in their own blood if they resisted, these panic stricken souls found their present cruel and demoralizing. A future uncertain, an immediate past unspeakably bad, a present crowded with bitterness and misfortune,—where is there hope?

The experience of Jacob becomes at once suggestive,—the ladder. The ladder! Hence the message of the song is: There are no situations which are so depressing, so devoid of hope, that the human spirit cannot throw itself into a realm in which these conditions do not exist, and live in that realm despite all the hell about them. And so they sang about a ladder reaching from the earth—a place of torture to them—to the sky—a place that represented release.

There is danger in this type of dreaming. It is a way of escape from present realities,—a defense mechanism, the symbol of cowardice and fear. Dangerous as it may be, there are times when it is the only thing that saves people from suicide. It is always the door of last resort which no one can shut,—it is the picture that Tennyson gives us of the man who wanders in the darkness trying to find a way out of his agonizing situation. He reaches his hand out into the darkness, but instead of getting a live faith, he gets a handful of straw. Exhausted he falls, and finds himself at the foot of a stairway that leads from darkness into light.[5]

Hence I call this a "spiritual" of great faith and optimism. Through it the slave says: "I am enslaved, I am beaten and brutalized by power-maddened men, but I shall see to it that my experiences and my environment do not crush me. I'll send my spirit clear through it all and live in a realm where the air is pure." Even as Jacob, "We are climbin' Jacob's ladder; every roun' goes higher and higher."

> I will fly in the greatness of God as the marsh hen flies,
> In the freedom that fills all the space 'twixt the marsh and the skies;
> By so many roots as the marsh-grass sends in the sod,
> I will heartily lay me a-hold on the greatness of God.—[6]

OCTOBER 16: MY SOUL IS A WITNESS

> My soul is a witness for my Lord,
> My soul is a witness for my Lord,
> My soul is a witness for my Lord,
> My soul is a witness for my Lord.
> You read in de Bible an' you understan',
> Methuselah was de oldes' man,
> He lived nine hundred and sixty-nine,
> He died an' went to heaven, Lord, in due time.
>
> O, Methuselah was a witness for my Lord,
> O, Methuselah was a witness for my Lord,
> O, Methuselah was a witness for my Lord,
> O, Methuselah was a witness for my Lord.
>
> Now Daniel was a Hebrew chile,
> He went to pray to his God awhile,
> De King at once for Daniel did sen'
> An' he put him right down in de Lion's den;
> God sent His angels de lions for to keep,
> An' Daniel laid down an' went to sleep.
> Now Daniel was a witness for my Lord,
> Now Daniel was a witness for my Lord.

O, who'll be a witness for my Lord,
O, who'll be a witness for my Lord,
O, who'll be a witness for my Lord,
O, who'll be a witness for my Lord!

It is amazing to me how in the past the creators of these songs felt so keenly their kinship with the people who are commonly called the Hebrew children. And yet it is not amazing! The Hebrew children were in bondage at various periods in their history. Their records, which have become ours, are filled with sorrow and suffering, most of which was either punitive or redemptive. The slaves very early seized upon these records as symbols of their own experiences. Even today some of their posterity seems to see in the teachings of Jesus much that is suggestive of the present relationship which they hold with a dominant white majority group.

The "spiritual" which we are considering this morning had its roots in the past experiences of the Jewish people as well as in the immediate experiences of the slaves themselves. It is the great missionary "spiritual." Every time we sing it, let us remember that we are confirming our faith once again in the genius of the missionary enterprise and the missionary spirit in life. It seems to sum up the whole philosophy of missions.

A witness is one who testifies to what he has seen and known. The more personal and thorough-going the knowledge, the more significance may be attached to the quality of the testimony. The "spiritual" begins with a personal testimony: "My soul is a witness for my Lord." "I know for myself that God is and that I am a sharer of His great spirit," it seems to say.

Then in the stanzas the appeal is much wider. The experience which the singers found for themselves is not an exclusive affair. They belong to a good company—there is Methuselah, Samson, and Daniel. The experience which these great Bible men had found fulfillment in their experience. The slave affirms his spiritual solidarity with the great religious figures of the Jewish religion.

On the basis, therefore, of what this experience meant to the slave himself and to the great figures in the past, a blanket challenge is thrown out to the rest of the world:

O, who'll be a witness for my Lord?
Who'll be witness for my Lord?

No doubt the slave felt that an experience universal enough to include him and the great lights of Biblical history must have in it that which would satisfy all. "If you want to come to yourself, become a witness for my Lord."

What these slaves found true for their religion is true for the entire missionary enterprise. Let me suggest it in outline:

People cannot share what they do not have. If I am to share God's spirit with men, I must be a possessor of that Spirit. This is a basic fact to any thought of missions.

The roots of thought which I have to share are deep within the life of the race. The past claims me; I claim the past!

That which I share and which has been shared so fully in the past, no one can afford to ignore.

If the missionary enterprise in America were true to the genius of this "spiritual" there would be a different situation obtaining in many of the great mission fields of the earth, including America.

"O, who'll be a witness for my Lord?"

OCTOBER 17: *HEAB'N, HEAB'N!*

> I got a robe, you got a robe,
> All o' God's chillun got a robe;
> When I get to Heab'n I'm goin' to put on my robe,
> I'm goin' to shout all ovah God's Heab'n.
>
> Heab'n, Heab'n,
> Ev'rybody talkin"bout Heab'n ain't goin' dere,
> Heabn, Heab'n,
> I'm goin' to shout all ovah God's Heab'n.
>
> I got a wings, you got a wings
> All o' God's chillun got a wings;
> When I get to Heab'n I'm goin' to put on my wings,
> I'm goin' to shout all ovah God's Heab'n.
>
> I got a shoes, you got a shoes,
> All o' God's chillun got a shoes;
> When I get to Heab'n I'm goin' to put on my shoes,
> I'm goin' to shout all ovah God's Heab'n.
> I got a crown, you got a crown,
> All o' God's chillun got a crown;
> When I get to Heab'n I'm goin' to put on my crown,
> I'm goin' to shout all ovah God's Heab'n.
>
> Heab'n, Heab'n,
> Ev'rybody talkin"bout Heab'n ain't goin' dere,
> Heab'n, Heab'n,
> I'm goin' to shout all ovah God's Heab'n.

Perhaps no "Spiritual" has been used by minstrels and fun makers more than this one. Its basic message is one leveled against hypocrisy. Many times has my grandmother told me about the old "slave row" in the master's church. It may have been the gallery or the last two rows in the rear of the church.

> "Heab'n, Heab'n,
> Everybody talkin'"bout Heab'n ain't goin' dere."

The genesis of this song must have been somewhat as follows: On Sunday the slave had heard his master's minister talk about heaven as the reward for goodness on earth. It puzzled him greatly.

"It can't be that both of us are going to the same place. There must be two heavens. No,—for there is only one God! I know! I know! This is it,—I am having my hell now: when I die I am going to have my heaven. He is having his heaven now; when he dies, he will have his hell."

So the next day, as he worked in the field with his mate, he said, "I got a shoes, you got a shoes, all o' God's chillun (pointing to the rest of the slaves) got a shoes. When we get to heab'n we're goin' to put on our shoes an' shout all ovah (no slave row, no discrimination) God's Heab'n. But ev'rybody talkin' 'bout Heav'n (pointing up to the big house where the master lives) ain't goin' dere."

This suggests two things to me. The first is that to these simple people the great gulf between the confession of faith and the quality of life of the master was most apparent. With remarkable insight he saw that the test of the religion of Jesus, in the last analysis, is to be made in the intimate, primary, face to face relationships of people who live together day in and day out. It was true then and it is true now. If the religion of Jesus cannot purify human relations, if it cannot teach men reverence for life and personality, then one of two attitudes is forced upon us: Men have misunderstood its genius and upon embracing it discover that it is impotent, or they have deluded themselves into believing that they have embraced it when they have not.

The second thing which is suggested is this: People who live under social pressure as in a master-slave society and its posterity find it almost impossible to be honest with each other. To my mind one of the most vicious results of human slavery is found in the fact that it robs people of the ability to be straightforward, honest, courageous. This is true alike of master and slave. It is very hard for a Negro man and a white man, especially in this section, to look each other in the face and tell the truth. It has made masters and the sons of masters, slaves and the sons of slaves monumental hypocrites.

One afternoon I was standing on a street corner waiting for a car. It was in Jacksonville, Florida. There were two Negro men standing about five feet away from me talking. Presently, a tall, well-developed white man, wearing a wide Texas hat, came up. As soon as one of the men saw him, the conversation stopped. One of them greeted him and then this followed:

"Hello there, Jim, you old — where have you been so long? We've been needing you up at the mill every day. When you coming up?"

"I've been a little puny. Be up there Monday."

The white man walked in the drug store. The Negro to whom he had been talking said to his companion, "Did you hear what that old — called me? He needn't think he can call me a — without paying for it." Then he walked into the drug store. I do not know what he told the white man, but whatever it was, it was a lie. He came out with a five dollar bill and with a broad smile he said, "I told you that — would have to pay for it." Monumental hypocrites, both of them!

Yes; this "spiritual" suggests that the master bows his knees to what his life denies, that the slave gives homage to one whom he despises and fundamentally regards as immoral. The master-slave ethic brought a moral famine in the land. Sometimes I think that it has made their heirs constitutionally weak.

> I would be true, for there are those who trust me;
> I would be pure, for there are those who care;
> I would be strong, for there is much to suffer;
> I would be brave, for there is much to dare.
> I would be friend of all, the foe, the friendless;
> I would be giving, and forget the gift;
> I would be humble, for I know my weakness;
> I would look up, and laugh, and love, and lift.[7]

OCTOBER 18: *DE BLIN' MAN*

> O de blin' man stood on de way an' cried,
> O de blin' man stood on de way an' cried,
> Cryin' O, Lawdy, save me, O Lawdy,
> De blin' man stood on de way an' cried.
>
> Cryin' dat he might receibe his sight,
> Cryin' dat he might receibe his sight,
> Cryin' O, Lawdy, save me, O Lawdy,
> De blin' man stood on de way an' cried.
>
> Cryin' Lawd, have mercy on my soul,
> Cryin' Lawd, have mercy on my soul,
> Cryin O, Lawdy, save me, O Lawdy,
> De blin' man stood on de way an' cried.

This "spiritual" has to do with one of the most common problems of human life, a problem which always baffles, a problem for which men find it very difficult to discover a solution which is satisfying. It has to do with the problem of human suffering.

We don't know why human suffering comes into our lives. There are almost as many answers to the query as there are human sufferers. We do not know! I can understand, however, why the story of the blind man would make such a tremendous appeal to the people who created this song. A man who had been blind for a long time, whether from birth we do not know, heard that Jesus was passing. We recall the story of Blind Bartimaeus, I am sure. When Jesus appeared in the synagogue at home he read the great passage from Isaiah: "The spirit of the Lord is upon me, for He has anointed me to preach the gospel to the poor, to heal the broken hearted, to open the eyes of the blind."[8] Bartimaeus heard that such a man was passing by and out of the depths of years of longing and suffering, he cried to Jesus for mercy. And who knows more about what mercy means than a blind man? As the story goes, Jesus stopped as soon as He heard the cry and urged that the blind man be brought to him. When Jesus and the blind man met there was silence.

Then, "What dost thou wish that I do unto thee?" asked Jesus.

"My-my sight," quivered Bartimaeus. What a great day in the life of a sufferer! When he received his sight, Jesus bade him go home, but the record says that "he became one of the followers of Jesus."[9]

The great difference between this "spiritual" and the Gospel story is perhaps the fundamental difference between peace that people can understand and the peace that passeth understanding. In the story Bartimaeus cries for his sight and receives it. The "Spiritual" begins with the blind man's crying and it ends the same way. This was true to the facts, because the people who created this song had been crying for a long time but their cry had not been answered. Thus they could not understand the joy of the answer! But they could understand his crying! That is the difference between the peace that we can understand and the peace that passeth understanding. If I am sick and find the strength coming back to me, I can understand that peace. If I am hungry and find food, I can understand that peace. If I am lonely and find a friend to comfort and to bless, I can understand that peace. But the peace that passeth understanding is the peace that comes when the pain is not relieved. It is the peace that comes shivering on the crest of a wave of pain. It is the spear of frustration transformed into a shaft of light. I cannot understand it, but I know what it is!

Why is there human suffering? I do not know. One thing I do know; I have learned it from life and the tragic story reflected in these songs. There is something in the human spirit—to me, it is God—which makes it possible for the most tragic experience to be transformed into that which is sacred and beautiful and blessed.

Do you recall the story, "The Sky Pilot"?[10] Gwendolyn had a severe accident. When the sky pilot came to see Gwendolyn, she asked him, "Did God let me fall? Just because I am a poor little girl and He is a great big man, He took advantage of me, I—I hate him!"

"Gwendolyn, did the doctor hurt you when he put you in the cast?"

"You silly man, you know it hurt."

"Do you mean to tell me that your daddy let the doctor hurt you?"

"Don't you see that the doctor had to hurt me in order to help me?"

"I want to tell you a story. One day the Master of the Prairie came seeking flowers from the prairie. Not being able to find any he sent the wind to scatter flower seeds everywhere. But when he returned sometime later there were no flowers because the birds and the heat had destroyed them. The prairie was greatly disturbed. Then the Master sent the lightning and the thunder to tear a great chasm through the heart of the prairie. Day and night the prairie groaned in agony. After a while the river that had been running around the edge of the prairie began pouring itself thru the great open sore, carrying with it rich sediment and soil. This time when the seeds were planted, they grew. Down along the banks of the river, flowers began blooming, beautiful columbine and clematis, and the open sore of the prairie became the Master's favorite resting place."

"De blin' man stood on the way and cried." What these slaves learned and what all others must learn is that God,—God is the answer to human suffering, and when He comes, sometimes the pain is relieved but very often it is not!

> The gray hills taught me patience,
> The waters taught me prayer;
> The flight of birds unfolded
> The marvel of thy care.
>
> The calm skies made me quiet,
> The high stars made me still;
> The bolts of thunder taught me
> The lightning of thy will!
>
> Thy soul is on the tempest,
> Thy courage rides the air!
> Through heaven or hell I'll follow;
> I must—and so I dare![11]
>
> Lawd, have mercy on my soul
> That I might receive me sight.[12]

OCTOBER 19: *DEEP RIVER*

> Deep River
> My home is over Jordan,
> Deep river,
> Lord, I want to cross over into camp ground,
> Lord, I want to cross over into camp ground,

Lord, I want to cross over into camp ground.
Oh, don't you want to go to that Gospel Feast,
That promised Land where all is peace?
Deep river,
My home is over Jordan,
Deep river.

I've known rivers:

I've known rivers ancient as the world and older than the flow
of blood in human veins.
My soul has grown deep like the rivers.

I bathed in the Euphrates when dawns were young,
I built my hut near the Congo and it lulled me to sleep.

I looked upon the Nile and raised the pyramids above it,
I heard the singing of the Mississippi when Abe Lincoln went
down to New Orleans, and I've seen its muddy bosom turn
all golden in the sunset.

I've known rivers:
Ancient, dusky rivers.

"My soul has grown deep like the rivers."[13]

This is perhaps the most philosophical of all the "Spirituals" that have come down to us. It has to do with life and with a particular philosophy of life. Viewed from one angle it may be considered a song of Pilgrims.

Life, a deep river! The analogy seems to be perfect. A river is always moving, always changing, always becoming, always fluid. Long ago Heroditus[14] observed that a man could not bathe twice in the same stream. Life is always moving, always changing, always in process. I can never get to the place that I can say, "This is it, this is life." The present is always becoming the past and the future the present. What I call the present is simply the point at which the past and the future meet— always moving, always temporary, always in transition. Therefore, whatever my present situation may be, I can afford to be quiet, calm, self-possesed, because Eternity is on my side! "Yet all experience is an arch where there gleams that untravelled world, whose margin fades forever and forever when I move."[15]

Yes, life is like a deep river!

In the second place the analogy seems to be perfect because life is exacting and revealing. It is the great Judge of all experience. When Jesus wished to pic-ture the climax of human history he thought of it as a time when the inner sig-nificance of the deeds of men's lives would be revealed to them. In other words, their history is their judgment. If I want to know the judgment of the Mississippi

River, let me examine a shovelful of the sand where the river dips into the gulf. In that sand is revealed the story of every tributary that has become a part of the Mississippi River in its long passionate drive for the gulf. The judgment which I pass upon the river is simply its history. The judgment of my life is simply the history of my life. Nothing is lost. Everything counts. Everything registers. Life is exacting. Life is revealing. Yes; life is like a deep river.

In the third place the analogy seems to be perfect because life has a goal. There is an end to all of its striving. The river has a goal. All the life of the river points to the sea. Many things may be put in its pathway; there may be an abundance of obstructions and hindrances; it may be shifted many miles from its course, but nothing can permanently keep the river from its goal, the sea. At last the river must come home to the sea. In a very profound sense life is a grand pilgrimage. We are all of us pilgrims, and the goal of all of life is God! It is small wonder that Augustine said so long ago, "Thou hast made us for thyself and our souls are restless till they find their rest in thee."[16]

> I've known rivers:
> I've known rivers ancient as the world and older than the flow
> of blood in human veins.
>
> My soul has grown deep like the rivers.
>
> I bathed in the Euphrates when dawns were young,
> I built my hut near the Congo and it lulled me to sleep.
> I looked upon the Nile and raised the pyramids above it,
> I heard the singing of the Mississippi when Abe Lincoln went
> down to New Orleans, and I've seen its muddy bosom turn
> all golden in the sunset.
>
> I've known rivers:
> Ancient, dusky rivers.
>
> My soul has grown deep like the rivers.
>   *Spelman Messenger* 45 (October 1928): 4–12.

1. "Religious Ideas in Negro Spirituals," *Christendom* 4 (Autumn 1939): 515–28. A somewhat shortened version of this article was published as "Concerning Backgrounds," the opening chapter of *Deep River: An Interpretation of Negro Spirituals* (Mills College, Calif.: Eucalyptus, 1945). The remainder of the volume contains, in separate chapters, elaborations of his 1928 treatments of "Jacob's Ladder," "De Blind Man," "Heab'n, Heab'n," and "Deep River" and discussions of "A Balm in Gilead" and "Wade in the Water, Children."

2. See, for example: Alain Locke, "The Negro Spiritual" in *The New Negro*, ed. Locke (New York: Boni, 1925), 199–213; James Weldon Johnson and J. Rosamund Johnson, *The*

Book of American Negro Spirituals (New York: Viking, 1925); James Weldon Johnson, *The Second Book of Negro Spirituals* (New York: Viking, 1926); and R. Nathaniel Dett, *Religious Folk-Songs of the Negro as Sung at Hampton Institute* (Hampton, Va.: Hampton Institute Press, 1927).

3. HT, *Deep River and The Negro Spiritual Speaks of Life and Death* (Richmond, Ind.: Friends United, 1975), 3.

4. Thurman would give another version of this series at Kings Mountain in the summer of 1929. "Student Confab Opens," *Pittsburgh Courier*, 15 June 1929, describes it as follows: "Thurman delivered a series of three very helpful lectures—two of them being on 'The Deeper Meaning of Some Negro Spitituals.' The two spirituals chosen were 'Deep River' and 'The Blind Man Stood on the Road and Cried.'" Among those in attendance at the Kings Mountain conference were the theologian Reinhold Niebuhr and Thurman's future wife, Sue Bailey, whom he would marry at Kings Mountain in 1932.

5. Thurman is referring to Tennyson's *In Memoria*, canto 54, stanza 4:

> I falter where I firmly trod
> And falling with my weight of cares
> Upon the great world's altar-stairs
> That slope thro' darkness up to God.

6. Sidney Lanier, "The Marshes of Glynn" (1878), 1.73–76.

7. Howard A. Walter, "I Would Be True," 1906.

8. This is a paraphrase of Luke 4:17–19.

9. This is a paraphrase of Mark 10:46–51.

10. From Ralph Connor, *The Sky Pilot: A Tale of the Foothills* (Chicago: Revell, 1899). Ralph Connor is a pseudonym for Charles William Gordon (1860–1937), a Canadian novelist and minister.

11. Allen Eastman Cross, "The Gray Hills Taught Me Patience," 1926.

12. This is a paraphrase of Mark 10:47, 51.

13. The lines starting with "I've known rivers" are from Langston Hughes, "The Negro Speaks of Rivers," 1921. The concluding part of the quotation is at the end of Thurman's text.

14. Heraclitus, from Plato, *Cratylus*, 402A, "Heraclitus says somewhere that all things are in process and nothing stays still, and likening existing things to the stream of the river he says that you would not step twice into the same river."

15. From Tennyson, *Ulysses,* lines 18–21. The original is:

> I am a part of all that I have met;
> Yet all experience is an arch wherethro'
> Gleams that untravell'd world, whose margin fades
> For ever and for ever when I move.

16. From *The Confessions of St. Augustine,* book 1.

*Building on an earlier work on religion and the development of young minds,
Thurman in this article in* Southern Workman[1] *considers how African American ministers might provide moral and spiritual guidance to the entire black community as it grappled with the complexities of modernity. He holds the view that the "extended crisis" of slavery and its aftermath led many African Americans to overvalue materialism, apocalypticism, and institutionalism. Hence, the task of Negro ministry is to encourage prophetically the cultivation of spiritual power over "the demand for things," to draw practical ethical meaning out of personal piety, and to ensure that the spirit of Jesus is not overshadowed by the institutions created to perpetuate that spirit. Thurman also sees a need for "creative synthesis" between religion and science, so that folk traditions do not stunt the possibilities for both intellectual and spiritual growth.*

In a recent article on "Higher Education and Religion" appearing in the *Home Mission College Review* I suggested that in order for the claims of religion to be made effectively to our developing youth, four characteristic attitudes must obtain:

1 We must refuse to be caught in the current demand for things and must find our security in the reality of God and the spiritual tasks to which He has set our hands.
2 We must put a vast faith in the contagion in the Spirit of Jesus rather than in the building of organizations to perpetuate his Spirit.
3 We must seek to demolish the artificial barrier between religion and life.
4 We must not allow any phase of human knowledge to lie outside our province, but must provide a creative synthesis, in the light of which all the facts of science or whatnot may be viewed.

In this paper I shall use these four suggestions as the basic outline for my discussion of an aspect of the present task of the Negro ministry.

I

We must refuse to be caught in the present demand for things and must find our security in the reality of God and the spiritual tasks to which He has set our hands.

Negroes are poor. Despite the phenomenal increase in houses and land during the last decade or two; despite the relatively large amount of economic power that has come under their control. Negroes are poor. They are a part of a social system in which the dominant group is represented by vast economic power and the social security it brings. To counsel a minority group, such as Negroes represent in this country, to put greater confidence in values than in material possessions, *per se,* is to seem to urge the development of a kind of defense mechanism which may be the result of a mere protective philosophy. Further, it seems to play into the hands of many crafty persons who are ready to take advantage of the unsuspecting by securing for themselves more than a gentleman's share of this world's goods.

As a result of a period of extended crisis, Negroes have discovered that a rare spiritual beauty and insight are much more possible if the thing that gives meaning to one's life is not grounded in economic power. The slave worked for his master but he did not carry the burden or responsibility for economic survival. Once deprived of rancor (a superhuman feat in itself under the circumstances) his soul was free to grow with utter abandonment of the cotton which he hoed. There developed a simple disregard for possessions in terms of what they could bring as security. The tyranny of things did not entrap the vast majority of these people.

The problem became greatly complicated when the slave became an economic competitor. He was swindled and cheated because he had developed no mentality for making his interest in economic goods so keen that the possession of them would give him security. To this day the adjustment has not been adequately made. In a desperate attempt to make the adjustment there is an almighty danger of overemphasis.

It is at this point that the task of the Negro minister becomes very clear. He must interpret the deadening effect upon American life of the growing dependence upon things and what they may accomplish. He must lay bare the awful truth that where the highest premium is put upon the possession of things, human life is relatively cheapened. And where life is cheap, ideals languish and the souls of men slowly die.

> "Shall I ask my God Sunday by Sunday to brood across the land and bind all its children's hearts in a close knit fellowship;—yet when I see its people betrayed, and their jaw-bone broken by a strike from the hand of gold; when I see freedom passing from us, and the whole land being grasped by the golden claw, so that the generations after us shall be born without freedom, to labor for men who have grasped all, shall I hold my peace?"[2]

II

We must put a vast faith in the contagion in the Spirit of Jesus rather than in the building of organizations to perpetuate his Spirit.

A member of a certain Foreign Mission Board was asked by a friend of mine why his board refused to send Negroes out as missionaries. He said that Negroes knew very little about technique of organization and the risk involved would be too great. Sometimes men who dispense millions of dollars in the interest of the Kingdom of God are very easily deceived as to the relation between the dollars and the machinery for spending them and the spirit of Jesus and its propagation.

The idea of large-scale production with its attendant economic advantages, due to centralization and the like, is having its bearing upon the institutional religious life of America.[3] There seems to be a growing passion for building temples and towering structures which call for bigger and better organizations—which in turn call for more dynamic energy to keep them "efficient." They almost always represent great spiritual waste. Negro churches seem inclined to follow the lead of white churches in this form of expansion. I heard a man say one day, "People always build their temples to their dead Gods."[4]

As this expansion becomes characteristic there is more dependence upon those in a community whose incomes make substantial giving possible. This may easily mean that the gifts of a person who makes $5.00 a week, let us say, will become less and less significant. Then what? For the most part, Negro churches in America have been built by the pennies, nickels, and dimes of simple toilers. For this reason, if for no other, there is a sense of possession which they feel for the church which is unique. As an old lady said to a passerby as she stood weeping because her church was being burned: "I wouldn't mind it, son, but that's blood money that's being burned. These old hands have been rubbed to the quick to get money to put on that altar."

The danger may be remote but the task of the Negro minister is clear. It expresses itself in a very interesting paradox. A dynamic idea cannot continue to persist unless it is housed in some form of organization. In order for it to become intelligible it must be couched in current concepts and the like. The disciples of Jesus were not long in discovering this fact. (It has always impressed me that Jesus did not seem to make the same discovery unless we think of his disciples as a form of organization. They had more of a fellowship.) It is also true that just as a dynamic idea is conserved in some form of organization, it is also destroyed by the very organization that preserved it. Hence the paradox: The power that makes it breaks it.

The minister must encourage the development of systematic procedure in the institutional religious life but it must be clear to him and he must make it clear to his people that the Spirit of Jesus grows by contagion and not by organization. One life aglow with the Spirit of Jesus is far more efficacious than a dozen organizational attempts to salvage society. In the final analysis a man's life is changed by contact with another life.

Dr. Albert Parker Fitch sums it up rather adequately: "The clergy are not business men. They are of a different order, and their primary office is not to be organizers. Men are not to be made good by machinery."[5]

III

We must seek to demolish the artificial barrier between religion and life.

Christianity in America has tended in its more practical bearing to be more theological than ethical. Mark you, I emphasize this as the tendency. This has been most noticeable in areas of conflict. It is often safer, as Rauschenbusch points out somewhere, to be eloquent about the immortality of the soul than about the ethical demand that the soul makes for a living wage. It may be a very strengthening exercise to be concerned about the Trinity and the Apostle's Creed but a precise theological statement of what is involved in these may make no ethical demands upon him who states it.

As the wife of the minister in "Trooper Peter Halket" says, "If it is necessary for you to attack someone, why don't you attack the Jews for killing Christ, or Herod, or Pontius Pilate; why don't you leave alone the men who are in power today?"

And the minister replied: "Oh, my wife, those Jews and Herod, and Pontius Pilate are long dead. If I should preach of them now would it help them? Would it save one living thing from their clutches? The past is dead, it lives only for us to learn from. The present, the present only, is ours to work in, and the future ours to create."[6]

Christianity in Negro churches has little to do with dogmatic controversy. Life has been too realistic for that. This intense realism has caused their soul to recoil into an overemphasis upon the other world. The emphasis has been more speculative than ethical. This has been offset somewhat by the fact that the conditions upon which the joy of the future has been meted out are ethical in their inferences. The net results on American life from the two groups of Christians has been well nigh identical. The ethical has gone a-begging in both instances. But not quite. The fact that the overemphasis on the other world on the part of the Negro Church sprang out of a situation of extended crisis has given to it a sense of reality which may not be found in a form of Christianity which has overemphasized the theological. The Negro minister must read, though through tears, the story of the spiritual strivings of his people. He would not underestimate the value and the validity of a quiet confidence in the other world, but with marked insight he will help his people to see that there is no clear cut cleavage between this world and the other world—that life and religion may not be separated without disaster to both. He must assert continually the ethical demands of the religion of Jesus upon those who would walk on the earth by the light in the sky.

IV

We must not allow any phase of human knowledge to lie outside of our province but must provide a creative synthesis, in the light of which all the facts of science or what not may be viewed.

There are more Negro young people in school today than ever before. More books and magazines and newspapers are being read than ever before. The facts and the pseudo-facts which are the burden of modern science are becoming increasingly intelligent to the man in the street. The Dayton Trial[7] did more to popularize the theory of evolution than tomes of manuscripts revealing careful scientific research could have ever done. Men everywhere are asking questions.

There is the development and the increasing perfection of the radio. Thousands of homes have brought to them through the air all kinds of lectures, sermons, etc. A new world is being opened up even to those who cannot read. Vast stirrings of inquiry which are faint now will be most articulate presently.

Add to all of this the general suspicion that "the letter killeth"[8] and the Negro minister is caught between the demand for preparation and the fear which many feel for what exhaustive preparation may do for one's spiritual insight.

The audience to which the Negro minister preaches is becoming more and more complex. He is called upon to give some word of hope to people who live and suffer in a hostile environment; to be a steadying influence to the business and professional men who are finding life to consist largely of a series of points of ethical confusion; to throw a gleam of light upon dark areas where men and women, high school and college boys and girls wander aimlessly because of bewilderment created for them by much reading and study.

The young people are a part of the present reaction against certain conventional standards of morality. They have questions about sex which their elders cannot or will not answer. The questions must be met. He who helps them there will gain their confidence and will be privileged to share in their spiritual rebirth, if he will.

The meaning of all these things is clear. The Negro minister must find how to interpret life in terms of a creative expansive idealism. Therefore, he must be a student. For instance, he must know what the problem of evolution is and must be prepared to think clear through it with the anxious ones who share their doubts with him. He must be aware of the findings in all the major fields of human knowledge and interpret their meaning in terms of the Kingdom of God.

He must be a thinker. He must sense the dilemmas which his people face in American life and must offer intelligent spiritual and practical guidance to them. To his eye must be clear the thin line between cowardice and fear and dynamic redemptive love. He must judge the ethical significance of the religion of Jesus in the light of the Zulu proverb: "Full belly child says to empty belly child, be of good cheer."[9]

He must be God-conscious. This will keep him close to life and will serve also as a valuational consciousness which will reveal the meaning of all the facts of experience. It will be to him a creative synthesis in the light of which all the facts of science or what not may be viewed.

Southern Workman 57 (October 1928): 388–92.

1. The *Southern Workman* was the official publication of Hampton Institute. Founded in 1871 to promote industrial education in the south, by the 1920s the *Southern Workman* was the primary forum for issues related to the economic condition of African Americans.

2. Olive Schreiner, *Trooper Peter Halket of Mashonaland* (Boston: Roberts Brothers, 1897), 129–30.

3. From the late nineteenth century to the first quarter of the twentieth, American Protestantism underwent a movement to make churches more efficient. This mirrored a similar movement in American business culture, most evident in the work of Frederick W. Taylor, whose *The Principles of Scientific Management* (New York: Harper, 1919) had a profound impact on the way in which American enterprises, including churches, conducted their daily operations. See Shailer Mathews, *Scientific Management in the Churches* (Chicago: University of Chicago Press, 1912); Clarence A. Barbour, ed., *Making Religion Efficient* (New York: Association Press, 1912); and Rufus Jones, "The Bearing of Mystical Experience on Organization and System," in Jones, ed., *New Studies in Mystical Religion* (New York: Macmillan, 1927).

4. This paraphrase echoes Friedrich Nietzsche: "What are these churches now, if they are not tombs and monuments to God?" *The Joyful Wisdom ("La Gaya Scienza"),* trans. Thomas Common (New York: Ungar, 1960), 169.

5. Albert Parker Fitch, *None So Blind* (New York: Macmillan, 1924), 27.

6. Schreiner, *Trooper Peter Halket,* 120–21.

7. In 1925, John Scopes, a high-school biology teacher, challenged a Tennessee law prohibiting the teaching of Darwinism in public schools. A Dayton, Tennessee, jury convicted Scopes, although the decision was later overturned on a technicality.

8. II Cor. 3:6.

9. Patrick Ibekwe, ed., *Wit and Wisdom of Africa: Proverbs from Africa and the Caribbean* (Trenton, N.J.: Africa World, 1999), 31.

 "'RELAXATION' AND RACE CONFLICT"

1929

This essay is an expanded version of "Peace Tactics and a Racial Minority," which appeared in the World Tomorrow *in December 1928. Published from 1921 to 1934,* World Tomorrow *was one of the most influential journals of the Christian left, close to Socialist Party leader Norman Thomas, a one-time editor of the magazine and an advocate of non-Marxist socialism and pacifism.[1] Pacifism in the Modern World collected fourteen essays from the* World Tomorrow *(often, like Thurman's, in altered form), under the supervision of Devere Allen (1891–1955), the longtime editor of the journal. The contributors,*

who include Rabindranath Tagore, Rufus Jones, A. J. Muste, and Reinhold
Niebuhr, all wrote on aspects of pacifism. Thurman was the only African
American contributor.

Thurman was a committed pacifist during the interwar years, though the
article here is concerned with domestic politics rather than international
relations. Thurman begins his article by pointing out that pacifism generally
ignores race relations, but a comprehensive view of pacifism needs to take into
account the relation between the dominant and subordinate racial and ethnic
groups. As Thurman analyzes the situation, there is a "will to dominate and
control the Negro minority" among whites in the United States. Among blacks,
the reaction to this can be an indiscriminate hatred of the majority group, a
sense of resignation, and, at times, an imitation of the worst aspects of the
dominant culture, which can lead to the replication within the black community
of a hierarchy based on class status or skin color.

Thurman's suggested solution is the adaptation of the technique of "relax-
ation," in which blacks and whites stand outside the usual contexts of power
relations to seek a new relation and creative methods of social interaction. The
"technique of relaxation" for Thurman likely had specific religious connotations,
following his study of mysticism in the late 1920s. Many of the writers in the early
twentieth century who described the psychology of mysticism wrote of a prepara-
tory stage akin to relaxation. George Coe, who was a major intellectual influ-
ence on Thurman, describes the spiritual satisfactions of relaxation in The
Psychology of Religion.[2]

I

It is a very simple matter for people who form the dominant group in a society
to develop what they call a philosophy of pacifism that makes few, if any,
demands upon their ethical obligations to minority groups with which they
may be having contacts. Such a philosophy becomes a mere quietus to be put
into the hands of the minority to keep them peaceful and controllable. A certain Zulu proverb summarizes the idea: "Full belly child says to empty belly
child, Be of good cheer."

The difficulty which a minority group faces is two-fold.

First, there is always present the danger which comes from the rather blind
imitation of the dominant majority. In its position as a minority it may live
vicariously the total life of the group which is contributing so largely to its discomfort. A careful study of the life of minorities usually reveals this imitation
of the majority. The latter stampedes the former with prestige and power. Often

when the dominant group is heartily hated, the imitation takes the form of compensation. That is, those who ride on top in a minority group may treat those below them, so to speak, as they themselves are treated by the dominant majority.

I know a man who is treated very contemptuously at the place where he works, and when he comes home he passes the treatment on to the family that is dependent upon him for its existence. This danger is certainly one which is, for example, facing the Negro in American life. It is entirely possible to love people so blindly that one becomes like them in details of conduct, especially those aspects of conduct that are revealed in intimate contacts. On the other hand it is equally possible and perhaps more feasible to hate people so bitterly that one becomes like them. The man who *attends* to evil that he may not fall heir to it becomes like it. As someone pointed out long ago, what gets your attention gets you. This general imitation, whatever may be its cause, tends to cover the whole gamut of experience, from the cut of clothes and small-town economic "imperialism" to religious ceremonials.

The second danger is even more immediate and deadly: a dread despair due to the overwhelming expressions of domination and control which emanate everywhere from a powerful majority. All the current symbols of "civilization" which reach their clammy hands into the most intimate social processes of Negro life bespeak the will of the majority. Everything that he possesses tends to lose its significance if it is not validated by those who are in control. Even if he wants to get a meal in a downtown restaurant in an Eastern city his chances are infinitely better if he enters as a guest of a member of the dominant group. He must be validated, approved of, sanctioned by those whose validation and approval are meritorious. In many areas this method of evaluation has become a part of *his* method of evaluation.

A sense of helplessness and despair is apt to work its way into the very soul of such a stigmatized minority group. This helplessness expresses itself in many ways. I was going through a section in Atlanta called Beaver's Slide[3] when my attention was attracted by a deep baritone voice singing this refrain:

> "Been down so long—
> Down don' worry me."

A Negro man whose soul had given up the ghost in the struggle! Or this helplessness may express itself as the motive (this is not always the motive, however), which drives a brilliant Negro holding two degrees from one of the dominant group's best symbols of "education" to become a dining-car waiter—the light has faded from his eyes! At the present time it is increasingly expressing itself in pessimism, bitterness, and tenseness. I shall return to this later in the discussion.

II

I have gone to great length before attempting to state the thesis of my paper. I have been asked to discuss the philosophy of pacifism as it applies to the relationship between Negroes and white people in America. Fundamentally this means as it may be applied to the relationship between a stigmatized minority and a dominant more or less hostile majority group.

A philosophy of pacifism implies the will to share joyfully the common life and the will to love all—healingly and creatively. It springs out of a sense of the unity, the basic interrelation and the vast sacredness of all life. It has its roots in a primary *self-estimate,* a self-awareness from which it gets its key to the life around it. Hatred seems to spring out of a warped self-estimate. Perhaps this is in the mind of the spiritual geniuses of the race who have felt that a man *ought* to love his neighbor as he *ought* to love himself.

This conception of pacifism means at least two things for Negroes and white people who must live together in America. First, it means that white people who make up the dominant majority in American life must relax their will to dominate and control the Negro minority. Second, Negroes must develop a minority technique, which I choose to call a technique of relaxation, sufficiently operative in group life to make for vast creativity, with no corresponding loss in self-respect. The meaning of these will become clearer as I discuss each in its turn.

III

At the present time in America the will of the dominant group is tense; it is increasingly concentrated on the domination and control of the minority group, utilizing all of the machinery at its disposal to that end. Nothing is spared: the press, including the comic sheet and the highbrow journals; the church, including the pulpit, much that goes by the name of charity and many of the *materials* of religious education; and for the most part, the technique and the philosophy of education.

The relaxation of this will to dominate and control would be very far reaching because it would demand an evolutionary, if not revolutionary, shifting of a group mind-set, and the discovery of a new basis for group security. In the mind of the group *the will to dominate* and *the will to live* are *one in the same.* It would be interesting, indeed, to trace the development of this fusion. But that is apart from our purpose. It is out of the depths of this fusion that the Negro is viewed as the "white man's burden," the "black menace," the nucleus of the "rising tide of color."[4] The situation in America is largely shaped by the historical relationship between the two groups.

Slavery would have been very difficult to maintain as a system if there had not been developed a stern, relentless will to dominate and control in minute detail the life of the slave group. For many generations the springs of such a will were fed by education, by religion, and by observation. The security of the group rested in the unchanging quality of this relationship. So important was this fact that the slaves themselves were deliberately trained to fit into the system. My grandmother has often told me how she was taught as a little child just who she was and where she fitted into the scheme of things on the plantation. Nothing was left to chance—she must be taught that she was a slave and that the will of the mistress must be the desire of her heart. As a nurse in the master's household she saw how careful the training was with reference to the status of the master and his family. The master was the lord of his plantation and held in his destiny the lives of all the members of his colony; his will must never be thwarted and he was responsible only to God. And shall I add, the God of his fashioning? The slave was not an underling, for that implies belonging to the same order, but lower in the scale. The slave was essentially a *body*—of course there were many exceptions to this point of view. The idea that the slave was a body has proved itself to be extraordinarily long-lived. As a small boy I remember being stuck with a pin, and when I reacted to it the little boy who had done it said, "Oh, that doesn't hurt you; you can't feel."

So thoroughgoing was this whole procedure that, far from questioning the ethics of the position, a master-slave ethic evolved which is still to be reckoned with. The sanction for this ethic was not far to seek. I quote here in outline the position as used by Mode in his *Sourcebook for American Church History* (p. 573 ff.):

> Slave-holding does not appear in any catalogue of sins or disciplinable offences given us in the New Testament.
>
> This fact, which none will call in question, is presumptive proof that neither Christ nor his Apostles regarded slave-holding as a sin or an offence. That we may give to this presumption its proper weight, we must take account of such facts as the following:
>
> First. That Catalogues of Sins and Disciplinable Offences, given us in the New Testament are numerous, and in some instances, extended and minute.
>
> Second. All the books of the New Testament were written in slave-holding states, and were originally addressed to—persons and churches in slave-holding states: One of them—the epistle to Philemon—is addressed to a slave-holder. . . .
>
> Third. The condition of slaves in Judea, in our Lord's day, was no better than it now is in our Southern states, whilst in all other countries it was greatly worse. . . .
>
> Fourth. Slavery, and the relations which it establishes are frequently spoken of, and yet more frequently referred to by Christ and his Apostles.

"The Apostles Received Slave-Holders into the Christian Church, and Continued them therein, without giving any intimation either at the time of their Reception, or Afterwards, that Slave-Holding was a sin before God, or to be accounted an offence by the Church." Proof: Eph. 6:9; Col. 4:1; I Tim. 6:2; Philem. 2. . . .

"Paul sent back a Fugitive Slave, after the Slave's hopeful Conversion, to his Christian Master again, and assigns his reason for so doing that Master's right to the services of his Slave." Proof: Philem. 10:19.

"The Apostles repeatedly enjoin the relative Duties of Masters and Slaves, and enforce their Injunctions upon both alike, as Christian Men, by Christian Motives; uniformly treating the Evils which they sought to correct as incidental Evils, and not part and parcel of slavery itself." Proof: Eph. 6:5–9; Col. 3:22–25, 4:1; I Tim. 6:1, 2; Titus 2:9, 10; I Peter 2:18, 19.[5]

Now let us put alongside this outline a very impressive statement written by Professor Coe in his *Social Theory of Religious Education:* "When we who pray to God as father, and call humanity a family and exalt the idea of service, nevertheless take unprotesting comfort in the anti-domestic, unbrotherly, caste-like inequalities of opportunity that prevail in the world, then, however unconscious we may be of compromising our religion, we actually become teachers of an anti-Christian ethic."[6]

On the surface it seems that the relaxation of the majority group's will to dominate and control the minority group is a very negative statement of the philosophy of pacifism as far as it concerns the dominant group. A more careful examination shows that this is not the case. The will to share joyfully the common life and to love all healingly and creatively cannot be the product of the tenseness that is born of fear. When the will to dominate and control is relaxed, then the way is clear for spontaneous self-giving, for sharing all gratuitously. This new spirit finds its direction in *the will to love.* A group so disposed finds its security in a new kind of relationship. The relaxation of the will to control and to dominate becomes something very positive and dynamic.

Nothing can take the place of or atone for this profound change of basic point of view. Anything less than this on the part of the dominant group is mere patronizing. "And Jesus said unto them, The kings of the Gentiles exercise lordship over them, and they that exercise authority upon them are called benefactors."[7]

How may this change be brought about? I am sure that I am not competent to answer this question. I am profoundly convinced, however, that the change must be an individual as well as a social one, if we may think of them separately for convenience. There must be individual creative experimentation along with the actual harnessing of social forces to that end. The process must be formal and informal, direct and indirect, studied and spontaneous. The springs which feed the school, the church, and the home must be tapped. This will mean a new philosophy of education, a more adequate philosophy of religion, and a higher quality of religious experience.

IV

In the second place Negroes must develop a minority technique which I choose to call a technique of relaxation sufficiently operative to make for creative living. And this without a corresponding loss in self-respect—perhaps an impossible synthesis.

The supposedly ignorant Negro who has done much of the heavy work of the South has mastered such a technique in some of its aspects. In the midst of a hostile, dominating, controlling white majority he relaxes and oftentimes becomes remarkably creative. When he swears or laughs or sings the gods tremble. Whatever our judgment may be of the advisability of the attitude, the fact is, such a Negro has transcended his environment and in that degree he is free. It is true that the attitude is often immoral, for sometimes it makes the man bow his knees to what his heart denies. It has given him an exterior defense mechanism which often is not in keeping with his true self. I am of the opinion that it is possible for a member of a minority group to live a relaxed life in the midst of a hostile majority without the apparent or real loss of self-respect and manhood. A faint glimmer of this realization is to be found in the experience of some unlettered Negroes in the South. "In the midst of his thralldom he has created the beautiful on earth; in the midst of his torments he has had so much surplus energy of soul that he has sent it radiating forth into the cold depths of space and warmed them with God."[8]

But what about the educated Negro and those who are in the schools? Ideally stated, it seems to me that the goal of education is to make people at home in the world so that they may live fully and creatively. It aims to put at their disposal a technique of mastery over themselves and over their environment, as far as possible. If the mastery of the environment includes the mastery of persons as well as things, then the way leads straight to a terrific struggle for survival. This makes for tenseness as against relaxation. Often it breeds fear. The members of both groups with the same slant as to education would tend to give each other no quarter.

The philosophy and technique of education which are the tools of the educated Negro are alike the tools of the educated white man. They are to be used by people who stand in society as keepers of the established order. Their skill is most fully revealed when one stands in society in a position of advantage. (I am referring to philosophy and technique rather than subject matter.) The Negro stands in a position of disadvantage—he is a member of a minority group with a dominant group technique. The net result is discouragement, despair, pessimism, and bitterness. The gulf between him and the great majority of his own group widens. He tends to look upon the lowliest members of his race as the dominant group looks upon them.

Under the circumstances this seems to be inevitable. But an education which tends to throw a member of a minority group out of sympathy with the life and struggles of the greater number of his group to whose fate his fate is also tied is suicidal. I am not here making a plea for a particularized type of education, but I am thinking of placing at the centre of whatever kind of education there may be *a unique concept* which would profoundly influence the whole sphere of education as it had to do with being at home in the world. This concept must be *indigenous;* it must spring out of the life of the minority group itself.

It was pointed out above that in the mind of the dominant group there has been a fusion of the will to live and the will to dominate and control. In the mind of the minority group a similar thing has taken place—there is a fusion of *the will to live* and *the will to hate* the man who makes living such precarious business. A minority technique which I am calling a technique of relaxation would put the group into a frame of mind that would make it possible to detach itself from the clash of minority and majority sufficiently to interpret the relationship between them in the light of a will to share and a will to love.

This is agonizingly difficult because, for the most part, individual and group experience is against it. It is difficult again because it is not a mere matter of relaxing a will, hard as that is, but it means a whole technique of relaxation running the entire length and breadth of experience. It means that the group itself must be relaxed. This requires a vast faith and an almighty affection. The moment the dominant group relaxes its will to dominate and the minority group relaxes, the way is cleared for summarizing the relationship on a new basis. To this end all social forces operating separately and jointly among both groups must be harnessed.

In my opinion, all our attempts to bring about brotherhood, sympathetic understanding, and goodwill are dashed to pieces against an adamant wall. On the one side it is labelled: The Will to Control and Dominate. On the other it is labelled: The Will to Hate the Man Who Tries to Dominate and Crush Me. When there is relaxation, then the way is clear for the operation of the will to share joyfully in the common life—the will to love healingly and creatively.

"'Relaxation' and Race Conflict," Devere Allen, ed., *Pacifism in the Modern World* (Garden City, N.Y.: Doubleday, 1929), 67–78.

1. On 5 September 1934, Thurman wrote to Kirby Page, one of the editors of the *World Tomorrow,* when the journal was absorbed into the *Christian Century:* "I am very sorry to hear that The World Tomorrow has gone out of business as such. I feel that there is no magazine that can quite take its place." HTC-MBU: Box 16.

2. William James, *The Varieties of Religious Experience: A Study in Human Nature* (1902; repr., New York: Library of America, 1987), chap. 16, 17; Evelyn Underhill, *Mysticism* (New York: Dutton, 1910); George Coe, *The Psychology of Religion* (Chicago: University of Chicago Press, 1916), 138–40.

3. Beaver's Slide was an impoverished black neighborhood in southwest Atlanta that bordered Atlanta University. The public housing project University Homes was built in this area. See Clifford M. Kuhn, Harlon Joye, and Bernard West, *Living Atlanta: An Oral History of the City, 1914–1948* (Athens: University of Georgia Press, 1990), 46–47.

4. The quoted phrases are references to Rudyard Kipling, *The White Man's Burden: The United States and the Philippine Islands* (1899) or Lothrop Stoddard, *The Rising Tide of Color against White World-Supremacy* (New York: Scribner, 1920).

5. Peter George Mode, *Source Book and Bibliographical Guide for American Church History* (Menasha, Wis.: Banta, 1921), 573. This is an excerpt from George Armstrong, *The Christian Doctrine of Slavery* (New York: Scribner, 1857).

6. George Coe, *A Social Theory of Religious Education* (New York: Scribner's Sons, 1917), 87–88.

7. Luke 22:25–26.

8. Johan Bojer, *The Great Hunger,* trans. by W. J. Alexander Worster and Charles Archer (New York: Moffat, Yard, 1919), 326.

❧ TO RUFUS JONES
4 JUNE 1929
LAGRANGE, GA.

In the spring of 1929 Thurman was a special student at Haverford College, studying with Rufus Jones,[1] the Quaker historian and scholar of mysticism. Thurman had weekly sessions with Jones and also attended a seminar on Meister Eckhart (ca. 1260–1327), the German mystical writer. Thurman wrote papers on the French Quietist Madame Guyon (1647–1717) and Saint Francis, mentioned in this letter. Although Thurman had been interested in mysticism for a number of years, his study with Jones enabled him to gain new historical and theological perspectives on mystic experience, and he regarded his study with Jones as a "watershed."[2]

My dear Friend,

Before I leave for California I must send you a word.

Please accept my personal, yes my most sincerely personal thanks for the huge share which you have had in the enrichment of my life during the past 5 months. I cannot now estimate the significance of the days with you at Haverford.

I do hope for you and Mrs. Jones a safe trip to England.

The paper on St Francis reached me all right—Thank you very much.

Will you arrange for me to get the letters to Heiler[3] and to certain outstanding Friends at Woodbrook and York before you sail or will there be time after I reach London in early November or the very last of October?[4]

My best wishes to you forever,

Very truly yours,

[*signed*] Howard Thurman

105 Fannin St

LaGrange, Ga.

June 4, 1929

ALS. RJ-PHC: Box 28.

1. Rufus Matthew Jones (1863–1948) was educated at Haverford College and Harvard University. In 1893 Jones became philosophy professor at Haverford College and editor of several Quaker periodicals. After a short period of graduate study, he returned to Haverford in 1901 and remained there for thirty years. Jones published many works related to mysticism and Quakerism, notably, *Studies in Mystical Religion* (1923) and *The Fundamental Ends of Life* (1925). Jones's *Finding the Trail of Life* (1926) deeply influenced Thurman.

2. *WHAH*, 77.

3. Friedrich Heiler (1892–1967) is an important figure in the development of the fields of history of religion and psychology of religion. A Catholic turned Lutheran, Heiler was a phenomenologist whose work sought to trace out the connections among the world's major religions. His most important works are *Prayer: A Study in the History and Psychology of Religion* (New York: Oxford University Press, 1932), *The Gospel of Sadhu Sundar Singh* (New York: Oxford University Press, 1927), and *The Spirit of Worship, Its Forms and Manifestations in the Christian Churches, with an Additional Essay on Catholicity, Eastern, Roman, and Evangelical* (New York: Doran, 1926).

4. There is no evidence that Thurman traveled to Europe in the fall of 1929. Presumably the worsening health of his wife led to a cancellation of his plans.

FROM HENRY PITNEY VAN DUSEN

1 NOVEMBER 1930

EDINBURGH, SCOTLAND

Henry Pitney Van Dusen,[1] the theologian who was among the leaders of the modern ecumenical movement, provides Thurman with a detailed summary of some of his anticipated research projects. It is likely that he and Thurman established their friendship while working with the student division of the YMCA and that Thurman had planned to meet with him and the group at some point in Edinburgh. Writing one month before Katie's death, Pitney expresses heartfelt concern for her recovery. Thurman's trip did not materialize as planned. In June of 1931, six months after Katie's death, he took a sea voyage to Europe in search of much-needed solace and restoration.

My dear Howard,—

This letter has been a long, long time in the writing—since long before your fine note came to me at Aurora. But I do not have your happy and right habit of sending just a line or two if there is not time to write as much as one wants to.

And now comes further direct word of you—from my sister who heard you at Vassar.[2] I can't forbear sending you her spontaneous tribute just as she had written it. Sometimes these quite indirect reflections of our work mean most to us, I think. You will appreciate it more when I say that my sister is by no means an easy enthusiast, especially about sermons.

Work here goes along quietly and slowly, but happily. It is a marvellous opportunity—to get away from the rush and "immediacy" of life at home, especially as we live it on Morningside Heights. The time between now and Christmas I have planned to spend largely in catching up on the backgrounds of modern thought—the development of scientific, philosophical and theological thought from Hume to the beginning of the twentieth century. This is material which should have been read long ago. All of this is preparatory to where my major concern lies—in the tendencies in contemporary thought. If I am lucky enough to carry on in study straight through the year, I shall try to get on to the writing of a thesis after Christmas.

I have two alternative pieces of writing in view, although there is no certainty when either of them will actually get done. One is a study of the main issue in contemporary theological thought—which, in one view, seems to me to be the relation between the realm of facts and the realm of value, the world of science and the world of art and religion: in another and more religious view, it is the attempt to think through the ways in which God is actively related to our life. The other bit of study, which may never come to fruition, would center on Von Hugel.[3] {You and I have talked about this!}

By all odds the richest discovery I have recently made is the writings of Von Hugel. I am sure you must be very familiar with them. I would think you would find your own spirit more at home with him than almost any other recent writer. Here we have the richest scholarship and hard intellectual labor in union with an absolutely undimmed religious experience. How in the world can we bring that sort of approach to religion and experience of religion home to our American college youngsters? The thing which {first} strongly directed me to Von Hugel was the arresting quotations from him in Oldham's Devotional Diary which I have found personally more helpful than any other book of devotions I have ever known, I think. As you well know, Doug Steere[4] is doing his doctorate on Von Hugel.

Enough of myself and plans. Forgive me for writing on so long, but I felt sure you would want to know a bit of what I am up to here. One further fact. There is some probability that I shall not take the full year in study but return at mid-year—only in order to be able to be away all of next year on a most interesting and important survey of the foreign mission field in the Orient. I have been invited to take part in the latter, and it will be a most unusual privilege, if the Seminary approves of my doing it.

We missed you greatly at Aurora. Many spoke of you. And I especially appreciated your little note of welcome to the Council. The meeting was a good one, I think. The Council group here in Edinburgh numbers six—Jack and Marietta Benton; Jack Thomas of Union Seminary, Richmond, and his wife; one of our own Union students, Doris Webster; and myself. We are to meet this coming Wednesday afternoon.

The last word I was able to get of Kate was most encouraging, and I am hoping with all my heart that the slow and tedious improvement has kept up. Give her my very dear and true love, won't you? If you can find time for one of those brief lines which say so much, you know how welcome it will be. I do think of you both (and the baby) very, very often, even though the long silences would give no indication of it. The Lord should have provided us with some method of communicating the fact to our friends whenever our thought turns seriously to them!! Perhaps he expected us to perfect some definite method of thought transference, and that we shall yet discover a way.

In any event, a great deal of love to you. And a prayer for Kate's health, for your work, and for your life and love together.

Ever loyally,

[*signed*] <u>H. P. V. D.</u>

P.S. I shall be here until December 10th. Then home for the Christmas holidays. And after that—??

TLS. HTC-MBU: Box 198.

---

1. Henry Pitney Van Dusen (1897–1975) received his AB from Princeton University (1919). He completed some graduate work at New College in Edinburgh (1921–22) and received his BD from Union Theological Seminary (1924). By 1932, he had completed his PhD from Edinburgh University. He taught at Union Theological Seminary from 1926 to 1975, serving in various capacities including dean of students (1931–39), Roosevelt Professor of Systematic Theology (1936–1959), and president from 1945 to 1963. After stepping down as president, he became Union's Lamont Professor of Christian Theology emeritus and traveling professor from 1963 until his death in 1975. A Presbyterian minister, Van Dusen was a delegate to almost every major ecumenical conference from 1937 to 1975. He authored such works as *In Quest of Life's Meaning* (New York: Association Press, 1926), *The Plain Man Seeks for God* (New York: Scribner's Sons, 1933), *God in These Times* (London: Student Christian Movement, 1935), *What Is the Church Doing?* (New York: Friendship, 1943), and *Dag Hammarskjold: The Statesman and His Faith* (New York: Harper, 1967).

2. See in the current volume Lester A. Walton, "Negro Minister Fills Pulpit at Vassar: Rev. Dr. Howard Thurston [*sic*] Is First of His Race to Do So," 1 April 1928, Walton's account of Thurman's 12 March 1928 lecture at Vassar College.

3. Friedrich Von Hugel (1852–1925), considered one of the great spiritual leaders of twentieth-century Roman Catholicism, called for the Church to be open to modern, critical

ideas. Deeply interested in the relationship between science and religion, he was a man in pursuit of holiness and a living encounter with God. Von Hugel held that personality is growth and movement outward and beyond the preoccupied self, and it is a gift and an achievement—the actuation of what was there at the beginning, as offered, as grace. Personality in Von Hugel's thought is not individualism but the process of constituting a self. For perspectives on personalism, see Walter G. Muelder, *The Ethical Edge of Christian Theology: Forty Years of Communitarian Personalism* (New York: Mellen, 1983) and Paul Deats and Carol Robb, eds., *The Boston Personalist Tradition in Philosophy, Social Ethics, and Theology* (Macon, Ga.: Mercer University Press, 1986).

4. Douglas Steere was a religious philosopher and Quaker mystic with whom Thurman corresponded over the years.

❧ FROM JOHN HOPE
15 JANUARY 1932
ATLANTA, GA.

Despite some temporary recoveries, Katie Thurman's prognosis steadily worsens, and she dies in Atlanta on 21 December 1930. A little over a year following Katie's death, Hope writes to congratulate Thurman on his marital plans to Sue Bailey. "You have told me in your letter what evidently was much in your mind" is perhaps a reference to Thurman's decision to leave Morehouse and Spelman colleges for Howard University. Thurman and Sue Bailey are married on 12 June 1932, at Kings Mountain in North Carolina. They move to their new home on the campus of Howard two weeks later.

Dear Mr. Thurman:

Your letter of January 4 has been received and read with much interest. I am sorry that we did not have a chance to talk before you left, but you have told me in your letter what evidently was much in your mind.

May I beforehand express my hearty wishes that your marriage will bring happiness to you both and result in even larger service to the great cause in which you have both enlisted.

I remember Mr. Henry B. Barnes very well. He was one of the most helpful men with whom I came in contact in France. If you see him again give him my kindest regards. I would like to have his address so that I may write a note and renew our acquaintance.

With kind regards and best wishes, I am

Sincerely yours

[*unsigned*]

Mr. Howard Thurman
715 South Hope Street
Los Angeles
California

            TLc. JLH-GAU: Box 25.

꙳ FROM FLORENCE M. READ
1 MARCH 1932
ATLANTA, GA.

In early 1932 Thurman accepted a position as associate professor of theology in the Howard University School of Religion, at a salary of $3,500 a year.[1] In this letter, President Florence Read accepts Thurman's resignation from Spelman College. Although Read had been accommodating to Thurman and his late wife during the latter stages of her illness, their relationship was strained, in large part because of Thurman's perception of her paternalistic attitudes toward her students.[2]

Dear Mr. Thurman:

Your letter of February 26, 1932, resigning from your position at Spelman College at the close of the present academic year, has been received.

I cannot accept your resignation without letting you know that I appreciate your fine devotion to students, here and elsewhere, and your many efforts and activities emphasizing the importance of spiritual qualities in an age when material welfare receives more attention than is its due. I value your friendship for Spelman College and your expression of faith in its future possibilities.

You have youth, physical vigor, keenness of mind, and earnestness of spirit. Whatever the position may be into which you have decided to throw your energies next year, it holds much promise, I am sure, for great usefulness. You have my good-will and my confidence in full measure.

I should like to talk with you at your convenience about your plans.

Sincerely yours,

[*signed*] Florence M. Read

Mr. Howard Thurman
Spelman College
Atlanta, Georgia

TLS. HTC-MBU: Box 17.

1. From Emmett J. Scott, 9 March 1932, HTC-MBU: Box 19.
2. *WHAH*, 79–80.

꙳ FROM WILLIAM J. FAULKNER
21 APRIL 1932
ATLANTA, GA.

Reverend William J. Faulkner,[1] the pastor of First Congregational Church of Atlanta, Georgia, thanks Thurman for the stirring address he delivered on the previous Sunday evening. Thurman's reputation as a theologically creative and prophetic preacher was not lost on prominent ministers like Faulkner.

Rev. Howard Thurman
Morehouse College
Atlanta, Georgia

My dear Mr. Thurman:

You were no doubt at your best on last Sunday night when you delivered that memorable address on "The Kind of Education the World Needs Most" at our annual College Night celebration.

God is bountifully blessing you as a teacher and prophet in pointing the way to the light for our people in these troublous times. It will be a keen personal loss to me to have you leave this community. I regret now more than ever that I have denied myself a closer fellowship with you during the past few years. But I shall always count it a source of genuine hope and inspiration that I have known you.

If I can be of any service to you at any time, please command me.

Yours very cordially,

[*signed*] W. J. Faulkner

TLS. HTC-MBU: Box 6.

1. William J. Faulkner (1891–1987) was a noted minister, folklorist, and educator. He received his BA from Springfield College, Springfield, Massachusetts, and his ThD from the Chicago Theological Seminary of the University of Chicago. He worked several years as a YMCA secretary in Philadelphia, Atlanta, and Washington, D.C. He also served as pastor of churches in Atlanta and in Chicago, where he was the first pastor of the Park Manor Congregational Church in the early 1930s. From 1934 to 1942, he was dean of men and ministry at Fisk University, Nashville, Tennessee, and from 1942 to 1953 he served as Fisk's dean of the chapel.

CHAPTER V

Howard University and Washington, D.C.

🐟 To Balamu J. Mukasa
AUGUST 1932
WASHINGTON, D.C.

Thurman responds to the request for financial assistance and advice from a Ugandan student who evidently is experiencing racism in his part-time job and is having financial difficulties at Morehouse. Thurman is unable to offer financial help and urges him to deal gracefully yet shrewdly with the racism and to discuss any difficulties with John Hope, Morehouse president, openly and without rancor. Thurman, offering what for him is an unusual comment about Africa, reminds Mukasa, "You are an African with the pure blood of a thousand generations of noble men in your veins."

The crisis behind Mukasa's correspondence to Thurman was resolved, and he graduated from Morehouse in 1935. The two men remained in correspondence, and when Mukasa received a Carnegie Fellowship to study at Yale University, Thurman congratulated him, though warned him somewhat cryptically, "You will enjoy Yale University, though a friend of mine calls it the Negroes graveyard."[1]

My Dear Makasa,[2]

I have just come in and I am leaving again tomorrow for a few days.

Your letter was very deeply moving and I am clearly at a loss to know exactly what to say to you.

In the first place my own obligations are of such that I cannot see my way clear until after Xmas. We have just taken to live with us a young fellow from out in Arkansas. He is to go to school just as you are and the money that I thought I would have had free goes into his upkeep etc.

There is just one possibility that I see and that is ~~you~~ I may be able to get my friend, Stuart Nelson,[3] the President of Shaw, to grant you all expenses there for next year. I am going to be with him this week and shall talk the matter over with him and let you know the outcome the last of the week.

You are up against a very difficult situation but you must try to see your way through it. You see, if you permit her to drive you away, you lose, she does not. What you want is your education. Suppose you do have to eat in the kitchen, get your food and bide your time, you will not have that to do always. You are young, youth is on your side—they are older. You are an African with the pure blood of a thousand generations of noble men in your veins.—Long before they and their forebears were on the earth—your forebears were rulers in the greatest continent of the earth. Do not let cheapness kill your soul—You above all else must be a man,—Do not crouch and cower, hold your ground and do not move an inch until Dr. Hope himself tells you that he is through with you. It is hard I know it. I do not say it is not but life will bless you if you start and see your way through. God bless you and keep you, my friend, and ~~do not~~ when you are able to endure with confidence and courage clear through to the end!

Tell the thing clear through with Mr. Hope when he returns. Speak quite frankly but always be a courteous Christian gentleman. I believe Mr. Hope wants to do a gracious and good part by you. Let me hear again real soon. If you must leave do not do so until Mr. Hope returns.

My love to you forever,

Your friend

[*signed*] Howard Thurman

ALcS. HTC-MBU: Box 12.

1. To "Baluma Mukosa," 18 March 1935, HTC-MBU: Box 12.

2. When he was twenty-five years old, Balamu Jaberi Mukasa (1904–19??), a native of Hoima, Uganda, came to the United States upon promise by John Hope in 1929 of a Morehouse Scholarship. According to Thurman (*WHAH*, 37–38), Mukasa was unable to make contact with Hope and was detained for several months on Ellis Island by immigration authorities and then deported. Other accounts offer an alternative story, that he arrived in New York City and, alone and bewildered after a few days alone in the city, decided to return as soon as possible to Africa. Whatever transpired in New York City, on the return boat to Europe, he met with John Hope, who was traveling on the same ship. Hope convinced Mukasa to return to the United States and Morehouse. After receiving an MA from Yale University (1937), Mukasa became head of the social science department at Makerere College in Uganda. In 1944, he was elected Minister of Agriculture of Uganda. In 1951, as prime minister of the province of Bunyoro in Uganda, he made a three-month tour of the United States at the invitation of the State Department to study social welfare, race relations, and education in the United States. See "African Youth Receives Degree at Yale's 236th Ceremony:

Belamu [*sic*] J. Mukasa Is Brilliant," *Chicago Defender*, 27 July 1937; "Uganda Premier Who Fled N.Y. as Boy Visits in D.C.," *Washington Post*, 29 August 1951.

3. William Stuart Nelson (1895–1977) served as president of Shaw University in Raleigh, North Carolina, from 1931 to 1935.

⨀ "Barren or Fruitful?"
28 August 1932
Washington, D.C.

This sermon, preached at the Plymouth Congregational Church in Washington, D.C., pastored by his friend, the Reverend Herbert King, is Thurman's first individually published sermon.[1] "Barren or Fruitful?" is based on Jeremiah 17, one of Thurman's favorite sermon texts. Thurman had previously preached on the same subject at United Church in Oberlin, Ohio, on 13 November 1927, and at Vassar College on 12 March 1928.[2]

Thurman's message was one of hard-earned affirmation through recognition of human limitation. False pride in family background, worldly success, and failure to recognize the instrumental role of God in one's achievements lead to spiritual undernourishment, like the parched desert shrubs that wither under difficulties. By contrast, those who know that God is near and within and that God is love are "like a tree planted by the waters," growing stronger despite the strains of life.

There are two remarkable pictures given us by the Prophet Jeremiah. With these two pictures as a background, I want each of you to think seriously about this question: To what do I appeal when I want to convince myself that I am somebody?

I

First—a curse on him who relies on man, who depends upon mere human aid. For he is like a desert scrub that never thrives; set in a salt solitary place in the steppes— a striking picture! A certain kind of man likened unto a desert scrub—undeveloped and underdeveloped, undernourished and emaciated, stubby, and stunted, acting on the theory that to breathe is to live![3] What a character analysis!

He is thus, says Jeremiah, because he relies on man. He has a false sense of security. When such a man wants to convince himself that he is somebody, his appeal, most often, is to those things that are of temporary and passing significance.

I am putting the question quite personal this morning: In what do you find your security? I shall review, in outline, three of the more commonplace bases of appeal. You may supply others and out of your experience make a fuller rendering of the details of the three which I shall mention.

In the first place, there are those who appeal to family connections and social position. They are quite proud of family background and take keen sweet delight in pointing out the fact that the leaves of their family tree are always green. A friend of mine has written some lines depicting such a man—

> He was proud of descent
> For he came from one of
> The best families.
> But as a man, he was
> Worth exactly forty cents an hour.

It is a very desirable thing to come from a good healthy vigorous family stock. But in the last analysis Life is not interested in the accident of birth. Life does not care who your father was or how far back you can trace your mother's roots! What about you? Every man must stew in his own juice. If your basic security is found in your family connections, you are leaning on a broken stick. A desert scrub that never thrives!

There are others who appeal to their training, their education. Education is very useful and necessary. More often, a good education is a commodity that has a very definite exchange value. For instance, a doctor charges a fee for his services, unique to him because of specialized training. In other words a doctor rents his skill to the public, for which he receives varying degrees of economic security. Superficially viewed, this may seem to be a true basis of security.

Very often when a man's stock begins to go down or the ground is being cut away from beneath his self-respect, the fact that he is educated does give him a certain sense of security. There *is* something marvelously sustaining about genuine education. But a man who appeals to the fact that he is a college graduate or a professional school graduate in order to convince himself that he is somebody—well, such a man is sailing under false colors. Life does not ask you from what college do you come, or if you have been to college at all. It wants to know *basically* what you are and in what direction you are going. Very often in the most rigorous and elemental experiences of life the differences between men resulting from training and background melt away. And behold, where are they? He who thinks to the contrary is fooled—a desert scrub that never thrives!

And then there are those who appeal to the peculiar quality of their righteousness. They are "I thank God I am pure" people. Jesus dramatized this quality very effectually in His picture of the two men who went up into the temple to pray. One man said in substance: "O God, I thank Thee I am not as other men. I pay my vows. I attend all temple services. I give of my means to charity. I thank Thee God that it is with me as it is. I pause in my busy life to let thee know how good I am."

In an obscure part of the temple another man prayed. He dared not lift his head above, but with deep contrition cried aloud, "Lord, Lord, have mercy on me, a sinner!"[4]

The tragedy of a self-righteous man is that he has an ideal that he can live up to—he has a goal that he has reached already. He who turns to his self-righteousness for security is doomed to fundamental defeat. In utter amazement he will discover one day that his life is barren—a desert scrub that never thrives!

What a revealing experience it is to step aside and see yourself go by. Try it! It will certainly make you humble!

Is your life barren? When you are most yourself do you know yourself to be a "desert scrub," a spiritual undernourished and moral emaciated individual—narrow, selfish, puny-souled, bigoted, living under a false sense of security?

II

The second picture is most inspiring. The prophet pictures the man who depends on God, who has God for his confidence, as a tree planted beside a stream sending his roots down to the water. He has no fear of scorching heat, his leaves are always green.[5] He goes on bearing fruit when all around him is barren and lives serene. In other words such a man looks out on life with quiet eyes!

Perhaps, in the last analysis the only thing to which a man may appeal for basic security is the high quality of his dedication and the supreme worth of that to which he is dedicated. If a man dedicates his life to the highest that he knows, that dedication at once gives to his life added worth and significance.

A man cannot dedicate himself to that which is outside of the realm of his experience at every point. I cannot conceive of that which does not have its roots within me. If you have no conception of the meaning of the word "fly," I could not explain the aeroplane to you. "If you have no thought of your own, those of other men will find nothing to which they can fasten themselves." So when a man dedicates himself to God, the Highest, the fact and the experience cannot be foreign to him originally but in some genuine sense it must be already present in him.

A man came to Jesus seeking help for his son. (Pathos is revealed in utter rawness when a strong man finds that his strength is powerless to help where his love dictates.) Jesus said to him, "It will be as you desire if you have faith." It was then that the man said, "I have faith—help Thou my lack of faith."[6] *The consciousness of a lack of faith springs out of faith itself.* If I had no faith in God, I could not know that I had no faith in Him. When a man dedicates himself to God it means that that dedication springs out of a genuine God-consciousness.

Your fundamental security then is not family, training, piety or the like but rather the supreme quality of your dedication to the highest there is in life—God.

To say, "I affirm my faith in God with my total personality" is one of the supreme affirmations of the human spirit.

The real atheist is not necessarily the man who denies the existence of God; but rather the man who, day after day and week after week, subscribes to a faith in God with his lips while *acting* on the vital assumption that there is no God.

I have deep respect for the man who with great sincerity reaches the conclusion that life has no meaning for him. Full of years he might conclude, no God, no sin, no future life—nothing but the survival of the fittest and every man for himself. To him I can only say, "Such is not my experience." Such a man, however, is not an atheist in the sense that many church-goers are. "They honor Me with their lips but their hearts are far from Me."[7] Acting every day as if there were no God while doing lip service to God.

Suppose we dare start today believing in God to the extent that wherever we went the Kingdom of God would be at hand. In a very short time the entire complexion of our city would be transformed!

There are three things that my faith in God teaches me about God. I shall mention these almost in outline. In the first place it teaches me that God *is*. Bear in mind ever, my friends, that faith is a way of knowing.

When Jesus prayed, all who heard Him were conscious that He was not talking to the air. When Jesus prayed He met Somebody. And when I am most myself and sigh my soul in prayer, I too meet Somebody—I know Jesus was right!

Have you ever tried to pray and could not connect up? So many details of living, so many carking cares loomed large before you that your words fell back dead.

> "My words fly up, my thoughts remain below,
> Words without thoughts never to heaven go."[8]

And then, sometimes, as if by chance, there is kindled in the heart an upmounting desire on the wings of which one mounts to the very presence of God!

To one who has a living, leaping faith, God is. There are no ordinary proofs—one has worked one's way through all such preliminary stages. It is like growing in love. At first there are many "tokens of testing," little ways of checking, but gradually there is an awareness that proofs are unnecessary—one knows and is relaxed! My faith *teaches* me that God is!

Again, my faith teaches me that God is near. Not away off, up above the sky, on a great white throne—an aged white man with blonde angels standing in mid-air to obey his command! Not that.

Isaiah says that in the year that King Uzziah died he saw the Lord on a great white throne, high and lifted up.[9] But Jesus funded the religious experience of all the prophets of Israel, erected a vast experimental pyramid, scaled the heights of it and brought God down out of the clouds and discovered Him pre-eminently as the main spring in the heart of man. An amazing insight it was that exclaimed, The Rule of God—it is within you![10]

> "Speak to Him, Thou, for He heareth
> And spirit with spirit may meet—"[11]

Do you remember the words on the Railway Station: He who seeks the wealth of the Indies must take the wealth of the Indies with him?[12]

God is here. In the midst of life, breaking through the commonplace, glorifying the ordinary, the Great, High God is near. One should tread the earth with a deeply lying awe and reverence—God is in this place!

Do not wait to hear His spirit winging near in moments of great crisis, do not expect Him riding on the crest of a wave of deep emotional excitement—do not look to see Him at the dramatic moment when something abnormal or spectacular is at hand. Rather find Him in the simple experiences of daily living, in the normal ebb and flow of life as you live it.

The final thing that my faith teaches me is that God is love. Not only that He is; not only that He is near; but that He is love; Fully do I realize how difficult this is. There is so much anguish in life, so much misery unmerited, so much pain, so much downright reflective hell everywhere that sometimes it seems to me that it is an illusion to say that God is love. When one comes into close grips with the perversities of personality, with studied evil—it might be forgiven one who cried aloud to the Power over Life—human life is stain—blot it out! I know all that. I know that this world is messed up and confused. I know that much of society stretches out like a gaping sore that refuses to be healed. I know that life is often heartless, as hard as pig iron. And yet, in the midst of all this I affirm my faith that God is love—whatever else He may be.

Why do I? The reason is not far to seek. When I love someone I seem to be at the center of all meanings and values. Life takes on a new significance and I seem to have a quality of experience which is or was the guarantor of all experience. Again, under the compulsion of love, I send my life forth to do and be things that nothing else is capable of inspiring. I do gladly for Love's sake, what no power in heaven or hell could make me do without it. Therefore, whatever else Ultimate Reality God is, He must be love.

When a man dedicates his life to God he begins at once to fulfill in his own experience the practical logic of that dedication. It is here that he finds a true basis for security. The measure of my dedication is the measure of my own stature. He who dedicates his life to God is like a tree planted beside a stream sending its roots down to the water. Its leaves are always green. It has no fear of scorching heat. It goes on bearing fruit when all around it is barren and it lives serene.

Which shall it be for you—a scrawny scrub in a desert—barren—or a fruitful tree that looks on life with quiet eyes? Which?

TD. HTC-MBU: Box 192.

1. In a 1978 letter to Frank White, who had written to Thurman about his vivid memories of the 1932 sermon preached at Plymouth Congregational Church in Washington, D.C., Thurman indicated that one of the church deacons was so impressed by the sermon that he had it privately printed. To Frank White, 11 August 1978, HTC-MBU: Box 162; Lester A. Walton, "Negro Minister Fills Pulpit at Vassar: Rev. Dr. Howard Thurston [*sic*] Is First of His Race to Do So," 1 April 1928, printed in the current volume.

2. By *New York World* reporter Lester A. Walton's description, the sermon delivered at Vassar followed closely "Barren or Fruitful?" though it was more political, and ended with a tribute to American socialist leader Eugene V. Debs.

3. Jer. 17:5–6: "This is the eternal's word: a curse on him who relies on mere human aid, turning his thoughts from the eternal! He is like some desert scrub that never thrives, set in a dry place in the steppes, in a salt land."

4. Luke 18:10–13: "Two men went up in to the temple to pray; the one a Pharisee, and the other a publican. The Pharisee stood and prayed thus with himself, 'God, I thank thee, that I am not as other men are, extortioners, unjust, adulterers, or even as this publican. I fast twice in the week, I give tithes of all I possess.' And the publican, standing afar off, would not lift up so much as his eyes unto heaven, but smote upon his breast, saying, 'God be merciful to me a sinner.' I tell you, this man went down to his house justified rather than the other: for every one that exalteth himself shall be abased; and he that humbleth himself shall be exalted."

5. Jer. 17:7–8: "But happy is he who relies on the Eternal, with the Eternal for his confidence! He is like a tree planted beside a stream, reaching its roots to the water, untouched by any fear of scorching heat, its leaves are ever green."

6. Mark 9:23–24.

7. Isa. 29:13.

8. Shakespeare, *Hamlet*, 3.3.

9. Isa. 6:1–3.

10. Luke 17:21.

11. Heb. 1:1–2.

12. When Union Station in Washington, D.C., was erected in 1908, its walls were inscribed with half a dozen quotations according to a program devised by Charles W. Elliott, president of Harvard University. On the western end of the station is the following quotation from James Boswell's *Life of Johnson*, "'[As the Spanish proverb says,] He, who would bring home the wealth of the Indies, must carry the wealth of the Indies with him.' So it is in traveling; a man must carry knowledge with him, if he would bring home knowledge." Boswell, *Life of Johnson*, ed. R. W. Chapman (Oxford: Oxford University Press, 1980), 954.

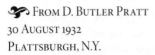 FROM D. BUTLER PRATT

30 AUGUST 1932

PLATTSBURGH, N.Y.

D. Butler Pratt,[1] the acting dean of the School of Religion, welcomes Thurman to Howard University. The letter suggests that President Mordecai Wyatt Johnson has made the appointment of Thurman as a full-time professor. Pratt's detailed description of teaching duties offers a glimpse of the stringent teaching load undertaken at the time by full-time faculty at predominantly black institutions of higher learning. Also, he points out that the school takes a modernist approach to theological studies, arguing for the critical study of the Bible and Christian history.

Rev Howard Thurman,
Howard University,
Washington, D.C.

My dear Mr. Thurman:

Unexpectedly, President Johnson has asked me to serve as acting dean of the School of Religion for another year. He informs me that you have been appointed a full time professor in the School in the general department of Theology with a teaching load of fifteen hours a week.

I congratulate you upon the appointment. All of us who have been associated with the work have a growing sense of its importance and of its fascination. It grips us and calls out our best endeavor. I am confident that a similar experience awaits you. May all the joy that I anticipate for you in this inspiring task be realized fully by you in the days to come—

I am writing of some details of the classwork that you may know what to expect and that certain possible alternatives may be considered. As you probably know much of the teaching has been done by pastors and others who have given us part time service. Our budget is very limited and it will be necessary for you to teach five classes, three hours a week, taking thus the work done by some of the part time men.

Normally, the class [*illegible line*] Theological College—the class in the Philosophy of Religion and the class in the History of Religions in the Graduate School would be under your care during the first quarter. As the number of students in the Graduate School is very small, it may be necessary to unite, for economy's sake the Junior & Middle classes. In that case, there would be only two classes which would strictly come under your department of theology. The course in systematic theology runs through the year three hours a week for each of the three quarters. It is designed to cover the general field in a way suited to the needs of students who are of senior college grade. They will have had for the most part the elementary courses in Philosophy and Psychology [*illegible*] in college and the preliminary Bible courses. Clarke's text book has been used as a guiding outline.[2] It has been my policy to assign a general task to a professor and give him freedom in its execution rather than to attempt to dictate details. You will, therefore, have a group of earnest students of average ability to instruct for one year in the field of Theology. Obviously, in so vast a field one cannot do all that would be desirable. A view point and an insight are about all that one can hope to impart. It may not be necessary to add—but I do so in order to avoid possible misunderstanding—that each teacher is absolutely free to express his opinions and to teach the truth as God gives him to see the truth, but that each teacher should avoid dogmatism and seek to cooperate with others in the faculty who may hold other views. Our faculty is distinctly modern in its attitude toward the Bible and theological questions, which means, as I understand it, that we have the attitude of searchers for the truth, rather than of the closed mind, even of some so-called modernists.

The courses in the Graduate School were prepared in cooperation with other members of the faculty, by President W. S. Nelson of Shaw University, who was then a professor in our school, The Philosophy of Religion and the History of Religion were arranged to cover two years—being so interrelated as to give the best training in the field of religion, its history and philosophy, possible under the limitations of time and faculty we are subjected to. As you come to your work, I wish that you would submit to the faculty a tentative outline of how you think the subjects should be treated with a division by quarters—The field is yours, what has been done is only suggestive and by no means a rut for you to follow. The brief statements in our bulletin will perhaps [illegible line].

We are to lose Prof. Moon of Johns Hopkins, who becomes Executive Secretary of the American Schools of Oriental Research. He was thoroughly trained in the Semitic field & read Egyptian inscriptions, besides being perhaps the most popular teacher we had—His going leaves a vacancy hard to fill. I refer to it to say that our greatest immediate need is in the O.T.[3] field—Introduction and Theology of the O.T., a one year course with the Juniors in the Graduate School and O.T. Exegesis in both divisions—In the Theological College we have a one quarter course in Introduction to Bible Study, to orient the first year men in Biblical subjects—the canon the versions—the literature—history of interpretation, and the like. It is elementary and must be adapted sympathetically to some who hold to the literal views of tradition and need, by actual study of the facts, to open their minds to the historical method of approach.

If you have preparation, as I know you must have, for these courses—viz. (1) Introduction to Bible Study—T. Col. 1st yr. (2) Introduction and Theology of O.T. Grad. Sch. Juniors—(3) O.T. Exegesis T. Col. 3rd. yr., it would be most happy for our present arrangement. There are other possible alternatives, but where a man has made good in a given field for several years, I dislike to remove him. The value of a teacher increases with the experience of years—There are several of these part time men who are well prepared in their special fields and I think it adds richness to our curriculum to have the personal slant of each on the great subjects of Theological study. I wish to retain in our service men like Clark in Psychology, Bentley in Relig Education and Washington in Pastoral Theology to mention only a few. King[4] is a live wire, as you know, and has brought an enthusiasm and the outlook of one fresh from the Seminary—So I might go on—There are other matters to discuss seriously like our correspondence school which is in a bad way and our evening class work which is well worth all the sacrifice of time and strength it has required—

More later—Please let me have your frank reaction to what I have so hur-
riedly written—
Cordially yours,
[*signed*] D Butler Pratt

ALS. HTC-MBU: Box 16.

1. Rev. Davie Butler Pratt (1861–1940), a graduate of Williams College (1883) and Union
Theological Seminary (1889), served as pastor of Union-Beecher Memorial Congregational Church in Brooklyn (1889–1900) and Faith Congregational Church in Springfield,
Massachusetts (1900–1908). Pratt taught Biblical literature at Talladega College (1908–13)
before moving on to Howard University, where he was professor of church history and
sociology (1913–34) and dean of the School of Religion (1917–34).
2. "Clarke's text book" may refer to a modernist work of William Newton Clarke, such
as *An Outline of Christian Theology* (New York: Scribner, 1906).
3. Old Testament.
4. Reverend Herbert King was a friend of Thurman and pastor of Plymouth Congregational Church in Washington, D.C., where Thurman preached "Barren or Fruitful?" on 28
August 1932.

🖎 FROM MORDECAI WYATT JOHNSON
8 OCTOBER 1932
WASHINGTON, D.C.

*During Thurman's first semester on the Howard faculty, Johnson appoints him
as chairman of the university's committee on religious life.*

Dear Mr. Thurman:
   On behalf of the Trustees and Faculties of Howard University, I am today
appointing you Chairman of the University-wide Committee on Religious Life,
which has charge of the weekly worship at the University and general supervision
of the religious life of the University community. The retiring Chairman, Mr. J. W.
Huguley,[1] is glad to learn of your willingness to accept this responsibility and has
given me his promise to remain on the committee and to give you all possible help,
during the current year. I am sure that you will find him cordial and very helpful.
I shall be glad to confer with you, when you are ready, about the membership of
the committee and about the plans for the current year. May I request that you
secure from Mr. Huguley at once a copy of the tentative schedule of preachers.
With great appreciation and with cordial regards, I am
Sincerely yours,
[*signed*] Mordecai W. Johnson
Mordecai W. Johnson
President

TLS. HTC-MBU: Box 8.

1. John Wesley Huguley, a professor of chemistry at Howard, received his doctorate from the University of Minnesota.

✒ To Lucy Diggs Slowe
3 November 1932
Washington, D.C.

In this letter to Lucy Diggs Slowe, dean of women at Howard University, Thurman requests her recommendations for women speakers.

My dear Dean Slowe[1]

To date our preaching schedule this year lists no woman speaker. I am wondering if you have any suggestions. I am very anxious to complete the schedule for the year. Personally, I wish we might secure some powerful Negro woman.

Many thanks.

Sincerely yours,

[*signed*] Howard T

Nov. 3, 1932

ALcS. HTC-MBU: Box 19.

1. Lucy Diggs Slowe (1885–1937) received her BA from Howard University (1908) and MA from Columbia University (1915). She taught at Armstrong High School in the District of Columbia from 1915 to 1919, was one of several key people charged with organizing the first junior high school (Shaw Junior School) in D.C., and was its principal from 1919 to 1922. Slowe became the first dean of women at Howard University, a position she held from 1922 until her death in 1937. She was also one of the founders of Alpha Kappa Alpha Sorority in 1908. In 1923, she became the first president of the National Association of College Women (NACW), an organization of black women graduates of accredited liberal arts colleges and universities.

✒ From Kirby Page
25 November 1932
New York, N.Y.

Kirby Page[1] responds to Thurman's request for a list of books on socialism. The booklist he enclosed is not extant. Thurman's interest in socialism was long-standing, dating to his undergraduate days at Morehouse when he first became involved in the socialist-oriented pacifist organization Fellowship of Reconciliation (FOR), and he retained this interest throughout the interwar years.

Dear Howard:

I am glad indeed to make up a short list of books on socialism, and will include it in this letter.

We are sending you the books which you have ordered.

Unfortunately, I cannot accept your invitation for January 8th as I am going to Asilomar[2] and will be on the Pacific coast at that time. I probably could get free for February 19th or February 26th if either of these dates are convenient for you. I wired you on Saturday suggesting these dates.

Cordially yours,

[*signed*] Kirby

Rev. Howard Thurman

Howard University

Washington, D.C.

KP:ST

{Feb. 19th is a go!}

TLcS. HTC-MBU: Box 16.

1. Kirby Page (1890–1957) was a leader of the Fellowship of Reconciliation (FOR), an active socialist, and an editor of *World Tomorrow*. He authored many books, including *Jesus or Christianity; A Study in Contrasts* (Garden City, N.Y.: Doubleday, 1929), *A New Economic Order* (New York: Harcourt, Brace, 1930), *Is Mahatma Gandhi the Greatest Man of the Age? A Biographical Interpretation and an Analysis of the Political Situation in India* (New York: Page, 1930), and *Religious Resources for Personal Living and Social Action* (New York: Farrar & Rinehart, 1939).

2. He refers to the annual YMCA student conference in Asilomar, California.

REVIEW OF GEORGE BERNARD SHAW, *THE ADVENTURES OF THE BLACK GIRL IN HER SEARCH FOR GOD*
MAY 1933
WASHINGTON, D.C.

Thurman gives a perfunctory review of a novel for which he has little regard, The Adventures of the Black Girl in Her Search for God, *by British socialist and Nobel Laureate George Bernard Shaw.[1]*

Any publication by Shaw gets attention. This particular book he must have written with tongue in cheek and twinkle in eye. Inspired by the intellectual and spiritual bankruptcy of a missionary lady, the Girl knocks at many doors seeking God. In her hand there is a very useful but devastating weapon, a knobkerry,[2] which she uses to dramatize in space and time what her mind does to most of the solutions offered. At length the girl encounters a philosopher who has learned to accept life and not worry about it. He has found escape or fulfillment in his garden. "God is at your elbow," he says, "and he has been there all the time. Make a little garden for yourself: dig and plant and weed and prune; be content when he jogs your elbow when you are gardening unskillfully, and blesses you when you are gardening well." She lays down her knobkerry and joins the philosopher in his gardening and reflections. Then she marries an Irishman, has copper-colored children, sees the travail of her soul and is not satisfied.

In an extended note at the close of the book, Mr. Shaw gives his apologia. There is nothing new and little that is fresh in what he has to say. The significance of the book is that Bernard Shaw wrote it.

Intercollegian 50 (May 1933): 232.

1. George Bernard Shaw (1856–1950) was a playwright and novelist. He created such famous works as *Pygmalion* (1913) and won the Nobel Prize for Literature in 1925.

2. A *knobkerry* is a short club.

⌇⌇ To Vernon Johns

2 May 1933
Washington, D.C.

Thurman invites Vernon Johns, the outspoken and celebrated preacher, to open Negro History Week at Howard University.

My dear Vernon:[1]

I am sending you a note to invite you to preach at the University on February 11, 1934. You will note this is the Sunday before Lincoln's birthday and I am, therefore, asking you to prepare a special sermon having to do with some aspect of the moral and spiritual challenge of either the life of Lincoln or Frederick Douglass. Incidentally, this will open the observance of Negro History Week.

I regret that we have not been able to get down there this year but the wolf has been at the back door. Someone left the door unlatched and he got inside. Sincerely,

[*unsigned*]

President Vernon Johns
Virginia Theological Seminary and College
Lynchburg, Virginia

TLc. HTC-MBU: Box 9.

1. Vernon Johns (1892–1964) attended Virginia Theological Seminary and College in Lynchburg (1911–12) but was expelled for insubordination. He talked his way into Oberlin Graduate School of Theology, despite having no bachelor's degree. In 1918 he earned a BD from Oberlin and then studied at the University of Chicago. In 1920, Johns became the pastor of Court Street Baptist Church in Lynchburg, where he developed a strong friendship with poet and social activist Anne Spencer. That same year, he established the Southern Mercantile and Development Company in order to organize black capital and reduce dependency on whites in the town. Fired from that job, he went to First Baptist Church of Charleston, West Virginia, succeeding Mordecai Wyatt Johnson. Johns preceded Martin Luther King Jr. at Dexter Avenue Baptist Church in Montgomery, Alabama. See Charles

Emerson Boddie, *God's Bad Boys* (Valley Forge, Pa.: Judson, 1972) and Samuel Lucius Gandy, *Human Possibilities: A Vernon Johns Reader* (Washington, D.C.: Hoffman, 1977).

☙ Review of Benjamin E. Mays and Joseph W. Nicholson, *The Negro's Church*
June 1933
Washington, D.C.

In this review published in the Intercollegian, *Thurman tells the reader very little about the book's content, save that it highlights the arrested development of black churches. Not only did segregation prevent their maturation by starving them of resources but it also produced racially separate institutions not found in other religions, which, for Thurman, attested to the ungodliness of the "American white man's religion."*

The Negro's Church is an indispensable handbook for one who would be intelligent in matters pertaining to the development of organized Christianity in the United States. It provides much of the material for the missing link in almost all of the works dealing with the history of the Church in America. The study is made specifically of 609 urban and 185 rural Negro churches but it involves an interpretation of social forces that antedate all Negro churches. Statistics abound; but they are woven into an interesting mosaic. The authors, Negroes themselves, give a rather disinterested interpretation of the data revealed. It is a pathetic picture; the churches seem to be lacking in almost everything except in vitality. What a criminal indictment they are to the American white man's religion in whose midst they were established and subsequently developed! The story is an eloquent dramatization of the tragedy of the segregated church. To preach the Kingdom of God from a segregated pulpit is one of the profoundest kinds of atheism. Loud must ring the laugh of Allah in his Mohammedan heaven as he beholds the spectacle of the First Baptist Church (Colored) and the First Baptist Church (White).

Intercollegian 50 (June 1933): 258.

☙ To John Hope
29 June 1933
Asilomar, Calif.

Writing to an ailing John Hope from the YMCA student conference in Asilomar, Thurman reveals his keen understanding of human suffering and loss.

My dear Mr Hope
Word came to me yesterday that you are ill. I am very sorry—I trust that it is not a critical illness and that the days will be useful for deep rest as well as healing.

One thing I learned from the long terrible illness through which I passed with Kate—The test of a man's life is to be found in the amount of pain he can absorb without spoiling his joy.

Sincerely,

[*signed*] Howard Thurman

June 29

ALS. JLH-GAU: Box 25.

To Reinhold Niebuhr

8 JANUARY 1934

WASHINGTON, D.C.

Thurman sends Reinhold Niebuhr a reminder letter in preparation for his upcoming speaking engagement at Howard University.

Dear Reinie:[1]

Just a note to remind you that you open the Week of Prayer here on Saturday night, January 20. I want you to talk about "Education and the Good Life"; this from the point of view of the increased moral responsibility that the advantages of education bring with them to the individual. Sunday morning in your sermon I would like you to talk about the significance of morality in the struggle for existence.

Of course Sue and I are planning for you to live with us. Come as early as you can Saturday afternoon or Saturday morning if possible. We promise you that Anne Spencer's crying will only disturb you until three in the morning, after that you may sleep.

My best to you and Mrs. Neibuhr for a hearty New Year.

Sincerely yours,

[*unsigned*]

Howard Thurman

Professor Reinhold Niebuhr

Union Theological Seminary

New York City

HT/m

TLc. HTC-MBU: Box 14.

---

1. Karl Paul Reinhold Niebuhr (1892–1971) was one of the leading figures in American religious and social thought during the twentieth century. He received his BA from Elmhurst College, Illinois (1910), and his BD from Yale Divinity School (1914). He was strongly influenced by his work for thirteen years as an evangelical and reformed pastor in a working-class Detroit neighborhood. An active member of the Socialist Party during the 1930s, he grew to embrace New Deal policies. A pacifist in 1919, he was one of the first in the United States to call for an active resistance to fascism worldwide. In 1928, his teaching

career began at Union Theological Seminary, where he remained until his retirement in 1960. A strong proponent of neo-orthodoxy or Christian realism, Niebuhr was a founder of the journal *Christianity and Crisis* and of the political group Americans for Democratic Action. Both groups were formed to give liberal Christian interventionists a voice. *Moral Man and Immoral Society* (New York: Scribner's Sons, 1932), his best-known work, significantly influenced the American movement of Christian realism, which registered strong belief in the Fall of Man, the dialectical nature of the self, and the primacy of sin and grace.

🐎 SUE BAILEY THURMAN TO SUSAN FORD BAILEY
12 FEBRUARY 1934
WASHINGTON, D.C.

Sue Bailey Thurman writes a Valentine's Day greeting to her mother in memory of her father, Isaac Bailey,[1] a prominent educator in Dermott, who cofounded with Susan Ford Bailey the Southeast Baptist Academy, one of the few existing secondary schools for blacks in the state of Arkansas. The strains of caring for her ailing mother-in-law and two young children, together with Howard's hectic schedule and frequent absences, are evident.

Dearest, dearest Mama![2]

This is my valentine greeting for 1934. I am thinking of our beloved one who left the world twenty long and short years ago, leaving behind a widow and three young children. I have his picture out now, the one that I brought up here to be framed. His memory is a beautiful thing to me, even tho I was scarcely twelve when he passed away. And you are thinking of him, too. They must be long, deep thoughts. I can understand your devotion for him and for us, since I now have a husband and child, too.

We have been blessed in every possible way. And to think that you have built a fine monument of work during these years which will stand forever, and honor to him and you and all your children. I am grateful to God that you are still with us. May you live long to continue your blessed work.

Howard & I have been discussing a way to honor papa in Dermott. If the high school were named for him, we would equip its play ground completely or give an annual scholarship to one of its graduates or do something at your suggestion to induce the school board to consider this. In this way we two can always keep up with the graduates and help them get into the various schools.

Mother Alice has been back from the hospital going on three weeks. Howard has been away almost two weeks of that time, coming in and going right out again on speaking tours. I am carrying a great load, physically, but I am now getting some help from a student who comes in for one hour each day.

We are planning for our summer. Shall we come to Dermott in June or August? Which will suit you best. The whole family wants to come.

Anne Spencer weighs 15 lbs. looks like a pumpkin or tomato. Olive is progressing wonderfully. Phillip[3] is in line for graduation in June. We are applying to H. U. for a scholarship for him. My! but I would rejoice to see you. {You aren't sick or anything are you. Please write. A line from my dear mother would cheer and relieve me wonderfully. And write Mother Alice.}

[*signed*] Baby

ALS. BTP-GEU: Box 3.

1. Isaac George Bailey (1847–1914) was born in Arkansas City to Perry Bailey, a slave from Eastern Shores, Maryland, and Virginia, a Cherokee who had traversed the 1838 Trail of Tears. Perry and Virginia were among those who founded Saint John Baptist Church, one of the first African American churches in Arkansas City. Educated at Branch Normal College in Pine Bluff, Arkansas, he served as pastor of First Baptist Church in Dermott, Arkansas, and Log Bayou Church in Tillar Station, Arkansas. He was also president of the Southeast District Industrial Baptist Academy in Dermott and moderator of the South-East District Baptist Association. Bailey was a major force within the Arkansas Baptist Convention and worked closely with the National Negro Business League and the Arkansas Baptist College. In 1866 he married Minnie White. They had two children: Charles H. Bailey and Maude Bailey Frazier, who served as assistant principal of the South-East Industrial Academy. In 1884 Isaac married Susie Ford, and they had nine children, six of whom died before adulthood. In the late 1880s he served in the Arkansas legislature.

2. Susie Elvie Ford (ca. 1870–1948) was the daughter of Elvie, a slave, and T. S. Ford, a Mississippi plantation owner. She attended Sumner High School and Normal School in St. Louis, Missouri. In 1883 she purchased land in Pine Bluff, Arkansas, where she built a home for her mother and herself. She served as president of the Southeast District Baptist Women's Association and as an agent for the Women's American Mission Baptist Home Mission Society.

3. Sue is referring to Phillip Miller, who was sent by Mrs. Bailey to live with the Thurmans while completing his education at Howard University, where he graduated with honors from the art department. Thurman recalls that Phillip "marked the beginning of a long line of young people, inspired and helped by Sue's mother, to leave the small town of Dermott to seek an education in the large world beyond." *WHAH*, 87.

✒ REVIEW OF E. S. WATERHOUSE, *WHAT IS SALVATION?*
MARCH 1934
WASHINGTON, D.C.

Thurman rarely discussed Christian salvation in public discourse, but this book review provides a glimpse of his thinking on the subject. Thurman concludes, as does Waterhouse, that salvation is "the process by which Christ possesses the life of a man." Thurman also finds resonance with the author's nontheological approach to salvation, deemphasizing atonement theology and opting, instead, for an understanding of salvation as a way of thinking and being in the world.

The author begins by calling attention to the nature of the problem precipitated by the fact that before any formal theology existed connecting the death of

Christ with the Christian experience of the forgiveness of sins, those who experienced the sense of forgiveness regarded the death of Christ as the ground of their experience. From the author's point of view, the death of Jesus opened the eyes of men to the true character of sin and awakened them to a belief in the love of God. Notwithstanding the fact that it is definitely stated that the treatment is from the point of view of psychology, there is no attempt to give a psychological explanation of two very important facts: that millions of people did and do connect the death of Christ and the forgiveness of sins; that therefore a unique significance is attached to the death of Christ.

Since the man who is saved exhibits certain signs of the fact, if one would know objectively what salvation is he must observe its fruits. For the individual this means finding a new and larger center of focus or integration, so that the mind of Christ functions practically in character. Obviously, since there are degrees to which this is true it must follow that there are degrees of salvation. It is the *process* by which Christ possesses the life of a man. What is true of the individual is true of the psychological climate in which the thought life of the individual develops. It is folly to think of a Christ-centered man continuing to function in a thought world alien to his own deepest experiences. Given enough time a synthesis is effected whereby Christ becomes indigenous.

In the chapter "The Transformation of Commerce" there is a scintillating discussion of the problems involved in the renovation of society. The remaining chapters deal with the universal nature of salvation, an interesting problem study of Judas, the attitude of the Bible toward salvation and a kind of prolegomena to what the author calls "A Galilean Society."

The volume's chief merit is its fresh simplicity and essentially non-theological character. It deals deftly and with a measure of originality with an old problem but one in which it is reasonable to suppose the human race will maintain a lively interest for years to come.
Intercollegian 51 (March 1934): 147.

꙳ To W. E. B. Du Bois
24 MARCH 1934
WASHINGTON, D.C.

Thurman informs W. E. B. Du Bois that he plans to attend the conference called by Du Bois on the "Negro Youth Movement."

Dear Dr. Du Bois:

Just a note to express my personal interest in your i̶t̶o̶m̶ {notice} concerning a Negro youth movement. My other plans for the month of July have not been completed but I assure {you} that if it is at all possible I shall be happy to attend the conferences that you have in mind.

Very sincerely yours,
[*signed*] Howard Thurman
Howard Thurman
Dr. W. E. B. Du Bois
Atlanta University
Atlanta, Georgia
HT/M

TLc. WEBD-MU: film D82625, reel 43, frame 29.

☙ To WINNIFRED WYGAL
24 MARCH 1934
WASHINGTON, D.C.

Winnifred Wygal, friend of the Thurman family and executive secretary of the National Student Council, had written Thurman earlier about the prospect for a united student movement in America. Thurman is unequivocal in his response, citing the need for the great spiritual issues of the day to be raised in new and fresh ways. Wygal was scheduled to speak at Howard University in May. The letter is insightful regarding Thurman's skepticism of national student movements and his convictions about the process for establishing a vital student organization.

My dear Winifred:[1]

It is simply outrageous that I have not answered your long letter of September 17. I was foolish enough to hope that we would have a chance to talk sometime during the winter. The way things are looking now that will not be possible. I do not have the kind of letter writing intellect that reveals its working to the greatest and best advantage. That is another reason why I have not addressed myself to the questions which you raise in your letter. The only thing that I wish to say about the United Movement in this country is this: What are we going to unite? In all of the movements there is a lot of deadness. And if you make the tragic error of attempting a vital connection between something that is dead and something that is less dead, we simply increase the sureness of death. Zero multiplied by infinity is still zero. I have no faith in the future of a united student movement in America that is simply a combination of the existing units. It seems to me Windy that we must undertake a fresh start. How to do it of course is the question. As you have long since known I am quite impracticle, but this is my suggestion: First, We must find out what the basic spiritual issues of our generation are, where the points of greatest tension are. Your letter seems to suggest some of them, perhaps the most pertinent of them.

Second, We need to discover a sound hypothesis with reference to our attack on the problems or issues as revealed in number one. Third, On the bases of number one and two, enlist the youth as to name and spirit in our enterprise. This will mean creating machinery as the need arises, Unless we are willing to make some such fresh start as the thing outlined above (I make no plea for what I am saying, it is only suggestive of what I mean by a fresh start), we shall simply go on as we are now. And if we unite it will simply mean just a reduction of overhead expenses and an increase in objective efficiency but the devil will continue undisturbed.

You ought to see Anne Spencer. She is a little dinosaur. We are looking forward to seeing you in May.

Sincerely yours,

[*unsigned*]

Howard Thurman

Miss Winifred Wygal

600 Lexington Avenue

New York City

HT/M

TLc. HTC-MBU: Box 21.

1. Winnifred Wygal (1884–1972) served as executive secretary of the National Student Council of the YWCA and was a professional staff member of the YWCA from 1919 to 1940. She was a prominent leader in international student conferences throughout Europe, Canada, and the United States during the 1930s and 1940s. Wygal graduated from Drury College (1906) and did graduate study at Columbia University, Union Theological Seminary, and the University of Chicago.

CHAPTER VI

Pilgrimage of Friendship

The Negro Delegation to India, Burma, and Ceylon

"THE PILGRIMAGE OF FRIENDSHIP": NEGRO DELEGATION

An epochal event in Howard Thurman's life was his participation in the Negro Delegation to India, Burma (now Myanmar), and Ceylon (now Sri Lanka) in 1935 and 1936. Thurman served as chairman of the delegation, and other members were Sue Bailey Thurman, the Reverend Edward G. Carroll,[1] and his wife, Phenola Carroll.[2] They arrived in Colombo, Ceylon, on 21 October 1935, and spent over four months in South Asia, delivering more than 250 addresses before departing Ceylon on 8 March 1936. Selected documents begin with the 16 May 1934, letter from Winnifred Wygal, executive secretary of the National Student Council of the YWCA, inviting Sue to become the second member of the delegation.

No one was more instrumental in bringing about the "Pilgrimage of Friendship" of the Negro Delegation than the Reverend A. Ralla Ram, then executive secretary of the Student Christian Movement of India, Burma, and Ceylon, at whose behest and invitation the delegation toured South Asia.[3] Ralla Ram had much experience in the International Student Christian Movement. He had given a speech in fall 1931 at Spelman College and met Thurman. The *Spelman Messenger* reported that Ralla Ram had a particular interest in "the social and class distinctions to which Negroes in America are subjected" because "they seemed to parallel, to some degree, caste distinctions in India." There, he had made a plea that "the colored people of America pray for India and identify themselves sympathetically with problems so nearly akin to their own difficulties in this country."[4]

African Americans had long had an interest in India. By the mid–nineteenth century, Frederick Douglass and other abolitionists railed against the practice of the "caste system" in the United States. African American Christians had been a presence in India at least since the 1880s, when the Fisk Jubilee Singers had an extensive Asian concert tour. The prominent Methodist Episcopal missionary Amanda Berry Smith, born a slave in Maryland, spent several years in India on a successful preaching mission. In the twentieth century, the interest in India was greatly heightened by the rise of Mahatma Gandhi as the charismatic leader of India's independence effort. For his part, Gandhi published a special message "To the American Negro" in 1929 in *Crisis*, the official magazine of the NAACP, in which he was introduced by W. E. B. Du Bois as "the greatest colored man in the world."[5]

The tour of the Negro Delegation highlighted a new urgency by the International Student Christian Movement to deal forthrightly with the issues of racism and colonialism. By the 1920s there was a powerful Protestant critique of the missionary enterprise that argued that the identification of the Christian message with the western and colonial powers was greatly reducing its scope.[6] The new emphasis on race within the Student Christian Movement was in part reflected by a new prominence of African Americans within the movement. Thurman's close friends Frank T. Wilson and Juliette Derricotte were the first prominent African American student Christians to visit India when they were part of a six-person United States delegation who attended the General Committee of the World's Student Christian Conference in Mysore, India, in 1928.[7]

Organizing the Pilgrimage of Friendship

By 1933, there was discussion between the American and Indian Student Christian movements about the tour of a Negro Delegation to South Asia.[8] Ralla Ram is reported as saying in a conversation with Luther Tucker, a member of the Committee on the Negro Delegation to India (hereafter the India Committee), "Since Christianity in India is the oppressors' religion, there would be a unique value in having representatives of another oppressed group speak on the validity and contribution of Christianity."[9] The India Committee, a six-person committee from the national YMCA and YWCA, was set up to handle the tour arrangements and included Tucker, Elizabeth Harrington, Warren Scott, Frank T. Wilson, A. Roland Elliott, and Marion Cuthbert. Harrington served as the committee's chair; two members, Wilson and Cuthbert, were African American. By April 1934, Wilson set forth the committee's criteria for selection to the Negro Delegation. As outlined in a statement of "General Principles," the delegation was to constitute a team with dovetailing talents and abilities. The delegation would have an equal number of men and women, with one member under the age of twenty-six.[10] Some leaders in the American Student Christian Movement wanted the delegation to be interracial, with two or three blacks and one white, but this was rejected in April 1934 on the grounds that it was contrary to the invitation from the Indian Student Christian Movement and would entail a revision of the purposes of the delegation.[11] The India Committee wanted the members of the Negro Delegation to have had "vital contact" with the Student Christian Movement in the United States, as well as an ability to deal with persons of other religious traditions, and to speak before large public gatherings and in intimate small groups. They also desired that members be able to convey "the philosophical, mystical approach of personal religion and the practical and ethically compelling demand for social justice."[12] The members of the delegation would have to agree to attend conferences, appear at colleges, and write articles about the tour, both to publicize their efforts beforehand and to share their experiences afterwards.[13] At times the Thurmans felt the India Committee's demands on their time for public speaking were excessive.[14]

The delegation's expenses were to be split between the American and Indian Student Christian Movements, with the Indian Movement handling expenses in India and the American Movement responsible for oceanic transportation and other related expenses. The India Committee estimated that a four-person delegation would cost about $2,400. There had been some interest in extending the tour to China and Japan. As late as May of 1935, there was still uncertainty about the possible extension of the tour, but in the end, there were not enough funds for this purpose.[15] The members of the delegation had to provide one hundred dollars for their own incidental expenses. Thurman complained in December 1935 that insufficient funds had been raised to cover a four-person delegation.[16] Additionally, Thurman was unable to arrange for a paid sabbatical from Howard University, resulting in the loss of a full year's salary, and the financial sacrifice required for the trip created what Thurman later described as an "overwhelming hardship."[17]

There were many details to be worked out by the India Committee in the United States and the Asian sponsors of the tour. The India Committee had planned on the tour taking place over the winter of 1934 through 1935.[18] But Ralla Ram made it clear that because of fundraising and the extensive preparation required, the tour could not take place until the fall of 1935.[19] In a letter to Harrington dated 13 May 1935, Thurman expressed concern about ensuring against discrimination in accommodations and transportation during the tour.[20]

The members of both the India Committee and the Negro Delegation were very concerned that the delegation be taken seriously as thoughtful African American representatives of American Christianity and not, as Wilson wrote, "on exhibition either as singers or anthropological specimens."[21] Originally the

Indian sponsors had wanted to ensure that the members of the delegation would be "expert singers." Writing to Harrington in August 1934, Wygal stated that the committee had made clear to Ralla Ram that "sending a good tenor or bass to India was no concern of ours."[22]

The India Committee and Thurman were also concerned that the Negro Delegation not be seen as having an evangelical focus. As Thurman recounted in his "Final Report to the India Committee" in 1938, he was worried from the beginning that the delegation would be considered "the spearhead of some kind of evangelistic movement from the West."[23] It was not easy to convince their Indian hosts that the delegation would not be "singing, soul-saving evangelists," as the prominent American missionary Stanley Jones in India had mistakenly described the tour in advance publicity.[24] Thurman's success in this regard was fairly limited, and he complained that the non-evangelical nature of the tour had to be explained to their hosts time and again.[25] During the tour many who heard the delegation's addresses were upset; Thurman related that a Sri Lankan convert in Kandy who spoke to him after a sermon, said, "You did not call my Master's name!"[26] In his report Thurman wrote, "If the pilgrimage of friendship was a disappointment at any point it was in connection with the whole question of evangelicalism," and many of their Indian hosts were deeply dissatisfied with the non-evangelical nature of the delegation's religious presentations. "It was not that we believed less in evangelism," Thurman explained, "but rather that our interpretation of evangelism differed profoundly from the one to which the Indians themselves were accustomed."[27]

Another delicate issue was the role that politics would play in the discussions of the Negro Delegation. The India Committee sought assurances that the delegation would have the political freedom to speak and discuss political issues with student groups.[28] Ralla Ram told the India Committee that while the delegation was free to speak on whatever topics they wanted, he hoped they would restrict sensitive topics to smaller meetings at which no journalists were present. Ralla Ram was concerned that a discussion of Indian politics in large public meetings would produce an intense negative reaction from British officials and could "defeat the primary purpose of the mission to India."[29] Thurman, who respected the constraints that Ralla Ram described, wrote in his final report that he was "determined also not to discuss or deal with questions of a political nature; our understanding was clear on this point before leaving the country."[30] Despite such precautions, Thurman recalls in his autobiography that the delegation was constantly worried about the monitoring by the British Criminal Investigation Department.[31]

Adding to Thurman's unease with the question of the limits to his political speech were concerns about the conservatism of the Student Christian Movement, a fear widely shared among blacks and progressives. Many wondered whether the delegation's message would be cautious and temporizing. The managing editor of the *Christian Century* questioned how the delegation would avoid "sentimental- ism" and a "false sense of representativeness."[32] Others were concerned that the delegates were chosen for their political docility,[33] and Thurman's friend Reverend Herbert King wondered what compromises were necessary on Thurman's part to be acceptable to the YMCA and YWCA. Although King found something "ines- timably hopeful" about the work of the delegation, this was "despite the auspices of the thing."[34]

Thurman's response to his own doubts and the doubts of others about the purpose of the delegation was to gather as wide a spectrum of views as possible on the state of black America, ranging from socialists to Robert Russa Moton, Booker T. Washington's successor at Tuskegee.[35] He also met with many who were familiar with India, including the Indian anthropologist P. Kodanda Rao, who was then studying at Yale.[36] Thurman also extensively prepared in other ways for the tour of South Asia. In the fall of 1934, he outlined an ambitious study of both the social conditions of American blacks and the political and religious history of South Asia and set up training sessions for the delegation and meetings with Indian students in the United States.[37] During the prepara- tion period, Thurman convinced Madeleine Slade, Gandhi's close associate, to speak at Howard University in October 1934 in the course of her American tour.[38] Thurman also made a cross-country train trip from Washington, D.C., to San Francisco for the express purpose of spending a few hours with Muriel Lester, an English pacifist and author on Indian affairs.[39] Sue's difficult trip to Mexico in March 1935 was undertaken in part to give her training in the presen- tation of American culture to foreign groups and to forestall any possible objec- tion to her presence on the delegation.[40]

SELECTING THE PERSONNEL

The personnel for the India delegation was chosen over a period of sixteen months. By far the easiest choice was that of Thurman himself. By 13 March 1934, the India Committee had contacted a number of black student leaders for suggestions for candidates. Fifteen names were under consideration, with Thurman topping the list.[41] Two weeks later, on 26 March, the committee submitted six names to the national headquarters committee of the YWCA and the executive committee of the YMCA: Thurman, Celestine Smith, Jane Saddler, Fenorah Bond Logan, Ben- jamin E. Mays, and Frank Wilson.[42] At a joint meeting of the YMCA and YWCA on 3 April, the first choice was Thurman. Also selected was Smith, who was at that time one of the most prominent African American female leaders within the YWCA. The other two members were less certain, though the committee was leaning toward selecting Wilson and Saddler. Reverend Carroll, who was then serving as pastor of John Wesley Methodist Church in Salem, Virginia, was added to the list of names for consideration. Harrington was authorized to negotiate with Thurman about his availability for the delegation,[43] and Thurman evidently accepted soon afterwards. The only opposition offered to Thurman's presence on the delegation had been that as a respected professor in his mid-thirties, he was on the outer limits of what might be considered a "student Christian."[44]

According to Thurman's 1938 final report, when he was first asked to serve, he felt that "under no circumstances would it be possible for me to accept." One of Thurman's reservations was primarily political; how could he, as a member of a discriminated-against minority, represent American Christianity to a foreign audience? Thurman's other main concern was that the tone of the delegation would not be evangelical. Wygal, who had been planning a trip to Howard to speak at Rankin Chapel on 6 May, was deputized by the India Committee to talk with Thurman about his reservations.[45]

While at Howard, Thurman and Wygal had what he described as an "exhaustive discussion" that assuaged his doubts and convinced him that his participation "fell within the range of my own life purposes."[46] It seems likely that the possibility of Sue's participation was also raised during the meeting with Wygal, especially as it appeared by then that Smith would not be joining the tour but instead accepting a position as director of the YWCA in Lagos, Nigeria. In a 16 May letter Wygal confirmed Thurman's agreement to participate in the delegation and extended the invitation for Sue to join. Shortly thereafter the India Committee extended invitations to Carroll and Grace Towns Hamilton, the national student secretary of the YWCA.

Matters grew more complicated when by the end of January 1935 Hamilton was contemplating withdrawing from the delegation, doing so by the next month.[47] The committee gave some consideration to limiting the tour to three persons but felt that a strong fourth person was needed.[48] In a letter from Harrington to Thurman dated 18 February 1935, she mentions that the India Committee hoped to have the decision finalized by the middle of March. But the decision dragged out until July. The candidacies of Saddler, Mamie Davis, and Marian Minus were considered and evidently rejected.[49] Although Thurman was a close friend of Davis, he was not very enthusiastic about her selection,[50] favoring Minus, a graduating senior at Fisk.[51] He had been led to assume that Minus would be selected.[52] In the end, the India Committee, without consulting Thurman and presumably at the behest of Carroll, selected Carroll's wife, Phenola.[53] Thurman thought Minus more qualified and felt that the selection of Phenola Carroll created the appearance that the wives were simply accompanying their husbands, rather than having been selected independently in their own right. The dilatory way in which the India Committee selected Phenola Carroll, six months after the resignation of Grace Towns Hamilton and a mere three months before the India Delegation left on their journey, surely made this delicate situation worse.

Travel Arrangements

Making the travel arrangements for the Negro Delegation, in an era of ocean liners, war scares, and widespread racial discrimination, was both prolonged and complex. What in the early twenty-first century is a one-day flight between New York City and Sri Lanka took an entire month in 1935 and touched four continents. The travel arrangements were complicated by questions of the treatment of African Americans on transportation carriers. In a letter written in May 1935, Thurman requested that the India Committee arrange second-class passage for the delegation and expressed concern about the treatment African Americans generally received as third-class passengers on Atlantic crossings. This request was not honored. The Negro Delegation traveled third class from New York City to Le Havre, France, but did travel second class on the SS *Chenonceaux* from Marseilles to Colombo.[54] The delegation evidently made the return trip on the same two ships.[55]

The Negro Delegation left New York City on the *Ile de France* on 21 September 1935.[56] Traveling with the Negro Delegation were Thurman's sister, Madaline, and his daughters, Anne and Olive. After arriving in France, the Thurmans accompanied Madaline and the children to Geneva, Switzerland, where Madaline would study eurhythmics and supervise the children.[57] Geneva was the headquarters of the World Student Christian Federation, and its president, Willem Visser't Hooft, had arranged many aspects of the stay of Thurman's sister and daughters.[58] Visser't Hooft had recently returned from India, and he and Thurman held discussions about India and Indian Christianity. The Thurmans and the Carrolls met again in Marseilles and embarked on 1 October 1935, passing through the Suez Canal and including a stop in Djibouti in French Somaliland. After a twenty-one-day sea voyage, they arrived in Colombo, Ceylon, on 21 October 1935.[59]

The pace of the 140-day tour was relentless, and Thurman's responsibilities as chairman were considerable. He had to handle all of the correspondence on arrangements and keep accounts of all expenses. Given all of the engagements, travel, and recordkeeping, it is hardly surprising that the members of the delegation were often near the point of exhaustion. There was the anxiety of having to make train connections every few days. Adjusting to the lifestyle in South Asia was also a challenge. Thurman complained about the hot, spicy food, and despite growing up in the pre–air conditioned south, he found the sultry weather enervating.[60] He evidently fell ill in Madura shortly after his arrival in India from Ceylon[61] and worried about his ability to keep up the pace of his engagements.[62] In February 1936, Thurman wrote to his secretary at Howard University, Ruth Taylor, "We are now in the last month of schedule. I do not see how I can possibly last until March 1st but I can, I know. These are very very hard days for us all."[63] Indeed, while in Delhi, the delegation cancelled all of their planned activities for several days because of illness and overwork. The most serious illnesses befell the Carrolls. Edward was unable to accompany the delegation to Rangoon, and Phenola was indisposed from 10 November to 20 November and again from 21 January to the end of the tour with a case of scarlet fever. Phenola's illnesses also required Edward to briefly take leave from the tour to tend to his wife.

Some records of the daily routines planned for the delegation survive, which give a sense of the pace of their activities. This is the planned itinerary for the delegation for 11 November 1935, in Madura, about the time Thurman evidently had an attack of nervous exhaustion:

8:00 a.m. To meet for an informal gathering with the College S.C.M. [*Student Christian Movement*]

9:00 a.m. College Chapel—Spiritual. Address by two of your number. This will be especially for the S.C.M., but there will certainly be a large number our students present, Hindus, and Moslems.

10:00 a.m. Visit the Madura College, our sister College in Madura, under Hindu Management. Two to speak.

10:45 a.m. Visit the American College, classes and hostels.

11:30 a.m. Free

12:30 p.m. Meal with the students

1:00 p.m. Rest.

2:45 p.m. Visit the Hindu Temple and Palace; other sights

3:15 p.m. Tea at the College, with the College Staff and prominent citizens of Madura. Be prepared to answer questions.

5:30 p.m. Free.

6:00 p.m. Meeting in the College Chapel—more in the nature of a public meeting, mostly students, but people of the community will also be invited. One short message if a number are present who do not understand English.

6:30 p.m. Meeting at the East Gate Church. The four of you to be present for the first part of the 6 o'clock meeting at the College and then two to be taken to East Gate. The address or addresses there will be interpreted. Christians, nurses, school children, and no doubt some non-Christians.

8:00 p.m. Dinner[64]

SIGNIFICANCE

The range of responses to the Negro Delegation was wide and to some extent in the eye of the beholder. An elderly Anglo-Indian woman in Calcutta lauded the delegation as bearing proof that "Jesus is alive and divine."[65] On the other hand, T. J. George wrote Thurman in early 1936, "I have been following with great interest the speeches you have been giving in different parts of the country, and it was a great disappointment when I was told plans to visit Trichur were dropped. . . . I feel that the great conflict in future will be waged more or less on racial or color lines. It will be a question of white races against brown or black. I am trying to study it as closely as possible and write on it from the point of view of an Asiatic."[66]

The question of race in America was the frequent subject of probing questions by Indian auditors. Many in the audience understood that Thurman's comments on the condition of African Americans implicitly spoke to the troubled situation of Indians under British rule. The response of an Indian journalist in Madras to Thurman's talk on "The Faith of the American Negro" is worth quoting at length:

> The like of it has not been heard before. The thrill that the audience felt was not because of the articulation of their own deepest and unexpressed feelings. Such stirrings have been known before, as for example, when Mahatma Gandhi in his pre-Indian career came as the messenger of suffering Indians in South Africa. It was rather the response of hearts that felt their linking up with another race as the lecturer proceeded with his interpretation of his people, defending them against false judgment, proclaiming the grit and character that was evolved under great stress, tracing the moods through which they have passed and expressing the bases of their confidence, while betraying no bitterness against their environment. It was no cold intellectual presentation of the incidents of a complex social history, but the soulful expression of the faith of the meek that rose conqueror over trials and suffering.[67]

The trip of the Delegation to India, despite its enormous strains and challenges, was one of the central events of Thurman's life. In his autobiography, Thurman devotes a quarter of the pages retelling his life through the early 1940s on his four months and seventeen days in India. Thurman's contact with Indians of all religious backgrounds helped push his conception of Christianity towards a largely non-creedal, experiential religion. Both the political and spiritual experience of India helped propel Thurman toward his later experiments in practical religion, notably the Fellowship Church. The Negro Delegation played a significant role in the furthering of the contacts between Indian colleges and African Americans. The year after the Negro Delegation returned to the United States, Thurman's close friends Channing Tobias and Benjamin Mays, under

Student Christian auspices, went to India in 1937 and like the delegation had a meeting with Gandhi. In the years following the delegation's trip, the Thurmans sponsored male and female students to various colleges in India. If World War II brought these contacts to a sudden end, it was not forgotten. For Bayard Rustin, Martin Luther King Jr., and other leaders of the Civil Rights Movement, the trip of the Negro Delegation and especially their meeting with Gandhi would continue to be an inspiration.[68]

1. Edward Gonzalez Carroll (1910–2000) was born in Wheeling, West Virginia. He earned an AB from Morgan College [now Morgan State University] (1930), a BD from Yale University (1933), and an MA from Columbia University (1941). At the time of the India Delegation planning, he was pastor of John Wesley Methodist Church in Salem, Virginia (1934–35), and in 1935 he was ordained an elder there. He then served as pastor of the Methodist Church in Grafton, West Virginia (1936–37). He was also an instructor in the Bible and philosophy at Morgan College (1937–41), a U.S. Army chaplain (1941–45), and associate student secretary of the YMCA in New York City (1945–49). He subsequently worked in New York City as associate pastor of St. Marks Methodist Church (1949–53) and pastor of Epworth Methodist Church (1953–55). From 1955 to 1962, he was pastor of Sharp Street Memorial Methodist Church in Baltimore. The Methodist Church's Northeastern Jurisdictional Conference elected him a bishop in 1972, and he served the Boston area until his retirement in 1980.

2. Phenola Valentine Carroll (1912–99) was born in Frederick, Maryland, and received her BA from Morgan College (1933). She was an analyst for the War Department during World War II, a caseworker for the Department of Welfare in New York City, and a social worker for the Baltimore Housing Department.

3. For more on the career of Reverend Augustine Ralla Ram (1888–1948), see Myra Skovel, *I Must Speak: The Biography of Augustine Ralla Ram* (Allahabad, India: North India Christian Literature Society, 1961).

4. "A Great Christian from India," *Spelman Messenger* 48 (October 1931): 24–25.

5. M. K. Gandhi, "To the American Negro, a Message from Mahatma Gandhi," *Crisis* 36 (July 1929): 225.

6. An influential work in this vein was Daniel Johnson Fleming, *Whither Bound in Missions?* (New York: Association Press, 1925). See also William R. Hutchinson, *Errand to the World: American Protestant Thought and Foreign Missions* (Chicago: University of Chicago Press, 1987).

7. Sudarshan Kapur, *Raising Up a Prophet: The African-American Encounter with Gandhi* (Boston: Beacon, 1992), 81.

8. See *Intercollegian,* June 1933.

9. Committee on the Negro Delegation to India, Minutes, 13 March 1934, HTC-MBU: Box 136.

10. Frank T. Wilson, "General Principles to Be Followed in Sending to the Student Christian Movement of India a Deputation of Negro Representatives by the Student Christian Movement of the United States," 6 April 1934, HTC-MBU: Box 136. For Wilson's authorship, see "Committee on the Negro Delegation," 6 April 1934, HTC-MBU: Box 136. W. A. Visser't Hooft, president of the World Student Christian Federation (WSCF), wrote to Wilson in June 1934 that the main point of the delegation was to strengthen the Christian impact in

Indian universities: "It needs very badly to be shown in Indian universities that Christian truth transcends the limitations of race." 5 June 1935, HTC-MBU: Box 191.

11. Frank T. Wilson, "Minutes Regarding the Decision of the Personnel of the Proposed Delegation to India," 19 April 1934, HTC-MBU: Box 136.

12. Wilson, "General Principles."

13. Ibid.

14. To Elizabeth Harrington, 10 April 1935 and To Frank T. Wilson, 15 April 1935, both printed in the current volume.

15. To Elizabeth Harrington, 13 May 1935, printed in the current volume.

16. To the Members of the India Committee, 20 December 1935, printed in the current volume.

17. *WHAH,* 108–9.

18. Wilson, Committee on the Negro Delegation to India, 1 March 1934, Minutes, HTC-MBU: Box 136.

19. A. Ralla Ram to Frank Wilson, 28 June 1934, printed in the current volume.

20. Minutes, Committee on the Negro Delegation to India, 26 March 1934, HTC-MBU: Box 136, and To Elizabeth Harrington, 13 May 1935, the latter printed in the current volume.

21. Wilson, "General Principles."

22. Wygal to Harrington, 14 August 1934, HTC-MBU: Box 136.

23. "Final Report to the India Committee," HTC-MBU: Box 136, to be printed in volume 2.

24. *WHAH,* 116.

25. "Final Report."

26. Ibid.

27. Ibid.

28. Minutes, Committee on the Negro Delegation to India, 13 March 1934, HTC-MBU: Box 136.

29. A. Ralla Ram to Frank Wilson, 28 June 1934, printed in the current volume.

30. "Final Report."

31. *WHAH,* 121.

32. Paul Hutchinson to Winnifred Wygal, 14 March 1935, printed in the current volume.

33. To Grace Virginia Imes, 5 December 1934, printed in the current volume.

34. From Herbert King, 11 October 1934, HTC-MBU: Box 10.

35. To Robert Moton, 30 August 1935, printed in the current volume.

36. P. Kodanda Rao to HT, 1 May 1935, HTC-MBU: Box 136.

37. To Elizabeth Harrington, 6 September 1934, HTC-MBU: Box 10.

38. Kapur, *Raising Up a Prophet,* 83–85. See also *WHAH,* 105–7.

39. From Muriel Lester, 21 January 1935, printed in the current volume.

40. To Members of the India Committee, 19 November 1935, printed in the current volume.

41. Minutes, Committee on the Negro Delegation to India, 13 March 1934, HTC-MBU: Box 136.

42. Minutes, Committee on the Negro Delegation to India, 26 March 1934, HTC-MBU: Box 136.

43. Minutes, Committee on the Negro Delegation to India, 6 April 1934, HTC-MBU: Box 136.

44. Minutes, Committee on the Negro Delegation to India, 10 April 1934, HTC-MBU: Box 136.

45. To Winnifred Wygal, 24 March 1934, printed in the current volume. Wygal was a close friend of Thurman's, and the two had previously shared their doubts about the direction of the Student Christian Movement.

46. "Final Report."

47. Minutes, Committee on the Negro Delegation, 30 January 1935, HTC-MBU: Box 136. Grace Towns Hamilton withdrew from the delegation because she did not want to be separated from her daughter, who was four years old at the time. She later told her biographers, "It was when Eleanor was still a baby and I just decided I couldn't do it." Lorraine Nelson Spritzer and Jean B. Bergmark, *Grace Towns Hamilton and the Politics of Southern Change* (Athens: University of Georgia Press, 1997), 63. Hamilton (1907–92), born and raised in Atlanta, lived in Memphis, Tennessee, from 1930 to 1941, where she taught at LeMoyne College and worked for the Works Progress Administration (WPA) and the YWCA. From 1943 to 1961, she was executive director of the Atlanta branch of the National Urban League. In 1965, she became the first African American woman elected to the Georgia General Assembly, the lower house of the Georgia legislature, serving until 1984.

48. Minutes, Committee on the Negro Delegation, 30 January 1935. HTC-MBU: Box 136.

49. Ibid. See also From Elizabeth Harrington, 18 February 1935, HTC-MBU: Box 136.

50. To Elizabeth Harrington, 13 May 1935, printed in the current volume.

51. Marian Minus to Elizabeth Harrington, 23 May 1935, printed in the current volume.

52. To Elizabeth Harrington, 11 July 1935, and To the Members of the India Committee, 20 December 1935, both printed in the current volume.

53. To Elizabeth Harrington, 11 July 1935, printed in the current volume.

54. From Open Road [travel agents], 19 September 1935, HTC-MBU: Box 136.

55. Compagnie des Messageries Maritimes to HT, 20 February 1936, HTC-MBU: Box 136.

56. "Report of the Negro Delegation," HTC-MBU: Box 136.

57. Initially, the plan had been to have the Thurman children spend the winter with a European family, but evidently Frank Wilson convinced him of the "possible moral embarrassment" this might cause, and Thurman looked into the possibility of Madaline spending the winter in Washington with the children. To Frank T. Wilson, 28 May 1935, printed in the current volume.

58. Willem Adolf Visser't Hooft (1900–1985), born in Haarlem, Netherlands, was appointed general secretary of the WSCF in 1932. He was general secretary of the provisional committee of the World Council of Churches (WCC) from its founding in 1938 and was the first general secretary of the WCC from its formal organization in 1948 until his retirement in 1966. For Visser't Hooft's visit to India, see "The Idol of Young India," *Student World* 27 (1934): 260–63. For the assistance he provided to the Thurmans in Geneva, see "Final Report."

59. *WHAH*, 112.

60. Ibid., 113.

61. S. W. Savarimuthu to HT, 19 November 1935, HTC-MBU: Box 136.

62. Benedicte Wilhjelm to HT, 14 November 1935, HTC-MBU: Box 136.

63. To Ruth Taylor, 12 February 1936, HTC-MBU: Box 136.

64. "Madura Itinerary," HTC-MBU: Box 136.

65. From Henrietta Wise, 14 January 1936, printed in the current volume.

66. T. J. George to HT, 14 January 1936, HTC-MBU: Box 136.

67. "One Who Met Them, the Negro Delegation in Madras," *Guardian (Madras),* 12 December 1935.

68. See Bayard Rustin, "Even in the Face of Death," in *Down the Line: The Collected Writings of Bayard Rustin,* ed. Bayard Rustin (Chicago: Quadrangle, 1971), 103.

❧ FROM WINNIFRED WYGAL
16 MAY 1934
NEW YORK, N.Y.

After her lecture at Howard University, Winnifred Wygal invites Sue Bailey Thurman to join her husband, Howard, on the delegation to India. Celestine Smith's decision not to take part in the delegation opened the way for Sue to join the group.

Mr. Howard Thurman
Howard University
Washington, D.C.

Dear Howard:

I have been very slow in acknowledging my delightful visit to Howard University on May 6. Circumstances of that visit were truly inspiring and my appreciation of your invitation and of the generous honorarium should have been made clear to you before this. You do indeed have a stimulating audience before whom to speak and I am greatly appreciative of the confidence you {re}pose in me to ask me to meet such a group.

I very much admire the way you and Sue handle the task in which you are engaged. I think you are doing a unique thing in a unique way.

I am overjoyed to hear that the committee, after the most careful consideration and in consultation with Celestine Smith whom as you know does not wish to be considered for India, are unanimous in hoping that not only yourself but your wife will be available for the India delegation.

Some recent developments make some of us more eager than ever that the delegation go. Perhaps it is honest to add that those same delegates do in some ways jeopardize the project for some of the various reasons which you and I recently discussed.

Cordially yours,
[*signed*] Winnifred Wygal
Winnifred C. Wygal
Executive Secretary
National Student Council
WCW:EGW

                                        TLS. HTC-MBU: Box 21.

❧ A. RALLA RAM TO FRANK T. WILSON
28 JUNE 1934
JAMNA, ALLAHABAD

Reverend A. Ralla Ram, executive secretary of the Student Christian Movement of India, Burma, and Ceylon, clarifies his views for a delegation of Negro Christians to visit India.

Frank T. Wilson, Esq.[1]
347 Madison Avenue
New York, U.S.A.

My dear Wilson:

I am afraid that my last letter has caused you some misgivings. Let me make some matters as clear as I can make them:—

1. The chief reason which has led me to suggest this mission of your students to India is that in the minds of our young people belonging to other faiths, Christianity is identified with western imperialism, and they all think that Christianity is a part and parcel of western cult. The purpose of suggesting a mission of this kind and several others is that our students throughout the country should see for themselves that Christianity is universal in its sweep, and when our Negro friends from America will come to India, (those who have suffered acutely at the hands of the white people), bearing witness before the students as to what Christ means to them, such a witness will carry with it an incalculably great importance and will help in pressing to the claims of Christ on the youth of modern India. This is the only motive which has made me suggest this mission.

2. What my colleagues and myself would expect from the mission would be that they should throughout the country bear witness to the work of Christ in their lives. The Christian message, to my mind, is meant for every individual in his own personal life, and at the same time it has to be brought to bear on all problems of life. I believe that the Christian message, if it remains unrelated to the problems of life as we face them, can never carry with it that all-sufficiency which is our great need today.

I would, of course, expect these fellow students to speak to us with their own background, and that their message should come to us from their own experience among the American people.

I would like to say that the relations between Britain and India are by no means satisfactory, but our own people will keep nothing from our fellow students from America. They will speak to them quite frankly about the situation in India, but I believe that this should be done in smaller groups at which no journalist should be present; for if our students from America should publicly express opinions on the relations between Britain and India and if their opinions should get into the press, the British Government may come down hard on them. I personally feel that they should be free to say whatever they like from public platforms, but facing facts as they are I feel that no public pronouncement should be made on this subject for they may defeat the primary purpose of the mission to India.

3. I was going over all the letters that have come to me from America, and so far the whole project seems to have been in the process of taking root, and no definite steps had been taken that the mission should come to India in the winter of 1934–35. It is only within the last two months that through your letters I noticed that you were planning to send this mission this winter. We need a great deal of preparation for this mission and we need the whole coming year to plan. I do hope that this will in no way damp your enthusiasm, and that taking these coming months for all our planning will only help to make this whole project a great success.

In conclusion, I want to write and assure you that this mission from America will do this country an immense amount of good in not only dramatizing the wide sweep of the Christian faith, but will also be a great adventure in healthy internationalism.

It is very interesting to find that Dr. E. Stanley Jones[2] in his recent visit to America was quite independently working at the same project. I am sending you a copy of the letter which I recently received from him. And, by the way, that reminds me to say that when I said in my last letter that we were expecting your delegates to be expert singers all I meant to say was that if they came to us singing their Negro Spirituals from the platforms of India they would enter our hearts through music and songs. I said this because Negro Spirituals have begun to be loved in India a great deal and our students sing them all over the country.

I hope that both of us will make up our minds to see that this project comes through and that we shall together set our shoulders to the task and that we shall meet any other difficulties that may arise with our objective clearly set before us. With my very kindest regards,

I am,

Yours very sincerely,

[unsigned]

A. Ralla Ram

ARR: YSS: CM

8/6/34

TLc. HTC-MBU: Box 22.

1. Frank Theodore Wilson (1900–1976) was one of Thurman's longtime, closest friends. He received an AB and STB from Lincoln University, and received an EdD from Columbia University (1937). He served as the student secretary of the national council of the

YWCA, New York (1923–26), and was a member of a research committee to study the service of the YMCA movement to black men in the United States. From 1936 to 1949 he was dean and professor of psychology at Lincoln University and in 1949 was appointed associate professor of religious education and dean of the School of Religion at Howard University. Wilson also served as secretary of education for the Board of Foreign Missions of the Presbyterian Church, USA.

2. According to Thurman, Eli Stanley Jones (1884–1973) had already raised expectations in India that the Negro Delegation, whom he had not met, would come to save souls, a point of view that the group carefully avoided. Jones, a well-known Methodist Episcopal Church missionary to upper-caste Indians, wrote *The Christ of the Indian Road* (New York: Abingdon, ca. 1925) and *Christ and Human Suffering* (New York: Abingdon, 1933), among others. See *WHAH*, 116.

 To Mordecai Wyatt Johnson
17 July 1934
Washington, D.C.

Thurman presents his vision for the growth of religious life at Howard University.[1] Much of the letter is administrative in detail, revealing the limited institutional resources at his disposal. Thurman envisions an expansive role for Rankin Chapel, both in the life of the university's students and staff, as well as in the larger community. Two of Thurman's chapel legacies, the published sermon and vesper services, find their geneses here.

My dear Mr. President:

I am sending you this letter setting forth certain details with reference to my plan for the religious life of Howard University for next year. I shall list them in order that your reaction to each may be simpler and clearer.

1. Booklet announcing preachers for the year. This should be done on a very good grade of manila enamel paper, carrying on the outside a well-designed cut of the entrance to the Chapel, that being backed by a word of welcome to the services. This word of welcome being followed by a complete list of preachers for the year. We would need about three thousand of these, so that each new student may have one for his guidance during the year, and as a memoir for his scrapbook. One, together with a letter, should be sent to all of the officials in the Federal Government.[2]

2. Do you have any plans for the dedication of the organ? My suggestion is that we should plan a twenty or twenty-five-minute dedicatory service as a part of the regular Sunday morning worship, September thirtieth. This is the opening service for the year, and you are the preacher. If this meets your approval, please advise me so that I can begin making plans quite definitely for the service.

3. Will you please notify all Deans of the University that matters, which have to do with the use of the Chapel on Sunday, will have to be cleared through the Chairman of the Committee on Religious Life.

4. Will someone be designated as official organist for next year or will it be left primarily in the hands of Miss Childers[3] to decide? As Chairman of the Committee on Religious Life, I would like very much to have the control of the organ on Sundays. This would reduce possible conflicts, and make cooperation both easy and simple.

5. I am suggesting to my Committee that we plan a series of perhaps five vesper services for next winter, one or two of which will be musical, featuring the organ primarily. It may be possible to interest several student groups in sponsoring these.

6. I am asking for a transfer of five hundred dollars of my budget from Sunday speakers and advertising for the two following items:

   (a) For inviting at least four persons to visit the University as our guests in order that they may work with student groups and faculty groups. For two years we have done this, but it has been paid out of the pockets of the Thurmans. Because there is one more mouth to feed in the Thurman family, we cannot do this any longer.

   (b) Extra stenographic help. As you know the School of Religion has {is} very generously sharing a part of its stenographic staff with the Committee on Religious Life. In the light of the work that will have to be done next year, it will hardly be possible for this to be sufficient without causing serious burdens to be placed upon the undermanned staff of the School of Religion. There are many things that I want to do that require mimeographing, the writing of letters, advertising, the sending of birthday notes to students and faculty, et cetera, that would take at least two whole days of work a week for some person who could do what I wanted done. Last year the Committee provided a tuition scholarship for a student who was my general assistant. He did some stenographic work, but in the very nature of the case it was most limited. Instead of offering a full tuition scholarship this year to the student, I would suggest that we offer a half tuition scholarship, letting the difference of seventy-five ($75.00) dollars be applied to the payment {expense} for the extra stenographic work. For this tuition scholarship, the young man would distribute placards, run errands, assist with the mimeographing, and the thousand and one other things that have to be done.

7. As yet, we do not have any one for the Week of Prayer. I plan to open the Week of Prayer on Sunday morning, December ninth, but there seems to be no one available for the other days during the week. Two weeks ago, I

tried to get John Haynes Holmes,[4] but was not successful. Do you think it advisable to try Fosdick for the Day of Prayer, December thirteenth? If not, do you have any other suggestion? I am now working on other plans.

8. Personnel of the Committee on Religious Life. Am I correct in asserting that the following members of the Committee on Religious Life will not be here next year: Mr. Browning, Miss Houston, Mr. Huguley, Mr. Hilyard Robinson? As for the new committee, I am suggesting the following: Dr. Washington, Dr. Gordon, Dr. Jason of the Medical School; Professors Darnaly Howard, Walter Daniels, T. J. Anderson; Director Childers, and Mr. Hansbury.[5]

9. The final suggestion that I am making is that I be permitted to arrange with someone for a verbatim stenographic transcription of the Chapel sermons, which transcription will be prepared as copy to be sent to the speaker for correction. After corrections have been made, the address will be mimeographed and distributed at cost. Copies will be filed and at the end of the year, the complete list of addresses will be bound as volume I of the Howard University Sunday Morning Series. It seems to me that this could be done without any additional cost to the budget if handled properly.

I am sure it is criminal to have you give your attention to all these details when the weather is ninety-four in the shade, but I wanted to have them placed before you in order that I can spend more time on my plans before the end of the summer.

Faithfully yours,

[*unsigned*]

Howard Thurman

President Mordecai W. Johnson

Howard University

Washington, D.C.

t.

TLc. HTC-MBU: Box 9.

1. Because a chronological order is maintained throughout these Thurman volumes, several documents in this section, especially in the beginning, are unrelated to the India trip and instead focus on Thurman's family life and other professional activities in the mid-1930s.

2. Howard University was chartered by Congress and received a significant amount of its funding from the federal government. Thus, many officials on Capitol Hill took an interest in the ongoing activities at the school.

3. Lulu V. Childers was director of the University's School of Music.

4. John Haynes Holmes (1879–1964) was a prominent minister in the Unitarian movement during the first half of the twentieth century. Best known for his stalwart pacifist

position, he was a civic and social activist who was heavily involved in the Community Church movement. Holmes was one of the founders of the Unitarian Fellowship for Social Justice in 1908, serving as its president until 1911. He was among the founders of the NAACP as well as a founding member and eventual chair of the American Civil Liberties Union. He also served as founder and pastor of the Community Church of New York, a diverse multicultural organization, from 1917 until his death.

5. The names and affiliations for members of the Committee on Religious Life are as follows: Joanna Houston, dean, School of Women; John Wesley Huguley Jr., instructor in chemistry; Hilyard Robinson, chair of the Department of Architecture; Robert S. Jason, faculty of the College of Medicine/Medical School; Walter Daniels, professor of engineering; Lulu V. Childers, director of the School of Music; and William Leo Hansberry, professor of African history. The department affiliations of committee members Browning, Washington, Gordon, Darnaly Howard, and T. J. Anderson are unknown.

ᔦ To Susan Ford Bailey
29 August 1934
Washington, D.C.

Thurman expresses concern for Susan Ford Bailey, his mother-in-law, who is living alone in Dermott, Arkansas.

My dear Mamma

I was very glad to get your letter which came in the morning's mail.

Sue is doing very well indeed and is in the best of spirits. We are very much concerned because you are alone in the house. Sue and I have talked about it and we decided that it would be a fine thing if you arranged to have the lady whom you suggested to Sue as a good person to come up to be with her, to come to live with you. (That is a terrible sentence but you get the idea.) We do not want you to live alone in the house so please have a good person come in to be with you, particularly at night. It will make it possible for us to have peace of mind being so far from you. We know how you feel about such a thing that you will be all right but we cannot keep from being anxious despite our faith. Won't you write us and tell us that you are having someone move in to take Johnet's place?

The University opens next week and my year's work will be upon me. All of this week I have been getting the house in shape—that is, I have been doing what the misses ordered. See! but Sue knows how to keep a fellow busy. When we were working last week I said, "my, you certainly have a technique for getting your day's work out of me." She laughed and said, "You ought to put in a day for Mrs. S. E. Bailey." And then she told me many interesting stories out of the past.

Olive is in first grade now and is doing well in school and seems to be quite happy about it all. Phillip is also in school and is doing nicely.

Next Sunday (tomorrow) I have my last Sunday morning service at a church in the city. The next Sunday I shall be presiding at the services up here at the University and the year will be on.

Now, mamma, please take care of your dear self and do not allow yourself to become too tired before you stop to rest. We are praying for you and thinking of you.

Often I think of you and your work there. I know of nothing that gives me more inspiration than the thought of the many lives you have blessed through the years and the way that God has used you to glorify His own highest ends. Often I look at Phillip and thank God for you. God bless you and keep you and give you peace,

Sincerely

[*signed*] Howard

ALS. HTC-MBU: Box 1.

✣ FROM LEWIS JONES
1 SEPTEMBER 1934
MARLBORO, S.C.

Fisk University professor Lewis Jones[1] outlines for Thurman the harsh conditions endured by black tenant farmers across the south. His insights provide a lucid portrayal of black economic and religious realities of the rural south of the 1930s.

Dear Howard Thurman:

I am about to close a summer chockful of work and experience. Early in June I set out on a study of the cotton tenant situation and have worked in Mississippi, Texas, and South Carolina. Coming through Atlanta about two weeks ago Gresham[2] told me that you were in Arkansas. I should like to hear of your summer.

I have had interviews with about 1,000 tenants in the course of the summer and have observed a great variety of working conditions. It proved much more interesting than my work during the winter. These areas in which I have been have been characterized by a majority of Negroes in the population, and they are dominated and exploited more than in areas where you have a large poor white population as we saw in the Tennessee Valley.

There have been areas in which we had to secure letters of recommendation from the sheriff and permission from landlords to talk to their tenants. Since I had to contact landlords I decided to have landlord interviews and found them illuminating the picture more than it would have been. I talked with the President of the Delta and Pine Land Company of Scott, Mississippi, which controls [*strikeover illegible*] 53,000 acres of cotton and has 800 Negro sharecroppers. Other owners ranged down in number of acres owned. I had from them such expressions as "The Nigger is nothing but a child and we have to treat him that way," "As long as God keeps them humble I'll keep them poor," "We get along all right with our tenants and we don't need you bothering them," "The government can't make laws for the tenant because they are in Washington and don't know the situation." There is one thing I thank them for—they were brutally frank and spared me nothing. They looked me in the face and told me directly what they thought of "niggers" and cited examples to prove their allegations.

I went so far down in Mississippi that tenants called me "cap'n" and "boss." There were life histories of tenants taken where they purchased as many as 15 pairs of mules—a pair of mules here that must be left when they move, and a life spent in repeating this process. The childlike simplicity of their stories in which they have been allowed simple necessities and worked hard and produced wealth in which they never shared.

The church in these areas is the strong institution enjoying much more support than it deserves. There were many families who gave more in contributions to the church than they spent on clothing in the year. It serves the old function as an escape and recreation center. Great throngs gather for the revivals and "meeting" days.

I visited Lucius Tobin[3] at Union. He is doing a most interesting piece of work. In his church he is aggressive and speaks in no uncertain terms about economic conditions. The direct approach he has is something I have never experienced in any church. He told me you were having some kind of conference this fall and that he is thinking of attending. What is it?

Give my very best wishes to the family. Ask Mrs. Thurman how my artistic tin cans are holding out. I hope to come in that direction this winter.

I am sorry to hear that Rev. Faulkner[4] is to be our Chaplain. I have promised to work with a student group this fall in fostering an aggressive program of education in labor problems and politics and active participation in Nashville in these things. I suppose I am young enough or too old to care about success in the venture, and if the propagandizing of the student is successful, I think the program stands a good chance of success. One object is the political organization of the city by the students. Another thing is the student committees responsible for New Deal enforcement so far as Negroes in Nashville are concerned. This will require knowing the codes and discussing labor legislation and economic principles. It is ambitious but if sufficient drive is put into the students, their experience in this sort of thing will mean a very great deal in their personal development. I will enjoy it. If the appeal to the students can be placed on a sufficiently strong emotional basis, they will be storm troopers in some such organization. Having zeal for the work and not being a toy to play with, it will be something about which lives may be enjoyed. I shall send you copies of plans when they are completed.

Yours for friendship

[*signed*] Lewis Jones

ALS. HTC-MBU: Box 9.

1. Lewis Wade Jones (1910–79), a sociologist, received his AB from Fisk University (1931) and an AM from Columbia University (1939). From 1932 to 1942 he worked at Fisk as a research assistant to Charles S. Johnson, the supervisor of field studies and instructor in the Department of Social Sciences, and he coauthored with Johnson *A Statistical Analysis of Southern Counties* (Chapel Hill: University of North Carolina Press, 1941). From 1952 to 1979 he was a professor of sociology and director of the Tuskegee Institute Research Development Center.

2. Clarence J. Gresham, a classmate of Thurman's at Morehouse, was professor of biblical literature in the School of Religion at Morehouse.

3. Lucius Tobin (1898–1984) was professor of religion at Morehouse College and pastor of Providence Baptist Church in Atlanta, Georgia (1944–69). A native of Greenville, South Carolina, Tobin earned a BA degree from Virginia Union University (1923), an MA in sociology from the University of Michigan (1928), and a BD from Rochester Theological Seminary.

4. William J. Faulkner then was dean of men and ministry at Fisk University.

> ✂ From Douglas V. Steere
> 4 September 1934
> Wallingford, Pa.

Douglas V. Steere,[1] the distinguished religious philosopher and Quaker mystic, writes to Thurman to solicit the name of a Negro youth to study at Pendle Hill,[2] a Quaker retreat center. Thurman, apparently disappointed by the community's rejection of persons whose names he had submitted in the past, is nevertheless asked to forward new names of persons possessing "exceptional qualifications."

Professor Howard Thurman
Howard University
Washington, D.C.

My dear Howard:

It has been a year since I have written you and the experiences of ten months abroad have come in between us. I am very eager to see you and to hear from you what fresh insights have come to you in this time.

I am staying at Pendle Hill for a week until our house is ready at Haverford, and Joseph Platt talked with me yesterday about the fact that Pendle Hill has not up to this time secured a suitable Negro student for the coming year. We feel very deeply that the experience of the past four years in having such a student or students here has been of immense worth and we wish to continue it if we can get students of sufficient calibre who are interested in this peculiar piece of work which we are doing here. Joe[3] told me that you had been a little put out about our committee's having refused certain people you had suggested in the past. I do not know the facts in any of these cases but you can believe me, Howard, that this year's committee are sincerely trying to locate the person who can fit into our group here and are prepared if need be to offer him or her a full scholarship. I believe the committee feel that the type of student who is coming to Pendle Hill must have exceptional qualifications and that in this case they would not feel prepared to offer a full scholarship unless they were assured that it was to be given to such a student in spite of their desire to have one or more Negroes in the group. What we want is another Richard McKinney[4] or St. Clair Drake.

I write you to ask if you do not have such a student in mind and whether you will take the time to sit down and write me about him or her. I believe the curriculum this year will be an exceptionally unified one and that such a person would be able to receive as well as give a good deal in this group. I enclose a program of the year and a list of the students who have enrolled up to date so that you can get some impression of them.

It seems so good to be back with our little daughter again. She is now almost two and a half and I need not tell you how interesting she is. Dorothy joins me in sending our love to you and your wife, and we certainly hope that this year will not pass without our families meeting one another, either in Washington or here.

Your friend,

[*signed*] Douglas V. Steere

TLS. HTC-MBU: Box 19.

1. Douglas Van Steere (1901–95) received a BS from Michigan State University (1923), MA from Harvard University (1925), BA from Oxford University (1927), and PhD from Harvard University (1931). He also received an MA from Oxford (1953). Steere spent much of his life in higher education, teaching from 1928 to 1964 at Haverford College in Haverford, Pennsylvania. A prominent Quaker, Steere served as chair of the board of managers at Pendle Hill School of Religion and Social Studies from 1954 to 1970. He authored a number of works on spiritual life, contemplation, and Quakerism, including *Prayer and Worship* (New York: Association Press, 1938) and *Introduction to Quaker Spirituality* (New York: Paulist, 1984).

2. Pendle Hill is an educational center for study and spiritual contemplation in Wallingford, Pennsylvania, founded in 1930 by members of the Religious Society of Friends (Quakers).

3. Unidentified person.

4. Richard Ishmael McKinney (1906–2005) received an AB from Morehouse (1931), BD and STM from Andover Newton Theological School (1934, 1937), and PhD from Yale (1942). He did postdoctoral studies at the Sorbonne, University of Chicago, and Columbia University. He taught at a number of institutions, including Virginia Union University (1935–44), Morgan State University (1951–76), and Storer College, where he served as president from 1944 to 1950. Among his publications are *Religion in Higher Education Among Negroes* (New Haven: Yale University Press, 1941) and *Mordecai: The Man and His Message* (Washington, D.C.: Howard University Press, 1997).

Thurman, for reasons unknown, wrote two reviews in the October 1934 issue of the Journal of Religion. *He had never reviewed a book for the journal before and would not review another book for the journal for six years. The longer review, which appeared as a "critical review," was of Mary Anita Ewer's* A Survey of Mystical Symbolism. *This was Thurman's first published discussion of mysticism and demonstrates his familiarity with much of the vast body of mystical literature. Thurman would make extensive use of Ewer's text in his later writings on the subject, and it would form the framework for much on his discussion in his 1939 lecture series "Mysticism and Social Change."*

In the same issue of the journal, under a section of shorter reviews listed as "recent books," Thurman reviewed two published volumes in the series of Ingersoll Lectures, an annual lecture presented at Harvard University on the "Immortality of Man."[1] This was Thurman's first published comments on survival after death, a subject he infrequently commented on. Of the two lectures, Thurman was more taken with the argument of William Pepperell Montague (1873–1953), a professor of philosophy at Barnard College and Columbia University, who argued from analogies to Einstein and recent developments in physics that the mind was a "field" separate from the body, capable of shaping space and time, and could in some sense have an independent existence. In the review, Thurman, likely inspired by but not directly quoting Montague, refers to the self as a "space and time binder," a phrase he would often use in his later career. In 1947, Thurman would become the first African American Ingersoll lecturer.

"Review of Mary Anita Ewer, *A Survey of Mystical Symbolism*"

Perhaps there is no word in our language that has been as completely misunderstood and as freely interpreted by unintelligent sincerity as "mysticism." According to popular conceptions mystic types range all the way from Houdini to Mahatma Gandhi; from a Kaffir[2] witch doctor to Jesus on the Mount of Transfiguration. Much of the confusion as to the meaning of mysticism is due to the fact that the language of the mystic is itself very often shrouded in much that is vague and misleading. The reality of the mystic's experience is much more clear cut to the mystic than the symbolism he employs in communication. Students of religion and of mysticism, in particular, will welcome *A Survey of Mystical Symbolism* by Mary Anita Ewer as a very useful guide in the interpretation of symbols employed by religious experience.[3]

The author undertakes to penetrate the heart of the major insights of mysticism by an examination of its characteristic symbolism. It is a very precarious business to attempt to get behind the thought forms and imagery with which any experience clothes itself, to the nature of the experience of which the forms and imagery are but expressions. This Miss Ewer has done with amazing skill and dexterity.

The major part of the discussion is an interpretation of the four general possibilities open to the mystic when he attempts to discuss in human language that which he believes to be "the nature of the spiritual realm and of human relationships within that realm." To use the author's outline: First, he may perceive an analogy between a simple sensory experience and a spiritual experience.... Second, he may see an analogy between a physical process and a spiritual process.... Third, he may try to express the nature of the Infinite Life-Giver Himself, in terms of those earthly entities and forces from which we derive our physical life and in whose grip we are so often helpless.... Fourth, he may attempt to express the relationship of the human soul to God in terms of some familiar physical or human relationship.

These four methods of symbolic expression of mystical experience correspond exactly to what Miss Ewer discloses as the four divisions of mystic insight: the momentary mystic experience, mystic growth and development, the Divine Other, the abiding mystic experience.

The volume abounds in much carefully selected illustrative material culled from the literature of mysticism, and on the whole supplies a clearly defined need.

One comment should be added to the author's discussion on mystical union. The observation is made that no other subject is as difficult as the one having to do with the union of the soul with God. This is true because we are dealing with two entities, one finite, the other infinite. It seems to me that this observation overlooks one of the most important assumptions which the mystic makes, namely, that there is in the human soul that which Meister Eckhart calls an "uncreated element."[4] It is the point at which the infinite enters the finite—it is given, and is not finite but infinite.

The selected bibliography is the most comprehensive grouping that I have seen on the subject. It helps to make the volume well-nigh indispensable as a handbook.

Journal of Religion 14 (October 1934): 457–58.

"Reviews of the 1933 and 1934 Ingersoll Lectures"

There will always be a lively interest in the question of survival after death. The reasons are more or less obvious and not far to seek. Many thoughtful persons have come to regard the "Ingersoll Lecture Series" of Harvard University as providing a definite source of reassurance on this theme. *The Chances of Surviving*

Death was the title chosen by Professor William P. Montague for the 1934 Ingersoll Lecture. It is a brilliant, daring analysis of the nature of the self as a space and time binder. On the basis of very apt analogy he establishes the case for the mind as something substantive in its own right. Developing this thesis in its many thrilling ramifications, taking time out for many wise cautions, Professor Montague suggests, rather convincingly, in conclusion that "the simple goodness which animals and men both *acquire* may be the main determiner of whether life continues after death; or at least, of whether such continuance would hold the promise of unending progress lacking which eternity would pall."[5]

Immortality and the Cosmic Process is the title of the lecture for 1933.[6] In this lecture Dean Shalier Mathews confines himself to the Christian basis for the assurance of immortality. His words are seasoned with the mellowness of sustained religious insight and experience. They do not present a particularly fresh and stimulating point of view, but this is not necessarily a point of condemnation.

Journal of Religion 14 (October 1934): 383–84.

1. The Ingersoll Lecture was first given in 1896, and some of the distinguished lecturers in the series before the early 1930s had included William James, Josiah Royce, and Harry Emerson Fosdick.

2. *Kaffir* or *Kafir* refers to a member of the Bantu-speaking peoples of southern Africa. Today, the term is regarded as pejorative.

3. Mary Anita Ewer, *A Survey of Mystical Symbolism* (New York: Macmillan, 1933).

4. The "uncreated element" to which Thurman refers is synonymous with Meister Eckhart's notions of "uncreated grace" and "divine spark." For Eckhart, the uncreated element is not the individual soul but rather a spark of the Intellect, the Son of God, uncreated and immutable. C. F. Kelly, *Meister Eckhart on Divine Knowledge* (New Haven: Yale University Press, 1977), 133–39.

5. William Pepperell Montague, *The Chances of Surviving Death* (Cambridge: Harvard University Press, 1934), 95–96.

6. Shailer Mathews, *Immortality of the Cosmic Process* (Cambridge: Harvard University Press, 1933).

꙳ TO GEORGE CROCKETT JR.
10 OCTOBER 1934
WASHINGTON, D.C.

Thurman writes a humorous and encouraging word to his friend George Crockett upon learning that Crockett took the Florida bar examination.

My dear friend:[1]

I know you have long since decided that of all Negroes in the world, I am the sorriest. My only word of wisdom to such a resolution is this, "Every judgment that you pass upon another is a self-judgment."

As soon as I get some time, I shall pen you a letter in my own inimitable style, but in order that you may know how deeply interested I am in your welfare and in your future, I am taking this time to send you a more formal word.

Hacker told me the other day that you were taking the Florida bar. What success did you have? It seems to me that you have a very great opportunity to develop an independent career for yourself in Jacksonville as in almost no other Southern city. In your profession you come into a tradition of skill and leadership. Ever since I can remember Jacksonville has had one or two very able Negro lawyers. It is only in recent years that the men have not been of outstanding significance.

Of course, West Virginia offers an excellent chance, because it is a border state and there is less overt racial prejudice and, therefore, the success that is won there is perhaps of more doubtful character.

Please know that I am vitally concerned about how you make it and under what conditions. You have had very excellent training. You have a good mind, and you know how to fight if life can make you mad enough. Here's hoping that it does.

Give my warmest personal regards to Mrs. Crockett, and you will hear from me again before many days pass.

Sincerely yours,

[*unsigned*]

Howard Thurman

Attorney George Crockett Jr.
610 West Duvall Street
Jacksonville, Florida

                                    TLc. HTC-MBU: Box 3.

1. George William Crockett Jr. (1909–97) was an attorney, judge, author, and government legislator. Born in Jacksonville, Florida, he received his BA from Morehouse in 1931 and his JD from the University of Michigan in 1934. After beginning his legal career in Jacksonville, Crockett moved to Fairmont, West Virginia, where he practiced from 1934 to 1939. In 1939 he became the first African American attorney in the U.S. Department of Labor (1939–43), and in 1943 President Franklin D. Roosevelt appointed Crockett as a hearing examiner of the wartime Fair Employment Practices Committee, making him the first African American examiner appointed to a government labor board. Crockett also represented Michigan's Thirteenth Congressional District in the U.S. House of Representatives (1980–91).

☙ TO MARY THORN GANNETT
11 OCTOBER 1934
WASHINGTON, D.C.

Thurman requests from Mary Thorn Gannett a list of publications by her husband, the late William Channing Gannett, a prominent Unitarian minister in Rochester, New York.

My dear Mrs. Ganett:[1]

I suppose when you read my signature, you will say that the dead is coming to life. Doubtless, you remember me for I was a student several years ago at the Rochester Divinity School, and have been the recipient of much generous hospitality in your home.

I am writing to ask you if you will send me a copy of all of the books or pamphlets or addresses that were written by your husband, Dr. Ganett?[2] I am teaching in the School of Religion at Howard University where Mordecai Johnson is, and I would like to use this material in connection with my personal preparation for certain aspects of my job. I hope you will not consider me presumptuous in making a request of this sort, but it comes out of a deep earnestness. If I am in Rochester again, I shall certainly come to see you.

Thank you and sincerely,

[*unsigned*]

Howard Thurman

Mrs. W. C. Ganett

23 Sibley Place

Rochester, New York

t.

TLc. HTC-MBU: Box 8.

1. Mary Thorn (Lewis) Gannett (1854–1952), an educator and social activist, was an 1880 graduate of the University of Pennsylvania. A close friend of Susan B. Anthony, she was dedicated to the cause of women's suffrage. The two worked together to encourage the University of Rochester to establish a college for women.

2. William Channing Gannett (1840–1923) had been a Unitarian pastor in Saint Paul, Minnesota (1877–83), and at the First Unitarian Church of Rochester, New York (1889–1908). He received his BA (1860) and MA (1863) from Harvard and afterward worked with the Port Royal Experiment for freed blacks in Port Royal, South Carolina. He went on to earn a BD (1868) and a doctorate (1908) from Harvard Divinity School and Harvard University, respectively.

To Henry Burke Robins

11 October 1934

Washington, D.C.

Thurman solicits advice from one of his seminary professors on how best to prepare for his upcoming experience in India.

Professor Henry Burke Robbins[1]
Colgate-Rochester Theological Seminary
Rochester, New York

My dear Professor Robbins:

Doubtless, you will be surprised to get a letter from me but I hope it will not be fatal. I have been asked to be the chairman of the delegation of American Negroes, four in number, to visit colleges and universities in India during the school year 1935–36. This delegation will concern itself with interpreting the spiritual significance of life against the background and experience of an under-privileged minority in American life. The invitation comes directly from the Indian students themselves, and the project is being financed on this end by American students in all sections of the country.

I am writing you to see if you have any suggestions to make to me with reference to preparation for the experience. During this winter the group is making a careful study of: First, comparative religion; second, historical Christianity; protestantism in America, primarily with reference to minorities in America; the relationship between Christianity and capitalism; the life, career, and teaching of Jesus; finally, the history of the British and Indian.

For the past two or three years, I have been making a study of the religion of the underprivileged. It seems to me that there is no more searching question that Christianity has to face than "What is its word to the most underprivileged and exploited individuals in society?"

Out of your experience and knowledge, will you make any suggestions to me that may occur to you? I shall appreciate whatever you say or do. I appeal to you because it is from you that I first received a warm stimulating appreciation of Indian religion and of Indian people.[2]

With kindest personal regards,

Faithfully yours,

[unsigned]

Howard Thurman

t.

TLc. HTC-MBU: Box 17.

1. Henry Burke Robins (1874–1949) received his BA (1902) and MA (1906) from William Jewell College, his BD from Rochester Theological Seminary (1905), and an MA (1911) and PhD (1912) from the University of Chicago. He pastored Baptist churches in Oregon and California from 1905 to 1909. Robins taught at Pacific Coast Baptist Theological Seminary (1907–13), Rochester Theological Seminary (1913–28), and Colgate Rochester Divinity School (1928–41), where he was professor of history and philosophy of religion. His publications include *Aspects of Authority in the Christian Religion* (Philadelphia: Griffith & Rowland, 1911) and *The Basis of Assurance in Recent Protestant Theologies* (Chicago: University of Chicago Press, 1912).

2. Robins is widely regarded as having a crucial impact upon Thurman's intellectual formation. Thurman took Robins's course "The Philosophy of Religion," but it was Robins's chapel meditations that made a profound impression upon him. According to Luther Smith in *Howard Thurman: The Mystic as Prophet,* Robins identified for Thurman "the religious essence which is found in all expressions of religion." 30. For Robins's works on India, see *Report of the Commission of 1928–1929 upon the Burma Baptist Mission* (Rangoon, Burma, 1928) and *Report of the Special Commission of the American Baptist Foreign Missionary Society on the South India Mission* (n.p., 1920).

◆ FROM HENRY BURKE ROBINS
15 OCTOBER 1934
ROCHESTER, N.Y.

In his response, Robins shows his affinities to the Social Gospel through his analysis of how both Christianity and Hinduism have been controlled by privileged and dominant social classes.

Professor Howard Thurman,
Howard University,
Washington, D.C.

My dear Thurman:

No; the surprise of your letter will not be fatal. It is, in fact, most agreeable, and for the reason that you have had my affectionate regard ever since your student days here. It is agreeable, moreover, because I am deeply interested in the project which you have outlined.

I am sure that I do not think of myself as possessed of any unusual qualification for the role of advisor which you ask me to assume. I have, however, had a very deep and genuine interest in India and in her underprivileged classes for years past, and particularly since I spent a winter in that land and had first-hand contact with some of them. I was there, you know, on mission deputation work, the winter of 1928–29.[1]

It seems to me that the fields which you have proposed for study as introductory to your specific task are well chosen and inclusive. Your query is general, so that my reply, I fear, may be too general. By and large, religion down to date, has been administered and even formulated by privileged classes in the various cultures. That perhaps lay in the nature of the situation. Privileged classes have as a rule regarded their own relation to the social scale as fundamentally indisputable, warranted by the sanctions of whatever powers there be, on earth and in the heavens. When the teaching of a particular religion, as Christianity, invaded and challenged this assumption, privilege elaborated its own apologetic, and, while paying deference to the new teaching in word, through acts of charity, by knightly service and what not, nevertheless refused to modify its fundamental assumption. It might go so far as to acknowledge its divinely imposed duty to father the "lower" classes; but that equity and right required anything more of them scarcely dawned above their spiritual horizon. At the same time, the seeds of a new conception of human relations lay securely embedded in the soil of historic religions, most notably of Christianity. Christianity, better than any religion of which I know, and for the reason that this absolute ethic of fraternity was explicit in it, illustrates in the course of its history what happens when explicit religious motives seek to operate through essentially pagan patterns: the patterns dominate the situation, and the religious motives find fugitive expression through ritual, mystic pursuits and hopes of amend in another world, instead of finding expression in the common life. Some such "half-way covenant" has characterized Christianity in our West, except for small communities which tried to break the spell of it. Thus it has adapted itself, or been adapted, I might better say, to the "divine right of kings," to rugged individualism and the rights of property, and what not, rather than to social justice and human rights. You know the story well enough.

Now our convictions must define themselves in the white light of the acknowledged principle, and not in the shadowy region of prevailing practice. When we put the acknowledged principle over against the prevailing practice, our western religious life stands condemned; at best it is a piecemeal and relatively ineffective expression of the acknowledged principle. "Christendom" is in many respects mongrel; it is neither devotedly Christian nor whole-heartedly pagan. Now into that sort of situation most of us, of whatever level, privileged or under-privileged, have been thrust. Our religious teachers have often been confused in their thinking and uncertain in their utterance, because of the mixed tradition into which they have come. They themselves have taken refuge in the escape-mechanisms which traditional Christianity abundantly supplies, and they have led us to do so. I am not saying that we are victims of circumstance, we privileged folk who want to be Christian, but that we are heirs of a spurious as well as of an essential Christianity, and we often confuse them. I do not, therefore, believe that the Christianity of the privileged, as privileged, has any word for the under privileged but "sweet charity" and exhortation to be content with the lot into which they are born. But I believe that the Christianity of Jesus actually focusses about the problem of the under-privileged. I do not mean that he held any modern social theory, but rather that he went so directly and so searchingly to first principles that the ethic of fraternity, with its corollary of mutuality, strikingly emerged, and will emerge for anyone who deeply ponders his teaching. The two commandments are so intimately bound together that I cannot love God without loving my neighbor as myself. I myself believe profoundly that religion has those two foci.

Most of the people in our world are under-privileged. As a member in some proper sense of a privileged section, a privileged minority, I feel condemned; I carry that feeling with me constantly. I also feel, as I am sure many another does, how ineffective I have been in righting the hoary wrong implicit in the assumption that a stratified society can be justified.

The religions of India have made sporadic and ineffective protest, from time to time, but, in general, the Brahmin-fostered tradition of a class world has dominated the situation. These rigid orthodox are today fighting Gandhi, who has on his side, in my judgment, the most fruitful elements in ancient Hinduism.

If you would like to raise any question, or ask my judgment on any phase of the problem, I shall be happy to do what I can for you. It is not without significance that John E. Clough, when he had both the privileged and the under-privileged on his compound asking admission to the Christian church, turned to the under-privileged, with the result that our South India Mission is an outcaste mission. Read his wife's "Social Christianity in the Orient."[2] By and large the Christian missions, around the world, have gone to the under-privileged.

Cordially yours,

[*signed*] Henry B. Robins

                                        TLS. HTC-MBU: Box 17.

1. For Robins's works on India, see *Report of the Commission of 1928–1929 upon the Burma Baptist Mission* (Rangoon, Burma, 1928) and *Report of the Special Commission of the American Baptist Foreign Missionary Society on the South India Mission* (n.p., 1920).

2. Emma R. Clough, *Social Christianity in the Orient: The Story of a Man, a Mission and a Movement* (New York: Macmillan, 1914). John E. Clough (1836–1910) and Emma Rauschenbusch Clough (1859–1938), the sister of Walter Rauschenbusch, were Baptist missionaries who worked among the Indic peoples of Telugu in southern India. They arrived in India in 1865 and by the end of 1879 had amassed a church of more than thirteen thousand members in Ongole.

🦋 To Francis A. Henson
18 October 1934
Washington, D.C.

Thurman invites Francis A. Henson from the National Council of Student Christian Associations to speak on the topic of religion and social change during Howard University's Week of Prayer.

My dear Francis:[1]

When I was in New York the other day I wanted to see you but it wasn't any time. I shall be back through there the last of the month and I hope to pick you up at that time. I think it is practically impossible for me to put on paper precisely what I want you to do during the Week of Prayer, but I will take a stab at it. The general topic to which the list of Sunday speakers (enclosed) are addressing themselves is "The Function of Religion in the Modern World." I would like to see you,

Francis, address yourself to what seems to you to be the relationship or the relevancy better, that religion (interpret in your own way) has to questions which have to do with social change. I am not interested in having you include religion in what you have to say in any formal sense, but I would like to see you share with us the spiritual significance that may be found in the struggle for a better and more clean-smelling world. You will not be thought of as a religionist in any direct sense, but you will be interpreted as a man primarily interested in social change, who derived some measure of inspiration from what may be described as religious insights. We will talk further.

I like your suggestion about the conference and you can count me in on it. December is a very, very crowded month for me, but I am sure that I can arrange to cooperate if the conference is not set for the first week-end.

I am very happy that you have agreed to be with us. It may be interesting to you to know that you will be the first white man to conduct this particular service in some twenty years. Sue sends her love and says she will see that you have plenty of good coffee and cigarettes that you may preach the truth with a clear mind.

Faithfully yours,

[*unsigned*]

Howard Thurman

Chairman, Committee on Religious Life

Mr. Francis A. Henson

8 West Fortieth Street

New York, New York

Encl.

t.

TLc. HTC-MBU: Box 9.

1. Francis A. Henson (1906–63) served as executive secretary of the student division of the YMCA from 1931 to 1934 and was a member of the executive committee on the revolutionary policy of the Socialist Party. He was also executive secretary of the National Labor and Religion Foundation and chair of the National Council's economic commission. Henson was a founding editor of two periodicals, *Race* (1935) and *Marxist Quarterly* (1936). The former claimed to be dedicated to dealing with "the problems of interracial conflict and cooperation from a vigorous class-conscious perspective." See "Books and Authors," *New York Times*, 27 October 1935, BR16, and "Socialism Favored by Religious Groups," *New York Times*, 28 April 1931.

༄ From Channing H. Tobias
1 November 1934
New York, N.Y.

The paths of Tobias and Thurman had crossed a number of times, dating from Thurman's student days at Florida Baptist Academy to a network of involvements in the YMCA. Here Thurman's longtime friend responds warmly to a letter from Thurman and outlines his reasons for not seeking the presidency of Tuskegee Institute in the wake of the resignation of his good friend Robert Moton.

Mr. Howard Thurman
Howard University
Washington, D.C.

My dear Howard:

Your note of a few days ago, referring to the resignation of Dr. Moton and the possibility of my succeeding him, I appreciate more than I can express.[1] The truth is, however, that as far as I can discover, the mention of my name in connection with the presidency of Tuskegee is wholly a matter of newspaper reports and the good wishes of personal friends.

While Dr. Moton and I are very good personal friends, we have never discussed the matter of his successor except to regret the unfortunate interest in the position taken by men who were ambitious to be considered. As a matter of fact, I think the Trustees will turn in their thinking toward a young man, possibly in his late thirties or early forties. This, of course, would be in line with the procedure followed at the University of Chicago and at Harvard. One very influential member of the Board told me that he was thinking along this line. Just how influential he will be in urging his views upon the Board remains to be seen. Somehow I find myself agreeing with the position of this Board member.

You may not realize it, but I am now in my fifty-third year and even if the position were offered to me I doubt seriously that I could possibly consider it favorably. While I have had interesting contacts and have developed some executive ability, I am not an educator. Moreover, my view of the course that the development of Tuskegee should take is a little out of line with the present program of the institution. As you probably know, the college work at Tuskegee, under the direction of W. T. B. Williams,[2] is merely a duplication of the kind of thing that is being done at Talladega, Atlanta, and other Southern colleges. In my opinion Tuskegee should emphasize agricultural and technological subjects on the college level and leave the liberal arts field to the other colleges. You can readily see how impossible it would be for me to attempt to develop the school along {such} lines when I have no knowledge of these subjects and less experience in these fields. A final decisive factor, I think, with me would be that all my life I have been primarily interested in the character education of youth and would not at this late date find it easy to pull away from my life-work.

I have gone thus far into this expression of my possible reactions to a consideration of the presidency of Tuskegee because I know that you were sincere in writing me as you did. I agree with you that it is of utmost importance that the right man be chosen, and I assure you that if I have an opportunity to cooperate even to the slightest extent with the Board in making its choice I shall point toward the type of man that I think you have in mind.

Please remember me very kindly to Mrs. Thurman and the children. Both of you should certainly be proud of that fine baby.

Feel free to drop me a confidential line on Mays' condition.[3] I sincerely trust that he is much improved.

With every good wish, I am

Cordially yours,

[*signed*] C. H. Tobias

C. H. Tobias.

CHT:ERR

TLS. HTC-MBU: Box 21.

1. Robert Russa Moton (1867–1940) graduated from Hampton Institute in 1890. For the next twenty-five years, while serving as commandant for military discipline at Hampton, he traveled across the northern part of the United States seeking contributions for predominantly black colleges and universities. In 1915 he succeeded Booker T. Washington as president of Tuskegee Institute, where he remained until he resigned in 1935 due to poor health.

2. William Taylor Burwell Williams (1869–1941) was a well-known educator and journalist. He graduated from the Hampton Institute (1888), the Phillips Academy in Andover, Massachusetts (1893), and earned an AB from Harvard (1897). From 1902 to 1904, Williams was a field agent for the Southern Education Board. He also served as a field director at Hampton Institute from 1902 to 1919 and was an editor of the *Southern Workman*. Williams was a dean at Tuskegee from 1927 to 1936 and vice-president from 1936 until his death.

3. In an attempt to complete his dissertation, Benjamin Mays pushed himself to his physical and emotional limits and was bedridden for a significant period of time.

🎕 FROM THOMAS HARDMON
6 NOVEMBER 1934
BOWLING GREEN, VA.

Reminiscent of the young Thurman's appeal to Mordecai Wyatt Johnson, a first-year high-school student solicits advice from Thurman about his under-standing of ministry as a vocation. He attaches to his letter a questionnaire on vocation for his class in "vocational guidance." Thurman's brief, yet humorous and insightful responses to Thomas Hardmon's questions in his 10 November letter are italicized in the questionnaire.

Union High School
Bowling Green, Va.

The Rev. Howard Thurman
Howard University
Washington, D.C.

My dear Rev. Thurman
I am a freshman in the Union High School and am fourteen years of age. My class in vocational guidance is making a study of various vocations in which to engage upon leaving school. I am interested in ministry. You have been reco-mended to me as a representative person in this field. I am enclosing a list of ques-tions on this vocation which I should like to have you answer before I make a choice. I shall appreciate any help or information which you might give me con-cerning this occupation.
Enclosed please find a self-addressed envelope for a reply.
Very respectfully yours
[*signed*] Thos. Hardmon
Questionnaire

1. Why did you become interested in Ministry?
   I became interested in the ministry because I felt that I could find the fullest expression for my life in that field.
2. How long have you been engaged in this vocation?
   I have been engaged in this vocation for more than ten years.
3. Would you recomend your vocation to a group of youngsters?
   I would recommend my vocation to any one who has enough courage and ability and religion to undertake it.
4. What educational preparation do you deem necessary for the pursuit of this vocation?

Four years high school, four years college, at least, three years graduate theological study.

5. What family obligations have you?
   Wife and two children.
6. If you are the head of a family have you been able to support them on the American Normal Standard of living from your annual income?
   Yes.
7. Is your vocation over-run?
   Depends upon your point of view.
8. Does the pursuit of this vocation require a large amount of capital?
   No. Just sense.
9. What advice have you to give me as one who might enter this vocation?
   Don't be in too big a hurry to make up your mind. Enter this vocation only if you feel you have no other choice for complete fulfillment.
10. Is this vocation interesting?
    Thrilling.

ALS. HTC-MBU: Box 8.

To Ralph Bunche
9 NOVEMBER 1934
WASHINGTON, D.C.

Under a new title of acting dean of the School of Religion, Thurman thanks his Howard colleague Ralph Bunche, founder and chairman of the Department of Political Science, for his critique of the New Deal program.[1]

My dear Dr. Bunch:[2]

Just a note to thank you for the excellent analysis which you gave of the New Deal. In my opinion, it was well done and clearly done. Your contribution to our thinking was quite pointed. I was most happy that you, too, were not an official of the New Deal. Thank you very much.

Faithfully yours,
[*signed*] Howard Thurman
Howard Thurman, Acting Dean
Dr. Ralph Bunch
Department of Political Science
Howard University
t.

TLS. RB-NN-SC: Box 25.

1. At the time, Bunche was very critical of the New Deal, lambasting programs such as the Agricultural Adjustment Act, which often forced sharecroppers off the land without compensation, and the National Recovery Act, which provided legal protection to the

discriminatory practices of labor unions. For the politics of Bunche in the 1930s and its influence on the social thought at Howard, see Jonathan S. Holloway, *Confronting the Veil: Abram Harris, Jr., E. Franklin Frazier, and Ralph Bunche, 1919–1941* (Chapel Hill: University of North Carolina Press, 2002).

2. Ralph Bunche (1904–71) received his BA from the University of California at Los Angeles (1927) and a PhD at Harvard University (1934), the first African American to earn a PhD in political science from an American university. He later went on to advanced studies at Northwestern University, the London School of Economics, and the University of Cape Town. Bunche taught at Howard University from 1928 to 1942. In 1944 he began his association with the State Department, specializing in African affairs, and in 1946 he moved to the United Nations, where he remained the rest of his career. In 1950, for his work in helping to arrange the armistice between Israel and neighboring Arab states, he was awarded the Nobel Peace Prize, the first African American to be honored with the award.

✒ To Hubert Herring
10 November 1934
Washington, D.C.

After Sue Bailey Thurman is selected as a member of the Negro Delegation to India, she and her husband decide that one of her chief roles would be as an interpreter of the arts in America. To facilitate this, she goes to the University of Mexico in early 1935 to study music and art in Mexico City. As Thurman later writes, Sue "put in ten weeks of intensive study in Mexico during the late winter and spring on the whole of American culture in preparation for the contacts we would make with a significant culture of the East."[1]

However, discriminatory practices by the Mexican government make the Thurmans leery that Sue's trip will run into serious problems.[2] The previous summer, a colleague at Howard had been asked to post a $500 bond, returnable when leaving Mexico, before the Mexican government would admit her as a tourist. On 17 October 1933, the Mexican Ministry of the Interior had ruled that persons of the "yellow, Negro, Malayan, and Hindu races" were prohibited from entering the country as immigrants. Thurman's friend Hubert Herring,[3] writing to Josephus Daniels, the U.S. Ambassador to Mexico, argues that the growing practice of the Mexican government in keeping African Americans from entering Mexico is not based on "formal law" but an "informal interpretation by some officials." Mexico's policies are part of a worldwide wave of ethnically and racially discriminatory practices in the 1930s. As an American consular official will write to Shaw University President William S. Nelson in early 1935 that given the severe restrictions in place in American immigration policy as regards to race and ethnicity, it would be hypocritical for the State Department to complain about Mexico's policies.

Herring, an expert on Latin America, had evidently suggested in a previous
letter to Thurman that rather than going overland through Texas (the route Sue
eventually takes), it would be easier to enter Mexico by steamship. Thurman
feels that the racial discrimination on the lines serving Mexico will likely make
this alternative impossible. Thurman draws on a wide range of contacts to try to
get his wife into Mexico without the embarrassment of having to post bond. In
addition to Herring, he seeks the assistance of Walter White, the executive
secretary of the NAACP, and Charles Houston, dean of the Howard University
School of Law. He also contacts Nelson, asking him to write to Ambassador
Daniels, who had been editor of the Raleigh News and Observer *for many*
decades. Thurman, wary of being rebuffed, is reluctant to appeal directly to the
Mexican embassy, though on White's urging, he follows this approach. At the
end of 1934, Sue applies for a tourist permit for a three-month stay in Mexico.
Although she waits almost two months before being issued a visa, with the help
of the State Department, the proper papers are obtained, and the bond is waived.

My dear Hubert Herring:

I wish I could share your optimism with reference to the Ward Line. But I
do not. I would not run the risk of subjecting Mrs. Thurman and Olive to terrific embarrassment unless I had some written statement from an official of the
Ward Line.[4]

A friend of ours in the University here was turned back at the Mexican border last summer unless she were willing to post a five hundred dollar cash bond
to guarantee the Mexican Government that it would run no risk in admitting
her as a tourist. There seems to be a clearly definite effort on the part of someone
high up in Mexican officialdom to keep American Negro tourists out of Mexico.
It seems to me that your Committee can do a very worthwhile service in clearing
this matter up. We are still planning the trip into Mexico as outlined to you and
I am wondering if we decided to go by rail, could your office secure the tourist
permit? I do not want to raise the question with the Mexican Embassy here
unless it is absolutely necessary, because the temptation to lie to me would be a
very real one. As a well-known friend to Mexico, you may be able to get the truth
about the situation with reference to my family and any other Negroes, for that
matter, directly. I know you are busy, but I would appreciate it if you would give
this matter your very careful, personal attention as quickly as possible.
Faithfully yours,
[*unsigned*]
Howard Thurman

TLc. HTC-MBU: Box 9.

1. To the Members of the India Committee, 20 December 1935, printed in the current
volume.

2. On Mexican immigration restrictions, see Gerald Horne, *Black and Brown: African Americans and the Mexican Revolution, 1910–1920* (New York: New York University Press, 2005), 183–92.

3. Hubert Clinton Herring (1889–1967) was a Congregational minister best known for his interest in Latin America, which eventually became his full-time vocation. He was a professor of Latin American Civilization at Claremont Graduate School of Theology for over twenty years. He also served as executive director of the Committee on Culture and Religion in Latin America, and he sponsored numerous trips to Mexico under the auspices of the Committee on Cultural Relations with Latin America. Herring is the author of *A History of Latin America from the Beginnings to the Present* (New York: Knopf, 1961) and the editor, with Herbert Weinstock, of *Renascent Mexico* (New York: Covici, Friede, 1935).

4. The Ward Line was one of the travel lines of the New York and Cuba Mail Steamship Company and was well-known for its discriminatory treatment of blacks and other minorities. It operated U.S. passenger and freight ships on the East Coast and Caribbean from 1881 to 1959.

❧ To Arthur L. James
10 November 1934
Washington, D.C.

Thurman writes to "Cousin Arthur," declining his invitation to speak at First Baptist Church, where James was pastor, because of his already full schedule.

My dear Cousin Arthur:

I am sending this note to say that after checking in every possible way, I find that I simply can't get away during this month. Because of a situation with reference to my house in Atlanta, I shall have to take my spare time to go down there; and this counts me out for any extra trips other than those that are scheduled. But you may depend upon it, the first chance I get I shall avail myself of the happy privilege of visiting my second home again. Please remember me to the congregation and particularly to my friends in the Sunday School. I shall never forget the church there and the spirit of religion which they shared with me during the two summers of my sojourn, I often go back in my mind to the hours that we use to spend together on the front porch late at night discussing all the problems of religion.

I was very glad that you came up here during your vacation. Sue likes you very much and hopes that when you come again, it will be possible for you to live with us. Kindly remember us most definitely to Miss Ada and the children. Let me hear from you again.

Sincerely,

[*unsigned*]

Howard Thurman
Mr. Arthur James
Roanoke, Va.

TLc. HTC-MBU: Box 9.

❧ FROM HOWARD KESTER
16 NOVEMBER 1934
NASHVILLE, TENN.

Howard Kester,[1] executive secretary of the Committee on Economic and Racial Justice, requests Thurman's leadership and presence at an upcoming conference, noting the innovative interracial character of the event. Christian ministers with left-leaning politics, like Kester, Reinhold Niebuhr, Francis A. Henson, and others, linked the nation's economic woes with the crisis in race relations. Kester makes mention of an investigation on behalf of the NAACP that he is conducting of the lynching of Claude Neal.

Rev. Howard Thurman
Howard University
Washington, D.C.

My dear Howard:

Several days ago I wrote you an urgent letter regarding the forthcoming Conference of Younger Churchmen of the South which is to be held in Chattanooga on December 4, 5 and 6. Since I have not heard from you I fear that the letter never reached you.

We are extremely anxious to have you at this conference to help in the seminars and to give from one to two platform talks. The theme of the conference is "Religion and the Struggle for Social Justice," and it is our intention to go at things with gloves off. I might say that we have advertised your coming and that you are one of our main drawing cards. People do want to hear you and meet you personally. The conference is to be interracial from beginning to end and it will be something new under the southern sky. Please come if you possibly can. I don't know what we will do without you. Niebuhr can't come and neither can Thomas.[2] I am doubtful about J. B.[3] but Francis Henson is coming. With you and Francis we can pull a really significant conference. We don't have much money but I will do everything in my power to defray all of your expenses. Please help us!

I am enclosing the announcements which have already gone out. Don't fail us! I've just returned from Marianna where I investigated the lynching of Claude Neal for the NAACP.[4] My seventeen-page-report will be available shortly. I am up-to-my-neck-over-my-head in work.

We all send our love.

[*signed*] "Buck"
Howard

TLS. HTC-MBU: Box 10.

1. Howard Anderson "Buck" Kester (1904–77) was born in Martinsville, Virginia. He was a graduate of Lynchburg College and Vanderbilt University School of Religion (1930).

Kester worked as a secretary of the YMCA at Vanderbilt University until 1926, when he was fired for his radical views on religion, race, and labor. From 1926 to 1929 he worked as a youth secretary for FOR. Kester went back to Nashville in 1929 to complete graduate work at Vanderbilt, and from 1929 to 1933 he was FOR's southern secretary. He also investigated lynchings for the NAACP and helped to organize the Southern Tenant Farmers Union. Kester became deeply involved in Socialist Party politics and in 1932 ran for U.S. Congress on its ticket for Tennessee. He was a staunch critic of the New Deal and wrote *Revolt Among the Sharecroppers* (New York: Covici, Friede, 1936), which lambasted the effect of New Deal agricultural policy on tenant farmers. See Robert F. Martin, *Howard Kester and the Struggle for Social Justice in the South, 1904–77* (Charlottesville: University of Virginia, 1991), John Egerton, *Speak Now Against the Day: The Generation Before the Civil Rights Movement in the South* (New York: Knopf, 1994), 124–26.

2. Norman Thomas (1884–1968), an ordained Presbyterian minister, was a pacifist and prominent advocate of non-Marxist socialism and who, between 1928 and 1948, ran six times for president as the Socialist Party candidate.

3. Joseph Brown Matthews (1984–1966), a native of Kentucky, was a Methodist minister and active in numerous pacifist and Christian organizations in the South in the 1920s and early 1930s. His politics turned sharply to the right in the late 1930s, and he would become a prominent investigator and witness for the House Committee on Un-American Activities; see J. B. Matthews, *Odyssey of a Fellow Traveler* (New York: Mount Vernon, 1938).

4. Claude Neal of Greenwood, Florida, was brutally lynched on 26 October 1934, after being accused of and arrested, though never convicted, for the rape and murder of Lola Cannady, a young white woman. See James R. McGovern, *Anatomy of a Lynching: The Killing of Claude Neal* (Baton Rouge: Louisiana State University Press, 1982).

〰 To V. D. Johnston
17 November 1934
Washington, D.C.

Thurman vents his anger and frustration in response to a rent-due letter from V. D. Johnston, treasurer of Howard University. Thurman insists that the university had not fulfilled its contractual obligation in the maintenance of his home. Beyond mere business, this is a moral matter to Thurman, and he reminds Johnston that there are "personal moral obligations that the University has to the individuals in it."

My dear Mr. Johnston:

I am in receipt of your letter of recent date advising me as to the balance due the University on my rent account. I am fully aware of my obligation to the University, and since I understand my budget arrangements better than you, you will have to trust my judgment as to what kind of adjustment can be made in my budget so as to absorb my obligation to you. I say this because you suggested in your letter that on the basis of a conference, you might be suggestive to me as to how to put this amount in my budget.

I wish to call your attention, Mr. Johnston; to the fact that as a renter from the University, I have not been treated with the kind of meticulous care in fixing my house that you seem to think that I should exercise in the promptness with which I pay my rental to the University. I was in the house nearly two years before it was finally put into shape. Since last spring the cement has been peeling off the walls of my kitchen due to a leak in the wall. I have sent in several trouble reports on this. I have written you about it. The hole is still in the ceiling and it is getting worse. I have received no recognition relative to this matter. In the light of the lackadaisical manner in which I have been treated as a tenant of the University, you do not have any moral right to demand that I be more punctual than I am in paying my rent.

I go thus into detail because I think it is well to remind you that even though the best and most up-to-date business methods would have to be used in an organization of this size, there are personal moral obligations that the University has to the individuals in it, as well as obligations that the individuals have to the University. It is on this point that I am insisting.

Faithfully yours,

[*unsigned*]

Howard Thurman

Mr. V. D. Johnston, Treasurer

Howard University

Washington, D.C.

t.

TLc. HTC-MBU: Box 9.

🐟 TO JOSEPH BAKER

4 DECEMBER 1934

PHILADELPHIA, PA.

With nine months remaining before the delegation begins its travels to India, Thurman summarizes the main points of a presentation he gave, along with T. Z. Koo, special secretary of the World Christian Student Federation, at a delegation luncheon in New York. He spells out for a diverse audience his views on American Christianity, which are at once an indictment of the prevailing social order and institutional forms of Christianity. Thurman concludes his letter to Baker with poignant humor.

My dear Joe:[1]

It was not possible for me to get enough money to defray your expenses to New York to cover the luncheon yesterday, but I am sending you the major facts in order that you may use them in any way you wish.

The luncheon was called by the India Delegation of the National Councils of the Y.W.C.A. and Y.M.C.A. There were about sixty carefully chosen individuals including Negroes, white people, Indian, Japanese, and Chinese. The luncheon was presided over by Miss Winnifred Wygal of the National Y.W.C.A. There were two speeches—one by me, and the other by Dr. T. Z. Koo, the special secretary of the World Christian Student Federation, of which the American Student Movement is a member. I shall give you an outline of what was said.

First, I pointed out that I was not going out to represent American Christianity, because I did not have any confidence in the aspect of American Christianity with which I was familiar. As an underprivileged man, I was interested in religion from the point of view of the needs of underprivileged peoples. This interest had driven me to a critical examination of the genesis of the Christian religion, and to my amazement I discovered that in this genesis Christianity was not a world religion, but a technique of survival for an underprivileged minority. The technique that it worked out was so fundamental that it became the basis of a world redeeming faith. In America it had its greatest opportunity since its beginning, because here it started on the ground floor with one of the most audacious political experiments in the history of the world.[2] Its present state of impotency is a set commentary upon the use to which it has been put, and a definite reflection upon its genius. Going to India I propose to share with the Indian students whatever secrets I may have learned about the meaning of life, and to have them share the same with me. This can only be done in an atmosphere of friendliness, which atmosphere is guaranteed both by the nature and content of their invitation.

Dr. T. Z. Koo, speaking for the World Christian Federation, said that the Federation expected three things from this kind of exchange. First, that those who make up the Delegation will have a primary experience and understanding of the meaning of God in their own lives. Second, they may bring inspiration to the Indians, because they know the secret of suffering and can speak more directly to the Indians as their brothers. Third, the Delegation will be a personal manifestation of an impersonal transcontinental organization, which too often has merely mechanical expressions of its life. He hoped that the Delegation would also visit China while in the Orient.

Dr. Rao[3] of Poona, India spoke words of felicitation to the Committee and the representatives of the Delegation. He said that India represented a paradox. They are underprivileged with reference to political freedom, et cetera, and yet among themselves they have a condition which makes some of their number more underprivileged than others. He was happy to welcome American Negroes to India, because he felt they had so much in common that the experience would result in profound enchantment for each. Dr. Rao is studying in New York. He is leader in a movement called "The Friends of India."[4]

At five-thirty in the afternoon, Sue and I attended a tea given on Park Avenue by a woman who is very much interested in the project. It was a very unusual affair in several ways. I can tell you all about it when we talk, but I simply wanted it mentioned in the publicity. Both T. Z. Koo and I gave addresses at this tea, also. We said substantially the same thing that I have outlined above.

By the way, I saw Roy Wilkins at the luncheon.[5] He is planning an article for the *Crisis* for the middle spring. I like him.

Please work this up into a good story and release it as soon as is possible for a busy man. It seems as if you don't know what the truth is, for you said you were coming down here Thanksgiving.[6]

So long.

[*unsigned*]

Howard Thurman

Mr. Joseph Baker
713 South Sixteenth Street
Philadelphia, Pennsylvania

TLc. HTC-MBU: Box 1.

1. Joseph Baker was a prominent *Philadelphia Tribune* reporter, businessman, and a pioneering and long-term African American public-relations specialist. He achieved power as a behind-the-scenes advisor to leading political and civic figures beginning with the New Deal. Thurman would officiate at his 1938 wedding. "Newsman Marries Teacher," *Pittsburgh Courier*, 26 February 1938.

2. Articulated here are themes central to Thurman's thinking that will inform his ongoing engagement with American Christianity's inability and unwillingness to deal with the issue of race. This thought is more fully developed in his books *Jesus and the Disinherited* (1949) and *The Luminous Darkness: A Personal Interpretation of the Anatomy of Segregation and the Ground of Hope* (New York: Harper and Row, 1965).

3. Pandurangi Kodanda Rao (1889–?) was an Indian anthropologist who was studying at Yale University and who met with Thurman as part of the preparation for the Negro Delegation. His works include *East versus West: A Denial of Contrast* (London: Unwin, 1939). For Rao's meetings with Thurman, see his letters of 1 May 1935 and 5 September 1935, "Negro Delegation to India," HTC-MBU: Box 17.

4. The Friends of India was a network of groups established during the 1930s and 1940s to raise cross-cultural awareness and advocacy of human and civil rights in India.

5. Roy Ottoway Wilkins (1901–81) at the time this letter was written had recently replaced W. E. B. Du Bois as editor of *Crisis,* the official magazine of the NAACP, and would remain editor until 1949. Wilkins joined the NAACP as assistant executive secretary in 1931 and became executive secretary in 1955, remaining in that position until 1977.

6. Thurman and Baker often engaged in jocular exchanges in their letters. In his letter of 29 October 1934, Baker wrote Thurman, "I shall try to have somebody meet you at the station, but in case they should not recognize His Highness, take an octoroon Cab and come up and see us sometime. Note: be prepared to go to my apartment for a bull session afterwards." In his letter of 30 August 1934, he wrote Thurman, "hoping that you enjoyed your vacation in Arkansas and that the sun did not burn you any darker, believe me." HTC-MBU: Box 1.

۶۳ TO GRACE VIRGINIA IMES
5 DECEMBER 1934
WASHINGTON, D.C.

In response to the charge that southern Negroes were chosen as representatives
for the India trip because of their relative docility, Thurman, in clear disagree-
ment, seeks an audience with and further clarification from Grace V. Imes.

My dear Mrs. Imes:

I was very happy to have the pleasure of meeting you at last. I have enjoyed
the fellowship which has come to me as a result of knowing your husband, and
had looked forward to the privilege of meeting you.[1]

In a conversation with Miss Elizabeth Harrington yesterday afternoon, she
told me and Mrs. Thurman in detail about your statements to her relative to the
choice of Negroes on the Delegation, and the attitudes and ideas which those
particular Negroes represented. Particularly pointed was the remark that they
had been chosen arbitrarily from the South because southern Negroes are noted
for their tolerant, kindly, more or less weak, stand with reference to the American white man; while northern Negroes are noted for their courageous, outspoken, firm, attitude with reference to the American white man. I appreciate
knowing how you feel in this matter, and as chairman of the Delegation I am
making one request of you. Will you be kind enough to put in writing precisely
what attitude you would like to see presented to the students of India, so that in
the seminars which we will be holding this year in preparation for the journey,
we may be sure to include the type of opinion which to you is most in order.

In addition to this, if you will give me an audience sometime in January, I
shall be glad to call to see you when I am in New York.

Please know that I appreciate {knowing} your attitude, and my only regret is
that I had to get it indirectly.

Faithfully yours,

[*unsigned*]

Howard Thurman

Mrs. William Lloyd Imes
St. James Presbyterian Church
St. Nicholas Avenue, at 141st Street
New York, New York
t.

                                                       TLc. HTC-MBU: Box 9.

1. Grace Virginia Imes (1888–1976) was the wife of William Lloyd Imes (1889–1986), the
well-known pastor of Saint James Presbyterian Church in New York City.

✎ To FRED L. BROWNLEE
21 DECEMBER 1934
WASHINGTON, D.C.

Thurman requests, in confidence, an opportunity to lease Kings Mountain.

My dear Mr. Brownlee:[1]

I am just now getting the opportunity to write you relative to our conference on October 12 at Howard University. In going over the memorandum, I am
a bit puzzled by item three with reference to the attitude of the small group
towards Mr. Ricks. I am puzzled because my understanding was that at the
close of our discussion relative to Mr. Ricks and the future program of Kings
Mountain as outlined, you suggested that the matter concerning Mr. Ricks was
one which was a problem of your Board and was not the concern of ours. For
that reason, it seems to me, that item Number three prepares the way for you
and your Board to act seemingly at the suggestion of this Advisory Committee.
If I were in Mr. Ricks' place and this action were known to me, I would feel that
I had been knifed in the house of my friends. I hope I have made myself clear at
this point, because I am convinced that any general statement coming from us
relative to Mr. Ricks would be most unwise.

I am wondering if the American Missionary Association[2] would consider
leasing Kings Mountain to me and Mrs. Thurman for, say, twenty years and
some arrangement be worked out whereby your interest will be continued in
the Lincoln Academy and its development. The lease would obtain so long as we
fulfilled the economic requirements, and so long as enterprises that were not
commercial but eleemosynary were conducted. I know this is a very unusual
proposition and you may disagree with it at once.

In making a proposition like this, I pave the way for great misunderstanding;
for it seems as if I am taking advantage of the Advisory Committee's proposal and
confidence. Or it may seem as if I am making an indirect bid, through this proposition, for the position to head up the Kings Mountain enterprises under the plans
discussed by this Advisory Committee. Nothing is farther from my mind. I am
very happy in my work here, and am doing what seems to me a fundamentally
significant job. I share the complete confidence of my superiors and have full
opportunities to experiment with religion in higher education. But if Mrs. Thurman and I had the opportunity to develop of our own initiative certain enterprises
which we have discussed for many months, without the limitations which may be
involved when a superior board has the power to veto, we would give up our

present work. In order that I may be acting in complete good faith, I am sharing this letter with the Dean of the faculty of which I am a part.

Season's greetings.

[unsigned]

Howard Thurman

Mr. Fred L. Brownlee

287 Fourth Avenue

New York, New York

TLc. HTC-MBU: Box 1.

1. Frederick Leslie Brownlee (1883–1962) served as general secretary of the American Missionary Association from 1920 to 1950.

2. The American Missionary Association (AMA) was developed to provide educational opportunities for blacks and other racial ethnic groups in the United States. See Ralph Luker, *The Social Gospel in Black and White* (Chapel Hill: University of North Carolina Press, 1991) and Joe M. Richardson, *Christian Reconstruction: The American Missionary Association and Southern Blacks, 1861–1890* (Athens: University of Georgia Press, 1986).

☙ FROM JOHN NEVIN SAYRE

26 DECEMBER 1934

NEW YORK, N.Y.

John Nevin Sayre,[1] chairman of the Fellowship of Reconciliation (FOR), details a new plan for the organization's efforts to expand the pacifist movement in the United States. He invites Thurman to join select members of FOR as the only African American field representative. Thurman accepts the volunteer position.

Dear Howard:

The purpose of this letter is to enlist your cooperation in building a powerful pacifist movement in the United States. We want especially to have you become a Volunteer Field Representative of The Fellowship of Reconciliation.

The plan is as follows: In order to present its message more effectively in the field and to cover more adequately the huge geographical area of the United States, the F.O.R. is adopting the plan of appointing volunteer field representatives to act for it in the following capacity.

Each representative will agree to visit at least five communities a year to present our message from the platform; recruit new members; council with local F.O.R. groups as to program of activities; promote Fellowship literature; and generally serve as field workers for the Fellowship, making connection between local groups and national headquarters. Details as to just how this can be done will be furnished later.

We are inviting outstanding members of the Fellowship to engage in such service on a volunteer basis; that is to say, there would be no salary. With regard to expenses, the aim would be to fit in the work with other engagements so that the Fellowship representative would be put to no personal expense, but would also derive no personal financial profit. Some money will be available from our budget for travel, but the less we have to pay out on this, the more can we extend the range of our whole project.

Kirby Page is leading the list with his promise to visit twenty communities for the Fellowship within the next twelve months. Among others who have already agreed to be field representatives are: Roswell P. Barnes, Edmund Chaffee, Albert Coe, Bernard Clausen, George Collins, Henry Crane, Bruce Curry, Allan Hunter, Paul Jones, Halford E. Luccock, Edwin McNeill Poteat, Frances Perry, Kirby Page, Arthur L. Swift, and myself.[2]

I hope you can accept this invitation because we are very anxious to have the particular and invaluable contribution which you can make. Our list would be incomplete without you.

Should you decide favorably about this matter, will you please wire me at once? We are printing our new folder which will contain the names of the field representatives and will be used by them in recruiting new members. Will you also send me a brief paragraph about yourself to be included in our Who's Who contained in this folder?

With the hope that you can serve,
Yours cordially,
[*signed*] Nevin
Chairman
Professor Howard Thurman
Howard University
Washington, D.C.
JNS:T

TLS. HTC-MBU: Box 19.

1. John Nevin Sayre (1897–1967) was an Episcopal priest and member of the faculty at Brookwood Labor College, Katonah, New York, from 1919 to 1939. In addition to his work with the FOR, he was a member of the American Civil Liberties Union and the National Peace Conference.

2. All of the individuals named in the list were among the most nationally prominent religious and ecumenical leaders and intellectuals of the period.

🌿 To Reinhold Niebuhr
28 December 1934
Washington, D.C.

Reinhold Niebuhr's speaking engagement in early January is confirmed. The letter demonstrates not only Thurman's friendship with Niebuhr but also his interest in Niebuhr's politics.

My dear Reini:

We are very glad that you are to be our guest for the weekend of January 6. We hope you will plan to get here for the late afternoon on Saturday, January 5, for we are planning an informal dinner with you as guest of honor, at which time we want you to talk informally about the ethical justification for coercion.[1] I am very anxious to have this in the form of a sort of round table conversation, rather than an elaborate address. We plan to have the faculty of the School of Religion and seven or eight other people present. The dinner is called for six o'clock and will last until a quarter of eight.

It is one of the traditions of the Thurman family to have an old-fashion Twelfth Night party on the twelfth night after Christmas in keeping with the ancient idea. This party begins at ten in the evening and continues until the clock sounds twelve that night. Since the twelfth night this year falls on Sunday, we are having the party Saturday night. One of the major features of this party is an imported fortune teller. Sue has asked me to urge you to accept this role. Your function will be to tell the fortunes of as many people as you desire, using whatever magical vehicle you may prefer. It has been done on the basis of tea leaves, palms, and handwriting. It is all done in the spirit of great hilarity and fun. Do you bite? Please let me know by return mail. You will, of course, be our house-guest while here.

I regret that I shan't be here all day Sunday, but I am trying to arrange to stay over to preside at your service Sunday morning. I must leave for Florida during the day.

Season's greetings to yourself and wife and St. Christopher.[2]

Faithfully,

[*unsigned*]

Howard Thurman

Professor Reinhold Niebuhr
Union Theological Seminary
New York, New York

TLc. HTC-MBU: Box 14.

---

1. In his germinal work *Moral Man and Immoral Society* (1932), Niebuhr broke with his previous pacifist stance, arguing that "all social co-operation . . . requires a measure of

coercion," and that coercion was involved even in acts of nonviolence, including Gandhi's campaigns against importation. 3, 172. As a consequence, Niebuhr argues, Christians and others trying to live moral lives need to recognize that using force against aggression is sometimes necessary.

2. Christopher is Niebuhr's son.

✎ FROM REINHOLD NIEBUHR
31 DECEMBER 1934
NEW YORK, N.Y.

Niebuhr confirms dinner plans and Sunday-morning worship service at Howard University but declines Sue's playful invitation to tell fortunes.

Dear Howard:

Thank you for your kind letter. I will arrive Saturday, on the 6:00 o'clock train so that I can be ready for your dinner. I shall have to leave immediately after the service on Sunday to speak at the Baltimore Forum at 3:00 o'clock and will have my Sunday luncheon on the train.

Tell Sue that I appreciate her confidence in me, but I have never performed the role she assigns to me in my entire life. Not being very imaginative I just don't think I could do it. It would take everything I have in time and energy to think up material for that kind of a role, and then I wouldn't succeed. I am sorry to let her down, but I am just too prosaic to make that kind of an effort.
Cordially yours,
[*signed*] Reini
Reinhold Niebuhr
Reverend Howard Thurman
Howard University
Washington, D.C.

TLS. HTC-MBU: Box 14.

✎ TO WILBUR C. WOODSON
15 JANUARY 1935
WASHINGTON, D.C.

Thurman responds to an invitation made by Wilbur C. Woodson, executive secretary of the Detroit YMCA, to return once again to conduct their Holy Week Services.

My dear Woodson:

I am sending you this note to say that I shall make my plans to come back to Detroit this year. You recall that when I left my mind was not made up, because I was of the opinion that it would be a very good thing if a new voice were heard. Even now, if you have any suggestion in the light of my conversation with you in the railway station last year, please do not hesitate to make it. My major interest is in the highest development of the spiritual life of the Negro community there. If the plans go through as in previous years, I shall spend from Wednesday through Sunday afternoon—April 17 through 21—in Detroit.

I hope the new year has moved off auspiciously for you, the work, and the family. I received a copy of the program that was sponsored by the Howard Thurman Club.[1] It is a very humbling feeling that is mine as I look it over.

I am sure that you miss Herb King, for he was an asset to your community.

May I hear from you by return mail, if possible?

Faithfully yours,

[*signed*] Howard Thurman

Mr. Wilbur Woodson

St. Antoine Branch Y.M.C.A.

636 East Elizabeth Street

Detroit, Michigan

TL. DHU-MS: Box 4045.

1. No records have been found on this organization, a clearly enthusiastic local response to the work of Thurman.

✒ FROM MURIEL LESTER
21 JANUARY 1935
LOS ANGELES, CALIF.

Muriel Lester,[1] the British social activist and associate of Mahatma Gandhi, heard about the upcoming Thurman-led delegation to India while in the United States on a speaking tour. In this, her first letter to Thurman, Lester provides an impassioned assessment of the mind and mood of India's people and the demoralizing impact of British imperialism.

Prof. Howard Thurman,

Howard University,

Washington, D.C.

Dear Mr. Thurman,

I am overjoyed to hear that you are going out with a few other Negroes to help the Indian people. I would like to talk to you about this, and oh!, how I wish we could meet, if it was only for half an hour, because I had four and a half months last year of real saddening experience while I was staying with Mr. Gandhi. You see I am "persona grata" with Indians because I entertained Mr. Gandhi in London for three months, so they talk very frankly to me and they would "let out" on my colleague, Agatha Harrison, and me the accumulated stores of bitterness that ~~they~~ {most of them, I believe,} have definitely hoarded, perhaps {even} cultivated, since they began to think for themselves, perhaps at the age of fourteen.[2] Sometimes Agatha and I would feel ~~actually~~ physically exhausted after listening to them, some boy perhaps, or girl, for two or three hours solid talking, not in any pattern going on from one position to another in order to make us understand, but round and round and round in a circle. Often a meal would become drawn out, dragged out, to weariness point by this sort of talk. We would try to thrust a way out of the ~~vicious~~ circle, suggesting suddenly some line of action, some inquiry we were willing to undertake ourselves, or perhaps a visit we might pay there and then to the chief villain of the story, the person responsible for the particular wrong that they were at the moment describing. But they would never countenance such action. It displeased them when we suggested any sort of action, even when we were willing to ~~come into~~ {cooperate in} it with them. And if, weighed down by responsibility for the ~~viciously~~ bad thing that they were reporting to us we announced our determination, ourselves and alone, to go straight to the seat of authority and "make a fuss," they would generally disapprove or look profoundly bored, and assure us that nothing we could do would be any use, nothing that anybody could do would be of any use. And so it went on, week after week. Some of the young people were obviously ~~throughly~~ poisoned physically by their own acidulated cynicism. They seemed to have little confidence in themselves, each other, life or God. We felt very ashamed to realize how much of the damage done them was due to the "British in India" but there were other factors which were there in the very heart of the Hindu social order before the British arrived in India. I am not trying to excuse ourselves. The ground of my hatred of Imperialism is the deterioration of character in the ruling race and the subject race.

It seemed that a new note was struck from an unexpected quarter and at a time when no one was expecting any relief from the discord, by Pierre Cérésole, when he arrived in the heart of Bihar, the earthquake-stricken area, to offer his expert engineering qualities and his International Volunteer Service Group to the succor of ~~suffering~~ the population there.[3] He is there now, care of Rajendra Prasad, The All India Earthquake Relief Foundation, Patna, Bihar. Rajendra Prasad is a man of God, a dear friend ~~of mine~~ {Mr. Gandhi's, President of the Indian National Congress.}[4] He wrote to Pierre Cérésole saying that the material help he was bringing from Europe would be {in}valuable, but <u>far</u> more valuable was the new outburst of hope and confidence that was noticeable among the people so soon as they knew that this European group was going to throw in its lot with the ~~relief workers~~ {coolies & peasants of} Patna, working side by side with them in the fields and villages, clearing away the sand, helping rebuild the huts and houses.[5]

Now I hear about your people going over. A very fine {N} ~~negro~~ minister here, Dr. Lightner, was at breakfast with me this morning and we were talking of the great contribution which your race has made to the rest of us ~~in the world~~, showing us how to cope with bitterness and turn suffering into strength and sweetness and humor.[6] I would like to hear from you, please, as to what your itinerary in India will be and whether you are going via London. I would like to give you some ~~instructions~~ {introductions}.

Yours Sincerely[7]

[*signed*] Muriel Lester

TLS. HTC-MBU: Box 11.

1. Muriel Lester (1883–1968), a long-time leader of the International Fellowship of Reconciliation (IFOR), first traveled to India in 1926 and returned throughout the 1930s and 1940s as the organization's traveling secretary. Her responsibilities included investigating injustices and campaigning for reform, as she did in India in 1934 when she traveled about the country with Gandhi, speaking against the problem of untouchability. She helped form the Indian chapter of the IFOR and was one of Gandhi's closest British associates. Lester published a multitude of works, including *My Host the Hindu* (London: Williams and Norgate, 1931), *Entertaining Gandhi* (London: Nicholson and Watson, 1932), and *Gandhi, World Citizen* (Allahabad: Kitab Mahal, 1945).

2. Agatha Harrison, a close British colleague of Lester and a Quaker, first met Gandhi in India in 1929. At Gandhi's suggestion, she worked for reconciliation between India and Britain. She also served as secretary of the Indian Concilation Group, formed in 1931. See Gertrude Bussey and Margaret Tims, *Pioneers for Peace: Women's International League for Peace and Freedom, 1915–1965* (London: Allen and Unwin, 1965).

3. Pierre Cérésole (1879–1945) was born in Lausanne, Switzerland. An engineer, he arrived in the United States in 1910 and began Christian pacifist work, later becoming a Quaker. From 1919 to 1920, he was the secretary of IFOR, and from 1934 to 1937 he was a volunteer in India.

4. Rajendra Prasad (1883–1963) was an Indian nationalist leader who worked closely with Gandhi, serving as a member of the Congress Party, the Indian Constitutional Assembly, and the first president of the Republic of India (1950–62). Prasad began his carrer by practicing law and founded *Bihar Law Weekly* in Calcutta. In 1920, he left legal practice to follow Gandhi's noncooperation movement and was founder and editor of *Desh,* a Hindi weekly.

5. The term *coolie* is derived from the Hindi *Kuli,* an aboriginal tribal name, or from Tamil *kuli,* wages, usually pejorative in European usage, referring to unskilled laborers or porters from the Far East hired for low or subsistence wages.

6. Lawrence H. Lightner (1884–1968), educator, journalist, and religious worker, was active in the YMCA, NAACP, and the National Negro Business League.

7. The closing is handwritten.

🪶 FROM ALLAN A. HUNTER

28 JANUARY 1935

HOLLYWOOD, CALIF.

Allan A. Hunter,[1] pastor of Mount Hollywood Congregational Church, requests to meet with Thurman after his return from India to discuss ways of bringing a greater spiritual emphasis on the work of FOR.

Rev Howard Thurman
Howard University
Washington DC

Dear Howard:

I see that you are scheduled, along with me, to work as field representative of the FOR. Kirby Page has asked me to take the chairmanship of the West coast FOR in addition, and I have decided to go ahead and do the work. The FOR will put in the church a part time stenographic secretary to relieve me of some of the unnecessary details. Sherwood Eddy before five hundred ministers, their wives and lay people, introduced the plan yesterday morning, so we are going ahead to make the FOR really function out here, facing economic, racial and international issues but also facing these issues on the basis of small intimate groups where there will be prayer and if possible daily discipline. The Tuesday evening group that meets here and that put through the November 11 youth mass peace meeting ... has just decided to throw its energy into the FOR and one or two other promising youth groups also.

I am writing you with this request: that on your way back from India or at any possible time you stop off in Southern California and let the FOR (on this new basis) work out a worthwhile schedule for you. I really believe we could do a great piece of work together. It would mean wonders for our effort to place the movement on a definitely spiritual basis. You have the good will of hundreds of young people and others in Southern California. We could assure you of a fine response. The financial arrangements I am sure could be worked out satisfactorily to yourself. We are developing efficient facilities. Anyway if you will drop me the enclosed card stating your tentative schedule and the possibilities of this, we can begin to plan.

I am working on a little book "Five Ways of Life."[2] Five persons each will write from one thousand to three thousand words stating their way of life. Muriel Lester has promised one. She is asking Schweitzer[3] and Gandhi to do one each, and I am asking Kagawa[4] and you to do the other two. Further details will come by mail later. What do you think? Will you tentatively promise to do one of these? I can't make promises on remuneration. The idea is mostly to broadcast among young people these five approaches to effective and joyous living. You will be interested in the enclosed by Muriel Lester. We will get a new one from her, possibly using snatches of the enclosed.

Your telegram just arrived. I immediately forwarded to Muriel Lester. I trust her intuition on this request to confer with you but of course am not in a position to assume responsibility. Best wishes
{She has written Gandhi about you.}
[signed] Allan

TLcS. HTC-MBU: Box 9.

1. Allan Armstrong Hunter (1893–1982) was a 1916 graduate of Princeton University and was ordained a Presbyterian minister in 1922. Hunter had long been active in FOR and was a deeply committed pacifist. From 1919 to 1920 and again from 1925 to 1926, he toured missions in India, China, Korea, and Japan. He was minister of the Mount Holly-wood Congregational Church from 1926 to 1963. See A *History of Mt. Hollywood Congregational Church* (Mount Hollywood, Calif.: Hollywood Congregational Church, 1981).

2. This was eventually published, entirely written by Hunter, as *Three Trumpets Sound: Kagawa, Gandhi, Schweitzer* (New York: Association Press, 1939). That Hunter saw Thurman's life as exemplary and worthy of comparison to Gandhi and Schweitzer is an indication of the esteem in which Thurman was held by liberal Christians in the mid-1930s.

3. See "Review of Albert Schweitzer's *Indian Thought and Its Development*," to be printed in volume 2.

4. Toyohiko Kagawa (1888–1960) was a Japanese Christian pacifist and a leader in the labor and cooperative movements. Hunter had recently written a book, published in Japan, about him: *Kagawa, Gambler for God* (Tokyo: Topping, 1934).

꜅ To ALLAN A. HUNTER
30 JANUARY 1935
WASHINGTON, D.C.

As a matter of personal preference and long memory, Thurman rarely flew, even after airplanes became a common mode of transportation for Americans, black or white.

My dear Allen:

I have at last completed arrangements, and am squeezing every pocket in sight dry. I am leaving tonight for Berkeley where I shall spend a few hours with Miss Lester and return the same night for Washington. I regret that I shall not have the opportunity to come down to Hollywood to see you and Elizabeth and the kiddies, but I have no choice because I am doing an unprecedented thing as far as my own work here is concerned. I did not take the plane trip because it is too uncertain as to weather, and in addition I did not feel like fighting with these proud, godless, American Christian gentlemen for the right to spend an English lady's money to ride in one of their aeroplanes. Thank you for your interest in this, and I would give worlds, Allen, to see you.

You must know that I think of you very often, and feel that knowing you provides a great source of strength to me, as the struggle between Negroes and white people in this country becomes more terrible every day. It is our plan to return from India by way of the Pacific, and I am asking to remain out there for a couple of weeks so that I can have a real visit with you.

I have enjoyed reading your recent book about the Far East.[1] Sue was deeply impressed with it, particularly by the artistry which you used in conveying your ideas.

Heartiest greetings to the whole family.

Faithfully,

[*unsigned*]

Howard Thurman

Mr. Allen Hunter

Hollywood, California

TLc. HTC-MBU: Box 9.

1. Allan Hunter, *Out of the Far East* (San Francisco, Calif.: R and E Research, 1934).

❧ To Muriel Lester

30 January 1935

Washington, D.C.

Thurman accepts Lester's invitation to Berkeley, California, for further dialogue about India. In his letter Thurman also offers a telling glimpse into the difficulties of domestic travel for blacks.

My dear Miss Lester:

I received your telegram last night, and I am arranging my plans so as to leave here late tonight arriving in Berkeley Sunday morning about seven-thirty. I take it that you are speaking Sunday morning, and I am wondering if it will be possible for us to have a good chat upon my arrival. At any rate, I shall go directly to Mr. Hunter's from the railway station.[1] I must get a train returning the same day. I hesitated a long time about making the decision to travel this great distance for so short a time. I wondered, too, whether it was quite ethical to have you spend such a huge sum of money in order that the trip would be possible. In the light of the total situation, however, I decided that perhaps we could both serve a larger good if the sacrifices were made at this time.

I was deeply moved by your letter, and I shall have several questions to raise with you.

A word about the expense. The round trip rate from here by rail is $160.60; the pullman is $21 each way, meals will cost an average of $3.25 a day going and coming, this will mean six days of train travel making a total of $19.50. This makes a total cost of $222.10, figuring it as closely as I can in the light of the handicaps of travel for one of my race. This is about $75 cheaper than by plane. I did not consider the plane, both because of the weather and because of the terrific difficulties involved due to my race.[2]

It will be a very great joy to meet you, and to have this opportunity of getting a profound insight into the heart of the problems of the Indian youth viewed through the heart of one who deserves to be called Christian.

I shall see you Sunday morning and shall be leaving in the afternoon of the same day. I don't quite know how I am going to stand up under the terrific wear and tear of the continuous travel, in view of the fact that I have just returned from a long jaunt, but my interest will take care of that.

Sincerely yours,

[unsigned]

Howard Thurman

Miss Muriel Lester

2901 Benvenue Avenue

Berkeley, California

TLc. HTC-MBU: Box 136.

1. Allan A. Hunter.

2. There were no institutional policies against blacks flying, although blacks undoubtedly faced difficulties arranging reservations or encountered hostilities of fellow white passengers. Perhaps for Thurman, interstate train travel, even under Jim Crow conditions, had the advantage that the role for black passengers was well defined. See C. Vann Woodward, *Strange Career of Jim Crow*, 3rd. ed. (New York: Oxford University Press, 1974), 117.

To Tzung Z. Koo
8 FEBRUARY 1935
WASHINGTON, D.C.

Many people are interested in the work of the India Delegation, and as a result, Thurman receives unsolicited advice from various segments of the Christian community. Not all the advice is helpful, in Thurman's view. Here, he learns that Koo, special secretary of the World Christian Student Federation, has accused him of unduly emphasizing the underprivileged status of Indians. In addressing Koo's views, Thurman indicates that his primary frame of reference is the experience of blacks in America. If Koo was worried that an emphasis on the "underprivileged" in India and the United States would unduly politicize the Negro Delegation, Thurman tries to assure him that the delegation will have no overt political agenda.

My dear Dr. Koo:[1]

The Chairman of the Committee on the Delegation to India, Mrs. Elizabeth Harrington, has very kindly passed on to me your suggestion relative to the seeming over-emphasis that I am placing upon the fact that the Indians are an underprivileged group. I appreciate very much your concern in this matter, and your willingness to share with us what has come to you through contact with the Indian people themselves. I am profoundly aware of the fact that the Indians consider themselves a "superior race" culturally, and am not interested in the merits of the assumption. I have never in public address or in private conversation referred to the Indian people as underprivileged. All my references have been to the American Negro as an underprivileged minority, and what from that experience he may be able to share concerning the meaning of life with any group. I am not concerned about trying to make common cause with the Indians or any group in America or outside of America merely on the basis of the accidents of political, economic, or social advantage or disadvantage. As important as these things are, to me, they do not go to the root of the matter.

I shall be very happy to get some word from you before you leave the country. Once again let me express my appreciation for the thoughtfulness which you manifested in passing on to Mrs. Harrington this word relative to the delegation.

Sincerely,

[*unsigned*]

Howard Thurman

TLc. HTC-MBU: Box 10.

1. Dr. Tzung Z. Koo (1887–1971) was a prominent Chinese Christian evangelist, scholar, and religious activist. He led the Chinese Student Christian Movement and was a member of the foreign missions committee. In 1956, he initiated a new course of studies at Bucknell University, Lewisburg, Pennsylvania, which became its Department of Oriental Studies.

HUBERT HERRING TO SUE BAILEY THURMAN

12 FEBRUARY 1935

NEW YORK, N.Y.

Herring sends a copy of his request for help from Ambassador Josephus Daniels to Sue Bailey Thurman. His letter offers a troubling look at Mexico's informal immigration policy toward African Americans.

Mrs. Howard Thurman
Howard University
Washington, D.C.

My dear Sue:

I inclose a copy of my letter to Uncle Josephus. I have a hunch that he will get action. Let me know the news.

I am really coming down to see you next week and will let you know how and when.

Sincerely yours,

[*signed*] Hubert Herring

JWG

February 12, 1935

Hon. Josephus Daniels[1]
Embassy of the United States of America
Mexico, D.F.

My dear Mr. Ambassador:

I have been applauding you from the sidelines for your handling of that ticklish church situation. Now that the lunatics are breaking loose in Washington it is good to know that you are on the job in Mexico. I hope you won't let the firebrands get us into trouble.

I have a little matter which I should like to put before you and see if there is anything you can do to help. Mexico, as you probably know, has been building up a tradition against allowing negroes from the United States to cross the border. I don't think that they have any very formal law. I suspect that it is an informal interpretation by some of the officials. The situation is now pointed up in the case of Mrs. Howard Thurman, whose husband is a professor in Howard University in Washington. Mrs. Thurman is an exceedingly able young woman and she wishes to spend several months in Mexico studying music and the dance. It is just the sort of thing which Mexico should encourage, but after struggling for two months, she is still unable to get the necessary permission from the Mexican embassy.

The issues raised are, of course, obvious. As a great admirer of Mexico I hate to see her fall into all of the stupid ways which we in the United States have built up. There is, after all, in Mexico, little race prejudice, and why should they go out of their way to persuade intelligent American negroes that Mexico is as stupid as the United States has often been?

Would it be possible for you to take the matter up with the Minister Gobernacion or whoever has charge of such matters and see whether they can be persuaded to take a definite line? The specific case of Mrs. Thurman is presumably before them. She made application through the Mexican embassy in Washington and in order that you may have the record before you, I inclose a copy of her application.

Mrs. Thurman is anxious to leave as soon as possible. I would, therefore, greatly appreciate it if you could delegate this matter to one of your associates and let me know how the matter stands.

I am, of course, anxious that the thing should be cleared up not only for Mrs. Thurman's sake, but also for the sake of others who face the same situation.

With best regards to Mrs. Daniels and yourself,

Sincerely yours,

[*unsigned*]

Hubert Herring

TLS. HTC-MBU: Box 9.

1. Josephus Daniels (1862–1948), a writer and diplomat, was editor of the Raleigh (N.C.) *State Chronicle* (1885–92) and *News and Observer* (1894–1933), U.S. Secretary of the Navy (1913–21), and U.S. ambassador to Mexico (1933–41).

From Arthur L. James

16 February 1935

Roanoke, Va.

As president of the Hampton Ministers' Conference, James was seeking to have Thurman and Adam Clayton Powell Jr. address that year's Hampton Conference, a major event among black preachers. James reports that individuals within the organization have rebuffed his efforts.

Rev. Howard W. Thurman

Howard University

Washington, D.C.

My dear Howard:

Your very nice letter came yesterday. We are glad to hear from you and your little family and to know that things are still going well with you.

We shall be happy to have you come whenever you find it possible. I have announced your coming at least twice and you have been prevented each time, so I will simply listen and wait for you to come whenever you can. Any time will suit us that suits you.

Refering to the Hampton Conference,[1] I urged that you and young Clayton Powell[2] be given places on the program: asking that you be given the devotions or the annual sermon but he failed to agree upon either of you. Giving some reasons which he said were confidential, but I will be glad to tell you what he said when we meet.

Dr. Tobias was here two weeks ago as guest and speaker for our Y.M.C.A. Annual meeting.[3] He stopped in the home with us and we had a good many interesting conversations. I referred to Devan's attitude toward you and Powell, and he said that two more capable persons could not have been found and that the Hampton man had given out the impression that he is somewhat of a crank.

I asked that Powell be asked to speak on either the problem of the city church or the place of Social Service in the Church. Who doubts that he is capable of helping the men on either of these subjects?

For the things I suggested for each of you, I doubt that any other two men in the country would have done them as well. He is a nuisance and I will be pleased to step down and out at the end of my three year term.

All along the president has meant nothing more than a mere figurehead but I am determined not to, Howard, allow myself to be used as such. Up to this time, the men say that I have exercised more manhood in the office than any other since the days of Dr. A. A. Graham,[4] but to go further it will cause disruption and since my term is out next June, I think I will just quietly endure it until time to give it up.

Love to Sue and the children. When I come to Washington I will let you know and will be glad to spend some of my time with you.

My work here is still moving along nicely. I am enclosing you a copy of the Church News.

Yours as ever,

[*signed*] A. L. James

Cousin Arthur

ALJ/IJ

TLcS. HTC-MBU: Box 9.

1. The Hampton University Ministers' Conference (HUMC), which began in the summer of 1914, was originally held in conjunction with the Hampton Institute Summer School for Teachers as a way for leaders of African American communities to gather for a week of reflection, inspiration, and exchange in an interdenominational setting. Currently, the HUMC is the largest interdenominational gathering of African American clergy, with more than seventy-five hundred members. Membership is drawn from the historically black denominations as well as black leadership within white denominations. *The History of the Hampton University Ministers' Conference: An Experience in Interdenominational Cooperation* (St. Louis, Mo.: Hodale, 1996).

2. Adam Clayton Powell Jr. (1908–72), a prominent minister and civil-rights activist, earned his undergraduate and graduate degrees from Colgate University and Columbia University. In 1937, he became pastor of the ten-thousand-member Abyssinian Baptist Church in Harlem, New York. He was elected to the New York City Council in 1941, the first black to hold the office, and in 1944 was elected to Congress, where he served until 1970. See Charles V. Hamilton, *Adam Clayton Powell, Jr.: The Political Biography of an American Dilemma* (New York: Collier, 1992).

3. Channing H. Tobias, a close friend of Thurman, was at this time secretary of the Colored Department of the National Council of the YMCA.

4. Archie Allen Graham (1873–?) was pastor of the Zion Baptist Church of Phoebus, Virginia. In 1919 he became the corresponding secretary of the Lott-Carey Baptist Foreign Society. He was elected president of the Hampton Minister's Conference in 1915 and served as a trustee of Virginia Union University, Richmond, Virginia.

✌ THOMAS D. BOWMAN TO WILLIAM S. NELSON
25 FEBRUARY 1935
MEXICO CITY, MEXICO

In response to his recommendation on behalf of Sue Bailey Thurman for a visa to Mexico, William S. Nelson receives a procedural letter from the American Consul General, specifying the process by which Sue was to make formal application. The consulate, for its part, refused to intervene on her behalf.

Mr. William S. Nelson,
President of Shaw University,
Raleigh, North Carolina.

Sir:

This Consulate General has received, by reference from the American Ambassador in this City, your letter of February 13, 1935, regarding the desire of Mrs. H. Thurman to enter Mexico for the purpose of studying in the University of Mexico.

There is quoted below for your information pertinent paragraphs of a circular of the Mexican Ministry of the Interior dated October 17, 1933, pertaining to the restriction of certain classes of aliens in Mexico.

"This Ministry believes it advantageous to summarize in a single circular all the circulars in force which prohibit or restrict the immigration of certain classes of aliens, and you are hereby informed of the races and individuals which are definitely subject to prohibition or restriction in their immigration to the country. These races and individuals are the following:

"First.—For ethnical reasons, the yellow, Negro, Malayan and Hindu races, with the exception of the Japanese while the International Treaty in this regard is in force."

This office understands that a special permit must be obtained from the Ministry of the Interior in Mexico City for any of the types of aliens, mentioned in the above quoted circular, to enter Mexico. Mrs. Thurman's proper procedure would be to make application to the nearest Mexican Consul (in her case probably New York City), who will be in a position to advise her. It is understood that the consuls are authorized to forward applications of this character to Mexico City.

In a somewhat similar, though not identical case, this Consulate General has made inquiry of the immigration authorities in Mexico City and has been informed that the central office here is not prepared to discuss a case until formal application has been received as each case must be treated upon its merits.

It may also be well to point out that, in view of our own stringent immigration regulations, consular officers are obliged scrupulously to avoid suggesting to local authorities departure from established rules and regulations.

Very truly yours,

[*signed*] Thomas D. Bowman

American Consul General

TLc. HTC-MBU: Box 15.

To Arthur L. James

27 February 1935

Washington, D.C.

Thurman confirms James's earlier assessment of his rebuff by the Hampton Conference and concurs with James's decision to step down from the presidency at the end of his term in June.

My dear Cousin Arthur:

It was certainly good to get your letter a few days ago, and I am making haste to send you a line in return.

Thank you for enclosing a copy of the "News." Sue's comment on the paper was that it looked like some aristocratic Nordic paper. I know you feel flattered.

I happened to find out the other day more precisely why the gentlemen at Hampton refused to follow your suggestion, particularly with regard to me. When I see you, I shall go into detail. I discovered, also, that there is considerable resentment of the fact that you are taking your position as president of the conference more seriously than it has been the custom so to do. I understand that you had the temerity to suggest speakers. In my opinion, it would be very wise if you did withdraw and have no more to do with it officially; but, getting the benefit of the programs whenever you found opportunity to do so.

I hope that my mother will be up to spend some time with me and Anne Spencer while Sue and Olive are disappearing to parts unannounced.

Thank you for your good letter, and the best real wishes to you and "Miss" Ada.[1]

Sincerely,

[*signed*] Howard Thurman

Reverend Arthur L. James

Roanoke, Virginia

---

1. A. L. James's wife.

TLc. HTC-MBU: Box 9.

⋙ SUE BAILEY THURMAN TO SUSAN FORD BAILEY
[MARCH 1935?]
MEXICO CITY, MEXICO

Sue Bailey Thurman informs her mother that she and Olive have arrived safely
in Mexico. Apparently they traveled to Mexico via the Bailey family home in
Dermott, Arkansas. Sue reports on their full schedule that included Mexican
folk dancing for Olive and her own activities with the YWCA women's leader-
ship on behalf of the Mexican youth. During the time of their absence, Anne
Spencer was cared for by Howard's mother, Alice Sams.

Dear Mama of mine,

This comes to let you know that "Miss Olive" and I have invaded Mexico, and here we are enjoying ourselves and the country immensely. Beginning back to the {time} when we departed from Dermott; We made the train about ten minutes ahead of time. But in Little Rock, we had to wait for 3 hours because the Texas train had been delayed because of a flood in Missouri. Olive played with the things you gave her. After a while along came the train and we were the only passengers all day, except for the short ride from Little Rock to Hope. Prof Childress was the other passenger for that distance. We had a good talk. He said he had known my family for many years. He discussed education in the state of Arkansas, and didn't think any too much of Watson! Ha! Ha!

We are learning a great deal here each day. Olive is going to a private school, and is learning how to swim. This week I am getting her a Mexican costume so she can be in the folkdancing and games that the little children have at the Y.W.C.A. each Wednesday from 5 to 6.

Last night I attended the annual banquet of the Y.W.C.A. in Mexico City. There were present any number of "high ups" in the government, at least a dozen women doctors, lawyers, teachers in the university and secondary schools. I understand much of the speech that was given in Spanish. I sat beside the president of the Y.W.C.A. I thought of your work at home and how in every country there are conscientious women doing the same thing. These women are laboring for their young people, in the hope that there will come a new day for Mexico. Howard writes that he has sent the report to you. Is it a good one? Do you like it? I wish I could see it, but I suppose I will, or will {have to} wait until I come back through Dermott.

Anne Spencer and Mother Alice seem to be getting along excellently! I think she is doing a better job than with Miss Olive. And she seems so very anxious this time to do well. I guess Howard told you that Anne Spencer walks a little every day. This is fine for her fat self. I know you sent the cap and other things. Thank you. You are a dear mother. I'm afraid I can't dream of being so dear and sweet a mother as you. For they come that way only "once and occasionally," as Mills says, and never more than <u>one</u> to a family. (Smile)

I can't say today when I will start home. There will be several weeks more here. My address is:

Asociacion Cristianna Femenina

Articulo 123 # 110

{Please write a good long letter and here after you will hear from me at once each week. Hope you continue well and allright. I love you <u>very</u>, <u>very</u>, <u>very</u>, <u>very</u>, much.}

[*signed*] Baby

Olive has written you a letter but I can't find it and she is in school. She will mail it when she comes.

ALS. BTP-GEU: Box 2.

❧ PAUL HUTCHINSON TO WINNIFRED WYGAL

14 MARCH 1935

CHICAGO, ILL.

Paul Hutchinson, managing editor of the Christian Century, *agrees to write an editorial supporting the pilgrimage to India, expressing some concerns that the Negro Delegation would blandly avoid sensitive political questions.*

Miss Winnifred Wygal

Secretary, Laboratory Division

Y.W.C.A. 600 Lexington Avenue

New York, N.Y.

My dear Miss Wygal:

I am very glad to have your memorandum.

I think that it will be possible for me to write an editorial along the lines you suggest some time in the near future, although at the present moment I find myself distracted with the number of editorial topics which are on my waiting list.[1]

There are two or three questions connected with this pilgrimage to India concerning which I am not quite clear. I wonder how it will be saved on the one hand from sentimentalism, and on the other from a false sense of representativeness. After all, I should think it would give all connected with this project a good deal to think about when they remember that its forerunner was Miss Derricotte.[2] Suppose the Indians begin to ask what became of her?

Faithfully yours,

[*signed*] Paul Hutchinson

Managing Editor

PH

CL

TLc. HTC-MBU: Box 8.

1. The *Christian Century* is a nondenominational ecumenical magazine that features articles on religion, theology, politics, and other current events. It is published under the auspices of the Christian Century Foundation in Chicago.

2. Hutchinson hopes the members of the delegation would remember the fate of Juliette Derricotte. She and Frank Wilson were the first two prominent African American student Christians to visit India as American representatives of the World Student Christian Conference in Mysore, India, in 1928. Derricotte's death in an automobile accident in Georgia in November 1931, amid widespread speculation and protest that her death could have been avoided if she had been transported to a nearby white hospital, became a cause célèbre. Thurman, a good friend of Derricotte's, delivered the eulogy at her funeral and probably would not have been reluctant to speak about her life and death.

❧ To Richard C. Cabot
15 March 1935
Washington, D.C.

Thurman writes Richard C. Cabot, a prominent Boston physician and humanitarian, a lengthy response to a proposal that would involve a black person traveling around the world to study race relations, with an eye toward improving black-white relations in the United States. Clearly evident is Thurman's conviction that international perspectives on race relations would broaden understandings of race relations in the United States. Cabot was considering sponsoring the project.

My dear Dr. Cabot:[1]

In a recent letter from Julian Steele, the executive of the Robert Gould Shaw House in Boston, he says that you are interested in having me write to you my reaction to a proposition, relative to the advisability of an American Negro studying various race problems in different parts of the world, with a view to being practically helpful in our own situation in America.

As doubtless you know, because of the present economic disturbances in our American life, and because of an increasing self-awareness on the part of young and old Negroes, the lines of tension between the races are much more clearly drawn and more keenly felt. From my own experience, intolerance among both groups is certainly on the increase. But what is more important to me is that there is little evidence of the fact that our present race situation is a part of a large world situation which, when we remember, gives to us a certain range of confidence in working out our own problem within the limitations of the American scene. It seems to me, therefore, if he had an opportunity to see and experience life at a few of the racial cross roads of the world, that a young, socially-minded, sympathetic, intelligent Negro would be able to make a profound contribution in the interest of justice and cooperation between the races in America. The question as to what he would do in America is one that can be worked out, I think. The important thing to me is to get the right man and give him the experience. It seems to me, that such a man would spend some time at the International Labor Office in Geneva; some time in South America, particularly in Brazil; some time in the Phillipine Islands and Honolulu; some time in South Africa and in West Africa; some time among the minority nationalities in the Soviet Union, and some time in India. The whole thing is profoundly staggering but of tremendous significance. Such an individual ought to be able, therefore, to do three things as a result of the suggestion above:

First, to publicize very widely among the masses in America the racial problems and techniques of various groups around the world. This would make for a certain international-mindedness, both with reference to suffering and with reference to reconciliation and hope.

Second, he ought to be practically suggestive to various groups—labor, religious, educational—as to practical techniques for working out harmonious relationships between minorities and minorities, and minorities and majorities in American life.

Third, through speaking and much writing to stimulate the colleges and universities in America to utilize, to a cultural and spiritual advantage, the resources of the people from other cultures who may be in their midst.

I may add one more thing, such a person would be able to give to Negroes expert advice as to travel in other lands; what countries have laws against their admittance, and under what conditions may they be admitted; to what extent they are discriminated against as travelers in different parts of the world; and finally, to establish contact whereby American Negro scholars may come into direct cultural relationships with scholars all over the world.

You will pardon this long letter, but it is an indication of the way I see the problem which Mr. Steele presented to you.

Our committee is very anxious to have you return to us next year.[2] I shall correspond with you in a few days about a date, if such can be arranged in your schedule.

Sincerely yours,

[*signed*] Howard Thurman

Dr. Richard C. Cabot

101 Brattle Street

Cambridge, Massachusetts

t.

1. Dr. Richard C. Cabot (1868–1939), scion of a distinguished Boston family, was chief of staff at Massachusetts General Hospital and a professor of Clinical Medicine at Harvard

University Medical School. He was also an active layperson in the Unitarian Church in Boston, and during the 1920s he was instrumental in introducing clinical pastoral education as a method of learning pastoral practice in a clinical setting. Cabot's work also reflected his longstanding interest in interracial issues.

2. The committee to which Thurman refers is Howard University's Committee on Religious Life.

🐟 FROM RICHARD C. CABOT
18 MARCH 1935
BOSTON, MASS.

Cabot quickly writes a letter of rejection to Thurman's proposal.

Dear Mr. Thurman,

After reading your letter, as was the case when I talked with Julian Steele, I am unable to picture in any realistic way the advantage to American Negroes that would accrue from Mr. Steele's going to the different countries that you mention. I have no doubt it would be a developing and interesting thing for him, but I doubt very much whether it would help the interests of justice and cooperation between the races in America. America has not been at all prone to take over ideas from other countries, and so far as I have seen the attempt in other matters more familiar to me, I have not felt that the attempt was likely to be successful. The differences in our situation as compared with any of the other countries are too great.

I remember very pleasantly my visit at Howard University, and should I ever be there again shall hope for a chance to have a talk with you.

Sincerely yours,

[*signed*] Richard C. Cabot

Professor Howard Thurman.

TLS. HTC-MBU: Box 3.

🐟 TO HUBERT HERRING
22 MARCH 1935
WASHINGTON, D.C.

Thurman thanks Herring for his able assistance in helping to make Sue and Olive's trip to Mexico possible. He does not, however, refrain from a final passing comment about the discriminatory attitudes and arrangements of the Mexican government.

My dear Hubert:

Thank you very much for your letter and the inclosures. Working through the State Department here, we were able to clear the whole matter and the bond was waived. Sue and Olive are already in Mexico and are having the time of their lives. If you have time, I am sure Sue would appreciate getting a note from you at the Asociacion Cristiana Femenina, Articulo 123-110, Mexico, D.F. Her mail is received here even though she is living with a Mexican family. She and our daughter are both studying, Sue in the University and Olive in some progressive school.

Thank you for your time and pains in this matter, and I hope that the Mexican Government will sometime understand that there is a relationship between the attitude that it takes towards other peoples whom it does not respect, and the attitude that other people take towards it because it is not respected. If you are passing through Washington again, please let me know.

Faithfully yours,

[*signed*] Howard Thurman

Mr. Hubert Herring

287 Fourth Avenue

New York, New York

TLc. HTC-MBU: Box 9.

✌ "THE MISSIONARY SPIRIT AND WORLD PEACE" AND "CAN WE BE CHRISTIANS TODAY?"

APRIL 1935

Thurman delivered the following two addresses at the Intercollegiate Missionary Conference at Gammon Theological Seminary on February 23 and 24, 1935. Several groups cooperated in the conference's sponsorship, including the interracial Georgia Student Union, FOR, the Interracial Commission of Atlanta, and the Stewart Missionary Foundation for Africa of Gammon Theological Seminary.[1] News of Thurman's impending journey to India was well known in both intercollegiate and missionary circles, and his selection as a speaker for the occasion was related to his upcoming trip.[2] In the first address, Thurman outlines three types of peace, with "real peace" through social contact and "Christian, intelligent sincerity" as the ultimate aim of Christian endeavor. Thurman's second speech acknowledges the power of evil and asserts that the only way to live a Christian life is to purify one's relationships. The tone is highly evangelical and somewhat uncharacteristic of Thurman. It also can be read, however, as reflecting Niebuhr's influence on his thinking, particularly in his comments on the difficulty of realizing the "Kingdom of God" in this world. The extent to which Thurman's original message was altered in this redaction is not known.

The following two articles are summaries of the final addresses of the Intercollegiate Missionary Conference, delivered by Dr. Howard Thurman of Howard

University, Washington, D.C. Those who are acquainted with the dynamic personality of Dr. Thurman will realize that in such brief statements much of the forcefulness of the spoken address is lost. However, we are glad to share with all of the Gammon Family readers these pungent paragraphs which give something of an insight into the thought-life of one whose leadership is widely recognized.—Editor

"THE MISSIONARY SPIRIT AND WORLD PEACE"

There are three kinds of peace. First, is the peace between individuals and groups through restraint. One person may remain peaceful if after being knocked down with a club he sees a pistol in the other person's hand. He is constrained to be peaceful. This seems to be uppermost in the minds of many of our political leaders who advocate the construction of floating docks, and the general increase of armaments.

It is based upon the theory that it is possible for one nation to inspire all potential enemies with a reverential regard for their armed strength. In other words, it is the modernization of the law of the jungle. It is much easier for the League of Nations to practice virtue on helpless Liberia by investigating their slavery situation than upon the stronger powers who may foster equally as criminal practices which destroy the liberties of the people within their borders.[3]

Second, is the peace which is maintained by the arrogance or false pride of those who do not desire to contaminate themselves by contacts. It reminds one of the utter aloofness of a huge bull dog that just walks on while the little feist goes about nervously barking himself hoarse. In such a manner the United States can easily destroy the spirit of the Monroe Doctrine. If nations get too obstreperous, send the marines then a commissioner extra-ordinary to be the Chancellor of the ex-chequer! This is the peace which exists between the powerful and the powerless.

Third, is the peace which obtains between nations when in the profound insight of their spirit, they salute one another as brothers. This is literally the peace which passes all understanding—when the "spear of frustration is transformed into a shaft of understanding."[4]

Real peace is marked by a great deal of intelligence and the cardinal virtue of sincerity.

When Albert Schweitzer was accepted for missionary service in Africa he was told that he could use all of his medical skill, but he should not preach because they did not agree with his theology. However, he found ways of being more effective than that of preaching. The people were dying "like flies" from rum drinking. An African woman asked Dr. Schweitzer to name her new baby and also the fetish.[5] This was a custom which was rigidly followed and the child was scrupulously cared for so as to be protected. Sometimes, because of the fetish, they were even deprived of certain kinds of needed food. But Dr. Schweitzer seized his opportunity. After naming the new-born baby, he said that the fetish was that the child should never touch alcohol.

It is the task of the Christian missionary to acquaint himself with the motivating forces in human life and utilize every opportunity to direct activity along lines wherein Christian, intelligent sincerity will find untrammeled expression in all human relationships.

I cannot give what I do not have. I do not have that which I have not discovered.

"Can We Be Christians Today?"

It is not a simple matter to be a Christian today. If by some act of God every human heart were purified at midnight tonight, every single person would awake in the morning in a sinful society. The only way to get a good world is to purify the relationships between men.

The Kingdom of God is not of this world. The goals of the Kingdom, according to Jesus, are always outside of this world and beyond man's power. When man has done his best he is still merely knocking at the door of the Kingdom. Man's best is less than the minimum requirement.

Can We Be Christians?

Man can be a Christian in our society only in the narrrowest possible meaning of this term. To be a Christian is to live every day in utter fulfillment of the complete demands of Jesus of Nazareth. This would require that a person should start with his roommate, or those nearest to him, in light of what seems to be the highest possibilities of that relationship.

He who would be Christian in the modern world lives in an endless series of compromises. An illustration of this fact is to be found in such experiences as that of the salesman of a cleansing fluid at a high price when the same could be purchased at a filling station for fifteen cents a gallon. Does that salesman consider himself under obligation to tell the truth? No! He considers his obligation to be to the one who makes his living possible. The Kingdom of God will never come by a moral appeal to people who must always live in an immoral society.

Can a Christian Seek?

Before a person's search for God can be fruitful, it is necessary to see to it that whatever he condemns in society does not exist in his own heart. Furthermore, he should always respond to opportunities which will help to bring about relationships in which the Christian can really function. There is no security in fear. You cannot trust anybody if you are afraid. Neither should we identify the Kingdom of God with society, because it is beyond anything that man's society can produce.

In this connection what happened during and after the world war. We were told that we were fighting to make the world safe for democracy. The forces of the Christian Church were enlisted to help. Christian Ministers asked God's blessing upon men going out to blow out others' brains, to slaughter them with bayonets, machine guns and poison gas. Now we are passing through a period of critical quiet like the man who has been hit on the head with a club, and the physician is waiting for him to pass the crisis. Since the end of the war, the nations have not asked the church, which had blessed their wholesale slaughter, what they should do with the spoils.

Stop Fooling Yourselves

If we cannot be Christians, we can at least stop fooling ourselves. We can begin to call everything by its right name and ask God to deal mercifully with the wretchedness of our souls. There is none whose life is without evil. There is none worthy. Perhaps it does not yet appear what we shall be. God loves us better than we know how to love ourselves.

No, we cannot be Christians today if we depend on ourselves and our society to make it possible. The Kingdom of God is not of this world. It is God's gift. While it is our task, we cannot by our own strength achieve it. Let us stop fooling ourselves and face the fact of our dependence upon God the Giver of all, and surrender ourselves to Him who has it within His divine power to help us become Christians.

Foundation (April 1935): 10–11.

1. This material appeared in the *Foundation*, which was the quarterly publication of Gammon Theological Seminary in Atlanta, Georgia. It served as the general alumni magazine, as well as the voice of the School of Missions and the Stewart Missionary Foundation.

2. From Claude Nelson, 22 December 1934, HTC-MBU: Box 14, and from Willis J. King, 22 December 1934, HTC-MBU: Box 10.

3. Allegations that the Liberian government was routinely forcing indigenous peoples into involuntary servitude were the subject of a League of Nations investigation in 1929 and 1930. The issue divided African Americans. Some, like George Schuyler in his 1931 novel, *Slaves Today: A Story of Liberia* (New York: Brewer and Warren, 1931), attacked the Liberian government for their policies. Others, including Thurman here, attacked the League of Nations for their selective indignation at one of the few countries in Africa not colonized by the west, while ignoring the greater injustices of imperialism. On the debate see I. K. Sundiata, *Black Scandal: America and the Liberian Labor Crisis, 1929–1936* (Philadelphia: Institute for the Study of Human Issues, 1980).

4. Phil. 4:7.

5. The term *fetish* is most commonly understood as "totem," but it may also be understood as "taboo." In this context, Thurman defines it as the latter.

🦋 To Frederick D. Patterson
8 April 1935
Washington, D.C.

In congratulating Frederick D. Patterson on his recent election to the presidency of Tuskegee Institute, Thurman reveals his commitment to black educational institutions and the encouragement of their leadership.

My dear Dr. Patterson:[1]

I am sending this letter of congratulation to you because of your recent election to the presidency of Tuskegee Institute. This information is carried in the Washington Post under date of April 8.

I do not know when I have been so heartened by any action of the Board of Trustees. I remember distinctly meeting you the first time down at Prairie View, Texas, and subsequently at Virginia State. As one young man to another, I hope that you will be able to fulfill in a profound fashion the deepest desires of your own heart, with reference to the way that an institution like Tuskegee can become increasingly meaningful in the lives of the masses of Negroes.

Your task will not be an easy one; but who wants an easy job, anyway. It is well to remember that the test of a man's life is found in the amount of pain he can absorb without spoiling his joy.

My very best to you.

Sincerely yours,
[*signed*] Howard Thurman
Dr. F. D. Patterson
Tuskegee Institute,
Alabama

TLc. HTC-MBU: Box 16.

1. One of the leading black educators of the twentieth century, Frederick Douglass Patterson (1901–88) graduated from Prairie View State College in 1919 and received his doctorate in veterinary medicine from Iowa State University in 1923. He earned his MS degree from Iowa State (1927) and PhD in veterinary medicine from Cornell University (1932). Patterson taught at Virginia State from 1923 to 1928, when he joined the faculty of Tuskegee Institute. From 1935 to 1953, he served as Tuskegee's third president. Patterson was founder and president of the United Negro College Fund, president of the National Business League, and during his presidency at Tuskegee secured the Negro pilot-training program that gave birth to the Tuskegee Airmen. He was awarded the Presidential Medal of Freedom in 1987.

⤳ To Elizabeth Harrington
10 April 1935
Washington, D.C.

Howard and Sue Bailey Thurman balk at accepting another speaking engagement for the summer of 1935 suggested by the India Committee.

My dear Betty:

I am in receipt of your letter under date of April 8. I agree very heartily with the judgment of the India Committee that it would be a fine thing for me and Sue to be in as many conferences as possible during the summer. In the light of this fact, we delayed acceptance to invitations unduly until we were reasonably sure that all requests were in. This was done because of our interest in the whole project. We are now signed up for the entire month of June, and it is too late to make any adjustments. We could not guess that people would want us; nor could we come to the conferences uninvited.

With reference to Roland Elliott's invitation to Eagles Mere, I explained to him in a letter that the request simply came too late and I do not see any point in his appealing to you; in fact, it is a very puzzling procedure.[1] I do not wish to give the impression that it is not central to my purpose to cooperate in every way, but April 1 is too late to make adjustment in conference commitments that were given weeks before. I hope you will understand our position in this matter and communicate the same to the Committee.

Sincerely yours,
[*unsigned*]
Howard Thurman

Mrs. Wells Harrington
600 Lexington Avenue
New York, New York

TLc. HTC-MBU: Box 136.

1. From Roland Elliott, 22 March 1935, HTC-MBU: Box 6. A. Roland Elliott served as executive secretary of the student division of the YMCA from 1934 to 1943. He also served as executive secretary of the War Emergency Council on Student Christian Work, an organization established in 1942 to assist colleges and universities with the readjustments on their campuses made necessary by the impact of World War II. The council collected and disseminated information, arranged regional consultative conferences, and worked as an intermediary between the U.S. military establishment and student religious movements.

❧ FROM J. OSCAR LEE
13 APRIL 1935
NEW HAVEN, CONN.

J. Oscar Lee,[1] a young divinity student enrolled at Yale University, expresses his interest in serving as the acting chair of Howard University's Committee on Religious Life and guiding the weekly chapel services while Thurman was on leave during the 1935–36 academic year. Upon Thurman's recommendation, Lee would be selected for this position and would go on to build a distinguished career in ministry, higher education, and race relations advocacy.

Prof. Howard Thurman
Howard University
Washington, D.C.

Dear Prof. Thurman:

I promised to write you as soon as I returned to school, in order to let you know about the dates of Convocation. Enclosed you will find a copy of the program. I hope you will find it possible to attend. Eddie Carroll is planning to be in New Haven during that time.

Frank Wilson sent me some literature on the Pilgrimage to India, and a group of us are getting together in order to attempt to work in interest of the project in this section. I hope that we shall be able to make a real contribution to it.

In reference to the matter that we talked about in Washington, I have written to Dean Mays asking that he take me into consideration as a possible candidate to carry on your work during your absence. In addition to this, the Dean and my major Professor, Jerome Davis,[2] have sent Dean Mays recommendations as to my scholastic ability.

I want to thank you again for speaking to Dean Mays for me. Again, I hope that you may find it possible to come to Convocation. With the very best wishes to you and yours,
I am, Sincerely yours,
[*signed*] J. Oscar Lee

TLS. HTC-MBU: Box 11.

1. J. Oscar Lee (1910–?) received his AB from Lincoln University (1931), BD from Yale Divinity School (1935), and MA from Virginia Union Theological Seminary (1946). Lee was an instructor of religion at Howard University (1935–36), assistant chaplain of Hampton Institute (1936–39), and teacher at Virginia Union Theological Seminary (1940–43). He also worked as associate secretary of the Connecticut Council of Churches (1944–46) and was a national field secretary of the department of race relations of the Federal Council of Churches beginning in 1946. In 1947 he served as executive secretary

of the department of race relations and was a member of the National Conference of Social Work and the Association of Council Secretaries. He was also executive secretary of the Federal Council of Churches (1949). Lee authored *The Christian Citizen and Civil Rights: A Guide to Study and Action* with Dorothy Height (New York: Woman's Press, 1949).

2. Jerome Davis (1891–1979) received his BA from Oberlin (1913), BD from Union Theological Seminary (1920), and PhD from Columbia University (1922). Davis occupied the Gilbert L. Stark Chair of Practical Philanthropy at Yale University from 1924 to 1936, when he was dismissed because of his labor activism. His books include *Contemporary Social Movements* (New York: The Century Co., 1930), *Peace, War and You* (New York: Schuman, 1952), *Citizens of One World* (New York: Citadel, 1961), *Disarmament: A World View* (New York: Citadel, 1964), and *Peace or World War III: a Symposium* (New York: Greenwich, 1969).

❧ To Benjamin E. Mays
15 April 1935
Washington, D.C.

Thurman's letter to Benjamin E. Mays, dean of Howard's School of Religion, illustrates the strong bond between these men dating back to Morehouse, when Mays was his psychology professor and served as coach of the debating team. Thurman recommends individuals he feels are suitable to replace him during the 1935–36 academic year, when he will be traveling in India. J. Oscar Lee, "the young fellow from Yale," was eventually selected. Mays, nearing completion of his work for the PhD in religion from the University of Chicago, has taken ill.

Dean B. E. Mays,[1]
School of Religion,
Howard University,
Washington, D.C.

My dear Bennie:

I am sending this note to say that I hope that you are all right and that the temperature has gone. I was greatly disturbed because I had to leave you in bed. I do not know when I have had such a struggle for it seemed that my major obligation was to stay in Washington to help in every way I could while you were retained at home. The only comfort I had was in the thought that spring recess came within a few days. Please go easy and do not strain your resources until you have a larger reserve.

I have been thinking about some one to do my work next year. My first choice is Herbert King for reasons with which you are already familiar. I would like for him to have the opportunity to turn it down if his plans warranted it. My second choice is Mr. Young at Virginia State.[2] He may be amenable to coming to the University for a year as a kind of lark. This strikes me as a real possibility. My third choice is the young fellow from Yale.[3] Personally, I am of the opinion that number one is already out of the picture just now but it would be worth trying; I think he is the best man for the job. My suggestion is that you act on this in any way that you see fit and let me know.

Please get a great deal of rest and let that thesis alone. There are other days in which you can work much more effectively without spending as much time on it. My best to Sadye.[4]

Sincerely,

[*signed*] Howard Thurman, Chairman

Committee on Religious Life

HT/s

TLc. HTC-MBU: Box 12.

1. Benjamin Elijah Mays (1894–1984) received his AB (1920) from Bates College and his MA (1925) and PhD (1935) from the University of Chicago. A member of the Morehouse College faculty from 1921 to 1924, Mays then went on to teach at South Carolina State College. In 1934, he became dean of the School of Religion at Howard University, and he was president of Morehouse College from 1940 to 1967. Mays also served as the first black president of the school board for the city of Atlanta, and he received the NAACP's Spingarn Medal in 1982. Among the books he authored are *The Negro's Church* (New York: Institute of Social and Religious Research, 1933), *The Negro's God as Reflected in His Literature* (Boston: Chapman & Grimes, 1938), *Disturbed about Man* (Richmond, Va.: John Knox, 1969), and his autobiography, *Born to Rebel: An Autobiography* (New York: Scribner, 1971).

2. Nathan Young.

3. Thurman is referring to J. Oscar Lee. See From J. Oscar Lee, 13 April 1935, printed in the current volume.

4. *Sadye* is Mays's wife, Sadie.

To Frank T. Wilson

15 April 1935

Washington, D.C.

Thurman expresses his strong displeasure with the liberties taken on the part of some committee members to pressure him and Sue Bailey Thurman into accepting more engagements to publicize the upcoming "Pilgrimage of Friendship" to India.

Mr. Frank T. Wilson,

99 Clairmont Avenue,

Apt. 313,

New York City.

My dear Frank:

I asked Miss Taylor to send you a copy of the letter I wrote to Betty relative to our attending more than three conferences during the month of June.[1] I did not mean to offend her and I hope I did not, but I am tired of the assumptions of proprietorship which seem to be working in the minds of some of the members of the committee relative to me.

A. R. Elliot invited Sue to Buckhill Falls last winter. Sue could not go. A. R. then appealed to Betty urging her to urge Sue as if pressure from Betty would make any difference. I wrote A. R. several weeks ago telling him why I could not go to Eaglesmere in June. He appealed to Betty and she, in turn, wrote to me as if she could do something that I could not do with regards to my disposition of my time. In my opinion the whole thing is disgusting, and I had to make it clear to Betty. I want to cooperate and to participate in every way that I can in the task to which the India Committee is dedicated but I am insistent that they will not disregard my personal judgment as an individual and a man.

If you go to Waveland, will you stop by Washington on your way back? I shall be getting home Monday, April 29.

Sincerely,

[unsigned]

Howard Thurman, Chairman

Committee on Religious Life

HT/s

TLc. HTC-MBU: Box 191.

1. Miss Taylor is Ruth Taylor, Thurman's secretary. The letter he is sending to Wilson is To Elizabeth Harrington, 10 April 1935, printed in the current volume.

❧ TO ELIZABETH HARRINGTON

13 MAY 1935

WASHINGTON, D.C.

Responding to an earlier letter from Harrington, Thurman reminds her that when making the delegation's reservations, careful consideration must be given to the poor treatment blacks typically experience in international travel. Thurman also speaks with candor about Mamie Davis, who was under consideration for the India Delegation.

My dear Betty:

Thank you for your kind word about my article for the Woman's Press.

I am making my arrangements for sailing September 21. I regret that I had gathered from a previous communication that we would be leaving early in September, and am arranging to rent my house beginning September 1. This mere fact makes a difference in sixty-five dollars, but I shall work it out in some way.

With reference to travel on the boat.—I await your word after you investigate third class accommodations on the Rex.[1] My experience in crossing the

Atlantic was that the tendency to discriminate against Negroes in third class is much more marked than in second class. It is not my purpose to be holding out for deluxe travel, but in the light of the rather terrific work that we have to do in India, we simply cannot afford to travel three weeks in relative discomfort. Please examine accommodations with great care. The testimony of some white person as to how he was treated crossing the Atlantic means absolutely nothing. He can only know the other side if he happens to be a Negro traveling without connections. About the second economical from Naples, I hope you will investigate it from as many sources as is possible.

Is the decision final about China and Japan? It is quite important that we know about this next month because if we go to China and Japan, we shall do one thing with our children; but if we are not going to China and Japan, we shall do another thing with them. Also there are several people on the Pacific coast who had asked me to remain there for a few weeks when we are landed next spring, and certain schedules are being thought of around that possibility. If we are not returning by way of the Pacific, then I can more easily make my plans for the summer, 1936. This is important because I have no money and shall have to earn enough from engagements to support my family until I am again on a payroll.

With reference to Mamie Davis.—I have known Mamie a long time and worked with her a great deal several years ago. I do not know what Sue thinks, for she has not returned home yet. But I am of the opinion, based upon experience that is not most recent, that Mamie Davis would have no definite contribution to make. I write to you in great confidence and utter frankness. We have one person with reference to whom it is not clear as to the contribution that may be expected, and I certainly would not like to see us take on another. I can talk to you in detail about this, but suffice it to say that I am not in favor of Miss Davis despite the fact that I consider her an intimate acquaintance and almost a friend. I am thinking of the work that we are commissioned to do rather than my personal likes or dislikes. Dr. E. Franklin Frasier[2] is giving me his opinion of Marian Minus today.

I hope to see you at Kings Mountain.

Sincerely,
[*unsigned*]
Howard Thurman
Mrs. Elizabeth Harrington
600 Lexington Avenue
New York, New York

TLc. HTC-MBU: Box 8.

1. The *Rex* is the Italian line's *SS Rex*; however, the delegation sailed on the *Ile de France*.

2. E. Franklin Frazier (1894–1962), the eminent sociologist, taught at Morehouse (1922–27), Fisk (1929–34), and Howard (1934–59). Frazier was Thurman's teacher at Morehouse. He had

presumably known Minus at Fisk. Another Fisk sociologist, Charles S. Johnson, gave Minus a sterling recommendation. He also had recommended her for a Social Science Research Council grant for study with Harvard sociologist Lloyd Warner. Charles S. Johnson to Elizabeth Harrington, 20 March 1935, HTC-MBU: Box 8.

✒ MARIAN MINUS TO ELIZABETH HARRINGTON
23 MAY 1935
NASHVILLE, TENN.

Despite Thurman's enthusiasm for Marian Minus's[1] candidacy and strong recommendations from her instructors at Fisk, the India Committee was delaying making a decision on her candidacy as a member of the delegation, evidently because of their concern about her religious unorthodoxy and lack of involvement in the organized student Christian movement.

My dear Mrs. Harrington:

Your letter gave me my first very definite information concerning the Negro delegation to India, and the first suggestion of exactly what my contribution should be in the event that I should be chosen. Since I first heard of it, there has been some doubt in my mind as regards my qualifications, and my interview with Mr. Dillingham[2] did little to lessen that uncertainty. For this reason I have found your letter a bit difficult to answer in that I have been trying to recapitulate, for myself as well as for you, those things about which you asked.

My major interests in the field of religion resolve themselves into one interest alone, and that is in the observation of human behavior in all its forms as it reflects the teachings of Jesus. Consequently, I do not lean toward denominations and sects or other organizational forms as the only mediums of religious expression and opinion. This failure to be more or less orthodox has left me unable to decide whether or not such an attitude makes my interest in religion secondary, but I don't believe that it does. Similarly, in the field of social relationships, I am interested in strengthening those forms in which the self respect of the individual is at its highest premium and, at the same time, forms in which the good of the greatest number of the group is emphasized, and in creating forms which will make these two things compatible.

The matter of the additional $100 does constitute something of a problem to me. There is a slight possibility, however, that I may be able to secure the money in the three months preceding the date of sailing if I am selected. I shall try, however vainly, in any event.

I have wondered about my being able to make the proper interpretation of the philosophy and activities of the Student Movement here in America. However, I am not entirely ignorant of the organization and its function. I should be very glad to attend all summer conferences possible. Final examinations here at Fisk are on the 7th and 8th of June and Commencement is not until June 12th. This will prevent any contemplated attendance at the Kings Mountain Conference.

I have talked with Mrs. Rambo, the dean of women here, about the project, and shall be very glad to talk with Mr. Kester, Miss Young, and Mrs. Hart.

This letter has probably left some things still unanswered but I have made some effort to clear up the more important things.

I want you to know that I can think of nothing that I'd like better than to make this "pilgrimage of friendship" to India, and I hope that my lack of experience in the National Student Movement will not seriously affect my chance for selection. Yours truly,

[*unsigned*]

Marian Minus

TLc. HTC-MBU: Box 12.

1. Marian Minus (1914–1972) was co-valedictorian (along with John Hope Franklin) of Fisk University in 1935. She subsequently went to the University of Chicago for graduate study where she became involved in a circle of left-leaning black intellectuals in the area that included Richard Wright and Dorothy West, and with West she edited in 1937 a short-lived literary quarterly, *New Challenge*.

2. John Dillingham was a 1925 graduate of Shaw University and received an MA from Yale University (1931) and a BD (1936) and MTh (1940) from Crozier Theological Seminary. He was a national student YMCA secretary and director of Lincoln Academy at Kings Mountain. In 1936 he joined the executive staff of the Emergency Peace Committee. In 1946 he founded an interracial church in Oakland, the Faith Presbyterian Church, and in 1950 became pastor of the Thirteenth Avenue Presbyterian Church in Newark, New Jersey. He was the author of *Making Religious Education Effective* (New York: Association Press, 1935).

❧ To Frank T. Wilson
28 May 1935
Washington, D.C.

Thurman apologizes to Wilson for any confusion caused by his own uncertainty about the childcare plans for his children in Switzerland. Thurman's sister Madaline accompanied them on the trip as far as Geneva, Switzerland, where she served as a surrogate parent for Olive and Anne while pursuing her own studies in eurhythmics at the Dalcroze School of Music, also in Geneva.

My dear Frank:

I have put off writing to you because I wanted to be sure of my own thought. We received your telegram several days ago and our discussions have gone on apace. I am sorry that I was not any more vocal the other night than I was, and that you could have very easily concluded that my own mind was not made up relative to the matter in question to the same extent that Sue's mind was. I take full responsibility for this apparent confusion. There were two factors responsible for it. In the first place, I had not thought about the possible moral embarrassment that would arise from the presence of our children in a family of European or American white people. When you raised the question it naturally threw all my order into disorder, and I did not recover in time to be articulate before you left. In the second place, I thought most of the ground had been covered before I got there and I did not want to seem to be going over the same material. In talking to Sue later, I found that there were things that I could have said.

It seems now that we shall get Madaline to take the children if it can be worked out for her to come to Washington to live next winter. Of this I am not sure, but we shall know within the next few days. If this works out, it will not be necessary to go further in our investigation of the other proposition.

Shaw University has agreed to take the entire Howard delegation to Kings Mountain for $15 round trip. I don't know {what} bearing this will have on the possibility of John Harris's[1] going, but I am sure it will be all right if the Howard delegation comes through. I have found at the last minute that I don't have any money in my budget and something will have to be done to get the money for the delegates if no money can be found. I shall send Tommy Hawkins out of my own pocket, for his presence there is indispensable as far as the future of the work here is concerned.[2]

I hope the Fletcher Farms was a tremendous experience for you and that you will return inspired and comforted in your new commitment.

Please know that Sue and I appreciate your coming down to Philadelphia to see us. We regret that it was not more rewarding.

Sincerely yours,

[*unsigned*]

Howard Thurman

Chairman Committee on Religious Life

Mr. Frank T. Wilson

99 Claremont

Apartment 313

New York, New York

TLc. HTC-MBU: Box 191.

---

1. John Henry Harris received his AB from the Howard School of Religion in 1933.

2. Thomas Earl Hawkins was the dean of men at Howard University beginning in 1933.

❧ "Good News for the Underprivileged"
Summer 1935

Thurman first presented "Good News for the Underprivileged" at the annual convocation on preaching at Boston University in 1935. He had presented an earlier version of the same lecture as early as 1932.[1] A version of the 1935 lecture was published in the summer edition of Religion and Life. *After reading a draft of the article in January 1935, the journal's editor, John W. Langdale, wrote Thurman that it was "the noblest expression that I have read from your race. It combines intelligence, self-respect, and magnanimity."[2]*

Thurman's theological argument here draws on the historical criticism of the late nineteenth and early twentieth centuries, which often pointed to the differing social statuses of Jesus, raised in relative poverty in the Galilee, and that of Paul, the well-to-do Greek-speaking cosmopolitan from the Diaspora. For many adherents of the Social Gospel, the process of taming the revolutionary message of Jesus into a complacent religion that upheld the status quo began with Paul.[3] Thurman also drew on the African American tradition of hostility to Paul because of his condoning of slavery. Thurman recounted that his grandmother, on this account, refused to quote from the Pauline epistles.[4]

In this article, Thurman lays the foundation for his ongoing inquiry into the religion of Jesus. He argues that the "distinguishing mark" between Jesus and Paul is their citizenship. While both were members of a "captive" Jewish community, Paul's ability to appeal to his Roman citizenship is ground for suspicion. On the other hand, Jesus was a poor Jew whose message to those of similar social status is only enhanced by his low social position.[5]

Thurman contends that in its "social genesis," Christianity was a "technique of survival for a disinherited minority." The religion of Jesus, he claims, solves the main problem facing oppressed minorities—a sense of fear stemming from low "self-estimate." But the religion of Jesus and religion in general restore one's self-esteem by placing one squarely in the family of God, therefore giving one a sense of belonging in a natural system that supersedes principalities.

"Good News for the Underprivileged" is a critical organ in the Thurman corpus for several reasons. First, it establishes Thurman's belief that "only the underprivileged man may bring the message to the underprivileged." Furthermore, it broaches the question as to the appropriate response of an oppressed community to violence, placing Thurman in the traditions of nonviolence and redemptive love. While recognizing the initial role of deception as a weapon of

the weak, he challenges its ultimate usefulness, because it requires a level of insincerity that is antithetical to the message of Jesus.

Thurman continued to draw on the subject of "Good News for the Under-privileged" in his sermons and lectures, and this was a staple of his talks in India.[6] His reflections on this theme culminated in his 1948 lecture series on the same subject—as the Mary L. Smith Memorial Lectures at Samuel Houston College, Austin, Texas. These lectures were published the following year as Jesus and the Disinherited, *arguably Thurman's most influential work.*

There is no more searching question that the individual Christian should ask himself than this: What is the message, the good news, that Christianity has to give to the poor, the disinherited, the dispossessed? In seeking an answer certain basic historical facts must be taken into account. First, Christianity is an historical faith, the result of a movement that was started in time, by an individual located in history. Setting aside for the moment all metaphysical and theological consider-ations, simply stated, this individual was a Jew. That mere fact is arresting. Did it simply happen that as a result of some accidental collocation of atoms, this human being came into existence so conditioned and organized within himself that he was a perfect instrument for the embodiment of a set of ideals of such alarming potency that they were capable of changing the calendar, redirecting the thought of the world, and placing a new sense of the rhythm of life in a weary nerve-broken civilization? Or was there something basic in the great womb of the people out of which he sprang that made of him the logical funding of a long development of race experience, ethical in quality and spiritual in tone? Doubtless there is wide-spread agreement with the latter position.

He was a poor Jew—so poor that his family could not afford a lamb for the birth presentation to the Lord, but had to secure doves instead (Leviticus 12:8). Is it too daring to suggest that in his poverty he was the symbol of the masses of men so that he could truly be Son of Man more naturally and accurately than if he had been a rich Jew?

As a poor Jew, Jesus was a member of a minority race, underprivileged and to a great degree disinherited. The Jews were not citizens of the Roman Empire and hence were denied the rights and privileges such citizenship guaranteed. They were a captive group, but not enslaved.

There were exceptions. The first great creative interpreter of the Christian reli-gion was a Jew, but a Roman citizen. This fact is instructive in enabling us to understand the psychology of this flaming, mystic tentmaker with his amazing enthusiasm. It is demanding too much of human nature to expect that a man who was by blood and ties deeper than blood—religion—a member of a despised group, could overcome that fact and keep it from registering in the very ground of his underlying interpretation of the meaning of existence. No matter where Paul happened to be located within the boundaries of the, then all inclusive, Roman Empire, he could never escape the consciousness of his citizenship. Whenever he was being beaten by a mere Roman soldier, doubtless hired to be the instrument of discipline and imperialism of the Empire, he knew that in the name of the Emperor he could demand the rights of citizenship of the Empire. He could appeal to Caesar in his own right and be heard. It is to his great credit and a decided tribute to the "fragrance of Christ," of which he called himself the essence,[7] that he did not resort to this more frequently. But there it stands, a distinguishing mark setting him off from his group in no uncertain fashion. Do we wonder then that he could say: "Every subject must obey the government authorities, for no authority exists apart from God, the existing authorities have been constituted of God, hence any one who resists authority is opposing the divine order, and the opposition will bring judgment on themselves. . . . If you want to avoid being alarmed at the government authorities lead an honest life, and you will be commended for it; the magistrate is God's servant for your benefit. . . . You must be obedient, therefore, not only to avoid the divine vengeance but as a matter of conscience, for the same reason that you pay taxes. Since magistrates are God's offering bent upon the maintenance of order and authority" (Romans 13).[8] Or again: "Slaves, be obedient to those who are your masters, saith the Lord, with reverence and trembling, with singleness of heart, as to Christ himself" (Ephesians 6:5). Other familiar references could be quoted. Why Paul could feel this way is quite clear, when we remember that he was a Jew—yes, but a free Jew. But Jesus was not a free Jew. If a Roman soldier kicked Jesus into a Galilean ravine, it was merely a Jew in the ravine. He could not appeal to Caesar. Jesus was compelled to expand the boundaries of his citizenship out beyond the paltry political limitations of a passing Empire, and establish himself as a Lord of Life, the Son of God, who caused his sun to shine upon Roman and Jew, free and bond. The implications of his insight had to be worked out on a narrow stage in the agonizing realities of the struggle of his people against an over-arching mighty power—the Roman Empire. *Christianity, in its social genesis, seems to me to have been a technique of survival for a disinherited minority.*

The meaning of his public commitment in the little Nazareth synagogue, when he felt himself quickened into dedication by the liquid words of the prophet of Deutero-Isaiah, is much to the point:

> The Spirit of the Lord is upon me:
> For he has consecrated me to preach the gospel to the poor,
> He has sent me to proclaim release for captives
> And recovery of sight for the blind, to set free the oppressed,
> To proclaim the Lord's year of favor. (Moffatt.)[9]

What, then, is the gospel that this underprivileged One would proclaim to the poor and the disinherited? The first demand it makes is that fear should be uprooted and destroyed, so that the genuine power of the dominant group may not be magnified or emphasized. Fear is the lean, hungry hound of hell that rarely ever leaves the track of the dispossessed.

The dispossessed are a minority, sometimes a minority as to numbers, always a minority as to economic power and political control. They happen occasionally to be the balance of power, but even then, it is a matter of playing one element of the powerful over against the other. Because of the insecure political and economic position of the dispossessed, they are least able to protect themselves against violence and coercion on the part of the powerful. The fear of death is ever present. Men with healthy minds and fairly adequate philosophies do not fear death as an orderly process in the scheme of life. But it is exceedingly difficult for individuals to accommodate themselves to cataclysmic death at the hands of other men, not nature, without associating it with some lofty ideal or great cause. This is the lot of the dispossessed. Without a moment's notice any one of them may be falsely accused, tried, sentenced without adequate defense and certainly without hope of justice. This is true because the dispossessed man is without political and economic status as a psychological *fact*, whatever the idea of the state may specify to the contrary.

Fear becomes, therefore, a safety valve which provides for a release of certain tensions that will ordinarily be released in physical resistance. Physical resistance is almost always suicidal, because of a basic lack in the tools of violence and the numbers to use them. Fear is a natural defense because it acts as a constant check on the activities which may result in clashes and subsequent reprisals. Psychologically, it makes certain costly errors impossible for the individual and thereby becomes a form of normal insurance against violence. But it disorganizes the individual from within. It strikes continually at the basic ground of his self-estimate, and by so doing makes it impossible for him to live creatively and to function effectively even within the zones of agreement.

Religion undertakes to meet this situation in the life of the dispossessed by seeking to establish for the individual a transcending basis of security which locates its center in the very nature of life. Stated in conventional religious terminology, it assures the individual that he is a child of God. This faith, this confidence, this affirmation has a profound effect upon the individual's self-estimate. It assures him of a basic status that his environment cannot quite undermine. "Fear not, those who can kill the body, but rather fear him who can destroy both soul and body,"[10] says Jesus. To say that this is merely a defense mechanism is not to render it invalid. Granted that it may be, although I do not think so, the practical results of such a conception are rich and redemptive.

This kind of self-estimate makes for an inner-togetherness, carrying within it the moral obligation to keep itself intact. It gives to the inner life a regulation that is not conditioned by external forces. In its most intensified form it makes of men martyrs and saints. Operating on the lower reaches of experience, it gives to them a wholeness and a simple but terrible security that renders fear of persons and circumstances ridiculous.

Again, this kind of relaxation at the center of life, growing out of a healthy self-estimate, gives to the individual an objectivity and detachment which enable him to seek fresh and unsuspecting ways for defeating his environment. "Behold, I send you out as lambs among wolves, you must be as wise as serpents and as harmless as doves."[11] Often there are things on the horizon that point logically to a transformation of society, especially for the underprivileged, but he cannot co-operate with them because he is spiritually and intellectually confused. He mistakes fear for caution and caution for fear. Now, if his mind is free and his spirit unchained, he can work intelligently and courageously for a new day. Yes, with great calmness and relaxation, as sons of God, the underprivileged may fling their defiance into the teeth of circumstances as they work out their salvation with fear and trembling *as to God*.

Religion also insists upon basic sincerity and genuineness as to attitude and character. Let your words be yes and no; you must be clear and transparent, and of no harm to any one; have your motive so single that your purpose is clear and distinct—such are the demands of religion.

This emphasis in Christianity creates the most difficult problem for the weak. It is even more difficult than the injunction to love your enemies. This is true because it cuts the nerve of the most powerful defense that the weak have against the strong—deception. In the world of nature, the weak survive because in the regular process of natural selection ways of deceiving the enemy have been determined upon and developed. Among some lower animals and birds the techniques are quite uncanny. The humble cuttlefish is supplied with a tiny bag of sepia fluid, and when beset by an enemy he releases the fluid into the water, making it to turn murky and cloudy. Under the cover of this smoke screen he disappears, to the utter confusion of his enemy.

Among many American Negroes, self-deception has been developed into an intricate subtle defense mechanism. This deception is often worked out with deliberate unerring calculation. A classic example is to be found in the spiritual, "All God's Chillun." The slave heard his master's minister talk about heaven as the final abode of those who had lived the good life. Naturally, the terror of his present existence made him seek early to become a candidate for a joyous tomorrow, under a very different order of existence. Knowing how hard and fast the lines were drawn between him and his master in this world, he decided that there must be two heavens; but no, for there is but one God. Then an insight occurred to him. While on earth, his master was having his heaven; when he died, he would have his hell. The slave was having his hell now; when he died, he would have his heaven. As he worked the next day chopping cotton, he sang to his fellow-slave: "I got shoes, you got shoes, all God's chillun got shoes (pointing to the rest of the slaves); when we get to heaven we're goin' to put on our shoes, and shout all over God's heaven. (No lines, no slave row there.) But everybody talkin' bout heaven (pointing to the big house where the master lives) ain't goin' there."[12]

There are three possible solutions to the dilemma of genuineness as the under-privileged man faces it. First, deliberate deception and a naive confidence that God will understand the tight place in which the individual is caught and be merciful. It is needless to point out what such a course may do to the very foundation of moral values. Traffic along this avenue leads to the quicksand of complete moral break-down and ineffectiveness. The second possibility is an open frankness and honesty of life projecting itself in a world-society built upon subterfuge and deceit. It is the way that is taken by the rare spirit in response to the highest demands of his nature without regard to consequences; for the average individual completely outside of the range of his powers as yet developed. It will mean stretching himself out of shape for the sake of ends that are neither clear nor valid. The third means accept-ing an attitude of compromise. The word is a bad one. No man can live in a society of which he does not approve without some measure of compromise. The good man is one who often with studied reflection seeks to reduce steadily to a vanishing point the areas of compromise within and without—while the bad man is one who often deliberately increases such an area without and within. The third attitude stated categorically is, absoluteness as to the ideal; compromise in achievement. This means that the battle must be fought to the limit of one's power in areas not fundamental to one's self-estimate and integrity. A line must be drawn beyond which the underprivileged man cannot go in compromising. Religion, with its car-dinal virtue, sincerity, inspires the individual to become increasingly aware of, and sensitive to, the far-reaching significance of many of his simplest deeds, making it possible for him to act, in time, as though his deeds were of the very essence of the eternal. This type of action inspires courage and makes for genuineness at increas-ingly critical points. He is made to know that out of the heart are the issues of life and that life is its own restraint. With an insight overmastering and transcending, he becomes spiritually and practically convinced that *vengeance belongeth to God.* It becomes clear to him that there are some things in life that are worse than death.

The third demand that religion makes upon the underprivileged is that they must absorb violence directed against them by the exercise of love. No demand has been more completely misused. The keenest discrimination is quite necessary in the exercise of this prerogative of the spirit. It belongs in the same category as grace, the outpouring of unasked for and unobligated kindness without chartering it on the basis of objective merit. For the underprivileged man this often seems to mean cowardice and treason to his own highest group and personal interest. This particular emphasis of Christianity has many times been used by the exploiters of the weak to keep them submissive and subservient. For the man of power to tell the powerless to love is like the Zulu adage which says: "Full belly child says to empty belly child, be of good cheer!"[13]

In examining the basic roots of the concept there are revealed three elements which are fundamental. Love always implies genuine courage. It is built upon an assumption of individual spiritual freedom that knows not the limitations of objective worthiness and merit. It means acting contrary to the logical demands of objective worthiness and character—hence the exercise of a kind of bold power, vast and overwhelming!

It means the exercise of a discriminatory understanding which is based upon the inherent worth of the other, unpredictable in terms of external achievement. It says, meet people where they are and treat them as if they were where they ought to be. Here we are dealing with something more than the merely formal and discursive, rational demand. It is the functioning of a way of knowing that Paul aptly describes as "having a sense of what is vital."[14] Love of this sort places a crown over the head of another who is always trying to grow tall enough to wear it. In religion's profoundest moments it ascribes to God this complete prerogative.

It widens the foundations of life so that one's concept of self increasingly includes a larger number of other individual units of life. This implies the dramatic exercise of simple, direct, thoroughgoing imaginativeness rooted in an experience of life as one totality. Years ago, I encountered this quotation: "The statement, 'know thyself,' has been taken more mystically from the statement, 'Thou hast seen thy brother, thou hast seen thy God.'"[15]

In this third demand religion gives to the underprivileged man no corner for individual hatred and isolation. In complete confidence it sends him forth to meet the enemy upon the highway; to embrace him as himself, understanding his limitations and using to the limit such discipline upon him as he has discovered to be helpful in releasing and purifying his own spirit.

Only the underprivileged man may bring the message to the underprivileged. No other can without the penalty of the Pharisee. Jesus, the underprivileged One of Palestine, speaks his words of power and redemption across the ages to all the disinherited:

Come to me, all who are laboring and burdened,
And I will refresh you.
Take my yoke upon you and learn from me, for I am gentle and humble
    in heart,
and you will find your souls refreshed;
My yoke is kindly and my burden light.[16]

Religion and Life 4 (Summer 1935): 403–9.

1. In 1932, Thurman had spoken on "The Kinds of Religion the Negro Needs in Times like These" in Atlanta. An article in the *Atlanta World* recounted the speech: "The speaker called attention to the fact that the religion espoused by the 'lowly Nazarene' [unlikely to be a phrase Thurman used] got much of its basic significance for underprivileged people from the fact that its exponent was a member of a despised minority group. It therefore becomes significantly the spiritual survival economy of a minority group before it became a world religion." "27 Club Forum Draws Mammoth Crowd in Spite of Rain; Thurman Speaks," *Atlanta World*, 24 February 1932.

2. From John W. Langdale, 21 January 1935, HTC-MBU: Box 11.

3. Notably Walter Rauschenbusch depicts Paul as a "social conservative" and the determined opponent of the "radical social spirit" of the Palestinian followers of Jesus. Rauschenbusch, *Christianity and the Social Crisis* (1907; repr., New York: Harper and Row, 1964), 102, 99.

4. HT, *Jesus and the Disinherited*, 30.

5. See Thurman's argument in "A 'Native Son' Speaks," printed in volume 2 of this series, which makes a similar use of citizenship as a category of political and spiritual analysis by contrasting blacks and whites in America rather than the religion of Jesus and Paul.

6. See "Why Negroes Are Christians," *Times of Ceylon*, 27 October 1935.

7. 2 Cor. 2:15.

8. The complete citation is Rom. 13:1–6.

9. Luke 4:18–19.

10. Matt. 10:28. Thurman omits the reference to hell at the end of this verse "destroy both body and soul in hell." A slightly different wording of this text appears in Luke 12:5.

11. Luke 9:3.

12. This discussion draws on Thurman's similar analysis of the same spiritual in "The Message of the Spirituals," October 1928, printed in the current volume.

13. This is one of Thurman's favorite proverbs. See also his use of it in "The Task of the Negro Ministry," October 1928, and "'Relaxation' and Race Conflict," 1929, printed in the current volume.

14. Phil. 1:9–10.

15. This is close to John 4:20, "He that loveth not his brother whom he hath seen, how can he love God whom he hath not seen."

16. Matt. 11:29–30.

🐟 To Mabel E. Simpson
14 June 1935
Washington, D.C.

Thurman corresponds with an admirer of Gandhi, appreciative of her insight into aspects of Indian culture and life. Thurman clearly identifies a connection between the social condition of the untouchables—here called by Gandhi's term the Harijans—and that of American blacks.

My dear Miss Simpson:

I received your very fine letter many weeks ago, and have waited to reply when there was sufficient time to say many things. Since that time has not come, I must write any way.

I was deeply impressed by your discussion of the Harijan peoples.[1] Due to my daily experiences as an American Negro in American life, I think I can enter directly into informal understanding of the psychological climate in which these people live. While the details of our experiences differ, they do not differ in principle and in inner pain.

It was very kind of you to take time to write me so fully and with such understanding. I would be happy to send you a letter from India after the first impressions have been made. It is my plan to take along a motion picture camera and to keep many notebooks.

We are sailing from New York, September 21, and will be going almost directly to Colombo. We shall be in the south of India until after Christmas. The plan is to sail for America about the 15th of March.

Thank you again for your kind letter, of which this is an acknowledgement but not an answer.

Sincerely,

[unsigned]

Howard Thurman

Chairman Committee on Religious Life

Miss Mabel E. Simpson

Ingomar, Montana

                                        TLc. HTC-MBU: Box 19.

1. Gandhi coined the term *Harijan*, meaning "people of God," for those persons previously cast as "untouchables" by the elite.

❧ FROM WILLIAM STUART NELSON
18 JUNE 1935
[*RALEIGH, N.C.*]

William Stuart Nelson congratulates Thurman on receiving an honorary Doctor of Divinity from Morehouse College. It was the first of many such accolades he was to receive over the years. Colgate Rochester Divinity School also conferred upon him the DD in 1935.

Mr. Howard Thurman
Howard University
Washington, D.C.

Dear Howard:

I have read with great joy word of the conferring upon you of the D.D. degree by Morehouse College and of your commencement address there. Morehouse College chose very appropriately when it selected you for the D.D. degree this year. I think you understand what I feel concerning your present contributions to the field of religion but I want to make it very emphatic that I believe you are making an eminent contribution to the religious thought of our times, and what is more important to the building of character in our youth. One of our students who was at the Kings Mountain Conference remarked that the conference was very fine but that when you left the conference seemed to leave. I have also read the report of your commencement address; your theme was eminently appropriate and the treatment most thoughtful.

On yesterday Mr. Martin and I talked for sometime about the Kings Mountain Conference; the conference evidently did a great deal for him. He suggested that he had talked with you and had expressed his appreciation to you for urging him to come. I suppose you saw Mr. Watson[1] and know now that he is to be our dean of men next year.

We are giving wide publicity to your place on our Ministers' Conference program. I hope this will be sufficient to frighten away during the period of the conference the possible ill effects of the treatment which you plan to take. I hope you will keep in mind not only that we want you to come for the conference but that I am looking forward to eight or ten hours of talk with you myself. Mr. Tilley has been asked to write you concerning your place on the program.

Incidentally, Mr. Robinson is to be on the Ministers' Conference program. You probably prefer to come by train but I suggest this so that if you wish to have company you might ask him concerning his plans. At any rate please keep in mind that there are two trains arriving in Raleigh in the morning, one at 5:05 and the other at 9:45; beware of any error in your choice.

I am expecting to see you in July.

Sincerely,

[*signed*] Stuart

{Can you send us a photograph immediately? Please!}

TLS. HTC-MBU: Box 14.

---

1. Melvin Hampton Watson (1908–2006) was one of Thurman's dearest friends. He received an AB from Morehouse College (1930), MA from Oberlin College (1932), BD and STM from Oberlin Graduate School of Theology (1932, 1934), and ThD from the Pacific School of Religion, Berkeley, California (1948). Watson served as dean of men and professor

of religion at Shaw (1934–38), dean of men and professor of religion at Dillard University (1938–44), acting dean of the chapel and professor of religion at Howard University (1944–46), chair and professor of religion and philosophy at Morehouse (1946–80), and professor of theology at the Interdenominational Theological Center, Atlanta (1958–68). He was pastor of Liberty Baptist Church in Atlanta from 1958 to 1990.

⟫ To Elizabeth Harrington
11 July 1935
Washington, D.C.

In a surprising turn of events, the India Committee names Phenola Carroll, the wife of Reverend Edward G. Carroll, as the fourth member of the delegation. Thurman protests her selection and the undermining of his position as chair of the delegation. Thurman states that he will ask his wife to resign from the delegation and holds open the possibility that he will do the same.

My dear Betty:

Your communication advising of the appointment of Mrs. Carroll to the delegation to India has been received. As Chairman of the India delegation, I think the New York Committee has broken faith with me completely by selecting Mrs. Carroll without giving me any warning or advice that this was about to be done. The selection of Mrs. Carroll changes the complexion of the whole undertaking; for while she is a very lovely person I cannot understand the basis on which the selection was made. It cannot be because of her Student Movement history nor can it be because she stood head and shoulders over the other persons considered in ability and personality. It seems, therefore, that without any narrow, personal element entering in she cannot be counted upon to team-mate with those of us in the delegation who hold the venture to be of a two-fold sacredness to the millions of Negroes in America, to American students in general and to the advanced guard in the Student Movement whose vision has led us all to make such an undertaking at tremendous sacrifice. When I was at Kings Mountain there was not the slightest word of this possibility. You told me that the decision had narrowed down to Miss Minus and that she was considered an excellent find except for her lack of Student Movement experience. The communication from you received at Maqua indicated that there would probably be no fourth person. The Committee has taken its plea to the country through the Crisis for the remaining $1,200 needed for the venture. It seems to me that it is reasonable to expect a storm of protest from both groups, Negroes and whites, if the Committee throws away the chance for this being a very significant venture by exercising poor wisdom in the choice of a fourth person. I do not like to think that this is a hasty move due to the fact that time is no longer on our side and that in the judgment of the Committee the fourth person was absolutely necessary.

If the personnel stays as it is in the light of the latest decision, I shall ask Sue to resign her place on it. It is extremely unwise and of very poor judgment to have two couples making up the delegation. It will be impossible to convince anyone that the selection of the team plus the responsibility reposing on each member has not been done because they are man and wife and because they are four individuals who in the judgment of the Committee are the four persons best able to do this particular job.

I would like to be thoroughly understood in this matter and take full responsibility for my words. I confess to you that this action of the Committee with all that it represents has seriously affected my own enthusiasm for the journey. Inasmuch as three of the people have been selected for over a year and inasmuch as the New York Committee has given me the responsibility as Chairman of the group, the whole thing leaves no place for surprise moves of this sort. To travel together for a month en route and to work together in a foreign land doing one of the most difficult jobs in the world require the greatest esprit de corps and fundamental understanding on the part of all the parties in the undertaking. These facts apparently have been ignored by the Committee.

I would like to get some word from you as quickly as possible so that if the decision of the Committee is final, I can make the necessary readjustments with reference to my own personal plans.

Sincerely yours,

[*unsigned*]

Howard Thurman

Mrs. Elizabeth Harrington
600 Lexington Avenue
New York, New York

TLc. HTC-MBU: Box 136.

❧ FROM FRANK T. WILSON

20 JULY 1935

NEW YORK, N.Y.

Sue Bailey Thurman has resigned from the Negro Delegation. Wilson offers an apology to his friend for the way the India Committee handled the selection of Phenola Carroll.

My dear Howard:

These have been very terrifying days. I can feel nothing other than a very profound sense of regret that the Committee has so sadly mismanaged the affairs of the India Delegation just at the time when enthusiasm was at its height, and when opportunities for correcting errors are practically impossible. I repent of my share of responsibility for the mistakes that have been made and would find relief from remorse only in my ability to straighten out the whole affair. This I cannot do.

Sue's resignation makes the tragedy complete. Eddie's[1] letter to you reveals the point at which our judgment first went astray. Whatever we fail to recover in terms of mending a shattered hope may we nevertheless find something in the depths of our certainties of one another that keeps our mutual confidences unimpaired.

We must plan our time for seeing each other very soon. Love to all. Your Friend

[signed] Frank

ALS. HTC-MBU: Box 191.

1. Eddie is Edward Carroll, the husband of Phenola.

🐟 FROM J. G. ST. CLAIR DRAKE JR.
4 AUGUST 1935
PHILADELPHIA, PA.

J. G. St. Clair Drake Jr.,[1] later an eminent sociologist and anthropologist, invites Thurman to speak to a study group in Philadelphia. The group comprises African Americans interested in Gandhian nonviolence as a way of fostering interracial relations.[2]

Rev. Howard Thurman
Howard University
Washington, D.C.

Dear Rev. Thurman,

Some of us who have been studying the relationship between pacifism and social change for several years are becoming increasingly interested in getting a group of Negroes together for discussion and study of non-violent coërcion as used in the Satyagraha movement and the philosophy of non-violence. This group would attempt to relate the philosophy to our American Negro-white relations. We have envisioned a preliminary meeting near Christmas which would consider planning a work-study camp for next summer devoted to this problem. As a nucleus we have thought of you, "Dick" Hill,[3] "Eddie" Carroll, Dr. Virginia Alexander,[4] Prentice Thomas,[5] and a few other persons. We consider your advice invaluable; and since you are planning to be abroad in December we are very anxious to secure your opinion and counsel before you go. With this in mind, as well as for the ~~general~~ benefit of our general camp group, Wilmer Young, our camp director, is extending you an invitation to visit us this summer.

I am a graduate of Hampton (class of '31) and spent a year at Pendle Hill School. Both last summer and this I have been working in Friends' Camps.

During the summer of 1931 I was a peace caravaner in N.C., S.C., Ga., Ala.[6] For the last three years I have been teaching at Christiansburg Inst.[7] in Virginia. I have thus been doing some thinking on the problem. "Eddie" Carroll, who pastors about 25 miles from Christiansburg, and I have also done some thinking and talking this past school session. Now our desire is to get a dozen or more persons with this point of view to discuss some of the further implications of a non-violent approach to our racial problems.

I hope you can find it convenient to come for a few days before we close camp here, both for discussing this plan and to lecture.

Please give my regards to Mrs. Thurman, who, as Sue Bailey, Y.W. secretary at Hampton, was one of the first persons to stimulate my interest in labor problems and broader social problems.

Sincerely yours,

[signed] J. G. St. Clair Drake Jr.

ALS. HTC-MBU: Box 5.

1. John Gibbs St. Clair Drake Jr. (1911–1990) graduated from Hampton University in 1931 with a degree in biology and taught sociology at Roosevelt University in Chicago, Illinois. His 1945 work detailing the social conditions of working-class blacks in Chicago, *Black Metropolis: A Study of Negro Life in a Northern City* (New York: Harcourt, Brace), coauthored with Horace Cayton, is widely considered a classic in social anthropology.

2. For early African American involvement with Gandhian nonviolence, see Sudarshan Kapur, *Raising Up a Prophet* (Boston, Mass.: Beacon Press, 1992).

3. Richard Hurst Hill was the assistant to Howard University President Mordecai Johnson from 1935 to 1938.

4. Virginia Alexander, a graduate of the Medical College of Pennsylvania specializing in obstetrics and gynecology, served as medical advisor for Howard University from 1937 to 1941.

5. Prentice Thomas, a Thurman protégé, received a degree from the Howard School of Religion before attending and graduating from Howard Law School. He worked as an attorney for the Southern Tenant Farmers Union before briefly joining the NAACP as a civil rights attorney in the early 1940s.

6. The term *peace caravaner* means a disarmament caravan, which were small speaking groups sponsored by pacifist organizations who toured, speaking on pacifism and disarmament in the late 1920s and 1930s.

7. The Christiansburg Institute, in Christiansburg, Virginia, was founded in 1866 as an educational institute for freed slaves. By 1947 both the primary and secondary schools were incorporated into the local segregated public-school system. With the coming of integration in 1966, over the objection of many local black residents, the Christiansburg Institute was closed.

 To Mary McLeod Bethune
30 August 1935
Washington, D.C.

Thurman congratulates Bethune, a friend and role model since childhood, on her receipt of the NAACP's prestigious Spingarn Medal. He also continues his effort to obtain as wide a possible range of opinions on the state of African American life before his trip to India.

My dear Mrs. Bethune:

All the summer Sue and I have been planning to get some word of felicitation to you because of the Spingarn Medal.[1] This has been without doubt the busiest summer of our life, for we are completing our plans for sailing September 21 on the *Ile de France*. In this connection, I am wondering if you have any message that you would like to have us convey to the women of India. If so, please send it to me before the 21st.

The Spingarn Medal comes as a remarkable climax to a long sustained effort that has been yours in connection with the development of Negro womanhood. I am sure that it gives you a feeling of validation which will be a source of tremendous inspiration to you in your hours of discouragement and despair. We are both happy for you.

Sincerely,
[*unsigned*]
Howard Thurman
Mrs. Mary McLeod Bethune
Bethune-Cookman College
Daytona Beach, Florida

TLc. HTC-MBU: Box 1.

1. The Spingarn Medal is the prestigious award given annually by the NAACP to African Americans of distinction. It was created in 1914 by Joel E. Spingarn (1875–1939), a white author, critic, and one of the founders of the NAACP. Bethune was the second woman to win the Spingarn medal, after Mary B. Talbert in 1922.

 To Nathan W. Collier
30 August 1935
Washington, D.C.

Three weeks prior to his departure for India, Thurman writes Collier, now president of Florida Normal and Industrial College, in fondness and appreciation for the exemplary high-school education he received at Florida Baptist Academy and to inform him of his pilgrimage.

My dear President Collier:[1]

If I wrote you as often as I thought of you you would hear from me every week, for I grow daily into a more meaningful appreciation of the four years that I spent there in high school. You may take this for what it is worth, but I count my four years at the Academy as the four most significant years in my academic career. My high school education was much more cultural and much more thorough than my college education. This is saying a great deal and it is a voluntary expression of an experienced fact.

September 21, Mrs. Thurman and I are scheduled to sail for India where we, together with two other Negroes, will be the guests of the Indian Student Movement. I have agreed to take the major responsibility as Chairman of the delegation and it will be my work to interpret the significance of the religion of Jesus as over against Christianity in the life of people who have their backs against the wall and in the light of the background of the social struggle in American life. We shall visit all of the principal colleges and universities in India and shall remain in the country about five and one-half months. I wanted you to know this detail even though I am very late in sending it to you.

I do hope that your work is moving along clearly defined lines of development, and your own deepest aspirations in its regard will come into increasing fulfillment. My best regards to Miss Blocker.[2]

Sincerely yours,

[unsigned]

Howard Thurman

President N. W. Collier

Florida Normal and Industrial College

St. Augustine, Florida

TLc. HTC-MBU: Box 3.

1. Nathan W. Collier (1875–1942) received his AB (1894) and AM (1906) degrees from Atlanta University. He became president of the Florida Baptist Academy in 1896 and served until 1941 as president of the Florida Normal and Industrial Institute, as it was known after its move to Saint Augustine in 1918. Now known as Florida Memorial University, it is located in Miami.

2. Sarah Ann Blocker (1857–1954) was one of Florida's pioneer black educators. In 1879, she cofounded the Florida Baptist Academy with Reverend J. T. Brown and Reverend Matthew Gilbert. Blocker was a longtime administrator and teacher at Florida Baptist Academy when Thurman was a student there.

🪶 To Robert R. Moton
30 August 1935
Washington, D.C.

Seeking out as wide a range of opinions as possible on the issues facing blacks in America prior to leaving for India, Thurman tries to arrange an interview with Robert Russa Moton, the recently retired president of Tuskegee Institute and the ideological successor to Booker T. Washington.

My dear Dr. Moton:

I am sure you do not know me, but my name is Howard Thurman and I am connected with Howard University.[1] As the Chairman of a delegation of four Negroes who are to sail for India September 21 in response to an invitation from the students of India, I am exceedingly anxious to talk with you about certain problems affecting Negro life viewed from your particular vantage point. You have had a long public career and have had many, many experiences. I am sure it would be a source of tremendous inspiration to me personally to have the opportunity to talk with you unhurriedly.

I am wondering, therefore, if I can arrange to come to Capahosic sometime during the first two weeks in September, could you see me? I have no car and would, therefore, be compelled to come on the train. Can you direct me as to how to get there from here?

Thank you for whatever consideration you may give me in this matter. I am

Sincerely yours,
[*unsigned*]
Howard Thurman
Dr. Robert R. Moton
Capahosic, Virginia

TLc. HTC-MBU: Box 13.

1. According to Thurman's autobiography, he preached at the Tuskegee Institute chapel in the spring of 1929, after which Moton invited Thurman to take the chaplaincy at Tuskegee. *WHAH*, 77–78.

🪶 To Mahatma Gandhi
9 September 1935
Washington, D.C.

Thurman seeks an audience with Gandhi[1] during the delegation's pilgrimage to India. The groundwork for such a conversation began shortly after the announcement of the tour in 1934, when one of Gandhi's English disciples, Madeleine Slade, spoke at Howard University at Thurman's invitation and promised to arrange a conversation with the great Indian leader. Muriel Lester had also urged Gandhi to meet with Thurman and his associates.

My dear Mr. Gandhi:

I am the Chairman of a delegation of four American Negroes who will be the guests of the Student Christian Movement of India during the months from October through a part of March. Doubtless our mutual friend, Miss Muriel Lester, has talked with you of our proposed visit. I am exceedingly anxious to spend sometime visiting you in your Ashram if this is convenient for you. For years I have read about you and have heard many mountains of words piled up relative to you and your work. There are many things that I should like to talk through with you and covet the privilege very, very keenly.

Miss Madoline Slade[2] was a guest on our campus and spoke to an audience at our University when she was here during the last school year. I told her then that when we came to India, I should certainly like to see you. Will you drop me a note c/o A. Ralla Ram, Student Christian Association, Jumna, Allahabad?

Sincerely yours,

[unsigned]

Howard Thurman

Chairman American Delegation to India

Mr. M. K. Gandhi Gandhi Ashram

Wardha, C.P., India

TLc. HTC-MBU: Box 8.

1. Mohandas Karamchand "Mahatma" Gandhi (1869–1948) was a central figure in the movement for Indian independence, a longtime leader of the Congress Party of India, and a renowned advocate of nonviolent resistance as a means of social change.

2. Madeleine Slade (1892–1982), the daughter of an English admiral who adopted the Indian name of Mirabehn, was one of Gandhi's closest disciples.

🐟 TO MURIEL LESTER
9 SEPTEMBER 1935
WASHINGTON, D.C.

Thurman comments on the political tension in the Mediterranean that would soon lead to the Italian invasion of Ethiopia. His prediction of hostilities beginning by the end of September 1935 was only off by a few days; hostilities began on 3 October. The SS Chenonceaux, which carried the Negro Delegation to Colombo, left Marseilles on 1 October and made a port of call in Djibouti, French Somaliland, at about the time the war was beginning in neighboring Eritrea.

My dear Miss Lester:

In two weeks we are to sail for India by way of Europe. As you doubtless know the Mediterranean may be a war zone before the end of the month. How terrible it is that we have moved few steps in advance of where we were in 1914. In fact, it seems to me that hatred and bitterness are moving rapidly to the surface of life in so many relationships that have worn thin since the beginning of the depression. There never has been a time when the peace and love testimony of individuals was so critically needful.

We shall arrive at Colombo about the 23rd of October. My mailing address will be,

c/o A. Ralla Ram
Student Christian Association
Jumna, Allahabad.

Please drop me a note telling me when it will be our privilege to see you. Blessings upon you.

Sincerely,
[unsigned]
Howard Thurman
Chairman American Delegation to India
Miss Muriel Lester
c/o Mr. M. K. Gandhi
Gandhi Ashram
Wardha, C.P., India

TLc. HTC-MBU: Box 11.

❧ FROM W. E. B. DU BOIS
10 SEPTEMBER 1935
ATLANTA, GA.

In 1934 the Phelps-Stokes Fund named W. E. B. Du Bois¹ editor-in-chief of the "Encyclopedia of the Negro." Du Bois writes to Thurman requesting that he contribute to the project. Unable to attract sufficient support, the project soon runs into financial difficulties, and only a brief, preliminary volume is published.²

Atlanta University
Atlanta, Ga.
September 10, 1935

Mr. Howard Thurman
Howard University
Washington, D.C.

My dear Mr. Thurman:

About three years ago, a number of persons representing institutions of learning and other organizations, met in Washington and laid tentative plans for publishing an Encyclopaedia of the Negro. I am enclosing an abstract from the memorandum which these persons adopted showing in general the plan which they had in mind. The industrial depression naturally halted their plans, but it seems now that the time is ripe for trying to carry this project through. We have not as yet secured the sum necessary for the financing of the Encyclopedia, but we think that the prospects are good.

I have, therefore, been asked by the Board of Directors to correspond with a number of persons whose interests we want to enlist and to ask for their co-operation.

First, I should be glad to know if you agree with us that the time has come when some authoritative collection of articles concerning the Negro race in the form of an Encyclopaedia is in demand; and secondly, I want to ask if you would be willing to contribute a short article or articles on some subject to be decided upon later which could be published in the Encyclopaedia. I would be glad if you would suggest the subjects in which you are interested and which you think would be needed in this publication. All the contributors would, of course, be paid at the usual rates.

All this is tentative and no final and definite plans have yet been adopted, but in this preliminary survey, I hope very much I can be assured of your interest and willingness to cooperate in the way in which I have indicated.

Very sincerely yours,

[*signed*] W. E. B. Du Bois

W. E. B. Du Bois

WEBD/DW

Enclosure 1.[3]

TLS. HTC-MBU: Box 5.

1. In 1935 William Edward Burghardt Du Bois (1868–1963) was chairman of the sociology department of Atlanta University, having left his long-term position as the editor of the *Crisis* the previous year. In 1935 Du Bois published his most important historical work, *Black Reconstruction In America* (1935; repr., New York: Russell & Russell, 1966).

2. The preliminary volume was W. E. B. Du Bois and Guy Johnson, *Encyclopedia of the Negro: Preparatory Volume with Reference Lists and Reports* (New York: Phelps-Stokes Fund, 1945). For the tangled history of the encyclopedia project, see Kenneth Robert Janken, *Rayford W. Logan and the Dilemma of the African American Intellectual* (Amherst: University of Massachusetts Press, 1993), 89–96, and David Levering Lewis, *W. E. B. Du Bois: The Fight for Equality and the American Century, 1919–1963* (New York: Holt, 2000).

3. The enclosure is not included among Thurman's papers.

🦋 FROM MAHATMA GANDHI

6 OCTOBER 1935

WARDHA, INDIA

This postcard invites the delegation to meet with Gandhi. It is waiting for Thurman when the party disembarks in Colombo, Ceylon, on 21 October 1935.[1]

Dear Friend,

I thank you for your letter of 9th Sept. just received. I shall be delighted to have you and your three friends whenever you can come before the end of this year. After that my movement will be uncertain though you will be welcome at this place whenever you come. Reverend Rallaram will be able to tell you how simply we live here.[2] If therefore we [strikeover illegible] {can} not {provide} [strikeover illegible] western amenities of life, we will be making up for the deficiency by the natural warmth of our affection.

Muriel had prepared me to receive you here—[3]

Yrs sincerely—

[signed] M. K. Gandhi

ALS. HTC-MBU: Box 136.

1. It is presumed that this note is the one that Thurman describes receiving upon his arrival in Colombo in *WHAH*, 107.

2. Gandhi is referring to Reverend A. Ralla Ram.

3. Gandhi is referring to Muriel Lester.

🐟 DETAILED SCHEDULE OF THE NEGRO DELEGATION IN SOUTH ASIA
21 OCTOBER 1935–1 APRIL 1936

The delegation, in South Asia for 140 days, visit about fifty-three separate cities,[1] with extensive travel by train and at least one trip (from Masulipatam, India, to Rangoon, Burma) by boat. The network of Christian colleges in the region forms the basis of the tour schedule, and the Negro Delegation visits almost all of the approximately thirty-two Christian colleges in India, Burma, and Ceylon. The delegation's agenda explains in part why they travel so extensively in what will be Kerala State, in the south of India, the area with the greatest number of native Christians and Christian institutions.

According to the Detailed Schedule, counting joint appearances as a single engagement, the Negro Delegation gives at least 264 lectures, sermons, and talks while in South Asia.[2] As Thurman cautions in his concluding comments on the schedule below, this does not include discussion groups, interviews, formal receptions, or teas. Neither does it include meetings outside of the regular schedule, such as the meeting with Gandhi. Counting all of their appearances on the schedule, Thurman speaks at least 135 times, having almost twice as many engagements as Sue Bailey Thurman (69) or Edward Carroll (65). Phenola Carroll speaks publicly at least 23 times.

The delegation delivers a number of different types of addresses. The size of the meetings vary widely, from small meetings in chapels to groups of twenty-five[3]

Negro Delegation in Negombo,
Ceylon (from right, Edward and
Phenola Carroll, Sue Bailey and
Howard Thurman), October 1935.
Courtesy of the Thurman family and
Arleigh Prelow/Howard Thurman
Film Project

NEGOMBO. 27.10.35

Howard and Sue Bailey Thurman in
Indian dress, October 1935–March
1936. Courtesy of the Thurman family
and Arleigh Prelow/Howard Thurman
Film Project

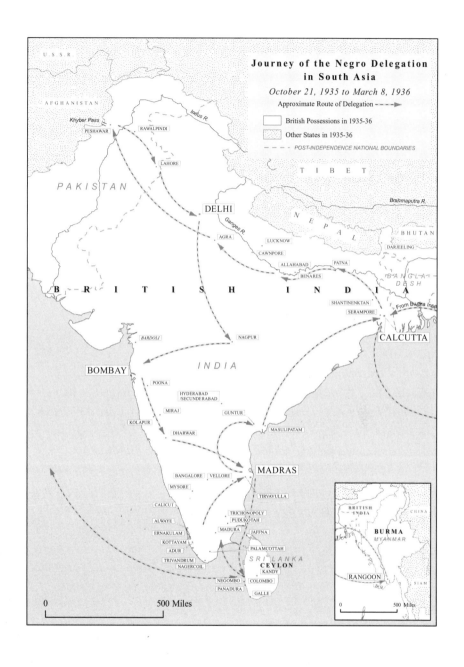

Journey of the Negro Delegation
in South Asia
October 21, 1935 to March 8, 1936

Approximate Route of Delegation

British Possessions in 1935-36

Other States in 1935-36

POST-INDEPENDENCE NATIONAL BOUNDARIES

U.S.S.R.

AFGHANISTAN

Khyber Pass
PESHAWAR
RAWALPINDI
Indus R.

LAHORE

PAKISTAN

DELHI

Ganges R.
AGRA
LUCKNOW
CAWNPORE
ALLAHABAD
BENARES
PATNA

TIBET

Brahmaputra R.

NEPAL

BHUTAN
DARJEELING

BANGLA-
DESH

SHANTINENKTAN
SERAMPORE

From Burma Inse

BRITISH INDIA

CALCUTTA

BARDOLI
NAGPUR

BOMBAY

POONA

INDIA

HYDERABAD
/SECUNDERABAD
MIRAJ
GUNTUR
KOLAPUR
DHARWAR
MASULIPATAM

BANGALORE   VELLORE
MYSORE
CALICUT
ALWAYE
ERNAKULAM
KOTTAYAM
ADUR
TRIVANDRUM
NAGERCOIL

MADRAS

TIRVAVULLA

TRICHONOPOLY
PUDUKOTAH
MADURA   JAFFNA

PALAMCOTTAH
SRI LANKA
CEYLON
KANDY
NEGOMBO   COLOMBO
PANADURA
GALLE

BRITISH
INDIA
CHINA

BURMA
MYANMAR

RANGOON
SIAM

0   500 Miles

0   500 Miles

and question-and-answer sessions at YMCAs, to large public meetings (invariably Thurman handles these) that attract crowds of up to four thousand. The delegation also makes occasional radio broadcasts and is filmed in a performance of spirituals in Bombay.[4] Thurman's talks are divided between religious and secular topics, with the latter aimed at the public meetings with large numbers of Hindus and Muslims in attendance. Although many of the addresses listed in the Detailed Schedule lack titles, those that are named provide a sense of the range of their talks.

Although the delegation deliberately avoids any discussion of Indian politics during the tour, especially in the larger meetings, Thurman speaks extensively on American political topics, including "American Negro Political Questions" and the "Education of the Negro in America."

Despite its title, the speech "Faith of the American Negro," which Thurman gives at least six times in India, is a lecture of the political sort, to judge from surviving newspaper accounts, printed in the current volume. He provides a brief overview of African American history since emancipation, with both an appreciation and critique of the role that Booker T. Washington played in black education and politics. Thurman speaks of how black society has progressed since the end of World War I and of the oppression and discrimination that are holding African Americans back from a full participation in American society.[5] The account of Thurman's meeting with Gandhi in "With Our Negro Guests," in the current volume, provides another version of this kind of address.

Given the concern of the delegation and their American sponsors that the delegation not be primarily singers or entertainers, it is interesting how much of their programs concern spirituals—either singing them directly or Sue training native choruses to sing them or Thurman lecturing on them.[6] Thurman, for example, speaks on the spiritual "Deep River" at least six times. Sue, an expert musician with an excellent singing voice, perhaps was chosen for the delegation in part for those qualities. If Americans see the request for a tour of trained musicians as reducing the delegation to something akin to a minstrel show, for many in South Asia the spirituals are a distinctive, non-European form of Christian expression, which they rarely hear from authentic performers. Gandhi asks the delegation to perform spirituals when they meet with him, as do representatives from a number of the colleges they visit. As W. A. Visser't Hooft wrote to Frank Wilson in 1934, "Burmese Christians love to sing these spirituals because they express to them Christianity more congenial than Western music does."[7] In many cities there evidently is a compromise between the desire of the delegation to avoid the trappings of a vaudeville turn and the interest of Asians in hearing spirituals sung by African Americans.

The version of the Detailed Schedule published here was compiled in 1938 from handwritten notes taken by Thurman while the delegation was in South Asia.⁸ The schedule does not include the dates of the stops of the delegation; these dates, where available, are added in square brackets and italicized. A date that is conjectured is indicated by a question mark. Also noted in square brackets and italics when appropriate are the current names of South Asian cities and postcolonial borders. Place names and institutions mentioned in the Detailed Schedule have not been annotated.

Detailed Schedule Exhibition "A" as executed by Negro Delegation from Student Christian Movement of America to Student Christian Movement of India, Burma and Ceylon

October 21st, 1935, to March 1st, 1936

CEYLON [*NOW SRI LANKA*]
COLOMBO [*21–27 October?*]⁹

S.C.M.—(University Students) Formal Addresses—Mr. and Mrs. Thurman
University Student Union—(Students of all religions)
Mr. Thurman—Address: "Negro in American Life"
Mrs. Thurman briefly on "American Coeducation"
University Law Student Body—Mr. Thurman—"American Negro Political Questions"
Sermons—English Baptist—Mr. Thurman
English Methodist—Mr. Carroll
University Assembly—Mr. Thurman—Address: "Deep River"
Y.M.C.A.—Address: Mr. Thurman—Message of Jesus contrasted with theory and doctrine of Paul.
Y.W.C.A.—Mrs. Carroll—"Adult Education under New Deal. F.E.R.A. project in Salem, Virginia."
Mrs. Thurman—"Internationalism in the Beloved Community"
Teacher Training College—Mr. Carroll—"American Negro Achievements"
Mrs. Carroll—"Education of Negro in America"
Evening of Music—Audience of 800—Singing and playing of Negro Music
High School Talks.
Methodist (girls) Mrs. Carroll—Introductory poem
Mrs. Thurman—Devotional talk
Methodist H.S. (boys) Mr. Carroll—Devotional talk

Buddhist H.S. (girls) Mrs. Thurman—Reading of Poetry of Younger Negroes
Anglican H.S. (girls) Mrs. Thurman—Reading of Poetry of American Negro Women
Anglican H.S. (boys) Mrs. Thurman—Address: "Philosophy of Life for Youth"
Baptist H.S. (girls) Mrs. Carroll—"Negro Girls in America"

GALLE

Two addresses in Dutch Reformed Church—Mr. Thurman and Mr. Carroll
High and Training School—Mrs. Thurman
Boys School (Richmond Hill)—Mr. and Mrs. Carroll

KANDY

Public Meeting—Mr. Thurman—Delegation sang Spirituals
Kingswood College—Mr. and Mrs. Carroll
Men's S.C.M. meeting—Mr. Carroll
Girls Anglican Chapel Service—Mr. Thurman
Methodist H.S. (girls)—Mr. and Mrs. Carroll

JAFFNA

Retreat for S.C.M. Workers and Sympathizers—Mr. Thurman leading Worship Service
Sunday Services—Two Sermons—Mr. Thurman
Two Sermons—Mr. Carroll
One Devotional Talk—Mr. Carroll
St. John's College—Mr. Thurman
Uduvil Training School—Mrs. Thurman
Uduvil High School (English)—Mrs. Thurman
Uduvil Vernacular School—Mrs. Carroll
St. John's College—Mrs. Thurman
Public Meeting—Mr. Thurman and Mr. Carroll
Point Pedro School—Mrs. Thurman
Kopay School—Mr. Thurman
Public Meeting—Mr. Thurman "Deep River." Delegation sang Spirituals
Hartley College—Mrs. Carroll
Catholic College—Mr. Thurman
Jaffna Central College—Mr. Thurman
St. John's College—Mr. Thurman
Jaffna College—Mr. Carroll
Chundikuli College—Mrs. Thurman

PANADURA

Mr. and Mrs. Carroll spent a day with Christian group—both addressing audiences on phases of Negro in American Life. Institutions addressed: St. John's, Buddhist School and Prince of Wales, including Public Meeting in local Church, Mr. and Mrs. Thurman in Colombo.

NEGOMBO

Mr. Carroll—Sunday afternoon sermon in Methodist Church

[*INDIA*]

TRICHINOPOLY[10] [*now Tiruchirapalli, 7–10 November*]

Public Meeting[11] (presided over by British official—Collector of City). Audience of 4,000. Delegation sang one Spiritual. Mr. Thurman gave address: "Contribution of Negro to American Life."
Public Meeting: sponsored by S.C.M.—Mr. Carroll—"Youth and Peace"
Mrs. Thurman—"Social Significance of the W.S.C.T."
Bishop Heber H.S.—Mr. Thurman
National University (Hindu)—Mr. and Mrs. Thurman "The Negro in Literature"

MADURA [*now Madurai, 10–16 November?*][12]

Public Meeting: Sponsored by S.C.M. Sunday afternoon. Mr. and Mrs. Thurman on "The Social and Spiritual Emphasis of the American Student Movement"
Meeting for Madura Public—Mr. Thurman—"Deep River"
Mr. Carroll "Youth and Peace"
S.C.M. Morning Meeting—Mr. Thurman on "American Movement"
American College Chapel—Mr. Thurman—"Tragedy of Dull-mindedness"
Hindu University—Mrs. Thurman—Interpretation and Reading from Negro Poets
American College Chapel—Mrs. Thurman "Worship through Negro Music"
Two Sermons: Mr. Carroll in local Madura Churches
Madura Woman's Meeting—Mrs. Thurman—"Social Work among Women in America"
Teacher Training College for Men (Pasumalai)—Mr. Carroll—Chapel address
Mrs. Thurman—S.C.M. group meeting
Teacher Training College for Women:
Mrs. Thurman—College group—"Education through the Arts"
H.S. group—"Around the World with Music"

Evening Meeting for Community Public: Mrs. Thurman—"Explanation of
    Negro Spirituals"
Women's Union—Mrs. Thurman—Question Hour on "Negro Women"

PALAMCOTTAH [*now Palayamkottai*][13]

Public Meeting: Mr. Thurman—"Faith of the American Negro"
Men's chorus trained by Mrs. Thurman to sing Spirituals for the occasion.
St. John's College (Anglican men)—Mr. Thurman
Sarah Tucker College—Mrs. Thurman—"Worlds Week of Prayer" address

NAGERCOIL [*19 November*][14]

S.C.M. Meeting—Mr. and Mrs. Thurman—"Message of the American Movement"
Sermon—Mr. Thurman
Women's Meeting—Mrs. Thurman—"Women's Organizations"
College Chapel—Mr. Thurman—"Deep River"
Public Meeting—Mr. Thurman—(specially trained chorus to sing spirituals)

TRAVANCORE STATE [*now in Kerala and Tamil Nadu States*]

TRIVANDRUM [*now Thiruvananthapuram, 21 November?*][15]

Women's College—Mrs. Thurman—"Internationalism through Music"
Public Meeting—Mr. Thurman—"Faith of American Negro"
S.C.M. Meeting—Mr. Thurman—"American Movement"
S.C.M. Meeting—Mr. Carroll—"Youth and Peace"
Y.W.C.A. Meeting—Mrs. Thurman
Song Service—Chorus trained to sing Spirituals
Science College—Mr. Thurman
Teacher Training University Assembly—Mr. Thurman—"Education of the
    Negro"
Women's Assembly—Mrs. Thurman
Address—Mr. Carroll—"The Negro Church"

ADUR[16]

Public Meeting—Mr. and Mrs. Thurman—"General"

TIRIVALA [*Tiruvalla, 22 November*]

Public Meeting: Mr. Carroll and Mrs. Thurman—"General"

KOTTAYAM [*22–25 November*]

Anglican High and Training School for Girls—Mrs. Thurman
Public Meeting—Mr. Thurman

Women's Meeting—Mrs. Thurman (using map of U.S.)
Seminary address—Mr. Thurman
Chapel address—Mr. Carroll
Sunday Sermon—Mr. Thurman
Song Service—Chorus trained to sing Spirituals (Delegation sang solo parts)
Mar Thoma Chapel—Mr. Carroll—Sermon
Seminar of Education (Mr. Thurman and Mrs. Thurman)

ERNAKULUM[17]

Public Church Service—Mr. Thurman—"Deep River"
Public Meeting—Mr. Thurman
Address in Cochin Church—Mr. Carroll
Women's Meeting—Mrs. Thurman
S.C.M. Meeting—Mr. Carroll and Mrs. Thurman (talks and singing of Spirituals)
Women's Student Meeting—Mr. Carroll—"Self-Support Movement of American Students"
Mrs. Thurman—"American Student Organizations in U.S."

ALWAYE [now Aluva]

Chapel Address—Mr. Thurman
Chapel Address—Mr. Carroll
Social Settlement School—Mrs. Thurman (for poor children)
High and Training School for Girls—Mrs. Thurman
Professors' Group—Mr. Thurman
Song Service—(chorus of men's voices trained to sing Spirituals). Delegates sang solo parts, Mr. Thurman giving poetic interpretation of Spirituals.

CALICUT [now Kozhikode]

Girls School—Mrs. Thurman
College Chapel—Mr. Thurman
College Chapel—Mr. Carroll
Public Meeting—Mr. Thurman—(Chorus trained to sing Spirituals)
Sermon—Mr. Carroll

MADRAS [now Chennai, 1–8 December][18]

Madras Christian College Student Union—Mr. Carroll—"General"
Queen Mary's College—Mr. Thurman—"Deep River"
Madras Christian College—Mr. Thurman—"Tragedy of Dull-mindedness"
Kellet High School—Mr. Carroll—Negro Boy

Y.M.C.A. Meeting—Mrs. Carroll read Poem (Introductory)
Mr. Thurman—"Negro Education"
Y.W.C.A.—Mrs. Thurman—"Social and Religious Forces among Women in
    America"
Mr. Carroll—Closing Devotions
Danish Mission Reading Room—Mr. Carroll—Address—Negro Church
Guntukal Theological College —Mr. Thurman
Kellett Hall—Mr. Thurman—"Deep River"
Ramakrishna Mission—Mr. Thurman—Negro Life
Women's Christian College—Mrs. Carroll—Interpretation and reading of
    Negro Poetry
St. George's Cathedral—Mr. Thurman—"What Shall I Do with My Life?"
Methodist Church Saidapet—Mr. and Mrs. Carroll—"Negro's Church"
International Fellowship—Mrs. Thurman—"Negro in American Civilization"
Public Meeting, Godhale Hall—Mr. Thurman—"Faith of American Negro"
Zion Church Sermon—Mr. Thurman
Baptist Church Sermon—Mr. Carroll
St. Mary's Chapel—Mr. Carroll—Devotional Address
St. Andrew's Church—Mr. Thurman—Sermon

VELLORE [9–10 December][19]

Students Meeting at Cobb Hall Training School—Mr. Carroll
Public Meeting—Mr. Carroll—"Negro Church"
College Hill Medical College—Mr. Thurman
Ladies' Ashram Meeting—Mrs. Carroll
College Hill Medical College—Mrs. Thurman
Theological Seminary—Mr. Carroll
Voorhees College—Mr. and Mrs. Carroll

MYSORE

Wesleyan Church—Mr. Carroll—"Youth and Peace"
College Quadrangle—Mr. Thurman—"Faith of American Negro" (Public
    Meeting)

BANGALORE [13–14 December][20]

General Meeting for Students: Mrs. Carroll—Reading Negro Poetry
Mr. Thurman—"Education of the Negro"
Special Y.W.C.A. Group Meeting—Mrs. Thurman
Public Meeting—Mr. Thurman

HYDERABAD [*14–18 December*][21]

Two Sermons—Mr. Carroll
Women's Meeting—Mrs. Thurman
Public Meeting—Mr. Thurman
Two Worship Series—Mr. Thurman
Public Meeting—Mr. Carroll (Mrs. Carroll giving introductory remarks with
    reading of Negro Poetry)

SECUNDERABAD

Public Meeting—Mr. Thurman
Public Meeting—Mr. Carroll
S.C.M. Meeting—Mr. Thurman

MASULIPATAM [*now Machilipatnam, 19 December*][22]

Sunday Public Meeting—Mr. Carroll
College Chapel—Mr. Thurman
Public Meeting—Mr. Thurman
Sunday Sermon—Mr. Carroll (Church of India)

GUNTUR [*18 December*][23]

Andra S.C.M.—Mrs. Thurman
College Chapel—Mr. Thurman
Undra Christian Council—Mr. Thurman
Women's Meeting—Mrs. Thurman
College Chapel—Mr. and Mrs. Carroll

BURMA [NOW MYANMAR]

RANGOON [*now Yangon 29 December–9 January 1936*][24]

Burmese Women's Meeting—Mr. Thurman and Mrs. Carroll
Y.M.C.A.—Town Branch—Mr. Thurman—"Meaning of Negro Spirituals"
St. Gabriel's Church—Mr. Thurman (Sermon)
Union Hall Student Assembly—Mr. Thurman on Booker T. Washington
Judson College Chapel—Morning Worship—Mrs. Thurman—"Worship
    Moods in Negro Music"
Judson College Chapel—Morning Worship—Mr. Thurman (completing series
    for Mrs. Thurman)
Judson Evening College Worship—Three addresses—Mr. Thurman
Divinity School—Mr. Thurman on "Leadership"
Mrs. Thurman—brief demonstration and address, two on the singing of Negro
    Spirituals

Judson All-College Assembly—Mr. Thurman
Sunday morning College Sermon—Mr. Thurman
United Rally of Christians—Mr. Thurman
Evensong Service—Mr. Thurman interpreting Negro Music and Poetry
Mrs. Thurman training Judson choir to render programme of Worship music
Anglican Divinity School—Mr. Thurman
Women's Meeting—Mrs. Carroll—Devotional Talk
University Students Union—Mr. Thurman

INDIA

SERAMPORE [now Shrirampur]

College Chapel—Mr. Thurman
Special Student-faculty group—Mr. and Mrs. Thurman—"Meaning of Negro
    Spirituals"
College Chapel—Mr. Carroll—Sermon

CALCUTTA [now Kolkata]

Student Fellowship—Mr. Thurman—All S.C.M. Meeting. Both general
    secretaries for India present, i.e., Mr. Ralla Ram and Miss Gavin
Thoburn Church—Mr. Carroll (Sermon)
Union Chapel—Mr. Thurman
St. Paul S.C.M.—Mr. Carroll
Public Meeting (Y.M.C.A.)—Mr. Thurman
Bishop's College—Mr. Carroll
Y.W.C.A. Women's Meeting—Mrs. Thurman
Lady Jane Dundas Hostel—Mrs. Carroll

SANTINEKETAN (Tagore's School) [16–17 January][25]

Meeting of Faculty and Students—Mr. Thurman on "Negro in American
    History."
Music Department Lecture—Mrs. Thurman—"History of Negro Music" (Mrs.
    Thurman remained three extra days at Santineketan to visit Music
    Departments). Other delegates proceeded to Patna and Benares.

PATNA

Public Meeting—Mr. Thurman
University Students' Meeting—Mr. Thurman and Mr. Carroll
Church Assembly—Mr. Thurman

BENARES [now Varanasi]

Hindu University—Mr. Thurman
Methodist Church Union Meeting—Mr. Carroll

LUCKNOW [*21–25 January*][26]

Public Meeting—Chand Bagh Hall—Mr. Thurman—"Faith of Negro"
Vespers—Opening Day of Prayer Series—Isabella Thoburn College—Mrs.
    Thurman
Isabella Thoburn College—Day of Prayer—Mr. Carroll
S.C.M. Meeting—Mr. Thurman
Lucknow Christian College for Men
Chapel address—Mrs. Thurman
Methodist Church—Mr. Thurman
Political Science Club of Lucknow University—Mr. Thurman
University Student Union—Mr. Thurman
Isabella Thoburn Chapel—Mr. Thurman

CAWNPORE

Public Meeting—Mr. Thurman

ALLAHABAD

Union College Chapel—Mr. & Mrs. Thurman
University Students' Union—Mr. Thurman

AGRA

Chapel Address
St. John's College—Mr. Thurman
2 Public Evening Meetings—Mr. Thurman
Mixed chorus trained to sing spirituals each evening.
College H.S. and Medical faculty and students—Mrs. Thurman
English Baptist older boys' Conference—Mr. Thurman
Halman Institute—Mrs. Thurman
Boys H.S.—Mr. Carroll

[*Now Pakistan*]
PESHAWAR [*7–8 February*][27]

Public Meeting—Mr. Thurman
College Chapel (Edwardes)—Mr. Carroll & Mrs. Thurman

RAWALPINDI

Public Meeting—Mr. Thurman—"Faith of Negro"
    "   "   —Mr. Thurman on Negro Spirituals (Mr. Thurman and Mrs.
    Carroll singing)

LAHORE [*10–12 February*][28]

Annual Y.W.C.A. Meeting—Mrs. Thurman
Public Meeting—Mr. Thurman
D. V. College—Mr. Carroll
Kinnaird College Chapel—Mrs. Thurman
S.C.M. Meeting—Mr. Thurman
Service of Song conducted by members of delegation (Y.M.C.A. Hall)
Former Christian College Chapel—Mr. Thurman

[INDIA]

DELHI

Public Meeting—Mr. Thurman
St. Stephen's College—Mr. Carroll
Special S.C.M. Group—Singing of Negro Spirituals by delegation

NAGPUR

Training School Assembly—Mrs. Thurman
Vernacular Primary School Group—Mrs. Thurman
Nagpur University Union—Mr. Thurman
Song Service (Mr. Thurman interpreting spiritual significance of Negro Poetry
     and Music)
Evening Service in Scotch Church annex—Mr. Thurman
Anglican College Chapel—Mr. Carroll
S.C.M. Group Meeting—Mr. Thurman
Non–Christian Student group meeting—Mr. Carroll

BOMBAY [*now Mumbai, 19–24 February*][29]

International Fellowship—Mr. Thurman
Broadcast on "Negro Spirituals"—Mr. Thurman
Sunday Morning Church
Wilson College—Mr. Thurman
St. Columba School Assembly—Mrs. Thurman
St. Columba Church—Mr. Thurman
S.C.M. Meeting—Mr. Thurman, Mr. Carroll & Mrs. Thurman addressing
     group.
Sunday evening Community Song Service (made into moving picture film).
     Three delegates speaking. Mrs. Thurman giving explanation of Negro
     Spirituals.
Public Meeting—Mr. Thurman
Sunday evening Church Service—Mr. Carroll

POONA [*now Pune*]

S.C.M. Meeting—Mr. & Mrs. Thurman
Harijan Meeting—Mr. Thurman
Ashram Meeting—Mr. Thurman
Public Meeting—Mr. Thurman
College Girls Hostel Meeting—Mrs. Thurman

MIRAJ

Medical College—Mr. Thurman
Willydon College—Mr. Thurman
Women's Meeting—Mrs. Thurman
Union X'n Meeting—Mr. Thurman

KOLAPUR

S.C.M. Meeting—Mr. & Mrs. Thurman
Public Meeting—Mr. Thurman
Union X'n Meeting—Mr. Thurman

DARWHAR [2 *March*][30]

K. College—Mr. Thurman
Public Meeting—Mr. Thurman

HUBLI
Y.W.C.A. & Too H.—Mr. & Mrs. Thurman
Union X'n Meeting—Mr. Thurman

Remarks: Discussion groups and interviews which were included in each day's
assignment have not been listed above—Nor is there mention made of the
formal receptions and teas given upon the arrival of the delegation or which
[*illegible*] the Chairman of the Delegation [*illegible*] greetings from the
American Movement. The time given to teaching groups to sing Spirituals has
been indicated only by reference to occasions when Song Services were given.

B. Illnesses during the Pilgrimage.
All suffered much from colds and fatigue
Mrs. Carroll [*illegible*] Madura our schedule Nov. to November 20. Scarlet
Fever January 21st to end of schedule March 1st.
Entire schedule suspended after [*illegible*] for while Thurman in quarantine
January 26 to 30.
Mr. Carroll recovered with Mrs. C. [*illegible*] Madura November 14–20. Mr. T
illness Dec. 29–Jan 9 Calcutta Jan 23 to Feb 3 Quarantine M [*illegible*]
schedule or Bombay to travel with Mrs. C. to Colombo.

1. The precise number of cities visited can be calculated in different ways and is complicated by some visits to twin cities. The Detailed Schedule printed below lists fifty-three separate cities, a number seconded in Thurman's March 1936 article "'Our Delegation' in India," printed in the current volume.

2. Statistics are compiled from the Detailed Schedule. It is not always clear from the schedule how many members of the delegation spoke or sang at the presentations at which spirituals were sung and discussed.

3. "Peshawar Itinerary," HTC-MBU: Box 136.

4. Possibly another film of the delegation was made in Madura. See From Edward Notling, 21 January 1936, HTC-MBU: Box 14.

5. See From Henry W. Luce, 12 February 1936, printed in the current volume.

6. For Sue Bailey Thurman's training of choruses, see Thurman's letter, To the Members of the India Committee, 19 November 1935, printed in the current volume.

7. W. A. Visser't Hooft to Frank Wilson, 5 June 1934, HTC-MBU: Box 191. Indeed, after hearing of the delegation's reluctance to sing spirituals, representatives of Judson College in Rangoon, Burma, wrote to Thurman begging the delegation to relent and sing some spirituals in their performances because "we cannot do justice to the deep religious experience which they express for we cannot enter into the soul of your people." From Judson College (Rangoon, Burma), 18 December 1935, HTC-MBU: Box 136.

8. Detailed Schedule as Executed by Negro Delegation, HTC-MBU: Box 136.

9. Thurman spoke at the Colombo YMCA on 26 October. *Times of Ceylon*, 29 October 1935.

10. "The Christian Young Men of Pudokotah State" greeted the Negro Delegation at 5:15 in the afternoon of 7 November at the Pudukotah Railway Station. In their prepared remarks they stated it was a privilege "to be the first to welcome you in our country," so it is presumed that this was the initial stop in India. The Detailed Schedule gives no indication of a stop in Pudokotah (fifty miles from Trichinopoly), though perhaps this was a stop at a railway station at which the delegation gave no formal addresses, HTC-MBU: Box 136.

11. Schedule for Madura has the Negro Delegation leaving Trichinopoly at 7:30 a.m. on 10 November "Madura Itinerary," HTC-MBU: Box 136.

12. "Madura Itinerary," HTC-MBU: Box 136; *Hindu (Madras)*, 13 November 1935.

13. "Madura Itinerary," HTC-MBU: Box 136.

14. To the India Committee, 19 November 1935, HTC-MBU: Box 136.

15. *Statesman (Calcutta)*, 28 November, 1935.

16. *Hindu (Madras)*, 26 November 1935. According to the newspaper account, the delegation arrived in Adur mid-morning, gave a short address, and then arrived in Tirivala at 2:30 p.m., gave an address, and left for Kottyam at 4:00 p.m.

17. *Hindu (Madras)*, 27 November 1935. During their time in Ernakulam, the Negro Delegation visited the neighboring city of Cochin, touring its sixteenth-century synagogue.

18. Printed itinerary for Negro Delegation in Madras, HTC-MBU: Box 136, indicating the stay would be from December 2 to December 8; handwritten railroad schedule by Thurman indicating that the delegation traveled from Calcutta to Madras on December 1. While in Madras, they visited the international headquarters of the Theosophical Society in Adyar.

19. The delegation probably left Madras in the evening of 8 December. See printed itinerary for Negro Delegation in Madras, HTC-MBU: Box 136. The delegation left Vellore on 10 December. See handwritten schedule by Thurman, HTC-MBU: Box 136.

20. The delegation traveled from Bangalore to Hyderabad on 14 December. Handwritten railroad schedule by Thurman, HTC-MBU: Box 136.

21. Handwritten railroad schedule by Thurman, HTC-MBU: Box 136.

22. For the reversal of Guntur and Masulipatam in the Detailed Schedule, see the comments on Guntur in note 23. After the stop in Masulipatam, the Negro Delegation probably broke for their Christmas vacation. In the lengthy December 20 letter to the India Committee, written in Calcutta, Thurman tells the India Committee he was enjoying "the first breathing space we have had since arriving in Colombo." To the Members of the India Committee, 20 December 1935, printed in the current volume. From Calcutta he changed trains to Darjeeling [now Darjiling], near the Nepalese border, where the Thurmans and the Carrolls spent Christmas with some Indian and American friends. *WHAH*, 126. While in Darjeeling, Thurman climbed to the foothills of Kinchinjunga [now *Kanchenjuanga*], at 28,208 feet, the third-highest mountain in the world. After the vacation, the delegation returned to Masulipatam and from there sailed to Rangoon. *Behar Herald*, 16 January 1936. Thurman, in his handwritten schedule, indicates that the date of embarkation was 29 December. Edward Carroll did not accompany the delegation to Burma.

23. The Detailed Schedule is probably in error in placing the stay of the Negro Delegation in Guntur after that of Masulipatam. Thurman's handwritten railroad schedule has a trip from Hyderabd to Guntur on 18 December, and the logistics of the travel (to go from Hyderabad to Masulipatam, one would likely have had to pass through Guntur) makes this version of the itinerary more likely than the Detailed Schedule. This is further complicated by the uncertainty about the stay in Darjeeling (see below).

24. HT, handwritten schedule, HTC-MBU: Box 136.

25. *Times of (Bombay) India*, 16 January 1935. The delegation met with Tagore on each of the two days of their stay in Shantiniketan. Sue Bailey Thurman stayed behind three days to study Indian music. *WHAH*, 130–31; handwritten itinerary, HTC-MBU: Box 136.

26. *Hindustani Times*, 26 January 1936. In the 13 January 1936 letter from S. Chakko (Isabella Thoburn College), there is a four-day itinerary for Lucknow, HTC-MBU: Box 136.

27. From A. M. Dalaya, 9 February 1936, HTC-MBU: Box 136. The letter from the vice-principal of Edwardes College was written just after the delegation departed. The delegation was scheduled from 10:30 a.m. to 2:00 p.m. to visit the Khyber Pass on the first day of their stay, presumably 7 February.

28. From Henry W. Luce, 12 February 1936, printed in the current volume.

29. *Times of (Bombay) India*, 20 February 1936. On 21 February, three members of the delegation (without Phenola Carroll) met with Gandhi at Bardoli.

30. From G. T. J. Thaddaeus, 21 February 1936, HTC-MBU: Box 136. The Detailed Schedule mentions that the four members of the delegation reassembled in Madras on 2 March traveled to Ceylon, and embarked from Colombo on 8 March.

◢ COLOMBO JOURNAL
[OCTOBER 1935–DECEMBER 1935?]
COLOMBO, CEYLON

This excerpt from Thurman's trip journal concerns the opening weeks of the delegation's work in Ceylon. The rest of the journal is not extant. The journal chronicles Thurman's distrust of British colonial officials, his dismay at the delegation being perceived as having an evangelical focus, the design of the local toilets, and his difficulty with hot, spicy curries. He also discusses his first visits to Hindu and Buddhist temples in Ceylon. The journal also provides Thurman's first account of the Colombo lawyer who challenged Thurman to explain how an African American could profess the religion of the slave masters.

Colombo, Ceylon.

Delegation reached Colombo on Monday morning October 21, exactly 30 days after setting sail from America. There were many misgivings as to whether we would be able to land because of the general rumor that the B. G.[1] would give us trouble. ~~When~~ The entrance to the [*illegible*] harbor at Colombo was very interesting. A long breakwater stretches over from the shore within which the vessels come as a kind of haven from the direct roughness of the sea. We arrived at the very end of the Monsoon, and the last dying gasps of it were shown in the high sprays that rose in the morning sunlight as the waves dashed madly against the breakwater. Small fisher boats were everywhere in the harbor— they were long narrow boats carrying only one man, occasionally two—they rode the waves like toothpicks.

As soon as we were anchored to a buoy in the harbor, our hotel de maitre told all to go up to 1st class smoking parlor for passports and for permits to land. We knew now that the moment had arrived. When we reached the deck of the office of the Port, he said, How long will you be staying in [*illegible*] Colombo [*illegible*] Ceylon—10 days. What is your address in Colombo—I do not know my address in India; Student Xn Mvmt, Jamna Allahabad—That is not sufficient I must know where you will be in Ceylon during your ten day interval before going to India.—We are being met by a group of people this morning (this was a stab in the dark for me. I had sent a cable to Ram announcing the time of our arrival but had not idea as to what to expect because the N.Y. committee had left so many things at loose ends)—Very well, when the persons arrive, you come back and I'll give you your passport. He turned away and then he called me back saying—I'll stamp your passport and give it to you but if the person arrives before I leave the ship, kindly bring him up here before you leave—With this I turned away ending my first contact with B.G.

When I returned from upstairs, a note was delivered to me coming from the acting chairman of the Local Colombo Committee—a Rev. J. A. Lee, a Wesleyan Missionary. In this note he said that a committee would meet us by [*illegible*] aboard at 9 a.m. This brought to each of us immeasurable relief. At 9:10 they appeared—Mr. Lee, an Englishman, [*illegible*] Mr. Buell, local YMCA. General Secretary, a Senholese,[2] a student, and 3 women, one of whom was actg General Secretary of Y.W.C.A. and one a hostel warden who had just returned from 5 years study in University of Toronto. We were brought ashore on a launch with our luggage and then proceeded through customs. We had to declare our luggage but had little trouble because [*illegible*] the Customs officer said, "You come as bearers of peace, so we do not suspect you."

I found that we were not expected until Friday and we had arrived on Monday. Hence some plans had to be remade. The first night I spent in Colombo I was the guest of the Y.M.C.A.—Mrs. T[*hurman*] & C[*arroll*] went to local YWCA hostel and Mr C.[*arroll*] went to Wesley College as the guest of the principal.

After the first day we were reunited. Mrs. C. joined Eddie, & I joined Sue at the Hostel where we remained until Friday when we moved into the home of Mr. & Mrs. [*illegible*], an Indian Civil Servant, a "Senholese."

It was at the YMCA that I received my first introduction to Indian food. The rice and curry were very good but the curries were extremely hot. The Y.M.C.A. is a modern building extremely well used by hundreds of men—it is much like an American bld, except there is a nicer court and much more ventilation for the country is very hot. I lived in a dormitory room—it was much like our own. The one thing that was different was the arrangement of toilets—for defecation one squatted, a much more rational and natural arrangement.

Newspaper reporters came around to take photos and to interview me. Before I was through customs I was tipped off by an Indian to go easy on the interviewers and do not say anything to offend the white man lest our journey be cut off before it started. My reply was that I understand the situation. The reporters asked much about America, and for the most part they were quite good questions. There was much about Negroes, Joe Louis,[3] etc. They wanted know about Negroes who had achieved things in life—I mentioned several but true to the mentality of the white world they did mention only Booker T. W. & Carver.

A Civil servant, an Indian together with a young woman, the daughter of an American woman and Indian, a graduate of University of Toronto, carried us to see a Budd. Temple, a Hindu Temple and an old Dutch church. The Bud. Temple was small with a very large Banyan Tree on the side. There was much symbolism that I need not recount. Hindu Temple & school were both built by our guide's father. The masonry was monolithic—the temple was not very clean but there was present there a strange kind of serenity. The old Dutch church was severe, stolid, cold—It impressed me with its austerity and its lack of any warmth or kindness. It did not stir a single emotion related to worship or religion in my own mind or heart.

~~Over~~ the next day we began our retreat. Our first lecture was by Dr. [*illegible*]. He gave the high points about the History of Ceylon. I have his books so I need not recount details. The most impressive thing was the way that the old & new existed side by side in the place. Ceylon is at the Crossroads between the Far East & the Near East between the East and the West. It has been a prey to all rovers who had courage and who sought its wealth. The Language of the people is largely Senholese—in Joffna—Tamil because of the families who have migrated from South India.

The next lecturer was the Minister of Education. He told of the educational scheme, the English School, Vernacular School and the Bilingual schools. I have one of his reports. I asked him, what is the purpose of education in Ceylon? "Oh, you are from America and you naturally think of education in terms that are utilitarian. We do not in England. An Englishman is educated broadly and then he takes his place to work in the Engine, somehow. There is no purpose in our education over here in the sense you mention." Well said I, how does your finished product look when your system has succeeded? He said many general things and then finished by admitting he could not answer my question. This was my first real shock.

The next lecturer was from the Wesleyan Church, he talked about Xnity in the Island. Of course he meant Prot. X-nity. The Methodist, Baptist Church of Ceylon and a few other groups are there. Much emphasis was put upon members etc but there was the first [*illegible*] of the major problem that the church people are not Xns and never they could not make an impression for Jesus X. I was not impressed with him or with what he said.

The final meeting was a worship service lead by one of the students. It was a complete surprise. He was pentecostal in his emphasis and said that the second coming of X was universal because we had come in fulfillment of the word, thus before the end of time the gospel would be preached to all people. It was a wretched disappointment and I saw trouble ahead if there were many like him ahead. I appreciated his seriousness but it was all so sad because he had been completely duped. He gave Stanley Jones credit for his insight.

The first meeting that impressed me profoundly was a meeting at the Law College. Here I lectured to the Law Club. The subject—some aspects of the Racial Parity in America. The interest in [*illegible*] was most keen. I spoke a little about it. When the whole thing was over, there were many keen questions. I found that they knew all about Scottsboro and knew also the status of the case. When the hour was up I was invited downstairs for more questioning and then the first bombshell was thrown!

A young lawyer said, "What are you doing here? This is what I mean—Africans were taken to America as slaves, by Xns.—they were sold in America to other Xns—they were held in slavery for 300 years by Xns—They were freed as a result of economic forces rather than Xn idealism and now you are held in by many [*illegible*] all once American and I understand that you are lynched in America by Xns. In the light of all this, I think that for a young intelligent Negro such as you to be over here in the interest of a Xn enterprise is for you to be a traitor to all the darker peoples of the earth. Such I consider you to be. Will you please account for yourself and your very unfortunate position?"

"Yes—. Let me thank you for what you have said. Particularly am I deeply moved by your frankness, it is an excellent measure of your confidence in me. I am not here to bolster up a declining or disgraced Xn faith in your midst. I do not come to make converts of Xny nor do I come as exhibit A as to what Xnity has done for me & my people. I am Christian because I think that the religion of Jesus in its true genius offers me very many ways out of the world's disorders. But I make a careful distinction between Xnity and the religion of Jesus. In my opinion the churches & all so-called Xn institutions are built prevail upon the assumption that the Strong man is superior to the weak man and as such the sound right to exploit the weak & be served by him. I am dead against most of the institutional religion with which I am acquainted. I belong to a small minority of Xns who believe that society has to be completely reorganized in a very definite egalitarian sense if life is to be made livable for the most of mankind. To us Xnity was a way out, originally, for an underprivileged minority in the Greco Roman Empire and became a world religion officially under a banner other than the banner of Jesus X. Finally I admit even more relative to slavery & Xnity than you indict but I see also that in all of this practice not one time was there an appeal to the central teaching of Jesus to bolster up the existing order. The work of the minority in America interested as I am in changing society is just as much a fact as the iniquity of the majority.

"Thank you, Dr. I feel much better relative to in all and I hope to come to see you again before you leave.

A very unusual conversation with the Warden of Union Hostel. He is a Buddhist. The point of our discussion was Xnity and its influence upon Buddhist students. "I look with alarm upon the number of Buddhists who are attending Xns schools. Not because I fear that they will become Xns. Not at all. Because I think that there is very little difference between the two religions. My concern is this. I notice that our students who attend Xn Schools fall out with their own faith but tend to refuse to become Xns. If the Xn schools made them into Xns, I could have no quarrel but they make it easy for them to become merely drifters." I said at this point, "It seems to me Xn education has succeeded if it makes a man a ~~good~~ {true} Xn or makes of him a better and more completely intelligent Buddhist. For I believe that Jesus reveals to a man the meaning of what he has already." [*illegible*]

Miss [*strikeover illegible*]—a [*illegible*] young Danish woman—buxom, ruddy faced, tendency to plumpness. Has a good face—keen mind—zealous—business like. In a job that does not represent her ideal of relationships of European & Ceylons but does not admit this even to herself. Anxious to be evangelical. Blind to the possibility of native women because if she were not, she would lose her self-respect in her job. Has a sense of beauty and glimpses of the vision of God. Miss E., Senholese—quiet—subdued inarticulate. Understands much but does not become effective. Admires the advantages of being European, wishes she were at times and yet underneath carries a burning bitterness against all the things that hold her and her women back which bitterness is gradually killing her soul.

L. Fairly intelligent Englishman—enjoys his work—has a keen sense of institutional values—respects the Senholese more than is usual. Believes that a line should be drawn between the social life . . . [*page missing*]

On the whole the days in Colombo were not very satisfying. It was my first contact with the East. I was impressed and deepened by more of what I said. The outstanding fact was the irreverent regard for the [*illegible*] of the peoples. Servants were everywhere. Rickshas pulled by men were everywhere. Servants were called "Boys." Shades of Southern United States. We were thrown into the arms of a people expecting us to be evangelical, to win souls for X. We did not see much of the students. Stanley Jones had prepared the way for us and what a preparation—we were to be singing soul-saving evangelists full of the grace of God. The net result of our stay there: 1 Deepen the knowledge of the people concerning Negroes. 2 Appreciation of our music, culture and literature. 3 Revealed ourselves to be non-evangelical. 4 The true nature of ~~our~~ {the} problem of the pilgrimage pointed up—A to be true to America N.B. to be true to Jesus and at the same time to steer clear of the obvious need of Xnity to be bolstered up by members of the colored race C. to speak about our own problems and not say anything in favor of or against the present in India. D. to dispel the suspicions in the minds of the native people that we were here to fit into the schemes of Western Civilization of which Xnity is a part. E. to pitch our discussions on a plan above [*illegible*] & Modernism. F. though is to learn all we could about the problems and the life of the people and to make personal friends.

AD. HTC-MBU: Box 139.

1. The term *B.G.* stands for British Government.
2. The term *Senholese* is "Sinhalese" or "Singhalese."

3. The African American boxer Joe Louis (1914–81) established himself as the dominant heavyweight in the summer of 1935 by defeating two former champions, Primo Carnera on 25 June with a knockout in the sixth round and Max Baer on 24 September with a knockout in the fourth round. Louis did not become heavyweight champion until 1937, a title he retained until 1949.

❧ "The Faith of the American Negro"
19, 28 November 1935; 21 February 1936
India

Thurman and the other members of the Negro Delegation prepared a number of talks specifically for South Asian audiences. These talks provide an overview of some of the principles of American and African American history tailored for Indian audiences. Probably the most popular of Thurman's talks is "The Faith of the American Negro," which Thurman delivers at least eight times. This talk, which describes the dilemmas faced by American blacks after emancipation, "created the most uneasiness in the American colony," according to Thurman in his autobiography.[1]

No text in Thurman's hand of "The Faith of the American Negro" survives, and Thurman often extemporized when he spoke. Two newspaper accounts, printed below, of Thurman delivering "The Faith of the American Negro" survive, clearly describing similar though distinct versions of the same talk, though whether this reflects differences in Thurman's presentation or in the perspectives of the newspaper reporters is impossible to say. Also included is Sue Bailey Thurman's version of a similar talk from a female perspective, delivered while the delegation was in the adjoining cities of Cochin and Ernakulum.

"The Faith of the American Negro: Prof. Howard Thurman's Address"
Tinnevelly, November 16, 1935

Under the auspices of the YMCA Palamcottah, a public meeting was held last evening at the Centenary Hall, Palamacottah, where Professor Howard Thurman of the American Negro Delegation delivered an address on "The Faith of the American Negro." [*after the introduction*] . . . Mrs. Thurman then sang the piece, "We are climbing Jacob's Ladder" to the accompaniment of a chorus.

Prof Thurman

Prof. Howard Thurman in the course of his speech said that in 1st January 1938 they would be celebrating in America the 75th anniversary of the liberation of the Negro, marking three quarters of a century during which period the Negro had been free in America, and had been working his way into the life and development of the civilization in the new world. More than 300 years ago, these people were taken from their homeland, carried to America and were sold there as chattel and were distributed in the different parts of the country and in the several plantations of America. The Negroes then had no common language. The people who came first in the slave ships did not speak the same dialect. Now, the common language of the American Negro was English, the language of the American people. During the period of liberation, the American Negro was faced with the most difficult task of developing for himself economic stability, that would bring them reasonable comforts and resources in life and would help them in the future development of their families.

People here in India, he added, might very well imagine, continued the speaker, the magnitude of the Negro problem and how difficult it was to plant in the minds of Negroes the free ways of thinking and feeling and looking at their lives as endowed with responsibility and to make them think that they had their own destiny to fulfill in the life of the country. Steps were taken by the great Negro leaders to uproot soon the slave mentality of the race. They soon brought into existence a new way of knowledge and thinking and understanding. They developed in the minds of the Negroes a deep faith in their own strength and abilities.

After referring to his ancestry, and training, the speaker said that the American Negro had been trained to look forward and not backward, to look up and not down. He observed that the Negroes even while slaves had a certain knack and skill for adjusting themselves to their environments. After their liberation, the Negroes developed a quick, persuasive and persistent confidence in their ability and integrity.

The speaker then said that what he wanted to refer to was the firm religious faith of the American Negro. This faith had taken deep root in the Negro race. It was this faith that inspired them to realize their own destiny.

Mrs. Thurman then sang "Were you there when you crucified my Lord?"

Hindu (Madras), 19 November 1935.

"THE THREE FAITHS OF THE NEGRO: BELIEF IN HIS ABILITY, IN LIFE, AND IN GOD"

BOMBAY, FEBRUARY 21, 1936

A large gathering was present at the Sir Cowasji Jehengir Hall, Bombay, on Thursday Evening, when Dr. Howard Thurman, leader of the American Negro Delegation now visiting Bombay, delivered an address on the "The Faith of the American Negro." The Rev. Dr. J. MacKenzie presided. Dr. Thurman discussed the many problems that had confronted the American Negro during and after his release from slavery, and examined the effect of these problems on contemporary Negro life. . . .

Dr. Thurman said the American Negro on gaining freedom had been left to shift for himself. Unlike American Indians, who had been placed in reservations, the Negro found himself faced overnight with the practical problem of earning his food, guaranteeing for himself economic security, and participating in ordinary American life. The story of the struggle for bread was one of the most fascinating stories in the life of the Negro, Dr. Thurman declared.

Another practical question which had confronted the Negro released from bondage was to develop a constructive outlook—a way of thought in new relationship so as to relieve himself of the feelings of insecurity and inferiority caused by the system of slavery. The part that education played in solving that problem was of tremendous importance to the development of the race.

The fundamental ideals of the Negro, Dr. Thurman declared, expressed themselves in three important ways. They were the faith of the Negro in his own abilities, a faith that lived through three centuries of slavery; the faith of the Negro in life itself; and the faith of the Negro in God.

The Negro's faith in himself was not an emotional type, but was the positive registration of the personality of the individual which made him act in the present with reference to the present. In the years of their bondage they had lived in the midst of pain and frustration, but they had borne their sorrows with a quality of courage which belonged to men who were not bound with chains.

Though bound by shackles and deprived of education, the Negro had lived through the centuries of his travail with his courage undaunted, and today in many parts of America were yet to be seen beautiful examples of handicraft; the work of thinkers and designers—though they had been slaves. Dr. Thurman was deeply moved when he made a brief reference to the life of his grandfather, who as a slave had been a calculator on an American estate.

The second practical aspect in the life of the Negro was to give him a kind of elemental laughter. Rumour and propaganda had made the American Negro the greatest clown of all, but there was something much deeper, and that was the laughter in the heart of the group life. It was the laughter of the strong man who struggled out of defeat to struggle again.

In the expression of the religious life of the Negro there was an abiding confidence in the personal element.

Dr. Thurman analysed the philosophy of the Negro in relation to his thought and life, was contained in every Negro mother's song to her child—"shut your eyes to nothing that seems to be the bitter truth, though your life be unheralded, and perhaps a failure."

Times of India (Bombay), 21 February 1936.

"Emancipation of the Negroes: Mrs. Thurman's Address"
Cochin, November 27
Address at Y.W.C.A.

Addressing yesterday a meeting of the Young Women's Christian Association, Mrs. Bailey Thurman gave a vivid picture of how the Negroes were taken to America as captives and said that Negroes had become full-fledged citizens of America after the abolition of slavery 75 years ago. They were now able to shoulder the economic responsibilities of life, of supporting the family and they were striving hard to imbibe and assimilate everything good in the culture of America as their own. The Negroes had achieved such a rapid progress that to-day over a hundred of them held very important positions in American society and public life. There were as many as 40,000 Negroes, men and women, who were employed as teachers and this showed what progress had been made in education. There were several hospitals financed and manned entirely by Negro physicians and surgeons.

Negro Women's Work

Continuing, she said that it was the Negro women who kept alive the courage of their men during their days of trial and tribulation. Their struggle to bring themselves abreast of the civilized nations of the world was still in progress. There were two women's organizations in American, one strictly limited to college graduates, which was always eager to find out the hidden talent in Negro boys and girls who had not the opportunity to get themselves educated. They had discovered that the most talented boys and girls did not come from wealthy families. This organization raised funds to have the highly talented Negro boys and girls properly educated and strived its utmost to see that they were fixed up later in life in places of position and importance. Lately, they had sent some of their students for higher studies to some of the greatest educational centres of Europe.

The other organization, continued the speaker, was the National Association of Negro Women. This Association was conducting a magazine which reflected the life and thought of American Negro women. There were many first-rate women poets among them. Their poetry gave them a unique place amongst the greatest people of the day. The Negro women took great care to see that her home was a lovely place and she paid greater importance to the education of girls than even of boys. The educated Negro women engaged themselves in village reconstruction, handicrafts, and cottage industries and they helped producers in collecting their goods and selling them to advantage. The only religion prevalent in America was Christianity. America would never become truly Christian as long as there was poverty and ignorance in the land as differences of race suggesting an inferiority complex were perpetuated.

She concluded her address by extending an invitation to Indian women to visit America to come into closer contact with them and study their life and environments. She said they had great reverence for the hoary culture and civilization of India. They derived their knowledge of India from books written by Indian authors, and likewise, she exhorted Indians who were desirous to know about the Negro problem to read books, written by Negroes themselves.

Hindu (Madras), 28 November 1935.

1. *WHAH*, 123.

꙳ To the Members of the India Committee
19 November 1935
Nagercoil, India

Thurman, in his first correspondence to the committee since arriving in Ceylon, provides an overview of the delegation's first few days.

To the Members of the India Committee

Greetings:

The first day of our arrival the programmes began. In the afternoon of the first day we were taken on a tour of several of the temples and during the next two days we had a rather stiff seminar on the life and history of the people of Ceylon. This proved to be very valuable because it gave to us some ideas as to the actual background of the people to whom we would be talking during our stay on the island. Mr. and Mrs. Carroll lived at the home of a Methodist Missionary from England and Mrs. Thurman and I lived at the home of a Sengalese[1] family.

Colombo is the only real college center on the island. It was there that we met the students of college and university training. All the days were crowded and during three nights there we did not get dinner until eleven o'clock in the evening. It was here that we received our first taste of the tremendous difficulties inherent in the nature of the job which is ours. The Law College Society invited me to give a lecture to them as an extra thing. I went over for an hour but remained for three hours, there were so many questions. The first real question was this: The African slaves were brought to America by European Christians; they were sold to other Christians who in turn sold them to other Christians. Slavery was given the blessings and the sanction of Christian ministers (here he quoted from Sherwood Eddy[2]). Emancipation came as a result of economic forces rather than Christianity. Negroes are segregated and discriminated against not only by nominal Christians but also by the Christian Church and by official Christians. You are here as a part of a Christian organization that segregates you and your people.

In my opinion, and you will pardon me Dr. Thurman, I think you are a traitor to the highest good not only of the Negroes in America but also of the darker peoples of the earth. What have you to say in defense of the position in which you find yourself? I answered the question fully and upon his admission to his satisfaction. I wonder what you, my friends, would have done with that question? I find that at every point I am using whatever is mine as a result of a lifetime of thought and study. No harder job will ever be mine in this world.

We visited Colombo, Galle, Kandy and Jaffna in Ceylon. From Ceylon we came to India and our first stop was at Trichinopoly; from there to Madura where there is a large American college; from there to Palemcottah; from there to Nagercoil from which place this letter is being written. Mrs. Thurman is teaching groups to sing our songs and these groups at the various places furnish music for our public meetings. Our welcome is warm and enthusiastic on every hand and nothing is being left undone to guarantee a genuine welcome. The audiences are large and responsive and for this we are very grateful. More anon.

[*unsigned*]
Howard Thurman
SC:CM
1/31/36

TLc. YWCA: Box 134.7.

1. The term *Sengalese* means "Sinhalese" or "Singhalese."
2. The work of Eddy's that is quoted is unknown (and it is possible that Thurman was not implying a literal quotation from Eddy's work), but Thurman notes the irony of Eddy's research into the toleration of slavery by Christian divines being used to undermine Eddy's (and Thurman's) conception of a nonracist Christianity.

🐟 CH. JOHN TO MEMBERS OF THE INDIA DELEGATION
21 NOVEMBER 1935
WALTAIR, INDIA

The tour of the Negro Delegation greatly appeals to Asian Christians who, like Thurman, are seeking ways to reconcile their religious beliefs with their disgust at the complicity of Christianity with imperialism and racism. This letter to the delegation from an Indian Christian schoolmaster demonstrates both the avidity with which Indian Christians follow the progress of the delegation and the depths of their suspicion of white promoters of Christianity. Thurman's reply is not preserved.

My Dear Commerades in Christ,

Though it is late, I welcome you heartily to our mother-land, India. When at first your names appeared in the December 1934 issue of "The Inter Collegian, and Far Horizons," I have been praying for you all that you might have a successful and fruitful fellowship in India.

You wrote a poem on"God I need thee" in April 1935 issue of the above magazine, and I have the rare previlege of reading and meditating on it. I sometimes read the magazines such as "The New-York Age,"[1] "The Southern Workmen," etc and also read something about the world's most famous Institute Tuskegee, founded by your illustrious Leader late Mr. Booker T. Washington.

I have the great heart and head sympathy for you Breathren & Sisters, for the treatment accorded to you in U.S.A. particularly in Alabama, Florida, South Carolina, Georgie, at the gregerous[2] imperialistic animals of the white Americans. Your economic exploitation, political disfranchisement, Educational inequalities lynching etc are a sheer mockery to the brute force of the White race. Your insight, charm, and above all spontanious christian Character are known to students in all parts of the country (U.S.A.) who have met you in conferences or else where.

We ask you to do an effective job in India. The Indian Movement knew that and asked for you and no others. You are well qualified to speak to the Indian situation, because of the comparable position to which you are subjected in your own country. Like the Indians you are concerned with the liberation of your people. White Americans on the other hand as just one more example of patronising oppressers preaching love. Indians will listen to you as American Negroes; You will command respect and [illegible] admi {ration} as few white men could.

I beg to introduce myself to you as an insignificant and humble but faithful follower of the crucified and risen Christ of Nazareth. I am running [illegible] school which has about 100 children. It is an indignious effort.

I see your tour program in "the Students Outlook." You will leave Bezwada[3] on the 23rd December by rail and it arrives at Waltair and stops for about 35 minutes. So I shall arrange a car for you to come and go, and kindly spend 10 minutes in my school, and give your choicest blessings to it and to its servants. With kind regards to all {of} you
Yours in the service of the master,
[signed] Ch. John
Manager,
N.B.: I extend a very cordial Welcome, to you Grace[4], Sue Baily, Edward, and Howard: and awaiting for an early reply.
    *Prof Howard Thorman's Poem,

ALS. HTC-MBU: Box 136.

1. *New York Age*, published from 1887 to 1960, was for most of that time the leading black newspaper in New York City.

2. Egregious.

3. Bezwada Junction, near Madras, was one of the largest railway stations in India. The date in the letter is not compatible with other information on the stops of the tour, though

presumably the Thurmans, after visiting Madras and neighboring cities on the east coast of India like Vellore and Masulipatam, went through Bezwada Junction on their way to Calcutta and their Christmas vacation.

4. The writer is referring to Grace Towns Hamilton. Ch. John was relying on out-of-date information about the composition of the delegation.

To the Members of the India Committee
20 December 1935
Calcutta, India

Thurman takes the opportunity at the beginning of his Christmas break from the work of the delegation to explain again why he was so opposed to the selection of Phenola Carroll as a member of the delegation and complains about her lack of preparedness for the duties assigned to her. He further complains that the financial support for the delegation by the American sponsors has not been adequate. Thurman intends this letter to be his definitive statement on his disagreement with the India Committee on the selection of Phenola Carroll, and he circulates copies to his close friends, among them Channing Tobias.[1]

The only known response to the letter came from Elizabeth Harrington, who, among other matters, is suspicious that Thurman has circulated the letter to others outside of the India Committee. Her 7 February 1936 response to Thurman is excerpted below:[2]

> I want to acknowledge receipt of the letter of Dec 20th as one member of the India Committee. I do not feel that there is any value in repeating all that has been said to date by way of explaining the committee's actions since my previous explanations are evidently invalid ones in your judgment. I deeply regret that you and Sue feel as you do to the work of the committee and I hope you feel that in some measure, as I do, that in spite of the misunderstandings and pain that the total experience has been of enough worth to have made all of us glad of the part that we have had in it.
>
> I wonder if you would give me the names of the persons to whom you sent copies of your letter. I am assuming that it did go only to members of the India Committee, but if it went to other persons I should like to know who they were.

To the Members of the India Committee—
Greetings:

During the first breathing space that we have had since landing in Colombo, October 21, I am taking the time out to write a full letter to the Committee setting down in order certain matters concerning my relationship to the committee, and proposing herewith to give a final statement which you may have before your committee actually and technically dissolves, March 1, 1936. This letter has special significance for me, because I want you to know directly and exactly what my position is at present, and was, and also because we are now actually face to face with the practical results of the unwise action of the committee over which so much friction arose back home and because of which so many friendships were irrevocably impaired.

Ever since my acceptance of the responsibility of coming to India on a mission like this I have been deeply impressed with the colossal nature of this particular assignment and the responsibility involved therein. In the first place, I was painfully conscious as all thinking Negroes would be, of the many false impressions that people all over the world have been given of the American Negro, sometimes through the press, sometimes through travellers bent on spreading this propaganda, et cetera. I knew that it was generally known that Negroes were lynched by white Americans and that Christianity in America had proven itself impotent to date to do anything practical about it. I knew that we would have to face this in India, and the facts by which it is surrounded. It was clear to me in the beginning that we would be scheduled to go into all or most of the largest and most influential colleges and universities in India, meeting many of their foremost people in intellectual training, culture and refinement. I sensed also that there would be many delicate and difficult aspects of our pilgrimage which would require the utmost taste, skill and understanding of many relationships so as not to have them prove embarrassing to our friends in India and ourselves. Because of all this and several other things that I need not go into here, I was insistent all the time that the very best people available in America, only should be accepted for this pilgrimage. And I thought then as I think now that the whole committee's attitude toward this matter would have been very different if it had been called upon to carry out the assignment in India. I am more sure of this when I think of the careful, painstaking methods of several members of the committee which they always employ when called into action on jobs for which they have the responsibility. The fact of this great concern proved embarrassing. I was forced, as a member of the delegation, to contend for the highest possible representation for the delegation, which contention should not have been necessary for any member of the delegation itself. It seems that from interpretations given out by some members of the committee during the summer, I had represented myself as a "judge" to veto any and all suggestions that came in relative to personnel. The one time when I was advised that the committee was going to vote on Mrs. Hamilton's successor and the name of the Fisk undergraduate, Miss Minus, was intimated, I wired my approval to the chairman. The chairman of the committee had tacitly promised me that when the person would be selected to take Mrs. Hamilton's place I would be advised beforehand so that, as leader of the delegation, I would have some share with the committee in knowing just how the person being considered would fit into the plan for the delegation's work here in India—which plan was being devised in my own mind at the time. Nevertheless this understanding was set aside and I was advised only after the invitation was extended to Mrs. Carroll, that she was the last-minute and final choice. Despite the fact that I was not well I made two separate trips to New York at my own expense to try to clear up the misunderstanding. The reasons given on the second of these trips were two-fold: The understanding that existed between the chairman and myself was considered by the chairman as merely an understanding between us to which the committee itself was not committed; second, in a conversation between the two of us, during which a personal question was raised as to a person whom she had considered suggesting, a person who was one of my dearest friends—I had replied that I feared the strain of executing this difficult assignment would be too taxing because of temperaments. Any two close friends who knew their responses and reactions to be similar in given situations would have raised the same questions. Sue and I had done so regarding ourselves many times before. We deplored what we anticipated to be the inevitable and distressing result of our working and travelling together for six months on a job which demanded that people be not emotionally at one under stress and duress. We have found that our prognostications were only too correct. I thought I knew the chairman sufficiently well to expect her to have discernment delicate enough to understand this point. But in any case in what happened later, her actions were based on an unofficial question and answer which had no bearing on any action, or proposed action of the committee itself. It was during this same conversation that I expressed myself as feeling that the delegation should remain at three members because it seemed too late for a third[3] person to get ready for the pilgrimage. Practically all of the summer conferences were over and there were only two months and a half remaining before time to sail.

But finally when the delegation was at last completed it consisted of two married couples. My reaction to this fact was determined by what I had experienced from people who had raised the question relative to Mrs. Thurman and myself. So anxious were we that there would be no grounds for criticism of the committee for naming the two of us in one family we sought every conceivable way to guarantee our "individual" kinds of preparation. This is one of the primary reasons why Sue put in ten weeks of intensive study in Mexico during the late winter and spring, on the whole of American Culture in preparation for the contacts we would make with a significant culture of the East. For considerations touching this particular aspect of the final choice, I felt as leader of the delegation that the situation would be relieved if some one of the married couples would withdraw. I had no power or right to ask any one to do so other than Mrs. Thurman or myself. She was of the same opinion as I and later resigned. Her reasons were two: The first as stated above relative to the couples; the second, the fact that all along she had felt very deeply that there was no undergraduate representation in the delegation. The latter fact was made clear in a letter to the chairman in which she stated that she would quietly resign giving no reasons to any one outside of the committee so that an undergraduate might have the chance to be reconsidered. This step would be taken so that the Negro student population of the movement would not know that it was not the committee's final plan to select one of them as substitute for Mrs. Hamilton.

Now with the four of us in India what is the situation? We have discussed for hours on end in trains, in hostels, and in private homes, the best possible ways for meeting the demands of this situation. We find that it is assumed by our presence here, since we are not students, that we are in our own right a cross section of the intellectual, cultural and religious life of America. Rightly or wrongly, we are expected to speak with thoughtful maturity on a broad range of interests. Explanations, if they should be given, would be beside the point. There are many people there who have studied in America and who understand enough about the American student movement to know that our delegation is composed of people some of whom would not have been sent by the movement to do a platform job in our most insignificant Negro colleges, to say nothing of white colleges—and to have them used in conference leadership would have been out of the question entirely. In a meeting of the delegation in preparation for Madras, the center of education and culture for South India, we put aside all personal considerations and looked squarely at ourselves and our equipment. We looked at the programme for Madras (enclosed) and saw at once that here we would have to use all of our resources. The training and experience of each one of us was reviewed in turn. The four of us saw at once that the person who was in the most embarrassing predicament was Mrs. Carroll. If she had been given six or eight months in which to prepare herself she could have developed something definite to give in India. As it was, according to her own statement she was reassured by members of the committee that at the time of her appointment she was quite ready for what she had to do here. The facts simply stated at the conference together were as follows: the actual experience upon which she may draw for her work here is her college course at Morgan College with a major in Mathematics—her work as a teacher is limited to one term in an F.E.R.A.[4] night school in Salem, Virginia—she clerked in a five and ten cents store in Baltimore for several months during the active vigilance of the Negro Alliance—she had casual relationships with the Y.W.C.A. at her own college where membership is automatic. When the four of us had a long meeting in Washington, shortly after her appointment, I had suggested that she work in the field of Rural Education in the light of information that had been given me by the committee relative to her preparation. In Ceylon, our first field of activity, she undertook to speak on the subject assigned. It was not long before she herself discovered that there was a demand for a knowledge of the subject which she did not possess. At the present time in this country (India), there are many of the keenest minds in the field of Education desperately concerned about rethinking the whole problem of National education in India. They use their knowledge of foreign indigenous schemes, particularly those of America and Britain, as a point of departure for general comparison. I found in the end that Mrs. Carroll had had some training in elocution and had been interested in dramatics at Morgan. It occurred to me, therefore, to ask her to learn to recite some of the poetry of American Negroes. She has given two such readings since we have been in India and I shall schedule her in this capacity as often as it is practical.

Mr. Carroll has worked over his subject several times since we have been here. After two months it has shaken down to an appreciative discourse on the Negro Church. Whenever it is opportune he gives an informal talk on his experiences in the student movement and on student life.

Sue is taking the Y.W.C.A. meetings and Women's meetings, as such. She has found the women of India terribly "Movement" conscious. In addition she has been training local groups of faculty and students to sing American Negro songs hoping to make it possible for them to share concretely in some experience definitely related to our life in America. Because the women students in the colleges of India are just joining in with the men in a united student Movement, it is necessary to talk at length in each college center about the work of other movements and their various objectives and accomplishments. In my opinion this is the most fundamental piece of work that is being done by the delegation for the student Christian movement of India, as such.

I am taking all public meetings (as you will see on the programs) for cities and towns. These are extremely large audiences of Christians, Muslims and Hindus. They make a point here in India of having these meetings presided over by the highest Indian or British official available. You may be sure that there will always be three or four representatives of the press present. We have had battles with reporters ever since we have been here. Once a statement I had made regarding Howard University was given the spot the next day as information concerning Harvard University.[5] In Madras, Sue had a speech completely changed for her.

About the outcome of finances—Mr. Carroll and I understood that $600.00 would be allowed for each person's travel and that the difference left from this amount after purchasing tickets and visas would be applied to incidentals such as tips, taxi, et cetera. We were never told what the cost of tickets and visas was, nor that the money left after their purchase would really have to be applied to honoraria rather than incidentals. If we had been advised of this change in the plan, some arrangement would have been made to take care of the situation before leaving America.

I suppose all of this should end with the conclusion that the American Movement did not have quite funds enough to finance four delegates to India. India itself is being strained to take care of four, and in practically every place it becomes necessary to resort to taking public collections to help with the expenses.

I need not say that we find India teeming with many things—discussions with professors and leaders of thought carry us far into the night. Indian students complain that there is no one in the delegation who can see life at their level and hobnob with them in their hostels and dormitories as fellow undergraduates. It so often happens that the president of the local union is the principal or president of the college and that students themselves get only the minor job of keeping the minutes as secretary, et cetera. So the students are especially interested to hear about a movement in which undergraduates play important and official parts. We are trying to find ways and means of making it possible for some of our undergraduates to come here for study and also to establish exchange professorships for Negro and Indian schools.

Personal greetings to each member of the committee: To "A. R." as he journeys through the land[6]—to Luther Tucker who is remembered by many friends out here—to Marion who will be hearing soon about the exploits of Anne in Geneva—to Francis Henson about whose winter work we wish we could hear a word—to Frank as he begins the new life at Talladega—to Betty who becomes a full-time "hausfrau" after March 1.

During the Christmas holidays we shall write something for the *Intercollegian*. Sue is writing an article for the Woman's Press on Indian Instruments. Our days are so completely scheduled and the places follow each other in such rapid succession that there is very little time for writing at all. We shall be reaching America the last of April unless, as some of us dream, it will be possible to return by way of the Pacific.[7]

Sincerely yours,

[*signed*]Howard Thurman

Howard Thurman

TLcS. HTC-MBU: Box 136.

1. See Channing H. Tobias to Ruth Taylor, 9 March 1936, printed in the current volume. It is not known who else was included in the circulation list of the 20 December letter.

2. From Elizabeth Harrington, 7 February 1936, HTC-MBU: Box 9.

3. This should read "fourth person."

4. The Federal Emergency Relief Act, or FERA, was the first of the New Deal programs. Under the FERA forty thousand teachers eligible for relief were employed in nursery schools and, in this instance, various forms of adult education.

5. This was a common mistake among Indians unfamiliar with American higher education. See "With Our Negro Guests," 14 March 1936, by Mahadev Desai, in the current volume.

6. A. Roland Elliott.

7. Months after this possibility was seemingly rejected, Thurman was still thinking about returning by the Pacific and stopping in China on the way.

⁓ FROM BENJAMIN E. MAYS
26 DECEMBER 1935
WASHINGTON, D.C.

During Thurman's absence from Howard, Mays writes to brief him on the School of Religion's activities and reflects upon receiving the PhD from the University of Chicago. He also indicates that he will recommend to Howard University that Thurman be promoted to the rank of full professor upon his return.

Dr. Howard Thurman
India

Dear Howard:

I hope that you and Sue had a very fine Christmas and that the same was true of Madolina and the children in Geneva.[1] Things are moving along smoothly here, and though we are busy during the holidays we are taking it more leisurely than we do during the regular session. We spent a quiet Christmas at home yesterday and I believe that we were able to bring a degree of cheer and happiness to Sadie's mother and to my parents. They had been fairly good children during the year and Santa Claus was somewhat generous in his gifts to them. My mother insists that it was the finest Christmas that she has ever experienced. I am sure that all three of the parents got more than they have customarily received. Though it requires good common sense and the artistic touch to bring together two sets of aged parents under the same roof we are enjoying the experiment, and I am glad that they are here in that we are convinced in our own minds that we have not chosen the easier part by having them somewhere else with our furnishing the money. I do not know how long it will last because mother Gray has already drawn her money out of the Post Office and threatens to return to Georgia at any moment though there is no house on the place. And my mother is beginning to say that she has never said she was going to stay in Washington always—notwithstanding the fact that she had already indicated previously that she would want to stay with us always.

We had a very fine Convocation. Both Dean Pratt and Dr. Gordon[2] agreed that it was one of the best Convocations that the School of Religion has ever put on. Dr. Gordon says that the music was the best of any Convocation. This being true the Convocation must have been as good as in previous years. It is the belief of the students and teachers in the School of Religion that the attendance this year was more uniform than in previous years. That is, there were no lean sessions. We had a good attendance from beginning to end. Many people seem to believe that the regularity of attendance of city pastors was better than before and that possibly a larger number of the outstanding pastors attended. Although the Convocation was not in every particular what I had dreamed for it to be, I am certain that it was truly representative of the best that we could have found anywhere.

Mr. Lee, Miss Taylor and I had planned to send you and yours Christmas greetings by cable, but after discovering that it would have cost fifty-five cents a word we got cold feet and felt that you would understand that we were thinking about you on Christmas Day. Yesterday Sadie and I had to dinner Miss Taylor and the lone, single men in the School of Religion who are away from home. It was an ambitious undertaking, but I think we were able to supply sufficient for all who came.

I read a portion of your letter to our assembly Monday of last week, particularly that part where you expressed the view that you found use for every idea that has ever come {in} to your head, and then your admonition to the students here to go deep in the field of religion. I am sure that you are having an invaluable experience and that you are not only making a fine contribution to the people of India but that you will return to America better equipped because of your wide contact in India.

I would suggest that you write Dr. Johnson reminding him of the letter which you wrote him just before you sailed concerning your wishes and desires for the Committee on Religious Life. In conference with him the other day, he advised me to include half of your salary in the School of Religion budget and he felt sure that he could get the University to swing the other half. I will put two thousand dollars in my own budget which says to the University that they are to match that. I also plan to recommend to the University that you be given the rank of professor.

Though you are kept very busy, I hope you will find it convenient to write from time to time. The enclosed clipping indicates that the PhD degree has been conferred. The final examinations consisted of two days of writing and another two hours of oral examination on the thesis. This was more than I had expected but I came through in fine shape and there was never a moment when I felt doubtful, for I was able to make a comprehensive, intelligent approach to every question put to me. I came through as I had hoped that I would with my head high above the waters for I have never wanted to be a border line case in anything. I would have preferred not to have had the degree if I had barely gotten by.

Neither Miss Taylor nor I have heard anything from Madoline. I hope they are well.

With kindest personal regards from Sadie and me to you and Sue, I am Ever your friend,

[*signed*] Benjamin E. Mays

Benjamin E. Mays, Dean

N.B. no fever since you left.

TLS. HTC-MBU: Box 12.

1. Madolina is Madaline, Thurman's sister.
2. Dr. William C. Gordon was professor of homiletics from 1922 to 1934.

☙ FROM SUSAN FORD BAILEY

31 DECEMBER 1935

DERMOTT, ARK.

Susan Ford Bailey writes to her daughter and son-in-law while they are in India. Her dedication to the children in her community is evident.

Dear children

You will see that I started this letter before Christmas. But it has sleeted and snowed and kept me in for a week, and I have to get my letters mailed when Batts feels like getting out. My community children have misplaced the letter that I wanted to send to you. But the ladie's name was Mrs. Jenness of New York, she wanted me to send her your history Baby, so she could get out a book before you came back. Josie is spending a few days with. Please print your address and date of the month on some of your letters. I succeeded in having my boys to distribute about one hundred Christmas gifts to needy children in the community. This was aside from my Sunday school gifts. Well I am tired yet. But I am glad to make others happy. Write me soon. I have had only one letter from you since you been in India. May the dear Lord richly bless each of you.

lovingly

[*signed*] Mama

ALS. HTC-MBU: Box 198.

☙ FROM HENRIETTA WISE

14 JANUARY 1936

CALCUTTA, INDIA

Inspired by the India delegation's visit, Henrietta Wise praises them for their Christian witness. Despite their efforts the work of the Negro Delegation was often seen through an evangelical perspective.

Dear Dr. Thurman,

Please excuse the liberty I take in addressing you, but I have loved your people ever since, as a little girl, I heard here in Calcutta, the Fisk Jubilee Singers; I
never will forget the generosity of Mr. Londen, the leader, who gave us, school-
girls, a free entrée to one of his sacred concerts.[1]

The work of Booker T. Washington has been a source of inspiration also, and
as you spoke last Sunday evening, it came over me that you are a proof to the non-
believing world that Jesus is alive and divine, and that yours is a unique opportunity to witness to the worth of Jesus Christ as you and your companions address
our non-Christian brothers and sisters; for in spite of wrong interpretations of His
Gospel, the all powerful influence of His Personality has finally triumphed and
you today stand by His Grace where you do.

May they see the value of a Christian environment of 373 years as yours has
been, as against almost 2000 years of heathen surroundings in India, and
believe that Christ and He alone is able to lift man till he becomes in his turn a
lifter-up of men as you and your friends are in your community. May God's rich
blessing rest upon you.

I shall deem it a great favour if you will kindly accept the enclosed gift of
Indian embroidery work as a small token of friendship, from
Yours for the increase of International friendliness,
[*signed*] (Miss) Henrietta Wise
Henrietta Wise

ALS. HTC-MBU: Box 21.

1. The Fisk Jubilee Singers, who obtained worldwide fame as singers of Negro spirituals and work songs, were founded in 1867 by Fisk University treasurer and vocal music
instructor George L. White. The success of the eleven-member choir spread to the
northeast and to Europe, and they performed concerts for notables like President
Ulysses S. Grant in Washington, D.C., and Queen Victoria in England. The original
Fisk Jubilee singers disbanded in 1878. The next year, though, a reorganized group by
the same name (though lacking any connection to Fisk University) was formed under
the direction of White and Frederick Jeremiah Loudin. Loudin, free born, grew up in
Ravenna, Ohio, and had been a member of the original group. Under his direction, the
reorganized Fisk Jubilee Singers staged a six-year world tour starting in 1884, which
took them through India.

🐦 FROM MAHADEV DESAI
26 JANUARY 1936
WARDHA, INDIA

The high point of the delegation's journey to India is a three-hour private
meeting with Mahatma Gandhi at Bardoli. Thurman comes away from the
meeting deeply impressed with the urgency of rescuing American Christianity
from the historical and cultural grip of segregation. He asks Gandhi for a piece
of cloth in remembrance of the occasion. It arrives in the mail one year later.

Dear Friend,

Mr Gandhi has your letter of the 18th. He will certainly be delighted to give you a piece of cloth {woven} out of yarn spun by him on his wheel, but he is not sure that such cloth is at present available. I am trying to secure it for you and to give it to you when you meet him in Delhi about the middle of February.

Yours Sincerely

[*signed*] Mahadev Desai[1]

ALS. HTC-MBU: Box 136.

1. Mahadev Desai (1892–1942) was, like Gandhi, a native of Gujarat State. A lawyer by training, he became a close associate of Gandhi in 1917 and spent the rest of his life as his personal secretary. Frequently incarcerated with Gandhi on the latter's nationalist crusades, Desai died suddenly of natural causes in prison in 1942.

🐦 FROM CLARENCE J. GRESHAM

5 FEBRUARY 1936

ATLANTA, GA.

Clarence J. Gresham sends news on family, friends, and Morehouse College. He notes that word is getting back to the United States of the warm and enthusiastic response of Indians to the Negro Delegation.

Morehouse College

Atlanta, Ga.

My dear Howard,

I was so happy to get a letter from you and to learn about the rest of the family. Mother Sams has written me several times & I have also heard from Mrs. Bailey. Both were well. It is such a fine opportunity for Madeline, Olive & Anne Spencer. I knew you & Sue were busy so I have patiently waited for my letter yet I looked for it in every mail.

The Christian Century for this week Feb. 5th, in Mr. P. Domman Philip's[1] correspondence from India, mentions the fact that the American Negro Delegation covers India or student centers in south India and "Everywhere they have been received with great cordiality & enthusiasm, not only by Christian groups, but also by the general public." He does not mention the names.

I am doing nicely in my work, although the day your letter came I was in with a cold. Morehouse is here. We are more or less drifting no one seems to know where. Our enrollment was the largest this year than we have had in sometime. Mr. Archer is well but doesn't know what to do with this place and would be most happy if his time were up tomorrow.[2] And of course Dean Brazeal is of no account.[3] He is the most pitiful. Tillman was away studying the first semester but is back. Reid & Chivers are with government on a white collar survey of Negroes in the main cities.

The winter has been unusually cold this year with our heaviest ice storm in which we were without lights & street car service for a week.

We had our largest snow last week, ten inches.

Mattie is improving nicely. She was walking everywhere on crutches when I was over Xmas. She could do a bit of getting around in the house without crutches. She now writes me that she goes outdoors without crutches & hopes with in a month or so to put them aside all together. I shall get over to see her during spring recess. She will come home this summer.

The exams are just over and I don't know how Johnett came out in his subjects.[4] We have gotten on pretty well together. I had to do most of the cooking for he didn't know very much about it. He cleans & washes the dishes. He is very quiet. Seldom says anything. He will do anything you ask him to but he would never take the initiative in doing things. He is quite different from Philip. He could be taught but I am a poor teacher when it comes to cooking. There was some misunderstanding about his scholarship and Mrs. Bailey has had to get money for his room rent. Mr. Archer either forgot what he promised you or did not understand.

A Miss Mary Jenness of New York was gathering facts about the lives of you & Sue to be included in a missionary year book. I told her to let Miss Taylor at Howard read the final copy.

Shall be anxiously waiting your return. Mattie & many friends join me in love to you & Sue.

Ever

[*signed*] C. J. Gresham

ALS. HTC-MBU: Box 8.

1. Dowman Philip, "American Negro Delegation Covers India," *Christian Century*, February 5, 1936.

2. Samuel H. Archer served as president of Morehouse College from 1931 to 1937, during the most financially difficult years in the college's history due to the Depression. Beginning in 1931 the college underwent a sharp decline in enrollment, which did not improve until the 1936 academic year.

3. Brailsford R. Brazeal was professor of economics and served as dean of men at Morehouse until 1942, when he was appointed academic dean by president Benjamin E. Mays.

4. Johnett was a youth in Dermott, Arkansas, who had at one time lived with Susan Ford Bailey and who probably attended Morehouse.

🦋 BENJAMIN E. MAYS TO MARY JENNESS
12 FEBRUARY 1936
WASHINGTON, D.C.

Mary Jenness is asked by the Missionary Education Movement to provide a biographical sketch of Howard and Sue Bailey Thurman for one of its annual booklets.[1] Mays, Clarence J. Gresham, and some of Sue's YWCA friends supply Jenness with insightful information in the Thurmans' absence.

Miss Mary Jenness
Our Cooperative House
433 West 21st Street
New York, New York

Dear Miss Jenness:

My first teaching was done at Morehouse College, Atlanta, Georgia. Mr. Thurman was a Junior the year I began my teaching there and he was enrolled in my class in Psychology. Sixty young men and women were enrolled in that class and Mr. Thurman had the second highest mark. A young woman in the class beat him by a very small margin. He was by far the best student in his class as evidenced by the fact that he graduated as valedictorian. Out of a group of students numbering around four hundred, there was certainly no one who had a finer mind than Mr. Thurman. In human sympathies and social imagination, I am of the opinion that he was superior to most of them. He was so interesting and stimulating that I associated with him at Morehouse more than I did many of the professors.

He did not participate in athletics but he was kept extremely busy with other extra-curricula activities such as the Y.M.C.A., Debating Council, and other student organizations. He represented the college in many student conferences. He was a member of the debating team that I coached and was, without doubt, an inter-collegiate debater of the first magnitude. I believe that he showed signs then of possessing more mysticism in his religion than the average person, so much so that I am inclined to think that he was considered queer by some of the students and professors. This did not interfere with his general popularity because he possessed a mind and an integrity of character which they were forced to respect.

As a student at Morehouse, I believe he was less interested in social affairs than most students were. He did not join the college fraternities, though all of the fraternities would have been glad to have him as member. His refusal to join fraternities represented an independence which has displayed itself in subsequent years. He was able then to appraise and evaluate fraternities, and I feel that he doubted their value. I believe he did not have the desire for constant city social contacts as most of the students had.

As member of the faculty of Morehouse and Spelman previous to his coming to Howard University, there could be no denying the fact that he was one of the most popular teachers with students and possibly the most popular. They had great confidence in him and they would talk to him about their intimate problems and would seek him for help on delicate matters that they would have been afraid to discuss with other members of the faculty. They also believe that he was sufficiently interested in them as to make a sympathetic approach to whatever problem they presented to him.

Mr. Thurman has maintained the same kind of sympathetic understanding in student problems here at Howard University, and is one of the greatest factors for good on Howard University campus. He is an able teacher in the School of Religion of Howard University. He is constantly sought for conferences and consultations by students in the University at large, and he has built up a Sunday service at Howard University that compares favorably with the service held anywhere in America.

Mrs. Thurman and I worked together as student secretaries of the National Council of the Y.W.C.A. from 1928 to 1930. I believe you stated in your letter that you have sufficient information about her, but I might add that I found her very cooperative in spirit. During these years the Y.M. and the Y.W.C.A.s worked together in perfect harmony. We had a Christian student movement in five states in which we worked together. We did this at a time when it was thought impossible in many sections of the country. Mrs. Thurman made a profound impression upon the students and had a good following in the colleges. This was due, I think, to three things: her ability to take care of herself intellectually, her ability to get along with students in a democratic way, and her personal charm.

I hope these items will be of value to you and I urge you to use your judgment in changing or cutting out anything that I have said. I am sorry that I am so late getting this to you.

Respectfully yours,

[*signed*] Benjamin E. Mays, Dean

TLc. HTC-MBU: Box 191.

1. Juliette Derricotte and William Lloyd Imes are also featured in the volume by Mary Jenness, *Twelve Negro Americans* (New York: Friendship, 1936). Sue Bailey Thurman receives but brief mention in the chapter. For more on Mary Jenness see Thurman's letter of 15 April 1936 to be printed in volume 2.

🌱 FROM HENRY W. LUCE

12 FEBRUARY 1936

LAHORE, INDIA

As Thurman writes in his autobiography, his lectures in India on the theme of "The Faith of the American Negro" creates uneasiness for white Americans who heard him. It is in response to one of Thurman's public lectures on this subject in Lahore that he receives a letter from Henry W. Luce, an American missionary and the father of Henry R. Luce, the founder of Time *and* Life.[1] *Luce, in his own way, is wrestling with the dilemmas of race in America. Thurman includes Luce's letter in his autobiography. Due to the illegibility of much of the surviving facsimile, the letter is reprinted from Thurman's autobiography.*

Dear Mr. Thurman:

I listened with a good deal of interest to your address last night at YMCA (as also in the one given by your colleague yesterday morning at Arya-somaj

College). I shared also in the pleasure of the delightful group as your wife sang to them at the lovely home of Mr. and Mrs. Rollia Rama.

I have also been a missionary in China for thirty years, am an ardent internationalist and inter-racialist. From boyhood up I (and some millions of other whites in the United States also) have been interested in doing all I could to assist your group to attain the highest possible best.

That gives you my background and my friendly interest. Nevertheless, at the close of your address I had the feeling (shared by at least a few others) that, doubtless quite unintentionally, you had probably left a wrong impression on some of the thinking minds present.

The strong impression left upon me was that you felt the Negro race in America had suffered all it has suffered at the hand of the American whites—that they had not lifted a finger to help, and that your people, so far as they had gone, had attained all by their own inherent power. Not as much in what you said as in what you omitted was the impression given; and this could have been relieved by a very few sentences here and there.

Every since I traveled as a Student Volunteer Secretary in 1895, covering southward the Mason and Dixon Line for the first time and going from Texas to Virginia I had some real interest and knowledge of your problems. I think of the millions of dollars and hundreds of lives which have been given in sacrificial service to your people and the many colleges and schools established.

I think of thousands of Negroes who have been helped to the highest education and opportunities; it might be that the very fact that you and your colleagues were personally capable of going on a mission to India (and having a journey which many of your supporters would gladly but will never be able to take) has been partly due to the interest of some of your white friends.

I think also of how few of those of your peoples who stayed in Africa have arisen as high as the majority of your people who came to America.

That night before you were, no doubt, Muslims; and you *could* have said, if it had been tactful, that it was largely Arab Muslims that brought the slaves to the court.

I thing of Livingstone and Stanley and many another man or woman who gave their lives to stopping the slave trade at its source.

While no doubt the idea of "non-secession" was a dominant motive for some in the war, there were millions who fought and died to free the slaves. Lincoln was animated by his belief that "no nation can exist half slave, half free."

I realize that one cannot put everything one thinks and feels into one address among several addresses. But it seemed to me there was many a place in your address where a sentence or two, or even a parenthetical phrase, might have led me to feel differently. As it was, I felt that your message, far from aiding peace might (as, I said, quite unconsciously on your part) have the opposite effect. As I see it in the light of my understanding of your otherwise fine and able address, I would not be willing to contribute in the interest of good will and peace toward making such an address widely known in India or anywhere else.

I write in the kindest spirit and with all good will, solely to suggest as an older man to a younger, that your work, so far as I can see, would be more vital and creative if it touched upon the emphasis which I seem to miss.

So can you come work to communicate with me?

Very Sincerely Yours,

[*signed*] H W Luce

WHAH, 123–24; ALS. HTC-MBU: Box 136.

1. Henry Wnters Luce (1868–1941) received his BA from Yale University in 1892. He went to Union Theological Seminary in New York, then interrupted his studies for a year of service in the Student Volunteer Movement. Luce received his BD from Princeton Theological Seminary in 1896. From 1897 to 1927 Luce held a variety of missionary and academic posts in China, including serving eight years as vice president of Yenching University. In 1928 he was appointed to a professorship in the Chinese department of the Kennedy School of Missions of the Hartford Theological Foundation in Hartford, Connecticut, where he remained until his retirement in 1935.

ꙮ From Dr. Jazz

18 February 1936

Bombay, India

"Dr. Jazz," an African American musician in India, has heard about the delegation's travels and requests the pleasure of a lunch engagement with the group. There is an active jazz scene in mid-1930s Bombay, with a number of African American musicians playing prominent roles. "Dr. Jazz" was likely the pianist Teddy Weatherford.[1] The Taj Mahal Hotel had what is probably the best-known jazz club in India at the time.

Mongini's Restaurant
Churchgate Street
Bombay

Dr. Howard Thurman
care of Wilson College
Chowpatty (Bombay)

Dear Dr Thurman:—

I suppose by now, you know that there are very few Colored Americans in Bombay. Leon Abbey and his boys at the Taj Mahal Hotel are the only ones I know.[2] I am the only other one here. So, during your stay here, I should like to have you have lunch here at the place where I am engaged, which is mentioned above.[3]

It is understood that you will be pestered with engagements and appointments from all sides, but if such is possible, I should like very much for you and yours to come over and see me anytime before you leave Bombay.

It is good to meet someone from home. Which, I am sure you will admit is right.

Wishing you and yours every success in your venture, I am,

Cordially Yours,

[*signed*] Dr Jazz[4]

{p.s. When you have decided when you can come, please inform me. Also inform me if it is for four or more. Telephone.20325. If I am out or busy when you phone, please leave the message.}

ALS. HTC-MBU: Box 136.

1. Teddy Weatherford (1903–45) was one of the leading pianists on the Chicago jazz scene in the 1920s. After 1934 his career was in Asia, and he played extensively in Bombay from 1936 to 1940.

2. Leon Alexander Abbey (1900–1975), a Minneapolis-born bandleader and violinist, played extensively in Europe and Asia in the 1920s and 1930s, touring India in 1935 and 1936.

3. In June 1936, on his return to the United States, Thurman wrote to Mary Louise Jackson in St. Louis, telling her that her piano playing brother would be engaged through the fall in what was "perhaps the largest and most swanky restaurant in the city." Thurman also wrote that during their stay in Bombay, he and Sue had visited the restaurant for ice cream and a meeting with "Dr. Jazz." To Mary Louise Jackson, 23 June 1936, HTC-MBU: Box 9.

4. "Doctor Jazz," a well-known composition of the New Orleans pianist Jelly Roll Morton, was first recorded in 1926. It has been subsequently recorded numerous times and often adopted as a cognomen.

✺ "OUR DELEGATION' IN INDIA"
MARCH 1936
INDIA

From June 1933 on the Intercollegian *was a primary source of information about the Negro Delegation to India, Burma, and Ceylon, and publicized the forthcoming tour in editorials, news briefs, and longer articles. The most extensive account of the tour written by the delegates appears in the March 1936 issue. Three photographs with captions accompany the article.[1]*

A "mid-way" letter of impressions—affording an insight into the Indian student mind

The trip across the Atlantic seemed brief and was uneventful.[2] During the seventeen days and nights on the Mediterranean it was pure ecstasy to discover that a growing moon was cruising with us, everywhere we went![3] Italy itself was in the distance for sometime, and then old Corsica, Sardinia and the small volcanic plateaus of *Notre Mare*.[4] At night always music, the moon, and passing ships! . . . Then Port Said and the Suez.[5] The canal itself is a narrow waterway permitting boats to line up and creep through, keeping careful distances as they inch along. Djibouti,[6] the French African town, was one of our ports of call. The women of the delegation went over to see the city. So fascinated were they by the charming brass anklets and gay dark eyes of the damsel who accosted them in French with "*Danse, Mesdames*?" that they forsook all and hurried back to the ship so as not to lose their hearts forever in Africa, before reaching beautiful India!

The four of us learned to spend the days en route in most agreeable fashion. Each afternoon before tea we met for a few hours of creative communion. Sometimes there would be music, or poetry, or delightful short stories when Mr. Carroll was the performing artist. Reaching Ceylon, we spent several weeks in four of its principal cities: Colombo, capital and famous port; Galle, important stronghold of the early Dutch;[7] Kandy, noted for the Temple of the Tooth,[8] and Jaffna, homeplace of D. T. Niles, spirited Student Movement leader of Ceylon. The complete union of the men and women students in one All-India, Burma and Ceylon Movement is in the process of becoming. They are emerging from the past period when they had affiliations with the Y.M.C.A, and Y.W.C.A. such as we have had, and still have, in America.

All of our time since the middle of November we have spent in India itself, save for five days in Rangoon. We shall visit some fifty-three college and university centers before we conclude the schedule. In every contact we have found the Indian student keen and penetrating. He inherits a background of traditions and customs which, to us, is illimitably rich and strange. He is coming forth to form his own leadership in the tedious way ahead and he has excellent equipment in his own mind and soul.

Already we have spent long hours with the Executive Secretaries—Mr. A. Ralla Ram, of boundless enthusiasm and energy for his S.C.M. which he loves as his child, and with Miss Gavin, of New Zealand, a most capable person whose heart is made up all through of exquisite fibers of kindness. In the travels through South India we had the delightful escort of Mr. Matthew, a regional secretary of Travancore, a Native Indian State; and Mr. Duraisamy, of vigor and conviction, who directed the tour through his region, the Madras Presidency. Also in South India we were received by the Misses Isaiah, Matthew, and George, whose achievements suggest the possibilities of the young college women in the Movement to whom they are giving secretarial leadership.[9]

We have met questions that tax the minds of the greatest students of American life and thought. We are expected, and rightly so, to know almost everything about many subjects, and something about every subject touching on the Christian Movement, our national life and our own people. A few of them are entered here for you to have now, and probably for inclusion in conference discussions this summer. (Questions are usually asked from the floor or put into writing and directed to the speaker at the close of a platform address.)

What kind and method of social work is employed by the women of America?
Does it make any difference in race feeling on the part of white Americans
    when Negroes become Christians?
Do you have caste distinctions in the Christian Church in America? What is
    the American scheme of government?
Why is it that the constitution grants franchise to all citizens but is powerless
    to give legal redress to the technical disfranchisement of Negroes in
    Southern states?
Why were Negroes barred from jury service in the South until the recent
    Supreme Court decision about the Scottsboro Case?[10]
What is the illiteracy scale of America, Negroes, Whites and Indians?
Are American Indians included in your student movement?
What provision is made for them?
How do you account for the fact that lynching seems to be a "natural" expres-
    sion of the national life of America?
What is the unique cultural contribution of the various races and nationalities
    of America to the total life?
Would four white Americans have consented to visit Indian student groups?
Would they feel the same prejudices—eating with us, etc.—as with Negroes?
What are the instances of strength or weakness in your co-educational system?
Are undergraduates active in the American Student movement?
Do they participate in the conduct of its affairs?
Do you have unemployment problems among your graduates?
Do American students know anything about religions other than their own?
Why is it the policy of American mission boards not to send Negroes to the
    foreign field?
If Christianity has the answer to materialism, why has it not been effective in
    this regard in the civilizations of the West?

It is needless to say that the warmest reception has been tendered us everywhere. We have been decorated with sequins, flowers and spice—like the custom in Hawaii, but rendered more beautiful, in this atmosphere, by the Old

World charm of India. In the places where the citizens are not Christians, as often is the case, these extend a cordial friendship and in the contacts give us the finest demonstration of the spiritual genius of their religion.

Intercollegian (March 1936).

1. The photographs in the *Intercollegian* article are not reproduced in the current volume, but their captions are: "In India—Flowers and questions figure prominently on a college visit" for a photograph of the delegates, wearing flowered wreaths, as described in the article, and Indian faculty and students; "Keen and penetrating" under a photograph of three smiling South Asian men in western dress; and "At the Great Mosque there are spaces for 25,000 Mohammedan worshipers" to describe a photograph of a large crowd of white-garbed worshippers prostrate in prayer.

2. In his autobiography Thurman remembers the crossing differently as a stormy passage in which the ship "was flung recklessly up and down and from side to side—passively—as if at last we would be swallowed or demolished." *WHAH,* 109.

3. The seventeen days refers to the entire passage from Marseilles to Colombo and not merely the time in the Mediterranean. In his autobiography Thurman describes this trip as lasting twenty-one days. *WHAH,* 112. There was a new moon about 28 September and a full moon on 12 October, so if the delegation left Marseilles on 1 October the moon would have been waxing until the delegation was in the Indian Ocean.

4. *Notre Mare* is the French version of *Mare Nostrum,* a common name for the Mediterranean and Latin for "our sea."

5. Port Said in Egypt is the Mediterranean entrance to the Suez Canal.

6. Djibouti, on the East Africa coast on the Gulf of Aden, south of the Red Sea, was founded by the French in 1888 as the capital of French Somaliland. It is now the capital and largest city in the Republic of Djibouti.

7. Galle was under Dutch control from 1640 to 1795, when control passed to the British. The old Dutch fort still guards the entrance to the harbor.

8. The Temple of the Tooth houses a molar of the Buddha.

9. In 1934–35, Doris Gavin was the student secretary of the YWCA of India, Burma, and Ceylon. K. A Mathew and John Duraiswamy were the traveling secretaries of the Student Christian Movement of India, Burma, and Ceylon; Elizabeth George was associated with the Women's Christian College in Madras; Sosa Matthew was associated with the YWCA in Travandum. Travacore State, *Directory of Christian Missions in India, Burma, and Ceylon 1934–1935* (Nagpur, India: National Christian Council, 1934), 294, 204, 227. Miss S. Isaiah was listed as a traveling secretary on the stationery of the SCMIBC in 1935. HTC-MBU: Box 136.

10. The multiple trials during the 1930s of nine young black men from Scottsboro, Alabama, accused of raping a white woman focused intense attention on the blatant practices of racial discrimination in the administration of justice in the southern states. See Dan Carter, *Scottsboro: A Tragedy of the American South* (London, New York: Oxford University Press, 1969). In one of the Scottsboro cases, *Norris v. Alabama* 294 US 587 (1935), the Supreme Court decided eight to zero that the systematic exclusion of African Americans from juries constituted a violation of the Fourteenth Amendment.

🖎 CHANNING H. TOBIAS TO RUTH TAYLOR
9 MARCH 1936
NEW YORK, N.Y.

Ruth Taylor, Thurman's personal secretary, solicited advice from Channing H. Tobias on the sensitive matter of confidentiality relating to Thurman's 20 December letter to the India Committee. Tobias reminds her of the imperative to maintain such confidences in Thurman's absence, even when pressed by committee members, in this instance A. Roland Elliott.

Miss Ruth Taylor
Office of the Dean
School of Religion
Howard University
Washington, D.C.

Dear Miss Taylor:

Thank you for letting me see these programs. I note what you say about the confidential character of the letter written by Mr. Thurman to the India Committee, and shall be guided by Mr. Thurman's request.

I also note the request that Mr. Elliott made of you for information as to persons to whom the confidential letter had been sent. I think it very important that you not comply with this request, for I feel that it would be going over the confidence enjoined by Mr. Thurman.

Sincerely yours,

[*signed*] C. H. Tobias

C. H. Tobias.

Enclosures

CHT:ERR

TLcS. HTC-MBU: Box 21.

🖎 "WITH OUR NEGRO GUESTS"
14 MARCH 1936
POONA, INDIA

The highlight of Thurman's tour to India, Burma, and Ceylon as chairman of the Negro Delegation is his meeting with Mahatma Gandhi, the leader of the Indian independence movement and advocate of nonviolent social change. Gandhi's campaigns against British colonial rule had brought him worldwide fame, and he is widely revered among African Americans as the most prominent non-white critic of imperialism and racism.

Thurman recounts in his memoir that never in his life has he been examined in such a persistent fashion about the history and current realities of African

Americans. In their interview Gandhi wants to know about "voting rights, lynching, discrimination, public school education, the churches and how they functioned. His questions covered the entire sweep of our experience in American society."[1]

Although the meeting of the Negro Delegation with Gandhi is extensively covered in the black press and throughout the United States, the actual interview, written by Mahadev Desai and published in Gandhi's English weekly Harijan[2] has never before been reprinted in its entirety.[3] Gandhi's final comment, "It may be through the Negroes that the unadulterated message of non-violence will be delivered to the world," takes on a life of its own and will become a watchword in the Civil Rights Movement.[4]

The meeting with the members of the American Negro Delegation was the first engagement of an important nature undertaken by Gandhiji[5] since the breakdown in his health.[6] He could not think of letting them leave our shores without meeting them, and I had the honour one early morning to receive them at Navsari station and to escort them to Bardoli.

It was a privilege to meet these friends, and even a two hours' concentrated conversation with them did not seem to tire Gandhiji, who asked Dr. Thurman all kinds of questions about the American Negroes, in order to acquaint himself a little with his subject before he could talk with them with confidence. One of the best alumni of the Negro Universities, Dr. Thurman explained to Gandhiji, with the cautious and dispassionate detachment characteristic of a professor of philosophy, the various schools of Negro thought. Booker T. Washington represented the economic school which had its place when America was less industrialized than it is today and there was more demand for skilled labour. A young man of thirty-four is now in charge trying to adjust Tuskegee to the new situation.[7] Du Bois, the mulatto representative of the "Talented Tenth" was still directing part of the intellectual section of the Negroes, teaching Sociology in the Atlanta University, and offering a challenging intellectual solution of the Negro problem through his latest book—*Black Reconstruction*. He was now editing a big Encyclopaedia of the American Negro, giving the entire story of the American Negro from 1619 to the present time.[8] Dr. Thurman explained the State theory of the separate but so-called "equal" education of the Negro and told how Harvard University[9] in Washington was the only illustration of the Federal Government participating directly in the running of a Negro University, giving 80 percent of the expenses of its running. Up to ten years ago the whole of the teaching staff were European, now most of them are Negroes. "The President Dr. Johnson," said Dr. Thurman with kindly emotion, "is one of the greatest of your admirers."[10] He explained how the situation in the Southern States was still difficult, as the flower of the aristocratic

Mahatma Gandhi and Sue, in Bardoli, India, February 1936. Courtesy of the Thurman Family and Arleigh Prelow / Howard Thurman Film Project

Whites were all killed in the War of 1861–64 and as soon as the armies of occupation moved to the North the economic structure was paralysed, leaving the whole structure in the hands of the poor Whites who smarted under the economic competition of the Negro.[11]

"Is the prejudice against colour growing or dying out?" was one of the questions Gandhiji asked. "It is difficult to say," said Dr. Thurman, "because in one place things look much improved, whilst in another the outlook is still dark. Among many of the Southern White students, there is a disposition to improve upon the attitude of their forbears, and the migration occasioned by the World War did contribute appreciably to break down the barriers. But the economic question is acute everywhere, and in many of the industrial centres in Middle West the prejudice against the Negro shows itself in its ugliest form. Among the masses of workers there is a great amount of tension, which is quite natural, when the White thinks that the Negro's very existence is a threat to his own."

"Is the union between Negroes and the Whites recognized by law?" was another question. "Twenty-five States have laws definitely against these unions, and I have had to sign a bond of 500 dollars to promise that I would not register any such union,"[12] said Mr. Carroll who is a pastor in Salem. "But," said Dr. Thurman, "there has been a lot of intermixture of races as for 300 years or more the Negro woman had no control over her body."[13]

But it was now the friends' turn to ask, and Mrs. Thurman, nobly sensitive to the deeper things of the spirit, broke her silence now and then and put searching questions. "Did the South African Negro take any part in your movement?" was the very first question Dr. Thurman asked. "No," said Gandhiji, "I purposely did not invite them. It would have endangered their cause. They would not have understood the technique of our struggle nor could they have seen the purpose or utility of non-violence."[14]

This led to a very interesting discussion of the state of Christianity among the South African Negroes and Gandhiji explained at great length why Islam scored against Christianity there. The talk seemed to appeal very much to Dr. Thurman, who is a professor of comparative religion. "We are often told," said Dr. Thurman, "that but for the Arabs there would have been no slavery. I do not believe it."[15] "No," said Gandhiji, "it is not true at all. For the moment a slave accepts Islam he obtains equality with his master, and there are several instances of this in history."[16] The whole discussion led to many a question and cross-question during which the guests had an occasion to see that Gandhiji's principle of equal respect for all religions was no theoretical formula but a practical creed.

Now the talk centered on a discussion which was the main thing that had drawn the distinguished members to Gandhiji.

"Is non-violence from your point of view a form of direct action?" inquired Dr. Thurman. "It is not one form, it is the only form," said Gandhiji. "I do not of course confine the words 'direct action' to their technical meaning. But without a direct active expression of it, non-violence to my mind is meaningless. It is the greatest and the activest force in the world. One cannot be passively non-violent. In fact 'non-violence' is a term I had to coin in order to bring out the root meaning of Ahimsa.[17] In spite of the negative particle 'non,' it is no negative force. Superficially we are surrounded in life by strife and bloodshed, life living upon life. But some great seer, who ages ago penetrated the centre of truth, said: It is not through strife and violence, but through non-violence that man can fulfill his destiny and his duty to his fellow creatures.[18] It is a force which is more positive than electricity and more powerful than even ether. At the centre of non-violence is a force which is self-acting. Ahimsa means 'love' in the Pauline sense, and yet something more than the 'love' defined by St. Paul, although I know St. Paul's beautiful definition is good enough for all practical purposes.[19] Ahimsa includes the whole creation, and not only human. Besides love in the English language has other connotations too, and so I was compelled to use the negative word. But it does not, as I have told you, express a negative force, but a force superior to all the forces put together. One person who can express Ahimsa in life exercises a force superior to all the forces of brutality."

q. And is it possible for any individual to achieve this?

Gandhiji: Certainly. If there was any exclusiveness about it, I should reject it at once.

q. Any idea of possession is foreign to it?

Gandhiji: Yes. It possesses nothing, therefore it possesses everything.

q. Is it possible for a single human being to resist the persistent invasion of the quality successfully?

Gandhiji: It is possible. Perhaps your question is more universal than you mean. Isn't it possible, you mean to ask, for one single Indian for instance to resist the exploitation of 300 million Indians? Or do you mean the onslaught of the whole world against a single individual personally?

Dr. Thurman: Yes, that is one half of the question. I wanted to know if one man can hold the whole violence at bay?

Gandhiji: If he cannot, you must take it that he is not a true representative of Ahimsa. Supposing I cannot produce a single instance in life of a man who truly converted his adversary, I would then say that is because no one had yet been found to express Ahimsa in its fulness.

q: Then it overrides all other forces?

Gandhiji: Yes, it is the only true force in life.[20]

"Forgive now the weakness of this question," said Dr. Thurman, who was absolutely absorbed in the discussion. "Forgive the weakness, but may I ask how are we to train individuals or communities in this difficult art?"

Gandhiji [said,] "There is no royal road, except through living the creed in your life which must be a living sermon. Of course the expression in one's own life presupposes great study, tremendous perseverance, and thorough cleansing of one's self of all the impurities. If for mastering of the physical sciences you have to devote a whole life-time, how many lifetimes may be needed for mastering the greatest spiritual force that mankind has known? But why worry even if it means several lifetimes? For if this is the only permanent thing in life, if this is the only thing that counts, then whatever effort you bestow on mastering it is well spent. Seek ye first the Kingdom of Heaven and everything else shall be added unto you.[21] The Kingdom of Heaven is Ahimsa."

Mrs. Thurman had restrained herself until now. But she could not go away without asking the question with which she knew she would be confronted any day. "How am I to act, supposing my own brother was lynched before my very eyes?"

"There is such a thing as self-immolation," said Gandhiji. "Supposing I was a Negro, and my sister was ravished by a White or lynched by a whole community, what would be my duty?—I ask myself. And the answer comes to me: I must not wish ill to these, but neither must I co-operate with them. It may be that ordinarily I depend on the lynching community for my livelihood. I refuse to co-operate with them, refuse even to touch the food that comes from them, and I refuse to co-operate with even my brother Negroes who tolerate the wrong. That is the self-immolation I mean. I have often in my life resorted to the plan. Of course a mechanical act of starvation will mean nothing. One's faith must remain undimmed whilst life ebbs out minute by minute. But I am a very poor specimen of the practice of non-violence, and my answer may not convince you. But I am striving very hard, and even if I do not succeed fully in this life, my faith will not diminish."[22]

Mrs. Thurman is a soulful singer, and Dr. Thurman would not think of going away without leaving with us something to treasure in our memory. We sat enraptured as she gave us the two famous Negro spirituals—"Were You There, When They Crucified My Lord," and "We Are Climbing Jacob's Ladder"—which last suited the guests and hosts equally, as it gave expression to the deep-seated hope and aspiration in the breast of every oppressed community to climb higher and higher until the goal was won.

And now came the parting. "We want you to come to America," said the guests with an insistence, the depth of love behind which could be measured as Mrs. Thurman reinforced the request with these words: "We want you not for White America, but for the Negroes; we have many a problem that cries for solution, and we need you badly." "How I wish I could," said Gandhiji, "but I would have nothing to give you unless I had given an ocular demonstration here of all that I have been saying. I must make good the message here before I bring it to you. I do not say that I am defeated, but I have still to perfect myself. You may be sure that the moment I feel the call within me I shall not hesitate."

Dr. Thurman explained that the Negroes were ready to receive the message. "Much of the peculiar background of our own life in America is our own interpretation of the Christian religion. When one goes through the pages of the hundreds of Negro spirituals, striking things are brought to my mind which remind me of all that you have told us today."

"Well," said Gandhiji, bidding good-bye to them, "if it comes true it may be through the Negroes that the unadulterated message of non-violence will be delivered to the world."[23]

M.D.[24]

Harijan 4 (14 March 1936): 38–40.

1. *WHAH*, 132.

2. *Harijan* was an English-language weekly published from 1933 to 1956 (published in Poona 1935–36) by the Harijan Sevak Sangh, a society founded by Gandhi to help untouchables.

3. For earlier published versions of the interview, see M. K. Gandhi, *Non-Violence in Peace and War* (Ahmadabad, India: Navajivan, 1948), 1.131–34; D. G. Tenduklar, *Mahatma: Life of Mohandas Karamchand Gandhi* (Delhi: Ministry of Information and Broadcasting, Government of India, 1960), 6.48–51; and Homer A. Jack, ed., *The Gandhi Reader: A Source Book of His Life and Writings* (Bloomington: Indiana University Press, 1956), 313–16.

4. See Bayard Rustin, "Even in the Face of Death," in *Down the Line: The Collected Writings of Bayard Rustin* (Chicago: Quadrangle, 1971), 103.

5. *Ji*, from the Hindi, is a mark of respect and is usually added to a name.

6. Gandhi was diagnosed with high blood pressure in early December 1935. See *Collected Works of Mahatma Gandhi* (Delhi: Ministry of Information and Broadcasting, Government of India, 1958–84), 62.171–73.

7. Frederick D. Patterson was the third president of Tuskegee Institute, remaining in the position until 1953.

8. See From W. E. B. Du Bois, 10 September 1935, printed in the current volume.

9. *Harvard University* should be "Howard University."

10. Moredecai Wyatt Johnson was one of Gandhi's major American supporters and made frequent references to him in his addresses starting in the late 1920s. In 1930 he called Gandhi the most important religious figure in the world. Sudarshan Kapur, *Raising Up a Prophet: The African-American Encounter with Gandhi* (Boston: Beacon, 1992), 44, 86, 144–47.

11. For this argument, see W. E. B. Du Bois, *Black Reconstruction*, 349–52.

12. Edward Carroll underestimated the scope of antimiscegenation laws in the United States in 1936. At the time, at least thirty states barred interracial marriages. It was from Virginia, the state that required Carroll to post a $500 bond, that a successful challenge to antimiscegenation laws was finally raised. In *Loving v. Virginia* (1967), the U.S. Supreme Court declared all antimiscegenation statutes, still on the books then in sixteen states, to be unconstitutional.

13. One aspect of Gandhi's teaching that disturbed many African Americans was his apparent criticism of interracial marriage in the widely circulated summary of his teachings that appeared in 1930. See C. F. Andrews, *Mahatma Gandhi's Ideas, Including Selections from His Writings* (London: Allen & Unwin, 1929), 36–37, 57–59, 128.

14. Gandhi did not extend his campaign for civil rights among Indians to include native Africans. See Robert A. Huttenback, *Gandhi in South Africa: British Imperialism and the Indian Question, 1869–1914* (Ithaca, N.Y.: Cornell University Press, 1971), 43–44, 138.

15. In his letter of 12 February 1936, in the current volume, Henry W. Luce suggested that Thurman emphasize the complicity of Muslims in the African slave trade.

16. Thurman quotes Gandhi as saying to the delegation, "The Moslem religion is the only religion in the world in which no lines are drawn from within the religious fellowship. Once you are in, you are all the way in. This is not true in Christianity, it isn't true in Buddhism or Hinduism. If you had become Moslem, even though you were a slave, in the faith you would be equal to the master." *WHAH*, 132.

17. *Ahimsa* is Gandhi's term for *nonviolence*, derived from Jainist thought; *Satyagraha* is the term for *civil-disobedience campaigns*.

18. Given that Gandhi was speaking to Christian leaders, he was most probably referring to Jesus, perhaps Leo Tolstoy's pacifist interpretation of Jesus in *The Kingdom of God Is within You: Christianity Not as a Mystic Religion but as a Theory of Life* (London: Heinemann, 1894). Gandhi was, in his own words, "overwhelmed" by Tolstoy's work, which he read as a young man shortly after its appearance in English, and its impact was lasting. Judith M. Brown, *Gandhi: Prisoner of Hope* (New Haven, Conn.: Yale University Press, 1989), 78. Tolstoy's work opens with an extensive tribute to the Quakers, William Lloyd Garrison, and the American pacifist tradition: "'Christ's teaching, which came to be known to men, not by means of violence and the sword,' they [the Quakers] say, 'but by means of non-resistance to evil, gentleness, meekness, and peaceableness, can only be diffused through the world by the example of peace, harmony, and love among its followers.'" *Kingdom of God Is within You*, 1.

19. I Cor. 13:4–8.

20. Thurman's account of this part of his conversation in his autobiography diverges from the *Harijan* text. Thurman remembers asking Gandhi, "Why has your movement failed of its objectives, namely, to rid the country of the British?" which has no counterpart in *Harijan*. According to Thurman, Gandhi's answer was that the success of *ahimsa* relied on "the degree to which the masses of the people are able to embrace such a notion" and that "it cannot be the unique experience of the leaders." According to Thurman, Gandhi argued the failure to embrace *ahimsa* was a consequence of the lack of vitality by the Indian people caused by a lack of economic self-sufficiency and a lack of self-respect caused by the continuing scandal of untouchability. *WHAH*, 132–33. In the *Harijan* interview, Gandhi argues conversely that one person, fully enlightened, could "resist the exploitation of 300 million Indians." As Gandhi explained later in the interview, he still needed "to perfect himself" to become an adequate representative of the principals he was advocating. Gandhi's deep belief that his own example, especially when fasting, could transform India and the world was one the justifications for his frequent fasting. Brown, *Gandhi*, 187–88.

21. Matt. 6:33.

22. The difficult doctrine of "self-immolation" was the subject of many queries by those who talked to Gandhi. In 1937 in discussion with Benjamin E. Mays and Channing H. Tobias, Gandhi argued the resistance of Ethiopians to the Italian invasion would have been much more effective if "they had retired from the field and allowed themselves to be slaughtered." Of German Jews, writing shortly after Kristallnacht in 1938, he controversially counseled, "Suffering undergone voluntarily will bring . . . an inner strength and joy." Jack, *Gandhi Reader*, 310, 319.

23. Thurman's two versions of the end of the interview differ slightly from the *Harijan* interview. In a 1958 talk Thurman gave to Indian students, he described the end of the meeting as follows: "Just as we were about to take our leave he made one request. He asked that we sing 'Were You There When They Crucified My Lord?' adding that it is in suffering that the full-orbed meaning of Truth stood most utterly revealed. We sang as his few companions were in the attitude of prayer." It was after the long silence that the latterly oft-quoted statement was made: "It may be that through your people and their suffering, America may be saved." Thurman, "Talks to Students from India," HTC-MBU: Box 203. In his autobiography, however, Thurman writes that Gandhi made a different final statement, that the biggest obstacle to the spread of Christianity in India is "Christianity as it is practiced, as it has been identified with western civilization and colonialism. This is the greatest enemy Jesus Christ has in my country—not Hinduism, or Buddhism, or any of the indigenous religions—but Christianity itself." *WHAH*, 135.

24. Mahadev Desai.

APPENDIX

Academic Transcripts

Thurman was always a superb and attentive student who obtained marks in the high 90s, with many perfect scores. Math, with a few marks in the 80s, was apparently his weakest subject. Thurman was also a model student in his deportment. Although his transcripts for college and seminary are without any evaluation for his behavior, he continued his excellent academic record, and in every institution of learning he was formally enrolled—middle school, high school, college, and Rochester Theological Seminary—he graduated as valedictorian of his class.

7th Grade, R. H. Howard, Teacher (1913–1914)

Attendance Deportment Studies	1	2	3	4	Ex.	5	6	7	8	Ex.	Av.	G.Av.
Absent (Unexcused)												
Tardy (Unexcused)												
Times Tardy												
Days Present	20	17	14	18		20	18	19	18			
Days Absent												
Deportment	98	90	100	95	100	100	90	100	100			
Reading	80	85	90	90	91	90	98	100	100			
Spelling	90	91	90	95	90	91	100	100	90			
Writing	95	90	91	91	80	91	98	90	91			
Arithmetic	88	92	90	91	100	97	98	98	100			
Geography	91	95	96	91	90	91	98	100	100			
Grammar and Lang.	89	90	91	92	85	90	95	98	100			
U. S. History	90	98	90	100	100	95	98	100	100			
Physiology	90	100	90	100	80	85	91	90	100			
Agriculture	91	91	91	95	98	92	91	100	100			
Music												
Domestic Science												
Manual Training												
Home Economics												
Home Reading												
General Average												

8th Grade, R. H. Howard, Teacher (1914–1915)

Attendance Deportment Studies	1	2	3	4	Ex.	5	6	7	8	Ex.	Av.	G.Av.
Absent (Unexcused)												
Tardy (Unexcused)												
Times Tardy												
Days Present	20	19	20	19		20	19	18	20			
Days Absent												
Deportment	100	100	100	100	100	100	100	100	100			
Days Absent												
Reading	98	90	90	90	92	98	90	100	100			
Spelling	90	90	89	90	90	90	98	90	90			
Writing	90	91	90	90	92	90	91	98				
Arithmetic	91	90	91	92	95	91	96	91	98			
Geography	91	91	90	100	100	90	91	91	98			
Grammar and Lang.	90	91	92	98	90	91	91	91	90			
U. S. History	90	91	90	91	91	91	91	90	91			
Physiology	90	92	90	91	91	91	91	90	91			
Agriculture	91	91	91	90	91	92	91	92	91			
Music												
Domestic Science												
Manual Training												
Home Economics												
Home Reading												
General Average												

Note: The year on the original transcript (1915–1916) is in error and has been changed to the correct year.

Florida Baptist Academy (1915–1916)

MONTHS	1st	2nd	3rd	4th	5th	6th	7th	8th	9th	Yr.Av.	COMMENTS
Reading											1st Mo.
Writing											
Spelling											2nd Mo.
Arithmetic											
Geography											3rd Mo.
Grammar											
History	98	97	99	94	94	93				96	4th Mo.
Physiology											
Civil Government											5th Mo.
Literature	97	91	94	94	90	97	95			94	
Physical Geography											6th Mo.
Astronomy											
Algebra	90	91	92	90	91	92	98			92	
Latin	94	95	96	98	97	97	98			97	7th Mo.
Geometry	90	88	95	96	90	93	95			92	
Bible	95	90	93	90	90	95	97			93	8th Mo.
Days present											
Days absent											9th Mo.
Times tardy											
Average Scholarship										94	
Deportment	98	98	98	98	98	98	98			98	
Punctuality											
General Average										97	
Rank in Class											

Florida Baptist Academy (1916–1917)

MONTHS	1st	2nd	3rd	4th	5th	6th	7th	8th	9th	Yr.Av.	COMMENTS
Rhetoricals										96	1st Mo.
Writing											
Spelling											
Arithmetic											2nd Mo.
Geography											
Grammar											3rd Mo.
History Gen.	98	99	99	97	99	99	99	99		99	
Physiology											
Civil Government											4th Mo
Literature	99	99	99	97	97	99	99	98		98	
Physical Geography											5th Mo.
Algebra	88	95	94	96	89	94	96	98		94	
Physics		90	98	94	96	97	95	95		97	
Caesar	97	99	99	97	98	99	99	99		98	6th Mo.
Bible	100	98	98	99						99	
Days present											
Days absent											7th Mo.
Times tardy											
Average Scholarship										98	8th Mo.
Deportment										98	
Punctuality											
General Average										97	9th Mo.
Rank in Class											

Florida Baptist Academy (1917–1918)

MONTHS	1st	2nd	3rd	4th	5th	6th	7th	8th	9th	Yr.Av.	COMMENTS
Reading											1st Mo.
Writing											
Spelling											2nd Mo.
Arithmetic											
Geography											
Grammar											3rd Mo.
History											
Physiology											
Civil Government											4th Mo.
Literature	95	90	99	99	98	98	95	98		97	
Physical Geography											5th Mo.
Algebra	98	98	97	98	95	97	92	98		97	
Latin	98	98	98	98	98	99	99	99		98	
Zoology	95	98	98	98	98	99	99	99		98	6th Mo. Botany
Bible	75	85	90	95	95	97	95	98		92	
Days present											7th Mo.
Days absent	0	0	0	0	0						
Times tardy											
Average Scholarship										96+	8th Mo.
Deportment										100	
Punctuality											
General Average										98	9th Mo.
Rank in Class											

Florida Normal and Industrial Institute (1918–1919)

MONTHS	1st	2nd	3rd	4th	5th	6th	7th	8th	9th	Yr.Av.	COMMENTS
Reading											*1st Mo.*
Writing											
Spelling											*2nd Mo.*
Arithmetic											
Geography											*3rd Mo.*
Grammar											
History	85	90	90	90	88					89	*4th Mo.*
Physiology											
Civil Government											*5th Mo.*
Literature	88	90	88	90	90	85	92	93		91	
Psychology	98	98	98	98	97	98	95			97	*6th Mo.*
Chemistry				99	97	95	90	95		95	
Geometry					94	95	92	93		94	*7th Mo.*
Greek				98	94	94	94	96		96	
Latin	90	89	95	95	96	96	95	98		94	*8th Mo.*
Days present	10	9	31	31	28	31	30	28			
Days absent	12										*9th Mo.*
Times tardy											
Average Scholarship										94	
Deportment										96	
Punctuality											
General Average										95	
Rank in Class											

<u>MOREHOUSE COLLEGE, ATLANTA, GEORGIA</u>
Office of the Registrar
Official Transcript of the Record of <u>Howard W. Thurman, Daytona, Florida</u>
Form adopted by the Association of Colleges for Negro Youth.
Office of the Registrar
IV. College Credits.

DESCRIPTIVE TITLE OF COURSE	COURSE NUMBER IN CATALOG	FIRST SEMESTER SECOND SEMESTER HOURS PER WEEK	GRADE
REC. LAB.			
GRADE			
Year of 1919–1920			
French	1	5	90
		5	91
Greek	2	4	96
		4	96
English	5	4	90
		4	87
History	1	4	90
Bible	4	2	97
		2	97
History	5	4	87
Geometry (credited upon entrance)	2	4	94
1920–21			
French	2	4	89
		4	90
Economics	2	4	89
		4	88
Geology	3	2	87
	3	2	92
German	1	5	84
		5	87
English (Debating)	7	4	87
Greek	3	4	92
		4	87

MOREHOUSE COLLEGE, ATLANTA, GEORGIA
Office of the Registrar
Official Transcript of the Record of Howard W. Thurman, Daytona, Florida

Descriptive Title of Course	Course Number	First Semester Second Semester	
Rec. Lab.	in Catalog	Hours per Week	Grade
Year of 1921–22			
Money & Banking		4	91
		4	94
German	2	4	81
		4	81
Sociology		4	90
		4	90
English (public speaking)	7	4	91
English	6	4	96
		4	95
Psychology	1	4	92
Trigonometry		4	90
1922–23			
Ethics		4	91
		4	92
History	3	4	91
Music Appreciation		4	91
Social Theory		4	90
~~Teachers'~~ English		4	83

Columbia University
(summer session) 1922

Philosophy S1	2 points	A	grade Introduction to Reflective Thinking
Philosophy S2	2 points	A	grade Introduction
Government S2	2 points	C	grade American States

Passing Grades Are: 60   Total of credits secured   20½
                              Required for graduation: 18 credits

Issued
Registrar

Awards and Prizes

Howard W. Thurman

Scholarship award for 1st ranking student in Freshman Class, earned 1919–20.

    "   "   " 2nd   "   "   " Sophomore   "   "   1920–21.

    "   "   " 1st   "   "   " Junior   "   "   1921–22.

Edgar Allan Poe Short Story Prize, 1920.
F. J. Paxon Prize (Oratory & Elocution), 1921.
Willard Chamberlin Scripture Reading Prize, 1922
Starks (Best Man of Affairs) Prize, 1923.

Rochester Theological Seminary
Office of the Registrar
Rochester, New York

This is to certify that the following is a correct transcript of the courses and grades to the credit of Howard W. Thurman on the records of this institution.

Junior Year

First Semester, January 1924

Course		Hours	Grade	
Hebrew History	O.T.1	3	85	
Social Basis,	E&S 1	3	93	
Prin. Rel. Educ.	R.E.1	3	97	
Prep. of Sermons	P.Th.1	3	98	15 Hours,
Sermonic Expression	P.Th 3	3	89	92.4 Average for Semester

Second Semester, May 1924

Course		Hours	Grade	
Jewish Life	O.T.2	3	85	
Gen. Intro. to N.T	N.T.1	3	94	
Hist. Of Christianity	Hist. 1	3	94	
Psych. of Religion	R&M.1	3	92	
Christian Ethics				15 Hours
and Sociology	E&S 2	3	90	91 Average for Semester
				91.7 Average for year

Middle Year

First Semester, January 1925

Religion of N.T.	N.T.2	3	90	
Med. Christianity	Hist. 2	3	88	
Hist. of Religions	R&M.2	3	90	System of Grading Changed
Religious & Current Philosophies	R&M 5	3	90	15 Hours
Hebrew Cultus	O.T.7	3	90	89.6 Average for Semester

Second Semester, May 1925

Doctrine of Man	Syst.1	3	91	
Mod. Church School	R.E.2	3	90	
Life of Jesus	N.T.7	3	86	
New Testament Greek		3	80	15 Hours
Xity in Civilization	Hist.4	3	92	87.4 Average for Semester 88.5 Average for Year

Senior Year

First Semester, January 1926

Doctrine of God	Syst.2	3	92	
Modern Minister	P.TH.2	3	86	
Senior Preaching	P.Th.	1	95	
Xity in Mod. Civ.	Hist.4	3	92	13 Hours
Hebrew Family	O.T.6	3	92	Average for Semester 90.8

Second Semester, May 1926

Christian Finality	Syst.3	3	84	
Pastoral Theology	P.TH.1	1 ½	90	
Christian Ethics	E&S.1	1 ½	92	
Preaching Values	Hist.6	3	88	12 Hours
Genesis of Cath. and Prot. Orthodoxy	Syst.4	3	92	Average for Semester 88.8 Average for Year 89.8

Dated, June 8th, 1926   Earl B. Cross

INDEX

Page references in **bold** refer to photographs; page references in *italics* refer to biographical information contained in the notes.